The **Rough Guide** to

Den

written and researched by

Lone Mouritsen, Roger Norum
and Caroline Osborne

www.roughguides.com

Contents

Danish food and drink
colour section
following p.144

Denmark's great outdoors colour section
following p.272

◄◄ Lighthouse, Limfjord, North Jutland ◄ Bike on a cobbled street, Copenhagen

Introduction to

Denmark

Spread across some one hundred islands wedged between the northern tip of mainland Europe and the Scandinavian peninsula, once diminutive Denmark has in recent years evolved into a social, cultural and political powerhouse. Roughly the same size as the Netherlands and with comparatively few citizens (about as many as Scotland), the country offers one of the world's highest standards of living, a comprehensive social welfare system and an extremely efficient infrastructure with an excellent transport system and superb public services. Copenhagen, the capital, is now one of the most happening cultural destinations in the world, while the rest of the country – an unspoilt landscape of stunning beaches, thick forests, gently rolling meadows and beguiling little historic towns – rewards serious exploration. Danes, for their part, are extremely proud of what they have and – according to several recent surveys – happier in their day-to-day lives than anyone else on the planet. Get to know some of them, and their unique sense of warm, cosy cordiality known in Danish as *hygge*, and you'll quickly see why.

This is a conservative and very traditional country: Denmark's immigration policies are among the toughest in Europe, and its royal family is still held in high regard. But it's also a progressive nation, with legendarily liberal social values and forward-thinking attitudes that have made it one of the world's most environmentally conscious nations. And although Denmark's **history** is inevitably associated with the exploits of the Vikings, the country has long played a significant role in wider European and global affairs. The Danish

Fact file

• Denmark is one of the five Nordic nations, and with a total land mass of 43,560 square kilometres, it's by far the smallest. The **population** stands at just over 5.85 million, some 8.5 percent of which are foreign-born citizens and their descendants – a high number for the Scandinavian countries and one which has made immigration a major bone of political contention. Unemployment was 4.4 percent at the beginning of 2010.

• The **standard of living** in Denmark is one of the highest in the world – but income tax ranges from 45 percent to 59 percent, and 25 percent VAT is levied on most goods. In return Danes receive free, comprehensive social welfare, while the working week averages 37 hours.

• Though granted independence (in 1978 and 1948 respectively), the former colonies of **Greenland** and the **Faroe Islands** still have Danish as an official language alongside their native tongues, and the Danish government still provides them with total subsidies of some US$150 million each year.

• Denmark became a constitutional monarchy in 1849, and has been a **parliamentary democracy** since 1901; 36 percent of MPs are women.

• Denmark has more than twice the amount of **bicycles** than cars, with 4.2 million cycles and 1.8 million cars.

• **Copenhageners** pedal more than 1.13 million kilometres in total each day.

• Scandinavians are the world's highest per-capita consumers of **coffee**, with Danes (who drink on average four cups a day) coming third after Sweden and Finland.

• The Danish firm LEGO was founded in 1932, since when it has sold over 320 billion units of **Lego** – nearly sixty bricks for every human on the planet.

crown conquered England and drove out the Swedes to rule Norway for nearly five hundred years, and maintained colonial strongholds in South Asia, West Africa and the Caribbean until the early twentieth century. Since then, the country's energies have been turned inwards, toward the development of a well-organized yet hardly over-bureaucratic society that encourages national pride in the arts and fosters individual freedom.

Denmark is the easiest of the Scandinavian countries to explore in terms of travelling costs and distances: you can drive from Copenhagen in the east to Esbjerg in the west in well under three hours. The bulk of visitors are drawn to the principal **cities** of Copenhagen, Odense and Århus, but it would

be a shame not to explore the country's **great outdoors**. The landscape may not be hugely dramatic, but its gentle hillsides, vast meadows and forested valleys are unspoiled and graceful. Denmark's 7300km of **coastline** is perhaps the jewel in its crown, a bewitching mix of sandy beaches, chalk cliffs and placid fjords, with hundreds of islands and skerries just off its shores. Furthermore, as Denmark's countryside is crisscrossed by thousands of miles of cycling trails, it's one of the best places in Europe to explore by **bike**.

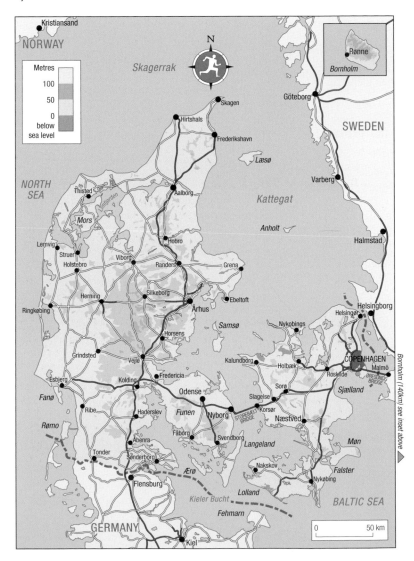

Where to go

Most visitors get their first glimpse of Denmark at the sleek international airport, just outside **Copenhagen** on the island of **Zealand**. One of the most cosmopolitan and culturally alive cities in Europe, bewitching **Copenhagen** boasts major national museums and art galleries and an enticing range of entertainment, from cosy cafés and bars to intimate clubs, rocking live music venues and, in summer, a bevy of outstanding arts and music festivals. Away from the urban verve, and within easy reach of the capital, northern **Zealand** offers enchanting royal castles and a string of superb beaches, with a smattering of posh bistros and restaurants to boot. South of the capital, picturesque and chipper **Roskilde** is best known for its unforgettable summer music festival, but also holds an imposing Gothic cathedral and Viking ship museum. The brick towers, stucco palaces and ruined fortresses of southern Zealand's medieval-era towns attest to a rich royal history, while the trio of large islands connected to the south coast by road and train links offer an appealing mix of lively beach towns and sleepy lakeside villages. Some 150km off Zealand's eastern coast in the middle of the Baltic Sea, **Bornholm** is a gorgeous and subdued place, its forests and winsome coastline bathed in a breathtaking light – it's obvious why the locals pledge allegiance first to their island and then to the Danish crown. With fetching harbour towns, white-sand beaches and hundreds of miles of cycling paths, this is the place to revel in *the* great outdoors.

Linked to Zealand by the awe-inspiring Storebælt bridge, **Funen** is Denmark's third largest – and by far its greenest – landmass, the countryside interspersed with fairytale castles, manicured gardens and small coastal outposts that, in

▲ The Øresund bridge between Denmark and Sweden

◄ Beach huts

the summertime at least, maintain a warm and friendly atmosphere animated by festivals, concerts and a prevailing bonhomie. The main urban draw is **Odense**, which makes much of its connections with locally born Hans Christian Andersen and holds a pair of superb art galleries, some excellent restaurants and a sizeable population of students and young professionals who ensure that its many bars and clubs rarely close before dawn. There's yet more rural appeal in the islands of the **south Funen archipelago**, with their gorgeous beaches, scenic cycling routes and lavish old estates.

West by bridge across the Lille Bælt is the expansive **Jutland** peninsula, jutting off from northern Germany in between the squally North Sea and the tranquil Baltic. Given its distance from Copenhagen, the peninsula has an appealingly no-nonsense, bucolic flavour that's evident even in the laid-back city of **Århus**, whose cultural delights rival those of the capital. Control of southern Jutland, which shares the border with Germany, was tossed back and forth between Denmark and Germany for centuries, a fact evident in the numerous castles built to stave off the invaders. The many bird species that inhabit the marshland and tidal flats of the **southwest coast** are a big draw for ornithologists, while the rolling, eastern hills at craggy, nose-shaped **Djursland** give way to some of the country's most spectacular white-sand beaches. The unrelenting winds that pummel the remote and rural **western coast** have thrashed the migrating sand dunes about for millennia, creating harsh living conditions for local farmers and fishermen as well as an incredibly striking coastline – and some of the world's best spots for windsurfing. Denmark's longest river, the lithe **Gudenå** bisects the pretty **Lake District** from south to north, and canoeing is the perfect way to explore. North of the river, Denmark's largest forest provides picture-perfect hiking and mountain biking, while valleys and fjord basins rich in Viking history terminate at atmospheric **Skagen**, whose magical oceanic light has attracted painters and creative types for decades.

When to go

Denmark has the least extreme **climate** of the Scandinavian countries, and though temperatures vary little across the country, wind conditions and proximity to the sea shake things up a bit – you'll notice the stiff breezes along Jutland's west coast in particular. Rainfall levels are more or less constant throughout the year, with an annual average of 61cm; the west tends to be wetter than the east, however.

Though **spring** usually brings bright sunlight and cloudless skies, the best time to visit Denmark is during the **summer** months of June, July and August, when the climate is warmest and the blossoming landscape at its prettiest, and when tourist facilities and transport services are operating at full steam. Bear in mind, though, that July is vacation month for Danes, who head en masse to the countryside or the coast – though even then, only the most popular areas are uncomfortably crowded. Summer is almost always sunny and clear, with temperatures rarely stifling: the warmest month is July, which averages 20°C (68°F), though highs of 26°C (78°F) are not unheard of. Copenhagen attracts visitors all year round and is a bit of a law unto itself; as the intake peaks during July and August, the best times to visit the capital are May, early June and September, though you'll find plenty going on throughout much of the year.

Birdwatching

Denmark is one of Europe's key destinations for birdwatching, and it's a very popular pastime for many Danes, too, who make good use of the tall, sturdy observation towers that you'll see in many of the country's nature reserves. The best birding site in the country is the Wadden Sea marshes and tidal flats on Jutland's southwest coast, where the receding tides provide a muddy refuge for flocks of wild geese, eider ducks and other aquatic birds. There are also regular visits from migratory species such as the red-breasted goose and barred warbler, while sundown and sunrise see nearly half a million starlings performing awe-inspiring aerial displays as they gather to roost. Throughout the country, the best time for birding is April, when many species don their handsome mating plumage – great crested grebes, ringed plovers and kingfishers are particularly eye-catching.

The museum of modern art, Arken

Autumn can also be a good time to visit, with the falling leaves providing a glorious golden show – though bear in mind that the coastal waters can get downright chilly as early as September, and that most sights and attractions maintain reduced hours outside of high season, from mid-September onwards.

Cold but rarely severe, Denmark's **winters** are decidedly less frigid than those of its northerly Scandinavian neighbours. Although temperatures can drop as low as minus 15°C (5°F), they usually hover around freezing, with the tail end of the Gulf Stream keeping the frost off in the coastal towns. Although the possibilities for outside pursuits are limited, winter isn't off-limits for visitors. During the darkest months, when daylight is in short supply, slugs of *snaps* and hot *gløgg* help to keep the cold at bay, and the Danish *hygge* comes into its own.

Average daytime temperature and rainfall

	Jan	Feb	Mar	Apr	May	Jun	Jul	Aug	Sep	Oct	Nov	Dec
Copenhagen												
°C	1.9	2.0	4.8	9.5	15.0	19.2	20.4	20.3	16.7	12.1	7.1	3.7
°F	35.4	35.6	40.6	49.1	59	66.5	68.7	68.5	62.0	53.7	44.7	38.7
mm	46	30	39	39	42	52	68	64	60	56	61	56
Aalborg												
°C	1.7	2.0	4.9	9.8	15.2	19.0	20.1	20.0	16.2	11.9	6.8	3.4
°F	35.0	35.6	40.8	49.6	59.4	66.2	68.1	68.0	61.2	53.4	44.2	38.1
mm	54	35	44	38	49	54	64	67	72	76	75	62
Odense												
°C	2.3	2.5	5.5	10.2	15.6	19.4	20.5	20.7	17.0	12.5	7.3	3.9
°F	36.1	36.5	41.9	50.4	60.1	67.0	68.9	69.2	62.6	54.5	45.1	39.0
mm	52	36	41	38	46	53	62	61	60	62	69	58
Bornholm												
°C	1.9	1.7	3.7	8.0	13.8	18.0	19.5	19.7	16.1	11.9	7.3	3.8
°F	35.4	35.0	38.6	46.4	56.8	64.4	67.1	67.5	61.0	53.4	45.1	38.9
mm	51	32	40	37	37	42	55	55	63	60	76	62

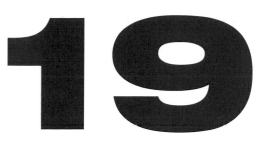

things not to miss

It's not possible to see everything that Denmark has to offer in a single trip – and we don't suggest you try. What follows is a selective taste of the country's highlights (in no particular order), from imposing castles and and world-class museums to unspoilt countryside and beguiling beaches. They're arranged in five colour-coded categories with a page reference to take you straight into the Guide, where you can find out more.

01 **Ny Carlsberg Glyptotek, Copenhagen** Page **72** • The Winter Garden of this fine art gallery holds an impressive collection of Egyptian and Roman sculptures, bedecked with blossoming flowers and plants all around.

02 **Jutland beaches** Pages **201, 262, 271** & **281** and *Denmark's great outdoors* colour section • The persistent westerly winds that thrash Denmark's western coast make for some wonderfully wild beaches, stunning vistas and excellent watersports possibilities.

04 **Hans Christian Andersen museums, Odense** Pages **158** & **159** • The museums dedicated to Denmark's most famous writer in his home town offer intriguing insights into this father of the modern fairytale.

05 **Smørrebrød** Page **28** and *Danish food and drink* colour section • This traditional open sandwich of dark rye bread topped with everything from smoked salmon or herring to salami or a fried egg is delectable and delicious.

03 **Louisiana Museum of Modern Art, Zealand** Page **97** • A crackerjack collection of contemporary art, housed in a nineteenth-century villa and with a sculpture garden overlooking the Øresund.

07 Vikingeskibsmuseet, Zealand
Page **115** • Denmark's most heralded museum showcases five magnificent Viking vessels, all dredged up from the fjord bottom where they lay dormant for nearly a thousand years.

06 Cycling
Pages **32** and *Denmark's great outdoors* colour section • With over 10,000km of well-maintained, waymarked cycling paths traversing coast, meadow and forest – not to mention the cities – a bike is the best way to get around this relatively flat and diminutive country.

08 Viking fortresses
Pages **121** & **242** • Built within a twenty-year period by Harald Bluetooth, these perfectly circular ring forts are amazing examples of Viking ingenuity.

09 Gudenå river canoeing, Jutland
Page **219** • Let the world float by as the current pulls you gently along Denmark's longest river, past stately manors, gardens and flocks of migrating birds.

10 Koldinghus, Jutland
Page **189** • The spectacular restoration of this former royal castle is a must-see while in Jutland, with imaginative lighting used to distinguish the old from the new.

11 Frederiksborg Slot, Zealand
Page **110** • Denmark's most grandiose castle, its marble and stucco rooms and ornate chapel complemented by gorgeous Baroque grounds replete with canals, fountains and a placid lake.

12 Designer shopping, Copenhagen
Page **90** • Head for the streets around Kronprinsensgade and off Amager Torv to pick up some of Denmark's hottest new designs of housewares, objets d'art and clothes.

13 **Christiania, Copenhagen** Page **66** • Although currently under threat of being "normalized", this self-governing hippie city, with its array of atmospheric cafés and restaurants and simmering nightlife venues, also excels in quirky, inventive public art.

14 **Tivoli, Copenhagen**
Page **71** • No trip to the capital is complete without a day at the world's oldest amusement park, smack dab in the city centre and offering daredevil rides, top-notch entertainment and beautiful landscaped gardens.

15 **Kronborg Slot, Zealand**
Page **105** • This fairytale sandstone marvel is better known as the Elsinore of Shakespeare's *Hamlet*, and is majestically located on a grassy promontory looking out to the sea.

16 **Rundkirke, Bornholm** Page **147** • These unique round churches served as defensive strongholds as well as places of worship, now dotting the island landscape with their unique, whitewashed forms.

18 **The Queen's Tapestries, Copenhagen** Page **62** • Denmark's history in one fell swoop, colourfully depicted on these glorious tapestries displayed at Christiansborg's Royal Reception Rooms.

17 **Roskilde Festival, Zealand** Page **113** • One of the best music festivals in Europe, with some 100,000 music fans pitching up for a long, drunken weekend of peace, love and lots of rock and roll.

19 **Sort Sol over the Wadden Sea, Jutland** Page **198** • During spring and autumn, the skies above the Wadden Sea marshes are painted with thousands of starlings performing their poetic pre-roosting aerial ballet.

Basics

Basics

Getting there

The most convenient way to get to Denmark from the UK and Ireland is to fly to Copenhagen or one of the country's smaller airports. There's a good range of scheduled and budget flights, and even the lowest scheduled fares are often a lot cheaper than the long and arduous journey by train, ferry or coach. From North America, a handful of airlines operate direct scheduled flights to Copenhagen, though it may be cheaper to fly to London and pick up an onward flight from there with a budget carrier, also the only option if you're travelling from Australia, New Zealand and South Africa, from where there are no direct flights.

Airfares depend on the **season**, with the highest between early June to mid-September; prices are reduced during the low season, November through to April (excluding Christmas, New Year and Easter, when prices are hiked up and seats are at a premium). Ticket prices from the UK don't vary seasonally as much as those from North America; note also that flying on weekends is generally more expensive; price ranges quoted below assume midweek travel booked a month in advance.

Flights from the UK and Ireland

Direct services **from London** to Copenhagen (roughly 2hr) are operated by SAS, British Airways, easyJet, Norwegian Air Shuttle, Cimber Air, German Wings and bmi. All of these carriers operate at least one flight a day, though services may be reduced at weekends. There are also numerous direct services to Copenhagen from the UK's **regional airports**, including Aberdeen (SAS), Birmingham (SAS and BMI), Edinburgh (Cimber Air, Norwegian Air Shuttle, bmi and SAS), Glasgow (SAS and bmi), Manchester (SAS, easyJet and bmi) and Newcastle (Cimber Air). Most of these carriers operate two to four flights a week.

There are also direct services from the UK to regional airports in Jutland. Denmark's second largest airport **Billund** is served by flights from London with British Airways, Cimber Air and Ryanair, from Birmingham with Ryanair, from Edinburgh with Ryanair, and from Manchester with BA. In addition **Esbjerg** has bmi with flights from Aberdeen. From London, Norwegian Air Shuttle also flies to **Aalborg**, and Ryanair to **Århus**.

At the time of writing, the lowest fares to Copenhagen from London are offered by easyJet and Norwegian Air Shuttle, both at around £50 return. Ryanair often has special offers for around £15 or less for its flights to Billund and Århus. Special offers and discounted tickets apart, the **scheduled fares** of the major airlines are pretty well matched; the cheaper seats tend to be found on smaller carriers such as Cimber Air and bmi. Expect to pay around £130 for a return ticket from Britain to Denmark with BA or SAS.

From Ireland, the most straightforward option is a direct flight to Copenhagen from Dublin with SAS or Norwegian Air Shuttle; Ryanair also flies to Billund from Dublin, while Aer Lingus flies from Dublin, Cork and Shannon to Copenhagen via London

Heathrow. Scheduled **midweek fares** to Copenhagen are around €200 year-round; flights with Ryanair from Dublin to Billund are around €50. If you're flying from one of Ireland's regional airports, it's usually cheaper to find one of the numerous special deals to London, and then take advantage of the more competitive airfares available from there.

There are no direct flights to Denmark **from Belfast**, so your best bet is probably to fly via London, Glasgow or Edinburgh.

Flights from the US and Canada

From the US and Canada, the majority of flights to Denmark involve changing planes at a European hub; you may save money by taking a cheap flight to **London** and travelling on to Denmark with a budget airline from there (see p.19). **Direct flights** to Copenhagen are only available from the US, from Chicago (SAS and United Airlines), Washington (SAS and United Airlines), Atlanta (Delta Air Lines and Air France) and New York (Continental Airlines, SAS and United Airlines).

Fares are fairly similar, whichever carrier you choose, though it's still worth shopping around. Flights from **Newark** (7hr 45min) costs $2900–3300 for a fully flexible return and $500–800 for an economy fixed return, depending on the season. Tickets from **Chicago** (8hr 15min) and **Washington** (8hr) cost $3000–3800 for fully flexible returns and $660–900 for economy fixed, while flights from **Atlanta** (9hr) cost $3200–3500 for a flexible, fully refundable ticket in high season, and $650–750 for a fixed low season return.

There are no direct flights from Canada, so the best plan is to fly to the UK, and take a cheap flight from there, or travel from a US hub.

Flights from Australia, New Zealand and South Africa

As there are **no direct services** to Denmark from Australia, New Zealand or South Africa, you'll need to change planes at a European or Asian gateway city. Fares are pretty steep, so if you're on a tight

budget it's worth flying to London, Paris, Amsterdam or Frankfurt, and picking up a cheap flight from there.

Airlines flying out of **Australia** and **New Zealand** often use SAS for connecting services on to Copenhagen and involve one stop en route. Other less direct routes involve a minimum of two stops en route, one Middle Eastern or Asian – Dubai, Singapore, Beijing or Bangkok – and one European – Frankfurt, Paris, Helsinki or London. Airlines such as Thai, British Airways, Finnair, Lufthansa, Emirates and Qantas ply these routes. For tickets from **Sydney**, **Melbourne**, **Perth** or **Auckland** expect to pay from AUS$1700/NZ$2100 in low season and from AUS$2500/NZ$3100 in high season. Flights from **Christchurch** and **Wellington** tend to go via Sydney or Auckland and cost around NZ$150–300 more.

The best deals from **South Africa** are from **Johannesburg** with Swiss via Zurich, Air France via Paris, KLM via Amsterdam and British Airways via London. Prices hover at the R8000 mark in low season and R9000 in high season.

Trains

Taking a **train** can be a relaxed way of getting to Denmark from the UK, though it's likely to work out considerably more expensive than flying, especially if you're over 26.

You can either cross over to mainland Europe by boat and pick up a train from there, or go via Eurostar through the **Channel Tunnel** from St Pancras International in London. Almost all ticketing for train travel within Europe is handled by **Rail Europe** (see p.22), which provides the fastest and most convenient routings via the Eurostar to Brussels, and then on to Denmark on an overnight train via Cologne. Rail Europe can sell you through-tickets from most UK starting points; through-tickets for the train/cross-channel ferry option are only available from a few agents (detailed on p.22) and larger train stations. You could, with careful planning, organize your own train and ferry tickets – a less expensive if more complicated process.

To get the **cheapest fares** with Rail Europe, you'll need to book a round-trip fourteen days

Six steps to a better kind of travel

At Rough Guides we are passionately committed to travel. We feel strongly that only through travelling do we truly come to understand the world we live in and the people we share it with – plus tourism has brought a great deal of **benefit** to developing economies around the world over the last few decades. But the extraordinary growth in tourism has also damaged some places irreparably, and of course **climate change** is exacerbated by most forms of transport, especially flying. This means that now more than ever it's important to **travel thoughtfully** and **responsibly**, with respect for the cultures you're visiting – not only to derive the most benefit from your trip but also to preserve the best bits of the planet for everyone to enjoy. At Rough Guides we feel there are six main areas in which you can make a difference:

- Consider what you're contributing to the **local economy**, and how much the services you use do the same, whether it's through employing local workers and guides or sourcing locally grown produce and local services.
- Consider the **environment** on holiday as well as at home. Water is scarce in many developing destinations, and the biodiversity of local flora and fauna can be adversely affected by tourism. Try to patronize businesses that take account of this.
- Travel with a purpose, not just to tick off experiences. Consider **spending longer** in a place, and getting to know it and its people.
- Give thought to how often you **fly**. Try to avoid short hops by air and more harmful night flights.
- Consider **alternatives to flying**, travelling instead by bus, train, boat and even by bike or on foot where possible.
- Make your trips "**climate neutral**" via a reputable carbon-offset scheme. All Rough Guide flights are offset, and every year we donate money to a variety of charities devoted to combating the effects of climate change.

in advance with one Saturday night away. With this type of ticket, the return fare to Denmark currently starts at £240 (more if you take a sleeper berth). The journey takes around 20 hours, via Brussels and Cologne. As always, check for special offers.

Buses

Taking the bus to Denmark can be an endurance test, and with such low airfares it can actually prove more expensive than flying. It's only worth taking the bus if time is no object and price all-important, or if you specifically do not want to fly.

The major UK operator is **Eurolines** (see p.22), which offers coaches to **Copenhagen** either via Brussels (24hr) or Amsterdam (30hr). **Fares** to Copenhagen start at £120 return, with discounts for those over 60 or under 26. Note that in the peak summer months, all fares increase slightly. Euroline tickets and passes are

bookable online via the company website (see p.22) and through most major travel agents (see p.22).

There are no through-services from anywhere in the UK outside London, though **National Express** buses from all over the British Isles connect with Eurolines services in London.

By ferry from Britain

There's just one direct **ferry** service between Britain and Denmark, run by **DFDS Seaways** (☎0871/522 9955, ⓦwww .dfdsseaways.co.uk) between Harwich and Esbjerg. Journey time is 18 hours and **fares** vary according to the season and type of cabin accommodation – which is obligatory on all crossings. Tickets start at £10 per person for a return ticket, plus at minimum a two-berth cabin with en-suite shower starting at £142 each way. Cars cost £80 each way.

Airlines, agents and operators

Airlines

Aer Lingus @ www.aerlingus.com.
Air New Zealand @ www.airnz.co.nz.
bmi @ www.flybmi.com.
British Airways @ www.ba.com.
Cimber Air @ www.cimber.com.
Continental Airlines @ www.continental.com.
Delta @ www.delta.com.
easyJet @ www.easyjet.com.
Emirates @ www.emirates.com.
Finnair @ www.finnair.com.
German Wings @ www.germanwings.com.
KLM (Royal Dutch Airlines) @ www.klm.com.
Lufthansa @ www.lufthansa.com.
Norwegian Air Shuttle @ www.norwegian.com.
Qantas @ www.qantas.com.
Ryanair UK ☎ 0871/246 0000, @ www.ryanair.com.
SAS (Scandinavian Airlines) @ www.flysas.com.
South African Airways @ www.flysaa.com.
Swiss @ www.swiss.com.
Thai Airways @ www.thaiair.com.
United Airlines @ www.united.com.

Agents and operators

North South Travel UK ☎ 01245/608 291, @ www.northsouthtravel.co.uk. Friendly, competitive travel agency, offering discounted fares worldwide. Profits are used to support projects in the developing world, especially the promotion of sustainable tourism.
Scantours UK ☎ 020/7839 2927, @ www.scantoursuk.com, US ☎ 1-800/223-7226, @ www.scantours.com. Huge range of package deals, hotel booking, customized itineraries, and city sightseeing tours.
STA Travel UK ☎ 0871/230 0040, US ☎ 1-800/781-4040, Australia ☎ 134 782, New Zealand ☎ 0800/474 400, South Africa ☎ 0861/781 781; @ www.statravel.com. Worldwide specialists in independent travel; also student IDs, travel insurance, car rental, rail passes, and more. Good discounts for students and under-26s.
Trailfinders UK ☎ 0845/058 5858, Ireland ☎ 01/677 7888, Australia ☎ 1300/780 212; @ www.trailfinders.com. One of the best-informed and most efficient agents for independent travellers.
Travel CUTS Canada ☎ 1-866/246-9762, US ☎ 1-800/592-2887, @ www.travelcuts.com. Canadian youth and student travel firm.
USIT Ireland ☎ 01/602 1906, Northern Ireland ☎ 028/9032 7111, @ www.usit.ie. Ireland's main student and youth travel specialists.

Rail and bus contacts

Eurolines UK ☎ 0871/781 8181, @ www.eurolines.com.
Europrail International Canada ☎ 1-888/667-9734, @ www.europrail.net. Rail passes and pre-booked tickets.
Eurostar UK ☎ 0870/518 6186, @ www.eurostar.com.
Rail Europe US ☎ 1-888/382-7245, Canada ☎ 1-800/361-7245, UK ☎ 0844/848 4064, Australia ☎ 03/9642 8644, South Africa ☎ 11/628 2319; @ www.raileurope.com.
The Man in Seat 61 @ www.seat61.com. Enthusiast-run site packed with information on all aspects of international rail travel.

Getting around

Although Denmark is largely made up of islands, travelling around the country is swift and straightforward. Public transport – trains, buses and the essential ferries – is punctual and efficient, and where you need to switch from one type to another, you'll find the timetables impressively well integrated.

And with Denmark being such a small country, you can get from one end to the other in half a day. Domestic airports are evenly spaced out, though given the ease of land transport, in-country flights are only really worth considering if you're really pushed for time or to catch connecting flights out of the country. Denmark is also very flat, with scores of villages linked by country roads that are ideal for effortless cycling.

By rail

With an exhaustive and reliable network run by the Danish state railway Danske Stats-baner (DSB; ☏70 13 14 15, ⓦwww.dsb.dk), **trains** are easily the most efficient and convenient way to travel in Denmark. InterRail and Eurail **passes** are valid on all routes except the few private lines that operate in some rural areas, on which they tend to afford substantial discounts (we've detailed these at relevant points in the Guide). There are just a few out-of-the-way regions that trains fail to penetrate, though these can be easily navigated by buses, which often run in conjunction with local train connections. Train passes are valid on bus services operated by DSB (for more on buses, see below).

Trains range from **inter-city express** services (**IC Lyn**), with a buffet car, to smaller **local trains** (**regionaltog**). Departure times are listed on notices both on station concourses and the platforms (departures in yellow, arrivals in white), and announced over loudspeakers. On the train, each station is usually called a few minutes before you arrive. Watch out for *stillekupé* – special quiet compartments where children, pets and mobile phones are prohibited.

Tickets should be bought in advance either from train stations – at ticket booths or automated machines; the latter take all major credit cards and only coins as cash – or online on ⓦwww.rejseplanen.dk although the actual purchasing page is in Danish only so you may need help from a local. Apart from on the train to Bornholm (see p.137) trains don't require advance seat reserva-tions (30kr; 25kr if bought online), but there's no guarantee that you'll get a seat if you don't make one. All trains have an inspector who checks tickets: he/she is almost certain to speak English and will normally be able to answer questions about routes and times. **Fares** are calculated on a zonal system. As a guide, one-way fares between Copenhagen and Odense cost 259kr; Copenhagen–Århus is 350kr. Both of these fares include the cost of a seat reservation, and your train ticket will also get you around on the local buses (and S-trains and Metro in Copenhagen)

in the departure and arrival town of your journey on the day the ticket is valid. The price of a return ticket is no cheaper than two one-ways. If you're under 26 and plan to do lots of train travel, it may be worthwhile buying a **DSB Wildcard** (180kr and valid for one year; only available online at ⓦwww.dsb .dk/wildcard – a Danish-only website), which gives you a fifty-percent discount Monday to Thursday and Saturday on normal cross-regional tickets (from Copenhagen to Lolland, for instance), and 25-percent discount when travelling Friday and Sunday. There are no other student discounts, but people over 65 qualify for the same discounts as Wildcard holders. Travelling in a group of eight or more also entitles you to a 25–30 percent discount – get details from any Danish tourist office. There are also great savings to be had with *Orange* tickets – a range of discount tickets that are available in limited numbers, at restricted times and routes. They are put on sale two months in advance of travel, so you'll need to be flexible with your travel times and book as early as possible in order to get one. Types of Orange discounts include one-day return tickets on journeys that involve crossing Storebælt; return tickets into Copenhagen from the commuter belt area; same-day return tickets to regional capitals from outlying areas; and discounted tickets to Bornholm. All but tickets to Bornholm can only be bought online (ⓦwww.dsb .dk – Danish only – click on the orange DSB Orange tab and enter your route and date, and it will come up with a list of options); an Orange ticket from Copenhagen to Århus, for instance, will only set you back 179kr while a standard costs 350kr.

Timetables detailing specific routes can be picked up for free at tourist offices and at train stations. Otherwise ⓦwww.rejseplanen .dk is easy to use.

By bus

There are only a handful of **long-distance bus** services in Denmark, though there are plenty of local buses that connect the regional centres with the surrounding countryside; all routes are detailed in the relevant Travel Details sections within the guide. Of the long-distance routes

Abildskous Rutebiler (☎70 21 08 88, ⓦwww.abildskou.dk) runs buses from Copenhagen to Århus (some via Ebeltoft), Aalborg (via Randers), Thisted (via Viborg and Nykøbing Mors), Silkeborg and Fjerritslev (via Randers, Hobro and Løgstør). As a guide to prices, a one-way ticket to Ebeltoft, Arhus and Silkeborg costs 280kr. **Bornholmerbussen** (☎44 68 44 00, ⓦwww.graahund bus.dk) runs a service between Copenhagen and **Bornholm** via the Øresunds Link and Ystad in Sweden (255kr one way). Some of the above offer discounts to students on less busy services. Fares represent quite a saving over full-price train tickets but, while just as efficient, long-distance buses are much less comfortable than trains.

Local buses really come into their own in the few areas where trains are scarce or connections complicated – much of Funen and northwest Jutland, for example. In Jutland, the excellent government-run **X-busser** (☎98 90 09 00, ⓦwww.xbus.dk) is especially useful, with a fast, efficient network that crisscrosses the peninsula.

By car

Given the excellent public transport system, the diminutive size of the country and the comparatively high price of petrol (around 9.90kr per litre at the time of writing), **driving** isn't really economical unless you're in a group. **Car rental** is expensive, though it's worth checking the cut-price deals offered by some airlines in conjunction with tickets. You'll need an international driving licence and must be aged at least 20 to take to the roads, although many firms won't rent to anyone under 25 – and some require you to be over 28. Costs start at around 3000kr a week for a small hatchback with unlimited mileage.

As for **rules of the road**, Danes drive on the right, and there's a speed limit of 50kph in towns, 80kph in open country and 110kph or 130kph on motorways. Dipped headlights need to be used at all times. There are random breath tests for suspected drunken drivers, and the penalties are severe. Note that in towns, a parking-time disc – which comes with all rental cars – must be displayed if you park anywhere that isn't metered; you can get the discs from petrol stations, police stations, and at banks,

where they have advertising on the back and are free; otherwise they cost around 20kr. You set the time when you've parked on the hands of the clock, then return before your allotted time (indicated by signs) is up.

The national motoring organization, Forenede Danske Motorejere, operates a 24-hour **breakdown service** (☎45 88 00 25) for AA members; if you're not an AA member, the Danish Road Directorate can be contacted from callboxes by the road, it will organize for the nearest roadside recue company to come and help you out. Call-out fees apply.

Hitching is illegal on motorways, but otherwise it's a fairly easy and reasonably safe way to get around, though thumbing a lift isn't very common these days.

Car-rental companies

Alamo ⓦwww.alamo.com.
Auto Europe ⓦwww.autoeurope.com.
Avis ⓦwww.avis.com.
Budget ⓦwww.budget.com.
Europcar ⓦwww.europcar.com.
Europe by Car ⓦwww.europebycar.com.
Hertz ⓦwww.hertz.com.
Holiday Autos ⓦwww.holidayautos.co.uk.
National ⓦwww.nationalcar.com
SIXT ⓦwww.sixt.com.

Cycling

If the weather is good, the best way to explore Denmark is to follow the locals and hop on a **bicycle**. The mostly flat, pastoral landscape lends itself beautifully to leisurely cycling, and a bike is also an easy and cheap way of getting around the towns. Traffic is sparse on most country roads, and all large towns have cycle tracks – though watch out for sometimes less-than-careful drivers on main roads. Remember also that **lights** are a legal requirement at night – you'll be stopped and fined if the police catch you without them. Bikes can be **rented** at nearly all youth hostels, campsites and tourist offices, at most bike shops and at some train stations for around 75kr per day or 300kr per week; there's often a 300kr–500kr refundable deposit, too. If you want to do some long-distance cycling (see p.32 for national cycle routes), take the frequent westerly winds into account when **planning**

your route – pedalling is easier facing east than west. The Danish cycling organization Dansk Cyklist Forbund (☎33 32 31 21, ⓦwww.dcf.dk) offers cycling advice and sells good informative maps of local and national cycling routes.

You can take bikes on all types of public transport except city buses. On trains, you'll have to pay according to the zonal system used to calculate passenger tickets – for example, 60kr to take your bike from Copenhagen to Århus, with 25kr on top if you reserve a place in advance, which you need to do at least two hours before departure; reserving is obligatory between May and August on all intercity express trains, and recommended all other times. The *Cykler i Tog* brochure (free from train stations) lists rates and rules in full. For a similar fee, long-distance buses have limited cycle space, while ferries let bikes on free or for a few kroner.

Ferries

Ferries connect all the Danish islands, and vary from the state-of-the-art catamaran linking Zealand and Jutland to raft-like affairs serving tiny, isolated settlements a few minutes off the (so-called) mainland. Where applicable, train and bus fares include the cost of ferry crossings (although you can also pay at the terminal and walk on), while the smaller ferries charge 25–75kr for foot passengers. We've detailed routes, fares and timings at the relevant places throughout the Guide.

Planes

Domestic flights are hardly essential in somewhere of Denmark's size, but can be handy if you're in a rush – it's less than an hour's flying time from Copenhagen to anywhere in the country. There are domestic airports at Aalborg, Århus, Billund, Karup, Sønderborg and Rønne, all of which are served by flights to and from Copenhagen. Billund has scheduled flights to Bornholm. **Airlines** operating domestic flights are SAS (☎70 10 20 00, ⓦwww.sas.dk), Cimber Air (☎70 12 12 18, ⓦwww.cimber.dk) and **Wings of Bornholm** (☎70 70 14 88, ⓦwww.wingsofbornholm.dk). **Fares** vary only slightly between the companies, although it can be worth looking for special offers. The longer in advance you book, the cheaper the flight, and you can get good deals, such as 261kr one-way from Copenhagen to Rønne on Bornholm. Weekend flights are generally cheaper than weekday ones.

Accommodation

Accommodation is going to be your major daily expense while in Denmark, and you should plan where you'll be staying carefully. Even if you're on a budget, hotels are by no means off-limits if you seek out the better offers, while hostels, sleep-ins and campsites are plentiful and of a uniformly high standard.

Note also that staying in a hotel means there won't be a curfew (common in some hostels in big cities), and that an all-you-can-eat breakfast – so large you won't need to buy lunch – is included in the rate, unless we've stated otherwise.

Wherever you stay (and especially in peak season), it's a good idea to bear in mind that rack rates are seldom charged if you **book in advance, online**. If you want to compare rates for specific dates, this is most easily done via the Danish tourist board website (see p.40). In less busy periods you can also save a fair deal by contacting local tourist offices for last-minute offers.

Accommodation price codes

The accommodation listed in this Guide has been graded according to the following price bands, based on the rack rate of the least expensive double room in summer.

❶ 200kr and under
❷ 201–300kr
❸ 301–400kr

❹ 401–500kr
❺ 501–600kr
❻ 601–850kr

❼ 851–1100kr
❽ 1101–1300kr
❾ 1301kr and over

Hotels

Visiting Denmark by way of a standard package trip, which includes accommodation as well as flights (see p.22 for operators) is one way to stay in a **hotel** without spending a fortune. Another is simply to be selective. Most Danish hotel rooms include TV and bathroom, for which you'll pay from around 700kr for a double (singles from around 450kr); going without the luxuries can result in big savings: in most towns you'll find hotels or hostels offering private rooms with access to a shared bathroom for as little as 400kr for a double (the same for a single). You'll find that rates may vary according to the season or day of the week, especially in the so-called "conference towns" where, outside the summer season (roughly mid-June to mid-Aug), hotels are packed with business travellers during the week (Mon–Thurs). In these towns, rates are reduced significantly during summer and on weekends. In the rest of the country, room rates tend to be some fifty percent higher during the summer season and over holidays.

Hostels and sleep-ins

Hostels (vandrerhjem) are Denmark's cheapest accommodation option bar camping. Almost every town has one, they're much less pricey than hotels, and they have a high degree of comfort – albeit basic. Most offer a choice of various sizes of private room, generally from two single beds to three bunk-beds, and often with private toilet and shower too; we've given price codes for these double rooms within the Guide, but expect to pay 300–650kr. All hostels also have shared dormitory-type accommodation with up to six beds in a room, for which you'll pay from 150kr per bed; dorms are only available during the summer season in some hostels. Nearly all hostels also have shared cooking facilities. Other than in major towns or ferry ports, it's rare for hostels to be full, but during the summer it's always wise to book in advance, and to check on location – some hostels are several kilometres outside the town centre.

As at all Scandinavian hostels, sleeping bags are not allowed, so you'll need to bring either a sheet sleeping-bag or rent hostel linen (45–55kr), which can become expensive over a long stay. It's a good idea, too, to get an **HI card**, since without one you'll be hit with either the cost of either an overnight card (35kr) or an annual Danhostel membership card (70kr). A year-long International HI membership costs 160kr and is available on the Hostelling International website (ⓦwww.hihostels.com). If you're planning on doing a lot of hostelling, it's worth contacting Danhostel Danmarks Vandrerhjem (☏33 31 36 12, ⓦwww.danhostel .dk) to get a copy of their free guide to Danish hostels, *Danmarks Vandrerhjem*, which is published in several languages including English; their informative free hostel/campsite map of Denmark is also useful.

Sleep-ins are a similarly cheap option if you're on a budget but don't want to camp. Originally run by the local authorities, sleep-ins are now just a more backpacker-oriented version of a hostel – privately run and generally full of young people. Some open between May and August only, but most now operate year-round. For bed and (shared) shower facilities, expect to pay around 120kr; bear in mind that you'll need your own sleeping bag, that in a few cases only one night's stay is permitted, and that there may be an age restriction (typically 16- to 24-year-olds only, although this may not be strictly enforced).

Private rooms and B&Bs

Tourist offices can supply lists of **private rooms** for rent in the homes of locals. Vaguely akin to British-style bed and breakfasts, these vary greatly in standard, but can be an easy way of getting to know the locals – whether you want to or not. The main thing to look out for is the distance to the town centre; some are far from the action, linked only by infrequent public transport options. Reckon on paying from 500kr for a double. Throughout the country, you'll come across places that call themselves **B&Bs** but are actually no different to private rooms; many of these are detailed online at ⓦwww .net-bb.dk, and there's also a separate B&B network on Funen. Note that despite the name, breakfast isn't included in any B&B or private room rates, and is only sometimes offered for an additional cost; there's often access to a kitchen, however.

Camping

Camping is by far the cheapest accommodation option in Denmark, and if the weather is good, it can really enhance the outdoor experience, as most sites are located near beaches or other beautiful natural landscapes. If you don't already have an International Camping Card from an organization in your own country, you'll need a Camping Card Scandinavia to camp in Denmark, which costs 100kr for both individuals and families, can be bought from any campsite and is valid on all official sites until the end of the year in which it was bought. A Transit Pass can be used for a single night's camping and costs 35kr. **Camping rough** without the landowner's permission is illegal and an on-the-spot fine may well be imposed. However, the Danish Forest and Nature Agency allows free (or max 15kr per person) low-impact camping in some 750 designated areas, so-called primitive campsites. Rules are strict: only two nights maximum at each site, only two tents per site, and the site has to be left as you found it. Go onto ⓦwww.friluftskort.dk for a map of designated areas and short descriptions – unfortunately this is only in Danish; local tourist offices should be able to advise if there are sites nearby.

Campsites (*campingplads*) can be found virtually everywhere. Most are open from April through to September, and a few all year round – we've indicated months of opening throughout the Guide. There's a rigid **grading system**: one-star sites have toilets and at least one shower; two-stars also have basic cooking facilities and a food shop within 2km; three-stars include a laundry; four-stars also have a shop and a TV room; while five-stars include a cafeteria and other facilities such as a swimming pool. **Prices** vary from 45 to 70kr per person, though you may pay more at city sites or those in other particularly popular locations. Most campsites also have **cabin accommodation**, usually small huts without bedding but with cooking facilities and some also with compact bathrooms; they're pleasant enough, and with prices from 2000kr for a six-berth affair for a week (350kr/day) they can represent a big saving especially for several people sharing, although on busy sites cabins are often booked up a year in advance. Most campsites also have full hook-ups for **trailers** and **camper vans**.

We've listed the best of the sites in the Guide, but any Danish tourist office can give you a free leaflet listing all the region's sites; there's also an official website ⓦwww .danskecampingpladser.dk where you can find details of all of the country's sites. For further information on camping, contact the national camping association, Campingrådet (☎39 27 88 44, ⓦwww.campingraadet.dk).

Holiday home rental

If you're planning to stay in the same area for a while, you may want to consider renting a **holiday home**. This is big business in Denmark with most of the country's picturesque coastline lined with homes only used by the owners for a couple of weeks a year, and rented out the rest of the time. Renting a holiday home is usually done through an agent, and you'll need to book months in advance for lets during the Danish holiday season. The local tourist office website will give you a list of agents in the area you want to be. A couple of well-respected countrywide **agencies** include Sol og Strand (☎99 44 44 44 44, ⓦwww.sologstrand.dk) and Dansommer (☎86 17 61 22, ⓦwww .dansommer.dk). The homes are usually well equipped (some even come with swimming pool and sauna) with duvets and pillows, but no covers. Holiday homes are rented by the week (from 2500kr), from Saturday to Saturday. The cleaning is up to you – either do it yourself or pay the agency to hire someone.

Food and drink

Although good food can be pretty pricey in Denmark, there are plenty of ways to eat well without breaking the bank, and with plenty of variety, too. Much the same applies to drink: the only Scandinavian country free of social drinking taboos, Denmark is an imbiber's delight – both for its huge choice of tipples, and for the number of places where they can be sampled.

Breakfast and brunch

Breakfast (*morgenmad*) can be the tastiest Danish meal – and the least meaty one, too. Almost all hotels offer a sumptuous breakfast as a matter of course – as do youth hostels, though the latter don't include breakfast in their rates, where you can often attack a buffet table laden with cereals, cheese, boiled eggs, fruit juice, milk, coffee and tea, and almost always freshly made bread, for around 50kr. Breakfast elsewhere will be far less substantial: many cafés offer a very basic set meal for around 30kr, but you're better off going for **brunch** instead. Served from around 10am until mid-afternoon, brunch is a delicious and filling option consisting of variations of international-style breakfasts (American, English etc), with plenty of fresh fruit and home-made bread – you'll spend upwards of 75kr, depending on your choices.

Lunch

You have two main choices when it comes to **lunch** (*frokost*) – hot or cold. In towns, the best way to find an inexpensive cooked lunch is simply to walk around and read the signs chalked up outside any café, restaurant or bar detailing the *dagens tilbud* or *dagens ret* – essentially the dish of the day – a plate of chilli con carne or lasagne for around 50kr, or a three-course set lunch from 90kr. You'll also find prices on finer dining significantly reduced at lunchtime compared to dinner, sometimes up to forty percent cheaper. The cold alternative is, for many, the highlight of a trip to Denmark – the delicious and quintessentially Danish **smørrebrød**, or open sandwich, best sampled in one of the many traditional smørrebrød restaurants, often open at lunchtime only. A selection of three or four slices (see *Danish food and drink* colour insert for examples) starts at about 110kr. A much less expensive alternative are the dedicated shops that sell readymade smørrebrød to take away (10–45kr per piece); many open until 10pm on weekdays. At cafés, you'll also be able to find a filling sandwich (30–50kr) or salad with fresh bread for 50–70kr, and in the winter there's always a daily soup on the menu (50–70kr).

Alternatively, eat on the hoof at one of the very popular **sausage stands** (*pølsevogn*) found on all main streets and at train stations. These serve various types of sausage (*pølser*) for 16–28kr: hot-dogs with trimmings such as roasted onion, remoulade and pickled cucumber; long, thin wieners; fatter *frankfurters*; or the dressing-soaked *franske* hot-dog.

Opening hours for cafés, restaurants and bars

Places that serve breakfast tend to open at 8am, if not earlier. For brunch, opening hours start from 9am onwards. Lunchtime service begins at noon and restaurants are open for the first dinner sitting at 6pm. Restaurant and café kitchens tend to be closed by 10pm, while bars stay open until midnight during the week, and until 2am or even 5am (if there's a dancefloor) during weekends. Most restaurants are shut at least one day a week, usually on Sundays or Mondays.

Throughout the Guide we have mentioned opening hours if they differ from what we list here.

Dinner

Dinner (*aftensmad*) can present a wide choice of cuisines, but the costs tend to be a lot higher than at lunch – although pizzerias and similar places charge the same in the evenings as during the day, and many youth hostels serve simple but filling meals for 50–75kr, though you have to order in advance. The most cost-effective dinner option (70–90kr), however, is usually an **ethnic restaurant** (most commonly Chinese or Middle Eastern, with a smaller number of Indian, Indonesian and Thai); as well as à la carte dishes, these often have a buffet table – ideal for gluttonous over-indulgence, and you usually get soup and a dessert thrown in as well. **Danish restaurants** that are promising for lunch often turn into expense-account affairs at night, offering an atmospheric, candlelit setting for the slow devouring of immaculately prepared meat or fish; you'll be hard-pushed to spend less than 200kr per person.

Danish pastries

One local speciality not to be missed is a **Danish pastry** (*wienerbrød*), tastier, lighter and much less sweet than the imitations sold abroad. Most cafés will serve reasonable versions, though they're best bought straight from the excellent and plentiful **konditorier** (patisseries) and eaten on the move or in the *konditori*'s coffee bar (see examples in the colour insert). **Coffee** (all Italian or French versions are widely available, as is freshly made filter coffee) or **tea** (including fruit and herbal brews) will cost 20–40kr.

Alcohol

If you've arrived in Denmark from near-teetotal Norway or Sweden, you're in for a shock. Not only is drinking **alcohol** entirely acceptable in Denmark, it's quite common to see people strolling along the pedestrianized streets swigging from a bottle of beer. Although extreme drunkenness is frowned upon, alcohol is widely consumed – albeit in moderation – throughout the day by all sections of society.

Bottled beer generally costs 20–30kr for a third of a litre, though the stronger **gold beer** (*guldøl*) costs 25–35kr per bottle. **Draught**

beer (*fadøl*) is more expensive, with a quarter of a litre costing 20–40kr, half a litre up to 80kr. It can be touch weaker than both types of bottled beer, but tastes fresher and is more popular. Most Danish beer is lager-style, the most common brands being Carlsberg and Tuborg, although a number of towns have their own locally brewed rivals. You'll also see special Christmas and Easter beers – stronger than normal to enhance the festive feel. The two days when they are released – "J-Day" and "P-Day" ("J" for "*Jul*" and "P" for "*Påske*" – Christmas and Easter respectively) see beer enthusiasts all around the country venturing out to taste the new offerings. If you prefer something weaker, there's also always a Lys Pilsner on offer, a very low-alcohol lager.

In recent years, an astounding number of **microbreweries** have popped up around the country, and produce a wide range of more adventurous ales, including some very similar to British-style bitter. Some of the best offerings are from Fur Brewery, Thisted Bryghus and GourmetBryggeriet in Roskilde. However, if you're after Guinness and genuine British draught beers, you'll find there's at least one themed Brit or Irish pub in most larger towns.

Wines and spirits

Most international **wines and spirits** are widely available in bars, a shot of the hard stuff costing 20–35kr, a glass of wine upwards of 25kr; but note that as most Danes drink wine with meals rather than socially, bars won't have the same range as restaurants. While in the country, you should also investigate the many varieties of **snaps**, a barley-based spirit that comes in various flavours, and is drunk ice-cold from a shot glass. Danes consume snaps eagerly, especially with smørrebrød, but more than two or three are likely to turn you pale if you're not used to it. A tasty relative is the gloriously spicy and strong Gammel Dansk Bitter Dram – snaps-based, but made with bitters, and drunk at breakfast time or as a pick-me-up during the day. In the winter, warm **gløgg** is also available in most bars. A spicy mulled wine prepared with snaps-soaked raisins and nuts, it's enjoyed with *æbleskiver*, deep-fried dough-balls with a slice of apple in the centre.

Festivals

Denmark's cities, villages and seaside towns come alive in the warmer months, when dozens of outdoor festivals and events are staged to take advantage of Scandinavia's extended daylight hours – and even the chillier months are made warmer with film, music and other cultural festivals to help get people out of their houses. The largest music festivals – and two of the biggest in Europe, in fact – are the Copenhagen Jazz Festival and the Roskilde Festival, held in late June/ early July. Equally, film festivals screening the latest arthouse movies alongside documentaries and features have become immensely popular over the last decade.

A festival calendar

January

Winter Jazz Festival ⓦ www.vinterjazz.dk. Late Jan to early Feb. With over 200 concerts in some fifty venues throughout the country, this ten-day winter festival attracts some of the biggest names in Danish and Scandinavian jazz.

March

Aalborg Opera Festival ⓦ www .aalborgoperafestival.dk. First two weeks. Denmark's only opera festival, with performances in concert halls, churches and cafés all over the city.
CPH PIX ⓦ www.cphpix.dk. Late March to late April. This two-and-a-half-week film festival featuring movies of all genres is the largest film event in Denmark, involving every single cinema in Copenhagen. Part of the programme is also screened in Odense, Aalborg and Århus.

April

Birthday of Queen Margrethe II, Copenhagen April 16. The queen's birthday is celebrated every year outside the Amalienborg Palace. Following the changing of the guard at noon, the royal family steps out onto the palace balcony to be greeted by thousands of flag-waving Danes chanting "Margrethe, Margrethe, kom nu frem, ellers går vi aldrig hjem" ("Margrethe, Margrethe, come on out, or we will never go home").

May

Aalborg Carnival ⓦ www.karnevaliaalborg.dk. Late May. Some 100,000 onlookers flock to this lively collection of parades and parties, when the city's canals are filled with groups of decorated boats, and music and dancing continues into the night in the central Kildeparken.
Copenhagen Carnival ⓦ www.karneval.dk. Late May. Samba and capoeira shows, salsa stages and kitschy, garish float parades, all held in the central Fælledparken park – Rio in Denmark.

June

Spot Festival, Århus ⓦ www.spotfestival.dk. Late May/early June. Staged at a dozen or so venues across central Århus and intended to promote pan-Scandinavian and Danish music, with concerts from around 100 groups over two days.
Riverboat Jazz Festival ⓦ www.riverboat.dk. Late June. Jazz played on and along the Gudenå River for five solid days. Predominantly traditional Dixieland and New Orleans jazz played in three large marquees in the town centre and on board a hugely festive riverboat.

July

Århus International Jazz Fest ⓦ www.jazzfest .dk. Mid-July. There's a small community feel at this ten-day festival, with concerts in small venues like cafés, tents, bars and arts-centre lobbies. Many of the musicians arrive straight from their shows at the larger Copenhagen Jazz Festival.
Copenhagen Jazz Festival ⓦ www.festival.jazz .dk. Early July. The capital's largest festival, with streets, outdoor spaces, bars and concert halls used as venues for everything from live bebop to post-industrial fusion, with spoken-word poetry and world music thrown in for good measure.
Langelandsfestival ⓦ www.langelandsfestival .dk. Late July. A coterie of mostly Danish rock bands play to an audience of around 25,000 on one of Denmark's most verdant islands.

Roskilde Festival ⓦ www.roskilde-festival.dk.
Late June/early July. One of the world's largest
music festivals, Roskilde is a massive party and loads
of fun. The lineup regularly features show-stopping
names such as Pink Floyd or The Strokes, plus
hundreds of smaller groups spread across six sound
stages over four days. See p.113.
Skagen Festival ⓦ www.skagenfestival.dk. Early
July. A lively festival featuring the latest in international
folk music, with dozens of groups playing Celtic,
bluegrass, zydeco and Scandinavian fiddle music.
Recent acts have included Runrig and Jim McCann.

August

Copenhagen Fashion Week ⓦ www
.copenhagenfashionweek.com. Early Aug. The
annual show for more than 2000 fashion designers
and clothing brands is the largest of its kind in the
Nordic countries. While the exclusive runway shows
are off-limits to the general public, the week is full of
associated events, talks and showings, and there are
sales at many of the city's clothes stores.
Copenhagen Pride ⓦ www.copenhagenpride
.dk. Early Aug. Annual gay pride parade with
thousands of spectators lining the streets while
gays and lesbians on colourful floats strut their stuff
through the capital.
Cultural Harbour ⓦ www.kulturhavn.dk. Early
Aug. Three days of dancing, music, theatre and
artistry aboard boats moored in Copenhagen's
harbour and on the quay.
Odense International Film Festival ⓦ www
.filmfestival.dk. Mid-Aug. One of Denmark's main
cinematic showcases, screening over 200 Danish and
foreign feature films, shorts and documentaries.
Skanderborg Festival ⓦ www.smukfest.dk.
Mid-Aug. Music fest in a gorgeous beech forest,
attended by some 50,000 people who come to hear
everything from folk to heavy metal and hip hop.
See p.215.
Tønder Festival ⓦ www.tf.dk. Late Aug. A superb
folk music festival held in Tønder on the banks of the
Vidå River, showcasing artists such as Steve Earle and
Arlo Guthrie. See p.200.

September

Architecture and Design Days ⓦ www.cphadd
.com. Early Sept. For five days, dozens of cultural

institutions and architecture firms lead tours of
Copenhagen's best buildings and pieces of fine
design.
Århus Festival ⓦ www.aarhusfestuge.dk. Early
Sept. One of Denmark's largest cultural events sees
dance, theatre, opera and art exhibitions take over the
city for ten days.
Copenhagen Golden Days ⓦ www.goldendays
.dk/festival. First three weeks of Sept. A unique
three-week festival that celebrates the influential
rule of Christian IV, and includes musical events,
theatre performances, exhibitions and city
walking tours.

October

Copenhagen Cultural Night ⓦ www
.kulturnatten.dk. Second Fri. Some 300 venues all
over the capital – churches, libraries, schools and
exhibition halls – open their doors and put on musical
shows, poetry readings, art exhibitions and other
cultural events.
Copenhagen Gay and Lesbian Film Festival
ⓦ www.cglff.dk. Late Oct. Copenhagen's oldest
film festival, this very popular event attracts a
diverse audience with its large number of dramas,
documentaries and animated shorts, to say nothing of
the legendary post-screening parties.

November

Copenhagen Irish Festival ⓦ www.irishfestival.
dk. Early Nov. A small festival that nonetheless
attracts some of the larger names in Irish and Celtic
folk music.
**Copenhagen International Documentary
Festival** ⓦ www.cphdox.dk. Mid-Nov. Denmark's
oldest documentary festival screens over 150
international films each year, and has established
itself as one of Europe's premier platforms for socially
conscious documentaries, many of which you'll be
hard-pressed to see anywhere else.

December

Copenhagen Christmas Fairs Nov–Dec. Not a
festival so much as a magical ethos that takes over
the entire city, with a prolific number of Christmas
markets and events, and the fairytale Tivoli Gardens
dressed in lights.

Sports and outdoor activities

Though it's connected to mainland Europe via a 68-kilometre border with Germany, Denmark is primarily made up of islands – over five hundred in total, a quarter of them inhabited – which, combined with scores of inland waterways, make for some excellent watery activities, from swimming, canoeing and kayaking to windsurfing and sailing. Denmark's interior consists of long stretches of undulating and varied terrain, with hedges, small trees and other flora providing shelter from the wind that blows in off the coast, allowing for invigorating coastal journeys by bike or on foot.

Cycling

Given its superb, rolling landscape of moors, hills and heaths, Denmark is easily the most enjoyable country in Europe for cycling, and riding is something of a national pastime here. You can find both leisurely and challenging riding on the network of eleven **national cycle routes**, which cover a total of 4325km. These lengthy, well-signed paths run along or near the country's major roadways and pass through some of its most important and interesting attractions, following lesser-trafficked tarmac, special cycle lanes or defunct rail lines. All are marked on the maps at the start of each chapter in this Guide.

A few **general rules** to keep in mind: lock up your bike even if you'll only be away from it for a few minutes, as bicycle theft is not uncommon, especially in the larger cities; there are cycle racks outside most commercial establishments in Denmark. Note also that cycling with a rucksack is very dangerous – instead, divide your luggage between side panniers (line them with plastic bags to avoid condensation). If you're cycling for long distances, remember to pack a pump, patches, a tyre lever, an extra tube, lights, a lock, sun cream, water bottles and of course a helmet. The churches along the national routes always have toilets and water and there are plenty of primitive campsites (see p.27) for kipping overnight. The Dansk Cyklist Forbund (Danish Cyclists' Association; ⓦwww.dcf.dk) has brochures and route maps on all aspects of cycling.

Hiking

Denmark currently has two designated national parks, Thy in West Jutland (see p.271) and Mols in East Jutland (see p.232) with three more imminent around Skjern Å in

---

Denmark's 11 National Cycle Routes

No. 1 The West Coast Route (560km; see maps on p.188, p.242 & p.268)

No. 2 Hanstholm to Copenhagen (420km; see maps on p.102, p.210 & 268)

No. 3 Hærvejen (450km; see maps on p.210 & p.188)

No. 4 Søndervig to Copenhagen (310km; see maps on p.102, p.210 & p.268)

No. 5 The East Coast Route, Skagen to Sønderborg (650km; see maps on p.188, p.210 & p.242)

No. 6 Esbjerg to Copenhagen (330km; see maps on p.268, p.154 & p.102)

No. 7 Sjællands Odde to Rødby (240km; see map on p.102)

No. 8 Rudbøl to Møn (360km; see maps on p.102, p.154 & p.268)

No. 9 Helsingør to Gedser (290km; see map on p.102)

No. 10 Touring Bornholm (105km; see map on p.136)

No. 11 The Limfjord Route (610km; see map on p.268)

West Jutland, the Waddensea area along the West Jutland coast (see p.198), and the north Zealand area (see p.108). These are all criss-crossed by bark- or gravel-covered **walking** or cycling paths. But there are numerous other protected and state-owned conservation areas and natural forests, such as Rebild Bakker in North Jutland (see p.244), which are ideal for a couple of days' hiking. See the *Denmark's Great Outdoors* colour insert for some recommendations. Check ⓦwww .haervej.dk for campsite details and maps. For more information, visit the Danish Ramblers' Association (ⓦwww.dvl.dk).

Swimming and beaches

Over 7000km of coastline – an amazing amount considering Denmark's relatively small landmass – allows for excellent **swimming** opportunities. Nearly all beaches are spotlessly clean, with wide stretches of silky sand and negligible undertow (except on Jutland's west coast) See the *Denmark's Great Outdoors* colour insert for our selection of the country's best beaches. The warm months of July and August are probably the most pleasant for swimming, though the water doesn't reach its peak temperature until September. Winter bathing is something of an institution among Danes, who hack through the ice, jump in, and then rush into hot saunas run by the local winter bathing club afterwards. There are clubs in Copenhagen (by Amager Strandpark), Århus (near the harbour) and most other large coastal towns. Ask at the local tourist office for information about nearby clubs. Note that **nude bathing** is fairly common, and that nudist beach areas are not always separate from standard ones, though most of them are signed in some way.

Canoeing and kayaking

Kayaking and canoeing along Denmark's many rivers and waterways is a popular summertime activity, and there are numerous outlets at which to rent equipment. **Canoeing** is best along the placid Suså river (see p.124), which wends its way through Zealand's central and southern heartland, and the Gudenåen (see p.219), Denmark's longest river. **Kayakers** are better off in inshore waters like the

Helnæs Bay, though if you're experienced you might want to try a trip across the Svendborg sound (see p.170) to one of the southern Funen isles. A more laid-back option is a canal kayak tour of Copenhagen (see p.51).

Windsurfing and paragliding

As suggested by the thousands of modern turbine windmills you'll see here, Denmark is a windy place, and boasts some of the best conditions for **windsurfing** on the continent. Beginners will want to head to the protected shores and inlets, while those with more experience will find more enjoyment on the open coast. Not all of the major beaches have places that rent out equipment, however, so it's best to head to Klitmøller (see p.271) or the northern edge of Hvide Sande (see p.276), both with established windsurfing scenes and places where you can have a lesson (around 400kr for 3hr, including equipment) or will rent you gear to head out on your own (000kr/day). There are also good spots in Fyns Hoved (see p.168), southern Langeland (see p.179) and Ebeltoft bay (see p.232). Given all the extra wind blowing around, **hang-gliding** and **paragliding** have become popular activities among Danes, as has **kite surfing**, this last best at either Klitmøller or Hvide Sande where lessons are available (250kr for two hours). For up-to-date information, contact the Danish Hang gliding and Paragliding Union (ⓦwww.danskdrageflyverunion.dk).

Fishing

With some of the best fishing in Europe, Denmark is a great place to go angling. To **fish** in Denmark's coastal waters, fjords and national rivers, you must first apply for a licence, available at most local tourist offices. These are valid for a day (35kr), a week (100kr) or a year (140kr). Natural lakes and streams are usually privately owned, but local angling societies will issue temporary angling passes for a nominal fee (40kr–150kr/day or 100kr–350kr/week). Note that you can fish from anywhere along the Danish coast as long as there is a public road which leads to the shore and a legitimate beach between the water and any farmland.

Several companies organize **sea-fishing** tours from Copenhagen, Helsingør, Korsør and Frederikshavn; for more on these, and general fishing information, enquire at tourist offices. Mackerel, cod and sea trout are the most common open-sea fish, though you will also find eel, turbot, plaice and flounder. Jutland's west coast is good for cod, flatfish, garfish and mackerel, and its east coast and Lake District are known for salmon, pike and bass; Limfjorden in the north tends to have more variety. Funen has sea trout and fat-bellied cod, best in the Langeland belt, and you can find herring in the Lillebælt, Storebælt and Langelandbælt. Zealand has larger varieties of cod, plus carp, whitefish pike and zander. Bornholm's various fjords, bays, inlets and open coastline are perfect habitats for silver sea trout.

For **freshwater** varieties, Denmark's many lakes and rivers are filled with pike, perch, zander and trout, most abundantly in the waterways of Jutland. For **fly fishing**, try the Gudenåen, Karup and Storå rivers in Jutland. The best resource on fishing is ⓦwww.sportsfiskeren.dk, the website of the Danish Angling Society.

Horseriding

Horseriding in Denmark can be a lovely way of seeing the country's spectacular scenery; head for the grasslands that front the north Jutland coast at Hirtshals, the trails along the island of Rømø or the multitude of paths in Zealand's deciduous Gribskov forest. Horseriding outfits are fairly common (we've listed them in relevant places in the Guide), with most charging around 100kr/hr for a ride on an Icelandic horse – the most common breed in Denmark and great for first-timers as they tend to be rather stocky and quite amicable.

Golf

Denmark's rippling landscape is perfectly suited to **golfing**, though you may find the greens on the country's seventeen courses far flatter than those elsewhere. Courses generally charge around 300kr for eighteen holes, though this may be a bit higher on weekends when the greens are at their busiest. You're likely to be asked for some documentation of your handicap or membership in a club at home, though such procedures are often waived for tourists. Be prepared to walk, as electric golf carts are rare. Of the country's best courses, there's the Copenhagen Golf Club, adjacent to lush woodlands just outside the city centre. The course in Odense is particularly large, and those at Harre Vig and on Bornholm are the most picturesque. The Danish Golf Union (ⓦwww.dgu.org) has details of the country's courses.

Culture and etiquette

Like its Scandinavian neighbours, Denmark is a modern European nation whose history has nevertheless brought about a number of subtle social and cultural differences that can throw even the most anthropologically aware of travellers.

Much social interaction among Danes is governed, at least to some extent, by the doctrine of **Janteloven** ("The Law of Jante"), a sort of unwritten code of behaviour coined by Dano-Norwegian author Aksel Sandemose in the 1930s, and based on his observations of Danish society. In general, Janteloven describes the sort of egalitarian comportment visible in Norway, Denmark and to some extent, Sweden, in which hubris, bragging and personal celebration are frowned upon, and sometimes even a difference of opinion will go unvoiced. The sentiment is that placing oneself higher than another member of society is a conceit that works against the values of the egalitarianism regarded as fundamental to Scandinavian societies, but many self-critical Danes – especially those who've made the choice to settle abroad – would argue that such conduct breeds mediocrity and stifles entrepreneurial thought and creativity. Such behaviour should, however, be understood in its historical context: there's a long tradition of social equality here, which has helped maintain a sense of solidarity in this territorially fractured country.

But all this talk of adherence to strict social mores shouldn't suggest that Danes are in any way unfriendly or antisocial. In fact, among the Nordic countries, they are probably the most welcoming to foreigners, a hospitality best described by the Danish precept of **hygge** (the oft-given English translation of "cosiness" doesn't quite do it justice), which sort of suggests a mixture of conviviality and intimacy. You'll sense *hygge* when you sit sipping hot *gløgg* in a toasty warm candlelit café while snow is falling outside, or around a midsummer's eve bonfire with people chitchatting and the odd traditional folksong being sung.

Danes often greet each other with a simple, informal "hej", a **standard greeting** that is a mite less colloquial than the English "hi". There is no single word in the Danish language for "please" – so when a Dane doesn't use it when speaking to you in English, it's not because they're rude – the word just doesn't come naturally. Danes are also renowned for being direct and to the point, which can sometimes be interpreted as impolite – if they want something, they'll for instance say "giv mig…" ("give me…").

Travel essentials

Children

Denmark is a child-friendly country and even the more exclusive cafés and restaurants have highchairs, changing facilities and a children's menu. The low level of traffic and many pedestrianized streets also mean Denmark is an easy country to explore with kids both on foot and, given the proliferation of dedicated cycle lanes and routes, by bike.

Top attractions for kids
Tivoli (p.71) **Legoland** (p.214) **Den Fynske Landsby** (p.160) **Den Gamle By** (p.225) **Bakken** (p.96) **Experimentarium** (p.78) **Zoos** in Copenhagen (p.75) Aalborg and Odense (p.160)

Danish beaches are also, on the whole, child-safe. The water tends to be shallow, and the waters at all (bar those on the west coast) are generally very calm.

Most of the country's museums cater for children in some way: many have dedicated children's sections, others are specifically geared towards children, so travelling with kids doesn't mean that you'll miss out on the country's cultural side.

Costs

There's no getting away from the fact that Denmark is an **expensive** country, although you can cut costs substantially if you spend wisely. If you stay in youth hostels or campsites and don't eat out, it's possible to get by on £35/US$60/€40 per day. Otherwise, staying in inexpensive hotels, moving around the country visiting museums, eating in a restaurant each day and buying a few snacks and going for a drink in the evening, you can expect to spend a minimum of £55–70/US$90–115/€60–75 per day. Going up a notch, staying in a mid-range hotel, eating lunch and dinner at restaurants and/or cafés, doing a couple of museums during the day, and maybe catching a club at night will set you back substantially more – expect to spend at least £110–135/US$180–225/€120–150 per day.

Crime and personal safety

Denmark is one of the most peaceful countries in Europe. Most public places are well lit and secure, the majority of people genuinely friendly and helpful, and street crime and hassle relatively rare. Like most large cities, Copenhagen, Århus, Aalborg and Odense have their share of **petty crime**, but keep an eye on your cash and passport and you should have little reason to visit the **police**. If you do, you'll find them courteous, concerned and usually able to speak English. If you have something stolen, make sure you get a **police report** – essential if you are to make an insurance claim.

As for offences you might commit, being drunk on the streets can get you arrested, and drinking and driving is treated especially rigorously. Drug offences, too, meet with the same strict attitude that prevails throughout the rest of Europe.

Disabled travellers

In many ways, Denmark is a model destination for disabled travellers: wheelchair access is generally available at hotels, hostels, museums and public places, and Danes are usually happy to assist in other ways. To see whether a place caters for travellers with disabilities, check the useful tourist-office-financed website W ww.godadgang .dk. Clicking the Inspiration tab at W www .visitdenmark.dk brings up the Disabled travel in Denmark page, with details about access to public transport and much more.

Electricity

The Danish electricity supply runs at 220–240V, 50Hz AC; sockets generally require a two-pin plug. Visitors from the UK will need an adaptor; visitors from outside the EU may need a transformer.

Entry requirements

European Union, US, Canadian, Australian and New Zealand citizens need only a valid **passport** to enter Denmark for up to three months. South African citizens must obtain **visas** from the embassy in Pretoria (see below) before travelling. All other nationals should consult the relevant embassy about visa requirements.

For **longer stays**, EU nationals can apply for a residence permit while in the country, which, if it's granted, may be valid for up to five years. Non-EU nationals can only apply for residence permits before leaving home, and must be able to prove they can support themselves without working.

In spite of the lack of restrictions, checks are frequently made on travellers at the major points of entry. If you're young and are carrying a rucksack, be prepared to prove that you have enough money to support yourself during your stay. You may also be asked how long you intend to stay and why.

Danish embassies and consulates abroad

Australia and New Zealand 15 Hunter St, Yarralumla, Canberra ACT 2600 ☎ 02/6270 5333, W www.canberra.um.dk.
Canada 47 Clarence St, Suite 450, Ottawa, Ontario K1N 9K1 ☎ 613/562-1811, W www .ambottawa.um.dk.
Ireland 7th floor Block E Iveagh Court, Harcourt Rd, Dublin 2 ☎ 01/475 6404, W www.ambdublin .um.dk.
South Africa Parioli Office Park, Block B2, Ground Floor, 1166 Park St, Pretoria ☎ 012/430 9340, W www.ambpretoria.um.dk.
UK 55 Sloane St, London SW1X 9SR ☎ 020/7333 0200, W www.denmark.org.uk.
US 3200 Whitehaven St NW, Washington DC 20008 ☎ 202/234-4300, W www.denmarkemb.org.

Gay and lesbian travellers

Denmark legalized **homosexuality** in 1930 and it was the first country in the world to legalise same-sex partnerships (in 1989). Danish society is accordingly very tolerant of homosexuality – many Danes pride themselves on their liberal attitudes, and heads won't generally turn if a gay or lesbian couple are seen kissing or holding hands. This liberal attitude has led to Copenhagen becoming one of the world's **premier gay cities** – its emancipated attitude is best illustrated by the way the main cruising spot, H.C. Ørstedsparken, has been equipped with "birdboxes" containing condoms and lubricating gel, while police patrols here are instructed not to chase out cottaging men, but to protect them from homophobic violence.

Paradoxically, Denmark's liberal traditions mean that there are fewer specifically gay and lesbian venues than in less tolerant cities, and that everything tends to be more mixed. For general **information**, the national organization for gays and lesbians, the Landsforeningen for Bøsser og Lesbiske (LBL), Nygade 7 In Copenhagen (☎33 13 19 48, ⊛www.lbl.dk), is an excellent place to pick up news of any gay- or lesbian-oriented events in the country. LBL runs a very useful listings website (⊛www.gayguide.dk). Readily available at all major gay hangouts is the monthly *Out and About* magazine – mostly in Danish – with dozens of handy listings, fairly easy to decipher even if you don't speak Danish.

Health

Health care in Denmark is superb. With the exception of some specialist hospitals in the capital (see p.94 for details of Copenhagen's provision), most hospitals **have emergency departments**, providing free treatment for EU and Scandinavian nationals, though citizens of other countries are unlikely to have to pay. For **medical emergencies**, call ☎112.

If you need a **doctor or dentist**, the local tourist office will give you details of those on call, and local practitioners are listed in each area's tourist office brochure. Outside tourist office opening hours, or if you don't have the brochure, call ☎112. Doctors' fees start at 250kr, to be paid in cash; dentist fees start at 200kr and can be paid with cash or cards. If you're an EU citizen and you have a European Health Insurance Card (EHIC) – available from post offices in your home country – you can claim back doctors' fees and charges for medicine from the local health department. You'll need to produce the relevant receipts and card.

Most larger towns and all cities have 24-hour **pharmacies**, which we've detailed throughout the Guide.

Insurance

A typical travel insurance policy usually provides cover for the loss of baggage, tickets and – up to a certain limit – cash or cheques, as well as cancellation or curtailment of your journey. Before paying for a new policy, it's worth checking whether you are already covered. Some all-risks home insurance policies may cover your possessions when overseas, and many private medical schemes include cover when abroad. In Canada, provincial health plans usually provide partial cover for medical mishaps overseas, while holders of official student/teacher/youth cards in North America are entitled to meagre accident coverage and hospital in-patient benefits. Students will often find that their student health coverage extends during the vacations and for one term beyond the date of last enrolment.

Rough Guides travel insurance

Rough Guides has teamed up with WorldNomads.com to offer great **travel insurance** deals. Policies are available to residents of over 150 countries, with cover for a wide range of **adventure sports**, 24hr emergency assistance, high levels of medical and evacuation cover and a stream of **travel safety information**. Roughguides.com users can take advantage of their policies online 24/7, from anywhere in the world – even if you're already travelling. And since plans often change when you're on the road, you can extend your policy and even claim online. Roughguides.com users who buy travel insurance with WorldNomads.com can also leave a positive footprint and donate to a community development project. For more information go to ⊛**www.roughguides.com/shop**.

Internet

Denmark has plenty of wireless hubs in cafés and bars and on board all trains. Most hotels and hostels – and even some campsites – offer wireless access (some for free) or some other form of internet access, and access is also available **free** at libraries (though not the Royal Library in Copenhagen). Larger airports, train stations and shopping malls also have wireless access zones.

Mail

Like most other public bodies in the country, the Danish **post office** runs an exceedingly tight ship – within Denmark, anything you post is almost certain to arrive the next day. You can buy stamps from most newsagents, and from post offices. Mail under 50g costs 8kr to other parts of Europe, and 9kr to the rest of the world.

Maps

The **maps** in this book should be adequate for most purposes, but drivers, cyclists and hikers will require something more detailed. Local tourist offices give out free reasonable city and regional maps, but for anything better you'll have to pay.

The best city maps are produced by Kraks, either in booklet or folding form and at various scales; they're updated yearly. Country maps are produced by Kümmerley & Frey (1:300,000), Ravenstein (1:500,000), and Baedeker (1:400,000). The Danish Youth Hostel Association also produces a very informative country map (including all hostels, campsites, ferry links and cycle routes), which you can order free of charge from ⓦ www.danhostel .dk. Detailed maps of all the **regions** are covered by the 1:200,000 Kort og Matrikel-styren map published by Aschehoug. The Danish Cyclist Organization, Dansk Cyklist Forbund (see details, p.32) also sells good

regional maps and booklets of recommended cycle routes.

Money

The Danish currency is the **krone** (plural kroner). It's made up of 100 øre, and comes in notes of 1000kr, 500kr, 200kr, 100kr and 50kr, and coins of 20kr, 10kr, 5kr, 2kr, 1kr, 50øre and 25øre. At the time of writing, the exchange rate was approximately 8.30kr to the pound, 7.40kr to the euro and 5.05kr to the US dollar. For the latest rates, go to ⓦ www.xe.com

Red Kontanten high-street cash machines (**ATMs**) give cash advances on credit cards and, if you've a Link, Cirrus or Maestro symbol on your ATM card, will allow you to withdraw funds from your own account in local currency (check with your home bank), which can work out cheaper than changing cash or travellers' cheques.

For the latter, banks (Mon–Wed & Fri 10am–4pm, Thurs 10am–6pm) charge a uniform commission of 30kr per transaction, so change as much as is feasible in one go. Copenhagen's airport and Central Station have late-opening exchange facilities, which charge a similar amount of commission. **Forex** exchange bureaux charge 30kr to exchange cash and only 20kr to exchange travellers' cheques, but are much rarer. See the relevant accounts in the Guide for details.

Newspapers and magazines

For a country of its size, Denmark has an impressive number of **newspapers**. Of most interest to non-Danish speakers is the **English-language** *Copenhagen Post* (ⓦ www.copenhagenpost.dk), which covers domestic issues and has an in-depth listings section; it comes out every Friday and costs 20kr. Of the main Danish-language dailies, *Politiken* and the Thursday edition of *Informa-tion* carry excellent entertainment **listings**.

Public holidays

New Year's Day; Maundy Thursday; Good Friday; Easter Sunday; Easter Monday; Common Prayer Day (fourth Friday after Easter); Ascension Day (fifth Thursday after Easter); Whit Sunday and Whit Monday (seven weeks after Easter); Constitution Day (June 5); Christmas (December 24–26).

Calling home from abroad

Note that the initial zero is omitted from the area code when dialling the UK, Ireland, Australia and New Zealand from abroad.

Australia international access code + 61
New Zealand international access code + 64
UK international access code + 44
US and Canada international access code + 1
Ireland international access code + 353
South Africa international access code + 27

The free **music** magazine *Gaffa* (monthly) lists most of the bigger concerts; you can find it in cafés, record shops and the like.

In Copenhagen, **overseas newspapers** are sold at the Magasin du Nord department store, Illum department store, the stall on the eastern side of Rådhuspladsen, and newsagents along Strøget and in newsagents at Central Station, which also stock foreign magazines. Most UK and US weekday titles cost 25–40kr and are available the day after publication.

Opening hours and public holidays

Shop **opening hours** are Mon–Thurs 9/10am–5.30/6pm, Fri 9/10am–6/7/8pm and Sat 9am–noon/1/2pm; hours are usually shorter outside the bigger cities. Supermarkets stay open a bit later, and some open on Sunday. Shops are allowed to open on the first Saturday of the month until 5pm, but it only tends to be inner-city shops that have taken this up. Shopping malls tend to stay open until 7/8pm during the week.

Most shops and businesses are closed on **public holidays** (see box opposite), when public transport services are also reduced.

Phones

You should be able to use your **mobile phone** in Denmark if it's been connected via the GSM system common to the rest of Europe, Australia, New Zealand and South Africa. Check with your phone company, however, as some mobiles are barred from international use. The North American mobile network is not compatible with the GSM system, so you'll need a tri-band phone that will be able to switch from one

band to the other. If you plan to make a lot of mobile calls while in Denmark, you could also invest in a Danish SIM card for use in your phone; these are available in all mobile phone shops. For 99kr, you'll get a Danish number plus about forty minutes of domestic calling time. The most commonly used network is TDC (the national landline network), but coverage with Telemore, Telia and others is just as good. Top-up cards can be bought in supermarkets, kiosks and phone shops.

Calling Denmark from abroad, the **international code** is ☎45; codes for international calls from Denmark are given above. To make a **collect international call**, dial ☎80 30 40 00 for the operator and ask to be connected to the operator in your own country, who will then put through the collect call – full instructions for this "Country Direct" system are displayed in phone booths (in English), and you can dial ☎80 60 40 50 for free assistance. For directory enquiries within Denmark your best bet is to try a phone book (there should be one in all public phone booths), the national phone company's website (@www .tdc.dk), or the online (Danish-language) yellow pages (@www.degulesider.dk).

Smoking

While Danes have made themselves known as some of Europe's staunchest opponents to **smoking** restrictions, the country has progressed more or less along with other European countries in public smoking reform, and you'll find fewer smokers than in, say, France or Italy. Cigarettes (around 40kr per packet) are sold at kiosks, grocers' shops and petrol stations. All trains and buses in Denmark are non-smoking, and smoke-free places are popping up everywhere as the country catches up with social health concerns. In January 2007, smoking was banned in all government ministries, shopping centres, cultural centres and many larger cafés, bars and restaurants, though these last are allowed to set up special sections for smoking patrons.

Taxes

A sales tax (MOMS) of 25 percent is added to almost everything you buy – but it's always included in the price. Non-EU citizens can claim a refund at the airport, provided you fill out a Global Refund Cheque at the point of purchase.

Time

Denmark is one hour ahead of GMT, six hours ahead of US Eastern Standard Time, and nine ahead of US Pacific Standard Time.

Tipping

Service is included on all restaurant, hotel and taxi bills, so unless you feel you've been given an exceptionally good service, adding anything on is not necessary – though a tip will obviously be appreciated.

Tourist information

Denmark's tourist offices (Ⓦwww .visitdenmark.dk) have heaps of free information leaflets and magazines that they will post out to you if you request them online. They can also point you in the right direction should you have any special travel requirements, or need information about special events. We've detailed local offices throughout the Guide.

Guide

Guide

① Copenhagen and around

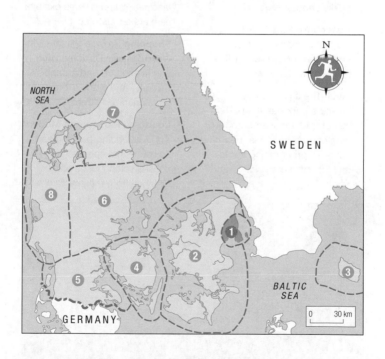

CHAPTER 1 # Highlights

* **Nyhavn** Enjoy a beer or lunch in one of the many lively cafés, restaurants and bars in the colourful gabled houses lining this picture-postcard canal. See p.65

* **Christiania** A beguiling sprawl of twisting paths lined with mural-bedecked houses, laid-back cafés and bars and quirky shops. See p.66

* **Rosenborg Slot** Check out the rich royal history and dazzling crown jewels at this fairytale castle. See p.67

* **Tivoli** The city's beloved pleasure park has the perfect mix of traditional and modern fairground attractions, beautiful gardens, great eating spots and lots of live music. See p.71

* **Ny Carlsberg Glyptotek** Rodin sculptures, Roman and Etruscan treasures and French Impressionist paintings as well as a stunning, palm-filled café. See p.72

* **The National Museum** From Viking treasure to Ancient Egyptian statues, Inuit harpoons to Chinese tea-sets, the fascinating and diverse exhibits here are a must-see. See p.73

* **Shopping** Browse the latest in world-famous Danish design and fashion on and around Strøget – the world's longest pedestrianized street. See p.90

* **Louisiana Museum of Modern Art** Outstanding painting and sculpture in a spectacular coastal setting just a short distance from the city. See p.97

▲ Nyhavn

Copenhagen and around

S ituated halfway down the eastern side of Zealand and just 11km from Kastrup International Airport, on the adjacent island of Amager, Denmark's small yet outward looking and vibrant capital **Copenhagen** (København) is the arrival point for most visitors to Denmark and, with its excellent transport connections, the natural starting point for onward travel. Even though it only has a population of around one million, it's Denmark's one truly large city and a stark contrast to the sleepy provincialism of the rest of the country. That said, it's a remarkably easy and relaxing place to spend time in – unlike most European capitals, walking between all of the major sights is a viable option, and large sections of the city centre are pedestrianized – and should you need it, there's a reliable and efficient public transport system. What's more, you're just a short ride away from some beautiful sandy beaches and open green countryside, while the city's lovely, revamped harbourfront and numerous canals and lakes offer plenty of options for waterside relaxation.

Historically, the city owes its existence to its position on the narrow Øresund strait, which separates Denmark from Sweden – one of the great trading routes of medieval Europe and now the site of the region's grandest engineering feat, the massive **Øresund bridge**, which connects the city by road and rail to the Swedish town of Malmö. It's this location, poised between Scandinavia and the rest of Europe, that gives Copenhagen its distinctive character. Compared to the relatively staid capitals further north, Copenhagen has a laid-back, European flavour; the freedom with which its most famous export, Carlsberg, flows in the city's hundreds of bars is in stark contrast to the puritanical licensing laws found elsewhere in Scandinavia. Yet Copenhagen is also a flagship example of the Scandinavian commitment to liberal social values – exemplified by its relaxed attitudes to everything from gay marriage to pornography – and its continued (if precarious) respect for the unique "free city" of Christiania.

Like most European cities, Copenhagen is facing modern changes. The most significant is a burgeoning immigrant community, which has brought on a degree of racial tension in certain areas of the city and a resulting rise in the success of right-wing politicians – both of which pose challenges to the city's tolerant image. For all that, it's worth remembering that the city's occasional smugness and resistance to change is the result of its citizens' pride in their capital – as a visitor, you'll be made to feel welcome wherever you go, especially since absolutely everybody speaks English.

The area **around Copenhagen** – either in its outlying suburbs or slightly further afield – offers some easily accessible sights well worth seeing on day-trips. Just to the north, along the Øresund coast, stretch a series of well-heeled suburbs: a visit to their attractions can be followed up by lazing on the adjacent beaches. Further north up the coast is the stunning modern art museum of Louisiana, while to the south of the city, another bastion of contemporary art, Arken, occupies an equally fabulous seafront location. All of this offers a taster for the rest of Zealand, covered in Chapter Two.

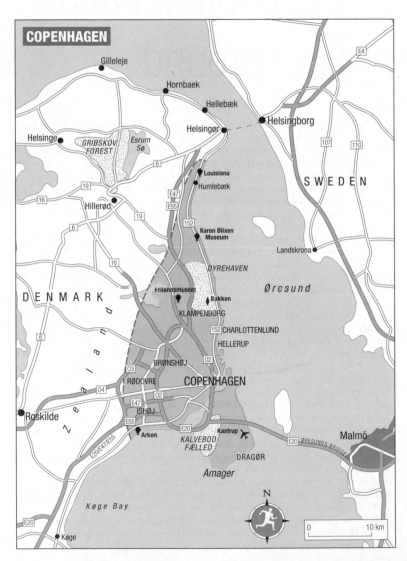

Copenhagen

Small, compact and easily explored **COPENHAGEN** (København) is a capital city on a thoroughly human scale with a skyline largely unchanged for centuries and a remarkably relaxed, unhurried vibe – people rather than cars set the pace here, with a multitude of pedestrianized thoroughfares, cycle lanes and pavement cafes. And though, Little Mermaid aside, most people would be hard pressed to name a landmark building or monument, that's just part of the city's understated charm – there's a cornucopia of historic royal palaces, museums, art galleries, sprawling parks and even beaches to be discovered, and, what's more, all are within walking distance or a short bus ride of each other. The vibrant harbourfront is undergoing a wave of renovations that has seen three new major cultural institutions built in the last decade; there's a renewed focus and leadership on environmental issues; while, at street level, the city boasts a range of chic hotels, an increasingly varied culinary scene, revamped museums and fabulous shops showcasing the country's outstanding design talent. What's more, there's a range of nightlife that belies the city's relatively modest size with plenty of cosy bars, intimate clubs and live music venues.

Much of Copenhagen dates from the seventeenth and eighteenth centuries, a cultured ensemble of handsome Renaissance palaces, parks and merchants' houses laid out around the waterways and canals that give the city, in places, a pronounced Dutch flavour. Successive Danish monarchs left their mark, in particular Christian IV, creator of many of the most striking landmarks including Rosenborg Slot and the district of Christianshavn; and Frederik V, who graced the capital with the palaces of Amalienborg and the grandiose Marmorkirken.

Arrival and information

However you **arrive** in Copenhagen, you'll find yourself within easy reach of the city centre. Copenhagen airport is just a few kilometres southeast on the edge of the island of Amager, while almost all trains and buses deposit you near the city's main transport hub, Central Station, right in the heart of the city.

By air

Getting into the city from Copenhagen **airport** (Ⓦ www.cph.dk), 11km southeast of the city in the suburb of Kastrup, couldn't be easier. A rail line runs regularly to Central Station (10–13min; 31,50kr), while the fast new metro line links the airport with Christianshavn (12min), Kongens Nytorv (13min) and Nørreport (15min) stations (all 31,50kr) in the centre. There's also a much slower city bus (#5A 31,50kr; #96N night bus, 63kr) to Rådhuspladsen and Nørreport station, which is only really convenient if you want to get off on the way. A taxi to the centre will cost about 180kr – there's a rank outside arrivals. There's a **left-luggage** facility in the walkway between terminals 2 and 3 (40kr per day, max one month), and small and large lockers for 30kr and 50kr per day respectively (max 3 days).

Inside arrivals, the helpful **information desk** (daily: June–Aug 5am–midnight; Sept–May 6am–11pm) has free maps of the city and runs an efficient **hotel booking service** (70kr) in conjunction with the tourist office (see p.49) with some very good last-minute deals. The airport also has two late-opening **banks** (daily 6am–10pm), ATMs, car-rental agencies (see p.93) and a post office.

By bus and train

All buses and trains to Copenhagen arrive at or near the **Central Station** (in Danish, Hovedbanegården or København H), the city's main transport hub, from where there are excellent connections to virtually every part of the city via bus or local train – but note, not the new metro (see p.52). The station is also home to an array of shops, a foreign-exchange bureau (daily 8am–9pm), a bicycle-rental service (see p.53), places

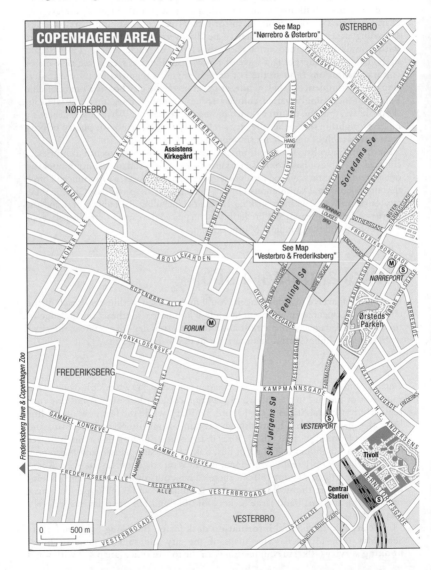

to eat and, downstairs, left-luggage lockers (Mon–Sat 5.30am–1am, Sun 6am–1am; 35kr or 45kr/24hr). The national train company, DSB, has a travel agency and information centre just inside the main entrance off Vesterbrogade (daily 5.45am–11.30pm; ☎70 13 14 15, ⓦwww.dsb.dk). Eurolines coaches (see p.21) from around Europe stop behind the station on Ingerslevgade, across from DGI-byen (see p.94).

Information and discount cards

The excellent Copenhagen Right Now **tourist office** (May–June & Sept Mon–Sat 9am–6pm; July–Aug Mon–Sat 9am–8pm, Sun 10am–6pm; Oct–April

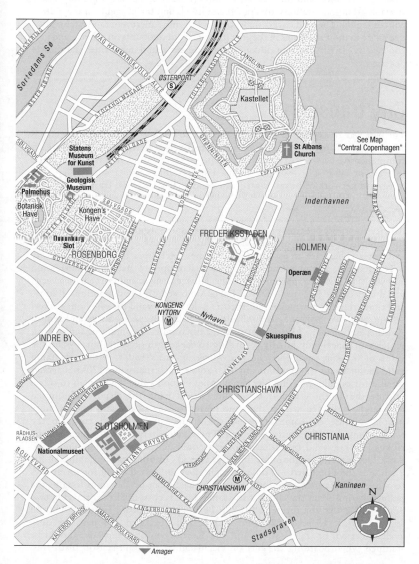

▼ Amager

Mon–Fri 9am–4pm, Sat 9am–2pm; telephone enquiries Mon–Fri 10am–4pm ☎ 70 22 24 42, ⓦ www.visitcopenhagen.dk), across from the Central Station at Vesterbrogade 4A, offers maps, general information and accommodation reservations (70kr). You can also book accommodation without a fee via a row of so-called Ispot computers locked into ⓦ ispot.wonderfulcopenhagen.dk. The office also distributes the free *Copenhagen This Week*, an up-to-date news and listings magazine.

If you plan to visit a lot of museums, either in Copenhagen or in nearby towns like Helsingør and Roskilde, you might want to buy a **Copenhagen Card**, which comes in versions valid for either 24 hours (225kr) or 72 hours (450kr) and is available from train stations, tourist offices, hotels and travel agents in the metropolitan region. The card covers transport on the entire metropolitan system, gives free entry to most museums in the area (fifty-percent discounts on others), and gets you twenty- to fifty-percent discounts on some car rental, ferry rides and theatre tickets.

City transport

The best way to explore Copenhagen is either to **walk** or **cycle**: the inner city is compact, much of the central area of Indre By is pedestrianized and there's a comprehensive network of excellent bike paths – you'll often find it's just as quick to walk or cycle as to wait for a bus. For travelling further afield, there's an integrated network of **buses**, **metro lines** and **S-Tog** and local **trains**.

Tickets

All city transport operates on an integrated **zonal system** extending far beyond the suburbs and encompassing S-Tog trains, the metro system, regional trains and buses. There are an astounding 99 zones (pick up a free leaflet from any S-Tog station); you may find it easiest at first simply to state your destination and you'll be sold the appropriate ticket. The city centre and immediate area, as you'd expect, are in zones 1 and 2. **Fares** are based on a combination of zones and time: the cheapest ticket (*billet*) costs 21kr and is valid for one hour's travel within any two zones, with unlimited transfers between buses and trains. Another option is the **klippekort** ticket, a discount card containing ten stamps, which you cancel individually according to the length of your journey and the value of the *klippekort*. The cheapest *klippekort* costs 130kr, with each stamp valid for an hour's travel within any two zones; each stamp in a 170kr *klippekort* is valid for one hour within any three zones – good value if you plan to travel outside the centre – and is also valid to and from the airport. Unlimited transfers are allowed within the time period of the ticket, and two or more people can use the same *klippekort* simultaneously, provided you clip the required number of stamps per person. There's also an excellent-value **24-hour ticket** (120kr), valid on all transport in zones as far away as Helsingør and Roskilde, as well as night buses. Finally, a good option if you're staying on for a while is the **FlexCard – 7 days**, which gives unlimited travel for seven days to whoever is carrying the card, meaning that it can be shared as long as the people sharing aren't travelling at the same time. It costs 205kr for travel in two zones and 250kr for three. *Billets* can be bought on board buses or at train stations, while *klippekort*, 24-hour tickets and FlexCard – 7 days are only available at bus or train stations and HT Kortsalg kiosks; *klippekort* should be stamped when boarding the bus or via machines on train-station platforms.

Except on buses, it's rare to be asked to show your ticket, but if you don't have one you face an instant fine of 750kr. Route maps can be picked up free at stations, and most free maps of the city include bus lines and a diagram of the S-Tog and metro network.

Guided tours

If you've limited time to see Copenhagen, a **guided tour** can be a good option. There's something to suit everyone.

Bike Copenhagen with Mike ☎26 39 56 88, ⓦwww.bikecopenhagenwith mike.dk. Guided bike tours (3hr 30min) starting from Central Station's Rewentlowsgade exit in front of the Københavns Cykler bike-rental shop. Charismatic Mike takes you past downtown Vesterbro, Amalienborg, The Little Mermaid, Christiania and more. No booking required. Tours depart daily at 10.30am and cost 165kr plus 85kr if you need to borrow a bike. Cash only.

Copenhagen Adventure Tours ☎40 50 40 06, ⓦwww.kajakole.dk. Original and challenging tours using well-designed, safe and easy-to-handle kayaks. Tours start April–Oct from Christianshavns Kanal, Strandgade 50 in front of *Restaurant Kanalen*, and give a unique view of the city from its canals. The standard ninety-minute tour (185kr) takes in Inderhavnen and the canals around Christianshavn (295kr); the longer two-hour trip includes the Holmen; the arm-shattering three-hour trip crosses Inderhavnen and circumnavigates Slotsholmen (345kr). The price includes a free drink in a canalside floating bar. A minimum of five people are required to do the tours.

Copenhagen Sightseeing Tours ⓦwww.sightseeing.dk. Eight different city bus tours (with multilingual headphone commentary; from 120kr per person) departing from Rådhuspladsen in front of the Lure Players statue. Other tours cover the rest of Zealand, taking in places such as Helsingør (5hr trip costing from 330kr) and Roskilde.

DFDS Canal Tours ☎32 96 30 00, ⓦwww.canaltours.dk. Two one-hour options (daily: April–Oct every 30min from 10am–5pm; Nov & Dec hourly from 10am–3pm) start from Nyhavn or Gammel Strand and take in various city sights, including the Little Mermaid, Amalienborg Palace and the Operaen; however, at 60kr, you'll get more for your money with Netto-Bådene (see below). DFDS also run three hop-on, hop-off **waterbus** routes (daily mid-May to Aug, roughly hourly from 10am–5pm), one going north to the Trekroner fort/island, one going south to the Fisketorvet shopping complex, and one going around the canals of Christianshavn. A two-day unlimited-use ticket, which includes the open-top bus tours (see Copenhagen Sightseeing Tours above), costs 220kr, a one-day ticket 60kr, and a single trip 40kr. Bring a raincoat and warm clothing if the weather is bad, as the boats are quite exposed.

Netto-Bådene ☎32 54 41 02, ⓦwww.havnerundfart.dk. Offering a combination of the two DFDS tours listed above, Netto-Bådene's one-hour trip for only 30kr is a lot better value. Tours start at Holmens Kirke across from Børsen, pass Nyhavn, Holmen, Nyholm, Amalienborg Palace and the Little Mermaid on the way, and end up circumnavigating Slotsholmen before finishing back at Holmens Kirke. Tours depart daily from April to mid-October between 10am and 5pm (July & Aug 10am–7pm) two to five times an hour.

Walking Tours A number of English-language guided tours are available from various points throughout the city. Most unusual is the "Watchman's Round" starting at dusk (Thurs, Fri & Sat: mid-July to mid-Sept 9pm; rest of the year 7pm; 75kr) from Gråbrødre Torv in front of *Peder Oxe* restaurant. The tour (roughly 1hr 15min) follows an "eighteenth-century watchman" on his round, while he tells tales (in English) of the old city. Check ⓦwww.nattevaegterne.dk for more info. Otherwise, the, Copenhagen Right Now office (see p.49) has a list of tours taking in most of the city-centre highlights.

Rail and metro

The **S-Tog train** service (Ⓦwww.s-tog.dk) is a metropolitan network laid out in a huge "U" shape covering Copenhagen and the surrounding areas. Six of its seven lines stop at Central Station (in Danish, Hovedbanegården or København H), while the remaining line runs a circular route around the centre. Each line has a letter, from A to H (some letters are not used), and is also colour-coded on route maps. Services run about every ten to fifteen minutes between 5am and 12.30am, and stations are marked by red hexagonal signs with a white "S".

The state-of-the-art underground **metro system** (Ⓦwww.m.dk) opened its first section in 2002 and has gradually grown ever since. Fast and efficient (departures every couple of minutes), it circumvents the Central Station in a "U" shape, connecting the island of Amager and Copenhagen Airport with west Copenhagen via two new stations conveniently located at Christianshavn and Kongens Nytorv. The metro's two lines – M1 and M2 – cross the S-Tog trains at Nørreport. Metro stations are marked by aluminium pillars bearing a large red underlined "M".

By bus

The city's **bus** network (Ⓦwww.moviatrafik.dk) is much more comprehensive than the S-Tog system and can be a more convenient way to get around once you get the hang of finding the stops – marked by yellow placards on signposts – and as long as you avoid the rush hour (7–9am & 5–6pm). The excellent free city map produced by Wonderful Copenhagen includes all of the bus routes in the centre. The city's bus terminal is a slick black building adjacent to the Rådhus, on the big open Rådhuspladsen, a block from both Central Station and Tivoli; you can pick up bus-route maps here, and get general information about the metropolitan transport system. Other useful buses leave from Central Station's Vesterbro side entrance, the

Useful bus routes

#1A DGI-byen (near Kødbyen), Central Station, Tivoli, National Museum, Christiansborg, Kongens Nytorv (near Nyhavn), Bredgade (near Amalienborg) and Esplanaden (near Kastellet and the Little Mermaid).

#2A Central Station, Rådhuspladsen,Christiansborg and Christianshavns Torv (near Christiania).

#3A Trianglen (near Fælledparken), Sankt Hans Torv, Enghavevej (near Vega).

#5A Assistens Kirkegård, Nørrebrogade (near Skt Hans Torv and Blågårdsgade), Nørreport Station, Nørre Voldgade, Rådhuspladsen, Central Station, Copenhagen Airport.

#6A Sortedams Dosseringen (the lakes), Statens Museum for Kunst (Royal Museum of Fine Arts), Nørreport Station, Gammel Torv-Nytorv, Rådhusstræde, Vester Voldgade, Rådhuspladsen, Vesterport Station, Vesterbrogade (City Museum) Roskildevej, Frederiksberg Slot and the City Zoo.

#10 Rådhuspladsen, Hovedbanegården, Istedgade, Enghavevej (for Vega Nightclub)

#26 Valby Langgade, Carlsberg Brewery, Pile Allé, Frederiksberg Allé, Vesterbrogade, Central Station, Rådhuspladsen, Vester Voldgade, Kongens Nytorv, Dronnings Tværgade, Øster Voldgade, Østerport Station, Indiakaj, Langeliniekaj and the Little Mermaid.

#40 Central Station, Christiansborg, Christianshavns Torv, Refshaleøen and Halvandet.

#66 Åboulevard, Vesterport Station, Tivoli and Central Station, Christians Brygge on Slotsholmen, City Hostel, Christianshavns Torv, Christiania, Operaen.

Tivoli side entrance, and the bridge at the end of the tracks. Buses with an "S" suffix only make limited stops, offering a faster service – check they make the stop you require before you get on. Buses with an "A" suffix indicate that the bus runs frequently. All buses have a small electronic board above the driver's seat displaying both the zone you're currently in and the time – so there's no excuse for not having a valid ticket. There's a skeletal **night-bus** service (running once or twice an hour), though fares are double daytime rates. Night-bus numbers always end with "N"; stops are well marked by yellow signs on major routes into and out of the city.

Harbour buses

A fun option for getting around are the city-run yellow **harbour buses**, which sail along the harbour between Nordre Toldbod (near the Little Mermaid) and the Royal Library, stopping six times en route (three times on the Christianshavn side). Services leave daily every twenty minutes from about 7am to 7pm (unless the harbour area is frozen) and cost the same as a normal bus fare (21kr).

Taxis

Taxis are plentiful but expensive with a flat starting fare of 24kr, plus 12,50kr per kilometre travelled (13,50–16,80kr after 4pm and at weekends). There's a handy taxi rank outside Central Station, or phone Taxamotor (T 38 10 10 10). Alternatively, just hail one in the street – if it's showing a green "*Fri*" sign on top, it's available. New on the scene are rickshaw-styled **cycle taxis**, which operate from April till October. Carrying a maximum of two people, they operate a flat starting fare of 40kr if you flag them down on the street, with an additional 4kr per minute until you reach your destination. Alternatively, contact Copenhagen Rickshaw (T 35 43 01 22, W www.rickshaw.dk).

Cycling

The best way to see Copenhagen is to do as the locals do – up to 166,000 every day – and ride a **bicycle**. Cycling is also excellent for exploring the immediate countryside, as bikes can be taken for two hours on S-Togs for 12kr through any number of zones; you can also buy a special bicycle *klippekort*, valid for ten journeys and costing 105kr. The superb, city-wide cycle lanes make cycling very safe, though remember that lights are a legal requirement at night (you'll be stopped and fined if the police catch you without them) and helmets are recommended at all times.

There are a number of outlets for **renting bikes** in central Copenhagen including Københavns Cyklebørs, Gothersgade 157, Indre By (Mon–Fri 9am–5.30pm, Sat 10am–1.30pm; T 33 14 07 17, W www.cykelboersen.dk; 75kr per day, 285kr per week, 300kr deposit) and Københavns Cykelcenter, Reventlowsgade 11, along the side of Central Station (Mon–Fri 8am–5.30pm, Sat 9am–1pm, July–Sept also Sun 10am–1pm; T 33 33 86 13, W www.rentabike.dk; 85kr per day, 375kr per week, 500kr deposit). Also bear in mind the summer-only free **City Bike scheme** (W www.bycyklen.dk), when two thousand free bikes (easily recognized by the advertisements painted onto their solid wheels) are scattered about the city at S-Tog stations and other busy locations; a refundable 20kr deposit unlocks one. The rules are simple: leave the bike in a rack when you've finished with it (you get your coin back automatically as you re-lock the bike), or just leave it out on a pavement, in which case someone else will happily return it and pocket the coin. Don't secure one with your own lock and don't take one outside the city limits (the old rampart lakes mark the border) or you risk a fine.

Parking

The city's **parking** rules take some deciphering. A **pay-and-display system** operates from 8am on Monday to 5pm on Saturday on the centre's streets (the area inside the lakes), with rates depending on the colour-coded zone you're in and the time of day. Stretching out from the centre, the zones are red (8am–6pm 26kr per hr, 6–11pm 9kr per hr, 11pm–8am 3kr per hr), green (same time slots, 16kr, 9kr and 3kr) and blue (9kr, 9kr and 3kr). Each pay-and-display meter has a zone map on it. Outside the centre, there's one hour's free parking (Mon–Fri 8am–7pm), but you have to use a **P-disc** (rental cars come with them). You set the time you park on the hands of the clock, returning before your allotted time (indicated by signs) is up. Outside this period, there are no restrictions. "STOPFORBUD" means no stopping, whilst "PARKERING FORBUDT" means no parking unless a time limit is displayed, in which case you must use a P-disc. It's usually not too difficult to find a street parking space, but note that your car will be towed away if you overstay or park where you shouldn't. Downtown **car parks** are thin on the ground: there's a handy one at Statoil on Israel Plads by Nørreport Station, one at Industriens Hus at Rådhuspladsen near Tivoli, and another attached to the Q8 station near Vesterport Station at Nyropsgade 42.

Accommodation

Accommodation in Copenhagen is plentiful but expensive, and in high season (July, Aug & Christmas) you'll need to book ahead. If you're willing to take a chance, you can make great savings if you book via the **hotel-booking service** at the Copenhagen Right Now office (see p.49) or at the tourist office at the airport (see p.47) on the day you arrive. Queues for this service can be lengthy, however, and there is a charge of 100kr. The **tourist office** also has a dedicated phone line (☏70 22 24 42; see p.50) and a website (Ⓦwww.bookcopenhagen.dk) – plus free internet terminals – via which you can make reservations without a fee (see p.50). **Room rates** are generally at their highest in summer, though in the majority of big hotels prices rise and fall on a daily basis according to demand, and you can get excellent weekend rates in business hotels. It's always worth checking hotel websites for **special rates** and packages.

A more affordable **guesthouse** sector is slowly starting to develop (from 325kr per night), but rooms fill quickly in summer; check out Ⓦwww.bedandbreakfast. dk (though note that despite the name breakfast isn't always on offer or included in the price). If you're on a budget you can choose from a number of **hostels** scattered around the city centre and suburbs, while **campsites** provide an alternative if you're really watching the pennies. For stays longer than a couple of weeks, an **apartment** will be most cost-effective. The efficient and friendly agency HAY4YOU, Vimmelskaftet 49 (☏33 33 08 05, Ⓦwww.hay4you.dk) has a range of central options.

Note that we list a few **gay and lesbian-friendly** accommodation options on p.92.

Hotels

Copenhagen has experienced a **hotel** boom in recent years. Several new, exciting designer hotels in great, central locations offer an interesting, more stylish, alternative to the chains. Most of the budget and mid-range options are just west of Central Station, in Vesterbro, with the majority of the inexpensive ones clustered along ever-so-slightly seedy (though rarely dangerous) streets of Helgolandsgade, Colbjørnsensgade and Istedgade. Further mid-price options can be found out towards the suburb of Frederiksberg.

Indre By

The following hotels are shown on the map on pp.60–61.

Copenhagen Strand Havnegade 37 ☎ 33 48 99 00, ⓦ www.copenhagenstrand.dk. Bus #29. Located on the waterfront in a converted 1862 warehouse, this is a friendly and comfortable option in a quiet spot. Standard rooms are a bit small but cosily furnished. Larger options are also available – only suites have harbour views. Rates reduced substantially at weekends. ❾

First Hotel Skt Petri Krystalgade 22 ☎ 33 45 91 00, ⓦ www.hotelsktpetri.com. Bus #6A. Housed in a former discount department store on a quiet street in the heart of the trendy Latin Quarter, there is nothing cut-price about the five-star *Skt Petri*, the only Danish member of Design Hotels (ⓦ www .designhotel.com). It's slick, classy and glamorous throughout – from the black-liveried porters to the ultra-trendy lobby and café. Rooms, from small to suite, feature large beds, stylish furnishings, wooden floors and bright prints on the walls – some have balconies, so ask when booking. All have wi-fi, internet and cable TV. There's a brasserie serving French classics, and a cocktail lounge, *Bar Rouge*. ❾

Kong Arthur Nørre Søgade 11 ☎ 33 11 12 12, ⓦ www.kongarthur.dk. Bus #5A or #350S. In a largely residential area by Peblinge Sø, this lovely hotel has recently been completely refurbished. Its comfortable lobby doubles as a bar (open 24/7) and is beautifully furnished. Rooms (all with internet and cable TV) are tastefully decorated, though some are quite small and views are limited. There's a courtyard where you can relax with a drink and the spa is free to guests. Breakfast buffet is organic and costs extra (135kr). The hotel is Carbon Neutral and electric cars can be rented from reception. Free parking. ❾

Sømandshjemmet "Bethel" Nyhavn 22 ☎ 33 13 03 70, ⓦ www.hotel-bethel.dk. Bus #29; Kongens Nytorv metro. This former seamen's hostel right in the heart of Nyhavn is an excellent budget option in this often expensive area. The decor is a little dated, but rooms are clean and comfortable and the atmosphere welcoming. Corner rooms have great views and are worth paying a bit more for. A small breakfast cafe serves cakes and coffee throughout the day. ❻

🏃 **Hotel Twentyseven** Løngangstræde 27 ☎ 70 27 56 27, ⓦ www.hotel27.dk. A recent addition to the city's designer hotels, this

is an edgy and exciting place to stay, with risqué artwork, a dildo-vending machine in the ladies' toilets, the glamorous *Honey Ryder Cocktail Lounge* and the *IceBar CPH* next door (see p.85). The rooms are pure Scandinavian style with light oak floors, fluffy rugs, red-lacquer wardrobes and black slate bathrooms. There's free tea, coffee and fruit, and you can also pay for half-board and have the evening buffet. Rates are surprisingly reasonable. Free wi-fi. ❼

Christianshavn

The following hotel is shown on the map on pp.60–61.

CPH Living Langebrogade 1C ☎ 61 60 85 46, ⓦ www.cphliving.com. If you fancy being lulled to sleep by the gentle rolling of waves, this new hotel boat might be just the place. With just twelve beautifully decorated rooms, this sleek, fully automated option (there's no reception; you check in using your credit card), moored in Inderhavnen, has its own floating restaurant, and a private sundeck with views of the Black Diamond. Breakfast not included. ❼

Frederiksstad

The following hotels are shown on the map on pp.60–61.

Comfort Hotel Esplanaden Bredgade 78 ☎ 33 48 10 00, ⓦ www.choicehotels.dk. In a lovely, quiet spot near Kastellet and the Little Mermaid, this pleasant and relatively small, no-frills hotel – one of the *Choice Hotels* chain – has decent, plain en-suite rooms, with the choice of bath or shower and all with wi-fi. Breakfast (95kr) is not included. Great offers during weekends and winter. ❾

Copenhagen Admiral Toldbodgade 24–28 ☎ 33 74 14 14, ⓦ www.admiralhotel.dk. Housed in an impressive 200-year-old granary in a great location on the waterfront and only 2min from Nyhavn, this large, handsome hotel exudes comfort, style and professionalism. The six-storey building has kept its rustic maritime interior with impressive vaulted brick ceilings and huge wooden beams throughout. Rooms are comfortable and classy with oak beams and furniture by top Danish designers Trip Trap; half have great views of Inderhavnen and cost around 250kr more. Doubles come in variable sizes. The breakfast buffet (115kr) is not included. There's a classy Conran-designed restaurant, *Salt*, and the *Salt Bar* on the ground floor. ❾

Rådhuspladsen and around

The following hotels are shown on the map on pp.60–61.

Hotel Alexandra HC Andersens Bld 8 ☎33 74 44 44, ⓦwww.hotel-alexandra.dk. This homely and charming hotel offers something different with its retro theme of Danish design from the 1930s, 40s and 50s. The beautifully furnished rooms all boast real Danish furniture classics – a few (for which you'll pay around 500kr extra per night) have even been done out completely in the style of designers such as Arne Jacobsen, Hans Wegner and Finn Juhl. ⓽

Cab-Inn City Mitchellsgade 14 ☎33 46 16 16, ⓦwww.cabinn.com. The only budget option in the area, offering a reasonably comfortable place to bed down in a central location near Tivoli and Central Station. Small, functional ferry-cabin-style rooms (for 1–3 people) with bath, TV, phone, internet and kettle (and free tea and coffee). Breakfast 60kr. ⓺

Hotel Fox Jarmers Plads 3 ☎33 13 30 00, ⓦwww.hotelfox.dk. Great-value, funky, friendly little hotel – the 61 rooms have been individually decorated and furnished by a team of young European designers, and though some may find (1960s psychedelic movies, Manga) may be too garish to live with for long, they all use their space creatively and with flair. Doubles come in medium, large and extra large; some have showers, some baths, so state your preference when booking. Breakfast – great coffee and pastries – is served on aeroplane-style compartmentalized trays in the bright lobby, while drinks can be taken up to the roof terrace. Part of the same chain as *Kong Arthur*, with free entrance to its spa (see p.55). Bikes and rollerblades for rent. ⓼

Marriott Kalvebod Brygge 5 ☎88 33 99 00, ⓦwww.marriott.com/cphdk. Bus #8. In a great harbourfront spot at the end of Bernstorffsgade, the high-rise *Marriott* offers all the American-style amenities you could want – large, plush, well-equipped rooms (many with harbour or city views), restaurant, terrace café (summer only), bar, gym, sauna and solarium, and expensive shops. Prices vary considerably according to demand and drop at weekends, so check website for special deals. Breakfast not included. ⓽

The Square Rådhuspladsen 14 ☎33 38 12 00, ⓦwww.thesquare.dk. Great hotel, slap-bang in the centre (hence no parking) and offering significant discounts (around 20 percent) at the weekends. The spacious, stylish lobby is scattered with gorgeous, red Arne Jacobsen swan chairs; the modern design is carried through into the smartly decorated, comfortable rooms. Those overlooking the square experience some traffic noise, so if you like quiet, request a room further back. Breakfast (there's no restaurant) is served on the sixth floor with views over the city. ⓽

Vesterbro

The following hotels are shown on the map on pp.76–77.

Absalon Helgolandsgade 15 ☎33 24 22 11, ⓦwww.absalon-hotel.dk. Bus #10; Central Station. On the corner of Istedgade, this large but friendly three-star family hotel, with a one-star annexe, offers a wide choice of rooms (some en suite), plus a number of deluxe doubles and suites. It's nothing special but it's reasonably priced, convenient and clean, and soundproofing keeps things nice and quiet. Free internet access in the lobby and charge-able wi-fi throughout. ⓺–⓻

Axel Hotel Guldsmeden Helgolandsgade 7–11 ☎33 31 32 66, ⓦwww.ibishotel.com. Bus #6A; Central Station. The newest member of the Danish Guldsmeden hotel chain, *Axel* is a four-star boutique hotel at the nice end of Colbjørnsensgade. Beautifully decorated rooms feature traditional Balinese wooden furniture and modern accents – including free wi-fi. The light and cheery public areas house an organic courtyard bar and restaurant, and there's a spa to die for. ⓼

Carlton Hotel Guldsmeden Vesterbrogade 66 ☎33 22 15 00, ⓦwww.hotelguldsmeden.dk. Bus #6A or #26. This small, charming hotel occupies a nineteenth-century building almost opposite the Københavns Bymuseum. All rooms are done out in French colonial style, with a laudable attention to detail, and some have small balconies, though the view isn't that enticing. There's free wi-fi in the café and lobby area and a beautiful breakfast from *Emmery's* (see p.91). Parking 95kr. ⓽

Centrum Helgolandsgade 14 ☎33 31 31 11, ⓦwww.dgi-byen.dk. Bus #10; Central Station. One of the trendier options in this area, the recently revamped *Centrum* has cool, modern decor – black leather sofas and cosy lighting in the lobby, tasteful whites, creams and pale wooden furniture in the modestly sized rooms (all en suite). Guests get free access to the DGI-byen swim centre. ⓽

Copenhagen Island Kalvebod Brygge 53 ☎33 38 96 00, ⓦwww.copenhagenisland.com. Dybbelsbro S-train. With stupendous views across Inderhavnen, this sparkling new large hotel, designed by the famous Utzon team of architects, is difficult to fault. Rooms are stylishly furnished with Scandinavian design, there's free wi-fi throughout and a free fitness centre on the top floor. ⓽

Løven Vesterbrogade 30 ☎ 33 79 67 20, ⓦ www .loeven.dk. Bus #6A or #26. One of central Copenhagen's real bargains, offering affordable, no-frills accommodation in plain but pleasantly decorated rooms sleeping up to six (mostly en suite). Breakfast isn't included, but there's a large and well-equipped kitchen and a good breakfast café downstairs. The major drawback is the noise – rooms facing the courtyard are quieter. En suite 690kr, shared 490kr. ❹–❻

Missionshotellet Nebo Istedgade 6 ☎ 33 21 12 17, ⓦ www.nebo.dk. Bus #1A, #2A, #6A. Next door to Central Station – take the back exit – this well-run Danish Mission hotel (profits go to a homeless shelter on Vesterbro) is one of the best deals this close to the centre. Rooms – some en suite – are simple but adequate and clean, and staff are friendly. There's also free internet access in the lobby, chargeable wi-fi in the rooms, and bike rental (100kr a day). ❻–❼

Tiffany Colbjørnsensgade 28 ☎ 33 21 80 50, ⓦ www.hoteltiffany.dk. Bus #10; Central Station. Small, charming and welcoming hotel, a cut above most in the area – the large, well-furnished double or family rooms come with free wi-fi and mini-kitchens comprising a microwave, fridge and toaster. Continental breakfast is left in the fridge, with freshly baked rolls delivered to your door each morning. Non-smoking. ❾

Frederiksberg

The following hotels are shown on the map on pp.76–77.

🏃 **Avenue** Åboulevard 29 ☎ 35 37 31 11, ⓦ www.avenuehotel.dk. Bus #67, #68, #250S; Forum metro. Comfortable and welcoming place on the border between Frederiksberg and Nørrebro, with spacious rooms tastefully decorated in classic Scandinavian style. There's a breakfast buffet (served outdoors in the summer), free wi-fi throughout and free parking. Rates often fall at weekends. ❽

Sct Thomas Frederiksberg Allé 7 ☎ 33 21 64 64, ⓦ www.hotelsctthomas.dk. Bus #26. In a great location just beyond the junction with lively Vesterbrogade, near the delis and foodshops on Værnedamsvej and a 10min walk from Frederiksberg Have. The friendly owners, pleasant rooms (some with shared facilities) and easy-going atmosphere have made it popular, so be sure to book ahead (a couple of months in high season). Tea and coffee and buffet breakfast are included in the price. Wi-fi in the room costs 50kr per day and they rent out bikes for 100kr per day. Parking 75kr per day. ❼

Nørrebro and Østerbro

The following hotel is shown on the map on p.79.

🏃 **Rye** Ryesgade 115, Østerbro ☎ 35 26 52 10, ⓦ www.hotelrye.dk. Bus #1A, #14 or #15. Near Fælledparken, Parken Stadium and busy Østerbrogade with its array of good places to eat and drink, *Rye* is a home away from home. On the second and third floors of an old apartment block, the sixteen comfortable rooms (one shower for every two rooms) – come with slippers and housecoat, and free wi-fi. There is also a large breakfast buffet with home-made bread. One of the best budget hotels in Europe. ❻

Hostels and sleep-ins

Copenhagen has a great selection of hostels and sleep-ins, though some are a little way out of the centre. Space is only likely to be an issue in the peak summer months when you should call ahead or turn up as early as possible to be sure of a bed.

Indre By & Radhuspladsen

The following places are shown on the map on pp.60–61.

Danhostel Copenhagen City HC Andersens Blvd 50 ☎ 33 11 85 85, ⓦ www.danhostel.dk. Central Station or bus #5A. Trendy and bright HI "design" hostel in a multistorey building overlooking the harbour and the green copper spires of the city. With over one thousand beds in four-to-six person rooms (all en-suite) and dorms (single-sex and mixed), it's the largest city-hostel in Europe. Linen/towel rental 60kr. Breakfast 69kr. No curfew, and open all year. Rooms with 1–4 beds 740kr. Dorm beds 185kr.

Danhostel Copenhagen Downtown Vandkunsten 5 ☎ 70 23 21 10, ⓦ www.copenhagendowntown .dk. Great, new, central hostel with a fun, cultural vibe – they host live music and art exhibitions. The café serves great coffee, breakfast (65kr), reasonably priced snacks and evening meals, and there's also a kitchen and TV room. With a range of two-to-four person rooms (some en suite) and dorms – all light, bright and newly renovated – it's very popular, especially with students and families. Bike rental, safety boxes, internet access and bedsheet/towel rental (60kr). Book ahead, especially at weekends. No curfew. En-suite double 549kr. Dorm beds 75kr per person.

Jørgensen Rømersgade 11 ☎33 13 81 86,
ⓦwww.hoteljoergensen.dk. Bus #5A, #14, #40,
#42, #43 or #350S; Nørreport S-Tog/metro. Great
hostel-cum-hotel offering three dorms with six to
twelve beds, with a TV in each room and breakfast
included. You can rent sheets for 50kr. Very central,
and popular with gay travellers. Open all year.
150kr per person.

Vesterbro

The following places are shown on the
map on pp.76–77.

City Public Hostel Absalonsgade 8 ☎33 55 00
81, ⓦwww.citypublichostel.dk. Bus #6A or #26.
Easy-going and handily placed hostel, 10min from
Central Station next to the Københavns Bymuseum.
There's a noisy 68-bed male dorm, a 24-bed
female dorm, and less crowded 6- to 32-bed
rooms, plus a kitchen and a barbecue. Open May–
Aug. 24hr check-in and no curfew. Bedding 40kr
extra, breakfast 30kr. 125kr–165kr. Cash only.
Sleep-In Fact Valdemarsgade 14 ☎33 79 67 79,
ⓦwww.sleep-in-fact.dk. Bus #6A or #26. In the
heart of Vesterbro, this is a sports centre out of
season and its facilities are available to rent in
season. The eighty beds are divided between two
large hall-type rooms, which can get very noisy.
Open July & Aug only; reception 7.30am–noon
& 3pm–3am. Small breakfast included in the
price. 120kr.

Nørrebro

The following place is shown on the
map on p.79.

Sleep-In Green Ravnsborggade 18, Nørrebro
☎35 37 77 77, ⓦwww.sleep-in-green.dk. Bus
#5A or #350S. In the centre of hip Nørrebro, this
eco-conscious hostel is run by students and staff
of the training school for organic production that
lives here the rest of the year. It has bright rooms

with 8, 20 and 38 beds, free wi-fi, and organic
breakfast and snacks sold at the reception/chill-out
room. Extra charge for bedding (30kr). Max age 35.
No curfew, Open June–Oct. 125kr.

Around Copenhagen

The following places are shown on the
map on p.95.

Danhostel Copenhagen Amager Vejlandsallé 200,
Amager ☎32 52 27 08, ⓦwww.copenhagenyouth
hostel.com. Bus #30 or Bellacenter metro and a
500m walk. A large 155-room three-star HI hostel on
Amager, with simple but adequate two- to five-bed
rooms, about half with en-suite bathroom, plus
laundry, kitchen and net café (20kr per hr). Despite
its size *Amager* tends to be fully booked during
summer so it's essential to book in advance. There's
free parking, no curfew and reception is open 24hr.
Breakfast 55kr, sheets 40kr. Closed Dec. En-suite
doubles for HI members 510kr, others 580kr, dorm
beds for HI members 145kr, others 180kr.
Danhostel Copenhagen Bellahøj Herbergvejen 8,
Brønshøj ☎38 28 97 15, ⓦwww.youth-hostel.dk.
Bus #2A. More homely than its rivals, and situated
in a residential part of the city – a 15min bus ride
from the centre – *Bellahøj* has four-, six- and
fourteen-bed rooms (sheets 50kr). There's a fully
equipped kitchen and cheap laundry facilities, too.
Reception is open 7am–8pm, check-in 2–5pm; no
curfew, although there's a dorm lockout
10am–1pm. Breakfast buffet 55kr. Closed Jan. HI
members 140kr, non-members 175kr.
Danhostel Ishøj Strand Ishøj Strandvej 13, Ishøj
☎43 53 50 15, ⓦwww.ishojhostelt.dk. Ishøj
station then bus #300S. Out near Arken and some
beautiful beaches, this well-run and comfortable
five-star HI hostel has spacious en-suite rooms
sleeping up to six, plus a decent restaurant. No
curfew; check-in daily 2–6pm. Open all year. HI
members 175kr, others 210kr.

Campsites

Some of the campsites near Copenhagen are in peerless locations by beaches or in
woods, and all are easily accessible by public transport.

Charlottenlund Fort Strandvejen 144, Charlottenlund ☎39 62 36 88, ⓦwww.campingcopenhagen
.dk. Bus #14. Situated in the old fort at beautiful
Charlottenlund beach, this excellent campsite is the
best within easy striking distance of the city centre
(the bus stops right outside). There are also sites
for camper vans and trailers. If you're camping, try
to get a pitch around the back, where there's
greater protection from the elements. Open May to
mid-Sept. 95kr.

Copenhagen Camping Bachersmindevej 13,
Dragør ☎32 94 20 07, ⓦwww.copenhagen
camping.dk. Train to Tårnby station then take bus
#350S and get off at Store Magleby Strandvej,
from where it's an easy 5min walk (a 30min
journey in total). Brand-new campsite just outside
Dragør and 12km outside the city centre, with
beaches on one side and a bird reserve on the
other. The site includes luxurious self-contained
cabins sleeping up to six (from 575kr per day) plus

a few excellent-value cabins sleeping two (375kr). Open all year. 70kr.

Tangloppen Ishøj Havn, Ishøj ☎ 43 54 07 67, ⓦ www.fdmcamping.dk. Ishøj station, then bus #128. Right next door to Arken (see p.98), and facing onto a picturesque lagoon, *Tangloppen* is a wonderful place if you want a beach, modern art and not much else – shelter is minimal, and tents take a battering here in bad weather. There's also a cheap café selling grilled food, and a number of stunningly positioned cabins (460kr for up to 4 people; 670kr for up to 8). Open April to mid-Oct. 77kr.

The City

Copenhagen is a very manageable city, and you can walk right across the compact centre in half an hour. The historic core is **Slotsholmen**, originally the site of the twelfth-century castle and now home to the huge royal and governmental complex of Christiansborg. Facing Slotsholmen over the Slotsholmen Kanal is the medieval maze of **Indre By**, the bustling heart of the city, traversed by **Strøget**, the world's longest pedestrianized street, and packed with an abundance of shops, cafés and bars, as well as an eclectic clutch of museums and churches. On the opposite side of Slotsholmen from Indre By, the island of **Christianshavn** is one of the inner city's most relaxed and bohemian areas, and home to the "free city" of Christiania, Copenhagen's famous alternative-lifestyle community. Northeast of Indre By, the fairytale palace of **Rosenborg**, one of several royal residences in the city, sits at the heart of the inner city's greenest area – Kongens Have and the lush Botanical Gardens – and within striking distance of two excellent art museums. Abutting Kongens Have, **Frederiksstaden**, Frederik V's royal quarter, is dominated by the huge dome of the Marmorkirken church and centred on the royal palaces of Amalienborg. South of Indre By, close to the town hall and main square, Rådhuspladsen, you'll find the more earthy pleasures of the delightful Tivoli pleasure gardens, as well as the excellent **National Museum** and **Glyptoteket** art and sculpture gallery.

To the west of the city centre, multicultural **Vesterbro**, with its ethnic eateries and trendy nightlife, rubs shoulders with the genteel, villa-lined streets of **Frederiksberg**, where you'll find the tranquil Frederiksberg Have, the city's zoo, and the Carlsberg brewery visitor centre. To the north of the centre lies the formerly working-class but increasingly gentrified district of **Nørrebro**; to its east snooty **Østerbro** is home to Copenhagen's old money, as well as the city centre's largest open space, Fælled Park.

Slotsholmen

The small island of **Slotsholmen** is the historical and geographical heart of Copenhagen. It was here, in 1167, that Bishop Absalon founded the castle that became the nucleus of the future city, and it's been the seat of Danish rule ever since. A hotchpotch of sights crams into the area, from ruins to state and royal buildings, as well as a bunch of diverse museums. Dominating the island is the austere grey bulk of **Christiansborg Slot** (ⓦ www.ses.dk/christiansborg), a hefty granite-faced neo-Baroque building, constructed between 1907 and 1928 around what little remained of the previous palace, destroyed by fire in 1884. Its illustrious occupants include the Supreme Court, prime minister's office, the Royal Reception Rooms and the **Folketinget** (ⓦ www.folketinget.dk), home to the Danish Parliament, located in Christiansborg Slot's south wing (to the left as you face the entrance) – there are free guided tours of the parliamentary chambers in English (July to mid-Aug Mon–Fri & Sun 2pm; Oct–May Sun 2pm).

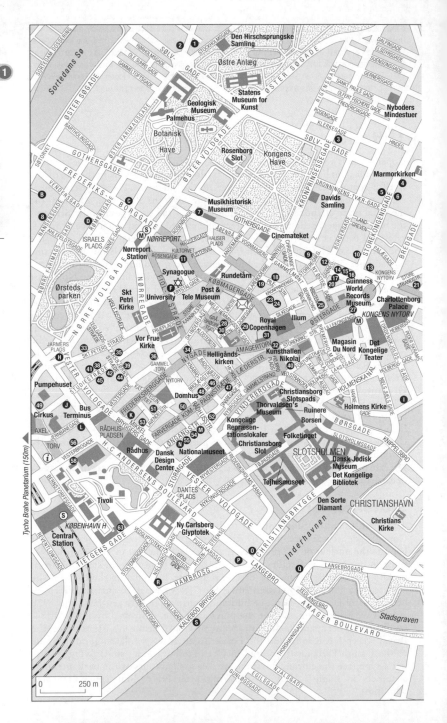

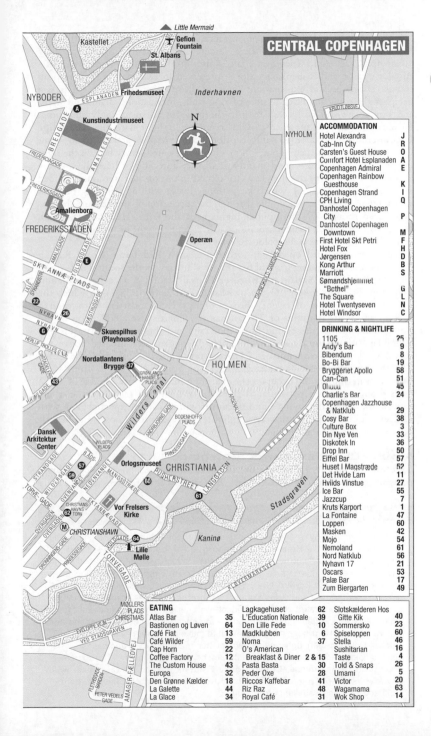

CENTRAL COPENHAGEN

Little Mermaid · Gefion Fountain · St. Albans · Kastellet · Frihedsmuseet · NYBODER · Kunstindustrimuseet · Inderhavnen · NYHOLM · Amalienborg · FREDERIKSSTADEN · Operæn · Skuespilhus (Playhouse) · HOLMEN · Nordatlantens Brygge · Dansk Arkitektur Center · Orlogsmuseet · CHRISTIANIA · Vor Frelsers Kirke · CHRISTIANSHAVN · Lille Mølle · Kaninø · Stadsgraven

ACCOMMODATION
Hotel Alexandra	J
Cab-Inn City	R
Carsten's Guest House	O
Comfort Hotel Esplanaden	A
Copenhagen Admiral	E
Copenhagen Rainbow Guesthouse	K
Copenhagen Strand	I
CPH Living	Q
Danhostel Copenhagen City	P
Danhostel Copenhagen Downtown	M
First Hotel Skt Petri	F
Hotel Fox	H
Jørgensen	D
Kong Arthur	B
Marriott	S
Sømandshjemmet "Bethel"	G
The Square	L
Hotel Twentyseven	N
Hotel Windsor	C

DRINKING & NIGHTLIFE
1105	25
Andy's Bar	9
Bibendum	8
Bo-Bi Bar	19
Bryggeriet Apollo	58
Can-Can	51
Charlie's Bar	24
Copenhagen Jazzhouse & Natklub	29
Cosy Bar	38
Culture Box	3
Din Nye Ven	33
Diskotek In	36
Drop Inn	50
Eiffel Bar	57
Huset I Magstræde	52
Det Hvide Lam	11
Hviids Vinstue	27
Ice Bar	55
Jazzcup	7
Kruts Karport	1
La Fontaine	47
Loppen	60
Masken	42
Mojo	54
Nemoland	61
Nord Natklub	56
Nyhavn 17	21
Oscars	53
Palæ Bar	17
Zum Biergarten	49

EATING
Atlas Bar	35	Lagkagehuset	62
Bastionen og Løven	64	L'Education Nationale	39
Café Fiat	13	Den Lille Fede	10
Café Wilder	59	Madklubben	6
Cap Horn	22	Noma	37
Coffee Factory	12	O's American Breakfast & Diner	2 & 15
The Custom House	43	Pasta Basta	30
Europa	32	Peder Oxe	28
Den Grønne Kælder	18	Riccos Kaffebar	41
La Galette	44	Riz Raz	48
La Glace	34	Royal Café	31
Slotskælderen Hos Gitte Kik	40		
Sommersko	23		
Spiseloppen	60		
Stella	46		
Sushitarian	16		
Taste	4		
Told & Snaps	26		
Umami	5		
Victor	20		
Wagamama	63		
Wok Shop	14		

As you head through the *slot*'s main entrance, an inconspicuous door on the right leads down to the **ruins** (Ruinerne under Christiansborg; May–Sept daily 10am–4pm; Oct–April Tues–Sun 10am–4pm; 40kr) from the previous castles – Absalon's castle and Københavns Slot – preserved in two massive subterranean rooms. Diagrams and explanations (and an informative short film) help you decipher the stone and brick jumble of ring walls, foundations, drains and wells, and though it's still fairly easy to lose the plot, it's all surprisingly absorbing. Nowadays, the royal presence at Christiansborg is limited to the **Kongelige Repræsentationslokaler** (Royal Reception Rooms; May–Sept daily 10am–4pm; Oct–April Tues–Sun 10am–4pm; 70kr) – look for the red sentry box on the right in the main courtyard – used mainly as a place for the royal family to wow important visitors. Try to time your visit to take in one of the entertaining guided tours (in English at 3pm), which keep things lively with a sprinkling of royal anecdotes and gossip as you amble through the succession of sumptuous, chandelier-decked rooms. The undisputed highlight is the Great Hall, adorned with Bjørn Nørgaard's wonderfully vibrant tapestries depicting the history of Denmark in a refreshingly modern and colourful way.

The inner courtyard opens out into the elegant **Ridebane** (Royal Riding Ground), still the training ground for the royal horses. In the south wing, you'll find the **Kongelige Stalde og Kareter** (Royal Stables & Coaches Museum; May–Sept Fri–Sun 2–4pm; Oct–April Sat & Sun 2–4pm; 20kr), in which the royal family's retinue of twenty horses occupy lavish quarters with vaulted ceilings and walls and cribs of Tuscan marble. There's also a collection of old riding uniforms, harnesses and horse portraits and the royal family's historic assemblage of coaches, carriages and cars. Incongruously situated above the Royal Stables, the **Teatermuseet I Hofteatret** (Theatre Museum in the Court Theatre; Tues & Thurs 11am–3pm, Wed 11am–5pm, Sat & Sun 1–4pm; 40kr; Ⓦ www.teatermuseet.dk) occupies the charming former Court Theatre of 1767. Each room explores a particular theme of Danish theatrical history – opera, pantomime, ballet and drama – and the **auditorium** is an unexpected gem, with its deep, sloping stage, plush velvet upholstery, elegant royal boxes and beautifully decorated oriental ceiling.

Around Christiansborgs Slotsplads

Back on Christiansborg Slotsplads, the graceful domed Neoclassical **Christiansborgs Slotskirke** (Palace Chapel; Easter, July & third week of Oct daily

The Danish monarchy

Denmark's **monarchy** is one of the oldest in the world, but the royal line of the current monarchs, the **House of Glücksborg**, dates back only to 1853 and the reign of Christian IX, who was nicknamed the "father-in-law of Europe" through having married off his female progeny to various European royals (including Alexandra, who wed Edward VII of England). Denmark's rulers were always men until the country's first and current queen, **Margrethe II** (1940–), came to the throne in 1972. Highly educated and independent, with her own interests and work (as a stage designer and translator), Margrethe – together with her French husband, the **Prince Consort Henrik II** – has done much to make the monarchy more approachable and human, although one aspect of her relaxed public demeanour – her chain-smoking – has come under criticism from some quarters. The extremely popular heir to the throne, **Crown Prince Frederik** married his Tasmanian wife, Crown Princess Mary, in 2005; they have two children, Prince Christian, born in 2005 and Princess Isabella, born in 2007.

noon–4pm; other times Sun noon–4pm; free; ⓦwww.ses.dk/christiansborg), was designed by C.F. Hansen, one of the most important Danish Golden Age architects. The lavish custard- and cream-coloured marble stucco interior is topped off by Thorvaldsen's magnificent angel frieze, which encircles the dome. At the southern end of Christiansborg Slotsplads, the flamboyant red-brick building with the distinctive gabled green copper roof and fanciful spire formed out of four entwined dragons' tails is Christian IV's **Børsen** (Stock Exchange); sadly, it's owned by the Chamber of Commerce and not open to the public.

Tucked behind Christiansborg's Slotskirke, the Neoclassical building with a striking ochre-coloured facade is **Thorvaldsen's Museum** (Tues–Sun 10am–5pm; July & Aug guided tours in English Sun 3pm; 20kr, free on Wed; ⓦwww .thorvaldsensmuseum.dk) housing the works and personal possessions (and the body) of Denmark's only sculptor of note, Bertel Thorvaldsen (1770–1844). While none of the pieces is famous in its own right, the collection makes for an enjoyable wander amid the roll-call of gods and mortals – Byron, Christian IV and Napoleon among others – set off beautifully by the richly coloured walls, mosaic floors and finely painted ceilings. Highlights include the enchanting *Cupid and Psyche* (room 2) and **Jason with the Golden Fleece** (room 5) – the piece that made his name.

South of Christiansborg

Halfway along Tøjhusgade, the exhaustive **Tøjhusmuseet** (Royal Danish Arsenal Museum; July daily noon–4pm; rest of year Tues–Sun noon–4pm; 30kr; free on Wed; ⓦwww.thm.dk), appropriately housed in Christian IV's old Tøjhus (Arms House), is reputedly the world's finest collection of eighteenth- and nineteenth-century armaments. Cannons, tanks and artillery line the 156-metre-long **Cannon Hall** – a handsome sight in itself, with its whitewashed arches and expanse of cobbled floor. On the first floor, the **Armoury Hall** displays endless rows of swords, suits of armour and firearms, including the breastplate and guns of Christian IV.

Adjacent to the Tøjhusmuseet, head through the **Bibliotekshaven** (Royal Library Garden) to the red-brick, Venetian-inspired **Det Kongelige Bibliotek** (Royal Library; entrance from the Black Diamond extension on the waterfront) whose left wing is home to the excellent Daniel Libeskind-designed **Dansk Jødisk Museum** (Danish Jewish Museum; June–Aug Tues–Sun 10am–5pm; Sept–May Tues–Fri 1–4pm, Sat & Sun noon–5pm; 40kr; ⓦwww.jewmus.dk). The museum recounts the peaceful co-existence of Jews and Danes in Denmark for over four centuries, and takes as its inspiration the concept of *Mitzvah* (good deed), as seen in one of the few Jewish success stories of World War II: the escape from deportation to concentration camps of seven thousand Jews, helped across the Øresund to safety in neutral Sweden by the Danish Resistance and scores of ordinary Danes. It's a fitting memorial to this proud episode in Denmark's history and the exhibition moves deftly on to broader themes such as the history of Jewish immigration to Denmark and the concept of "homeland", all amply illuminated by personal histories, possessions and a beautiful array of paraphernalia used in Jewish rituals.

Walk around the right side of the building to the library's stunning black-granite and glass extension, known as **Den Sorte Diamant** (Black Diamond; building Mon–Fri 8am–9pm, Sat 8am–5pm; library & exhibitions Mon–Sat 10am–7pm; exhibitions 40kr; ⓦwww.kb.dk; for guided tours in English contact ⓣ33 47 48 80 or ⓔbooking@kb.dk), which houses a concert hall, bookshop, restaurant, café and exhibition space.

Indre By

The heart of both medieval and modern Copenhagen, **Indre By** ("inner city") is where the city began, as the former site of the small, marshy fishing village of Havn, whose fortunes were transformed by the arrival of Bishop Absalon in 1167. Although it was subsequently ravaged by a series of fires and bombarded by first the Swedish and then the British, the medieval town's tangle of tiny streets, squares and ancient churches survived and is still very much in evidence today. Indre By is the hub of the city's day-to-day activity and its main shopping district – a maze of lively, attractive streets and squares, all the more enjoyable as its two main thoroughfares are pedestrianized. The first is **Strøget**, the colloquial name (it's not on any street signs) given to the series of connecting streets – Frederiksberggade, Nygade, Vimmel-skaftet, Amagertorv and Østergade – that run across Indre By from Rådhuspladsen in the west to Kongens Nytorv in the east. The other main street, **Købmagergade**, leaves Strøget at Højbro Plads, heading north towards Nørreport Station.

Along Frederiksberggade to the Latin Quarter

East from Rådhuspladsen, **Frederiksberggade** is the first – and tackiest – of the series of streets that make up Strøget, but you soon reach Kattesundet on the left, which leads to the altogether trendier area centred on the streets of **Larsbjørn-stræde**, Studiestræde and Skt Peders Stræde, overflowing with hip new and used clothes shops, independent music stores, secondhand bookshops and chic cafés. Shopping done, it's a few minutes' walk along to the more rarefied atmosphere of the **Latin Quarter**, home to **Copenhagen University**, founded in 1475 to train Catholic priests (though these buildings are now largely administrative), and the dusky pink **Vor Frue Kirke** (daily 8am–5pm), Copenhagen's cathedral. Built in 1829 to a design by the ubiquitous C.F. Hansen, it's largely unremarkable, though you might want to pop inside to see the weighty figure of Christ and the apostles – some crafted by Bertel Thorvaldsen (see p.63), others by his pupils.

Gammeltorv and Nytorv

At the junction with Nørregade, Strøget is flanked by the busy squares of **Gammeltorv** and **Nytorv** ("old" and "new" squares), two large, ancient spaces that mark the site of the first marketplace in Havn, when it was still a fishing village. The wide, gently sloping expanse and presence of the city's Hansen-designed **Domhus** (Law Courts), with its suitably forbidding row of Neoclassical columns, lend a faintly Roman whiff to Nytorv. Continue east down Nygade, then left just before reaching Helligåndskirken down cobbled Valkendorfsgade and through Kringlegangen to reach **Gråbrødretorv**, a charming, café-lined cobbled square that's a favourite spot with locals. Back on Strøget, **Helligåndskirken** (Church of the Holy Ghost; Mon–Fri noon–4pm), founded in 1296 as part of a Catholic monastery of the same name, is one of the oldest churches in the city, though largely rebuilt after the Great Fire of 1728. Entrance is through a beautifully carved sandstone portal dating back to 1620; inside, look out for an impressive altarpiece donated by Christian VI depicting the ascension of Christ. Past the church, at the busy junction with Købmagergade, **Højbro Plads** is always lively, with its two perennially popular cafés and abundance of street entertainers and buskers. To the right of the statue of Absalon is the delightful canalside stretch of **Gammel Strand** ("Old Beach"), its row of cafés and restaurants with outside tables and views over the canal are a great spot for lunch.

Købmagergade

From Hojbro Plads, Indre By's other main shopping street, **Købmagergade**, runs north. At no.37, the **Post & Tele Museum** (Tues & Thurs–Sat 10am–5pm, Wed

10am–8pm, Sun noon–4pm; 50kr, free on Wed; ⓦwww.ptt-museum.dk), charts the history of communication in Denmark, from Christian IV's 1624 decree establishing the Danish Royal Post Office to modern-day mobile phones with a well-displayed collection of old telephones, radio equipment, mock-ups of old post offices, philatelic displays and historical artefacts. The museum has a lovely, rooftop café. You might rather press on to the city's most intriguing landmark, the 42-metre-high **Rundetårn** (Round Tower; mid-May to mid-Sept daily 10am–8pm; mid-Sept to mid-May daily 10am–5pm; 25kr; mid-Oct to mid-March Tues & Wed also open 7–10pm; ⓦwww.rundetaarn.dk) looming two-thirds of the way up Købmagergade. It was built by Christian IV as part of the **Trinitatis** complex, which combined three important facilities for seventeenth-century scholars and students: an astronomical observatory, a church and a university library – the tower functioned both as observatory lookout and as the Trinitatis church tower. It's still a functioning observatory, and the public can view the night sky through the astronomical telescope in the winter period (mid-Oct to mid-March Tues & Wed 7–10pm). Inside, a wide cobbled ramp spirals its way to the top for a wonderful view of the hive of medieval streets below and the city beyond.

Just north of Kultorvet, at Åbenrå 30, the thoroughly entertaining **Musikhistorisk Museum** (Musical History Museum; May–Sept Tues–Sun 1–3.50pm; Oct–April Tues, Wed, Sat & Sun 1–3.50pm; free; ⓦwww.natmus.dk) has an impressive quantity of musical instruments and sound-producing devices spanning the globe and the last thousand years. There are recordings of most of the instruments to listen to.

Kongens Nytorv and Nyhavn

The final and most exclusive section of Strøget – **Østergade** – soon opens out onto the spacious grandeur of **Kongens Nytorv**, with an equestrian statue of its creator, Christian V, at its centre; in summer weary shoppers head for the outdoor seats of the square's high-ceilinged, glass-fronted cafés; in winter, for the cosy dens selling *gløgg* mulled wine and *æbleskiver* (see p.85). The southern end of the square is dominated by the grand late-nineteenth-century **Det Kongelige Teater** (Royal Theatre; guided tours in Danish only every Sun at 11am; 75kr; tickets must be bought in advance from BilletNet or the theatre box office; ⓦwww.kgl-teater.dk; see p.89). Next door, **Charlottenborg Palace** is home to the Royal Academy – the spacious, light rooms of the exhibition hall (Tues–Sun noon–5pm; 60kr, ⓦwww.kunsthalcharlottenborg.dk) at the back hold temporary exhibitions of contemporary art.

Heading off the northeast side of Kongens Nytorv, picture-postcard **Nyhavn** ("new harbour") – created in 1671 as a canal leading from the city's main port to Kongens Nytorv – is mostly known for its sunny northern side, with a long row of bars, cafés and restaurants set in brightly coloured and picturesque gabled houses, some dating back as far as 1681 – Hans Christian Andersen lived at varying times in nos. 18, 20 & 67. In summer, it's packed with locals and tourists alike, and on a sunny day here, drinking beer and snaps and eating plates of herring is about as good as it gets in Copenhagen. Or you can just grab an ice cream or hot-dog and wander along to the end of Nyhavn for a look at the stunning new **Skuespilhus** (Play House; Mon–Sat 8am–11.30pm, Sun 8am–3pm; ⓦwww.skuespilhus.dk; see p.89) and fine harbour views across to the opera house.

Christianshavn

Facing Indre By and Slotsholmen across the waters of Inderhavnen, and linked to them by Knippelsbro bridge, is the charming island of **Christianshavn**. Nicknamed "Little Amsterdam" on account of its pretty canals, cobbled streets and old Dutch-style houses with brightly painted facades, it's a laid-back area with a cosy, neighbourhood feel, and is a pleasant spot to hang out and watch the boats meander up and down the canals. Built on land reclaimed by Christian IV in the early 1600s, the area served two purposes: to protect the city from attack (hence the line of defensive fortifications) and to provide housing for Dutch merchants and local shipbuilding workers.

There are a couple of low-key sights here, though the island's main attraction is, without doubt, Christiania (see below). The **Orlogsmuseet** (Royal Danish Naval Museum; Tues–Sun noon–4pm; 40kr, free on Wed; ⓦwww.orlogsmuseet.dk), on the corner of Bådsmandsstræde and Overgaden Oven Vandet is devoted to the illustrious history of the Danish Navy and boasts a collection of four hundred **ship models** as well as an assortment of uniforms, weapons, nautical instruments and maritime art. Just to the south, soaring skywards through the trees on Skt Annæ Gade, is the unmistakable copper-and-gold spire of Christianshavn's famous landmark, the splendidly Baroque **Vor Frelsers Kirke** (April–Aug Mon–Sat 11am–4.30pm, Sun noon–4.30pm; Sept–March Mon–Sat 11am–3.30pm, Sun noon–3.30pm; ⓦwww.vorfrelserskirke.dk). It was completed in 1696, though the lavish **spire**, with its large golden globe carrying a three-metre Jesus waving a flag, was added later. You can climb the adrenalin-rushing spiral of four hundred slanted steps (11am–4pm, closed Nov–March and on wet and windy days; 25kr), for a fine view of Copenhagen and beyond.

Christiania

Stretching for almost a kilometre along either side of the moat and old ramparts that flank the eastern side of the island, the remarkable "Free City" of **Christiania** (ⓦwww.christiania.org) is living proof of Copenhagen's liberal social traditions. Ever since a group of young and homeless people colonized the complex of disused military barracks here in the spring of 1971, the area has excited controversy, sympathy and admiration in equal amounts. Declared a "free city" by its residents later that year with the aim of operating autonomously from Copenhagen proper, it inevitably became best known outside Denmark for its open selling of hash on "Pusherstreet", while its continued existence on some of Copenhagen's finest real estate has fuelled one of the longest-running debates in Danish society. Christiania has had a rollercoaster ride at the hands of successive governments, who either largely left it alone or tried to bring it under the municipal machinery. Its **future** remains in the balance under the current right-wing government.

From the **main entrance** on Prinsessegade, call in at **Infocaféen** (daily noon–6pm) for a copy of the excellent *Christiania Guide* (10kr). Don't be intimidated by the idea of wandering around by yourself: naturally, the area has a grungy, offbeat feel and you'll get more than the odd whiff of dope, but the atmosphere is welcoming and relaxed (cars aren't allowed). It's worth joining one of the **guided tours** (July & Aug daily 3pm; Sept–June Sat & Sun 3pm; 1hr 30min; 30kr), conducted by residents, that leave from the main entrance. Covering about 85 acres, Christiania spreads out in a loose network of unpaved paths and small green open spaces on both sides of Christian IV's old moat between Christianshavn and Amager (a bridge, Dyssebroen, connects the two sides), many of its ramshackle homes hugging the reedy water's edge in a picture of rural charm. It's a peculiar mix of huge old barracks and warehouses – livened up with vivid murals and now housing community projects like workshops, art centres and crèches – and small, colourful homes. To the right of the main entrance, the **Loppe building** houses the music venue *Loppen* (see p.88), and the highly rated *Spiseloppen* restaurant (see p.82). It also contains Gallopperiet, Christiania's art gallery and information centre (Tues–Sun noon–5pm), and the *Info* café and craft shop. Continuing straight ahead, you soon come to the closest Christiania gets to a commercial centre – **Carl Madsen Plads** – a small square lined with stalls selling snacks, cheap clothing, CDs, jewellery, incense and the like. The square marks the start of **Pusherstreet,** lined with stalls selling pre-rolled joints and an international selection of grass – and wildly popular with tourists. Just ahead, the small square on the right is crowded in summer with the chilled-out clientele of *Nemoland,* Christiania's most popular bar.

A few minutes' walk north of Christiania and occupying a prime waterfront spot is the striking **Operaen** (opera house), designed by Henning Larsen. To fully appreciate the building's unique architecture, including the lavish maple-encased auditorium with its gold-leaf ceiling, you'll have to get tickets for a performance (see p.89) or join a **guided tour** (July daily at 4pm in English, rest of year Sat & Sun 9.30am & 4.30pm primarily in Danish; 100kr).

Rosenborg, Frederiksstaden and Kastellet

There's quite a contrast between the narrow streets of Indre By and the open parks and boulevards of the more modern areas on the northeastern side of the city centre, which owe their character to two royal builders. The first, Christian IV, built the fanciful **Rosenborg Slot** and the fortress of **Kastellet** to the north. The second, Frederik V, gave his name to the district he created, **Frederiksstaden** – a sumptuous royal quarter boasting proud aristocratic monuments such as the **Marmorkirken** and the royal palaces of **Amalienborg.** Some of the city's main art museums are also found in these areas, principally the huge **Statens Museum for Kunst** (Royal Museum of Fine Art), the fine **Hirschsprungske Samling** and the **Kunstindustrimuseet** (Danish Museum for Decorative Arts) – the place to find out about the illustrious history of Danish design.

Rosenborg and around

Rising enchantingly from the carefully manicured lawns of Kongens Have is the Dutch-Renaissance palace of **Rosenborg Slot** (May, Sept & Oct daily 10am–4pm; June–Aug daily 10am–5pm; Nov–April Tues–Sun 11am–2pm, Treasury open till 4pm; 70kr, 90kr for a joint ticket with Amalienborg valid for two days; ⓦwww .rosenborg-slot.dk). Surrounded by a moat and decorated with spires and towers, this playful, red-brick palace was built by Christian IV in 1606. The castle was used as a royal residence until 1710 after which it became a storehouse for various royal collections, opening to the public in 1833. Today's museum covers the period from Christian IV to Frederik VII – the Oldenburg line – and is chronologically organized with rooms devoted to different monarchs.

The highlight of the **ground floor** is **Christian IV**'s private chambers – atmospheric, dark, oak-panelled and preserved largely intact. Room 3, his **bedroom,** is where he died; several personal belongings include his sword and, appropriately, his nightcap and slippers. Next door, in the **Dark Room** is a seventeenth-century armchair with hidden tentacles in the armrests that would grab the wrists of guests unlucky enough to sit in it. The victim would then be soaked with water from a container in the back of the chair before being released to the sound of a small trumpet. The **first floor** is rather less interesting, a labyrinth of ornate rooms in styles appropriate to the monarchs of the day, but don't miss the **Mirror Cabinet** (room 13A) – all four walls are covered in mirrors – commissioned by Frederik IV to indulge his erotic fantasies: the floor mirrors allowed him to peer up his partner's dress. Press on up to the **second floor** and the magnificent **Long Hall,** its walls covered with enormous tapestries showing Christian V's victories in the Scanian War of 1675–79. It's also home to one of the biggest collections of antique silver furniture in the world, including three fabulous silver lions guarding the king's throne. In the **basement**, the **Green Cabinet** houses a huge collection of royal riding regalia, armour and weapons, beyond which lie the dazzling jewels and precious artefacts of the **Treasury**; look out here for the silver Oldenborg Horn, allegedly dating from 989 AD, the **crown of Christian IV** – an exquisite latticework of gold, pearls and minuscule enamel figurines – and the present queen's **crown jewels**.

Adjacent to the *slot* lies central Copenhagen's oldest and prettiest park, **Kongens Have** (Royal Gardens; daily 6am–sunset; free). On the eastern edge, on Kronprinsessegade, the exquisite **Davids Samling** Islamic collection (David Collection; Tues, Fri, Sat & Sun 1–5pm, Weds & Thurs 10am–5pm; free; Ⓦ www.davidmus.dk) is an Aladdin's cave of Persian, Arabian and Indian antiques, some dating back to the sixth century, with everything from delicate embroidered silks and savage-looking daggers to illuminated manuscripts and Korans.

Across Øster Voldgade from Kongens Have, the glorious **Botanisk Have** (May–Sept daily 8.30am–6pm; Oct–April Tues–Sun 8.30am–4pm; free; Ⓦ www.botanic-garden.ku.dk) make for a lovely wander around the small coniferous forest, rock gardens and waterfalls, with further botanic thrills provided by the circular **palmehus** (palm house; daily 10am–3pm). At the northeastern corner of Botanisk Have, the **Geologisk Museum** (Tues–Sun 1–4pm; 40kr; Ⓦ www.geological-museum.dk) has the usual collection of minerals, meteorites and dinosaur bones.

Statens Museum for Kunst

The huge **Statens Museum for Kunst** (Royal Museum of Fine Arts; Tues & Thurs–Sun 10am–5pm, Wed 10am–8pm; free; Ⓦ www.smk.dk) is well worth visiting. The old building's second floor houses the main collection of **Danish Art from 1750–1900**; a central room offers a chronological taster and includes a fine selection of Golden Age works, with views of Rome by C.W. Eckersberg, landscapes by P.C. Skovgaard and views of Copenhagen by Christen Købke. The surrounding rooms explore certain artists and themes in more depth, including the Skagen painters, particularly P.S. Krøyer and Michael and Anna Ancher. One impressive room is dominated by the powerful work of Vilhelm Hammershøi – a mixture of empty, almost photographic scenes of Copenhagen buildings, and haunting portraits and nudes.

The **modern art** collections, to the right of the main stairs, highlight most of the major movements of the twentieth century. One huge room displays Danish painting and sculpture after 1960, with colourful canvases by Per Kirkeby and dramatic pieces by Asger Jorn, a member of the CoBrA movement (a group of mid-twentieth-century artists from *Co*penhagen, *Br*ussels and *A*msterdam). The rooms around concentrate on 1900 to the present day with a great selection of paintings by Matisse – the equivalent of many larger museums. Here too is work by Andre Derain, Braque, Dufy, Léger, Picasso and Gris, as well a couple of Modiglianis.

In the modern wing, **Foreign Art from 1300–1800** (mostly European) offers up a taster of Italian, Dutch and Flemish masters with some lesser-known Tintorettos, Brueghels, Rembrandts and Van Dycks. Some artists or movements get their own rooms, among them Lucas Cranach the Elder, Rembrandt and his workshop, Rubens and Jacob Jordaens, and the Italian Renaissance with works by Mantegna and Fra Filippo Lippi. The huge central room pulls all the themes together with paintings crammed floor to ceiling, old-style, and grouped by genre – still lifes, portraits and landscapes.

Den Hirschsprungske Samling

There's more art to be had nearby at **Den Hirschsprungske Samling** (Hirschs-prung Collection; daily except Tues 11am–4pm; 35kr, Wed free; ⑩ www .hirschsprung.dk), a gem of a gallery devoted to nineteenth-century Danish art – a particularly illustrious and productive period. The works were donated to the state in 1902 by second-generation German-Jewish immigrant and tobacco magnate Heinrich Hirschsprung. The **Golden Age** (roughly 1810–40) is initially reflected through a collection of pieces by C.W. Eckersberg, one of Denmark's first profes-sional artists, whose work was rooted firmly in romantic and idealistic traditions (*Woman Before a Mirror* is typical, with a poetic picture of a flesh-and-blood Venus de Milo); there are also plentiful gentle Danish landscapes by his students, such as Christen Købke and William Bendz. Other gallery highlights include Harold Slott-Møller's *Spring*, a simple but engaging painting of a young girl, her hair garlanded with yellow flowers, and the melancholy, haunting symbolism of the paintings of Ejnar Nielsen and Vilhelm Hammershøi. Room 20 contains a large collection of works by the **Skagen painters** from the town on the northernmost tip of the country renowned for its bewitching light – some of whom Hirschs-prung personally supported. P.S. Krøyer's paintings give a real feel for the qualities of Skagen's light, in particular the familiar *Self-portrait with Wife* and the enchanting *Summers Day on South Beach at Skagen*.

Frederiksstaden and around

Bordered by the harbourfront to the east and cut in two by the broad sweep of Bredgade, the **Frederiksstaden** district to the east of Rosenborg was commis-sioned by Frederik V and designed by Danish architect Nicolai Eigtved as a royal quarter fit for a noble elite. Rising majestically on the western side of Bredgade is the large green dome of the grandiose **Marmorkirken** (Marble Church; Mon–Thurs & Sat 10am–5pm, Wed 10am 6.30pm, Fri & Sun noon–5pm, free; ⑩ www.marmorkirken.dk). Frederik V himself laid the church's first stone in a grand ceremony in 1749, but the building took 145 years to complete, largely due to the expense of the original Norwegian marble – it was eventually finished using cheaper Danish marble. The **interior** of the church is grandly proportioned, if a bit drab – you can see the change from Norwegian to Danish marble about a quarter of the way up the walls. The real reason to visit, though, is to climb the 260 steep, twisting steps to the top of the **bell tower** (mid-June to Aug daily 1 & 3pm; Sept to mid-June Sat & Sun 1 & 3pm; 25kr). A guide will lead you to the summit where the grand vista of Copenhagen is laid before you; on a clear day you can see as far as Malmö, Helsingør and across the city to Roskilde.

Heading across Bredgade from Marmorkirken and along Frederiksgade, you reach Amalienborg Slotsplads. The square is surrounded by the four palaces of **Amalienborg**, centrepiece of Frederik V's Louis XV-inspired model town, and the home of the Danish royal family since 1794. The four almost identical palaces are functional rather than sumptuous. You're free to wander round the *slotsplads* and you might want to time your visit with the **changing of the guard** (daily at noon), during which the bearskin-hatted guards march back to their barracks beside Rosenborg Slot.

The first palace on the left from Frederiksgade – Christian VIII's Palace – is home to **De Danske Kongers Kronologiske Samling** (Royal Danish Collection; May–Oct daily 10am–4pm; Nov–April Tues–Sun 11am–4pm; 55kr, joint ticket with Rosenborg Slot 90kr; ⑩ www.amalienborgmuseet.dk), de facto shrine to the monarchy. It's a mishmash of family mementos and carefully preserved living quarters, the latter shielded behind glass screens yet still managing to transmit something of the character of the monarchs who inhabited them. Some are filled with assorted hunting regalia and military tackle, while others are more homely affairs, with family portraits, pipes and slippers. Diagonally across the *slotsplads*, past the enormous **equestrian statue** of Frederik V, is the Queen's current residence in Christian IX's (her father's) palace. To the right, Frederik VIII's Palace (also called Brockdorff's Palace) is home to the crown prince and his young family.

Kunstindustrimuseet

Housed in a sumptuous Rococo building from 1757, the **Kunstindustrimuseet** (Danish Museum of Art and Design; Tues–Sun 11am–5pm; 50kr; ⓦwww .kunstindustrimuseet.dk), Bredgade 68, traces the development of European (and particularly Danish) design from 1400 to the present day through its fine collections of furniture, ceramics, arts and crafts. It also examines the influence of Eastern styles on Western design. There are some really beautiful pieces here ranging from early Japanese porcelains to Chippendale furniture; look out, too, for the velvet-lined trunk containing a spectacular silver toiletry set given to the unfortunate Princess Caroline Mathilde by George III when she left England for Denmark. But it's the **twentieth-century design** wing that makes it really worth the visit – the place to see why Danish design is renowned throughout the world and how it all came about. There's plenty on the history and philosophy behind the work of the founding fathers – Kaare Klint, Hans Wegner, Arne Jacobsen and Poul Henningsen – and several rooms devoted to their iconic, still effortlessly stylish creations.

Kastellet and around

At the far end of Bredgade you'll find the green open spaces of Kastellet (see below) and Churchillparken, named after the British wartime leader. Within Churchillparken, the moving **Frihedsmuseet** (Museum of Danish Resistance; Tues–Sun: May–Sept 10am–5pm; Oct–April 10am–3pm; free; free guided tours in English May–Sept Tues, Thurs & Sun 2pm; ⓦwww.natmus.dk) offers a comprehensive account of Denmark's role in World War II, grasping the thorny issue of the Danish government's collusion with German rule. Exhibits take you through the slow build-up of resistance, beginning with the first acts of sabotage carried out in 1942 by a remarkable group of teenage boys from Århus called the **Churchill Gang**, whose courage and spirit spurred on other groups (mostly made up of Danish communists). The covert 1943 mass evacuation of Denmark's **Jewish population** (see p.63 & p.294) is also documented. Just past the museum stands the incongruous British St Alban's church and the completely over-the-top **Gefion fountain**.

Past Churchillparken, the star-shaped fortress of **Kastellet** (daily 6am–10pm; free) was conceived by Christian IV as the key element in the city's defences – occupied by troops since 1660, it remains the only part of the city's ancient defence system and is still in use, if only for administration. You enter via one of two gates – Kongensporten, near Churchillparken to the south, and Norgesporten, at the opposite end near the Little Mermaid. Kastellet's principal attraction has for generations been the chance for a leisurely stroll around its grassy bastions, moats and ramparts. A stone's throw from Kastellet (take Norgesporten gate) on the stretch of coastline called Langelinie, and poised on a pile of carefully positioned rocks by the harbour's edge, is the statue of the **Den Lille Havfrue**, better known as the **Little Mermaid**. Created in 1913 by Edvard Eriksen, this rather plain bronze figure has become the city's most enduring symbol despite its modest dimensions, and continues to exert an inexplicable magnetism on Danes and visitors alike. Inspired by the 1837 Hans Christian Andersen story of the same name, the statue was commissioned by Carlsberg brewery boss and art lover Carl Jacobsen after he had seen a performance of a ballet based on the story at the Royal

Theatre; the face is that of the prima ballerina, Ellen Price, the body that of Eriksen's wife (Price wouldn't pose nude).

Rådhuspladsen and around

Sandwiched between Indre By and Vesterbro, the area around the buzzing **Rådhuspladsen** town hall square is Copenhagen at its most frivolous, touristy and sometimes downright tacky. Top of the bill are the wonderful pleasure gardens of **Tivoli** – tagging along for the ride are plenty of other mass-appeal family amusements of varying quality. That said, the area is far more than an enormous fairground. Just south of the Rådhuspladsen lurk a few of the city's cultural heavyweights: the **Ny Carlsberg Glyptotek**, with its soothing collections of sculptures and paintings; the unmissable **Nationalmuseet**, home to many of Denmark's historic treasures; and the slick **Danish Design Centre**.

Rådhuspladsen

Flanked by two busy roads, **Rådhuspladsen**, Copenhagen's principal square, is dominated by the enormous Italianate red-brick **Rådhus** (Mon–Fri 10am–4pm, free; guided tours Mon–Fri 3pm, Sat 10am & 11am; 30kr; Ⓦ www.copenhagen city.dk). Designed by Martin Nyrop and completed in 1905, it's worth a little exploration, though given the building's size, you're better off joining a guided tour, which takes you behind locked doors to a series of impressive wood-panelled rooms such as the Banqueting Hall, lined with the coats of arms of Denmark's merchant towns. At 106 metres, the Rådhus's **tower** (guided tours Mon–Fri 11am & 2pm, Sat noon; 20kr) is Denmark's highest. It's about three hundred steps up to the balcony, and a further fifty through a narrow passageway to the spire (there is a lift too), but you'll be rewarded with a view along the length of Strøget to Kongens Nytorv. In a side room close to the entrance, what looks like a mass of inscrutable dials is in fact the astronomical timepiece of **Jens Olsen's Verdensur** (Jens Olsen's World Clock; Mon–Fri 8.30am–4.30pm, Sat 10am–1pm; 10kr). Set in motion in 1955, the clock features a 570,000-year calendar plotting eclipses of the moon and sun, solar time, local time and various planetary orbits – all with incredible accuracy.

Also on the square, on the northern side, at no. 57, **The Wonderful World of Hans Christian Andersen** (Jan to mid-June & Sept to Dec Mon–Fri 10am–6pm, Sat & Sun till 8pm; mid-June to Aug daily 10am–10pm, 87kr; Ⓦ www.topattractions .dk) offers a lighthearted jaunt through the life and works of the celebrated fairytale author, aimed squarely at the kids, with mock-ups of his childhood home and so on, and animated tableaux of some of his more popular tales.

A few minutes' walk southeast of the Rådhus, at Hans Christian Andersen Blvd 27, is the Henning Larsen designed, glass-fronted **Danish Design Centre** (Mon–Fri 10am–5pm, Wed open till 9pm & free from 5pm; Sat & Sun 11am–4pm; 40kr; Ⓦ www.ddc.dk). It's largely given over to temporary exhibitions but the **shop** makes it worth the effort, with an excellent range of books on design and architecture, plus drawers full of dinky designer gadgets.

Tivoli

With its main entrance at Vesterbrogade 3, Denmark's most popular tourist attraction is the delightful **Tivoli** (summer season: Mon–Thurs & Sun 11am–11pm, Fri & Sat 11am–midnight [from mid-June to mid-Aug open daily till midnight]; Halloween [October half-term] & Christmas season [mid-Nov to end Dec] Mon–Thurs & Sun 11am–10pm, Fri & Sat open till 11pm; adults 95kr, children 45kr; Ⓦ www.tivoli.dk), and though the relatively small number of **rides** here can't compete with the stomach-flipping thrills of modern theme parks, its popularity shows no signs of dimming – and to the Danes, Tivoli is nothing short of a national treasure. Since the gardens opened in 1843, the number of rides has grown from two to around twenty-five, but Tivoli has stayed faithful to its pleasure garden image – the delightful landscaped **gardens**, fairground stalls, plentiful restaurants, bandstands, theatres and concert halls as much a part of the experience as the rides. All in all, it's an expensive day out, with rides costing 20–80kr (best to opt for a multi-ride ticket at 205kr for adults, 170kr for children), high food prices and those for alcoholic drinks a white-knuckle ride in themselves, but a few hours wandering about here is time well spent, while on a fine summer's night, with the twinkling illuminations, it's almost magical. Tivoli has its historical aspect too, with a number of playful and well-maintained period buildings, notably the Chinese-style, open-air **Pantomime Theatre**, built in 1874. **Music**, some of it free with the admission price, plays a large part in Tivoli; check the programme for details of that day's events. In addition to the **Concert Hall** (ticket only, see p.89) there are several smaller venues and bandstands playing jazz and blues, while the open-air "Plænen" stage, given over most of the time to displays of acrobatics and dance, hosts Danish rock bands (and the occasional international rock and pop act) free every Friday at 10pm.

Tivoli has around thirty **food outlets** spanning the full range from hot-dog stands to a Michelin-starred restaurant. An undisputed favourite is the country-cabin style *Grøften* (☎ 33 75 06 75; booking advisable), which dishes up mouthwatering traditional Danish food, including an extensive smørrebrød selection. Alternatively, try *Restaurant Nimb* (☎ 88 70 00 10, ⓦ www.nimb.dk; booking advisable), a laid-back brasserie serving up delicious Danish classics in the glistening white Nimb complex – a faux-Moorish palace housing an upmarket hotel, several eateries, a wine bar and the tempting *Løgismose* deli (see p.92), whose gourmet hot-dogs put the rest of the park's bangers to shame.

Tycho Brahe Planetarium

At Gammel Kongevej 10, the **Tycho Brahe Planetarium** (Mon 1–9pm, Tues–Sun 10.30am–9pm; 130kr including exhibition, IMAX or 3D film; ⓦ www .tycho.dk), named after the famous sixteenth-century Danish astronomer, is home to a rather unexciting exhibition on the stars, planets and space travel. The only real reason to come here is the **IMAX cinema**, which shows hourly films (you'll need to rent headphones with English translations; 20kr), though they're more likely to be about ancient Egypt, deep-sea exploration or dolphins than anything astronomical.

Ny Carlsberg Glyptotek

Back on Hans Christian Andersen Boulevard, at Dantes Plads 7, the **Ny Carlsberg Glyptotek** (Tues–Sun 11am–5pm; 60kr, Sun free; ⓦ www.glyptoteket.com) was opened in 1897 by the philanthropic Carlsberg brewing magnate Carl Jacobsen to exhibit the collection of classical and modern art that he had generously donated to the state. Its focal point is the delightful glass-domed **Winter Garden** (*vinterhave*), filled with soaring palm trees, a fountain and statues, and with a superb **café**.

The building is somewhat confusingly made up of three sections; the entrance hall leads you into the oldest part, the **Dahlerup building** where, spread over two floors, you'll find the collections of **French and Danish sculpture**, with a bit of Danish painting thrown in. The undisputed highlight here is the particularly fine haul of **Rodins** – the largest outside France, including a version of *The Kiss* and the powerful *Burghers of Calais*. Head through the Winter Garden into the **Kampmann Building** for the recently revamped **Ancient Mediterranean** galleries, which seek to emphasize how the Ancient Greeks, Phoenicians, Etruscans and Romans influenced each other. It's pretty exhaustive, with thousands of exhibits ranging from sacrificial drinking cups found in Greek burial tombs to Roman coins. But it's the large and diverse **Etruscan** collection that really stands out, its impressive array of artefacts – votive offerings, sculptures, figurines, funerary items and jewellery – providing ample evidence of the Etruscans' mastery of gold, bronze, terracotta and stone. Finish off your classical tour with a stroll through the sculpture galleries, which kick off in rooms 1–4 with a small but excellent collection of **Egyptian** artefacts and continue with a seemingly endless procession of busts and statues of famous Greeks and Romans.

Occupying the modern Henning Larsen-designed **French Wing** (rooms 56–66; access from the Winter Garden), the museum's excellent collection of nineteenth- and twentieth-century **French painting** from Jacques-Louis David to Gauguin shouldn't be missed. The lower ground floor (rooms 56–60) displays works by the precursors of the Impressionists, with artists from the Barbizon school well represented via works by Corot, Delacroix, Courbet and Manet, including a version of the latter's well-known *Execution of Emperor Maximilian* and *The Absinthe Drinker*. The ground floor is given over to the **Impressionists** (rooms 61 & 62), with some exquisite Monets (notably *The Lemon Grove*), a few lesser-known Renoirs and a complete set of charming Degas bronze figurines. The exhibition continues upstairs with the **Post Impressionists** (rooms 63–66), including works by Toulouse-Lautrec, Pissarro, Bonnard and Van Gogh. **Gauguin** is particularly well represented (he was married to a Dane and spent a year in Copenhagen as a stockbroker) with over thirty paintings.

Nationalmuseet

To the east of Rådhuspladsen, on Ny Vestergade, the wonderful **Nationalmuseet** (Tues–Sun 10am–5pm; free; @ www.natmus.dk) is home to the country's finest collection of Danish artefacts, from the Ice Age to the present day, as well as fascinating ethnographic collections from around the world. For most, the highlight is **Danish Prehistory**, a thrilling trip through 14,000 years of prehistory, featuring a number of stunning treasures, most of them excavated from the country's peat bogs, which acted as a preservative on anything buried in them, often precious objects deliberately thrown in to curry favour with the marsh gods. Highlights include the 3500-year-old oak coffin and body of **Egtved Girl**, whose clothes, comb, bracelets and blonde hair have all survived eerily intact, the beautifully crafted **Trundholm Sun Chariot** (1400 BC), an enchanting model made by sun-worshippers that depicts a magical horse-drawn chariot pulling a gold-leaf sun disc across the heavens, and the dazzling solid-silver **Gundestrup Cauldron**, with its perfectly preserved reliefs of Celtic mythical figures and gods. The **Viking collection** makes a fine finish to the period, with everyday tools and artefacts, clothes and weapons as well as plentiful examples of shimmering filigree silver jewellery, coins and ingots, many of them from private stashes buried in times of unrest.

Upstairs on the first floor, there's an extensive display of religious and royal paraphernalia, weapons, furniture and household objects spanning the Middle Ages and Renaissance, while, up on the second floor, the exhaustive "**Stories of Denmark**" picks up the story from 1660 to the present, highlighting key historical and cultural events in the country's history. The bulk of the rest of the museum is taken up by the huge and exceptionally diverse **ethnographic collection** – a captivating journey through non-European art and culture with Africa, China, India and Japan particularly well represented. The fascinating section on **Inuit culture** shouldn't be missed for its impressive collection of whalebone carvings, harpoons, sealskin kayaks, furry boots and clothing, and spooky-looking sealskin whaling costumes.

Vesterbro and Frederiksberg

The two districts immediately west of the city centre, Vesterbro and Frederiksberg, couldn't be more different. **VESTERBRO** has always been determinedly working class, and also has a diverse racial mix, yet despite encroaching gentrification it remains one of the most colourful areas of Copenhagen, with the broadest selection of affordable ethnic restaurants and shops. There's a real sense of community here and a burgeoning new cultural scene centred on the historic buildings of the area's former meatpacking district, **Kødbyen**, and the adjacent square of **Halmtorvet**, with their hyper-trendy restaurants, bars, art galleries and venues. The area also boasts a vibrant street life along its three main thoroughfares – **Vesterbrogade**, **Istedgade** and **Sønder Boulevard**. Vesterbrogade is the district's major artery and one of the city's main shopping streets – more affordable than Strøget and with good restaurants and nightlife. The area around Istedgade by Central Station is the only part of the city where you might feel a little vulnerable at night – it's home to what's left of the city's red-light district, though a high police presence probably makes it one of the safest areas in the city.

At Vesterbrogade 59, **Københavns Bymuseum** (City Museum; Mon, Tues & Thurs–Sun 10am–4pm, Wed 10am–9pm; 20kr, free on Fri; Ⓦwww.bymuseum .dk) provides a slightly confusing but interesting introduction to Copenhagen's chaotic history (be sure to pick up an audioguide to get the most out of your visit); look out, in particular, for the sections on the impact of Christian IV's expansive building programmes on the city (some of his drawings are actually on display here); and, upstairs, the room devoted to **Søren Kierkegaard** (see box opposite), filled with his personal effects, caricatures of the man himself and paintings of his girlfriend Regine Olsen.

Continuing west for a couple of minutes along Vesterbrogade you come to **Værnedamsvej** – lined with speciality food shops of all kinds and the ideal place to put together a picnic before heading up to Frederiksberg Have (see p.75). From

---

Søren Kierkegaard

Søren Kierkegaard (1813–1855) – one of the most famous, if not the most comprehensible, philosophers of all time – is inextricably linked with Copenhagen, yet his championing of individual will over social conventions and his rejection of materialism did little to endear him to his fellow Danes. Weighed down by his puritanical father's lectures on the suffering of Christ and the inevitable misery of the world, the young Kierkegaard developed a morbid, depressive and, at the age of 25, deeply religious personality, which led him to end his engagement to the love of his life, Regine Olsen, for fear of drawing her into his melancholy and himself away from God. The resulting emotional trauma saw him flee to Berlin where he turned feverishly to writing, with the publication in 1843 of his first book, **Either/Or** – a philosophical examination of the conflicting emotions of his doomed love affair – and a concerted writing spell that lasted ten years. Few people understood *Either/Or*, with its discussion of the two worlds – the "aesthetic" (man's love of the bodily, sensory, material world and all its sins) and the "ethical" (man's relationship with the spiritual and eternal) – and the individual's resulting "dread" or angst at trying to reconcile the two. Kierkegaard, however, came to revel in the enigma he had created, becoming a "walking mystery in the streets of Copenhagen" (he lived in a house on Nytorv). His greatest philosophical works – *Either/Or*, *The Concept of Dread* and *Fear and Trembling* – are often claimed to have laid the foundations of **existentialism**.

here, it's a twenty-minute walk west along Vesterbrogade, then a left turn along Pile Allé, to the **Carlsberg Brewery Visitor Centre** (Mon–Wed & Fri–Sun 10am–5pm, Thurs 10am–7.30pm; 60kr; Ⓦwww.visitcarlsberg.dk) at Gamle Carlsberg Vej 11 – an entertaining ramble through the history of beer brewing in Denmark and the role of beer in Danish social history. Sadly, the bulk of the company's beer isn't brewed here any more but Carlsberg have retained the tradition of handing out a free beer at the end of your visit, in the bar overlooking the Jacobsen Microbrewery, which brews relatively small quantities of gourmet lager. While here, take a look at the beautifully carved **Elephant Gate**, around the corner from the visitor centre on Ny Carlsberg Vej.

In stark contrast to Vesterbro, **FREDERIKSBERG**'s wealthy residents tend to stay behind the doors of their grand villas, and the spacious and leafy roads here are relatively lifeless. Just beyond the City Museum (see p.74), the wide, tree-lined Frederiksberg Allé branches off Vesterbrogade and slopes gently up to the expansive English-style gardens of **Frederiksberg Have** (daily 6am–sunset; free), which stretch out in a network of pathways, lakes and canals that crisscross beautiful lime-tree groves. The grassy slopes, ponds and fountains attract hordes of picnicking locals in summer and intriguing follies, temples and grottoes abound. At their southern end, the gardens take on a distinctly more ordered, French-inspired look as they slope up to the pale yellow **Frederiksberg Slot**, the royal family's summer residence until the mid-1800s, when it was taken over by the Danish Officers' Academy. Next to Frederiksberg Slot, **København Zoo** (March Mon–Fri 9am–4pm, Sat & Sun 9am–5pm; April, May & Sept Mon–Fri 9am–5pm, Sat & Sun 9am–6pm; early to mid-June & mid to end-Aug daily 9am–6pm; end June to mid-Aug daily 9am–9pm; Oct daily 9am–5pm; Nov–Feb daily 9am–4pm; 130kr; Ⓦwww.zoo.dk) has the usual array of primates, huge bears and big cats; don't miss the grand Norman Foster-designed **Elephant House** and the open-plan African savannah area, where giraffes, impala and okapi look relatively at home.

Nørrebro and Østerbro

To the north and east of the city centre, the districts of Nørrebro and Østerbro both developed mainly during the mid-nineteenth century, but have deeply contrasting histories. **Nørrebro**'s roots are staunchly working class, and its residents have a reputation for political activism and rebellion. In the 1980s, immigrants started to arrive here, bringing much-needed cultural diversity to the city; they now rub shoulders with Danish yuppies lured by the low property prices. Though rather short on specific sights, Nørrebro is one of the most exciting, up-and-coming parts of the city – a great mix of markets, ethnic food stores and restaurants, designer and secondhand shops and hip cafés, bars and clubs. At the heart of Nørrebro, the small square of **Sankt Hans Torv** is a hub of Parisian-style cafés and bars catering to the city's bright young things, while two streets close by are well worth a wander. **Ravnsborggade**, just to the east, is lined with secondhand furniture and knick-knack shops interspersed with Danish designer clothes shops; while **Elmegade**, leading south off the square, has a mass of small, quirky deli-bars, selling all sorts of food from eastern European to Japanese sushi. Southeast across busy Nørrebrogade, you come to the intersection with **Blågårdsgade**, a pleasant, pedestrianized street and the heart of Copenhagen's immigrant and alternative communities – there's an intriguing multicultural mix of inexpensive restaurants and bars along here, and in the adjacent tree-fringed square of Blågårds Plads, with its own cluster of cafés.

Northwest of Blågårdsgade, heading along Nørrebrogade for around half a kilometre takes you to the unmistakable, graffiti-covered yellow walls of

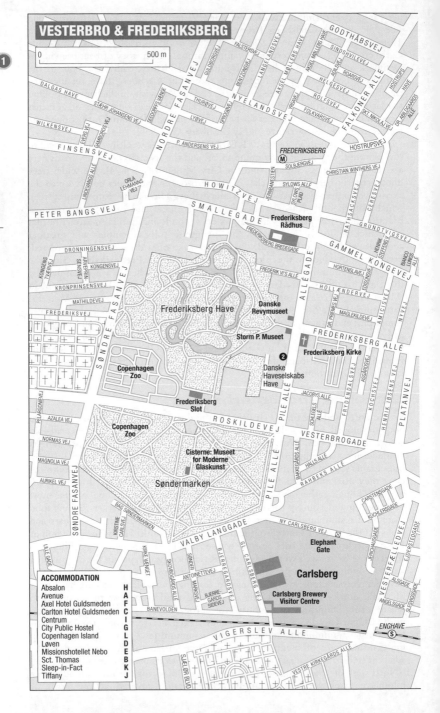

VESTERBRO & FREDERIKSBERG

0 — 500 m

GODTHÅBSVEJ

FALSTERSVEJ · LANGELANDSVEJ · AKSEL MØLLERS HAVE · SINDSHVILEVEJ
GULDBORGVEJ · BATZONSVEJ · ADIL TOFTS VEJ · ROARSVEJ
DALGAS HAVE · NORDRE FASANVEJ · THURØVEJ · HELGESVEJ
STÆHR JOHANSENS VEJ · SEEDORFFS VÆNGE · NYELANDSVEJ · ROLFSVEJ · FALKONER ALLE
WILKENSVEJ · EVERSVEJ · GAMBORGS VEJ · SPERGELVEJ · TRANEVEJ · FOLKVARSVEJ · HOSTRUPS HAVE
LYØVEJ · SKT. NIKOLAJ VEJ · DR. ABILDGAARDS ALLE
FINSENSVEJ · P. ANDERSENS VEJ
ORLA LEHMANNS VEJ · FREDERIKSBERG **Ⓜ** · SOLBJERGVEJ · CHRISTIAN WINTHERS VEJ · HOSTRUPSVEJ
LINDEVANGS ALLE · HØWITZVEJ · BERNHARD BANGS ALLE · SYLOWS ALLE · SYLOWS PLADS · RATHSACKSVEJ · CERESVEJ
PETER BANGS VEJ · SMALLEGADE · **Frederiksberg Rådhus** · GRUNDTVIGSVEJ
DRONNINGENSVEJ · FREDERIKSBERG BREDEGADE · GAMMEL KONGEVEJ · HENRIK STEFFENS · BIANCO LUNOS ALLE
KONGENS TVÆRVEJ · ARVEPRINSENSVEJ · KRONPRINSENSVEJ · KONGENSVEJ · FREDERIK VI'S ALLE · HORTENSIAVEJ
MATHILDEVEJ · SØNDRE FASANVEJ · **Frederiksberg Have** · **Danske Revymuseet** · HOLLÆNDERVEJ · DR. PRIEMES VEJ · MAGLEKILDEVEJ · AMICISVEJ · NYVEJ
FREDERIKSVEJ · **Storm P. Museet** · FREDERIKSBERG ALLE
❷ · **Frederiksberg Kirke** ✝
Copenhagen Zoo · Danske Haveselskabs Have · ASGÅRDSVEJ · FRYDENDALSVEJ · KOCHSVEJ · HENRIK IBSENS VEJ · PLATANVEJ
Frederiksberg Slot · JACOBYS ALLE · SCHLEGELS ALLE
Copenhagen Zoo · ROSKILDEVEJ · PILE ALLE · VESTERBROGADE
PELARGONIEVEJ · AZALEA VEJ · **Cisterne: Museet for Moderne Glaskunst** · BAKKEGÅRDS ALLE · HALLS ALLE
NORMAS VEJ · MAGNOLIA VEJ · **Søndermarken** · RAHBEKS ALLE
AURIKEL VEJ · SØNDRE FASANVEJ · BAG SØNDERMARKEN · CARSTENSGADE · KÜCHLERSGADE
ULLE VOLD · KIRSTINE CARLSENS VEJ · NY CARLSBERG VEJ · JERICHAUSGADE · ENGHAVEVEJ · EJDERSTEDGADE
VALBY LANGGADE · **Elephant Gate** ✉ · ALSGADE
KIRKE VÆNGET · BJERREGÅRDSVEJ · GL. CARLSBERG VEJ · **Carlsberg** · ESTRIDSGADE · ANGELSGADE · VESTERFÆLLEDVEJ
SKOVBOGÅRDS ALLE · SØNDER MARKVEJ · ANTOINETTEVEJ · BJERRE-GÅRDS SIDEVEJ · **Carlsberg Brewery Visitor Centre**
BANEVOLDEN · VIGERSLEV ALLE · ENGHAVE **Ⓢ**
SLAELØR BLVD · VESTRE KIRKEGÅRDS ALLE · VESTRE KIRKEGÅRDS ALLE

ACCOMMODATION	
Absalon	H
Avenue	A
Axel Hotel Guldsmeden	F
Carlton Hotel Guldsmeden	C
Centrum	I
City Public Hostel	G
Copenhagen Island	L
Løven	D
Missionshotellet Nebo	E
Sct. Thomas	B
Sleep-in-Fact	K
Tiffany	J

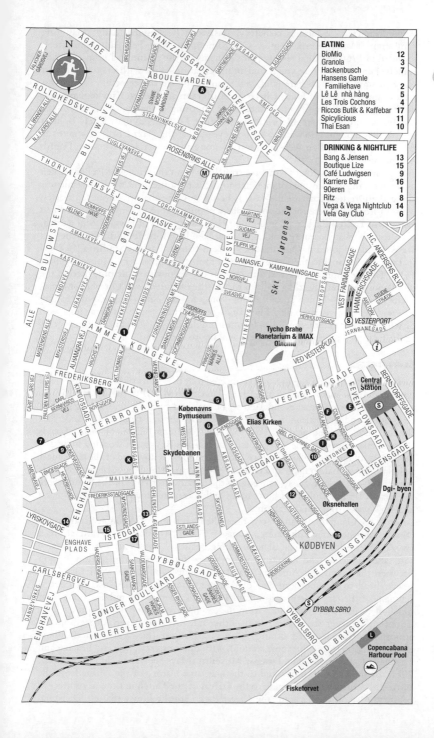

EATING

BioMio	12
Granola	3
Hackenbusch	7
Hansens Gamle Familiehave	2
Lê Lê nhà hàng	5
Les Trois Cochons	4
Riccos Butik & Kaffebar	17
Spicylicious	11
Thai Esan	10

DRINKING & NIGHTLIFE

Bang & Jensen	13
Boutique Lize	15
Café Ludwigsen	9
Karriere Bar	16
90eren	1
Ritz	8
Vega & Vega Nightclub	14
Vela Gay Club	6

Tycho Brahe Planetarium & IMAX Cinema

Københavns Bymuseum

Elias Kirken

Skydebanen

Øksnehallen

KØDBYEN

Dgi- byen

Central Station

Copencabana Harbour Pool

Fisketorvet

Copenhagen's most famous cemetery, **Assistens Kirkegård** (daily: May–Aug 8am–8pm; March, April, Sept & Oct 8am–6pm; Nov–Feb 8am–4pm; free); founded in 1760 and final resting place of many of the country's luminaries. The Kapelvej entrance, where you'll find an information office with maps, is the best place to start. Close to here (and well signposted) are the cemetery's two most famous graves, those of **Hans Christian Andersen** and **Søren Kierkegaard**, but don't expect anything grand. Rather more imposing is the owl-topped tomb of the Bohr family, where Nobel Prize-winning Danish physicist Niels Bohr is interred; you might also want to keep an eye out for the "Jazz Corner", where the American musician Ben Webster is buried alongside several lesser-known Danish jazz players.

The salubrious suburb of **Østerbro**, stretching from the fringes of Fælled Parken in the west through to the commercial docks, warehouses and wealthy residences along the Øresund coast to the east, is home to Copenhagen's moneyed classes. Most visitors head here for the enormously popular green expanses and tree-lined avenues of **Fælled Parken** (Community Park), with acres of lawn, a scent garden, playgrounds, skateboarding rink, and, at weekends, informal football matches (all are welcome to join in). On the park's eastern fringe, **Parken Stadium** (Ⓦwww .parken.dk) is home to the Danish national football team and FC Copenhagen or FCK. The area's only other real attraction is the **Experimentarium**, sited in the old Tuborg brewery bottling hall on the northeastern edge of Østerbro (Mon & Wed–Fri 9.30am–5pm, Tues 9.30am–9pm, Sat & Sun 11am–5pm; 145kr; Ⓦwww.experimentarium.dk). This hands-on "science centre" is great fun, with or without kids, and there are also lectures and demonstrations on a wide range of scientific topics (anything from cheese-making to dissection).

Amager

Just southeast of the city centre, and connected to it by a series of lifting bridges (and the superb new metro line), is the large island of **AMAGER** (pronounced *Ama*), home to some lovely beaches and stretches of park and currently undergoing gradual renovation and gentrification. Crossing Langebro bridge from H.C. Andersens Boulevard and Rådhuspladsen (bus #5A, #12, #33 or #250S; or metro Islands Brygge) takes you onto the harbour strip of **Islands Brygge**; a working industrial harbour until the mid 1980s, it's since had a facelift and is now one of the city's most popular summer hangouts, with a harbour pool (see p.94) and the adjacent Havneparken, a 400-metre long grassy strip edging the northwestern side of the island where the Islands Brygge Kulturhus hosts bands and entertainment year-round and has a laid-back waterfront café/restaurant.

Across the island on its eastern coastline, the **beach** area of **Amager Strandpark** (Ⓦwww.amager-strand.dk; metro Amager Strand) is another big attraction, a two-kilometre-long artificial island boasting beautiful – and extremely popular – soft sandy beaches, and kayaking and other watersports in the shallow lagoon between the island and Amager "mainland". Once you've had your fill of the beach, head to the southern end of Amager Strandpark and **Kastrup Fort**, a remnant of the city's fortification from 1886. It's open to the public, though not much of its past is evident, apart from the casemate and some old cannons.

South of Amager Strandpark, on the other side of Copenhagen Airport, lies the atmospheric cobblestoned fishing village of **Dragør** (bus #30 from Rådhuspladsen, #350S from Nørreport station), with quaint streets, peaceful beaches and a couple of attractions. The **Dragør Museum** (May–Sept Tues–Sun noon–4pm; 20kr), by the harbour, is devoted to the maritime history of the village from the thirteenth-century herring trade to the arrival of the Dutch in the early sixteenth century. Also on the harbour, the *Dragør Røgeri* **smoke house** (Easter–Christmas

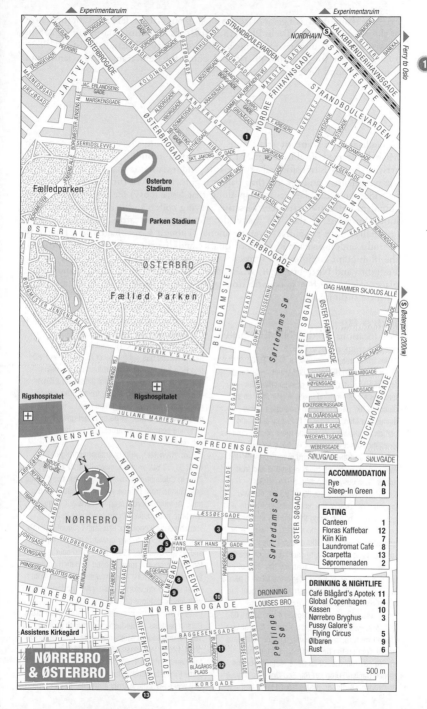

www.roughguides.com

ACCOMMODATION
| Rye | A |
| Sleep-In Green | B |

EATING
Canteen	1
Floras Kaffebar	12
Kiin Kiin	7
Laundromat Café	8
Scarpetta	13
Søpromenaden	2

DRINKING & NIGHTLIFE
Café Blågård's Apotek	11
Global Copenhagen	4
Kassen	10
Nørrebro Bryghus	3
Pussy Galore's Flying Circus	5
Ølbaren	9
Rust	6

NØRREBRO & ØSTERBRO

Fri–Sun 10am–3pm) is a great place to stock up on seafood delicacies. In the centre of the old village on Dr Dichs Plads, the **Mølsteds Museum** (May–Aug Sat & Sun noon–4pm; free) displays paintings by local celebrity Christian Mølsted (1862–1930), known for his atmospheric and colourful depictions of the land- and seascapes around Dragør.

Eating

Copenhagen's **restaurant** scene runs the gamut from cheap ethnic eateries to Michelin-starred establishments of international repute. As soon as summer arrives, the city is transformed as those cafés and restaurants that can, spill out onto the pavements – and for less than balmy nights, most will turn on gas heaters or provide you with blankets to help along that *hygge* (cosy) feeling. Copenhagen's abundant **cafés** are extremely versatile, serving coffee and cake, and brunch and lunch for most of the day; many also double as bars after dark, and serve a (generally more expensive) evening menu. Though Copenhagen is a long way behind London or Paris in terms of quality and diversity of **ethnic restaurants**, the immigrant community's impact is increasingly being felt, particularly in the Vesterbro and Nørrebro areas, where there's a large array of Turkish and Indian places, along with a good selection of (slightly pricier) Thai restaurants and Japanese sushi joints.

Indre By

For locations of the following places see the map on pp.60–61.

Atlas Bar Larsbjørnsstræde 18 ☎33 15 03 52, ⊛www.atlasbar.dk. In the basement underneath *Flyvefisken* restaurant, the popular *Atlas Bar* features a globetrotting menu (lunch 95kr plus, dinner 120kr plus) of exotic (and often spicy) dishes like Manila chicken, Pakistani lamb and ostrich on skewers, alongside more sedate options like fishcakes and lasagne. Portions are large and delicious, and the blackboard menu changes daily. Also serves excellent, fresh vegetable and fruit juices. Gets busy at lunchtime. Closed Sun.

Cap Horn Nyhavn 21 ☎33 12 85 04, ⊛www.caphorn.dk. One of the more reliable, friendly and good-value options along this touristy stretch. Sit by the canal and tuck into a lunch of herrings or gravadlax for around 54kr or, more substantially, tasty organic burgers with salad and potatoes for 129kr. The evening menu features the likes of pasta dishes, leg of lamb, steak and lobster, plus a vegetarian option. For dessert, you can't beat the home-made chocolate truffles.

The Custom House Havnegade 44 ☎33 31 01 30, ⊛www.customhouse.dk. Terence Conran's Danish venture, in the renovated former customs house right on the harbourfront. is a typically stylish gastrodome. Of its three restaurants, the clubby Danish/European *Bar and Grill* steakhouse (daily lunch & dinner; mains from 150kr) is the most informal, with decent steaks and burgers and a short menu of starters and other meat and fish dishes fuelled by regional Danish produce. The Italian *Bacino* has lighter decor and a classier vibe (Mon–Fri lunch & dinner, Sat lunch only; mains from 155kr), while the elegant Japanese *Ebisu* (Tues–Sat dinner only; mains from 160kr) offers great sushi, teriyaki and grilled meat and fish mains cooked on the large charcoal grill, There's quayside seating in summer, and two bars and a deli on site.

L'Education Nationale Larsbjørnsstræde 12 ☎33 91 53 60, ⊛www.leducationnationale.dk. Paris in Copenhagen: everything in this cosy, rustic café comes from France – even the butter on the table. At lunch there's croque-monsieur, baguettes, omelette and *moules frites*, for dinner hearty French country cooking, like rabbit ragout or lamb casserole. Expect to pay upwards of 49kr for lunch and, in the evening, 199kr for a main course, 325kr for a three-course meal. Closed for lunch on Sun.

Europa Amagertorv 1 ⊛www.europa1989.dk. In a great spot, overlooking bustling Amagertorv and with ample outdoor seating, the stylish, large, glass-fronted *Europa* serves excellent coffee, great Danish pastries, breakfasts and brunch (from 159kr), delicious salads and sandwiches for lunch (from 125kr) and classic fish and meat mains in the evening (from 159kr).

Café Fiat Kongens Nytorv 18 ☎33 14 22 77, ⊛www.f-i-a-t.dk. A truly authentic Italian food experience with a delicious lunch menu of antipasti, pasta (from 125kr) and wood-fired, thin-crust Neapolitan-style pizzas (from 115kr); for dinner there's also *secondi piatti* like braised rabbit leg with polenta, osso bucco, or grilled steak fiorentina, from around 195kr. Three-course menu 375kr. Takeaway available. Closed for lunch Fri & Sat.

La Galette Larsbjørnsstræde 9 ⓦ www.lagalette .dk. Tucked away in a backyard with outdoor seating in summer, this cosy, excellent-value and authentically Breton pancake joint offers the savoury and sweet buckwheat kind with a range of fillings, and jugs of Breton cider. Prices 35–110kr. Closed for lunch on Sun.

La Glace Skoubogade 20. In the city's oldest patisserie, primly dressed waitresses serve beautifully sculpted, cream-heavy cakes and pots of real hot chocolate to a genteel clientele.

Den Grønne Kælder Pilestræde 48 ☎ 33 93 01 40. "The Green Kitchen" is a busy but relaxed vegetarian cellar place, serving scrumptious hot seasonal dishes like vegetable stews and mushroom and spinach lasagne and unusual salads. Dinner is relatively cheap, starting at 95kr for very generous portions. Also serves organic wines, beer and home-made bread. No foreign credit cards. Closed Sun.

Pasta Basta Valkendorfsgade 22 ⓦ www .pastabasta.dk. Big, central and a good late-night option (the kitchen stays open till 1.30am), *Pasta Basta* is a favourite final stop for partygoers and extremely popular with young locals at all times. The all-day buffet of pasta and salads for 89kr is great value and there are plenty of other pasta dishes and fish and meat mains from around 159kr. Open till 2am.

Peder Oxe Gråbrødretorv 11 ☎ 33 11 00 77, ⓦ www.pederoxe.dk. In a charming, old, ochre-coloured building on a picturesque square, this French-inspired café/bistro is a local favourite and has outdoor seating in fine weather. It serves up a small menu of brasserie staples like *moules frites* and steak as well as a few Danish-inspired fish and shellfish options. The main attraction, though, is the juicy organic "oxe-burger" made with finest beef (129kr) – for an extra 45kr you can also help yourself to the salad buffet. The lunchtime smørrebrød option is good value at 138kr for three plates.

Riccos Kaffebar Studiestraede 24. This cosy, friendly little basement coffee house on funky Studiestraede attracts locals with its delicious filled rolls (baked on the premises), smoothies, milkshakes and great coffee. Healthy, homely breakfasts like boiled eggs, muesli or bread

and cheese set you up for the day; there's also internet access and special seating at the rear where you can plug in your laptop. This is the sister branch of the original, *Riccos*, on Istedgade (see p.83). Takeaway available.

Riz Raz Kompagnistræde 20 ⓦ www.rizraz.dk. *Riz Raz's* hot and cold Mediterranean veggie buffet is one of the city's best (and healthiest) budget options – all the fresh salads, pasta, falafel, rice and feta cheese you can eat for 79kr (89kr in the evening). There's also a more carnivorous menu. It's usually packed, but turnover is high and there's outdoor seating available. There's another branch at Store Kannikestræde 19.

Royal Café Amagertorv 6 ⓦ www.theroyalcafe.dk. In a small courtyard next to Royal Copenhagen Porcelain (see p.91), the high-ceilinged, quirkily decorated *Royal Café* is a chic place to stop for coffee or a pot of tea (lots of varieties on offer) with a delicious cake or biscuit. Alternatively, try the café's innovative "smushi" concept – mini-smørrebrød at 45kr each or 165kr for four, including a shot of snaps. While you wait you can read the glossy magazines or browse the eclectic and pricey merchandise. Some outdoor seating.

Slotskælderen Hos Gitte Kik Fortunstræde 4. It may not look much from the outside but this cosy, old-fashioned basement restaurant is one of the best places in town to sample smørrebrød. There's no menu – just walk up to the table, presided over by Gitte herself, pick your toppings from the heaped plates of delicacies, and the made-up smørrebrød will be brought over to you. Prices from 46–95kr per piece. Lunch only. Closed Mon.

Sommersko Kronprinsensgade 6 ⓦ www .sommersko.dk. Friendly, laid-back, Parisian-style café/brasserie on a boutique street attracting a young and trendy clientele. Great for morning coffee and croissant or hold out for the delectable brunch (80–115kr) or the wide-ranging lunch options including French classics like onion soup and steak frites, and regular staples like sandwiches, burgers, omelettes and salads. In the evening, innovative pasta dishes, fish and meat mains are served till 11pm.

Stella Kompagnistraede 18 ⓦ www.cafestella.dk. Cosy, low-lit, late-opening (kitchen closes midnight), corner café/bar (some outdoor seating) on pedestrianized Kompagnistraede, serving up generous portions at reasonable prices to a largely young crowd. Brunch, wraps, burgers, salads and sandwiches at lunchtime (from 74kr), as well as some hot food like nachos and noodles. In the evening, mains start at 99kr for standards like pasta, steak and fish; you can start the evening off with a cocktail (40kr on Thurs).

Told & Snaps Toldbodgade 2 ☎ 33 93 83 85, ⓦ www.toldogsnaps.dk. Just off Nyhavn, this traditional, family-run lunchtime smørrebrød restaurant focuses on high-quality food rather than fashion, with a vast range of possible toppings. The curried herring and home-made meatballs are delicious, especially washed down with the home-made aquavits or a beer from the Norrebro brewery. Closed Sun.

Victor Ny Ostergade 8 ☎ 33 13 36 13, ⓦ www .cafevictor.dk. Something of an old timer on the Copenhagen food scene, this large, bustling, French-style brasserie with smart, efficient waiters offers something for everyone from its French/Danish menu, be it lunchtime herring, coq au vin or croque-monsieur (from 95kr) or, in the adjacent restaurant, evening fare such as oysters, fish dishes and foie gras (from around 165kr).

Wok Shop Ny Adelgade 6 ⓦ www.wokshop.dk. Excellent Thai eatery with plenty of seating and a huge menu of fresh, fragrant, spicy soups, satays, noodle dishes and curries, most of them available for takeaway. Closed Sun.

Christianshavn

For locations of the following, see map, pp.60–61.

Bastionen og Løven Voldgade 50 ☎ 32 95 09 40, ⓦ www.bastionen-loven.dk. Set in the old miller's house, up on the ramparts and with outside seating, this is a charming, relaxed spot for traditional Danish food. The lunchtime menu offers delicious salads or smørrebrød from 65kr – try the delectable *kalveleverpostej* (calves' liver paté) and soups in winter; in the evening, main courses start at 185kr. Avoid the overpriced weekend brunch. Closed Sun evenings.

Café Wilder Wildersgade 56. Popular and relaxed locals' café, great for coffee and croissant, sandwich or a range of salads, and usually packed on Sundays with brunch junkies tucking into the "Wilders Brunch" (10am–2pm; 95kr) – a generous helping of egg, bacon, sausage, yoghurt, cheese and fruit.

Lagkagehuset Torvegade 45 ⓦ www .lagkagehuset.dk. At the absolute epicentre of Christianshavn – both geographically and socially – this fantastic bakery/café is always buzzing. Laden with a mouthwatering array of home-made Danish pastries, fruity muffins and cakes, it's also a great place to pick up a sandwich to eat by the canal. A large notice board advertises everything from lift-shares to rooms for rent and, with free wi-fi, the counter seating by the large windows is always packed.

Noma Strandgade 93 ☎ 32 96 32 97, ⓦ www .noma.dk. Housed in a former warehouse, recently voted the world's third best restaurant, and with two Michelin stars, *Noma* is *the* place for modern, inventive and unusual Scandinavian cuisine. It uses only seasonal ingredients from the North Atlantic countries cooked by traditional methods, so there's a good deal of pickling, salting and drying. Menu regulars include musk ox, lumpfish, Danish blood sausage, funghi and berries. With set three-course dinner menus costing upwards of 845kr, the three-course lunch menu at 395kr might be the way to go. Booking three months in advance for dinner. Closed Mon.

Spiseloppen The Loppe Building, Bådsmandsstræde 43, Christiania ☎ 32 57 95 58, ⓦ www.spiseloppen.dk. Upstairs from the music venue *Musikloppen*, this excellent evening-only restaurant has a reputation far beyond Christiania's borders for serving superb food from a changing but always imaginative small menu of international dishes. Meat and fish mains start at 165kr; there's always a good vegetarian option. Very popular, so book ahead. Closed Mon.

Rosenborg and Frederikstad

For locations of the following places see the map on pp.60–61.

Coffee Factory Gothersgade 21. Small, friendly coffee bar serving fine coffees from around the world, perfect for the *feinschmecker* (someone who can taste which estate a coffee comes from). It also does cakes, pastries and sandwiches. Closed Sun.

Den Lille Fede Store Kongensgade 15 ☎ 33 33 70 02, ⓦ www.denlillefede.dk. Literally "the little fat one", this cosy, good-value, little restaurant serves excellent Mediterranean-inspired food, in five or seven delicious courses at 325kr/448kr respectively. You can opt to add wine for an extra 225kr/350kr, in which case you'll get a different and perfectly chosen glass of wine to accompany each dish. It's not cheap, but the food is really good and the service is excellent too. Dinner only, closed Sun.

Madklubben Store Kongensgade 66 ☎ 33 32 32 34, ⓦ www.denanden.info. A trendy yet relaxed atmosphere, rustic Danish cooking with a modern twist, and good portions at reasonable prices have helped make this relative newcomer a madly popular choice. The menu changes frequently but features delicious starters like lumpfish roe or pork with smoked crackling, followed by unpretentious mains like leg of chicken with home-made sausage or braised beef with beetroot. One- to four-course menus at 100–250kr. Side dishes are 25kr extra but big enough to share. Booking advisable. Dinner only, closed Sun.

Sushitarian Gothersgade 3 ☎33 93 30 54, ⓦwww.sushitarian.dk. Among the city's best sushi places, with a small upstairs section where you can sit on cushions on the floor; also has tables and chairs and counter seating. À la carte dishes from 75–165kr; sushi assortments from 175kr for eight pieces. Vegetarian options. Also does takeaway. Closed for lunch on Sun.

Taste Store Kongensgade 80-82 ⓦwww.tastedeli .dk. This small, exquisite French-owned café/ bakery/deli/chocolate shop near the Marmorkirken serves largely organic sandwiches, wonderful tarts, salads, soups and home-made cakes, muffins and cookies. The daily hot special (95kr, 65kr to go) is a bargain. Takeaway available (and much cheaper). Closed Sun.

Umami Store Kongensgade 59 ☎33 38 75 00, ⓦwww.restaurantumami.dk. One of the trendiest restaurants in town with sleek, ultra-modern decor and a fabulous menu of Japanese food with a French touch. With food ranging from the relatively inexpensive soup and noodle dishes (from 125kr) to prime Japanese wagyu beef at 200kr per 50g – *Umami* caters for most budgets and should be experienced – you'll find no other place like it. Takeaway available. Dinner only.

Rådhuspladsen and around

Wagamama Tietgensgade 20 (see map, pp.60–61). Large, bright branch of the ubiquitous chain, dishing up steaming bowls of unfailingly delicious Asian soup, curries or noodles at very reasonable prices (all 80–110kr), with several good veggie options.

Vesterbro & Frederiksberg

For locations of the following options, see the map on pp.76–77.

BioMio Halmtorvet 19. Brand-new, fully organic restaurant on the outskirts of Kødbyen. A bit concepty – you order and check out with a plastic card and it's all self-service (they call you when your food is ready) – but the limited menu is very seasonal. A good bet is the spicy beef noodles for 125kr washed down with a draught Jakobsen beer.

Granola Værnedamsvej 5. Superb 1930s-style coffee bar/ice-cream parlour done out in pretty pastels with authentic old coffee grinders and the like, serving excellent early-bird breakfasts (60kr without coffee) and delightful sandwiches from 65kr. Also does excellent fresh fruit smoothies.

Hackenbusch Vesterbrogade 124 ☎33 21 74 74. Laid-back place serving three types of brunch (one veggie) until 2pm (from 85kr), and burgers and sandwiches, heaped with salad, in the café-bar at the front. The excellent Mediterranean-style restaurant at the back has steak and fish mains, with a daily special for 98kr and always one veggie option. Try the spicy and delicious 75kr "frog burger" (don't worry: it's actually made of beef) on offer on Tuesdays (65kr including a beer) in the restaurant. Closed Sun evenings.

Hansens Gamle Familiehave Pile Allé 10–12 ☎36 30 92 57. This historic outdoor all-day restaurant (under a sliding roof in winter) dishes up some of the city's most stunning open sandwiches, with a fantastic spread of herring, cold meats and cheeses, all lavishly decorated with fresh salad, pickles, fried onions, and other smørrebrød essentials. Beautifully prepared traditional hot meals, such as *biksemad* (109kr) and *flæskesteg* (168kr) are also on offer.

LêLê nhà hàng Vesterbrogade 40. Hugely popular Vietnamese restaurant with simple French colonial-style decor and equally simple (but elegant and tasty) food. Lunch starts at 70kr for six pieces of wonton with turkey and crab, or you can choose dishes such as rice-noodle soup, cold rice-noodle salad, and beef, pork or chicken baguettes with pickled vegetables dowsed in fresh herbs. At dinner, the choices are more varied and prices max out at 165kr. Arrive early for dinner (they don't take bookings) or prepare for a long wait at the *Tiger Bar.* There's a takeaway up the road at Vesterbrogade 56 where you can get the same salads plus some sushi-style Vietnamese fast food.

Les Trois Cochons Værnedamsvej 10 ☎33 31 70 55, ⓦwww.cofoco.dk. Part of the popular Cofoco (Copenhagen Food Company) chain, this French-style brasserie offers excellent-value three-course evening meals for 275kr. Starters and desserts are pre-set, and for mains you choose between beef, fish and veal – no veggie option – all freshly made and rustically presented. If there are two of you, you both have to pick the same mains. For lunch, there's a choice between six Danish and French classics such as the open potato sandwich (85kr) and *moules marinières* (95kr). Booking essential. Closed for lunch on Sun.

Riccos Butik & Kaffebar Istedgade 119. One of the best coffee joints in town, also serving cakes and Italian ice cream, with a small seating area. The owner describes himself as a coffee nerd and if he's not behind the counter, he's trotting the globe in search of the finest beans. Open till 11pm.

Spicylicious Istedgade 27 ☎ 33 22 85 33. Great Thai/Vietnamese restaurant overlooking the livelier end of Istedgade. The name says it all: the food is spicy and delicious (mains between 115kr for beef noodle soup and 120kr for Bahn Xeo – crispy prawn and chicken pancakes). Evenings only.

Thai Esan Lille Istedgade 7 ☎ 33 24 98 54. Taking advantage of fresh ingredients from the numerous Thai food shops in the area, the very popular and often crammed *Thai Esan* serves a wide range of cheap, hot food in a fairly authentic Thai atmosphere. Good choices are the chicken in oyster sauce for 85kr, or the Tom Yom shrimp soup for 80kr.

Nørrebro and Osterbro

For locations of the following, see map, p.79.

Canteen Nordre Frihavnsgade 52, Østerbro. Consistently voted the city's best brunch spot by local newspaper surveys, this friendly corner café serves light and delicious lunches prepared with the utmost attention to detail. Arrive early if you want to try the popular brunch (until 3.30pm; 60–115kr). Closed Mon.

Floras Kaffebar Blågårdsgade 27, Nørrebro. Easy-going café on the sometimes tense

Blågårds Plads, with many exotic coffees and an array of daily specials, soups, sandwiches and home-made cakes. Brunch is dished up daily until 3pm (98kr). Come back at night for cheap beer.

Kiin Kiin Gulbergsgade 21, Nørrebro ☎ 35 35 75 55. Nørrebro's wonderful Thai restaurant gained a Michelin star in 2008. Choose between the early bird four-course theatre menu (5.30–7.30pm) for 450kr, or the full-on six-course menu from 6pm for 750kr which features dishes such as Thai caviar with lime. It's all extraordinarily delicious. Booking essential. Dinner only, closed Sun.

Laundromat Café Elmegade 15, Nørrebro. Icelandic café with a laundry out the back. Basic brunch starts at 85kr (125kr for a larger portion at weekends), salads and sandwiches/burgers are 72–110kr.

Scarpetta Rantzausgade 7, Nørrebro ☎ 35 35 08 08, ⓦ www.cofoco.dk. Newest member of the popular Cofoco chain, this Italian serves only starter-sized dishes on its excellent menu, so you can sample tapas-style. Alternatively go for the five-dish combo (275kr). Hugely popular so book ahead. Dinner only.

Søpromenaden Sortedam Dosseringen 103, Østerbro. Lovely lunchtime spot in a tranquil lakeside setting, specializing in Danish smørrebrød. Select your bread and toppings (from 49kr) from a long list or go for the 139kr platter.

Drinking

Copenhagen's drinking holes run from dingy *kaffebars* to ultra-hip cocktail places. Most serve some kind of light food and it's worth bearing in mind that the distinction between bars and cafés is often blurred. Opening hours vary, though you'll be able to find somewhere to drink at any time of day or night.

Indre By

The following places are shown on the map on pp.60–61.

1105 Kristen Bernikows Gade 4. Great cocktail bar near Kongens Nytorv with large comfy sofas that could easily swallow you up – especially once the drinks start kicking in. Cocktails are a delight, and the famous bartender Hardeep Rehal – winner of two Danish cocktail-mixing championships – has a huge following. Wed–Sat only.

Bibendum Nansensgade 45. Small, crowded wine bar in a Nansensgade cellar, with a huge selection of wine, mostly served by the glass (from 45kr). Also great tapas. Closed Sun.

Bo-Bi Bar Klareboderne 14. Home to Copenhagen's oldest bar counter – an idea first

introduced to the city by a New York-returned sailor in 1917 – this small, atmospheric drinking hole is now patronized by inner-city professional types, artists and journalists.

Charlie's Bar Pilestræde 33. The only bar in Denmark to be awarded the prestigious Cask Marque for its vast selection of high-quality real ales, the vast majority from the UK and Ireland. A small crowded place so arrive early if you want a seat. Smoking permitted.

Hviids Vinstue Kongens Nytorv 19. Proper old-fashioned *vinstue* dating back to 1723 – Hans Christian Andersen, who lived just around the corner, was a regular – with many tiny crowded rooms patrolled by uniformed and respectful waiters. There's a good selection of Danish beers

(27 at last count) and a great lunch deal – three pieces of smørrebrød and a Tuborg – for 55kr. Outdoor seating on Kongens Nytorv square in summer, and justifiably famous *gløgg* in winter.

Ice Bar Løngangstræde 27. Part of the trendy *Hotel 27* next door, *Ice Bar* is the city's most unusual drinking spot. Don your designer cape and gloves and enter the sub-zero room made completely out of Swedish ice – the walls, the bar, tables, chairs, stools, even the glasses. Entrance is in 45-minute timed slots; the entrance fee of 150kr includes the gloves and cloak, plus one free cocktail.

Nyhavn 17 Nyhavn 17. A cross between a British pub and a maritime museum, with old iron diving helmets, ships' figureheads, anchors and rudders scattered around the dimly lit interior – the gleaming brass bar fittings are the only bright feature. Popular among tourists and Danes alike, with moderately priced draught beers and an excellent selection of Scottish single malt whisky.

Palæ Bar Ny Adelgade 5. Around the corner from Kongens Nytorv, a classy neighbourhood bar with the usual range of beer and live jazz every third Sun. Smoking permitted.

Christianshavn

The following places are on the map on pp.60–61.

Eiffel Bar Wildersgade 58. Next door to the smart *Café Wilder* (see p.82), this traditional drinking den couldn't be more different. Rumours of its shady past – featuring assorted sailors and can-can girls – add to the atmosphere, while the old carved mirrors and the tricolour hanging outside evoke 1930s Paris. Smoking permitted.

Nemoland Christiania. One of Christiania's two main watering holes, and among Copenhagen's most popular open-air bars, with occasional live gigs in summer, when it's packed with tourists and shoppers enjoying their purchases from nearby Pusherstreet. It's quieter in winter, with regulars playing backgammon or billiards.

Rosenborg & Frederikstad

The following places are on the map on pp.60–61.

Andy's Bar Gothersgade 33B. A so-called morning-pub, where the city's partygoers head when they can dance no more. Always crowded and noisy; you'll soon be chatting to your bar companions like they're long-lost friends.

Kruts Karport Øster Farimagsgade 12. Small Parisian-style neighbourhood café that has

Denmark's largest whisky selection (mainly Scotch single malts) and for years has been the only bar in Copenhagen selling Absinthe. Whisky tastings and cigar evenings in winter – smoking is still allowed here. Closed Sun evenings, and all Aug.

Rådhuspladsen and around

The following places are on the map on pp.60–61.

Bryggeriet Apollo Vesterbrogade 3. Close to Central Station, this place offers *Bryggeriet's* home-brewed beer amid gleaming vats, copper kettles and heavy wooden tables; food is available, too, in the bright upstairs section. Each month, with much brouhaha, a new brew is launched and judged by a beer-loving celebrity. This, plus a pilsner and a strong beer is all that's on offer. If you want more excitement, you can have it served in a Belgian litre *kwak*, similar to a short-yard glass. It's all a tad pricey.

Zum Biergarten Axeltorv 12. Lively Bavarian *bierstube* housed in the old waterworks building in front of Palads cinema by Vesterport station, offering Oktoberfest atmosphere with long rickety wooden tables and huge litre-mugs of delicious German microbrewery beer. When the weather allows, you can sit in the beautiful secluded beer garden, and food is prepared on an open grill. Closed Sun.

Vesterbro and Frederiksberg

The following places are on the map on pp.76–77.

90eren Gammel Kongevej 90, Frederiks-berg. Famous for its painstakingly pulled draught beer, an operation that takes roughly 15min, *90eren* is the only bar in Copenhagen to serve uncarbonated Carlsberg beer (from the nearby brewery). The strong hops flavour is reminiscent of English real ale and – supposedly – very similar to the original Carlsberg beer produced in the mid-nineteenth century.

Bang & Jensen Istedgade 130, Vesterbro. High stucco ceilings and a mahogany counter left over from its former incarnation as a pharmacy add to the character of this place, which is usually packed before concerts at *Vega* (see p.88) and on Saturday nights when *Ingeborgs Cocktail Saloon* takes over, and the in house DJ plays electronic jazz grooves. One of the pricier places in Vesterbro.

Boutique Lize Enghave Plads 6, Vesterbro. Heaving cocktail bar across the square from *Vega*

(see p.88) with a good selection of draught beer as well – both imported and from local micro-breweries. Prices are reasonable, possibly because the cocktails aren't that strong. The Tokyo Iced Tea comes especially recommended. Wed–Sat only.

Café Ludwigsen Sundesvedsgade 2, Vesterbro. One of those outrageously popular late-night bars (despite the "café" in the name, there's no food) where the young, free and on-the-pull congregate in the small hours for no good reason. If you want to meet the locals, this is your best bet.

Karriere Bar Flæsketorvet 57, Vesterbro. Hugely trendy bar-club-art space in the equally trendy Kødbyen meatpacking district. Packed most nights with hipsters, beautiful people and their acolytes. Great for celeb-spotting. Fri & Sat only.

Ritz Viktoriagade 22, Vesterbro. On the corner of Istedgade in the basement beneath *Shezan* restaurant this grungy new Berlinesque place has quickly become Copenhagen's party capital. With DJs every night – mostly rock on Thursday, mainly electronic the rest of the week – it has a refreshingly unpretentious feel, with cocktails are served in plastic cups. Thurs–Sat only.

Nørrebro

The following places are on the map on p.79.

Café Blågård's Apotek Blågårds Plads 20. Homely bar, still patronized by some of the left-wing activists who used to clash on this square with the police during the 1970s. They're now joined by a less committed crowd who come to sample the bar's many wines and Urquell draught beer. Gets jam-packed during weekends, when there's also live jazz, blues or rock.

Kassen Nørrebrogade 18. A stone's throw from *Nora* hotel, this small place is one of the city's top cocktail bars, preparing its own unique array of very tasty drinks for around 60–70kr each. The Friday happy hour(s) (3–10pm) offers two-for-one cocktails and beer. Smoking permitted. Wed–Sat only.

Nørrebro Bryghus Ryesgade 2. Immensely popular brewpub in an old factory, with a range of homebrews that sell out quicker than they can be bottled. Pricey restaurant, too.

Pussy Galore's Flying Circus Skt Hans Torv 30. Named after the nubile heroine of the James Bond movie *Goldfinger*, you'll be stirred if not shaken by delicious cocktails and outdoor seating on one of Nørrebro's hippest squares – definitely a place to be seen.

Ølbaren Elmegade 2. A small, crowded place frequented by beer enthusiasts, with a wide range of beer from all over the world, and absolutely no Tuborg or Carlsberg. Tell the bartender what flavours you like, and he'll find a beer to suit. Unfortunately, this personal service can be – endearingly – slow. Closed Sun. In summer Thurs–Sat only.

Nightlife and entertainment

Copenhagen is Scandinavia's party town, with a great array of **live music** and a wide range of **clubs** spanning every sort of music from bebop to bhangra; entrance is usually around 60kr. On the live music scene **jazz** has traditionally been the city's liveliest – a legacy of the number of respected American jazz musicians who lived here during the 1960s and 1970s – while the annual jazz festival is world-renowned. There's also a healthy local **rock** scene; many big-name international acts include Copenhagen on their tours.

The city is undergoing something of a renaissance in the high arts. Until recently, the grand old Det Kongelige Teater (Royal Theatre; ⓦ www.kglteater .dk) in Kongens Nytorv was home to the royal ballet, opera and theatre; with the recent construction of two stunning new venues – the **Skuespilhuset** (Playhouse) and the state-of-the art **Operaen** – the old theatre is now predominantly given over to ballet. The city puts on a wide range of **classical music** and is home to a number of top-class ensembles, including the Zealand Symphony Orchestra and the excellent Danish National Symphony Orchestra/DR, now also in new, purpose-built premises in Amager. Look out, too, for classical music concerts in many of Copenhagen's grandest churches and larger museums – the tourist office will have details. For **ballet** lovers, there's the fairly traditional repertoire of the Royal Ballet, staged at Det Kongelige Teater and occasionally at Operaen, as well as at Tivoli during the summer and at Christmas, while modern dance, though still limited to a handful of venues, has developed a stronger presence in recent years. Copenhagen has a diverse **theatre** scene, though as most productions are in Danish they're unlikely to be of interest to most visitors. You could see whether there's anything being staged by the **London Toast Theatre** (Ⓦwww.londontoast.dk), a well-established English theatre company which performs in the city's mainstream theatres. The monthly *Teater Kalenderen*, available from the tourist office and performance venues, has complete listings of theatre and modern dance, while Det Kongelige Teater produces its own glossy brochure listing productions across its various venues.

Danes are keen **cinema**-goers and most films are screened in their original language, with Danish subtitles. For the latest mainstream international releases head for the Imperial, Ved Vesterport 4, Vesterbro (Ⓣ70 13 12 11, Ⓦwww .biobooking.dk), Copenhagen's largest cinema, and the usual site for gala openings and premieres, or Grand Teatret at Mikkel Bryggers Gade 8, Indre By (Ⓣ33 15 16 11, Ⓦwww.grandteatret.dk). Alternatively, the city's **arthouse cinemas** have a good selection of more offbeat offerings, both Danish and international. A few of the best are Cinemateket at Filmhuset, Gothersgade 55, Indre By (Ⓣ33 74 34 12, Ⓦwww.cinemateket.dk), home to the Danish Film Institute; Gloria Biografen at Rådhuspladsen 59 (Ⓣ33 12 42 92, Ⓦwww.gloria.dk) and Vester Vov Vov, Absalonsgade 5, Vesterbro (Ⓣ33 24 42 00, Ⓦwww.vestervovvov.dk). At weekends, it's worth booking ahead. Check out the free listings calendar *Film Kalenderen* available from the tourist office and cinemas.

You can buy **tickets online** or by **phone** for most of the ticket-only larger venues listed below. Their websites will either link you through to **Billetnet** (Ⓣ70 15 65 65, Ⓦwww.billetnet.dk; Mon–Sat 10am–8pm) which can post it to you for a fee (30–85kr depending on ticket type) or let you pick it up, for 10kr, at its outlets (there's one at Vesterbrogade 3 beside Tivoli's main entrance and at all post offices), or **Billetlugen** (Ⓣ70 26 32 67, Ⓦwww.billetlugen.dk; Mon–Fri 10am–5pm) which gives you the option of printing the ticket at home for free or having it posted (15–85kr). Det Kongelige Teater holds back around 25 tickets for that evening's performances at each of its three venues but you have to go in person to the box office at August Bournonvilles Passage 1, just off Kongens Nytorv, to buy them. You might want to chance it and wait till 4pm when spare tickets for that night's performances are sold off half-price.

For **listings** information on all entertainment and nightlife, pick up a copy of the English-language *Copenhagen Post* (Ⓦwww.cphpost.dk; 20kr) from the tourist office or bookshops, or check out its website, Ⓦwww.cphpost.dk; alternatively there's English-language listings at Ⓦwww.aok.dk and Ⓦwww.kulturnaut.dk. For more details of festivals and annual events in Copenhagen see Basics, pp.00-00.

Live music venues

The places listed below are shown on the maps on pp.60–61, pp.76–77 and p.79.

Café Blågård's Apotek Blågårds Plads 20, Nørrebro Ⓣ35 37 24 42, Ⓦwww.kroteket.dk. Low-key place catering for a slightly older crowd with live jazz, blues, rock or world music every Mon, Fri and Sat, when it gets packed. Mon is jazzjam and free; Fri & Sat 20kr.

Copenhagen Jazz House Niels Hemmingsens-gade 10 Ⓣ33 15 47 00, Ⓦwww.jazzhouse.dk. Copenhagen's premier jazz venue, this large,

smart, two-level club draws jazz-lovers of all ages. Gigs start at 8pm weekdays and 9pm Fri and Sat, and range from trad to fusion to world music at its best. On Fri and Sat the *Natklub* nightclub (see p.89) takes over at midnight (or whenever the gigs finish).

Din Nye Ven Sankt Peders Stræde 34 Ⓦwww .myspace.com/dinnyeven. Homely, rustic café that transforms into a packed live-music venue one or two nights a week, generally with pop-rock and urban-hip hop. Also a nightclub. Closed Sun.

Drop Inn Kompagnistræde 34 ℡ 33 11 24 04. A cosy café-cum-jazz bar with live jazz, blues or folk music nightly from 10pm – often for free. In the summer, there's indoor and outdoor seating, and sandwiches and light meals available all day.

DR-byens Koncerthus Emil Holms Kanal 29, Ørestaden ℡ 35 20 62 62, ⓦ www.dr.dk /koncerthuset. Stunning state-of-the-art concert venue mainly devoted to classical music but also hosting the occasional rhythmic band and posh pop acts. From 150kr.

Global Copenhagen Nørre Allé 7 ⓦ www .globalcph.dk. Excellent world-music venue run primarily by volunteers as a not-for-profit organization. Gigs cover such diverse genres as reggae, Balkan fusion, Afrocuban rumba and Russian folk. Tickets from 60kr; 20kr discount for students. Fri & Sat 9pm–1am.

La Fontaine Kompagnistræde 11 ℡ 33 11 60 98, ⓦ www.lafontaine.dk. The city's oldest jazz venue, with live jazz Fri & Sat 11pm–3am & Sun 9pm–1am, largely featuring up-and-coming Danish hopefuls, this is the place to head if you're into small smoky rooms and surprise appearances by visiting big names. Later in the evening the stage is thrown open to aspiring performers in the audience. Daily 7pm–5am.

Huset i Magstræde Rådhusstræde 13 ℡ 33 69 32 00, ⓦ www.husetmagstraede.dk. Loads of different cultural venues under one roof with jazz at *1.Sal* on the first floor and newish, mostly Scandinavian bands at *Musikcaféen* on the third floor (both around 60kr). Gigs nightly at around 9pm. Advance tickets for *Musikcaféen* through ⓦ www.gaffabillet.dk.

Det Hvide Lam Kultorvet 5 ℡ 33 32 07 38. Traditional jazz in a small, dark basement bar with no stage but loads of atmosphere, and musicians giving it all they've got most nights. During the day you can eat your packed lunch here as long as you buy drinks.

Jazzcup Gothersgade 107 ℡ 33 15 02 02. An ingenious arrival on the Copenhagen jazz scene, this original café-cum-CD-shop-cum-music-venue has live jazz every Fri (3.30pm) and Sat

(2.30pm). Some of the best Danish and international musicians play here, including names from the world music circuit. 40–60kr. Mon–Thurs 11.30am–5.30pm, Fri 11am–7pm, Sat 10am–6pm.

Loppen Christiania ℡ 32 57 84 22, ⓦ www .loppen.dk. Most nights – around 9pm – this cool converted warehouse on the edge of Christiania hosts both established and experimental Danish rock, jazz and performance artists, and quite a few visiting British and American ones, too (some free, others 60–200kr).

Mojo Løngangstræde 21C ℡ 33 11 64 53, ⓦ www .mojo.dk. Live music nightly in this small venue with plenty of down-at-heel ambience, popular with blues aficionados of all ages. Music starts around 9.30pm and is followed at weekends with a DJ until closing. Less-established local acts get things going before the big names come on stage. Either free or around 60kr.

Pumpehuset Studiestræde 52 ℡ 33 93 19 09, ⓦ www.pumpehuset.dk. The city's spacious former pumphouse is one of its best concert venues, holding 600 people. A broad sweep of up-and-coming or fading international rock acts and big Danish names perform about eight times a month. 60–250kr.

Rust Guldbergsgade 8, Nørrebro ℡ 35 24 52 00, ⓦ www.rust.dk. One of the best-known venues in town, this multifaceted place on busy Skt Hans Torv hosts emerging indie rock, hiphop and electronic music acts from across the globe. Downstairs is the hip *Rust Natklub* (see p.89). Over-20s only after 11pm. 30kr–300kr. Wed–Sat 9pm–5am.

Vega Enghavevej 40 ℡ 33 25 70 11, ⓦ www .vega.dk. In a former union hall, this top music venue retains its 1950s and 1960s decor while showcasing plenty of modern alternative rock. There are two stages: Store Vega, accommodating 1500, hosts international names; Lille Vega, with room for 500, is used for smaller bands or when the big names want an intimate atmosphere. At the weekends it becomes *Vega Nightclub*. Keep your eye out for local and visiting luminaries: Björk apparently loves the place. Up to 400kr.

Clubs

The places listed below are shown on the maps on pp.60–61, pp.76–77 and p.79.

Culture Box Kronprinsessegade 54 ℡ 33 32 50 50, ⓦ www.culturebox.com. Dedicated to electronic music – techno, electro, electronica, drum'n'bass and dubstep – played by up-and-coming DJs, this is Copenhagen's most

happening club. You may have to queue. Around 60kr. Thurs–Sat 11pm–5am.

Diskotek In Nørregade 1 ℡ 33 11 74 78, ⓦ www .discotekin.dk. Three nightclubs under one roof: *La Hacienda*, a Spanish-inspired club playing soul and R&B, *The Dance Floor*, which is more electronic, and *The Jukeboksen* where you can make requests from lists on the tables. All three – you can move freely between them – are pretty mainstream, catering for a young audience. The free-bar concept – you pay a fixed fee (women pay about half what men do) and then drink your fill of beer, wine and champagne all night – is wildly popular. 75–150kr. Fri 11pm–8am, Sat 11pm–10am.

Natklub Niels Hemmingsensgade 10 ☎ 33 15 26 00, ⓦ www.jazzhouse.dk. When the live gigs are finished at *Copenhagen Jazz House* (see p.87), *Natklub* takes over with in-house DJs spinning Latin, house, acid jazz, bossa nova and old-school disco tunes. 65kr. Fri & Sat midnight–5am.

Nord Natklub Vesterbrogade 2E ⓦ www .nordlounge.dk. Fun nightclub across from Tivoli for the over-30s that's heaving after midnight, primarily playing 1980s and 90s rock and pop. Also an excellent cocktail bar with table service. 90kr. Sat 10pm–5am.

Rust Guldbergsgade 8, Nørrebro ☎ 35 24 52 00, ⓦ www.rust.dk. This small basement nightclub offers serious underground electronic dance music. Upstairs, there's a laid-back, minimalist cocktail bar and a larger main stage and dancefloor where guest DJs play hip-hop, house and cool, funky grooves. Only over-21s after 11pm. 60kr. Wed–Sat 11pm–5am.

Vega Natklub Enghavevej 40, Vesterbro ☎ 33 25 70 11, ⓦ www.vega.dk. One of the top clubs in the city, part of the immensely popular *Vega* (see p.88) and offering all you could want for a fantastic night out. The actual club is based in *Lille Vega* and sees resident and internationally renowned guest DJs raising the roof with funky beats and soulful sounds. There's also an upstairs chill-out lounge with soothing tunes and fancy cocktails, and out front, *Ideal Bar*, which becomes *Zoot Suit* every Thursday between 8pm and 5am – a swing club with free lessons until midnight. Gets very busy after 1am. 60kr after 1am. Fri & Sat 11pm–5am.

Classical music, theatre, opera and dance venues

Dansescenen Øster Fælled Torv 34, Østerbro ① 35 43 20 21 (Mon–Fri 5pm–7pm), ⓦ www .dansescenen.dk. The only place in Copenhagen with regular performances of modern dance, showcasing top Scandinavian ensembles on its two stages plus the work of the current choreographer in residence. The Dansescenen programme (available from the Tivoli ticket office) has a section in English.

Koncerthuset, DR-Byen Emil Holms Kanal 20, Ørestad. ⓦ www.dr.dk/koncerthuset. DR-Byen metro. This, the new National Concert Hall, is home to DR's collection of orchestral, choral and ensemble companies. There are four concert halls – three smaller ones hosting performances of choral works and chamber music, and a main one for symphony concerts and guest performances. Tickets from DR-butikken, the on-site shop and box office (☎ 35 20 62 62; open Mon–Wed & Fri noon–5pm, Thurs noon–6pm, Sat 11am–2pm), or from Billetnet.

Det Kongelige Teater Kongens Nytorv, Indre By ☎ 33 69 69 69 (Mon–Sat noon–4pm), ⓦ www .kglteater.dk. Copenhagen's oldest theatre provides all the gilt and velvet pomp you could ask for (see also p.65). Since the arrival of the new opera house and playhouse the "old stage", as it is affectionately known, is now largely given over to

the Royal Danish Ballet, with the occasional classical concert. Note that some ballet is also performed in the new opera house (see below). See p.87 for ticket information.

Operaen Holmen ☎ 33 69 69 69, ⓦ www .kglteater.dk and ⓦ www.operaen.dk. The city's new opera house has two stages – the opulent "Store Scene", with seating for up to 1700, and the much more intimate "Takkelloftet" (Tackle Loft), used for more experimental productions.

Skuespilhuset Skt Annæ Plads 36, Frederikstad ☎ 33 69 69 69, ⓦ www.kglteater.dk and ⓦ www .skuespilhus.dk. The city's stunning new playhouse offers a wide-ranging programme of drama across three stages.

Den Sorte Diamant Koncertsal Christians Brygge 9, Slotsholmen ☎ 33 47 47 47, ⓦ www.kb.dk. This stunning waterfront venue is a regular on the classical music scene, with frequent performances by solo pianists and string ensembles. Tickets from Billetnet or at the entrance one hour before the concert begins.

Tivolis Koncertsal Tietgensgade 20, Indre By ☎ 33 15 10 12, ⓦ www.tivoli.dk. Inside Tivoli, the recently revamped concert hall stages a variety of classical performances and some opera, often featuring the major national orchestras.

Shopping

Shopping is one of the highlights of a visit to Copenhagen, with Denmark's fine tradition of innovative design evident in products as diverse as furniture, clothing, lighting and stereo equipment. Most of the city's top shops are in Indre By: for clothes shopping, **Strøget** and **Købmagergade** are mostly lined with international chains. **Kronsprinsensgade** (off Købmagergade) is home to many of the best and most internationally recognized modern **Danish designer clothes** shops, though the streets stretching further east towards Gothersgade are also rich hunting grounds for up-and-coming labels. If your taste is for vintage, Larsbjørnstræde, Studiestræde and Skt Peders Stræde, all adjacent to the Latin Quarter, have the broadest selection of cheap **secondhand** and **ethnic clothes** shops. Good **interior design and furnishing** is important to the Danes and you'll find a range of shops selling imaginative and stylish furniture, glassware, kitchenware, crockery and table decorations – for an all-under-one-roof style taster, you can't do better than the outstanding **Illums Bolighus** (see p.91).

Copenhagen has no shortage of delis and excellent bakeries. There's also a good selection of centrally located **supermarkets** – opening hours are usually Monday to Friday 8 or 9am–7pm, Saturday 8 or 9am–4pm, with some open on Sundays too. Netto, the cheapest chain, has central branches at Nørre Voldgade 94 and Landemærket 11. The more upmarket Irma City (also open 10am–9pm Sun) has branches at Rådhusarkaden, Vesterbro 1, Falkoner Allé 13 and Nørrebrogade 3 (also open Sun); or there's a Superbrugsen at Christianshavns Torv 2 and Halmtorvet 25 (this branch also open Sun 10am–4pm) in Vesterbro. Note too that both Illum and Magasin (see p.91) have supermarkets in their basement, though you'll pay over the odds for the privilege.

We've detailed Denmark's retail **opening hours** in Basics (p.39).

Designer clothes and accessories

Alli C Læderstræde 1, Indre By ⓦ www.alli-c.dk. Women's shoes and handbags – expensive but unusual one-off designs. Also a stockist of Danish "Sanita" clogs, which come in everything from regular black to pink or furry.

Bruuns Bazaar Kronprinsensgade 8–9, Indre By ⓦ www.bruunsbazaar.com. Denmark's first fashion house, Bruuns is one of Europe's trendiest designer clothes shops, catering for both men and women, though it's as expensive and exclusive as you'd expect.

Flying A Kronprinsensgade 5, Indre By. Lots of ultra-trendy men's and women's gear from a variety of Danish and international labels, both well-established and up and coming, with everything from funky t-shirts to party frocks and jackets.

Ilse Jacobsen Kronprinsensgade 11, Indre By. From glam stilettos to her trademark natural rubber lace-up boots with warm cotton fleece lining – now a Scandinavian design icon and the ultimate in practical yet stylish footwear for the great Danish outdoors.

Munthe plus Simonsen Grønnegade 10, Indre By ⓦ www.muntheplussimonsen.com. Hot fashion to burn a hole in your pocket. The clothes are by Danish designers Naja Munthe and Karen Simonsen, who have established an international reputation with garments that blend Far Eastern influences with Scandinavian simplicity.

Nørgaard på Strøget and Mads Nørgaard Amagertorv, Indre By. A family business with two generations of designers, each catering for a different group. Nørgaard på Strøget – the oldest shop – houses women's and teenage wear in all price brackets. Mads Nørgaard is geared towards the trendy man.

Pede & Stoffer Klosterstræde 15 & 19, Indre By. Casual, trendy gear for men (no. 15) and women (no. 19) featuring a range of up-and-coming designer labels.

Stig P Kronprinsensgade 14, Indre By and Ravnsborggade 18, Nørrebro. The first designer shop to find its way to Kronprinsensgade in the 1970s and still going strong. A broad selection of jeans and smarter wear from well-known designer labels like See by Chloe and Sonia Rykiel as well as Danish designers and Stig P's own designs. The Indre By branch is for women only, whereas Ravnsborggade has a large men's section and also sells its own unique lingerie collections and kimonos.

Furniture, design and interiors

Designer Zoo Vesterbrogade 137, Vesterbro ⓦ www.dzoo.dk. This large, bright two-storey gallery sells the glassware, ceramics, art, jewellery and clothes made by the designers in eight workshops out the back. They're happy to come and talk to you about their designs – all contemporary and individual.

Georg Jensen Amagertorv 4, Indre By. The world-famous Georg Jensen silversmiths, which features works by many others besides the great man himself, has been turning out simple yet stylish silverware – from jewellery and cutlery to candlesticks and tableware – for over a hundred years.

Hay Pilestræde 29, Indre By ⓦ www.hay.dk. Funky, striking, colourful, totally modern furniture – some of the most cutting-edge names in modern Danish furniture design have their work on sale here. There's also a range of designer toys, ceramics and trinkets.

Illums Bolighus Amagertorv 10, Indre By. Four cool, elegant – and very Scandinavian – floors overflowing with an eye-catching assortment of Danish and international design, from fabulous kitchenware and glassware to Poul Henningsen lamps and Arne Jacobsen furniture classics, though such quality and refinement doesn't come cheap.

Normann Østerbrogade 70, Østerbro ⓦ www .normann.oøpønhagen.dk. Housed in a former cinema and a worthy rival to Illums Bolighus, this relatively new, supercool design emporium offers the best and latest in design all under one roof. Plenty of designer fashion from Danish names like Malene Birger and iconic international figures like Marc Jacobs and Ally Capellino, as well as great Scandinavian and Italian furniture, glassware, candlesticks, vases, lamps – the lot.

Royal Copenhagen Porcelain Amagertorv 6, Indre By. Even if you're not excited by the idea of china, it's worth a quick peep at one of Denmark's most famous exports, still being produced to centuries-old designs. Each piece is handmade and hand-painted, with the painter's signature as verification on the bottom – hence the extortionate prices.

Bookshops

Arnold Busck Købmagergade 49, Indre By ⓦ www.arnoldbusck.dk. Huge, central chain bookstore on three floors selling new titles and with a good English-language fiction section.

The Booktrader Skindergade 23, Indre By. On a quiet side street off Købmagergade, this rambling secondhand bookstore is filled with mostly Danish titles but has a good English-language fiction section (particularly crime) towards the back.

Nordisk Korthandel Studiestræde 26–30, Indre By ⓦ www.scanmaps.dk. Great guidebook and map store with friendly staff. Stocks a full range of Denmark maps for walking, cycling and driving.

Politikens Boghandel Rådhuspladsen 37, Indre By. Large, mainstream bookstore right on the town-hall square, with possibly the best range of English-language fiction and non-fiction in the city.

Tranquebar Borgergade 14, Frederikstad ⓦ www .tranquebar.net. This fantastic bookshop stocks a huge range of travel guides and travel literature – everything from *Rough Guides* to classic travelogues to glossy coffee-table tomes. There's a comfy café area where you can knock back a fairtrade coffee while thumbing through some of the stock.

Department stores and shopping centres

Illum Østergade 52, Indre By ⓦ www.illum.dk. The city's most fashionable department store, with almost 500 of the world's best and most luxurious brands on offer, including a good representation of Danish designers – a great place to get a feel for who you like before heading off to their own dedicated stores in the streets nearby. The Illum home department stocks a great range of interior furnishings and tableware and there are also two coffee shops, two bakeries, a good newsagent with some English-language magazines and an overpriced but convenient supermarket in the basement.

Magasin du Nord Kongens Nytorv 13, Indre By. Dating back to 1871, this grand and very classy place is Copenhagen's answer to Harrods or Bergdorf Goodman with seven floors of fantastic fashion, homewares and more besides plus a great deli, café, bakery, chocolate counter, newsagent and luxury supermarket Mad & Vin in the basement.

Food and drink

Emmerys Store Standstræde 21, Indre By ⓦ www .emmerys.dk. Trendy bakery where the young, rich and health-conscious queue up every weekend for their organic non-dyed, non-yeast bread, though there are plenty of scrumptious cakes on offer, too. Also outlets on Østerbrogade 51, Vesterbrogade 34 and Nørrebrogade 8.

Gammel Strand Ø log Vin Nabolos 6, Indre By. Over 200 different beers – Danish and international.

Lagkagehuset Torvegade 45, Christianshavn. Right opposite the metro station and easily identifiable by the ever-present queue, this sumptuous bakery produces amazing bread baked in traditional stone ovens, plus great pastries and cakes. There's another branch in the Copenhagen Right

Now tourist office on Vesterbrogade (see p.49). **Løgismose** Bernstorffsgade 5, Indre By. Bang opposite Central Station, this fabulous deli is part of the *Nimb* complex in Tivoli (see p.71) but there's also a street entrance for non Tivoli-goers. Aside from the inevitable jars of herring, cheeses, cured meats, remoulades, preserves and the like, you'll find more unusual delicacies to try or take home as souvenirs, and there's also the produce made by their own dairy and delicious home-made chocolates.

Rhein van Hauen Østergade 22, Indre By. The king of Danish bakeries, Rhein van Hauen has over 27 years of organic baking to its credit and serves up mouthwatering *rundstykker* (crispy bread rolls) and pastries. Also has branches at Store Kongensgade 45 and Gammel Kongevej 177.

Peter Beier Chokolade Skoubougade 1, Indre By. Delicious chocolates sold by weight and beautifully packaged.

Gay Copenhagen

Copenhagen is one of the world's **premier gay cities**. Paradoxically, though, Copenhagen's liberal traditions mean that there are relatively few specifically gay and lesbian venues. An excellent source of advice and general **information** on what's on in the city is Landforeningen for Bøsser og Lesbiske (LBL; see Basics p.37). Also readily available at all major gay hangouts is the monthly *Out and About*, mostly in Danish and published by Copenhagen Gay Life (Ⓦwww .copenhagen-gay-life.dk), a network of gay and gay-friendly businesses and organizations. They also publish a very useful *Gay map of Copenhagen*. The city's hugely popular annual gay pride march, **Copenhagen Pride** (Ⓦwww .copenhagenpride.dk) takes place in August, with a suitably flamboyant street parade followed by an all-night party. Also on the annual agenda are the Copenhagen Gay and Lesbian Film Festival in October (Ⓦwww.cglff.dk), and the legendary midsummer beach party at Amager Strandpark organized by LBL.

Accommodation

In addition to the places listed below, you can find rooms in gay or gay-friendly private accommodation by contacting the Germany-based Enjoy Bed & Breakfast (☎+49 30 23 62 36 10, Ⓦwww.ebab.dk). These places are marked on the map on pp.60–61.

Carsten's Guest House Christians Brygge 28, fifth floor (ring the bell marked "Carsten Appel"), Indre By ☎33 14 91 07, Ⓦwww.carstensguest house.dk. Bus #5A or #66; a 10min walk from Central Station or Rådhuspladsen. This guesthouse has a very friendly and international atmosphere, though the rooms are a bit small and the walls thin. There's a great roof garden, a comfortable and attractive lounge, and a kitchen for guests' use. Dorm beds 175kr. ❺

Copenhagen Rainbow Guesthouse Frederiks-berggade 25C, fourth floor, Indre By ☎33 14 10 20, Ⓦwww.copenhagen-rainbow.dk. Rådhuspladsen bus station. *Rainbow* is a gay and lesbian-only guesthouse in an excellent position on Strøget, just off Rådhuspladsen, with five rooms, three en suite, and all with queen-sized bed and tea- and coffee-making facilities. The rate includes a buffet breakfast, and there's free wi-fi. Two-night minimum. ❻

Hotel Windsor Frederiksborggade 30, Indre By ☎33 11 08 30, Ⓦwww.hotelwindsor.dk. Bus #5A; Nørreport station. On the second and third floor of a residential apartment block, this long-established and unpretentious gay hotel has some en-suite rooms. Continental breakfast buffet included. ❻

Bars and clubs

Unless otherwise stated, these places are marked on the map on pp.60–61.

Can Can Mikkel Bryggers Gade 11, Indre By. Small, friendly, inexpensive bar during the day, alive and bustling at night when mostly frequented by gay men.

Chaca Studiestræde 39. Indre By. Predominently lesbian bar spread over two floors with lots of different events; games nights, speed-dating and karaoke the most renowned. Good cocktails, too. Wed–Sat only.

Code Rådhusstræde 1, Indre By. This new addition to the scene attracts a good mix of lesbians and gay men. It's a café during the day and a lounge bar at night with DJ and dancefloor. Wed–Sat only.

Cosy Bar Studiestræde 24, Indre By. Popular dance and late-night/early-morning cruise venue (mostly gay men but a lot of straight people too) for the partygoer with stamina. DJ Tues & Thurs–Sat. Opens 10pm.

Masken Studiestræde 33, Indre By. Nearly every segment of the city's gay and lesbian population makes it to this raucous bar at some point during the week, possibly because of the cheap beer.

Oscars Rådhuspladsen 77, Indre By. A traditional first port of call on a night out, the very popular *Oscars* serves good, classic Danish food as well as every kind of soft and alcoholic drink imaginable.

Vela Gay Club Viktoriagade 2–4, Vesterbro. See map, pp.76–77. Hugely popular oriental-style place that began life as a predominantly lesbian venue – it serves "pussy-tails" as well as cocktails – but now attracts partygoers of all persuasions. Wed–Sat only.

Listings

Airport information For information on arrivals and departures visit ⓦ www.cph.dk.

Banks and exchange The airport and Central Station have late-opening exchange facilities, which charge a similar amount of commission. Forex exchange bureaux charge 30kr to exchange cash and 20kr to exchange travellers' cheques and are much rarer; there's one at Central Station (daily 8am–9pm), one at Nørre Voldgade 90, near Nørreport Station (Mon–Fri 9am–7pm, Sat 10am–4pm), and one at Gothersgade 8, near Kongens Nytorv (Mon–Fri 10am–6pm, Sat 10.30am–3.30pm).

Car rental Avis, airport ☏ 32 51 22 99, Kampmannsgade 1 ☏ 70 24 77 07, ⓦ www.avis.dk; Budget ☏ 33 55 05 00, airport ☏ 32 52 39 00, Vester Farimagsgade 7 ☏ 33 55 70 00, ⓦ www.budget.dk; Hertz, airport ☏ 32 50 93 00, Ved Vesterport 3 ☏ 33 17 90 20, ⓦ www.hertzdk.dk.

Dentists For dental emergencies, contact Tandlægevagten, Oslo Plads 14 ☏ 35 38 02 51 (Mon–Fri 8am–9.30pm, Sat & Sun 10am–noon), but be prepared to pay at least 200kr on the spot.

Embassies and consulates Australian: Dampfærgevej 26, 2nd floor ☏ 70 26 36 76, ⓦ www .denmark-embassy.gov.au; Canadian: Kristen Bernikows Gade 1 ☏ 33 48 32 00, ⓦ www.canada .dk; German: Stockholmsgade 57 ☏ 35 45 99 00, ⓦ www.kopenhagen.diplo.de; Irish: Østbanegade 21 ☏ 35 42 32 33, ⓦ www.embassyofireland.dk; New Zealand: Store Standstræde 21, 2nd floor ☏ 33 37 77 00, ⓦ www.nzconsulate.dk; Norwegian: Amaliegade 39 ☏ 33 14 01 24, ⓦ www.norsk.dk; South African: Gammel Vartov Vej 8 ☏ 39 18 01 55, ⓦ www.southafrica.dk; UK:

Kastelsvej 40 ☏ 35 44 52 00, ⓦ www.ukindenmark .fco.gov.uk; US: Dag Hammerskjölds Allé 24 ☏ 33 41 71 00, ⓦ www.denmark.usembassy.gov.

Fitness centres Scandinavia's leading health-club chain, SATS (ⓦ www.sats.com), has several branches in the city a day's membership costs 150kr and entitles you to use the full range of facilities. The most central branch is on the fifth floor of the Scala centre, just opposite Tivoli at Vesterbrogade 2E (☏ 33 32 10 02).

Internet Computer and wireless access is available free of charge at the city's libraries (though not the Royal Library). The city's main internet café is the huge Boomtown, Axeltorv 1–3 (daily 24hr; ⓦ www.boomtown.net).

Laundry Central places include: Istedgades Møntvask, Istedgade 45; Quickvask, Rosenørns Allé 37; Møntvask, Ranzausgade 62; and Vaske-teria, Dronningensgade 42. An average load costs about 30kr. Alternatively, head for the Laundromat Café, Elmegade 15, and eat while you clean (34kr; see p.84).

Libraries Most central are Københavns Hoved-bibliotek at Krystalgade 15, Indre By; Christianshavn Bibliotek at Dronningensgade 53; Blågårdens Bibliotek at Blågårdsplads 5, Nørrebro; and Østerbros Bibliotek, Dag Hammaskjölds Allé 19. Libraries tend to be open Mon–Fri 10am–7pm, Sat 10am–2pm.

Lost property The police department's lost-property office is at Slotsherrensvej 113, Vanløse ☏ 38 74 88 22. For items lost on a bus, contact the bus information office on ☏ 36 13 14 15; lost on a train or S-Tog, the central train information office on ☏ 70 13 14 15; lost on the metro, call ☏ 70 15 16 15; lost on a plane, contact the airline or Copenhagen Airport ☏ 32 47 47 25.

Mail The main post office is at Købmagergade 1 (Mon–Fri 10am–6pm, Sat 10am–2pm) and there's a late-opening one inside the Central Station (Mon–Fri 8am–9pm, Sat & Sun 10am–4pm).

Medical treatment If you need a doctor, call ☎33 15 46 00 (Mon–Fri 8am–4pm) and you'll be given the name of one in your area; outside these hours, call ☎70 13 00 41. Doctors' fees start at 250kr, to be paid in cash. For medical emergencies call ☎112. There are emergency departments at Amager Hospital, Italiensvej 1, Amager (☎32 34 35 00); Bispebjerg Hospital, Bispebjerg Bakke 23 (☎35 31 23 73) and Frederiksberg Hospital, Nordre Fasanvej 57, Frederiksberg (☎38 16 35 22).

Newspapers Overseas newspapers are sold at Magasin du Nord and Illum department stores (see p.91), the stall on the eastern side of Rådhuspladsen, and some newsagents along Strøget; the newsagents in Central Station stock a large range of foreign newspapers and magazines. The English-language *Copenhagen Post* newspaper (🌐www .copenhagenpost.dk) covers city issues and has an in-depth listings section; it comes out every Friday and costs 20kr.

Pharmacies Copenhagen's two main 24-hour pharmacies are Steno Apotek, Vesterbrogade 6C in front of Central Station (☎33 14 82 66) and Sønderbro Apotek, Amagerbrogade 158, Amager (☎32 58 01 40).

Police stations The central police station is at Polititorvet 14 (☎33 14 88 88), with additional stations at Halmtorvet 20 (☎33 14 14 48) and Nørrebrogade 88 (☎35 21 53 20), as well as Central Station (☎33 25 14 48).

Swimming pools The most central (and best) indoor pool is the one in the DGI Byen sports centre at Tietgensgade 65, Vesterbro (close to Central Station), with a gorgeous elliptical pool, children's pool and diving area. Entry is 58kr; swimsuit rental costs 30kr with a deposit of photo ID. The city also has two wonderful, free open-air harbour pools, at Islands Brygge, Amager (June–Aug Mon–Fri 7am–7pm, Sat & Sun 11am–7pm; Islands Brygge metro), which offers an adult pool, children's pool and diving pool; and one at Havneholmen, next to Fisketorvet shopping centre (June–Aug daily 11am–7pm; bus #1A, #30, #65E or Dybbølsbro S-Tog), which also has the mocked-up sandy "Copencabana" beach, complete with volleyball and other sports.

Around Copenhagen

Copenhagen's suburbs are, unsurprisingly, rather quiet, though there are a few attractions dotted about, along with a number of good sandy beaches and lovely tracts of open park and woodland, all within easy reach of the city centre. Along the coast to the **north of the city**, a trip to Charlottenlund and the **Danish Aquarium**, or Klampenborg, home to the amusement park **Bakken** and the wonderful **Ordrupgaard** art museum, can be combined with a lounge around on the adjacent sandy beaches. Inland from here lies the bucolic **Frilandsmuseet** open-air museum at Sorgenfri. A full day's jaunt further north up the Øresund Coast will allow you to take in the charming **Karen Blixen Museum** and spectacular **Louisiana** museum of modern art, with its superb coastal setting, while to the **south of the cit**y, there's more contemporary art at **Arken**, again in a stunning seafront location.

Charlottenlund and the Danish Aquarium

A few kilometres north of the city – a twenty-minute S-tog ride from Central Station or a forty-minute bus ride (#14) – and you're in the snooty suburb of **CHARLOTTENLUND**. From the train station it's a ten-minute stroll through woods to the immaculate tree-lined lawns of **Charlottenlund Slot** (closed to the public) and its gorgeous gardens (24hr; free). **Danmarks Akvarium**, in the white building on the eastern edge of the park (daily: Feb–May & Sept–Oct 10am–5pm, Wed open 10am–8pm; June–Aug 10am–6pm, Wed 10am–8pm; Nov–Jan

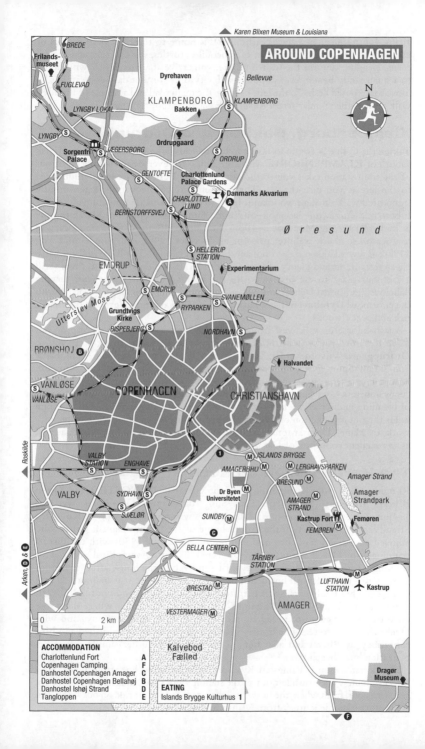

▲ Karen Blixen Museum & Louisiana

AROUND COPENHAGEN

BREDE

Frilands-
museet

I.FUGLEVAD

Dyrehaven

Bellevue

KLAMPENBORG

LYNGBY LOKAL

Bakken

KLAMPENBORG

LYNGBY

JÆGERSBORG

Sorgenfri
Palace

Ordrupgaard

ORDRUP

GENTOFTE

Charlottenlund
Palace Gardens

Danmarks Akvarium

CHARLOTTEN-
LUND

BERNSTORFFSVEJ

Ø r e s u n d

HELLERUP
STATION

EMDRUP

Experimentarium

EMDRUP

SVANEMØLLEN

Utterslev Mose

Grundtvigs
Kirke

RYPARKEN

BISPEBJERG

NORDHAVN

BRØNSHØJ

VANLØSE

COPENHAGEN

Halvandet

CHRISTIANSHAVN

VANLØSE

Roskilde

VALBY
STATION

ENGHAVE

ISLANDS BRYGGE

AMAGERBRHU

LERGRAVSPARKEN

Amager Strand

VALBY

SYDHAVN

Dr Byen
Universitetet

ØRESUND

Amager
Strandpark

Arken, D & E

SJÆLØR

SUNDBY

AMAGER
STRAND

Kastrup Fort

Femøren

FEMØREN

BELLA CENTER

TÄRNBY
STATION

ØRESTAD

LUFTHAVN
STATION

Kastrup

AMAGER

VESTERMAGER

Kalvebod
Fælled

0   2 km

ACCOMMODATION

Charlottenlund Fort	A
Copenhagen Camping	F
Danhostel Copenhagen Amager	C
Danhostel Copenhagen Bellahøj	B
Danhostel Ishøj Strand	E
Tangloppen	D

EATING

Islands Brygge Kulturhus	1

Dragør
Museum

10am–4pm; 100kr; Ⓦwww.akvarium.dk), is home to three hundred species of fish, plus the usual supporting cast of crocodiles, turtles, sharks, frogs and crustaceans. Heading towards the sea from here, you arrive at a stretch of lawn leading to a small sandy **beach**, ever popular with cityfolk – on hot days you can hardly move for exposed flesh. To the left, back on the main road and a couple of minutes' walk away is the popular *Jorden Rundt Café* – a great spot for lunch.

Klampenborg, Bakken and Ordrupgaard

Taking the C-line S-Tog to its last stop brings you to the wealthy and very stylish suburb of **KLAMPENBORG**, with something for everyone. Turning right out of the train station takes you to the very popular **Bellevue Beach** – nudist area to the left as you face the sea. Turning left out of the station, a ten-minute signposted walk through woodlands leads to the **Bakken** amusement park (daily: July to mid-Aug Mon–Sat noon–midnight, Sun noon–11pm; late March to June & mid- to late-Aug Mon–Sat 2–10pm, Sun noon–10pm; closing times vary in low season so check website; pass for all 34 rides 199kr, end June to mid-Aug 219kr; Ⓦwww.bakken.dk) – a noisier, brasher version of Tivoli – with beer halls, cheap restaurants and plenty of fairground rides. If you don't fancy it, there's still a fabulous place to eat just opposite the entrance – *Peter Lieps Hus*, serving delicious, traditional Danish lunches; alternatively pack a picnic and head off into the enormous **Dyrehaven** (Deer Park), a former royal hunting ground of ancient oak and beech woods.

A two-kilometre walk west from Klampenborg station, or a short hop on bus #388 towards Lyngby (left out of the station and across the road), takes you to **Ordrupgaard** (Vilvordevej 10; Tues, Thurs & Fri 1–5pm, Wed 10am–6pm, Sat & Sun 11am–5pm; 70kr; Ⓦwww.ordrupgaard.dk), a delightful art museum occupying a 1918 country manor house on the southern edge of Dyrehaven. The curvy concrete extension was designed by Zaha Hadid and does a pretty good job of blending in discreetly while surrendering none of its modernity. The museum holds the finest collection of **French Impressionist** art in northern Europe with works by Manet, Degas, Monet, Renoir, Pissarro and Sisley among others, as well as an excellent collection of Danish Golden Age painting.

The Karen Blixen Museum and Louisiana

Roughly 10km from Klampenborg, in the village of **RUNGSTED**, the **Karen Blixen Museum** (May–Sept Tues–Sun 10am–5pm; Oct–April Wed–Fri 1–4pm, Sat & Sun 11am–4pm; 50kr; Ⓦwww.karen-blixen.dk), at Rungsted Strandvej 111, is housed in the family home of the famous Danish writer who enjoyed a resurgence of international popularity in the 1980s with the Oscar-winning film *Out of Africa*, based on her 1937 autobiographical account of running a coffee plantation in Kenya. Blixen lived in the house after her return from Africa in 1931 until her death in 1962, and much of it is maintained as it was during her final years, with furniture, personal effects and photographs left as they were when she died. The light-filled study at the end is where she wrote most of her books, surrounded by mementoes of her time in Kenya and with lovely views out to sea. The house is backed by woodlands established as a **bird sanctuary** by Blixen and also her final resting place – her simple **grave** lies beneath a huge beech tree.

The closest station is Rungsted Kyst, on the regionaltog line, from where it's a fifteen-minute walk – turn left out of the station, right onto Rungstedvej, then right at the harbour, from where the house is signposted – or a short ride on bus #388. Bus #388 also makes the journey from Klampenborg S-Tog station.

In **HUMLEBÆK**, a sizeable coastal village 10km further north up the coast from Rungsted, and on the same train line, you'll find **Louisiana Museum of Modern Art** (Tues–Fri 11am–10pm, Sat & Sun 11am–6pm; 90kr; Ⓦ www .louisiana.dk), a compelling mixture of unusual architecture and outstanding modern art in a wonderful coastal setting. The **permanent collection** – divided between the museum buildings and the sculpture garden outside – reflects most of the important art movements of the second half of the twentieth century. Start walking clockwise around the gallery to reach a tall, purpose-built gallery that houses one of the museum's highlights – a striking collection of **Giacometti**'s gaunt bronze figures together with many of his original sketches. A little further on is the museum's outstanding collection of works by the **CoBrA** movement (named after the cities of Copenhagen, Brussels and Amsterdam), a left-wing collective of artists formed in 1948 and characterized by distinctive and colourful abstracts – there are works by Appel, Corneille and Heerup and a whole room devoted to the characteristically tortured abstracts of Asger Jorn, one of Denmark's most renowned artists. There's also a good representation of **Pop Art**, with works by Warhol, Rauschenberg, Robert Ryman and Lichtenstein providing the backdrop to Claes Oldenburg's models of oversized cigarette butts and a lunchbox, and Jim Dine's stark *White Bathroom*. **Contemporary art** is also well represented, boosted by the recent acquisition of *A Closer Grand Canyon* by David Hockney, a *Maman* spider by Louise Bourgeois and works by Sam Taylor-Wood, Jonathan Meese, Doug Aitken and video artists Gary Hill and Bill Viola, among others.

The beautiful grounds **outside** are dotted with a fantastic array of around sixty pieces of world-class sculpture from the likes of Max Ernst, Alexander Calder and Henry Moore, some of it specifically designed for this site.

Louisiana is on the northern edge of Humlebæk, at Gammel Strandvej 13; it's a short walk from the train station or bus #388 stops right outside.

The Frilandsmuseet and around

Half an hour north of the city on bus #184 from Nørreport, or B or B+ S-Tog lines to Sorgenfri station and a ten-minute walk (turn right out of the station, then left onto Kongevej) is the rural idyll of the **Frilandsmuseet** (Open-Air Museum; Easter to mid-Oct Tues–Sun 10am–5pm; free; Ⓦ www.natmus.dk), a wonderful mixture of heritage park and city farm spread across 86 acres of rolling countryside and displaying around eighty beautifully preserved buildings dating back to the seventeenth century from across Denmark and its former territories. The cottages and farmsteads are grouped together according to region, and furnished according to various trades – bakers, potters, millers, blacksmiths and so on – and offer a vivid picture of how rural communities lived in northern Europe in times past.

At the far northern end of the museum, on I.C. Modewegs Vej, is the equally rewarding **Brede Værk** (Industrial Works of Brede; same hours; free; Ⓦ www .natmus.dk) – a large textile mill and factory that operated here from 1832 to 1956. It's now home to a fine museum, devoted partly to the history of the mill and factory and partly to the wider story of the industrialization of Denmark. All of the buildings, from the huge brick bulk of the factory itself to the dye works, workers' cottages, children's nursery (many of the workers in the mill were women) and craftsmen's houses are well preserved and the museum works hard to bring history to life. Next to the factory, **Brede Manor**, the mill owner's grand Neoclassical residence (tours only; June–Aug Sun noon & 1.30pm; 50kr) reveals just how much wealth was made (for some) by the industry. From the nearby Brede train station you can catch a small, local train to Jægersborg (roughly every 20min), from where B and B+ S-Tog trains continue on to the city centre.

Arken

Situated 20km southwest of the city centre on a beautiful windswept beach near the suburb of Ishøj is the stunning **Arken** museum of modern art (Tues & Thurs–Sun 10am–5pm, Wed 10am–9pm; 85kr; ⓦwww.arken.dk). It's an obscure location – take S-Tog line A or E to Ishøj station, and then bus #128 – but worth the trip. The museum opened in 1996, its design the result of an open competition won by young Danish architecture student Søren Robert Lund. His striking deconstructivist creation – much criticized at the time for detracting from the art itself – pays homage to the maritime location, its intersecting white planes, angles and curves resembling some strange shipwrecked liner. The focus is on art from the 1940s onwards though the bulk of the works are post-1990 and by Nordic artists. Naturally, the big Danish names are here – a series of Asger Jorn's large, colourful canvases adorn the foyer and there are also works by Per Kirkeby among others – though seminal figures such as Jean Arp, co-founder of the Dada group also get a look in. Contemporary giants of the art world are represented, including Jeff Koons and **Damien Hirst**, who gets a room to himself with ten works on his favourite existential themes of life and death. On the first floor, there's a great restaurant with stunning views over the bay.

Travel details

Trains

Copenhagen to: Aalborg (29 daily; 4hr 43min); Århus (38 daily; 3hr 15min); Esbjerg (9 daily; 3hr); Frederikshavn (11 daily; 5hr 20min); Helsingør (every 20min; 45min); Hillerød (every 10min; 40min); Holbæk (2–3 hourly; 1hr 10min); (Kalundborg 2–3 hourly; 1hr 46min); Køge (every 10min; 42min); Næstved (2–3 hourly; 1hr); Malmö (3 hourly; 35min); Nykøbing F (hourly; 1hr 40min); Odense (every 30min; 1hr 30min); Ringsted (3–4 hourly; 40min); Rønne (3–5 daily; via ferry from Ystad; 3hr); Roskilde (every 5–10min; 25min); Slagelse (2–3 hourly; 1hr 15min).

Buses

Copenhagen to: Aalborg (3–5 daily; 4hr 45min); Århus (4–7 daily; 3hr 5min); Ebeltoft (2–3 daily; 3hr); Esbjerg (9 daily; 3hr); Fjerritslev via Grenå, Randers, Hobro and Løgstør (4–6 daily; 5hr 55min); Malmö (hourly; 55min); Thisted via Viborg and Nykøbing Mors (1–2 daily; 6hr 10min); Rønne via Ystad (2–4 daily; 2hr 30min); Silkeborg (2 daily; 4hr).

Flights

Copenhagen to: Århus (Cimber Sterling & SAS 3–6 daily; 40min); Aalborg (Cimber Sterling & SAS: 5–9 daily; 50min); Billund (Cimber Sterling & SAS: 2–5 daily; 45min); Bornholm, Rønne (Cimber Sterling & SAS 3–6 daily; 35min); Karup (Cimber Sterling & SAS: 2–9 daily; 50min); Sønderborg (Cimber Sterling & SAS: 2–4 daily; 45min).

2

Zealand

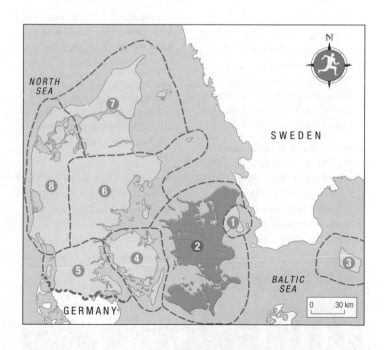

CHAPTER 2

Highlights

※ **Kronborg Slot** Best known as the home of Shakespeare's *Hamlet*, this pearl of a Gothic fortress sits on a grassy promontory overlooking the Baltic. **See p.105**

※ **Gilleleje and Tisvildeleje** These twin north-coast beach towns are among Denmark's swankiest places to swim and sunbathe, with great dining options, too. **See p.109**

※ **Roskilde** A mere half-hour from Copenhagen, this medieval town offers a striking Gothic cathedral, a superb museum of Viking shipbuilding and – every July – one of the world's largest music festivals. **See p.111**

※ **Viking plays, Frederikssund** These over-the-top dramatizations of Viking mythology feature hundreds of performers dressed to the nines and wielding medieval-style weaponry. **See p.117**

※ **Trelleborg Viking ring fortress** The ruins of this concentric ring fortress offer a fascinating insight into the complexities of Viking society. **See p.121**

※ **Storebælt bridge** Head to Korsør for superb vistas of this astonishing triumph of engineering and construction, then cross it to explore Funen. **See p.121**

※ **Holmegaard Glassworks** Make your own glass sculpture or kick back to watch the professionals at work. **See p.124**

※ **Møns Klint** Walk along these gleaming chalk cliffs, set between lush forest and the Baltic Sea, then explore the fascinating new nature museum. **See p.126**

※ **Marielyst** Every summer beach bums of all ages flock to this one-horse seaside resort town for sand, sea and a dab of hedonism. **See p.130**

▲ Trelleborg

2

Zealand

A s the largest of Denmark's islands and the home of its capital (covered in Chapter 1), **Zealand** (*Sjælland*) is the country's most important – and most visited – region. But while almost everyone who visits Zealand spends some time in Copenhagen, it's well worth venturing on from here to explore the towns and villages spread across the rest of the island to get a glimpse of how different, and how enjoyable, Denmark can be. Past Copenhagen's dormitory suburbs and beaches, things slide into the happily provincial, with woods and expansive parklands appearing almost as soon as you leave the city. And given the swiftness of the metropolitan transport network, which covers almost half the island – nowhere on Zealand is more than ninety minutes from Copenhagen – you can head out on day-trips and be back in the capital in easy time for an evening drink.

North of Copenhagen's suburban sprawl, the city's arterial ring road branches off to edge up along the sixty-kilometre long Kattegat coast, a dramatic landscape of healthy forests that's peppered with castles and royal palaces, not to mention a string of lovely beaches – some low-key, others decidedly modish – where Copenhageners have long come to swim, sunbathe and eat out at an excellent selection of restaurants. Other highlights of **northern Zealand** include **Helsingør**, site of the renowned **Kronborg Slot**, better known as the Elsinore Castle of Shakespeare's *Hamlet*, and the more eyecatching **Frederiksborg Slot** in nearby **Hillerød**. West of Copenhagen on the Roskilde fjord, **Roskilde** is Denmark's former capital and boasts an extravagant cathedral that's still the last resting place for the country's monarchs, as well as an engaging museum displaying five of the fourteen Viking ships salvaged from the fjord. The town is also within easy distance of the **Hornsherred** peninsula, ideal for cycling or lax days on the beach. South of Roskilde, the E20 motorway cuts straight through the more rural area of **central Zealand**, from the sandy Baltic beaches and well-preserved medieval centre of **Køge** on the east coast to the quaint town of **Korsør**, best known for its multi-billion-kroner **Storebælt bridge**, Zealand's link to the island of Funen. **Southern Zealand** is even more pastoral, with vast swathes of farmland and sloping hillsides prettied up by a handful of towns that hold some appealing accommodation and eating options. Just off Zealand's south coast and connected to the mainland by road bridge, the islands of **Møn**, **Lolland** and **Falster** are wonderfully bucolic, with first-class summer beach towns, medieval churches and plenty of opportunities for walking and cycling.

2

ZEALAND | Northern Zealand

Ebeltoft ◄

Århus ◄

Århus ◄

Samsø ◄

Nyborg (Funen) ◄

www.roughguides.com

102

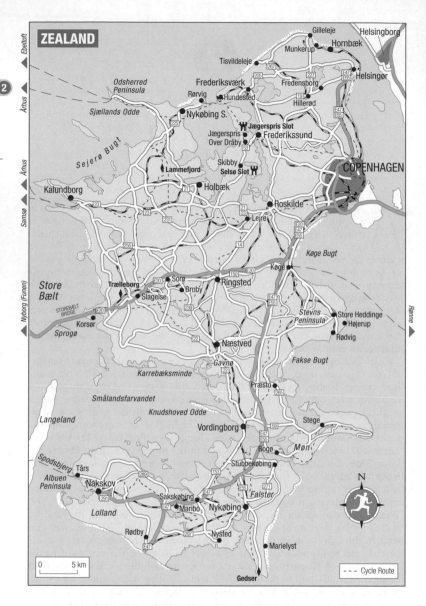

Rønne ►

Northern Zealand

The coast north of Copenhagen as far as Helsingør is tagged the "Danish Riviera", a label that aptly describes its line of tiny one-time fishing hamlets now inhabited almost exclusively by wealthy Danes. With its magnificent castle and pretty medieval streets, **Helsingør** is the perfect spot from which to start your exploration of the **north coast**, with its attractive villages and fantastic dune- and forest-backed sandy beaches at **Hellebæk**, **Gilleleje** and **Tisvildeleje**. Heading inland, **Hillerød** is home to the stunning Frederiksborg Slot and Museum of National History, precariously positioned across three small islands on an artificial lake.

Immediately west of Copenhagen, meanwhile, is the former Danish capital of **Roskilde**, home to a spectacular Viking ship museum and one of the most impressive cathedrals in Denmark. North of Roskilde and its namesake fjord, several waterside towns hold churches, castles or duned beachfronts that justify a diversion from the beaten path. The hilly **Hornsherred peninsula** offers **Skibby Kirke** and its stark medieval-era frescoes, while the nearby **Selsø Slot** preserves much of its pre-nineteenth-century charm. There are more frescoes further north within **Over Dråby**'s medieval church and **Jægerspris Slot**, former home of Frederik VII and filled with many of the idiosyncratic monarch's personal belongings, while just across the Roskilde fjord, **Frederikssund** is best known for the popular Viking plays staged outdoors in the summer.

All of these places are easily seen in a day-trip from the capital. The best means of exploring the areas north of Copenhagen is the #388 bus, which runs north to Helsingør from Klampenborg, itself the last stop on line C or F of the S-Tog system; you could also take one of the frequent trains between Copenhagen and Helsingør, but the views are obscured by trees for much of the journey. Transport to Hillerød from Helsingør and the north coast is limited to slow regional trains, with one line heading south from Gilleleje and one southwest from Helsingør. Roskilde is easily reached by regular train from Copenhagen; the fjord towns north of it are easily reached on regional bus routes or, if you have more time, by leisurely cycle.

Helsingør

Some 45km north of Copenhagen (45min by *regionaltog*), **HELSINGØR** is strategically positioned at the narrowest point of the Øresund, with the Swedish town of Helsingborg just 4km away on the opposite coast. Helsingør's wealth was founded on the Sound Toll of 1429, which was levied on ships passing through this narrow strait between the Baltic and the North Sea. With the toll long abolished, and the majority of traffic to Sweden now going via the bridge outside Copenhagen, things have slowed down somewhat, though it's still a popular spot for Swedes who come to take ample advantage of Denmark's easily accessible (and relatively cheap) alcohol. Booze-cruising apart, Helsingør's main draw is the mighty and ever-popular Kronborg Slot.

Arrival and information

The **train station** is on Jernbanevej, just a couple of minutes' walk from the town centre and ten minutes' walk from Kronborg Slot. Buses stop outside, and the **tourist office** (July–Sept Mon–Fri 10am–5pm, Sat 10am–3pm; rest of year Mon–Fri 10am–4pm, Sat 10am–1pm; ☎49 21 13 33, ⓦwww.visithelsingor.dk) is just across at Havnepladsen 3. As well as information on the town itself, it has ferry timetables for all of the companies.

Despite catering to so many ferry passengers and visitors to the castle, Helsingør is pretty low on **accommodation** options, so if you want to stay during the busy summer season, it's wise to book ahead.

Accommodation

Danhostel Helsingør Vandrerhjem, Nordre Strandvej 24 ☎49 21 16 40, ⓦwww .helsingorhostel.dk. Occupying a lovely restored villa and with lawns sweeping down to a beach, this is one of the best youth hostels in Denmark. There are double rooms (③) within chalet-type enclosures and a few large dorms (175kr), plus free wi-fi. It's a couple of kilometres out of town, either via a 20min walk along the coastal road (Nordre Strandvej), or via bus #340 from the station; get off just after the sports stadium. **Helsingør Camping** Strandalleen 2 ☎49 28 49 50, ⓦ www.helsingorcamping.dk. Lovely little campsite between Skt Anna Gade (known as Nordre Strandvej northwest of town) and the sea. There's a shop (May–Sept), bike rental and playground, as well as some cabins (from 250kr). **Marienlyst** Nordre Strandvej 2 ☎49 21 40 00, ⓦ www.marienlyst.dk. The top choice in town,

this modern hotel has a lovely seafront location, lavishly decorated rooms and resort-style amenities: restaurants, beach park, spa and pool. ❼

Skandia Bramstræde 1 ☎49 21 09 02, ⓦ www.hotelskandia.dk. Basic but comfortable rooms (some with harbour views, others with shared bathrooms), a central location (2min from the train station and main street) and the cheapest prices in town make this a popular option year-round. ❻

The Town

Helsingør is a lively and likeable town and, away from the hustle of the ferry terminals and tourist hordes at Kronborg, a quiet and relaxing place with a well-preserved **medieval quarter** and ample cafés and restaurants. The bustling pedestrianized main street, **Stengade**, is lined with shops and restaurants and linked by pretty, narrow alleyways of rickety half-timbered houses to **Axeltorv**, the town's small market square (markets on Wed, Fri & Sat mornings) and a good spot to linger over a beer. Toward the corner of Stengade and Skt Anna Gade is the town's cathedral, the red-brick, copper-spired **Skt Olai's Kirke** (daily: May–Aug 10am–4pm; Sept–April 10am–2pm), extensively remodelled and expanded over the centuries from its humble origins as a Romanesque church founded in 1200. Inside, there's a fussily ornate altar and some dark portraits of past rectors. Look out too for the font, to the left of the entrance, its balusters endowed by

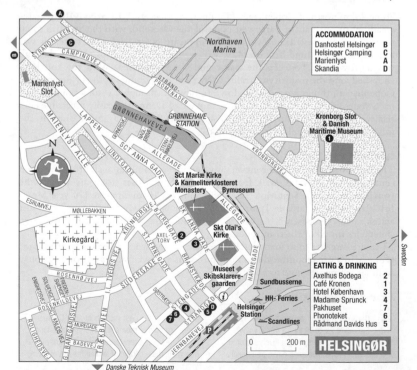

Danske Teknisk Museum

wealthy citizens and engraved with their children's names. Just beyond is the fifteenth-century **Sct Mariæ Kirke** (Mon–Sat 9am–noon, plus Thurs 4–6pm) with its pretty red-brick cloister, and the adjacent **Karmeliterklosteret Monastery** (guided tours only: June to mid-Sept daily at 2pm; 20kr), the best-preserved medieval monastery in Scandinavia. Erik of Pomerania gave the site to Carmelite monks in 1430; following the Reformation, in 1541, the monastery was turned into a hospital for the old and poor, during which time it gained some pre-eminence (and notoriety) for its innovative brain operations. The unnerving tools of this profession are still on show next door, at Skt Anna Gade 36, in the **Bymuseum** (daily noon–4pm; 20kr), an otherwise rather dry trawl through the town's history, with no English labelling. You'll get a better sense of what Helsingør was all about at the **Museet Skibsklarerergaarden** (Shipping Agent's House; Tues–Fri noon–4pm, Sat 10am–2pm; 30kr), Strandgade 91, a lovely eighteenth-century building once occupied by agents responsible for collecting the Sound Toll. The rooms have been reconstructed much as they were during the last days of the toll (it was abolished in 1857) and there's also a souvenir shop done out in period style, complete with a blackboard chalked up with the names of ships once present in the Sound and their captains' names.

A 25-minute walk northwest of town via Skt Anna Gade and Loppen, the stately Neoclassical pile of **Marienlyst Slot** was built in the eighteenth century as a royal summer residence, and is situated to make the most of the cooling sea breezes and stunning views. There's not much to see in the Louis XVI-style interior; the rooms are largely devoid of furniture, with just the odd gilt mirror and chandelier to set the tone, but the collection of paintings, mostly of local seascapes and the brooding Kronborg over the centuries, are wonderfully atmospheric and include a few by Golden Age painter C.W. Eckersberg. You can walk up behind the palace into the hilly gardens and forest (maps are available from the ticket desk), where you'll find a shady glade and a statue marking the supposed site of *Hamlet*'s grave, placed here in 1858 as a means of perpetuating the area's *Hamlet* associations; the views over the Øresund and Kronborg from the glade are stunning. The building is undergoing a seemingly interminable renovation, so for current opening hours and prices, contact the tourist office.

Kronborg Slot and the Maritime Museum

Tactically placed on a sandy curl of land extending seawards into the Øresund and a fifteen-minute walk from the train station, the spectacular castle of **Kronborg** (April & Oct to early Nov Tues–Sun 11am–4pm; May–Sept daily 10.30am–5pm; early Nov to March Tues–Sun 11am–3pm; Ⓦwww.kronborg.dk; 65kr, joint ticket with Maritime Museum 90kr) dominates Helsingør and is the town's main draw. It's famous principally as the setting – under the name of Elsinore Castle – for Shakespeare's *Hamlet*, though it's still uncertain whether the playwright actually ever came here (see box, p.106). Nonetheless, the association endures in *Hamlet* souvenirs and the annual staging of the play in the castle grounds, a tradition begun in 1816, with recent performers including Sir Derek Jacobi and Jude Law. In 2000, the castle was awarded UNESCO World Heritage Site status and a restoration project has been ongoing for well over a decade; don't be surprised if there's disruption in the odd room. **Guided tours** of the royal chambers take place in English daily at 11.30am and 1.30pm, and well-informed attendants hover ready to answer questions.

Originally constructed in the fifteenth century by Erik of Pomerania, the fortress of Krogen ("The Hook") was the key to control of the Øresund for hundreds of years. As Helsingborg on the other side of the strait was also under Danish rule, Denmark's monarchs were able to extract a toll from every ship that passed

Kronborg and Hamlet

The origins of the story of a tragic Danish prince stretch back far beyond Shakespearean times. The earliest mention of a character called **Amled** can be found in a story, derived from Icelandic and Celtic sagas, written around 1200 by one of Bishop Absalon's scribes, a certain Saxo Grammaticus. An earlier, Elizabethan version of the *Hamlet* story, thought to have been written by **Thomas Kyd**, had already appeared on the London stage twenty years before Shakespeare's **Hamlet** was produced in 1602. Quite how the semi-mythical Danish prince and the very real Danish castle became connected isn't entirely clear, though it's probable that Elizabethan England got wind of Kronborg from sailors who had passed through the Øresund, returning with stories of the mist-shrouded fortress that subsequently metamorphosed into Shakespeare's Elsinore. Another vague theory has it that Shakespeare spent part of his so-called lost years (1585–92) in Kronborg, rather than in Spain as was previously believed. That there are still conflicting stories has done nothing to diminish Kronborg's thriving trade in *Hamlet* souvenirs, nor the hundreds of requests for the whereabouts of "Hamlet's bedroom".

through it. The castle, which became the largest in Northern Europe, was rebuilt several times over, most recently by Christian IV, who had to double the Sound Toll to pay for it. Christian's castle sported lavish Baroque interiors – liberally sprinkled with his distinctive monogram – though the exterior is decidedly Renaissance, much like its predecessors. But his enjoyment of the castle (supposedly his favourite) was short-lived, however; only twenty years after the fire, it was bombarded and overrun by the Swedes, who carted off most of Kronborg's treasures. Over the next three centuries, it was largely given over to military use, being deemed too uncomfortable for the royals, but in 1924 the military moved out and a major restoration programme began.

Even now, as you enter the castle via a series of gates, bridges, moats, earthen ramparts and brick defences, you get a sense of the fortress's former power and invincibility, with antique cannons pointing menacingly out across the narrow sound. Crossing over the final bridge, you go through the forbidding Dark Gate, to the small forecourt and castle courtyard. The main keep is rather ornate, with plenty of Renaissance features, two spindly towers roofed with green copper jutting out into the usually blustery sky, and another tower providing a fully functioning lighthouse. The interior isn't as grand as you might expect, with white walls and wood floors replacing the former opulent fittings, but a few rooms are worth a look: the second-floor **King's and Queen's chambers**, adorned with magnificent fireplaces and fine circular ceiling paintings; the 62-metre-long **ballroom** on the third floor, its walls hung with paintings commissioned by Christian IV for Rosenborg Slot (see p.67); and the **Little Hall**, which has seven of the fourteen splendid tapestries woven in 1590 as part of a series depicting Danish kings. In the **Corner room**, part of a guest suite designed for James VI of Scotland (later James I of England) and his wife, who was Christian IV's sister, you can see the original black-and-white flooring that Christian had laid throughout the castle.

Be sure to see the beautiful **Chapel**, directly across the courtyard from the ticket office: the only part of the castle to survive the fire of 1629, its elaborate and colourful carving gives an idea of the richness of the castle's original Renaissance interiors. An altogether gloomier atmosphere pervades the dark, labyrinthine **casemates** (cellars; guided tours 11am & 1pm), where the body of Holger Danske, a mythical hero from the legends of Charlemagne, is said to lie in wait, ready to wake again when Denmark needs him – although the Viking-style statue depicting the legend detracts somewhat from the cellars' authentic aura of decay. The castle also houses the national **Handels og Søfartsmuseet** (Maritime Museum; same hours; ⓦ www.maritime-museum.dk; 50kr), a well-organized jaunt through the history of Danish seafaring up to the modern-day domination by the Maersk shipping dynasty; alongside the usual nautical trinkets and paintings, exhibits include the world's oldest ship's biscuit and figureheads of busty Viking maidens; look out also for the display on the valuable work done by the *SS Storebjørn* icebreaker, whose lovely 1920s wood-panelled officers' saloon, complete with table laid for dinner, is a sight to behold. From the museum, you can walk along the fortress wall to the **coastal batteries** (daily sunrise–sunset), which afford lovely views over the Sound.

Eating and drinking

You'll find plentiful **eating** options along the main drag, Stengade, a couple of which are located in preserved historic buildings. Wherever you eat, you might want to consider skipping dessert in favour of one of the immense home-made **ice creams** from *Café Brostræde*, Brostræde 2.

Given the proximity of the capital, **nightlife** is a rare commodity hereabouts, but for a relatively sedate evening drink, there are several decent bars along Stengade (rowdier boozing goes on at the top end of Axeltorv, popular with well-oiled Swedes living it up). Possibilities include *Axelhus Bodega*, a friendly, cheap local bar set just off Axeltorv at Sudergade 27, and *Hotel København*, Skt Anna Gade 17, with a lively atmosphere, good music and a pool table; look for the window stuffed full of beer steins.

Cafés and restaurants

Café Kronen Kronborg Slot ☏ 44 47 73 02. Superbly situated on the castle approaches, this is an excellent spot for coffee or lunch, with good salads and sandwiches from 89kr. Closed Mon.

Madame Sprunck Stengade 48 ☏ 49 26 48 49, ⓦ www.madamsprunck.dk. Atmospheric old timbered building in a tiny courtyard; the cosy café serves up good pasta, burgers and salads, while upstairs is a more formal restaurant (evenings only) with a small selection of traditional Danish mains (198kr). Outside seating in summer.

Pakhuset Stengade 26 ☏ 49 21 10 50. Excellent, cheap, authentic pizza and pasta in this friendly, unpretentious trattoria-style place – think red-and-white check tablecloths and Chianti bottles suspended from the rafters. Family-friendly and great value.

Phonoteket Music & Café Stengade 36 ⓦ www .phonoteket.dk. Sitting at the small tables in this modern café, you can listen to any one of the 15,000 CDs sold in the adjacent music store whilst enjoying cakes from an excellent local *konditori*; try the divine *fragilité* nut cake. The coffee is also especially good.

Rådmand Davids Hus Strandgade 70 ☏ 49 26 10 43. This charming building dating from 1694 was once the residence of one of the king's councillors. By day, the café serves a delectable selection of smørrebrød; on Friday and Saturday nights it's a cosy, candlelit bar. Limited space so book ahead for lunch in busy times. Closed Sun.

Ferries to Sweden

Two ferry companies operate regular boats between **Helsingør** and **Helsingborg in Sweden**. The trip takes approximately twenty minutes and as tickets are rarely sold out, it's easiest just to buy at the terminal when you want to travel. HH Ferries (☏ 49 26 01 55, ⓦ www.hhferries.dk) has half-hourly return trips running virtually round-the-clock and costing 44kr for foot passengers, with open-return car prices at 550kr and including up to nine passengers. The ships operated by Scandlines (☏ 33 15 15 15, ⓦ www.scandlines.dk) run slightly more frequently but have the same prices. Both advertise regular special day-return deals (*dagsbillet*) on their websites.

The north Zealand coast

Helsingør is the gateway to the **north Zealand coast**, whose succession of fine sandy beaches and cute fishing villages has long made it a favoured spot for summer homes, and it's still a popular destination for weekending Copenhageners searching for sun, sand and sea. Driving along the lovely coastline provides pre-eminent glimpses of the shallow green waters and golden sand; the road is never more than a few blocks from the beach. A private railway operates from a small terminal adjacent to the main station in Helsingør and runs as far as the former fishing town and latter-day tourist hub of Gilleleje, stopping frequently along the coast. Alternatively, bus #340 from Helsingør covers the same stretch, as does cycle route No.47.

Hellebæk, Hornbæk and around

From Helsingør, the coast road (Nordre Strandvej) runs west past a string of fine beaches towards the sleepy village of **HELLEBÆK**, some 5km north, where there's a well-known (if unofficial) stretch of shoreline dedicated to nude bathing – and very little else. Trains from Helsingør stop at Hellebæk and then continue for 7km to the moderately larger **HORNBÆK**, a tiny fishing hamlet until the late nineteenth century, when the capital's middle classes discovered its beautiful sandy beaches, sand dunes and fabulous sea views, and set about building their holiday villas along its coastal paths. For a time, Hornbæk was also a favourite summer haunt of various Golden Age artists, who came to capture its ever-changing light, salty fishing scenes and seascapes. There's little here besides the small harbour and beaches, though you might peep in to the tiny white church on Kirkevej for its C.W. Eckersberg altar and the four finely detailed model ships suspended from the ceiling. To the east of town, the lovely **Hornbæk Plantage** pine forest is a great spot for walking or cycling; maps of the forest trails and information on bike rental are available from the small **tourist office** (mid-June to Aug Mon 1–7pm, Tues & Thurs 1–5pm, Wed & Fri 10am–5pm, Sat 10am–2pm; rest of year closed Tues; ℡49 70 47 47, Ⓦwww.hornbaek.dk), which is set in the library just off the main street.

There are a couple of worthy distractions around Hornbæk. Some 3km further west along the coast, just beyond the small village of **Dronningmølle** (bus #340; tell the driver you want to stop at Munkeruphus), the hamlet of Munkerup holds the **Munkeruphus** art gallery (mid-March to mid-June & Sept–Dec Fri, Sat & Sun 11am–5pm; mid-June to Aug Tues–Sun 11am–5pm; 40kr; Ⓦwww.munkeruphus.dk), Munkerup Strandvej 78, situated in a lovely colonial-style country house surrounded by beautiful landscaped grounds and with views out to the sea. The exhibitions focus on twentieth-century and contemporary Danish art and change frequently; there's a delightful café serving cakes and light lunches.

Just west of Munkerup, and signposted off to the right along Fyrvejen, a non-operational restored lighthouse built in 1771 houses the **Fyrhistorisk Museum på Nakkehoved** (Nakkehoved Lighthouse Museum; May–June & Sept–Oct Thurs–Sun noon–4pm, July–Aug Tues–Sun 11am–4pm, early Nov to mid-Nov & March–April Sun noon–4pm; 25kr), an exhibition on navigation and seafaring in the area – though the collection is of less interest than the stunning views over the Øresund and Kattegat, which you can enjoy with a drink from the little café here. If you're going further west, note that a coastal path runs the 2km from the eastern edge of town to the lighthouse at the outskirts of Gilleleje – heading along Hovedgade, the path starts just beyond the church at the junction with Klokkervang. Bus #340 also stops nearby.

Gilleleje

From Hornbæk, trains continue 9km along the coast to **GILLELEJE**, another appealing, and somewhat busier, fishing and tourism centre. The town's beaches aren't the best along the north Zealand coast, but there's a lovely working **harbour** cluttered with trawlers, dinghies, tour boats, ferries and a few old wooden ships, and surrounded by a half-dozen restaurants, fish shops and smokehouses serving the local catch. The shop-lined main street, Vesterbrogade, runs parallel to the beach; at its western end, about ten minutes' walk from the centre, is the **Gilleleje Museum** (June–Aug Mon & Wed–Sun 1–4pm; Sept–May Wed–Fri 1–4pm, Sat 10am–2pm; Ⓦwww.holbo.dk; 25kr), housed on the first floor of the public library at Vesterbrogade 56; it's notable really only for a small section on Gilleleje's role in the evacuation of eighteen hundred Danish Jews in 1943 (see p.294).

Before you reach the museum, at the intersection with Nordre Strandvej, a path heads off along the coast along the top of the dunes. Follow it and you'll be walking in the footsteps of the famed Danish writer and philosopher **Søren Kierkegaard** (see p.74) who, as a young man, took lengthy soul-searching walks here, mulling over the meaning of life and later recalling: "I often stood there and reflected over my past life. The force of the sea and the struggle of the elements made me realize how unimportant I was." A monument to him now stands a little way along the path bearing his maxim: "Truth in life is to live for an idea". The **tourist office**, Gilleleje Hovedgade 6F (mid-June to late Aug Mon–Sat 9am–5pm; Jan to late June & mid-Aug to Dec Mon–Fri 9am–4pm, Sat 9am–noon; ☎48 30 01 74, Ⓦwww.visitgribskov.dk), has a useful town map as well as maps of the different routes Kierkegaard used to walk. A little further east along Gilleleje Hovedgade is the pretty **Seamen's Church**, in whose attic many Jews were concealed in 1943 (see above); adjacent to it, at no.49, the **Skibshallerne & Fiskerhuset** (June–Aug Mon & Wed–Sun 1–4pm; 25kr) explores the town's fishing heritage — there's a reconstructed fisherman's home of the 1850s and exhibits on the history of North Zealand fishermen from the Middle Ages.

There's no real reason to stay in Gilleleje, but if you do want to linger, best option is the lovely *Gilleleje Badehotel* (☎48 30 13 47, Ⓦwww.gillelejebadehotel .dk; ❽), a grand but homely old beach hotel, renovated in true Scandinavian style with white walls, wood floors, wicker sofas and open fires. It's right on the beach (though it's a rocky bit) and away from the main town bustle, tucked away down a quiet residential road 1km west at Hulsøvej 15. Alternatively, the tourist office has a list of private rooms from 500kr for two people including breakfast (25kr booking fee), or you could **camp** at *Dronningmølle Strandcamping* (☎49 71 92 90, Ⓦwww.dronningmolle.dk; early April to mid-Sept), right at the beach at Strand-krogen 2B with a few log cabins.

Tisvildeleje

From Gilleleje, bus #363 largely follows the coast to the windswept village of **TISVILDELEJE**, its expanse of sandy beaches backed by **Tisvilde Hegn** (locally called simply "Hegn"), a forest of wind-tormented beech trees planted here during the eighteenth century in an attempt to anchor the drifting sands. You can wander up through the extensive forest – populated by foxes, deer and hares – on various trails (the tourist office can provide a map) leading off from the beach car park; one of these emerges, after 4km, at a peaceful clearing containing the **Asserbo Slotsruin** – a jumble of stone walls surrounded by a little moat which comprise all that remains of a small castle built on the site of a twelfth-century Carthusian monastery. But the real reason to come to Tisvildeleje is its **beaches** – the main one is wide, duned and loaded with facilities – or to visit its many good restaurants and soak up some of its charming, upmarket atmosphere.

A summer-only **tourist office** (Mon–Fri 12.30–4.30pm, Sat 10am–2pm; ☎48 70 71 06) in the central train station at Banevej can help with accommodation (the town is the terminus of the Hillerød line so there is no coastal service from Gilleleje). Tisvildeleje's **restaurant** scene, meanwhile, epitomizes the posh-quaint aesthetic; reservations are highly recommended during peak season. Just to the west on the road into town, ⚶ *Tisvilde Bistro*, Hovedgaden 38 (☎48 70 41 91, ⓦwww.tisvilde-bistro.dk), has perfected the classic French bistro feel, with exposed beams, rustic-chic table settings and a Gallic-style menu. There are often live bands on weekend evenings, and films screen throughout the year in the attached cinema (60kr); it also serves the delicious local microbrew Ølfabrikken Porter. Just across the road at no.55, *Tisvildeleje Caféen* (☎48 70 88 86, ⓦwww .tisvildelejecafeen.dk; daily in summer, rest of year weekends only) is a tad less formal, with an all-you-can-eat grilled buffet of steaks and fish (250kr); it also has an inexpensive à la carte lunch menu.

Hundested and around

The marina town of **HUNDESTED** is best known as the former home of famed Danish polar explorer Knud Rasmussen, and the **Knud Rasmussens Hus**, Knud Rasmussens Vej 9 (early April to mid-Oct Tues–Sun 11am–4pm; 40kr; ⓦwww .krh.dk), has been turned into a museum dedicated to his life and work. Rasmussen was Scandinavia's most famous explorer after Thor Heyerdahl and Erik the Red. Born in Greenland, he led numerous expeditions across the Arctic, mapping the coastline and interior and penning ethnographic tomes about Eskimo society before building this well-preserved thatched cottage on a promontory 30m above Hundested's beach. Hundested is also the departure point for **ferries** across the Isefjord to Rørvig. Just south of here in Lynæs, an old fishing village that's one of the best locations for windsurfing in Denmark, is a small **campsite**, *Lynæs Camping*, Søndergade 57 (☎47 93 79 07, ⓦlynaes.dk-camp.dk).

Hillerød and around

Smack in the middle of northern Zealand, and reachable by S-Tog from Helsingør and Copenhagen, **HILLERØD** is best known as the location of the glorious **Frederiksborg Slot** (daily: late March to Oct 10am–5pm; Nov to late March 11am–3pm; 60kr; ⓦwww.frederiksborgmuseet.dk). Laid out across three small islands within an artificial lake and set within magnificent Baroque gardens, its fairytale grandeur, opulence and romance outstrip the more famous Kronborg. The castle was originally the home of Frederik II and birthplace of his son Christian IV who, at the start of the seventeenth century, began rebuilding the castle in an unorthodox Dutch Renaissance style. It's the unusual aspects of the design – a prolific use of towers and spires, Gothic arches and flowery window ornamentation – that still stands out, despite the changes wrought by a serious fire in 1859 and subsequent restoration.

You can see the exterior of the castle for free simply by walking through the main gates, across the seventeenth-century S-shaped bridge and into the central courtyard. The interior functions as a **Museum of National History**; rent an audioguide (20kr) to get the most out of the sixty-odd rooms charting Danish history since 1500. Along the walls of the spartan rooms are ranks of portraits – a motley crew of flat-faced kings and thin consorts who between them ruled and misruled Denmark for centuries. Of special note is **room 19** (to the left of the ticket office) with its low vaulted ceiling and imitation gilt leather, and the **chapel**, exquisite with its gilded and embellished vaults, pillars, arches and black marble gallery. From the chapel, head through room 23 along the Privy Passage to Christian V's **Audience Chamber** (room 24) – a Baroque salon of stucco and marble flourishes. The reconstructed, stark **Great Hall** – a ballroom in Christian IV's time – features gorgeous tapestries, wall reliefs, portraits and a glistening black marble fireplace. On the third floor is a portrait gallery of royals, politicians, scientists, writers and artists, including Karen Blixen, Niels Bohr, and a rather camp and gory self-portrait by Lars Von Trier (on the balcony section). Room 82 is devoted to the current royal family – look out for the portrait of Margrethe II by Andy Warhol.

Away from the often crowded interior, the intricate **Baroque gardens**, on the far side of the lake, offer a cascade of canals and fountains (summer only). To reach them, take the narrow Mint Gate to the left of the main castle building, which adjoins a roofed-in bridge leading to the King's Wing. In summer you can also do a thirty-minute **boat trip** on the lake aboard the *M/F Frederiksborg*, which leaves every half-hour from outside the castle (mid-May to mid-Sept Mon–Sat 11am–5pm, Sun 1–5pm; 20kr).

From central Hillerød, you can get to Frederiksborg via a **footpath** that runs from Torvet, the town's main square, and skirts the lake toward the castle – it's a pretty ten-minute walk; alternatively, buses #701 and #702 run from the train station, or you can follow the signs (*Slottet*) from the town centre.

Fredensborg

Whilst in Hillerød, it's worth hopping on the train to the small town of **FREDENS-BORG** to see a current royal residence, the picturesque **Fredensborg Slot** (July daily 1–4.30pm; guided tours 50kr), home to Queen Margrethe II for most of the year. Built by Frederik IV to commemorate the 1720 Peace Treaty with Sweden (the name means "fortress of peace"), this Italian Baroque palace is opened up to the public in July when the queen decamps to her summer home, Marsellsborg (see p.226). The lavish interior is filled with Baroque furnishings and features gorgeous stucco work and ceiling paintings, but unless you're a die-hard fan of Queen Margrethe, as are most of the visitors, you'd do better just to have a stroll around the lovely **grounds** including the adjacent Royal Family's private garden. There are also guided tours of the grand orangery and the Queen's veggie patch and herb garden (same hours; 50kr). The rest of the extensive gardens are open year-round (daily dawn–dusk; free): grand, seemingly endless tree-lined avenues radiate out from the palace to the waters of the beautiful bird haven of **Esrum Sø**, Denmark's second largest lake, where you can swim and rent boats. The gardens also hold **Normandsalen**, seventy life-sized sandstone statues of Norwegian and Faroese eighteenth-century peasant folk arranged in a grassy amphitheatre; the statues on display are replicas of disintegrating originals carved in 1773 and intended as an ethnographical record of the various folk costumes of the region. The on-site *Spisestedet Leonora* (daily 11am–4pm) serves fantastic smørrebrød, starting at 44kr a piece.

Practicalities

From Hillerød's train and bus station, it's a ten-minute signposted walk to the town centre. The **tourist office** is at Christiansgade 1 (June–Aug Mon–Wed 10.30am–5.30pm, Thurs–Fri 10.30am–4.30pm, Sat 10.30am–2.30pm; rest of year daily 10.30am–4.30pm; ☏48 24 26 26, ⊛www.c4.dk). Fredensborg station, meanwhile, is also a ten-minute walk from the town centre, where you'll find beautifully presented traditional Danish **lunches** at the lakeside *Restaurant Skipperhuset*, Skipperallé 6 (May–Sept Tues–Sun noon–6pm; book ahead ☏48 48 17 17, ⊛www.skipperhuset.dk).

Roskilde and around

Less than an hour by train from Copenhagen and some 35km due west, **ROSKILDE** has been the site of a settlement since prehistoric times, and was later inhabited by the Vikings, who exploited the Roskilde fjord (which extends nearly 40km north towards Frederiksværk) as a quick route to the open sea. But it was the arrival of Bishop Absalon in the twelfth century that made the place the base of the Danish church – and, as a consequence, the national capital for a while. Roskilde's importance waned after the Reformation, and it came to function mainly as a market for the neighbouring rural communities – much as it does today, as well as serving as an ersatz suburb for some Copenhagen commuters.

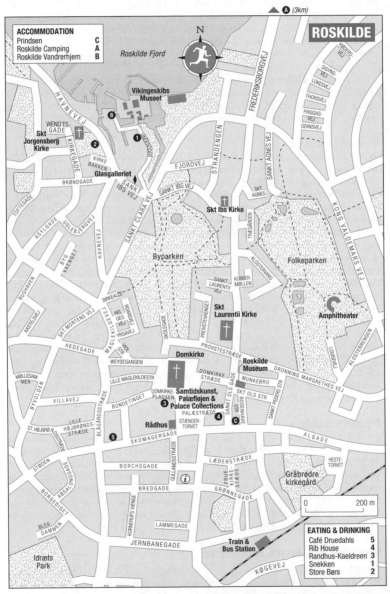

ROSKILDE

ACCOMMODATION
Prindsen   C
Roskilde Camping   A
Roskilde Vandrerhjem   B

EATING & DRINKING
Café Druedahls   5
Rib House   4
Randhus-Kaeldreen   3
Snekken   1
Store Børs   2

The Roskilde Festival

Held over four days and nights at the end of June, the **Roskilde Festival** (Ⓦwww
.roskilde-festival.dk) is the largest outdoor music event in Europe, regularly attracting
crowds of 100,000 strong. Nearly two hundred rock, electronica, hip-hop and world
music **bands** perform on six stages; recent guests have included Pink Floyd, Neil
Young, Coldplay, The Strokes and the Chemical Brothers. Most festival-goers pitch
their tents in the free camping grounds conveniently located nearby the stages,
where the festivities continue long after the bands stop playing at 2am, and it's all
remarkably peaceful (if rather inebriated) with even soft drugs little used – or at least
little seen – due in part to the extensive security measures taken by the festival organ-
izers. **Ticket prices** are high – upwards of 2000kr for a four-day pass – but nearly
always sell out several weeks in advance, so buy online early if you want to be
assured entry.

In high season especially, it can be crammed with day-trippers seeking the dual
blasts from the past supplied by its royal tombs and Viking boats, while the first
week of each July sees an onslaught of inebriated visitors when it hosts the
brilliant **Roskilde Festival**, Europe's biggest open-air rock event. Yet at any other
time the ancient centre and town museums make Roskilde one of Denmark's most
appealing towns, and the surrounding countryside is quiet and unspoilt, and holds
the absorbing **Sagnlandet Lejre**, a reconstructed Iron Age village.

Arrival, information and accommodation

Trains from Copenhagen arrive at the train station at the southern edge of the city
centre on Jernbanegade (where buses also arrive), a five-minute walk from the
tourist office, on the central Stændertorvet (Mon–Thurs 10am–5pm, Fri
10am–4pm, Sat 10am–1pm, Ⓣ46 31 65 65, Ⓦwww.visitroskilde.com), which
sells the Copenhagen card (see p.50), offering free or discounted entry to most of
Roskilde's museums.

As so many people visit Roskilde as a day-trip from the capital, there is a marked
paucity of places to **stay**. Best option is the sleekly designed, wooden **youth
hostel**, *Roskilde Vandrerhjem* (Ⓣ46 35 21 84, Ⓦwww.rova.dk; dorms 200kr,
doubles ❸), ideally located on the harbour at Vindeboder 7. If that's full, *Roskilde
Camping* (Ⓣ46 75 79 96, Ⓦwww.roskildecamping.dk; mid-March to mid-Sept),
on the forested edge of the fjord about 4km north of town (bus #603), has small,
clean cabins (❹) with furnished terraces, though with such a nice setting it too can
get very crowded at peak times. The best of Roskilde's few **hotels** is the pricey but
grand, central *Prindsen*, Algade 13 (Ⓣ46 30 91 00, Ⓦwww.prindsen.dk; ❾).
Finally, you could organize a stay in a **private home** through the tourist office
(450kr; breakfast extra).

The Town and around

Roskilde is laid out around its central square, **Stændertorvet**, from which the
pedestrianized Skomagergade and Algade extend west and east, lined with busy
cafés and boutiques. On the north flank of the square lies the major pointer to the
town's former status – its fabulous, UNESCO World Heritage-listed **Domkirke**
(April–Sept Mon–Sat 9am–5pm, Sun 12.30–5pm; Oct–March Tues–Sat
10am–4pm, Sun 12.30–4pm; 25kr), founded by Bishop Absalon in 1170 on the
site of a tenth-century church erected by Harald Bluetooth, and finished during
the fourteenth century – although portions were added right up to the twentieth.
The result is a mishmash of architectural styles, though one that hangs together
with surprising neatness. Every square inch seems adorned by some curious mark

or etching – the facade itself, with its slender Gothic spires and sunken Romanesque porticos, is a beauty to behold – but it's the claustrophobic collection of coffins containing the regal remains of twenty-one kings and eighteen queens in four large **royal chapels** that really catches the eye. The most richly endowed chapel is that of Christian IV, a previously austere resting place jazzed up – in typical early nineteenth-century Romantic style – with bronze statues, wall-length frescoes and vast paintings of scenes from his reign. A striking contrast is provided by the simple red-brick chapel just outside the cathedral, where Frederik IX was laid to rest in 1972. Try to get to the Domkirke just before the hour to see and hear the animated medieval **clock** above the main entrance: a model of St Jørgen gallops forward on his horse to wallop the dragon, and the hour is marked by the creature's squeal of death. Upstairs in the Great Hall, a small, recently renovated **Cathedral Museum** (tours April to mid-June Mon–Fri 11am, 1pm & 2pm, Sat 10am, Sun 1pm & 2pm; mid-June to Sept Mon–Fri every 30min between 11.05am & 2.35pm, Sat every 30min between 9.05am & 11.35am, Sun every 30min between 1.05pm & 3.35pm; Oct–March Tues–Fri noon & 1pm, Sat noon, Sun 1pm & 2pm) provides an engrossing introduction to the cathedral's colourful history.

From one end of the cathedral, a roofed passageway, the **Arch of Absalon** (off-limits to anyone not currently a member of the Danish clergy), feeds into the yellow **Bishop's Palace**. The incumbent bishop nowadays confines himself to one wing, while the others have been turned into showplaces for (predominantly) Danish art. The main building houses the **Museet for Samtidskunst** (Museum of Contemporary Art; Tues–Fri 11am–5pm, Sat & Sun noon–4pm; 30kr, Wed free), with diverse temporary exhibitions reflecting current trends. In the west wing, the **Palæfløjen** gallery (Tues–Sun noon–4pm; free), run by the local arts society, extends outdoors, turning up a striking collection of sculpture beneath the fruit trees of the bishop's garden. The less compelling **Palace Collections** (mid-May to mid-Sept daily 11am–4pm; rest of year Sat noon–4pm; 25kr) are made up of paintings, furniture and other artefacts belonging to the wealthiest Roskilde families of the eighteenth and nineteenth centuries.

From the cathedral, head east along Domkirkestræde to arrive at the tartan-painted doors of the **Roskilde Museum**, Skt Ols Gade 18 (daily 11am–4pm; 25kr), which open to reveal a mildly enticing array of anthropological and archeological goodies, with strong sections on medieval pottery, toys and textiles. The well-displayed collection includes the skeletal remains of a giant prehistoric ox found at the bottom of a nearby lake, where it drowned after jumping in to avoid the arrowheads of

Take my boats, please!

In 1997, while the Roskilde harbour was being dredged and ground broken for the Vikingeskibs Museet, archaeologists and museum curators around Scandinavia were astounded when building crews happened upon the intact remains of **nine Viking ships** just above the bedrock. Dating from the late Viking Age to the early Middle Ages (1025 to 1336), the vessels include the largest Viking ship found to date – 36m long, with plank seating for 72 oarsmen. Nearly all of the ships recovered were fully intact – preserved by the moisture and chemical properties of the soil – and they are now being held in on-site conservation chambers. Budgetary concerns notwithstanding, the museum has tentative plans to include the boats in the main museum collection over the next decade, but there is pervading speculation that once new buildings are dug to house them, further fleets of subterranean ships will be hit upon, ultimately with no place to store them, and the perpetual scenario will begin yet again.

approaching hunters sometime around 8600 BC. Look out also for the strange photos that satirist Gustav Wied (who lived in Roskilde for many years and whose rooms are reconstructed here) took of his family.

Heading north from the cathedral, past the green lawns of the **Byparken** city park, is the **Glasgalleriet**, Vindeboder 1 (Mon–Fri 10am–5pm, Sat 11am–4pm, Sun noon–4pm; free; Ⓦwww.glasgalleriet.dk), a good little glass gallery in the old Roskilde Gasworks building. However, the main draw hereabouts is the **Vikingeskibsmuseet** (Viking Ship Museum; daily 10am–5pm; May–Sept 95kr; rest of year 60kr; Ⓦwww.vikingeskibsmuseet.dk), one of the most enthralling and best-known attractions in Denmark. Set on the green fjord bank, the museum is centred around the reconstructed remains of five excellent specimens of Viking shipbuilding: a deep-sea trader, merchant ship, man-of-war, a ferry and a longship. Each was retrieved in 1962 from the fjord a few kilometres north of town at Skuldelev, where they had been sunk to the bottom of the narrow channel to block it against invading forces. The vessels give an impressive indication of the Vikings' nautical versatility, their skills in boat-building and their far-ranging travels to places as various as Paris, Hamburg and North America. Boat-building and sail-making **demonstrations** take place outdoors all year – the Vikings' sails were spun from a special wool produced from wild Norwegian sheep – and in the summer, you can also experience the seaworthiness of the reconstructed ships moored on the fjord by way of a boat jaunt: you'll be handed an oar when you board, and will be expected to pull your weight as a crew member (50min; 75kr on top of the museum ticket). There's also a decent gift shop, selling Viking-related books and more helmeted knick-knacks than you'll know what to do with.

From the adjacent docks, the **dinner boat** *M/S Sagafjord* (ⓣ46 75 64 60, Ⓦwww.sagafjord.dk; 95kr) sails up the pretty fjord for a three-hour tour during the summer on Thursdays, Fridays and Saturdays at 6pm; food is extra.

Around Roskilde: Sagnlandet Lejre and Ledreborg

If the Vikingeskibs Museet has put you in the mood for a bit of history, you might want to head 8km west of Roskilde to the village of Lejre, where Iron Age Denmark is kept alive and kicking at the **Sagnlandet Lejre** (Lejre Land of Legends; mid-May to late June & mid-Aug to late Sept Tues–Fri 10am–4pm, Sat & Sun 11am–5pm, late June to mid-Aug daily 10am–5pm; 95kr; Ⓦwww.sagnlandet.dk), a vast open space where volunteer families spend the summer living in a reconstructed Iron Age settlement, farming and carrying out domestic chores using implements – and wearing clothing – copied from those of the period. Modern-day visitors are welcome, and you can try your hand at grinding corn or paddling a dugout canoe. Trains from Roskilde go to Lejre, from where bus #233 runs the 4km to the historical centre's entrance. On your way back, hop off a few stops before Roskilde train station at **Ledreborg Slot** (July to early Aug Sat & Sun noon–3pm; 80kr; Ⓦwww.ledreborgslot.dk), a palatial eighteenth-century mansion with Baroque interiors of paintings, tapestries and furniture and imaginative French-style landscaped gardens, complete with a maze.

Eating and drinking

Eating well isn't a problem in Roskilde, with plenty of options in the maze of streets around the Domkirke and on Skomagergade and Algade. For more bucolic eating, stock up at the Irma supermarket, 21 Skomagergade, and picnic in the little park at the top of the steps behind the harbour, with good views of town. In the evening, serious party animals head to Copenhagen, but a few spots in town and by the train station offer less frenetic **entertainment**.

Cafés, restaurants and bars

Café Druedahls Skomagergade 40 ⓦwww
.cafe-druedahls.dk. A modern café on the pedestrianized strip offering salads, sandwiches and menu full of exotically flavoured teas (from 28kr), as well as some large brunch plates. In the evening it becomes a lively bar for local thirtysomethings. Daily 10am–11pm, plus Fri & Sat until 2am.

Rib House Djalma Lunds Gård 8 ⓣ46 36 36 46, ⓦwww.ribhouse-roskilde.dk. This spacious, multi-levelled restaurant is among the city's best deals, offering a carnivorous menu of steaks, burgers and club sandwiches (from 65kr) – though the real reason to come here is to chow down on the juicy spare ribs (from 125kr).

 Snekken Vindeboder 16 ⓣ46 35 98 16, ⓦwww.snekken.dk. Capacious,

ultra-modern café-lounge with black leather couches, abstract art and views onto the harbour. Main courses are few and pricey (around 200kr), so it's best to opt for the much cheaper sandwiches, salads or sushi dishes. The huge brunch spread (Sat & Sun 11.30am–4.30pm; 125kr), with sausages, scrambled eggs, Parma ham, muesli, gravadlax and a virgin bloody mary, should keep you full for most of the day.

Store Børs Havnevej 43 ⓣ46 32 50 54, ⓦwww.store-bors.dk. Located on the waterfront and across the docks from the Viking Ship Museum, this fish restaurant does great smørrebrød and home-smoked salmon specials, but the best menu choice is Den Klassiske Øl-menu, a four-course meal that's as Danish as they come, with beers from three separate local microbreweries (495kr).

The Hornsherred Peninsula and Frederikssund

West of Roskilde, the hilly **Hornsherred Peninsula** divides the thin, sheltered Roskilde fjord from the larger Isefjord further north. It conceals a series of idyllic little villages ranged around central commons and ponds and, along the western coast, to long, quiet beaches and hidden coves. The lack of a railway and the paucity of local buses mean the region is best toured by bike – the Roskilde tourist office (see p.113) has maps of suggested routes.

Skibby and Selsø Slot

About halfway up the peninsula some 25km from Roskilde in the village of Skibby, **Skibby Kirke** (Mon–Sat 8am–4pm) is Hornsherred's largest church, with original foundations dating back to 1100. It's worth visiting for its well-maintained frieze of medieval murals depicting wealthy princes enjoying leisurely rides atop spotted horses, the message being that decadence and secularism on earth will be punished accordingly in the afterworld.

Five kilometres east of Skibby, on the shore of pristine Selsø Lake, the stately **Selsø Slot** (May–Oct Sat & Sun 1–4pm; 40kr; ⓦwww.selsoe.dk) hasn't been renovated or modernized since the early 1800s – there is still no electricity, plumbing or heating – and its interior, packed with original marble and wood detailing, provides an authentic picture of early Danish aristocratic living. Today, its restored stucco-ceilinged **banquet hall** is adorned with four-metre-high marble panels, several large restored murals of battle scenes by Danish court artist Hendrick Krock and, most striking of all, two large gilded mirrors from 1733. The banquet hall is known for its fine acoustics, and between June and August classical music **concerts** (100kr) are staged here, spectacular events illuminated by candlelight.

Over Dråby and Jægerspris Slot

Some 9km north of Skibby, the peninsula's main road passes through tiny **Over Dråby**, whose eleventh-century **Dråby Kirke** (Mon–Fri 8am–4pm), Kirkevej 3, has vaults and walls adorned with mint-condition medieval chalk paintings that represent some of the best-preserved ecclesiastical frescoes in Denmark, painted in a naïve style in the mid-1400s by the so-called Isefjordsmester, one of

Denmark's many anonymous fresco painters. From here, continue 1km northwards to arrive at **Jægerspris Slot** (early April to late Oct Tues–Sun 11am–4pm; 50kr; ⓦ www.kongfrederik.dk), established during the fifteenth century as a royal hunting seat and last used by the eccentric Frederik VII in the mid 1800s. The castle rooms retain many of their original furnishings, including the King's impressive weapons collection and his beloved pipe, an item he almost certainly puffed on as he signed the Danish constitution on June 5, 1849, thereby ending absolutism in Denmark.

Frederikssund

Southeast of Jægerpris, where the east and west banks of the Roskilde fjord close in to a distance of a few hundred metres, a small bridge – the only place to cross over from Hornsherred to northern Zealand – leads to the sizeable town of **FREDERIKSSUND**, founded and named by narcissistic monarch Frederik III. A ferry crossing that doubled as a tax collection facility was in service over the fjord during the Middle Ages, after which a semi-permanent "bridge" of adjacent ships was used to cross the waters; the modern bascule drawbridge provides a decidedly less romantic crossing, and is much derided by locals for the regular traffic problems it causes. Frederikssund itself is best known for its extravagant summer **Viking plays** (Tues–Sat 8pm, Sun 4pm; 140kr; ☎ 47 31 06 85, ⓦ www.vikingespil.dk), staged for the last fifty years or so on the grassy Kalvøen lawns just south of the centre. Something of a cultural institution in Denmark, these elaborate dramas based on Viking mythology are well worth attending even if you don't speak Danish: the cast consists of several hundred amateur actors resplendent in medieval-style costumes, and performances feature burning longboats and lots of smoke bombs; written summaries of the plays are available in English. If you book in advance, you can get in the mood by reserving a place on a post-performance tour (190kr) to a nearby recreated Viking settlement to join in a communal feast – think steins of foaming beer and beef cooked on an open spit.

The only other point of interest in town, just east of the bridge at Jenriksvej 4, is the **J.F. Willumsens Museum** (Tues–Sun 10am–5pm; 40kr; ⓦ www.jfwillumsens museum.dk), a newly renovated exhibition space showing hundreds of works by Danish artist Jens Ferdinand Willumsen, best known for his mixed-media creations employing engraving, sculpture, ceramics, architecture and even photography. Pay special attention to *Jotunheim*, a wintry Norwegian landscape of wood, zinc and copper, and the radiant and explosive *Fear of Nature After the Storm, No.2*. Willumsen's own private art collection is also displayed on the premises and includes an El Greco, an artist with whom he shared an interest in dramatic use of light and expressive human figures.

Practicalities

Frederikssund is a mere 35min on the S-train from Copenhagen; the train station, which also receives buses, is right in the town centre. The **tourist office**, Havnegade 5A (Mon–Fri 10am–4pm, plus Sat 10am–4pm in summer; ☎ 47 31 06 85, ⓦ www.visitfrederikssund.dk), has information on the entire Hornsherred peninsula, and can help with finding (commission-free) rooms in nearby inns and B&Bs. One of the nicest places to **stay** is the *Villa Bakkely* (☎ 30 63 45 10, ⓦ www .villabakkely.dk; ❸), eight blocks south of the station at Roskildevej 109, which has seven lovely modern-rustic rooms with shared bathrooms; breakfast is 50kr extra. Hotels are limited to the central *Rådhuskroen*, Østergade 1 (☎ 47 31 54 55, ⓦ www.hotel-raadhuskroen.dk; ❻), with nine homely rooms and a good restaurant serving sizeable Continental and Danish dishes such as fried eel with white potatoes and parley sauce (189kr). Of other places to **eat**, the best option is *Toldboden* (T 47 36 17 77, W www.toldboden.info), at Færgevej 1 in the harbour's old customs house, with lovely views all around and very good Dano-French fusion cuisine; mains are around 200kr, but try the three- to five-course chef's surprise menu (285–382kr), for a bit of a gamble.

Central Zealand

Venture south of the peninsulas, fjord towns and Viking settlements that line Zealand's north coast and you're in the lush, rolling fields that characterize Denmark's heartland. This region holds a string of interesting towns, many still within easy day-trip range of the capital and all linked to one another via the **E20 motorway** that cuts clear across Denmark's midriff before traversing the *bælt* bridges to Funen and Jutland. Most interesting is **Køge** on the east coast, a thirty-minute S-tog ride from the capital, with busy beaches and a characterful medieval centre. At Køge, the road and rail network out of Copenhagen splits into two: one line heads further south to the islands of Falster, Lolland and Møn (see p.126) via Næstved, while the other heads westwards across the plains of central Zealand towards the laconic town of **Ringsted**, one of Denmark's most important early settlements, with a massive twelfth-century church that is the final resting place of a good number of Danish kings and queens. West of here is **Trelleborg**, site of one of the Viking age's most impressive administrative settlements, while further on lies the sleepy harbour town of **Korsør** on the west coast, where you'll find the brick remains of a great coastal fortress and the entry point to the multimillion-kroner **bridge and tunnel** that since 1998 has spanned the eighteen-kilometre-wide Store Bælt.

Køge and around

Not too long ago, **KØGE** was best known for the pollution caused by the chemical factories on its outskirts, and few ventured here to sample the sandy beaches of Køge Bay. Its more distant past is equally unpalatable, having been a centre for witch-burning in medieval Europe, and the spot where over three thousand Swedish soldiers died during the 1677 Battle of Køge Bay (see box below). The witches and warring are long gone today, and although a rubber plant does still dominate the massive harbour, the evocatively preserved medieval centre and the beaches have been cleaned up in recent years – and an extension of the S-tog network means that it's all within easy reach of the capital. It's also a good base for touring the **Stevns Peninsula**, which bulges into the sea just south of the town.

Trains and buses arrive at the **train station**, a short walk from the centre, first along Jernbanegade and then Nørregade, which takes you to the hub of the action, Torvet. Saturday is the best day to visit Køge, with free entertainment in the streets, and plenty of action in the harbourside bars as the day wears on. From the square, head for the cobbled streets and courtyards that lead off Brogade, which hold numerous old buildings as well as craft shops and cafés. Nearby, at Nørregade 4, the **Køge Museum** (June–Aug Tues–Sun 11am–5pm; Sept–May Tues–Fri 1–5pm, Sat 11am–3pm, Sun 1–5pm; 50kr joint ticket with the Kunstmuseum) contains remnants from Køge's bloody past, not least the local executioner's sword, said to have been wielded frequently on Torvet.

Once its market stalls are cleared away, a suitably spooky stillness falls over Torvet and the narrow cobbled streets that run off it. One of these, Kirkestræde,

The Battle of Køge Bay

The site of many naval skirmishes, **Køge Bay's** most famous battle took place on July 1, 1677, when 48-year-old **Admiral Niels Juel** won a decisive victory against the militarily superior Swedish fleet. Juel's victory was secured when he deftly surprised the Swedes by cutting through a dispersed configuration of Swedish battleships, thwarting communication between the Swedish commanders and securing the Danish fleet clear and direct longitudinal shots of the port and starboard flanks of the enemy ships. Danish firepower accounted for much of the damage inflicted, but a third of the Swedish fleet was maimed by friendly fire from its own battleships, which were maintaining their positions just opposite. After ten hours of fighting, the Swedes pulled back and conceded defeat, having lost 25 of their 36 vessels and a third of their regiment – some four thousand men; Denmark lost a few hundred sailors but no ships. It was the most decisive unassisted naval victory in the country's history, making Juel the most famous European admiral of his time. His prize money for the victory was ten percent of the value of the captured Swedish ships; when the king could not meet this amount in cash, he made up the difference in kind by granting him ownership of all the crown's land on Tåsinge, including the sumptuous Valdemars Slot (see p.175).

is lined with sixteenth-century half-timbered houses and leads to **Skt Nicolai Kirke** (June to mid-Aug Mon–Fri 10am–4pm, Sun noon–4pm; mid-Aug to June Mon–Fri 10am–noon), where pirates captured in Køge Bay were hung from the **tower** (July to early Aug Mon–Fri 10am–4pm; 10kr), which is opened up every half-hour to allow visitors to climb to the top and admire the lovely views. Along the 1450-era nave, look for the somewhat defaced faces of angels carved into the pew-ends; their noses were sliced off by drunken Swedish soldiers during the seventeenth century. On a more aesthetic level, the intriguing **Kunstmuseum Køge Skitsesamling** (Køge Museum of Sketches; Tues–Sun 10am–5pm; 50kr joint ticket with Køge Museum; ⓦ www.skitsesamlingen.dk), at Nørregade 29, holds a motley grouping of drawings and sculptures – as well as preparatory notes, musings and models – by important Danish artists of the twentieth century, plus temporary exhibitions of works in progress by both local and international artists. The pièce de résistance, on the third floor, is Bjørn Nørregård's colourful preparatory work for the Queen's tapestries, which are displayed at the Royal Reception Rooms in Copenhagen (see p.62).

The town's **beaches** stretch along the bay north and south of town. Søndre Strand is a short walk from the train station (head south on Østre Banevej), while the more expansive Solrød and Greve, which have watersports outlets, are just a few minutes' ride north on the S-train.

Practicalities

The **tourist office** (June–Aug Mon–Fri 9am–5pm, Sat 9am–2pm; Sept–May Mon–Fri 9am–5pm, Sat 10am–1pm; ☎56 67 60 01, ⓦ www.visitkoege.com) is on Torvet. To take full advantage of the local sands, visit Køge's slickest **hotel**, the *Hvide Hus*, Strandvejen 111 (☎56 65 36 90, ⓦ www.hotelhvidehus.dk; ⑨), a luxury design resort set just 100m from the beach. Otherwise, the town's **youth hostel** (☎56 65 14 74, ⓦ www.danhostelkoege.dk; April to mid-Dec) is 3km west of the town centre along Vamdrupvej, offering bunks (200kr) and some double rooms (⑨). To get here, take bus #210 from the train station and get off when the bus turns into Agerskovvej, from where it's a ten-minute walk. For camping near the sands, *Vallø*, Strandvejen 102 (☎56 65 28 51, ⓦ www.valloecamping.dk; April to early Sept), is your best bet, set between a pine forest and a small beach, with plenty of on-site activities and two dozen small cabins (from 325kr).

In terms of **eating** options, ⚔ *Slagter Stig & Co* (☎56 65 48 09, Ⓦwww
.slagterstigogco.dk), Carlsenvej 8, is one of the town's best – a butcher-cum-
brasserie with a buffet (Mon–Fri 5–11pm, Sat & Sun 1.30–11pm; 85kr), and
tasty plates of charcuterie for under 30kr. The atmospheric *Christians Minde*
(☎56 63 68 56, Ⓦwww.chrs-minde.dk), Brogade 7, is a half-timbered, smart
but relaxed spot serving novel Danish and Chinese specialities (from 148kr) such
as steak with a cognac-flavoured truffle sauce or white wine-smoked filet of
salmon. Just across at no.19, *Hugos Vinkælder* offers drinks in a cosy medieval
cellar, with dozens of international stouts and bitters on tap and warm *gløgg*
served in winter.

The Stevns Peninsula

Easily reached from Køge, the **Stevns Peninsula** is somewhat neglected in terms
of tourism largely on account of its rugged coastline, less suited to traditional
beachlife than the sandier spots north of Køge. It's worth a visit, however, for the
dramatic eighteen-kilometre stretch of white chalk and limestone cliffs, best seen
from the coastal settlement of **Højerup**, whose pretty cliffside church lost its
eastern section in 1928 when a landslide caused a good half of the building to
cascade into the sea, sending choir, altar and coffins filled with preserved skeletons
crashing onto the beach below. Now safe to visit, what's left of the church sits on
a promontory with spectacular views down to the water. You can reach many
towns in Stevns, including the main settlement of **Store Heddinge** and the
fishing harbour of **Rødvig** – a good place from which to embark on a coastal hike
– on the private train line from Køge (InterRail, ScanRail and Eurail passes not
valid). Bus #253 runs between all main peninsula towns from Køge. Rødvig has
a small **tourist information** centre at Havnevej 21 (Mon–Fri 9am–4pm, plus
July to late-Aug Sat 9am–4pm, mid-May to late June & early Sept to mid-Sept
Sat 9am–noon; ☎56 50 64 64, Ⓦwww.stevnsinfo.dk); staff can rent **bicycles**
and arrange stays at local B&Bs.

Ringsted

Though little more than a small rural town today, **RINGSTED**'s central location
made it one of the most important settlements in Zealand from the end of the
Viking era until the Reformation. It was the burial place of medieval Danish
monarchs as well as the site of a regional *ting*, the open-air court where prominent
merchants and nobles made the administrative decisions for the province. There's
little by way of traditional sights, but if you're en route to other parts of Zealand, it's
worth stopping for an hour or two to take a quick peek at its church. The three *ting*
stones around which the nobles gathered – and upon which the elders sat – remain
in Ringsted's market square, Torvet, but they're often concealed by the market itself,
or the backsides of weary shoppers. Instead, it's the sturdy brick **Skt Bendts Kirke**
(May to mid-Sept Mon–Fri 10am–noon & 1–5pm; mid-Sept to April Mon–Fri
1–3pm) that dominates Torvet, just as it has done for over eight hundred years. It's
the only structure remaining of the Ringsted monastery, a Benedictine cloister
levelled by fire in the eighteenth century, and is the oldest brick church in Scandinavia. Erected in 1170 under the direction of Valdemar the Great, the church was the
final resting place for all Danish monarchs until 1341 – there are at least a dozen royal
tombs marked by tablets in the floor – and many affluent Zealanders also had
themselves buried here, presumably so that their souls could spend eternity in the
very best company. During the seventeenth century, a number of the coffins were
excavated to dig more space for future coffins; the finds are collected in the **Chapel
Museum** within the church. Besides the lead slab found inside Valdemar I's coffin,
there's a decorative silk brocade found in that of his son, Valdemar the Victorious,

plaster casts of the skulls of Queen Bengård and Queen Sofia, and a replica of the Dagmar Cross, discovered when Queen Dagmar's tomb was opened in 1697 – the original is in the National Museum in Copenhagen.

Practicalities

Trains arrive at the local station, 15min from the centre; the **tourist office** (Mon–Wed 11am–3pm, Thurs 10am–6pm, Fri 11am–1pm; ☎57 62 66 00, ⓦwww .visitringsted.dk) is near to Torvet at Skt Bendtsgade 6. If you're planning on overnighting, the best option is the superb local **youth hostel** (☎57 61 15 26, ⓦwww.danhostel.dk/ringsted; May to mid-Dec), Skt Bendtsgade 18, set on a wooded cul-de-sac just alongside the church – clean, efficient and one of the more competently run hostels in the country, offering doubles (❷) and dorms (150kr). Ringsted is packed with places to **eat** and **drink**, most of them set around Torvet and just north on Nørregade. *Café Aspendos*, Møllegade 11 (☎57 67 05 09), is a cosy corner café great for brunch (60kr) or burgers, nachos and pasta dishes (around 100kr), while the popular *Rådhuskroen*, just next to the tourist office at Skt Bendtsgade 8 (☎57 61 68 97, ⓦwww.raadhuskro.dk), is an upscale gastro-pub with steaks, schnitzels and mountainous salads (around 225kr). The pick of the town's restaurants, however, is Italy & Italy at Torvet 1C (☎57 61 53 53, ⓦwww .italy-italy.dk), a pizza and pasta joint (dishes from 69kr) with country-style decor and a terrace looking onto the church lawn. It also serves larger main courses such as Norwegian salmon in cognac and tomato sauce that run upwards of 180kr; there's also a great ice-cream parlour just next door. Come evening time, *Løve Pub* at Nørregade 12, all dark pine tables and old bookshelves, pulls in a respectable crowd – and you might find after-hours dancing on weekends.

Trelleborg Viking fortress

Some 28km west of Ringsted, the Viking ruins at **Trelleborg** (April–Oct Tues–Sun 10am–4pm, until 5pm June–Aug; 55kr) are one of Scandinavia's most important historical sites. Located between two rivers on a hilly headland, the circular complex dates from 980. The eight thousand oak trees used for the original stocky constructions and tall fortress walls have long since rotted away, but it's still the best-preserved of Denmark's four Viking ring fortresses. The original complex had a main stronghold and an outer ring wall with four gates, and was intended for defence purposes as well as a centre of administration and trade. On the walk from the car park, a large reconstructed **longhouse** sporting bulky wooden doors and internal staved timber supports offers a vague sense of what things might have looked like then. The sixteen longhouses originally built here would have housed some four hundred people, the bodies of whom rest in the nearby burial grounds (alongside a mass grave containing the remains of some of their would-be attackers). The excellent on-site **museum**, with full documentation in English, has a scale model of the fortress alongside some of the findings from the site – swords, buckles and a sacrificial burial hole with the elfin skeletons of two children and a goat. During July, would-be Vikings from all over the country show up in full regalia to take part in lively **markets**, jousting matches and even a full-on dramatization of a historic Viking battle.

To get to Trelleborg, take the train to Slagelse, 5km east, then transfer to hourly bus #312 (free with train ticket), for the ten-minute journey.

Korsør

Separated from Funen by the Store Bælt, just 18km wide at this point, **KORSØR** has long served as western Zealand's connection to the rest of Denmark, though the ferries that once plied these waters have now been replaced by the impressive

Storebælt bridge and tunnel, some 3km north of town, which has been carrying all road and rail traffic west to Funen since it opened in 1998. Korsør isn't a hotbed of activity these days, but it's worth a quick diversion when travelling to or from Funen, with a couple of reasonable museums and a seventeenth-century fortress tower. Trains stop at the station close to the Storebælt bridge, from where buses into town terminate at Caspar Brands Plads, right in the centre next to the town hall. The two central intersecting pedestrianized streets, Algade and Nygade, hold what little action there is in Korsør, most notably its best-preserved building, the Rococo-style merchant's home of **Kongegården**, Algade 25 (daily 11am–4pm, Wed until 8pm; ⓦ www.kongegaarden.dk; free), now a gallery of sculptures and drawings by Jewish artist Harald Isenstein. A kilometre or so west of here, adjacent to the fishing harbour, is the **Korsør Søbatteri** (Korsør coastal battery; ⓦ www .byogoverfartsmuseet.dk; Tues–Sun 11am–4pm; free), locally known as the *Fæstningen* ("fortress"), a small grassy plot containing a handful of old buildings, the largest of which is now a **museum** (same hours as fortress; free), with displays on life in Korsør over the years and models of the liners that once made the Funen crossing. It's also worth climbing to the top of the **tower** (ask at the museum for the key) to take in the view down to the harbour.

Practicalities

Korsør's **tourist office** (June–Sept Mon–Fri 9am–5pm, Sat 10am–1/2pm plus Sun (July only) 11am–2pm; rest of year Mon–Fri 10am–4/5pm & Sat 10am–1pm; ⓣ58 35 02 11, ⓦ www.visitsydvestsjaelland.dk) is centrally placed at Nygade 7. If you're on your way to Funen, you're much better off looking for **accommodation** over the bridge in Nyborg or, better still, Odense, but Korsør's best option is the *Svenstrupgaard* youth hostel (ⓣ58 38 15 19, ⓦ www.svenstrupgaard.dk; dorms 150kr, doubles ❹), Svenstrup Strandvej 3, with sleek and spacious rooms, some with inlaid vaulted brick ceilings and exposed timbers. In terms of **food**, *Havfruen*, Algade 24 (ⓣ58 37 61 65), is one of the more atmospheric spots, with burgers (from 35kr) and good steaks (from 100kr) served in a spiffy modern setting.

Southern Zealand and the islands

Largely made up of yellow-green rolling farmlands, **southern Zealand** is seriously rural, though its prosperity and power during the Middle Ages is still evident in the imposing buildings of towns like such as **Næstved and Ringsted**, while **Vordingborg** castle and its attached museum offer tangible relics from Danish medieval history. Of the three sizeable islands off the southern Zealand coast, **Falster** has some of the most prized (and touristed) beachfront in the country, while **Lolland** is much more rural, home to quaint inland towns. The smallest of the three, and with gleaming white cliffs, quaint harbour villages and medieval churches, **Møn** is by far the most popular with visitors, though it never feels overrun. All of the islands are connected to mainland Zealand by road, and Falster and Lolland have rail links, too. Most of Southern Zealand is served by buses, though as services are infrequent outside of the main settlements, it's wise to rent a bike or car if you want to explore the far reaches of the islands.

Næstved and around

Some 25km south of Ringsted, **NÆSTVED** is easily the largest town in southern Zealand. Aside from a smartly restored medieval centre and a minor museum,

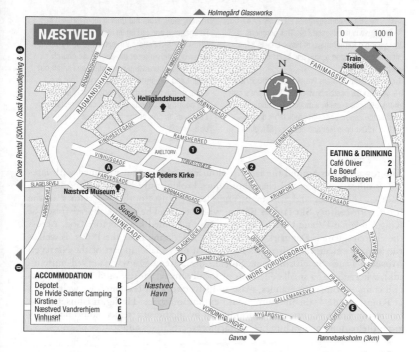

there's little to keep you here, though it is a good jumping off point for canoe trips down the peaceful, little-visited **River Suså**, as well as a visit to the agreeable **Gavnø slot**. Næstved's many brick buildings – a defining feature of many once-important cities along the Baltic coast – mark it out as one of the more powerful towns of the Hanseatic League, the trading alliance that dominated European commerce during the Middle Ages.

Arrival, information and accommodation

Transport links to Næstved are very good, with regular trains and buses from the north and south arriving at the **train station**, five minutes' walk east of the town centre along Ramsherred and Jernbanegade. Free parking is available at the harbour, in the southwest of town on Havnegade, where the **tourist office** is housed in the yellow Det Gule Pakhus, Havnen 1 (June & Aug Mon–Fri 9am–5pm, Sat 9am–2pm; July Mon–Fri 9am–6pm, Sat 9am–2pm; Sept–May Mon–Fri 9am–4pm, Sat 9am–noon; ☏55 72 11 22, ⊛www.visitnaestved.com). There's **bicycle rental** at Brotovets Cykler, Brotorvet 3 (Mon–Thurs 7am–5.30pm, Fri 7am–7pm, Sat 9am–2pm; 65kr/day). There's a decent selection of places to **stay** in the town centre, including a pair of grand old inns, and some good choices further afield.

Accommodation

Depotet Buen 18 in Skelby ☏45 26 20 97 19, ⊛www.depotet-susaa.dk. This quiet, wooded spot is located 12km northwest of Næstved with a dock right on the Suså river, and ideal for an overnighter during a canoe trip. The dirt-cheap lodgings feel hostel-like. May to mid-Sept. ❶

De Hvide Svaner Camping Karrebækvej 741 ☏55 44 24 15, ⊛www.dehvidesvaner.dk. The closest campsite to town, located on the coast by Karrebæksminde, 3km from a popular beach. Facilities include a large swimming pool and cabins (from 450kr), and it's very popular with families. April to mid-Oct.

2

Kirstine Købmagergade 20 ☎55 77 47 00, ⓦwww.hotelkirstine.dk. This gorgeous 250-year-old former mayoral home boasts 31 charming, well-sized rooms and loads of olde-worlde class. **❼**

Næstved Vandrerhjem Præstøvej 65 ☎55 72 20 91, ⓦwww.danhostelnaestved.dk. The town's only affordable option, set in a modern building just outside the centre and with predictable dorms (140kr; 190kr en-suite) and doubles (**❸**), but

friendly staff. From the train station, turn left into Farimagsvej and left again along Præstøvej.

Vinhuset Skt Peders Kirkeplads ☎55 72 08 07, ⓦwww.hotelvinhuset.dk. Set on the church square, this sprawling renovation has small but bright and delightfully dainty rooms that are some of the most atmospheric in this part of the country. Its medieval-style cellar restaurant, *Le Boeuf*, is one of the town's best eating options. **❼**

The Town

The town centres around the large, colourless Axeltorv square, lined with late-1960s office buildings and chain boutiques broken only by the Løve Apoteket, built in the 1640s and still in business today. Just south of Axeltorv is the fourteenth-century **Skt Peders Kirke**, whose chancel bears an elaborate fresco of King Valdemar IV and Queen Helvig, both on bended knees before God. Across the church square is Denmark's oldest town hall, dating from the 1400s, as well as the *boderne* – medieval craftsmen's stalls – that now make up part of the **Næstved Museum** (Tues–Sat 10am–2pm, Sun 1–4pm; free; ⓦwww.naestved-museum .dk), where there's a small collection of locally made, mostly modern Danish arts and crafts – primarily ceramics, glass and silverwork. A few minutes' walk north at Ringstedgade 4, the museum's main exhibition space, **Helligåndshuset** (same hours and ticket as museum), is dominated by medieval artefacts squirreled away from the region's many churches – altarpieces, crucifixes and statues of saints.

Eating

Næstved's **eating** options are somewhat spartan, though all the hotels have good restaurants. The modern *Café Oliver*, Jernbanegade 2, is a pleasant spot for a sandwich or salad (around 70kr), and has a terrace. A more enjoyable option is the *Raadhuskroen* (☎55 72 01 56, ⓦwww.raadhuskroen.com), Skomagerrækken 8, whose lunch menu features a dozen variations of smørrebrød, including a tasty one with asparagus on smoked salmon, with pricier fish and steak dinner dishes starting at 179kr. You can eat in the stately, wooded interior rooms or the covered terrace out back, there's live jazz Saturday afternoons in the summer, and the bar is a good spot for an evening drink.

Around Næstved

Næstved's surrounds hold several good possibilities for side-trips, most popular of which is a day or two spent paddling a **canoe** through the placid waters of the Suså river, a great way to get out into the dramatic landscape in this part of Denmark, from pasturelands to old water mills and chalk-white churches. The negligible current in this part of the river allows for leisurely progress – you could easily get to Bavelse Sø, 18km away, in well under a day – and there are basic camping places and a few B&Bs along the way for **overnighting**. Canoes are available from Suså Kanoudlejning (☎57 64 61 44, ⓦwww.kanoudlejning.dk; May–Sept; 370kr per day, 830kr per 3 days), whose launching spot is Slusehuset, a ten-minute walk northwest of Axeltorvet at Åstien 8; you can reserve online, though you should always book at least a day in advance.

The hi-tech **Holmegaard Glassworks** (July to mid-Aug daily 10am–6pm; mid-Aug to June daily 10am–4pm, Jan closed weekends; 95kr; ⓦwww.holmegaard .com) are also worth a visit, and are reachable via a fifteen-minute bus journey (#75) northwest of town to Fensmark. The professional glassblowers here have been producing household and decorative objects for nearly two hundred years, and tours allow you into their studios to watch them. For an extra 139kr, you can also test your own wind-power by blowing the molten glass to create your own unique piece. A museum showcases thousands of glass products, and there's a shop selling items produced here.

A few miles southwest of Næstved at the mouth of the River Suså, the island of **GAVNØ** is home to the eighteenth-century Rococo **Gavnø Slot** (daily: May 10am–5pm; June–Sept 10am–6pm; 85kr; Ⓦ www.gavnoe.dk), an imposing structure whose strategic location at the mouth of the river made it important for regulating shipping in and out of Næstved during the Middle Ages. The corridors and staircases are plastered with **portraits** depicting subjects from Sir Isaac Newton to Queen Margrethe I, and the rooms hold assorted diplays of Louis XVI antiquities, costumes and embroidery. The palace grounds (included in the ticket price) are enhanced by a delightful **tulip garden** and an exotic **butterfly preserve**. Gavnø is reached from Næstved by road or, in summer, via the *Friheden* ferry (Ⓣ 20 23 11 88, Ⓦ www.nord-line.dk; round-trip 120kr) which runs about three times a day between Næstved, the palace, and the small, touristy harbour town of **Karrebæksminde**, the latter known for its excellent **beaches**. Karrebæksminde is 12km southwest of Næstved; you can get here on bus #80 from the train station, or cycle along the banks of a canal which links the two towns.

Vordingborg

South of Næstved, the 22 motorway wends its way along the Dybsø fjord on its way to **VORDINGBORG**, a compact place whose protected harbour made it an ideal base for twelfth-century military raids into the Baltic to fight off the Wends. For several hundred years, the town was a frequent royal residence, and as the spot where the Jutlandic Code and the Danish constitution were both ratified, it maintains immense historical resonance for modern Denmark. Skulking behind dilapidated encircling walls at the easternmost end of the pedestrianized Algade, the town's one real draw is twelfth-century **Vordingborg castle** (June–Aug daily 10am–5pm; rest of year Tues–Sun 10am–4pm; 30kr or 45kr with museum entrance), looming over which – and dominating the entire town – is the 36-metre-high **Gåsetårnet** ("Goose Tower"), the sole remaining of nine such towers built hereabouts to serve as lookouts. This one was constructed in 1365 by King Valdemar IV, and its spire is crowned with a shiny gold-plated goose, said to have been placed there by the king as a slight on the Hanseatic League, with whom Denmark was fighting at the time: with its beak pointing towards the League's headquarters at Lübeck, the subtle implication was that the Hanseatic states were as much a threat to Danish power as a flock of wild geese. You can enter the tower's cellar, used as a prison in the nineteenth century, or climb up four floors to the top and sneak a panoramic peek through the small embrasured openings. In its heyday, the fortress was surrounded by a massive brick and stone **ring wall**, some 8m high and 800m long, as well as a complex arrangement of individual moats that encircled the wall from the outside. Only the foundations are still visible, but a rich array of archeological items found on the site are on display at the museum inside **Danmarks Borgcenter** (The Danish Castle Centre; same hours as castle; 30kr or 45kr with castle entrance; Ⓦ www.museerne.dk), housed in the seventeenth-century former barracks. Each June, museum archeologists set **digs** around, which usually turn up old bits of the fortress and various household items from the Middle Ages. If you're interested in helping out digging, even for a few hours, contact the museum for specific information. The only other thing to see in Vordingborg is the fifteenth-century **Vor Frue Kirke**, Kirketorvet 14A (10am–2pm; April–Oct open until 3pm), whose facade sports a fetching patchwork of red and yellow brick; inside highlights are the Renaissance pulpit from 1601 and a very ornate Baroque altarpiece from 1642, monogrammed with Christian IV's initials. Standing at the nave, crank your head back to spot the faint chalk **frescoes** that cover the triumphal arch, where several nativity scenes are overshadowed by a caricature painting of local bricklayer Jeppe Murer, wearing a dunce's cap and imbibing from a chalice on a breakfast break.

Practicalities

Trains, which arrive from central Zealand as well as from Falster, disembark at the town's station, a few minutes' walk west of Algade. There's a small, helpful **tourist office** in the Danmarks Borgcenter (June–Aug daily 9am–5pm; Sept–May Tues–Sun 10am–4pm; ☎55 34 11 11, ⓦwww.visitvordingborg.dk); staff can suggest local bicycle tours in the area – the Knudshoved Odde peninsula is especially nice – and will rent out bikes (50kr per day). Though **accommodation** choices are better on Møn or in Næstved, Vordingborg does have an acceptable **youth hostel** at Præstegårdsvej 18 (☎55 36 08 00, ⓦwww.danhostel.dk/vordingborg; dorms 150kr, doubles ❸), while just opposite the tower at Slotstorvet, there are sixty drab rooms at the *Hotel Kong Valdemar* (☎55 34 30 95, ⓦwww.hotel kongvaldemar.dk; ❻). In terms of **eating**, *Snekken* (☎55 37 05 74; April–Sept Tues–Sun noon–10pm; Oct–March Tues–Thurs 5–10pm, Fri–Sun 1–10pm) is an inexpensive Chinese restaurant offering nice views of the boatyard. Most of Vordingbord's restaurants, however, are overshadowed by a distinguished five-star establishment just north of town. ⌥ *Babette*, Kildemarksvej 5 (☎55 34 30 30, ⓦwww.babette.dk; closed Sun & Mon), is a snazzy, professionally run Franco-Danish fusion place that serves innovative fish, meat and vegetable dishes, and its sleek, modern interior is a perfect setting in which to enjoy the changing three-course menu (625kr). Reservations are required.

Møn

Connected to Zealand (and Falster) by the Queen Alexandrine bridge, the oblong island of **MØN** is one of the most popular destinations in southern Zealand, with sandy beaches that make for some great walking and a handful of inviting bed and breakfasts, and it's well worth making the effort to visit. Its main town, **Stege**, is a good place to start exploring, with a helpful tourist office and the lion's share of the island's restaurants. Over on the east coast, you're sure to want to spend a few hours at the famed **Møns Klint** cliffs, either exploring the excellent nature centre or strolling through the clifftop forest or along the beaches below. Elsewhere on the island, highlights include the fourteenth-century frescoes within the **medieval churches** at Fanefjord, Keldby and Elmelund, as well as a visit to the tiny, car-free islet of **Nyord**.

There's no train service to Møn, so if you're travelling by public transport, take bus #62 or #64 from Vordingborg.

Stege

If you don't have your own transport, **STEGE** is the best base from which to explore Møn, since it's the hub of the island's minimal bus service. Buses drop you by the tourist office, on the north side of the drawbridge which leads to the town centre. From here, Stege is bisected by its long, pedestrianized main street, Storegade, which runs from up the harbour past the looming burnt-umber Gothic roof of the town church, and terminates at the **Mølleporten** medieval gates – Stege's name is derived from *stike*, wooden poles rammed into the sea inlet as a supplementary defence against intruders. Connected to the Mølleporten is **Empiregården**, Storegade 75 (Tues–Sun 10am–4pm; 30kr; ⓦwww.empiregaarden.dk), a town museum within a

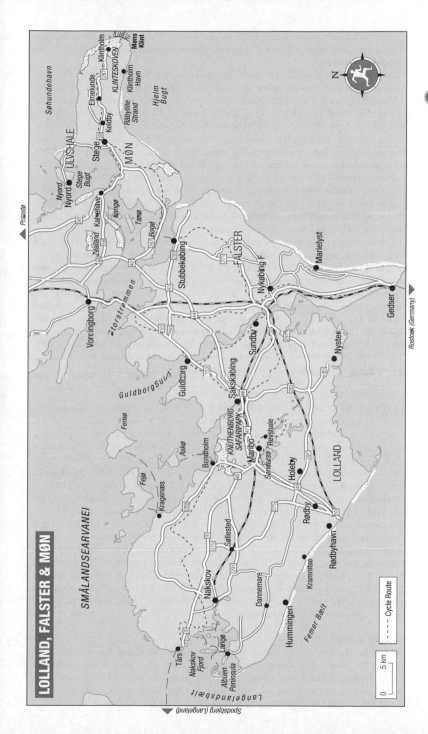

LOLLAND, FALSTER & MØN

SMÅLANDSEARVANEI

Søhundehavn

Præsto ▲

Rostock (Germany) ▶

Spodsbjerg (Langeland) ▼

Møns Klint

Klintholm

KLINTESKOVEN

Klintholm Havn

Råbylille Strand

Hjelm Bugt

Elmelunde

Keldby

MØN

Stege

ULVSHALE

Nyord

Stege Bugt

Kalvehave

Tærø

Bøgø

Zealand

Stubbekøbing

FALSTER

Nykøbing F

Marielyst

Storstrømmen

Vorcingborg

Sundby

Gedser

Nyster

GuldborgSund

Guldborg

Sakskøbing

KNUTHENBORG SAFARIPARK

Maribo

Revshale

Søndersø

Holeby

LOLLAND

Femø

Askø

Bandholm

Fejø

Kragenæs

Søllested

Rødby

Rødbyhavn

Kramnitse

Dannemare

Hummingen

Femer Bælt

Nakskov

Nakskov Fjord

Albuen Peninsula

Langø

Tårs

Langelandsbælt

0 5 km

- - - - Cycle Route

N

former merchant's house dating back to the 1780s. The collection here includes archeological and ethnographic exhibits covering everything from fossilized fauna to fresco-filled churches.

Once you've had your fill of Stege, it's a good idea to prime yourself for exploring Møn at the superb **tourist office** at Storegade 2 (late June to mid-Aug Mon–Fri 9.30am–5pm, Sat 9.30am–12.30pm & 2.30–5pm; mid-June to late June & mid-Aug to late Aug Mon–Fri 9.30am–4pm, Sat 9.30am–12.30pm & 2.30–4pm; May to mid-June & Sept–March Mon–Fri 9.30am–4pm & Sat 9am–noon; ☎55 86 04 00, ⓦwww.visitvordingborg.dk), where knowledgeable staff hand out a dozen excellent English-language brochures and cycling maps of the island, and can help with B&B **accommodation** across the island. The only **hotel** option in town is the *Motel Stege* at Provstestræde 4 (☎55 81 35 35, ⓦwww.motel-stege.dk; ❹), a friendly place next to the town's church with twelve basic rooms – half with cooking facilities – and a garden out back. Otherwise, there's the inexpensive *Stege Camping* on Falckvej 5 (☎40 30 45 75; May to mid-Sept). In contrast to its poor choice of accommodation, Stege does offer the best **places to eat** on Møn, most of them lining Storegade and catering to a diverse range of tastes. *David's* at Storegade 11 (closed Sun) is a slick, modern café with a terrace, serving juices, cakes and very good coffee, while at *Støberiet*, a deli-cum-restaurant down the road at no.59 (☎55 81 42 67, ⓦwww.slagterstig.dk), you select ingredients from the deli counter, watch them being prepared and then enjoy the results in the spacious, airy atrium or out back in the quiet, tree-lined garden; try the *inbagte rejer* – deep-fried baby prawns. The best place to eat, though, is ⅍ *Café Laika* at Havnen 1 (☎55 81 46 07, ⓦwww.cafe-laika.dk), a quaint dockside restaurant-bar with picnic tables and a sizeable menu of dishes such as wine-steamed mussels (75kr), as well as pricier steak and fish plates, and a popular weekend brunch (11am–3pm; 98kr). For evening **drinks**, try *Café Anden*, Møllebrøndstræde 2, just by the medieval gates in the north of town, with cheap draughts and bottles.

Ulvshale and Nyord island

To the northwest of Stege, the **Ulvshale** ("wolf's tail") peninsula is a dense, lush forest of beech, ash, and rowan trees that provide a suitable habitat for the venomous – and rare – black adder. The forest presents a handful of pleasant, signposted paths, ideal for leisurely walks; one path ends a few hundred metres east of the bridge to **Nyord island**, a landscape of grazing pastures, agricultural fields and salt meadows whose main draw is the tiny village (also called **NYORD**) in its the southwestern corner. In 1769, Christian VII sold Nyord to the island's twenty tenant farmers in exchange for their adept piloting services, and for the next two hundred years or so they lived completely self-sufficient lives here, more or less in isolation from the rest of Denmark. As a result, Nyord retains a uniquely rural charm, and it's well worth spending an hour or so walking among the sickle-shaped cottages and farmhouses down to the rustic harbour. A few streets up from here, you can have a **meal** at the island's central meeting point, *Lolles Gård* (☎55 81 86 81), Hyldevej 1, which serves a few simple Danish dishes from around 125kr. You can also **camp** at *Ulvshale Camping* (☎55 81 53 25, ⓦwww.ulvscamp .dk; April–Oct), just on the Nyord side of the bridge and right on a wide, duned beach – a superb spot for **swimming**.

Møns Klint

Backed by the dense Store Klinteskov woodlands, the **Møns Klint** chalk cliffs stretch for about 8km along Møn's eastern coast, and offer some extremely scenic walking. The forest along the top is home to some twenty species of orchid as well as peregrine falcons, while the sparkling white cliffs provide a gorgeous contrast to the turquoise waters below and the sea breeze keeps things

Møn's churches

Møn's many well-preserved **medieval churches** are notable mostly for their vibrant **frescoes**, painted by an anonymous fifteenth-century artist known simply as *Elmelundmesteren* ("The master of Elmelund"). They depict the objects of everyday medieval life in sometimes humorous scenes, and were painted in a naïve, unprepossessing style for the benefit of rural peasants, whom it was thought would have little appreciation for more ornate, representational work. The paintings are characterized by human figures with triangular faces and sleepy eyes amidst magical environments of stars, flowers and miniature trees. Just east of Stege, the church at **Keldby** (daily: April–Sept 7am–4pm; Oct–March 8am–4pm) has several notable frescoes, including one showing Joseph making porridge for the baby Jesus, though the best of the paintings are a few kilometres further on at **Elmelunde** (same hours); here, inside Møn's oldest church, the frescoes include some handsome scenes of Adam tilling his field with a horse-drawn plough – many of the motifs were taken from pictorial bibles of the late Middle Ages. Southwest of Stege, the large church at **Fanefjord** (same hours) sports fresco-covered arches in its western vault depicting local women being warned against the devilish nature of town gossip. The church is reachable via bus #62 (get off at Store Damme, then walk). Elmelunde and Keldby are connected to Stege via bus #52.

cool. The paths that thread through the trees have plenty of lookout points that afford some dazzling coastal views; there are also steps leading down to the stony beach below. It's hard to miss the **GeoCenter Møns Klint** at Stengårdsvej 8 (daily: late June to Aug 10am–6pm; early May to late June & Sept–Oct 10am–5pm; early Feb to mid-Feb 10am–4pm; 115kr; W www.moensklint.dk), an ultra-modern nature centre at the entrance to the cliffs walk. Nor should you: this outstanding museum presents the interesting geological history of the cliffs and surrounding landscape and has a great terrace restaurant; guided nature walks are planned, too – check the website or contact the tourist office in Stege for up-to-date information.

Bus #52 runs between Stege and the nature centre four to five times a day depending on the season. If you want to stay and soak up the atmosphere, you could try the excellent, spacious *Møns Klint* **youth hostel** (T 55 81 20 30, W www.danhostel.dk/moen; early April to Aug; dorms 165kr, doubles ❸), fifteen minutes' walk from the cliffs at Langebjergvej 1. The management are very friendly and the dorm rooms have no more than four beds each; many of them overlook the placid Hunosø lake (no swimming), where there are picnic tables right by the water. A few hundred metres south of the hostel at Klintvej 544, *Camping Møns Klint* (T 55 81 20 25, W www.campingmoensklint.dk; April–Oct) is the best campsite on the island, in an enclosed, hedged area just by the roadside; it has some newish cabins (550kr) too, though in high summer they're only available by the week. The *Bakkegård Gæstgiveri* (T 55 81 93 01, W www.bakkegaarden64.dk; ❺), at Busenevej 64 at the southernmost edge of the Store Klinteskov forest, has twelve simple rooms and picture-perfect views over the fields to the sea, while just north of Møns Klint is the *Liselund Slot* (T 55 81 20 81, W www.liselundslot.dk; ❾), Langebjergvej 6, a late eighteenth-century estate hotel with a dozen stylish rooms, many overlooking a lush lawn. For the best **eating** options, head 6km southwest of the cliffs to **KLINTHOLM HAVN** (bus #52 from Stege); there's zero charm at this unkempt harbour village, but authentic Italian meals (especially the lasagne) at *Porto Fino*, Thyravej 4A (T 55 85 51 81). There's also pricier Danish food next door at *Hyttefadet* (T 55 81 92 36), where the speciality is the scrumptious fried flounder (109kr).

Falster

In 1914, Franz Kafka visited the eastern coast of Falster, describing the area as having "a really awful beach with some terribly peculiar Danes". To be fair to Kafka's aesthetic sensibilities, **FALSTER** isn't southern Zealand's most stimulating destination, but its Baltic (eastern) coast has some excellent and clean (if very crowded) beaches. Trains and buses arrive at the island's main town, **NYKØBING** – usually written Nykøbing F (for Falster) – which has a decent attraction in its **Medieval Centre** (June–Aug daily 10am–4pm, plus July Wed & Thurs open until 6pm; May & Sept Tues–Sun daily 10am–4pm; 95–105kr; Ⓦ www .middelaldercentret.dk), an experimental open-air museum set in a recreated village, which aims to provide an insight into the hardship of medieval life, though on summer weekends it is primarily a place for Danes to run around dressed like their forefathers. If you want to continue on to Funen, bus #800 runs from Nykøbing to Langeland (via ferry), then continues on to Svendborg and eventually up to Odense (see p.153). There's no real reason to stay in Nykøbing, however, and you're much better off heading south to **MARIELYST**, one of the few towns in Denmark that can actually justify its reputation as a fully fledged seaside resort. It's home to the best beaches in the country – some 28km of them – which, as you'd expect, are hugely popular in summer, when the island's population more than doubles and the nightlife gets pretty lively. Although the sands are packed in season, finding a secluded spot is fairly easy, especially if you have a bike, since a path runs parallel to the shore for the entire stretch. Bathing spots are sandy and clean for most of the shoreline, with sandbars extending several metres out in many places; the best ones are a few minutes' walk east of the town centre, or south towards the forested nature reserve of Bøtø. At the very southern end of the strip, 4.5km south of the town centre, the Fribadestrand stretch is a designated nude area.

The helpful **tourist office** at Marielyst Strandpark 3 (Mon–Fri 9am–4pm plus Sat June–Aug 10am–2pm; Ⓣ 54 13 62 98, Ⓦ www.visitlolland-falster.com) is just off Skovby Ringvej as you enter Marielyst from Nykøbing; staff hand out detailed beach maps, provide a list of private rooms and rent bicycles (50kr per day). While most **accommodation** is comprised of holiday cottages with a minimum rental period of one week, there a few good options for shorter stays. The best hotel is the 🍴 *Nørrevang*, Marielyst Strandvej 32 (Ⓣ 54 13 62 62, Ⓦ www.norrevang.dk; ❼), with eighty A-frame bungalows, studios and double rooms and a popular, decently priced restaurant. Much cheaper are the simple cream and beige rooms at *Ellens* (Ⓣ 55 81 54 54, Ⓦ www.ellenskjoerupskro.dk; ❻), closer to the beach at Bøtø Møllevej 2. Of the five **campsites** in the area, the most central is *Marielyst Camping*, Marielyst Strandvej 36 (Ⓣ 54 13 53 07, Ⓦ www.marielyst-camping.dk; early April to early Sept), with pitches 200m from the beach.

You'll have no trouble finding somewhere to **eat** or **drink**. The most popular option is *Larsens Plads* at Marielyst Strandvej 57 (Ⓣ 54 13 21 70), a massive establishment with seating for seven hundred that focuses around its large buffet of grilled steak, ham and salads. Though the meat sits for a while under the heat lamps and isn't always full of flavour, the 139kr all-you-can-eat dinner buffet is still a very good deal. It's a great place to come after the beach, as you can catch the sunset from the tables out front. Just south, *Tannhäuser*, Bøtøvej 1 (11am–10pm), has simple pizzas and burgers from 40kr. **Bars** and **clubs** are plentiful, with several places within a few hundred feet of each other along Marielyst Strandvej. The bar at *Larsens Plads* (daily 10pm–4am) is where the fun starts for younger Danes, especially after someone's plugged the karaoke machine in. Across the street, *Klein* (daily 8pm–late), is the best-run bar and disco in town, with two rooms of music.

Lolland

Larger and less crowded than Falster, **LOLLAND** is otherwise much the same: wooded, with good beaches and lots of quiet, explorable corners. It's a lovely place to visit, and feels the least overrun of the southern islands. For years, however, it was dubbed the "social disaster of Denmark" when the closure of Nakskov shipyards resulted in the country's highest unemployment rate. These days, it's a centre for renewable-energy research into biogas, biomass and wind power – the world's largest offshore wind farm (90 windmills, each 200m in height) lies off the coast of southern Lolland – and unemployment is among the country's lowest (three percent).

A private railway (InterRail, ScanRail and Eurail passes not valid) runs to Lolland from Nykøbing on Falster, taking in lakeside **MARIBO**, Lolland's most scenic setting for a short stay. Handsomely positioned on the Søndersø lake, this sleepy town centres around Torvet, mostly modern and characterless save for a few Norwegian maple trees and the white stone town hall which houses the island's largest **tourist office** (Mon–Fri 10am–4pm, Sat 10am–noon; ☎54 78 04 96, Ⓦwww.visitlolland-falster.com), a good place to pick up brochures detailing cycling tours around Lolland. **Trains** and **buses** arrive at the Jernbanepladsen square, several blocks north, where you'll also find the excellent **Museum Lolland-Falster** (Tues–Sat noon–4pm; 30kr; Ⓦwww.museumlollandfalster.dk), which displays local archeological finds and costumes, and has several rooms covering the experience of Polish immigrants who settled here in the late eighteenth century to work in the cane fields and the sugar-processing plants. Otherwise, you could wander around the spectacularly located **Maribo Domkirke**, back in the centre of Maribo, just east of Torvet and reachable via the picturesque Kirkestræde or Smedestræde. Originally a Bridgettine abbey founded in 1418, its excavated foundation walls alongside the church mark the site of two large cloisters that once overlooked the lake. From here, a sand-sprinkled path runs the circumference of Søndersø lake and offers some lovely walking or cycling; a dock halfway around offers good **bathing** opportunities.

The best place to **stay** in Maribo is the lakefront *Hotel Maribo Søpark*, Vestergade 29 (☎54 78 10 11, Ⓦwww.maribo-soepark.dk; ❼), with spacious rooms (some with balconies) that look out onto the lake as well as an outdoor swimming pool and a very good restaurant. The town's lakeside **youth hostel** (☎54 78 33 14, Ⓦwww.danhostel.dk/maribo), with dorms (150kr) and doubles (❷) is at Sdr Boulevard 82B. *Maribo Sø Camping*, Bangshavevej 25 (☎54 78 00 71, Ⓦwww.maribo-camping.dk; April to mid-Oct), boasts one of the best locations in Zealand, on a grassy knoll on the west bank of the lake a few minutes' walk from the town centre, and has six brand-new cabins (❹). In terms of **food**, you need head no further than *Bangs Have*, Bangshavevej 23 (☎54 78 19 11, Ⓦwww.bangshave.dk; Tues–Sun 11am–3pm & 5–10pm); in addition to a variety of fish dishes, it serves up a massive Sunday brunch plate (155kr) that includes home-made jams, pesto chicken and artichoke hearts.

Travel details

Trains

Frederikssund to: Copenhagen (every 10 min; 40min).

Helsingør to: Copenhagen (every 20min; 45min); Gilleleje (every 20min; 45min–1hr 15min).

Hillerød to: Helsingør (every 30min; 30min); Hundested (every 30min; 40–50min).

Korsør to: Ringsted (every 30min; 25min); Roskilde (every 30min; 45min).

Nykøbing Falster to: Gedser (every hour; 30min); Nakskov (every 30min; 45min); Rødbyhavn (every 30min; 1hr 20min).

Nykøbing Sjælland to: Holbæk (every 20min; 1hr).

Næstved to: Køge (every 30min; 40min); Vordingborg (every 30min; 15–20min).

Roskilde to: Copenhagen (every 30min; 20–30min); Korsør (every 30min; 40min); Køge (every 30min; 25–40min); Nykøbing Falster (every 30min; 1hr 20min–1hr 40min).

Vordingborg to: Nykøbing Falster (every 30min; 20–25min); Næstved (every 40min; 15–20min).

Buses

Klintholm Havn to: Stege via Keldby and Elmelunde (hourly–several daily; 45min)).

Køge to: Store Heddinge (7 daily; 45min).

Maribo to: Vordingborg (hourly; 1hr).

Nykøbing Falster to: Gedser (hourly; 35min); Marielyst (9–10 daily; 30min); Odense via Rudkøbing, Langeland (Mon–Fri hourly, Sat & Sun 4–6 daily; 3hr 45min); Stege (7 daily; 55min).

Nykøbing Sjælland to: Rørvig (hourly; 15min).

Næstved to: Køge (hourly; 40min); Ringsted (hourly; 40min); Slagelse (every 30min–7 daily; 50min); Vordingborg (hourly; 35min).

Ringsted to: Køge (hourly; 45–55min); Næstved (hourly; 40min), Slagelse (every 30min–7 daily; 55min).

Rørvig to: Nykøbing Sjælland (hourly; 15min).

Slagelse to: Næstved (every 30min; 50min); Ringsted (every 30min; 55min); Roskilde (every 30min; 1hr 50min).

Stege to: Klintholm Havn via Keldby and Elmelunde (hourly–several daily; 45min); Nykøbing Falster (7 daily; 55min); Vordingborg (hourly; 50min).

Store Heddinge to: Køge (7 daily; 45min).

Vordingborg to: Maribo (hourly; 1hr); Næstved (hourly; 35min); Stege (hourly; 50min).

Ferries

Gedser to: Rostock, Germany (6–9 daily; 50min).

Helsingør to: Helsingborg, Sweden (frequent; 20min).

Hundested to: Rørvig (hourly; 45min).

Køge to: Bornholm (2 daily; 6hr 30min).

Sjællands Odde to: Århus (5–9 daily; 1hr); Ebeltoft (5–9 daily; 45min).

Tårs to: Spodsbjerg (hourly; 45min).

Bornholm

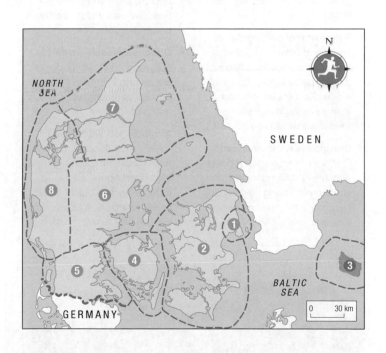

NORTH
SEA

SWEDEN

GERMANY

BALTIC
SEA

0   30 km

CHAPTER 3

Highlights

* **Bornholmer Clocks** The Bornholms Museum in Rønne holds several pristine examples of these traditional, tall grandfather clocks, many of them still ticking away. See p.140

* **Hammershus** The largest castle remains in northern Europe, set high up on a grassy knoll overlooking the Baltic. See p.142

* **Svaneke market** The Saturday crafts and farmers' market at this tiny harbourside village is a great place to pick up hand-made glass sculptures and sample *æbleskive*, delicious fried dough-balls. See p.142

* **Bornholms Kunstmuseum** This superb art museum boasts a stunning clifftop location and some breathtaking paintings by Denmark's foremost modern masters. See p.144

* **Christiansø** Once a tactical stronghold of the Danish navy, this tiny, sparse island with its single charming guesthouse is the epitome of blissful seclusion. See p.147

* **Rundkirke** Designed to inspire religious awe as well as fend off marauding pirates, these fortified, round medieval churches are some of Scandinavia's most distinctive buildings. See p.147

* **Dueodde Beach** These gorgeous chalk-white dunes are among Denmark's finest, popular with families, couples and nudists alike. See p.149

* **Almindingen woodlands** Take a walk through this idyllic forest, crisscrossed with trails, then learn about the island's compelling geological history at the nearby NaturBornholm centre. See p.149

▲ Hammershus castle

3

Bornholm

Surrounded by the Baltic Sea and closer to Sweden than to Denmark, **Bornholm** is said to have been formed when God cobbled together the most beautiful parts of Scandinavia and flung them into the middle of the ocean. Set some 200km southeast of Copenhagen, this landscape of stark granite cliffs, flowing wheat fields, bucolic harbourside towns and long dune-lined beaches is known to Danes as *solskinsøen*, or "island of shining sun". With a near-Mediterranean climate that provides more hours of sunlight than anywhere else in the country, a string of gorgeous beaches and an unspoiled interior criss-crossed by several hundred kilometres of well-marked cycling and hiking trails, Bornholm has become a haven for lovers of the outdoors. These natural attributes, combined with a tasty regional cuisine, some pristine medieval churches and an excellent modern art museum ensure that the island is well worth a detour from the mainland.

All but one of Bornholm's major towns lie along the coast, which is soft and sandy in the south, jagged and rocky to the north. At the southwestern tip, the capital town of **Rønne** is a busy transportation hub with limited charm but all the major facilities and amenities of a proper centre. From here, it's an easy bus ride up the coast to the northwest corner, where the ruins of **Hammershus** offer some captivating insights into a thousand years of military history and even more captivating views out to sea. Continuing clockwise, the appealing seaside towns of **Sandvig**, **Allinge** and **Gudhjem** are home to several excellent hotels and restaurants, and are well placed for a visit to one of Scandinavia's best art museums as well as the tiny and remote island of **Christiansø**, some 20km distant and a haven for eider ducks and day-tripping tourists. Back on Bornholm itself, harbourside **Svaneke** has a charming weekend market and a convivial microbrewery; its proximity to the island's central woodlands also makes it a good point of departure for walking and cycling the well-manicured trails and picnicking in the huge **Almindingen** forest, as well as visiting Åkirkeby's fascinating natural history centre and the island's fortified **rundkirke** churches. In the southeast, the beaches at **Dueodde**, **Snogebæk** and **Balka** represent some of Europe's finest stretches of white sand and are justifiably popular during the summer.

As locals will proudly tell you, summer in Bornholm lasts longer than anywhere else in Denmark, and is by far the **best time to come** – if you can, try and time your visit for mid-May or late September, when the weather is still superb but the bulk of the crowds are gone. The Baltic waters are usually warm enough for a quick dip as late as October, but winter is very cold and well near untenable for most visitors, with many of the towns pretty much shutting down. Spring is chilly but gorgeous, with cherry blossoms contrasting beautifully with patches of late snow on the hillsides.

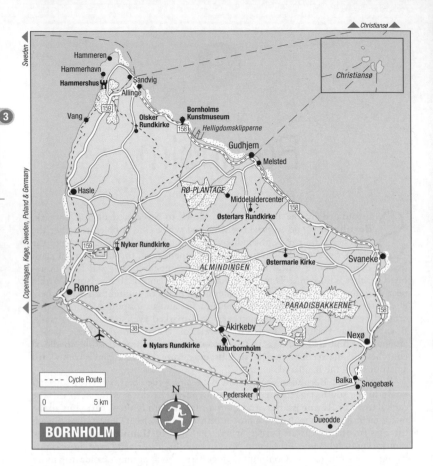

Some history

Bornholm has been inhabited since as early as 5500 BC, though its strategic location in the Baltic has ensured a fairly turbulent history, characterized by repeated attacks by Viking pirates, Hanseatic despots and neighbouring Scandinavian kings. In the sixteenth century, it was established as a **fiefdom** under the Danish crown, with small outposts of royal control set up across the island. Following the Swedish-Polish war, in which the Polish-aligned Danes lost dearly to Sweden, the 1658 **Treaty of Roskilde** awarded sovereignty to the Swedish king – but Bornholmers, by then fiercely Danish at heart, soon rebelled against their occupiers, killing the Swedish commandant, disarming his soldiers and swiftly winning back their Danish nationality. The island remained fairly peaceful until **World War II**, when its strategic position saw it occupied by German forces and used as a lookout post and a base from which to prevent Allied warships and submarines from entering Nazi-occupied waters. During an extended Soviet occupation at the end of the war, hundreds of buildings in Rønne and Nexø were destroyed, requiring extensive postwar periods of reconstruction, which was swiftly followed by the arrival of **tourism**, today central to the island's economy. These days, Bornholm receives some half a million visitors annually – roughly ten times its native population – but rarely feels overcrowded, even in high season.

Arrival, transport and accommodation

Nearly all visitors to Bornholm arrive by **ferry**; these dock at the main harbour town of Rønne, just steps from the main bus station and a five-minute walk from the town centre. The **airport** is 5km east of Rønne, and connected to it by bus #7. From Rønne's bus station, Bornholm Amts Transport (BAT; ☎56 95 21 21, ⓦwww.bat .dk), operates nine **bus** routes around the island, which depart roughly hourly and pass through Rønne's centre en route to destinations across the island, the longest of which – Rønne to Svaneke – takes just under an hour. Fares are priced per zone, with the furthest possible travel distance being five zones; tickets cost 11kr per zone, and are valid for unlimited rides within one zone for thirty minutes; fifteen minutes are added on to the ticket's validity for each additional zone. You can save money by purchasing a *RaBATkort* multi-ride ticket, which gives a ten- to thirty-percent discount on fares and can be used by more than one person. There are also one-day (140kr) and week (480kr) passes; all tickets are available on board the bus. If you're here for only a short time, or just want to get a sense of the island, hop on bus #7, which makes a four-hour counter-clockwise circumnavigation of Bornholm, stopping

---

Getting to and from Bornholm

Bornholm's main – but still tiny – port at **Rønne** is busy year-round, with daily **ferry** services to Copenhagen and Køge, as well as cities in Sweden, Germany and Poland. Most of the Denmark-bound ferry routes time well with **bus** and **train** connections to destinations further on. If you want to take your car to Bornholm, the best option is to drive to Køge and take the ferry from there.

From Copenhagen

The best and quickest way to travel overland from the Danish mainland to Bornholm is by the **DSB train-ferry** combo journeys that run to Rønne via Ystad, Sweden. Trains depart Copenhagen's Central Station several times daily, the first departing at 6.39am and the last at 10.22pm. The schedule occasionally changes, so you'd do well to check with either the Bornholm or Copenhagen tourist offices (see p.492 & 139) or DSB (☎70 13 14 15, ⓦwww.dsb.dk/bornholm) for up-to-date details. Tickets start at 281kr, the journey takes about three hours including the ferry and, during the week, seat reservations are obligatory. **Buses** run by **Gråhundbus** (☎44 68 44 00, ⓦwww.graahundbus.dk; 3hr; 255kr) represent a slightly less comfortable option, with daily services to Rønne from Central Station which also make use of the ferry. Another alternative is a flight with **Cimber Sterling** (☎70 10 12 18, ⓦwww.cimber.dk), which runs several flights daily (35min) from Copenhagen to Rønne; buy tickets online a few weeks in advance to take advantage of discounted saver fares of as little as 195kr each way – normal apex fares for one-way flights generally start at 860kr.

From Køge

Bornholms Trafikken (☎56 95 18 66, ⓦwww.bornholmstrafikken.dk) operates regular ferries to Rønne from Køge, 30km south of Copenhagen and easily accessible by S-Tog (see p.52). The trip takes six and a half hours and one-way tickets cost 257kr, but buying at least a week in advance gets you a return for 386kr (256kr from mid-Aug to late June). In peak season, there are two ferries daily, one early in the morning and one around midnight; off-season, there is only one late-evening boat. Though it's less direct and can be a bit pricier than some of the other options, taking the overnight ferry will save you on a night's hotel. Bringing along a bike will cost an extra 17kr, while prices for a car and up to five passengers start at 1483kr. Booking online gets you a 100kr discount if you're taking a car.

Cycling around Bornholm

Bornholm's extensive network of **cycle routes** was established in the early 1980s, and today the island boasts over 235km of coastal roads, bark-covered paths and gravelled forest roads that wend their way through the island's fields, moors, woods and sandy coastline. All routes are clearly marked with green and white signs that indicate directions and distances, and with bikes given right of way in nearly all situations, they're all safe for riders. Seven-speed cycles can be rented in most towns for around 70kr per day, 300kr per week, and bikes can be taken on local buses for a 25kr fee. We've listed the major rental outlets below, most of which are open year-round Monday to Friday from 8/9am to 5/6pm, and Saturday from 9am to noon – the outlet in Rønne is open daily from May to mid-Sept 8am–5.30pm (with slightly irregular hours in the off-season).

For more on biking on the island, visit the superb ⓦbike.bornholm.info, which has detailed pages on what to pack, how to ride and where to put the kids, in addition to plenty of interactive 3-D maps of dozens of suggested cycling routes.

Bike-rental outlets

Åkirkeby Åkirkeby Cykler, Storegade 21 ⓣ56 97 00 47, ⓦwww.lejcykler.dk.

Allinge Nordbornholms Cykelforretning, Pilegade 1 ⓣ56 48 02 91, ⓦwww .nordbornholmscykelforretning.dk.

Balka Boss Cykler, Kannikegårdsvej 10 ⓣ56 49 44 74, ⓦwww.bosscykler.dk.

Dueodde *Bornholms Familiecamping*, Krogegårdsvejen 2 ⓣ56 48 81 50, ⓦwww.bornholms-familiecamping.dk.

Gudhjem Sct Jørgens Gård, Ejnar Mikkelsensvej 14 ⓣ56 48 50 35, ⓦwww.danhostel-gudhjem.dk. May–Sept only.

Rønne Bornholms Cykeludlejning, Nordre Kystvej 5 ⓣ56 95 13 59, ⓦwww.bornholms-cykeludlejning.dk.

Svaneke Boss Cykler, Søndergade 14 ⓣ56 49 75 74, ⓦwww.bosscykler.dk. May–Sept only.

at all the major settlements. This daily route departs Rønne harbour roughly every two hours from 8am and costs 140kr. **Bicycles** are the most popular and efficient way to get around the island, which is crisscrossed by some 235km of bikeable roads and paths (see above); we've detailed rental outlets throughout the chapter. Finally, the short **sightseeing flights** operated by BAS, located at the airport (ⓣ56 95 35 73, ⓦwww.bornfly.dk), are a novel way to see the island, and start at 210kr per person.

Accommodation is plentiful but pricey (and often booked up throughout the season, when Danish youth groups descend on the island en masse), but a handful of youth hostels and good camping facilities can help to cut costs, and you can also camp out at Bornholm's half-dozen *lejrpladser* open camping areas for 15kr a night. Note that many of Bornholm's smaller hotels and pensions open from May to September only and do not include breakfast in their rates; we've highlighted exceptions to this in our reviews. **Bornholms Booking Centre**, Postgade 2 in Tejn, 5km south of Allinge (Mon–Fri 9am–5pm; ⓣ56 48 00 01, ⓦwww.bbc.dk) can locate vacancies for an 85kr fee.

Rønne and around

Though it holds the lion's share of the island's accommodation and restaurants **RØNNE** is not what draws visitors to Bornholm, and few locals consider it to be truly "*bornholmsk*". But with its quiet cobbled streets and pretty old houses, the town does merit a little of your time. Founded in 1327, Rønne functioned mostly as a small port town until the seventeenth century, when the island's administrative centre was moved here from Åkirkeby. Today, it's Bornholm's largest settlement and the centre of most of the island's commercial activity.

Information and accommodation

Rønne's spacious and helpful **tourist office**, the Bornholms Velkomstcenter, is just opposite the ferry terminal at Nordre Kystvej 3 (April–May & Sept–Oct Mon–Fri 9am–4pm, Sat 9am–noon; June–Aug daily 9am–7.30pm; Nov–March Mon–Fri 9am–4pm; ☎56 95 95 00, Ⓦwww.bornholm.info). It sells a great selection of booklets and maps of hiking and cycling routes around Bornholm (for bike-rental outlets, see opposte), and can book last-minute accommodation for no fee. **Internet** access is available across Nordre Kystvej inside the Snellemark Sentret (Mon–Fri 9.30am–9pm, Sat 9am–6pm, Sun 11am–6pm). Though **cycling** is the best way to get around the island, if you do need a **car**, Bornholms Biludlejning, Snellemark 19 (☎56 95 22 08, Ⓦwww.bornholmsbiludlejning.dk), offers them from 600kr a day.

There are plenty of places to **stay** in and around the centre, but many are booked up from May to September. If you're stuck, the tourist office has details of a few inexpensive rooms in private houses; alternatively, contact Bornholms Booking Centre (see p.138).

Accommodation

Galløkken Camping Strandvejen 4 ☎56 95 23 20, Ⓦwww.gallokken.dk. A great campsite about 1km from Rønne, at the edge of a patch of lushly forested coastal land and just a few minutes from the beach. Excellent facilities and some now four person wooden cabins (from 550kr). Open early May to Aug.

Griffen Ndr Kystvej 34 ☎56 90 44 45, Ⓦwww .hotelgriffen.dk. Only 500m from downtown Rønne, this spacious seaside hotel offers 140 rooms, many with a balcony or terrace and all with the expected mod cons, including use of the sauna, pool and spa. Open May–Sept. Ⓖ

Radisson Blu Fredensborg Strandvejen 116 ☎56 95 44 44, Ⓦwww.radissonblu.com. A few kilometres south of the centre, this mid-level chain hotel is a bit off the beaten path, but very comfortable, with Ikea-esque furniture and balconies overlooking the Baltic. The attached restaurant, Di 5 Stâuerna (see p.142), is expensive but superb. Bus #7. Ⓖ

Rønne Vandrerhjem ☎50 95 13 40, Ⓦwww .danhostel-roenne.dk. This well-run hostel is located 1km southeast of town on Arsenalvej 12 and offers both dorms (115kr) and private rooms (⓸). Open April–Oct.

Sverres Small Hotel Snellemark 2 ☎56 95 03 03, Ⓦwww.sverres-hotel.dk. The only place in the town centre, just around from the tourist office, is this pension that fancies itself a hotel. Its pricey rooms (some with shared bathrooms) are light and airy, but have little in the way of furniture or amenities. Ⓖ

The Town

Finding your way around compact Rønne is relatively uncomplicated. From the harbour, Snellemark cuts through the town centre, passing along the southern end of **Store Torv**, originally a training ground for the Danish military and today the town's market square; main market days are Wednesday and Saturday, and the stalls sell a good range of picnic fare – fresh breads, cheeses, fruit and so on. Between here and the smaller Lille Torv, a block east, lie most of the shops, restaurants and conveniences. Rønne is characterized by its colourful and well-preserved half-timbered, brick-tiled buildings, which comprise Denmark's largest collection of eighteenth- and nineteenth-century **wood-framed houses**. The most picturesque of these quaint, bright two-storey structures line the crooked, cobbled streets that branch off Store Torv to the west. In the bombardment of 1945, ten percent of Rønne's buildings were levelled, but the so-called *bombehuse* ("bomb houses"), red- and yellow-brick replacement homes built around the ones that survived, manage to blend in quite well with the original buildings. Once you've had your fill of the architecture, head to the **Bornholms Museum** (July & Aug daily 10am–5pm; Sept to mid-Oct Mon–Sat 10am–5pm; mid-Oct to mid-May Mon–Sat 1–6pm; 50kr, combined ticket with Ceramic and Erichsens Gård museums 125kr; Ⓦwww .bornholmsmuseum.dk), set in a former hospital at Skt Mortensgade 29. Despite the abundance of dusty glass cases, it nevertheless presents an engaging social and cultural history of the island, with laminated English-language sheets supplementing the displays. The ground floor is dedicated to **prehistoric** and **religious artefacts**, displaying finds from the remains of several dozen Stone Age dwellings near Åkirkeby, a handful of Runic stone carvings that once decorated local churches and a large golden clothes pin found in a local field in 2002. Upstairs, the most interesting exhibit is the large selection of prized **Bornholmer grandfather clocks** (for more on which, see below), all in mint condition – the earliest dates from 1770 and stands alongside a reconstructed clockmaker's workshop. Other intriguing exhibits include a wistful section on Bornholm's now-defunct railway, which served nearly the entire island for seventy years – it was closed down for good in 1968, when cars and buses took over; and a room covering the history of Bornholm's tourist industry, with some fetching 1930s posters advertising the romance of Danish steam travel.

Rønne's other museums are less engaging, but still worth a quick look. Three hundred metres west of the Bornholms Museum, across Store Torv at Krystalgade 5, is the **Hjorths Fabrik** (Ceramic Museum; July & Aug daily 10am–5pm; mid-May to June & Sept to mid-Oct Mon–Sat 10am–5pm; Dec Mon–Sat 10am–5pm, March to mid-May & mid-Oct to Nov Mon–Fri 1–5pm, Sat 10am–1pm; 50kr, combined ticket with Bornholms and Erichsens Gård museums 125kr), where two busy floors display a representative – if cluttered – collection of Bornholm's traditional brown stoneware, renowned all over Scandinavia for its simple, rustic design. From here, head north to Laksegade 7 for the **Erichsens Gård** ethnographic museum (mid-May to mid-Oct Mon–Sat 10am–5pm, plus Sun July & Aug; 50kr, combined ticket with Bornholms and Erichsens Gård museums 125kr), a mostly missable collection of housewares and knick-knacks that's mainly worth visiting to partake of a plate of tasty *stønnkager* pancakes, cooked up on a cast-iron stove out in the garden area. The only other sight to make for, ten minutes' walk south of Store Torv past the old customs house at Toldbodgade 1, is the impressive **citadel** of Kastellet, dominated by a round, bloated tower that vaguely recalls Bornholm's *rundkirke*. Construction on the fortress began in 1687 at the behest of Frederik V, but the project was abandoned mid-build, leaving only the turrets and storehouses completed. Today, it houses the **Forsvarsmuseet** (Defence Museum; May–Oct Tues–Sat 11am–5pm; 40kr), whose motley assortment of military gear and armaments includes an interesting exhibit on Bornholm's role in World War II.

The Bornholmer clock

Grandfather clocks have been associated with Bornholm since 1744, when a Dutch ship containing five specimens from England ran aground off the Rønne coast and the salvaged pieces were repaired and restored by local craftsmen. They learned enough about the construction of the longcase enclosures, cast-iron weights and internal mechanisms to begin making their own – by the turn of the century, Bornholm had developed its own rich tradition of handcrafted clockmaking. Each component of a **Bornholmer clock** – from the pendulum to the glass face and the pastel-painted or gilded wooden body – was meticulously crafted by hand, and the finished pieces were exported to the rest of Europe and beyond. Today, original Bornholmer clocks are proudly displayed in local homes, and if in good condition, older models can fetch upwards of 60,000kr.

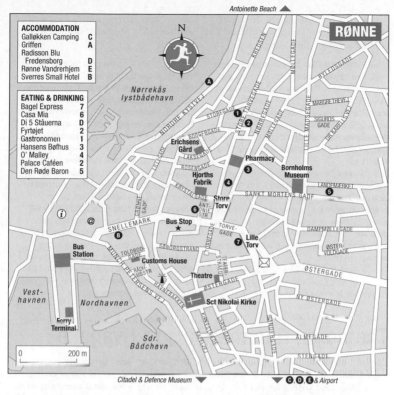

RØNNE

ACCOMMODATION
Galløkken Camping   C
Griffen   A
Radisson Blu
  Fredensborg   D
Rønne Vandrerhjem   E
Sverres Small Hotel   B

EATING & DRINKING
Bagel Express   7
Casa Mia   6
Di 5 Ståuerna   D
Fyrtøjet   2
Gastronomen   1
Hansens Bøfhus   3
O' Malley   4
Palace Caféen   2
Den Røde Baron   5

N

Nørrekås
lystbådehavn

Erichsens
Gård

Pharmacy

Bornholms
Museum

Hjorths
Fabrik

Store
Torv

Bus Stop

Lille
Torv

Bus
Station

Customs House

Theatre

Vest-
havnen

Nordhavnen

Sct Nikolai Kirke

Ferry
Terminal

Sdr.
Bådhavn

0   200 m

BORNHOLM | Rønne and around

3

    Though **swimming** is best on the eastern side of the island, Bornholm's southern coast holds plenty of good, sandy tracts, the nearest of which is at Galokken, 2km south of town. From here, the coast stretches another 30km east, offering hundreds of secluded spots for bathing, easily accessed from the main road. Bus #7 follows this route, but it's much more convenient to take a bike.

Nylars Rundkirke

Some 10km southeast of Rønne, the **Nylars Rundkirke** (May to mid-Oct Mon–Sat 9am–6pm) is the best preserved of Bornholm's four medieval *rundkirke* (for more on which, see box, p.147). Built in 1165 to honour St Nicholas (from which Nylars is derived), it has changed little since the sixteenth century, when it underwent a major restoration, and sports the typical tri-level *rundkirke* construction that allowed it to be used for both defensive and religious purposes. Look out for the two runic stones at the south entrance and, inside, several elegant frescoes on the nave's column depicting the Garden of Eden, which date back to 1250. The church is reachable via bus #6 from Rønne – get the driver to show you where to get off, then walk several hundred metres north along Kirkevej. If you're on a bike, you can get to the church from Rønne via the Rønne–Åkirkeby path in half an hour or so.

Eating

Rønne has a number of very good places to **eat**, from picturesque waterside restaurants to takeaways. Bornholm's limited **nightlife** scene is also centred in

www.roughguides.com

141

Rønne, the picks being the Irish pub *O'Malley*, Store Torvegade 2, the trendier *Palæ Caféen*, Store Torvegade 20, and *Den Røde Baron*, Skt Mortens Gåde 48, a disco popular amongst the younger set.

Bagel Express Lille Torv 10 ⓦ www.bagelexpress
.dk. Simple, airy café selling fresh, salads, bagels and ciabattas spread with any number of toppings.
Casa Mia Antoniestræde 3 ☎ 56 95 95 73, ⓦ www.casamia-bornholm.dk. Very good pizzas and pasta dishes (from 68kr) served in a homely Mediterranean-style setting and presided over by a friendly Italian-born Bornholmer. Daily except Tues 4.30–10pm.
Di 5 Ståuerna Strandvejen 113 ☎ 56 90 44 44. Though this sophisticated restaurant, attached to the swank *Radisson* hotel, is a bit out of the centre, its fine continental food is some of the best on the island. Beautifully presented dishes like mushroom steak with chilli sauce or gorgonzola filet of veal with garlic start at around 200kr, and there are also plenty of fish options.
Fyrtøjet Store Torvegade 22 ⓦ www.fyrtoejet.dk. Large, bright and done out in classy wood accents, this rustic-style restaurant serves tasty lunch

dishes from 35kr – try the great shrimp smørre-brød. The dinner buffet (5–9pm; 159kr) includes steamed fresh vegetables, cuts of roast beef and various rice and pasta dishes. Closed Sun mid-Jan to March, Mon April–June & mid-Aug to mid-Dec.
Gastronomen Torvegade 29 ☎ 21 48 75 77, ⓦ www.gastronomen.dk. Run by one of Bornholm's best-known chefs, who bases the evening's experi-mental meals on available ingredients and diners' suggestions, mixing island and Italian recipes to create some special dishes (798kr). Reservations recommended. Closed Mon & Tues.
Hansens Bøfhus Nørregade 2 ☎ 56 95 00 69, ⓦ www.hansens-beufhus.dk. Traditional place serving excellent lunch plates of *æggekage, Sol over Gudhjem* and pan-fried plaice. It's more popular at dinnertime, with its menu of fourteen different steak and beef dishes that includes the yummy speciality, a porterhouse steak with horse-radish sauce and redcurrants.

The north: Hammershus to Svaneke

Looking out towards Sweden, Bornholm's north coast is astoundingly rocky, the jagged, exposed bedrock and snaggled cliffs barbed with grottoes and ravines at water level, and with a series of cliffs that reach nearly a hundred metres in some places. A century ago, all this igneous rock made the island the hub of Denmark's once-raging granite industry, a fact made dramatically clear in the barren, bored-out landscape of inland quarries and a handful of deep, artificial lakes. At the north-western tip of the island, the evocative remains of the **Hammershus** castle, the largest fortress complex in northern Europe, are well worth a visit, while the nearby **Hammerknuden** cliffs and **Slotslyngen** forest provide for hours of invigorating walking. Working east along the coast, past the thriving neighbouring towns of **Allinge** and **Sandvig, Gudhjem** is a perfect base for explorations around the island, with a good choice of places to stay and eat. The town also receives a breath-taking light off the sea, which has made it a haven for Bornholm's great landscape artists, many of whose works are on display at the nearby **Bornholm Art Museum**. East of here, the land softens somewhat, with a few paths along the pebbled and rough-sand beaches, while at the far eastern tip, **Svaneke** is perhaps the most picturesque and alluring town on Bornholm, best known for its delightful weekend market and thriving craft galleries.

Hammershus and around

Sitting pretty atop a beautiful coastal hillock nearly 100m above the sea, the craggy ruins of the once-majestic **Hammershus castle** (unrestricted access; free) are Bornholm's biggest tourist attraction. Built around 1260, the stronghold was the home of the island's sundry Swedish rulers until 1658, when a number of Bornhol-mers armed themselves and overtook it, thereby returning rule of the island back to Denmark. The castle was abandoned in 1743 and partially dismantled, after which islanders hauled away its stone to build homes. There was a partial restoration in 1900, though you'd never know it, as much of the original structure is largely in rubble, but the craggy outlines of the tower, armoury, chapel and stables still give a sense of Hammershus in its heyday.

You enter the castle grounds from the bus and car park to the northeast, where a **visitor centre** (May to late Oct daily 10am–6pm) doles out information on the history and layout of Hammershus, has a small exhibition (10kr) and runs recommended English-language guided tours on demand. From here, a path leads across a dual-arched Gothic brick bridge – the only intact medieval bridge still standing in Denmark – over what was once the outer moat, and continues up past a weapons and goods store to the **fæstningsporten**, the main gatetower. Slightly further ahead is the massive square **manteltårnet** tower, at the top of which Christian IV's illegitimate daughter Leonora Christina and her husband Corfitz Ulfeldt were imprisoned after being convicted of treason; at one point they managed to escape by climbing down the outside walls via knotted bedsheets, but were recaptured soon after. While the tower itself stands largely intact, much of the rest of the brickwork in and around here has crumbled away; you can see out to the surrounding headland, encircled by the ruins of a 1km-long perimeter wall that once protected the entire fortress grounds.

Exiting the fortress grounds to the south takes you along any of three two-kilometre paths that wind through the **Slotslyngen forest** down to the fishing village of Vang, where there's a good restaurant (see p.144) and a stop for bus #1 south to Rønne or north to Allinge. The hike closest to the coast offers the best views out to the sea. On the opposite (northern) side of the fortress, an equally narrow path heads north for 1.5km to the enclosed harbour of **Hammerhavn**, from where you can hop on a motorboat for a forty-minute trip along the coast (T56 48 04 55, Wwww .hammerhavnensbaadfart.dk; 60kr), which gives a good perspective on how intimidating Bornholm must have looked to would-be attackers, whose cliffs must have seemed a formidable obstacle to soldiers weighed down by their chain-mail armour and heavy weaponry. The boats only seat a dozen passengers, and so are small enough to enter some of the narrow gorges creviced into the cliffs.

Allinge and Sandvig

The largest settlements along Bornholm's northwestern coast, Allinge and Sandvig were established as medieval fishing villages, later serving as the centre of Bornholm's thriving quarrying industry. There's little to do or see in either town, but both offer a pleasant stopoff on the way to or from Hammershus. **ALLINGE** is the larger of the two, its harbour (the departure point for boats to Christiansø; see p.147) dominated by a slew of restaurants and cafés; smack in the town centre, look out for the sizeable runic stone out in the churchyard of the sixteenth-century Gothic church. Just outside town, past the tall, brick-red *tårnhuset* tower, with its small glass observation room, a small path leads to the rocky mound of **Madsebakke**, where a sloping ridge overlooking the sea holds Denmark's largest extant display of Bronze Age *helleristinger* (rock engravings), small boulders covered with simple carved figures of ships, animals, footprints and crosses. The small cove of **SANDVIG**, another kilometre or so on, has a fine sandy shallow beach that's good for a dip and offers access to the escarpment of **Hammerknuden**, a grassed-over mass of rounded rock topped with heathy vegetation that complements the stark views out to sea.

Practicalities

Buses #1 and 7 run to Hammershus, while both Allinge and Sandvig are served by routes #1, 2, 7 and 9. **Tourist information** can be found at Nordbornholms Turist-bureau, Kirkegade 4 in Allinge (Mon–Fri 9am–3pm, plus June–Aug Sat 9am–2pm;

T 56 48 64 48, W allinge.bornholm.info), which also books hotel rooms for an 85kr fee. A good range of **accommodation** hereabouts makes this a good base for exploring Bornholm's northerly pockets. Of the two towns, Allinge has the best selection, and its shining star is the ℞ *Hotel du Nord*, Storegade 4 (T 20 95 12 53, W www.hotel-du-nord.dk; late June to mid-Aug; ⑥), a newly built, thoroughly modern and intimate hotel set a few hundred metres from Naes beach, and offering seven bright rooms with sea views that are the embodiment of rustic chic. Also fairly upscale is *Hotel Romantik*, Strandvejen 68 (T 56 48 03 44, W www.hotel-romantik .dk; ⑦), set right on the water with a range of atmospheric sea-view rooms. Slightly more middle-of-the-road is *Byskrivergaarden*, Løsebækgade 3 (T 56 48 08 86, W www.byskrivergaarden.dk; early May to late Sept; ⑦), a fetching half-timbered farmstead also at the water's edge that even has a small beach for wading and sunning; the rooms tend towards the basic, but some have sea views. Finally, *Gæstgiveren*, Theaterstræde 2 (T 56 44 62 30, W www.gaestgiveren.dk; late June to mid-Aug; ⑦), is a really lively place, with colourful, musical-themed rooms, great organic barbeques and lively music events throughout the summer season. Sandvig, meanwhile, boasts one of the island's best cheapies, the *Sjøljan Hostel*, Hammer- shusvej 94 (T 56 48 03 62, W www.cykel-vandrerhjem.dk; open April to late-Oct), offering dorms (150kr) as well as a few private rooms (③); it's 1.5km southwest of town opposite a small lake. *Lyngholt Familiecamping* (T 56 48 05 74, W lyngholt -camping.dk), at Borrelyngvej 43, 5km south of Allinge in the Slotslyngen forest near Vang, is a large and lively campsite offering a vast swimming pool – though its cabins are usually only available by the week.

In terms of **eating**, check out the barbeque events at *Gæstgiveren* (see opposite) in Allinge or the good smoked salmon dishes at the quiet *Blomster Cafeen*, Hammer- shusvej 2. For something a bit classier, venture just south of Hammershus to the harbourside settlement of Vang, where ℞ *Le Port*, Vang 81 (daily 11am–10pm; T 56 96 92 01, W www.leport.dk), is an upmarket spot that's perfect for a romantic dinner, with delicious French cuisine, appropriately blasé service, and spectacular sunset views from tables on the terrace; the garlic-fried prawns are especially tasty. Count on 900kr for dinner for two with wine, or arrive before 4pm to order off the 90kr lunch menu. Bus #1A stops just below the restaurant at Vang's harbour.

Bornholms Kunstmuseum and Helligdomsklipperne

Nine kilometres east along the coast from Allinge, the outstanding **Bornholms Kunstmuseum**, Søndre Strandvej 95 (April–May & Sept–Oct Tues–Sun 10am–5pm; June–Aug daily 10am–5pm; Nov–March Tues & Thurs 1–5pm, Sat & Sun 10am–5pm; 70kr; W www.bornholms-kunstmuseum.dk), is one of the most impressive art museums in Denmark. Its streamlined stone and glass structure is appealingly placed just inland from the Helligdomsklipperne cliffs (see opposite), and maintains some interesting architectural features, including a small observa- tion tower and a stream trickling through the main gallery, fed by water from nearby springs. The **galleries** hold a grouping of early- to mid-twentieth-century paintings by artists from both Bornholm and mainland Denmark, with particular focus given to the **Bornholm School**, whose painters – of which Karl Isakson, Kræsten Iversen, Olaf Rude, Edvard Weie and Oluf Høst are among the best repre- sented – made inventive use of pure, muted colour to produce work exploring new aesthetic directions in Danish painting. The hues and forms in works like Rude's *Still Life* and Kristian Zahrtmann's *Leonora Christina Receives her Oldest Daughter Anna Cathrina at Maribo Cloister* paint a clear picture of the strong current of modernism which defined Danish painting in the early twentieth century. Look out, too, for

Danish food and drink

If there is something rotten in the state of Denmark these days, it's certainly not the food. Since the turn of the millennium, Denmark has been at the forefront of a Scandinavian culinary renaissance, and its capital now boasts a total of fourteen Michelin stars – more than anywhere else in the Nordic countries. For most Danes, eating is inextricably linked with the sense of social occasion and cosy bonhomie known as "hygge" – great pride is taken in preparing delicious meals, perfect for lingering around the table late into the evening. In terms of drinking, you'll find a very relaxed and healthy attitude to alcohol here, and plenty of tempting bars in which to taste marvellous locally produced beers.

Herring in a smokehouse ▲

Smørrebrød ▼

Danish cuisine

Whether at a five-star restaurant or a harbourside smokehouse (*røgeri*), fish and seafood is one of Danish cuisine's strongest suits, and classic dishes like fresh fried plaice served with new potatoes and a buttery parsley sauce are surefire winners. Caught, salted, dried and smoked here for centuries, herring is central to Danish cuisine. The most popular preparation, and a fixture of the smørrebrød table, is **marinated herring** – raw herring left in a salt solution for several years (the longer it's left, the softer it becomes), and then marinated in sweet white vinegar flavoured with anything from onion and black pepper to cloves, sherry, dill or a hot tomato mixture. Though Denmark is known abroad for its bacon, locals prefer the more sophisticated concoctions – flavour-packed salamis and cold cuts – laid out on smørrebrød tables. Hearty hot **pork** dishes include *medister pølse* (a thick, spiced pork sausage eaten with sweet and sour pickled red cabbage) and the festive *flæskesteg*, roast pork with crackling.

Smørrebrød

The quintessentially Danish open sandwich, **smørrebrød** is delicious and utterly addictive, and you'll find no shortage of restaurants dedicated to this culinary phenomenon. It consists, simply enough, of a thin slice of dark, dense rye bread (*rugbrød*), loaded up with delectable combinations of hot or cold meat or fish and garnished with dollops of sauce and thin slices of fresh or pickled vegetables; we've listed the most common combinations below. A smørrebrød meal is usually served in three courses – a herring starter, a hot and cold

Rullepølsemad

Dyrlægens natmad Liver paté (*leverpostej*) with thin slices of salted beef and squares of meat aspic, garnished with raw onion and cress.

Stjerneskud Fried plaice and shrimp topped with a dollop of mayonnaise, red caviar, a sprig of dill and a slice of lemon.

Rullepølsemad Thin slices of *rullepølse* (rolled pork belly seasoned with herbs), topped with horseradish and cress.

Ribbensteg Slices of cold roast pork with sweet-and-sour pickled red cabbage (*rødkål*), garnished with a slice of orange.

Spegepølsemad Slices of salami topped with rémoulade (mayonnaise laced with pickles and capers) and crispy roasted onions (*ristede løg*).

Sol over Gudhjem Smoked herring with chopped raw onions and capers, topped with a raw egg yolk – a speciality of Bornholm.

▲ Outdoor eating in Copenhagen

▼ Choosing cakes

meat option, and a cheese board at the end – and traditionally, each course is washed down with a shot of ice-cold **snaps**, a strong, clear spirit typically flavoured with caraway or aniseed and intended to cleanse the palate.

Smørrebrød is generally eaten at lunchtime, and there's a certain etiquette to be followed when ordering. In specialized smørrebrød restaurants, the traditional way is to tick off your choice of pre-set pieces (*stykke*) from a long list (*smørrebrøds seddel*). In less traditional restaurants, you can usually get a **smørrebrøds platter** consisting of a selection of four to five pre-combined pieces; other places just lay out the three courses of toppings **buffet-style** (*det kolde bord*), so you can get creative and make up your own.

Danish pastries ▲

Copenhagen brewpub ▼

Café, Louisiana Museum of Modern Art ▼

Danish pastries

Light, flaky and best bought straight from a bakery in the morning, a real **Danish pastry** melts in the mouth and makes the perfect accompaniment to a cup of coffee. Here, "a Danish" is known as Viennese bread (**wienerbrød**) – the recipe was introduced by a Viennese baker in the mid-nineteenth century. *Wienerbrød* come in all shapes and sizes, and are flavoured with a variety of spices and fillings – and each has its own nickname. Look out for **hanekam** ("rooster's comb"), comb-shaped, with almonds and icing, and **bagerens dårlige øje** ("the baker's infected eye"), a delicious buttery confection with a glob of jam or custard at its centre.

Skål!

The list below details some of Denmark's best beers, and where to try them.

▶▶ **Jacobsen Dark Lager**, Carlsberg's Jacobsen microbrewery, Copenhagen. A dark, Bavarian-style lager brewed using an original 1847-era recipe, this is the inspiration for all Danish beers. See p.75

▶▶ **Hancock Dark Gambrinus**, Hancock Bryggerierne, Skive. A heavy, inky lager that in spite of its strength (9.5 percent) doesn't taste overly alcoholic. See p.273

▶▶ **Nørrebro Northbridge Extreme**, Nørrebro Bryghus, Copenhagen. US-inspired ale from Copenhagen's most popular brewery-restaurant. See p.86

▶▶ **Fur Ale**, A delightful lager brewed with water filtered through the cliffs of north Fur. See p.274

▶▶ **Brøckhouse IPA**, Brøckhouse, Hillerød. From one of Denmark's oldest modern microbreweries, this award-winning pale ale has a strong, hoppy flavour; best sampled at Copenhagen beer parlours such as *90eren*. See p.85

▶▶ **Thy Pilsner**, Thisted Bryghus, Thisted. Among the best of the classic Danish pilsners brewed using techniques borrowed from the Czechs. See p.269

three of Høst's best-known works, stark and ghostly sketch-like portraits of life at his Bognemark farmhouse, just east of the museum grounds. More modern trends in local painting, sculpture and graphic arts are also represented, and the museum houses the largest collection of Danish handicrafts outside Copenhagen, though these are still much less interesting than the paintings. Just behind the museum, there's a good spot from which to take a look at the 22-metre-high **Helligdom-sklipperne** ("Sanctuary Cliffs") that characterize Bornholm's northern coast, and which sheltered ships during stormy weather for centuries (hence the name).

To get to the museum, you can take bus #7 from Rønne, Allinge and Gudhjem via the coastal Helligdomsvej; be careful along this busy stretch of road if you're walking or cycling. There is also a knobbly, rutted six-kilometre route from Gudhjem (allow at least 90min) and regular boats from Gudhjem harbour to the base of the Helligdomsklipperne, from where steps lead up to the museum.

Gudhjem

For hundreds of years, Danish artists have been attracted to the gorgeous light that falls on the diminutive fishing village of **GUDHJEM** ("God's Home"). With its steep streets lined by brightly coloured, red-roofed houses scenically spread between two harbours, Gudhjem is one of Bornholm's more picturesque villages, and its central position along the north coast makes it a great base for seeing the rest of the island.

Information and accommodation

Getting to Gudhjem is straightforward, as many island buses stop just along Ejnar Mikkelsensvej opposite the harbour. Gudhjem's good range of places to stay makes it pretty popular with visitors, so it's always worth reserving rooms in advance. If you're stuck for a bed, the small **tourist office** (May to early Sept Mon–Fri 9am–3pm; ☎56 48 52 10), Åbogade 9, can locate rooms in private homes.

Gadegård Gudhjemvej 52 ☎56 48 52 85, ⓦwww .pfunch.dk. Part of a picturesque farmhouse run by a charming couple a few kilometres south of Gudhjem towards Østerlars, this spiffy, furnished apartment sleeps up to four and is a great option if you fancy a whole week on the island. 4000kr per week.

Gudhjem Vandrerhjem Ejnar Mikkelsensvej 14 ☎56 48 50 35, ⓦwww.danhostel-gudhjem.dk. This year-round youth hostel, with dorms (175kr) and doubles (④) has an enviable location right at the harbour and bewitching sea views from most of the rooms. It also has laundry facilities and rents out bicycles (70kr per day) and a few old pieces of fishing gear (85kr, including licence and lure).

Jantzen's Hotel Brøddegade 33 ☎56 48 50 17, ⓦwww.jantzenshotel.dk. Some of the island's classiest digs are these sixteen

smallish but extremely charming rooms in a creaky fin-de-siècle building; some have sea views and small cast-iron balconies. The sumptuous breakfasts are divine, and are included in the rate. ⓞ

Melsted Badehotel Melstedvej 27, Melsted ☎56 48 51 00, ⓦwww.melsted-badehotel.dk. Just east of Gudhjem in the small town of Melsted, this upscale waterfront spot does Gustavian chic well, with pale oak flooring and terraces off comely rooms and a sprawling lawn with lounge chairs. Dramatic views of the crashing waves, too. Mid-April to mid-Oct. ⑧

Strandlunden Melstedvej 33 ☎56 48 52 45, ⓦwww.strandlundencamping.dk. The facilities at this sheltered beachfront camping spot, 1km east of town, are more spartan than other campgrounds, but its spectacular waterside location offers access to a sandy small beach. Mid-May to mid-Sept.

The Town

The town is centred around an assortment of boutiques, cafés, restaurants and galleries lining the lively Brøddegade, a street so steep that cycling on it is banned. Once you've had a wander, head west to the **Oluf Høst Museum**, Løkkegade 35 (early May to mid-June Tues–Sun 11am–5pm; mid-June to late Sept Mon–Sat 10am–5pm, Sun 2–5pm; 60kr; ⓦwww.ohmus.dk), which pays homage to the island's best-known artist, famous for his colourful explorations of local life, from sunsets to summer bathers and wintry sea views. Høst lived and painted here until his death in 1966, and the studio has been converted to display a collection of his lesser-known works (the more famous ones can be seen at the Bornholms Kunstmuseum; see p.144). From the museum, Nørresand takes you around to the small harbour, where the waterside smokehouse is a great place to try the local speciality, a **Sol Over Gudhjem** sandwich, a herring fillet topped with an egg yolk and onion ring, served with radishes, chives and salt; the taste vaguely calls to mind a steak tartare.

Eating

Gudhjem has several excellent **restaurants** and **cafés**. *Pandekagehuset*, Brøddegade 15 (April–Oct daily 8am–midnight), is a great little crêperie (most around 30kr) with a small terrace; it also serves beer, wine and delicious coffee. Even more casual – and much more atmospheric – is ⅍ *Gudhjem Røgeri*, Ejner Mikkelsensvej 9, the local smokehouse and the best place to try the Sol over Gudhjem sandwich. There's a sizeable buffet lunch (noon–4pm), but you're better off buying some fresh shrimp or smoked fish by the kilo and eating on the benches outside. Slightly more upscale is *Bokulhus*, Bokulvej 4 (☎56 48 52 97, ⓦ www.bokulhus.dk; July–Aug daily 11.30am–9pm; May–June & Sept–Oct Thurs–Sun 5.30–9pm), set just up from Gudhjem within a spectacular estate, which offers half a dozen elegantly prepared Danish dishes with a French twist (200kr) on a terrace – try the house speciality, bacon-baked cod. Otherwise, the restaurant inside *Jantzens Hotel* is run by a great local chef who does some amazing takes on Danish cuisine. For dessert, *Karamel Kompagniet*, Holkavej 2 (ⓦ www.karamelkompagniet.dk), sells delicious home-made toffee.

Østerlars

Some 6km south of Gudhjem, **ØSTERLARS** is worth a visit to see the **Østerlars rundkirke** (Mon–Sat 9am–5pm; 10kr) on its northern outskirts. The largest and best-known of Bornholm's *rundkirke* (for more on which see box opposite), the building features the distinctive conical roof as well as slanting external buttresses tacked on in the Middle Ages to support the walls. Inside, the elegant restored pulpit and altarpiece both date from the seventeenth century, while twelve lovely fourteenth-century frescoes, fully restored in 2006, are worth a peep. The church is located immediately east of Gudhjemvej, halfway between Østerlars town and the **Bornholms Middelaldercenter** (Medieval Centre; May to mid-Oct Mon–Fri 10am–4pm, July until 5pm; 95kr; ⓦ www.bornholmsmiddelaldercenter.dk), a reconstructed fourteenth-century Scandinavian village where various re-enactments of period life are staged in the summer. Buses #3 and #9 stop just outside.

Svaneke

With a picturesque market square lined with cafés, tiny boutiques and craft galleries and spectacular scenery of steep cliffs, **SVANEKE** places high in the list of Bornholm's most charming towns. Since the island's now-defunct railway never reached this far east, the town remained relatively isolated from modern development, and today's residents champion Svaneke's rich past with strict laws prohibiting any building taller than three storeys. Until a few years ago, the town was a favourite haunt of Danish retirees, but recent years have seen a massive influx of **craftsmen** – mostly potters and glassblowers – whose workshops now dominate the town.

Start by exploring the large Torvet which, on Saturday mornings, hosts one of the most atmospheric (and eccentric) **markets** in Scandinavia, with crowds of locals and visitors perusing the stalls selling knitwear, jewellery, knick-knacks, and *æbleskive* – scrumptious fried balls of dough dabbed with jam and powdered sugar – while enjoying accordion players and mime acts. From here, head east along Brænderigænget to visit some of Svaneke's craft workshops, many of which are opened up to visitors so that you can watch the craftsmen as they work. At the **Pernille Bülow glassworks**, at no.8 (June–Aug Mon–Fri 9am–9pm, Sat & Sun 9am–6pm, Sept–May Mon–Fri 9am–6.30pm, Sat 9am–5pm, Sun 9am–4pm; Ⓦ www.pernillebulow.dk), you can try your hand at making your own glass vase or buy a professionally blown one fashioned by Pernille herself. For ceramics, try the studios a block north of here at Nansensgade 4 and 8.

Practicalities

Svaneke's **tourist office**, which also covers the beach towns of Dueodde and Snogebæk, is 100m northwest of Torvet at Storegade 24 (Mon–Fri 10am–5pm, plus Sat 9am–2pm May–Aug; ☏ 56 49 60 40, Ⓦ svaneke.bornholm.info). Though there isn't much in the way of **accommodation**, one sure bet is ⚡ *Siemsens Gård*, Havnebryggen 9 (☏ 56 49 61 49, Ⓦ www.siemsens.dk; April–Oct; ⑤), a former merchant's home across the harbour that's now a well-run hotel offering antique-furnished rooms, some with a terrace looking onto the leafy yard out back, others with views across a large courtyard straight out to sea. Other options include a **youth hostel**, 500m south of town at Reberbanevej 9 (☏ 56 49 62 42, Ⓦ www .danhostel-svaneke.dk; April–Oct; dorms 160kr; ③), and a **campsite**, *Svaneke Familiecamping*, Møllebakken 8 (☏ 56 49 64 62, Ⓦ www.svaneke-camping.dk; mid-May to mid-Sept), set on a quiet bit of land 500m north of town, with a few small wooden cabins (from 300kr; late June to early Aug weekly rentals only).

In terms of **eating** and **drinking**, the cosy bar and restaurant inside the ⚡ *Bryghuset* brewery, Torvet 5 (Ⓦ www.bryghuset-svaneke.dk), is a worthy choice, both to try the draught beers – best are the hoppy, golden ale and fresh-tasting, unfiltered pilsner – or for a **meal**, with several beef dishes (from 169kr). Across the square at Brænderigænget 3, *Pakhuset* (Ⓦ www.restaurantpakhuset.dk) has a remarkably similar menu, though with a bit more variety, including a few seafood and vegetarian dishes. For lighter fare, the popular restaurant at the *Siemsens Gård* hotel serves a dozen or so novel takes on smørrebrød.

Christiansø

A rugged, grassed-over speck in the middle of the Baltic, some 18km northeast of Bornholm, **CHRISTIANSØ** is the largest island in the remote Ertholmene ("Green Pea") archipelago, and makes a lovely day-trip from Bornholm spent walking the abandoned battlements and having a meal at the lone – and lovely – inn. Characterized by its enclosing fortress wall and fortified stone tower, Christiansø has a population of around a hundred and measures just 710m across, crisscrossed by some fetching manicured paths that can make for a very pleasant afternoon stroll.

With a view to keeping a close watch on the militarily superior Swedes, Christian V established a **naval base** on Christiansø in 1684, erecting two blocky stone towers surrounded by bastions and enclosing walls abutting the rough sea. The island served as a resting point for Denmark's navy during its eighteenth-century military incursions in and around the Baltic, but in 1855, when relations with Sweden had improved, the base was decommissioned, and many of the soldiers who had come to call the island home chose to stay on as fishermen. Today, the island is largely bankrolled by Denmark's **Ministry of Defence**, which has kept the island's grounds and fortress buildings in rather good nick.

At the top of the steps that lead up from Christiansø's boat dock is the island's combined inn, restaurant and provisions shop (see below), though the best way to start exploring is to head straight over the bridge to tiny **Frederiksø**, a neighbouring island holding the **Lille Tårn** stone tower and its ragtag **museum** (daily 11am–4pm; 10kr) detailing these islands' naval past – including a scale model of the fortifications as they looked in 1855 – as well as some information on the bird species that inhabit the area (mostly auks, guillemot and eider ducks). Once you've had your fill, cross back over to Christiansø, where you can climb up the craggy stairs of the larger **Store Tårn** (Mon–Sat 11.30am–4pm, Sun 11am–2pm; 10kr) and take in a lovely panorama of the archipelago from the lighthouse at the top. The only other thing to do here is head out on a leisurely stroll along the island's fortifying perimeter wall, taking time to admire the mighty black **cannon** that guards the southwestern edge of the parapet and the well-tended gardens and pretty half-timbered or stone cottages in which the islanders live – though you'll rarely need much more than an hour or so. On the eastern side of the island is a **bathing jetty** from where you can wade around a cool inlet of the Baltic. If you want to take back a bit of Christiansø, look out for the locally made *slåensnaps*, a tasty, tart snaps made from sloe berries that grow here – you can pick up a bottle at the small grocery adjacent to the inn.

Practicalities

Between May and September, regular Christiansøfarten **boats** (☎56 48 51 76, ⓦwww.christiansoefarten.dk) ply the choppy waters between Christiansø and Bornholm, leaving from Gudhjem (Mon–Fri 10am, 12.30pm & 3.05pm, Sat & Sun 12.30pm) and Allinge (daily 10.45am, plus Tues–Thurs 1pm & 3.30pm, Sat & Sun 3.15pm); journey time varies from thirty minutes to one hour and each boat returns roughly four hours later. Out of season, a postal boat makes the trip from Gudhjem only (Mon–Fri 10am). Round-trip tickets cost 220kr between July and early August, and are slightly cheaper off-season.

Since Christiansø is so small, you only need a few hours (at most) to fully explore it, but if you're in the mood for some real seclusion, the island is a peaceful place to **stay**. The wonderful ⅍ *Christiansø Gæstgiveri* (☎56 46 20 15, ⓦwww.christiansoekro.dk; ❼; closed Jan) has six rustic-style rooms, each with private bath, and its outstanding **restaurant** serves scrumptious seafood dinners and lunches, and is very popular with day-trippers. There is also a small **campsite** (☎24 42 12 22) on the eastern side of the island. In summer, you'll need to book well in advance for both options.

Åkirkeby and the interior

The oldest merchant settlement on the island, **ÅKIRKEBY** was founded in 1346 as a trading centre for local farmers, and served as the island's administrative and religious centre until the honour was passed to Rønne in 1660. Today, it offers little of interest besides **NaturBornholm** (daily April–Oct 10am–5pm, last entry

4pm; 95kr; Ⓦwww.naturbornholm.dk), a few minutes' walk from the town centre at Grønningen 30. The Henning Larsen-designed museum is filled with fascinating environmental and geological exhibits that take you through billions of years of Bornholm's history – there's everything from dinosaur fossils to a sample of the oldest rock in the world, forged an unimaginable 3.85 billion years ago in Greenland. By no coincidence, the museum is located on the Klintebakken hills atop the faultline where the island's granite and gneiss northern half is fused with the soft and supple sandstone of the south; just out behind the building, you can visit the remarkable quarry where the two separate seismic plates meet. A few kilometres south of here is **Vingården Lille Gadegaard**, Søndre Landevej 63 (daily 4–9pm; ☎56 97 80 63, Ⓦwww.a7.dk), the island's best-known liquor producer; the small, rustic café offers the perfect excuse to sample some whiskey.

Unless you're headed to the island's woodlands for some hiking, you'll have little use for the town's **tourist office**, Hans Romersvej 1 (Mon–Fri 10am–4pm, plus Sat mid-May to mid-Aug 9am–1pm; ☎56 97 37 20), and with ample coastal inns and hotels splayed out from Åkirkeby in all directions, there is little real reason to **stay**. **Food**-wise, your best bet is *Gåsen*, Jernbanegade 1, which serves tasty Danish meals in a 200-year-old former school.

Almindingen forest

The third largest woodlands in Denmark and occupying most of Bornholm's central highlands, **Almindingen forest**'s six thousand acres are peppered with lakes, ponds and bogs that help support a rich array of flora and fauna. The forest is dense in some parts, less so in others, and latticed by a dozen or so trails that are perfect for an afternoon of leisurely, sheltered walking or cycling. Several of Bornholm's arterial roads pass through Almindingen, so getting to and around it by bike, bus or car is easy, and there are numerous car parks at the various forest entrances. The eastern and western portions of forest offer the best **hiking**; you can pick up detailed free trail maps at the Åkirkeby tourist office (see above).

The southern beaches

Bornholm's southeastern tip, known as the "golden seaside" for its wide, clean stretches of sand, is the island's **beach** country, with several kilometres of sandy strand that run from Dueodde on the south coast to Balka, nearly halfway up the eastern shore. The beaches are busiest in July and August, but you should be able to find a quiet spot; most facilities in the beach towns are open from May to September only.

Beachbum-types head straight for **DUEODDE** (pronounced "doo-AWE-uuh"), one of Denmark's best-known **beaches** and the most popular on the island. The powdery sand here is some of the finest in Europe and was long used in the production of hourglasses, while the shoreline encompasses a variety of terrain, from towering dunes and extensive coastal sandbars in the south to places just north of town where the dense forest reaches all the way to the water's edge. Note that the point from which the beach narrows has been designated Bornholm's only (semi-) official **nudist beach**, Jomfrugård. Looming over the coastline is a stark 47-metre-high **lighthouse** (May–Oct dawn to dusk; 5kr), which you can climb to get some breathtaking views, especially beautiful when the sun is setting over the plains just west. Just north of Dueodde, the small hamlet of **SNOGEBÆK** is mostly dominated by newer homes, summer cottages and a couple of rather good restaurants. For more beach, it's best to continue just north to **BALKA**, which has an extensive sandbar that's ideal for young children but makes swimming a chore.

Practicalities

Information and maps on all the beach towns can be found at the **tourist office** several kilometres north of Balka in Nexø, Sdr Hammer 2A (Mon–Fri 10am–5pm, plus May–Aug Sat 9am–2pm; ⓣ56 49 70 79, ⓦnexoe.bornholm.info). The beaches' popularity means that there's plenty of **accommodation** around Dueodde, though this is often dominated by long-stay, apartment-style places. For shorter sojourns, best bet is *Dueodde Badehotel*, Sirenevej 2 (ⓣ56 48 86 49, ⓦwww .dueodde-badehotel.dk; May to late Oct; ❼/❾), just minutes from the beach, with sparkling-white apartment-style rooms, some with kitchenettes. The rustic apartments at the *Hotel Bornholm* (ⓣ56 48 83 83; ⓦwww.borntours.dk; May–Sept; ❼), just 300m from the beach at Pilegaardsvejen 1, have full kitchens, terraces and access to a pool, and you can usually swing a discount if you stay for a few days. Elsewhere, *Dueodde Vandrerhjem og Camping*, Skrokkegårdsvejen 17 (ⓣ56 48 81 19, ⓦwww.dueodde.dk; May–Sept) has perfectly acceptable doubles (❼), some en suite. **Camping** is best at *Møllers Dueodde Camping*, Duegårdsvej 2 (ⓣ56 48 81 49, ⓦwww.dueodde-camp.dk), whose prize location is set right in the pines just beside the beach and excellent facilities, including a large pool, bike rental, cafeteria, laundry and **two-person** cabins (❷) that you'll need to beg to rent for less than a week. In Balka, try the *Hotel Balka Søbad*, Vestre Strandvej 25 (ⓣ56 49 22 25, ⓦwww.hotel-balkasoebad.dk; ❼), a modern hotel complex right on the sand offering well-sized rooms, a sauna, a large pool and a private beach.

For **food**, Snogebæk has the best options hereabouts: ✳ *Æblehaven*, Hovedgaden 15 (ⓣ56 48 88 85, ⓦwww.aeblehaven.com; closed Tues), serves traditional Scandinavian dinners with good wines on a pebbled terrace, while the smokehouse at the harbour (May–Oct 10am–6pm, until 8pm June–Aug) is a great place to have a drink and try the catch of the day. For dessert, there are delicious and expensive chocs at *Kjærstrup Chocolate by Hand*, Hovedgaden 9 (ⓦwww.kjaerstrup.dk), which also sells organic ice cream. In Dueodde, try the grilled fish at *Dueodde Badehotel* or the large salmon buffet (180kr) at *Granpavillonen*, Fyrvej 5 (May–Sept).

Travel details

Trains

Rønne to: Copenhagen (3–5 daily; 2hr 50min inc. ferry).

Buses

The frequencies below relate to the peak summer season (late June to mid-Aug); outside of that time, services are reduced during the weekend.
Allinge/Sandvig to: Hammershus (every 30min; 15min), Rønne (every 30min; 45min–1hr), Vang (4–7 daily; 20min).
Dueodde to: Rønne (hourly; 45min).
Gudhjem to: Allinge/Sandvig (hourly; 20min); Rønne (12 daily; 35min).
Hammershus to: Allinge/Sandvig (every 30min; 15min); Rønne (every 30min; 55min).
Rønne to: Allinge/Sandvig (every 30min; 45min–1hr); Åkirkeby (hourly; 30min); Dueodde (hourly, 45min); Hammershus (every 30min; 55min);

Gudhjem (hourly; 35min); Nexo (every 20min, 50min–1hr 10min); Svaneke (hourly; 55min); Vang (hourly; 35min).
Svaneke to: Dueodde (hourly; 45min); Rønne (hourly; 55min); Allinge/Sandvig (hourly; 25min).
Vang to: Allinge/Sandvig (7 daily; 20min); Rønne (hourly; 35min).

Ferries

Allinge to: Christiansø (1–2 daily; 1hr 10min).
Christiansø to: Allinge (1–2 daily; 1hr 10min); Gudhjem (2-3 daily; 30–1hr)
Gudhjem to: Christiansø (2–3 daily; 30min–1hr).
Rønne to: Køge (2 daily; 6hr); Ystad (3–6 daily; 1hr 15min–2hr 30min).

Flights

Rønne to: Copenhagen (3–6 daily; 35min).

4

Funen

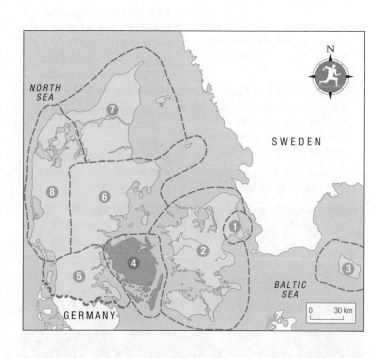

CHAPTER 4 Highlights

✳ **Åfart canal boat** This trip along the placid Odense canal stops off at several interesting attractions, including one of Denmark's most engaging open-air museums. **See p.160**

✳ **Odense nightlife** This lively city of students and yuppies is one of Funen's most happening spots for getting out and partying. **See p.162**

✳ **Ladby Boat** The burial vessel of a Viking chieftain, preserved in situ in a hi-tech subterranean museum. **See p.167**

✳ **Svendborg Harbour** Filled with dozens of wooden ships, this atmospheric harbour is a brilliant place to soak up some maritime flavour. **See p.168**

✳ **Egeskov Slot** Built on a bed of thousands of oak timbers, this fifteenth-century fairytale castle is surrounded by dazzling gardens. **See p.171**

✳ **Valdemars Slot** Soak up a bit of sumptuous noble ambience and stroll around the gilded corridors, plush salons and opulent sitting rooms of this mid-seventeenth-century castle . **See p.175**

✳ **TICKON Park, Langeland** Tranekær's striking vermilion castle is surrounded by a vast parkland speckled with dozens of eccentric modern sculptures. **See p.178**

✳ **Ærøskøbing** This beautifully preserved medieval town boasts scores of entrancing gabled buildings and some wonderfully rustic places to lunch. **See p.179**

▲ TICKON Park sculpture

Funen

C hristened "the garden of Denmark" by locally born Hans Christian
Andersen, **Funen** (*Fyn*) is the smaller of the two main Danish islands, and
one which lures its visitors with its bucolic feel, gorgeous coastline and
the mythology of Andersen himself. Unlike Zealand and Jutland, attractions here are mainly low-profile, consisting of a myriad remote **castles** and
manor houses – 124 to be precise – many of which maintain tree-lined avenues,
landscaped gardens and fertile agricultural fields that are often as enjoyable to visit
as the buildings themselves. Towns and villages are also small-scale, their
thatched, half-timbered buildings fronted by hollyhocks and orchards. Funen
maintains a well-developed **bus** network (though less in the way of **trains**) that
facilitates access to most of the major sites, plus a few of the minor ones, though
given their diminutive size, "mainland" Funen and its southern archipelago are
better explored by **bicycle**, with well-marked paths that circumnavigate much of
the coastline and pass through the major urban areas, all detailed in cycling maps
available from local tourist offices.

Arriving from Zealand across the massive Storebælt bridge, the towns of **Nyborg**
and **Kerteminde** hold a good collection of museums, while the isolated **Hindsholm
Peninsula** has several good beaches. South of here, **Odense** is Denmark's third-
largest city (though it feels more like an oversized town) and an obvious base.
Further south past the dazzling **Egeskov castle**, coastal Funen is dominated by two
towns: maritime **Svendborg** is the top scenic draw, with its sandy beaches, great
restaurants and interesting museums, while further west is the more rustic **Fåborg**,
with its pretty pastel period houses and superb art museum. The fragmented archipelago of pretty **islands** off Funen's south coast is summer vacation territory for
many Danes. The largest, **Tåsinge** and **Langeland**, are both accessible via road
bridge and offer plenty of opportunities for walking and swimming, as well as a
couple of grand old buildings. The smaller **Ærø**, accessible by ferry, holds a delec-
tably preserved medieval town and a slew of atmospheric inns and hotels, while the
tiny spits of land that make up the rest of the archipelago are beautifully unspoilt.

Odense and around

Funen's sole industrial centre, and one of the oldest settlements in the country,
ODENSE – named after Odin, chief of the Norse gods, and pronounced
"OWN-suh" – gained prominence in the early nineteenth century when its canal
was linked to the sea, making it the major transit point for produce of the island's
farms. Nowadays, Denmark's third-largest city feels much less industrial, a pleasant

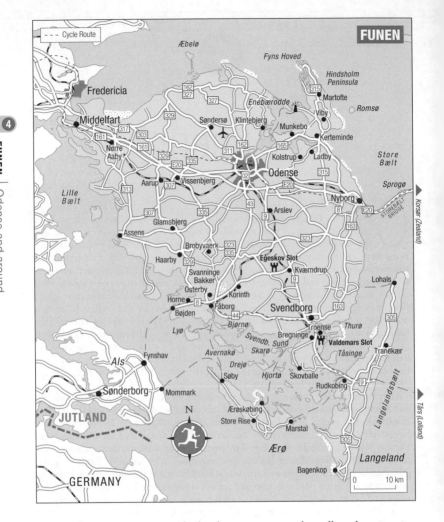

provincial university centre with absorbing museums and excellent shopping, its large manufacturing sector hugging the northern bank of the canal well out of sight of the compact old centre. The **old town** itself houses some fine museums and – thanks to the resident students – a surprisingly vigorous nightlife, and is great for a spot of aimless wandering. Odense is also known, throughout Denmark at least, as the birthplace of Hans Christian Andersen, a fact discreetly celebrated with souvenir shops and hotels. Elsewhere in town, it's worth making the effort to take in one of several absorbing **art collections** and check out the morbid contents of the crypt that lies beneath the city's **Gothic cathedral**. Odense, like Funen itself, is occasionally known as the "green garden of Denmark", and has an accordingly large number of **public gardens** – most notably in the southern part, where the lush Munke Mose meadow follows the narrow Odense canal. To the **north** and **south of town** lie a few other attractions, including the reconstructed nineteenth-century Funen Village and the Iron Age Village.

Arrival, information and city transport

Odense's **train station** is part of the large Odense Banegård complex, at the northern edge of the town centre along Østre Stationsvej. From here, it's a ten-minute walk to most city sights and hotels, as well as one hostel. **Long-distance buses** terminate behind here at the bus station on the northern side of the train tracks, while **city buses** depart just east on Dannebroggade. Odense **airport** (ⓦ www.odense-lufthavn.dk) is 10km north of town, though is not reachable by public transport. Odense's centre is 5km north of the E20 motorway, though much of it is pedestrianized and so off-limits to cars. Moreover as the jumble of one-way streets that are actually driveable can confuse and irritate even the most patient driver, you're best off leaving your car in one of the numerous, well-signposted metered city **car parks**, the largest of which is around Vindegade and Slotsgade (8kr per hr), just south of the train station. There is no charge for parking on most city streets between 6pm and 8am weekdays, after 2pm on Saturday and all day Sunday.

The **tourist office** (mid-June to Aug Mon–Fri 9.30am–6pm, Sat & Sun 10am–3pm; rest of year Mon–Fri 9.30am–4.30pm, Sat 10am–1pm; ☏ 66 12 75 20, ⓦ www.visitodense.com) is centrally located within the Rådhus complex on Vestergade. In addition to booking accommodation (35kr charge), it hands out the helpful, free *What's On* guide, which has comprehensive listings of city happenings, with summaries in English.

Nearly all of Odense's key attractions are in the compact city centre, which is best explored **on foot**. For some of the outlying sights and accommodation, however, you'll need to take a city **bus**. Flat-fare tickets for travel within the city limits cost 16kr (pay as you board); if you have to use more than one bus, ask the driver for an *omstigning* ("transfer ticket"). Be sure you have exact change, as drivers won't.

The tourist office (see above) **rents cycles** for 100kr per day (plus 500kr deposit), and stocks three very useful cycling brochures: *Twelve Biking Tours in Southern Funen* (35kr), *Cycling Map Funen* (119kr) and *Cycle Routes in Odense* (free); this last offers comprehensive suggestions for touring in and around the centre and up the Odense canal – the city and environs hold over 350km of bikeable paths. An English-language website (ⓦ www.cykelby.dk) provides additional information about biking around Odense.

Accommodation

Thanks to the Hans Christian Andersen connection, Odense has no shortage of pricey **accommodation**. There are several affordable alternatives, though, including several hostels and campsites just outside the city centre and a number of central and affordable B&Bs. All fill up during the summer, so book ahead.

Hotels and B&Bs

Billesgade Billesgade 9 ☏ 66 13 00 74, ⓦ www .billesgade.dk. A few minutes' north of the train station, the rooms at this B&B are compact but gorgeous, with bright cushions and modern Danish *objets* on the sills. All share bathrooms. ❸

City Hotel Odense Hans Mules Gade 5 ☏ 66 12 12 58, ⓦ www.city-hotel-odense.dk. Bright, sparkling, upmarket option with a prominent yellow facade that resembles a modern church, just a 3min walk from the train station: continue straight along Østre Stationsvej. Though lacking any real character, the brown and beige en-suite rooms are cosy enough. ❻

Det Lille Hotel Dronningensgade 5 ☏ 66 12 28 21, ⓦ www.lillehotel.dk. Small hotel run by a friendly proprietor and his family; most of the pleasant, simply designed rooms are en suite. ❹

Pjentehus Pjentedamsgade 14 ☏ 66 12 15 55, ⓦ www.pjentehus.dk. Beautifully renovated old house in the heart of Odense's cobbled section, with a garden that guests can use. Rooms are fine, if on the small side, with shared bathrooms. Breakfast costs 45kr extra. ❸

Radisson SAS H.C. Andersen Claus Bergs Gade 7 ☏ 66 14 78 00, ⓦ www.radissonsas.dk. Ideally placed on the quiet cobblestone streets in the east part of town, and just 100m from

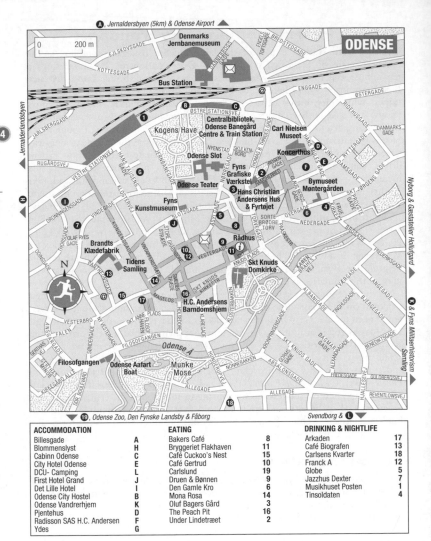

, Jernaldersbyen (5km) & Odense Airport

Denmarks Jernbanemuseum

ODENSE

0   200 m

Bus Station

Centralbibliotek, Odense Banegård Centre & Train Station

Kogens Have

Carl Nielsen Museet

Koncerthus

Odense Slot

Fyns Grafiske Værksted

Odense Teater

Hans Christian Andersens Hus & Fyrtøjet

Bymuseet Møntergården

Fyns Kunstmuseum

Rådhus

Brandts Klædefabrik

Skt Knuds Domkirke

Tidens Samling

H.C. Andersens Barndomshjem

Filosofgangen

Odense Aafart Boat

Munke Mose

19, Odense Zoo, Den Fynske Landsby & Fåborg

Svendborg &

Jernalderlandsbyen

Nyborg & Gæsteatelier Hollufgård

K & Fyns Militærhistorisk Samling

ACCOMMODATION		EATING		DRINKING & NIGHTLIFE	
Billesgade	A	Bakers Café	8	Arkaden	17
Blommenslyst	H	Bryggeriet Flakhaven	11	Café Biografen	13
Cabinn Odense	C	Café Cuckoo's Nest	15	Carlsens Kvarter	18
City Hotel Odense	E	Café Gertrud	10	Franck A	12
DCU- Camping	L	Carlslund	19	Globe	5
First Hotel Grand	J	Druen & Bønnen	9	Jazzhus Dexter	7
Det Lille Hotel	I	Den Gamle Kro	6	Musikhuset Posten	1
Odense City Hostel	B	Mona Rosa	14	Tinsoldaten	4
Odense Vandrerhjem	K	Oluf Bagers Gård	3		
Pjentehus	D	The Peach Pit	16		
Radisson SAS H.C. Andersen	F	Under Lindetræet	2		
Ydes	G				

H.C. Andersen's museum, this old-style chain hotel can feel a bit worn, but the rooms are spacious and have all necessary mod cons. Service is first-rate, there's a sauna in the basement and the buffet breakfasts are memorably lavish.

Ydes Hans Tausens Gade 11 ☎66 12 11 31, ⓦwww.ydes.dk. Inexpensive, basic place with smallish rooms, comfortable beds and extremely genial staff. Reception is located at its slightly more upscale sister hotel, *Domir*, just down the street at no.19.

Hostels

Odense City Hostel Østre Stationsvej 31 ☎63 11 04 25, ⓦwww.cityhostel.dk. Right next to the train station, this is an efficient, brightly decorated hostel with somewhat antiseptic dorms (265kr; June–Aug only) and doubles spread out over several floors. The helpful staff have loads of brochures.

Odense Vandrerhjem Kragsbjergvej 121 ☎66 13 04 25, ⓦwww.odense-danhostel.dk. Much quieter than its urban counterpart, offering dorms (235kr) and slightly cheaper doubles. The bland interiors are offset by the great setting in a wood-beamed farmhouse placed around a cobbled and grassy courtyard, some 2km southeast of the town centre; take bus #61 or #62 from the train station or cathedral south towards Tornbjerg or Fraugde and get out along Munkebjergvej at the junction with Vissenbjergvej. Open March–Nov.

Campsites

Blommenslyst Middelfartvej 494 ☎65 96 76 41, ⓦwww.blommenslyst-camping.dk. Facilities are pretty basic here, but the location, just next to a picturesque lake, is lovely. There are some extremely small cabins (320kr) that sleep four and have basic kitchenettes. The site is about 10km from Odense; half-hourly buses #830, #831, #832 or #833 from the train station make the journey in 20min.

DCU-Camping Odensevej 102 ☎66 11 47 02, ⓦwww.camping-odense.dk. This is the only campsite actually in Odense, fully equipped, with excellent cooking facilities and a few cute red cabins (❸). Take bus #21, #22 or #23 from the Rådhus or train station towards Højby, or take the Odense Åfart boat and it's 1km from the Funen Village stop.

The City

Since most of Odense is easily explored on foot, you should familiarize yourself with the half-dozen pedestrianized streets which wend through the centre, among them the **Vestergade** and a number of smaller streets off it, such as the cobbled passageways of the upscale Brandts Passage or the more down-to-earth Vintapperstræde; these narrow walkways have some of the city's best shops as well as many of its most popular bars and cafés.

Around the station

The first museum you're likely to see when you arrive to Odense – at least if you're coming by train – is more interesting than you might initially think. **Danmarks Jernbanemuseum** (Danish Railway Museum; daily 10am–4pm; 48kr; ⓦwww .railmuseum.dk), immediately behind the station, houses some of the state railway's most treasured artefacts, from aged train carriages to a recreation of an early twentieth-century station, all with excellent descriptions in English. The most notable of the carriages are those which belonged to Danish royalty, including Frederik VII's 1854 personal saloon, an old wooden jalopy found abandoned in a Jutland meadow. In much better condition are two sumptuous royal train cars from the 1870s, upholstered in thick silk brocade and furnished with plush velvet chaise-longues and recliners.

On the other side of Østre Stationsvej, just south across the manicured Kongens Have park, is the city's palace, **Odense Slot**, currently in use as a municipal office building but worth a quick glance. The adobe-roofed Italian Baroque structure was built in 1720 by Frederik IV just before he embarked on the much grander Fredensborg Slot (see p.111), a structure with which it shares some similarities – in the symmetrical layout, bevelled windows and colour scheme of its facade. During the early 1800s, when the *slot* was the royal residence of prince governor Christian VIII, H.C. Andersen's mother was employed here as a washerwoman and often brought young Hans to work with her so the shy youngster could play with other children – the future Danish king Frederik VII among them – in the front yard. The adult Andersen's maladroit likeness is prominently visible in the bronze statue out front.

Around the corner from the *slot*, there's a celebration of Odense's second most famous son in the **Carl Nielsen Museet** (June–Aug Fri–Sun noon–4pm; rest of year Mon–Wed 2–5pm; free), an hotchpotch of a museum inside the concert hall at Claus Bergs Gade 11. The **exhibits** detail the acclaimed composer's life and achievements, with mimeographed scores, photos, letters and even a crochet set he used to while the time away whilst bed-ridden after a serious heart attack. Nielsen's personal items are arranged in recreations of the rooms he used to compose in, and you can listen to some of his works on headphones, including excerpts from the polka he wrote when still a child.

Carl Nielsen

Born just outside Odense in 1865, **Carl Nielsen** displayed prodigious musical gifts from an early age, and went on to gain (posthumous) worldwide acclaim as a composer, particularly for his lush, sweeping symphonies; the musical cognoscenti in his own country later regarded him as having salvaged Danish music from a period of decline. Despite his travels, and long period of residence in Copenhagen, Nielsen championed the inspirational qualities of Funen's environment and the island's tuneful dialect, even writing a now-beloved essay romanticizing the landscape in which "even trees dream and talk in their sleep with a Funen lilt". If you've never heard of Nielsen, be assured that his music is nowhere near as half-baked as his prose: one of his greatest works was a cantata, *Springtime in Funen*, which he wrote in 1921 for the thousand singers of the Danish National Choral Society, and it's since become a key work in the repertoire of Danish national heritage. Nielsen was also well loved for his popular songs based on Danish folk poetry. An English translation of his well-written autobiography, *My Childhood on Fyn*, is on sale at the museum shop.

The H.C. Andersens Hus and around

Odense's showpiece museum is the **H.C. Andersens Hus** (June–Aug daily 9am–6pm; Sept–May Tues–Sun 10am–4pm; 60kr; ⑩museum.odense.dk), at Bangs Boder 29 in the house where the writer was born and which he described in *The Fairy Tale of My Life*. Oddly enough, Andersen was only really accepted in his own country towards the end of his life; his real admirers were abroad, which perhaps explains why he left Odense at the first opportunity and travelled so widely. Though he wrote novels and a few (best-forgotten) plays, it's his **fairy tales** that have gained most renown, partly autobiographical stories (not least *The Ugly Duckling*) that were influenced by *The Arabian Nights*, German folk stories and the traditional Danish folk tales passed on by inmates of the Odense workhouse where his grandmother tended the garden.

The darker aspects of Andersen's life are conspicuously neglected in the museum, but it is nevertheless stuffed with intriguing items: bits of school reports, his certificate from Copenhagen University, early notes and manuscripts of his books, chunks of furniture and his umbrella as well as paraphernalia from his travels, including the piece of rope he carried to facilitate escape from hotel rooms in the event of fire. A separate gallery contains a library of Andersen's works in seventy languages, and headphones for **listening** to some of his best-known tales as read by the likes of Sir Laurence Olivier. Nearby is a very mixed collection of illustrations and other art inspired by his writing, including Andersen's own meticulous paper cuttings and drawings, many of which were used to illustrate his books.

The Andersen theme is continued just next to the Hus at **Fyrtøjet** (Tinderbox; late June to early Aug daily 10am–5pm; early Aug to late June Tues–Sun 11am–4pm; 70kr; ⑩www.fyrtoejet.com), Hans Jensens Stræde 21, a sort of indoor cultural playground for kids based on Andersen's stories with costumes, fairytale sets, frequent storytelling events (in Danish) and other organized group activities.

Skt Knuds Domkirke and around

Immediately south of the tourist office, the thirteenth-century **Skt Knuds Domkirke** (Mon–Sat: April–Oct 10am–5pm; Nov–March Mon–Sat 10am–4pm; ⑩www.odense-domkirke.dk) is one of the finest Gothic churches in Denmark. The exterior is a riot of profiled bricks and layered silled windows, while inside, the main draw is the finely detailed sixteenth-century wooden altarpiece, rightly regarded as one of the greatest works of the German-born master craftsman, Claus Berg.

Commissioned in 1521 by Queen Christine, the massive altar is swathed in 23-carat gold, its central carvings depicting characters and scenes from the Old Testament; the outer sixteen panels show (horizontally, from left to right) the Passion and the events from Easter to the Pentecost. At the base of the altar, supporting the panels, rests a portrait of the royal family, kings Hans and Christian II on the left, their queens to the right, and a resurrected Christ in the centre to emphasize the role of religion in holy matrimony.

You might also want to visit the crypt to see one of the most unusual and ancient finds Denmark has to offer: the **skeleton of Knud II** (aka Canute), who was slain in 1086 by Jutish farmers angry at the taxes he'd imposed on them. The murder took place in the original wooden church that stood here, Skt Albani Kirke, in which the king was laid to rest in 1101, but the miraculous events of the following years (see p.286) resulted in his canonization as Knud the Holy, Denmark's first saint; his remains were subsequently moved to the present Domkirke. If you look closely at the skeleton, which rests on ninth-century silk pillows, you can observe some bone fragmentation in the pelvic region – it's believed that Knud was bludgeoned to death while genuflecting at the altar.

There's more (but not much more) about Andersen a few minutes northwest of the church at the tiny **H. C. Andersens Barndomshjem** (H.C. Andersen's Childhood Home; June–Aug daily 10am 4pm; Sept–May Tues–Sun 11am–3pm; 25kr), Munkemøllestræde 3–5, set in the house where Andersen lived from 1807 to 1819 before moving to Copenhagen, and the few austere rooms here, which hold little in the way of furniture or accoutrements, serve as a reminder of his childhood poverty.

Hans Christian Andersen

Few storytellers are as well-known for their poignant observations on the frailty of humanity as **Hans Christian Andersen**, the grandfather of the modern fairy tale and author of 156 stories, 800 poems, 43 plays and 11 novels. Born in Odense on April 2, 1805, Andersen grew up very poor and was, by all accounts, roughly brought up. Bright and ambitious, the young Hans read Shakespeare and Grimm at an early age, and began acting, singing and writing his own poetry and drama while still in primary school, though he regularly suffered humiliation at school because of his awkwardly gangly figure and less-than-masculine interests.

Andersen published his first collection of stories at the age of 24: **Tales, Told for Children** appeared in 1835 as a small, inexpensive booklet, and was followed two years later by a larger volume already containing classics such as **The Little Mermaid**, **The Emperor's New Clothes** and **The Princess and the Pea**. Andersen's style was initially criticized for being too vulgar and grotesque, but by the time he reached his early thirties, he had written his way from destitute child to wealthy adopted son of the upper classes, heralded across Europe as a literary sensation, winning unprecedented fame and cementing his place in the canon of great European literature.

Andersen's ability to identify and empathise with the outcast, the unfortunate and the hopeless undoubtedly helped to make his stories so compelling. The painful feeling of "being different" is a recurrent motif in his work, most notably in *The Little Mermaid*, whose central character takes her own life because she cannot be loved by a beautiful prince. Andersen's own relationships with women were perpetually tragic: his innumerable crushes were almost never reciprocated, something which drove him deep into a shell of self-pity. He never married and, as far as anyone can tell, died a virgin. Tall and lanky, with gaunt features highlighted by a long nose, close-set eyes and a well-receded hairline, Andersen may have believed he wasn't going to be anyone's prince charming, and despite all the admiration bestowed on him throughout his life, his loneliness made fame and critical acclaim something of a narcotic for him. He died at the age of 71, and is buried in a modest plot at Assistens Kirkegård, Copenhagen (see p.78).

Odense's art museums

Although most visitors come to Odense on the H.C. Andersen trail, the city also offers a couple of excellent art museums. Best is the **Fyns Kunstmuseum** (Funen Art Museum; Tues–Sun 10am–4pm; 40kr; Ⓦwww.museum.odense.dk), a few minutes' walk from the cathedral at Jernbanegade 13. The collection here gives a good sense of the region's importance to Danish art during the late nineteenth century, when a number of Funen-based painters gave up creating portraits of the rich in favour of impressionistic landscapes and studies of the lives of the peasantry. Highlights include Hans Brendekilde's enormously emotive 1889 *Udslidt* ("Exhaustion"), a tragic study of the lot of a peasant farmer, Helge Holmskov's 1968 larger-than-life, bespectacled iron bust of sculptor Adam Fisher and the mid-eighteenth-century Rococo portraits by islanders such as Jens Juel.

If you're in the mood for some more modern art, head along Vestergade, then Jernbanegade, and turn down Brandts Passage to reach the **Brandts Klædefabrik** (Ⓦwww.brandts.dk), an expansive former textile factory now given over to a number of cultural endeavours, including three museums (all Tues–Wed & Fri–Sun 10am–5pm, Thurs noon–9pm; visitable individually as detailed or on a combined 70kr ticket), a cinema and trendy cafés and restaurants. The **Kunsthallen** gallery (40kr) is a prestigious spot for exhibitions of high-flying new talent in art and design; close by are the varied displays of the large **Museet for Fotokunst** (35kr), taken from the cream of modern art photography and almost always worth a look. There's also the more down-to-earth **Danmarks Mediemuseum** (Danish Media Museum; 35kr; Ⓦwww.mediemuseum.dk), with its bulky machines and devices chronicling the historical development of printing and bookbinding. Further down Brandts Passage on the second floor of no. 29, the **Tidens Samling** (Old-Time Museum; daily 10am–4pm; 40kr; Ⓦwww.tidenssamling.dk) furnishes visitors with intimate insight into changing trends in interiors and fashion and home interiors since the beginning of the last century.

Out from the centre

While Odense's most famous sights are conveniently contained within walking distance of the city centre, the outskirts hold a couple of worthwhile attractions. In the summertime, one of Odense's most enjoyable activities is an afternoon jaunt aboard the **Odense Åfart** (Ⓦwww.aafart.dk; 50kr single, 70kr return), a small passenger vessel which sails daily along the Odense canal from Munke Mose park in the city centre, stopping at the Odense Zoo and ending up at Fruens Bøge, a short walk from Den Fynske Landsby. Bus #42 follows more or less the same route, but as services are infrequent, the boat is actually the most efficient way to travel. It departs on the hour from May to mid-Sept (10am–5pm). On Saturday afternoons from late June to mid-August, when passengers are serenaded by a jazz band, the fares go up a bit (60kr one-way, 120kr return), and it's best to book tickets in advance on ☎66 10 70 80.

The boat's first stop is at the **Odense Zoo** (check for hours; 130kr; Ⓦwww .odensezoo.dk), quite enjoyable as far as zoos go, with the usual lions, tigers and giraffes, but a more compelling time awaits a few minutes further on along the canal at the **Den Fynske Landsby** open-air museum (April to late June & mid-Aug to mid-Oct Tues–Sun 10am–5pm; late June to mid-Aug daily 10am–6pm; late Oct to late March Sun 11am–3pm; June–Aug daily 10am–7pm; 40kr, 60kr in summer; Ⓦmuseum.odense.dk). This reconstructed nineteenth-century country village is lent an air of authenticity by its period gardens and wandering geese. From poorhouse to farmhouse, all the buildings are originals sourced from other parts of Funen, their exteriors painstakingly reassembled and interiors carefully refurbished. In summer, traditional trades such as blacksmithing are revived in the former workshops, and there are free shows at the open-air theatre. An English-language film shown in the main building gives some good historical context. The village is located several kilometres south of the city centre on Sejerskovvej, and bus #42 runs to the village from the city centre (get out at the Den Fynske Landsby sign).

Jernalderlandsbyen

Some 5km northwest of Odense at Store Klaus 40, and easily reachable from the town centre (take bus #91 north towards Allesø), the **Jernalderlandsbyen** (Iron Age Village; late July to mid-Aug Mon–Fri & Sun 10am–4pm; mid-Aug to late June Mon–Thurs 8.30am–3.30pm, Fri 8.30am–2pm; 25kr; ⓦ www.jernalder landsbyen.dk) is one of many prehistoric collections in Denmark based on archeological findings from all over the country, but this one at least makes an effort to be a bit different. The recreated prehistoric dwellings are in active use as workshops where you can see such ancient trades as shoemaking and metalwork. There's also an interesting mock TV news broadcast covering events in Bronze Age Denmark, alongside displays describing how ancient symbols are used in modern times. Fans of jousting, chain mail and smithery all across Funen count down the days to the village's hugely popular Iron Age market, held every year on the third weekend in May.

Eating

Most of Odense's **restaurants** are squeezed into the central part of the city, which means there's a lot of competition and, potentially, some very good bargains – and many of the places listed here are also good for a **drink** in the evenings. Lazy, late-morning **brunch** is a well-established tradition, with many cafés offering weekend (if not daily) brunch menus or buffets; the greatest concentration of these places is around Gråbrødretorv and along Brandts Passage.

Duke.'s Café Fiskeiui vei 2. Excellent sandwiches and freshly baked pastries.

Bryggeriet Flakhaven Flakhaven 2 ⓣ 66 12 02 22, ⓦ www.bryggeriet.dk. This brewery-restaurant serves home-brewed pilsner, lager, ale and wheat beer, along with gargantuan meat dishes such as spare ribs (from 106kr) and juicy T-Bone steaks (319kr).

Café Cuckoo's Nest Vestergade 73 ⓣ 65 91 57 87, ⓦ www.cuckoos.dk. One of the few spots with any life early in the week, and one of the best places for Sunday brunch buffet (10am–2pm; 120kr). Lots of seating options, from settees to massive rattan divans, are set across two courtyards and smaller dining rooms inside. There's often live jazz out front on summer evenings and weekends.

Café Gertrud Jernbanegade 8 ⓣ 65 91 33 02, ⓦ www.gertrud.dk. Adorned with brass trimmings, dark wood and movie memorabilia, this Scandinavian bistro offers a great daily brunch (9am–5pm, Sun from 10am; from 56kr) which includes ham, home-made muesli, fruit and local cheese, with tables out front.

Carlslund Fruens Bøge Skov 7 ⓣ 65 91 11 25, ⓦ www.restaurant-carlslund.dk. Typical Danish restaurant which does delicious smørrebrød and is famous for its æggekage menus (from 175kr).

There's live jazz on summer Saturdays, and reservations are recommended. You can get here on the Odense Åfart (see p.160), but after 4pm or so, you'll need to either walk the 3km back to town or take the train from Fruens Bøge.

Druen & Bønnen Vestergade 15 ⓣ 66 11 18 13, ⓦ www.druenogboennen.dk. This café-cum-wine bar, with curious furry rawhide seats and chess and backgammon tables, offers very good coffee and Scando-Mediterranean breakfast plates – paté, salmon and charcuterie – in the morning, and freshly made brie, salmon and tomato sandwiches in the afternoons and evenings.

Den Gamle Kro Overgade 23 ⓣ 66 12 14 33, ⓦ www.den-gamle-kro.dk. Four dining rooms are packed into this creaky old 1683 inn, festooned with old-world stained glass, cast iron stoves and etched ceramic tiling. Meals are traditional Scandinavian and continental dishes like flambéed pepper steak run from 198kr to 338kr, the latter being the Tournedos Rossini, with foie gras, vegetables and truffle sauce. If you can, try to get a seat in the covered, leafy courtyard or the vaulted cellar. Reservations recommended.

Mona Rosa Vintapperstræde 4 ⓣ 65 91 49 13, ⓦ www.monarosa.dk. Summer evenings see this reasonably priced Mexican restaurant packed with families and couples, spread across two terraces that give onto the cobbles of Vintapperstræde. The lunch set menu is a very reasonable 79kr, while à la carte in the evening starts at around 125kr.

The Peach Pit Mageløs 1 ☎65 90 75 00. Pizza parlour offering huge and very tasty slices (15kr) as well as kebabs and burgers. Open till 6am on weekends, making it the destination of choice for the munchies.

🏃 **Under Lindetraeet** Ramsherred 2 ☎66 12 92 86, ⓦwww.underlindetraet. dk. Set in a picture-perfect restored inn dating back to 1771, this is easily the most atmospheric and lavish Danish restaurant in town. Considering the superb setting and the excellent food, the three-course menus (445kr) of traditional Danish dishes are a bargain, and lunch mains are a steal at around 125kr.

Drinking, nightlife and live music

After the sun sets, Odense's pedestrianized streets come alive as townies and visitors head out to take advantage of the ciy's superb nightlife. A surfeit of **late-opening cafés** have usurped the role of nightclubs as evening hangouts, several of them upscale, fashionable places attracting scantily clad Danish demoiselles and their hangers-on. Most of these establishments also function as restaurants, though the ones listed below are generally more known for their non-culinary goings-on.

Many bars put on **live music** on weekends, and several city music halls and concert spaces also host regular performances by bands from the Nordic countries – and occasionally further afield. On Thursdays in July between 7pm and 10pm there are live free rock concerts at Kongens Have, the public garden across from the train station, while the **Odense Symphony Orchestra** (☎63 75 00 50, ⓦwww .odensesymfoni.dk) puts on over one hundred classical music concerts each year at the Koncerthus, Claus Bergs Gade 9. The season stretches from September until April and tickets run between 70kr and 185kr, though students can get them for 25kr. The box office is open on concert days from 4pm onwards, plus Mondays to Wednesdays from 2pm to 5pm. Additionally, on Saturday mornings in August, orchestra members perform their much-loved **"Vegetable Concerts"** alongside the market stalls at Sorte Brødre Torv. For details of upcoming events, pick up the leaflets available at most cafés, music shops and the tourist office, check out Rytme-posten (ⓦwww. postenlive.dk) or grab a copy of the free *Odense Sommer Jazz* from the tourist office, which lists all of the city's summer jazz events.

For details on Odense's **gay and lesbian** scene, get in touch with the local organization Lambda (☎32 12 62 45, ⓦwww.lambda.dk).

Arkaden Vestergade 68 ⓦwww.cityarkaden.dk. If spring break ever took place in Odense, it would happen here. With six separate bars set in a mall-like arcade, this collection of loud and libidinous places to drink and dance is popular with both younger and older locals.

Café Biografen Brandts Passage 39–41 ☎66 13 16 16, ⓦwww.cafebio.dk. Enduringly fashionable and endearing Odense institution, decorated with a dazzling display of classic film posters. While the restaurant is quite popular, it's the bar that really gets going at night, mostly for a late-twenties to early-forties semi-professional crowd.

Carlsens Kvarter Hunderupvej 19 ⓦwww .carlsens.dk. Inexpensive, unpretentious pub serving fruity Belgian beers, English ales and a couple of *Fynske* microbrews. Danish folk music occasionally accompanies.

Franck A Jernbanegade 4 ☎66 12 27 57, ⓦwww.francka.dk. One of Odense's hippest places, this modern café is best known for its after-dinner boozing, when the DJs spin top-40 Euro hits for an over-30 crowd. Live music later in the week (usually Thurs). Cocktails start at 65kr.

Globe Asylgade 7–9. Odense's oldest disco, popular with twentysomethings and still *the* place to go after-hours, with live music, stand-up comedy and lots of dancing. Cover around 50kr.

Jazzhus Dexter Vindegade 65 ☎63 11 27 28, ⓦwww.dexter.dk. This expansive bar is a great place to hear some of the finest jazz in Denmark, from swing to fusion, four or five times a week until early morning. There is a cover (up to 120kr, but usually 50kr) all nights except Mondays, when students from Det Fynske Musikkonservatorium show off their licks at the open-mike jam sessions.

Musikhuset Posten Østre Stationsvej 35 ☏ 66 13 60 20, ⓦ www.postenlive.dk. Funen's prime live music venue, this converted post office hosts a lot of heavy rock bands. Tickets generally start at 100kr, though better-known bands can cost upwards of 220kr.

Tinsoldaten Frue Kirkestræde 3. This smoky dive-bar attracts early morning stragglers and is well known as Odense's last-ditch pick-up joint; the fun doesn't usually begin until well after 3am.

Listings

Banks and exchange There's a Den Danske Bank at Flakhaven 1, and a Nordea Bank at Vestergade 6; Forex is at the train station (Mon–Fri 9am–6pm, Sat 10am–3pm).

Bookshops Arnold Busck, Vestergade 54, and B.O. Bøger, Vestergade 59–61 both sell maps, guidebooks and some English-language titles.

Car rental Avis, Østre Stationsvej 37 ☏ 66 14 39 99; Europcar/Østergaard, Vestre Stationsvej 13 ☏ 66 14 15 44; PS Biludlejning, Middelfartvej 1 ☏ 66 14 00 00.

Hospitals There is an emergency department at Odense University Hospital, J.B. Winsløws Vej (☏ 66 11 33 33).

Internet access Free at the tourist office and at the city's library (Mon–Thurs 10am–7pm, Fri 10am–4pm, Sat 10am–2pm, plus Sun Oct–March 10am–2pm) in the train station complex, for which you must book in advance on ☏ 65 51 43 01. Also in the train station is Galaxy Netcafe (daily 9am–1am; 17kr per hr).

Laundry Møntvask at Vesterbro 44 (Sun–Fri 7am–8pm, Sat 7am–7pm) charges 30kr per wash including soap.

Left luggage The train station has both large (20kr) and small (10kr) lockers. You can also store bags in the building next to the tourist office for a pricey 15kr per day per item.

Pharmacy Apoteket Ørnen (☏ 66 12 29 70), Vestergade 80, is open 24hr.

Post offices The main office is in the train station at Dannebrogsgade 2 (Mon–Fri 8am–9pm, Sat & Sun 10am–4pm), and offers poste restante.

Swimming pools There is a central indoor public pool at Klosterbakken 5 (Mon–Fri 6.30am–7.30pm, Sat 7am–1pm; 28kr; ☏ 65 51 53 30), and an outdoor one 6km west of the city centre at Elsesmindevej 50 (May–Aug daily 10.30am–7pm, 28kr; ☏ 65 51 53 60).

Taxis Taxis can be hailed at the train station, or call Odense Taxa on ☏ 66 15 44 15. Initial price is 27kr, with 14.34kr added on for each kilometre driven. In addition, there are off-hours supplements tacked on between 8pm and 6am weekdays and all day Saturday and Sunday.

The northeast coast

Funen's easternmost town, **Nyborg** is connected to Zealand by the eighteen-kilometre **Store Bælt** ("Great Belt") road and rail link (see p.122). Most visitors see little more than its train station, but unless you're in a great rush it's worth sparing a few hours to take a stroll around the old town and thirteenth-century **castle**, the seat of Danish political power for two hundred years. North of here, **Kerteminde** is the home of one of Funen's most beloved wildlife painters as well as an aquarium that runs under the fjord, and is within easy distance of the meadows and forests of the **Hindsholm peninsula**, just north.

Nyborg and around

At the centre of the Store Bælt, **NYBORG** was strategically important as Funen's only fortified town, with large stockades and sinuous moats built to protect it against invaders approaching from both the Storebælt coast and from Funen's interior. Nyborg today is small and easily navigated, with dark red-brick buildings and what's left of the *slot* fortification reminders of a rich past. The central, pedestrianized Nørregade is home to most of the town's commercial action, with half a dozen cafes and boutiques that terminate at the town's main church, **Vor Frue Kirke** (June–Aug 9am–6pm, Sept–May 9am–4pm), Gammel Torv 1, dating from the late fourteenth century. The current structure is a late nineteenth-century rebuild, holding a few old fittings: a fourteenth-century crucifix at the chancel arch, the marble, neo-Gothic main font from 1876 and a post-Reformation wooden font from 1585, as well as an exquisite Baroque pulpit from 1653.

Head west from here on Nørregade to reach **Torvet**, flanked to the north and east by several stately looking municipal buildings, including Nyborg's original 1803 red-brick Gothic town hall and clocktower. After a fire in 1797 razed many of the town's buildings, the new limestone constructions were designed by Johan Jakob Encke, whose German background accounts for the Neoclassical feel of much of what's visible today. One exception, dominating the west side of the square, is the **Nyborg Slot** (daily: April–May & Sept–Oct 10am–3pm; July 10am–5pm; June & Aug 10am–4pm; 30kr; Ⓦwww.museer-nyborg.dk), Denmark's oldest intact castle, built around 1200 by Valdemar the Great as part of a chain of coastal fortresses to guard against piracy. For more than two hundred years, the summertime national assembly comprised of king, clergy and nobility known as the Danehof met here – most notably in 1282 to draw up Denmark's first constitution – which effectively made Nyborg the Danish capital until 1443, when power moved to Copenhagen. The castle bears little evidence of those years, however, and all that remains on view is a chunk of the front portal and a stubby, elongated building, its distinctive harlequin brickwork the result of a 1920s restoration. Inside, the first floor is by far the most impressive: check out the **Banquet Hall**, hung with a series of illuminated historical paintings and two massive genealogies of Christian III. To the south is the **Danehof Hall**, where the assembly met and discussed the constitution; the unusual geometrical wall pattern was added in 1520. Outside, you can climb up to the **ramparts**, now decked with replicas of the original cannon, or walk through the two posterns – brick, tunnelled passages that run under the ramparts – that allowed soldiers easy access between the lookout area and the stronghold. There is good documentation out here explaining the ruins, but try to time your visit to coincide with one of the informative English-language **tours** (June–Aug Wed & Sat 2pm; rest of year Sat 2pm; free). Between late June and August, the castle also hosts Danish and international musicians who perform choral, piano chamber and opera **concerts** in the Banquet Hall. Tickets (usually around 100kr) are available from the tourist office or on Ⓦwww.nyborgslotskoncerter.dk.

Practicalities

Nyborg sits at the base of the Nyborg fjord, dominated to the east by the mammoth Storebælt bridge linking Funen to Zealand; thanks to this bridge, the **train station** is now placed 1km outside of town. From here both trains and buses depart for destinations all across Funen. From the station, it's an easy walk to the town centre where the central **tourist office** is just opposite the castle at Torvet 9 (June to mid-Aug Mon–Fri 9am–5pm, Sat 9.30am–1pm; rest of year Mon–Fri 9am–4pm, Sat 9.30am–12.30pm; Ⓣ65 31 02 80, Ⓦwww.visitnyborg.dk). Although the bright lights of Odense are just 25km west, Nyborg isn't a bad place to hole up for a night, with a few inexpensive **accommodation** options in the centre and several pricier ones on the coast. Best of all is the resplendent *Hotel Hesselet* (Ⓣ65 31 30 29, Ⓦwww.hesselet.dk; ⑨), Christianslundsvej 119, with rooms in olde-worlde English style and upscale features like granite bathroom floors and immaculate period furniture, along with views out either to the Storebælt bridge or to the forest. A step down is *Villa Gulle*, Østervoldgade 44 (Ⓣ65 30 11 88, Ⓦwww.villa-gulle.dk; ④/⑤), a B&B with slightly stodgy but passable en-suite and shared rooms; it also rents out rowing boats (80kr per hr). *Nyborg Strandcamping* (Ⓣ65 31 02 56, Ⓦwww.strandcamping.dk; open April–Sept), Hjejlevej 99, is a lovely campsite on wooded grounds with a great beach, Fynsbadestrand, just south.

In terms of **food**, *Alanya*, Torvet 3 (☎65 31 13 23), is a Turkish restaurant set in a somewhat dark basement but with a courtyard terrace out back and a delicious 69kr lunch buffet; dinners are a bit pricier. Otherwise, a block away on Nørregade, *Central Caféen* (☎65 31 01 83) is a tad fusty on the inside, and much better at the back on the pleasant covered terrace, where you can enjoy traditional Danish dishes from 150kr. If you have your own transport, though, you'd do better to head to the atmospheric *Teglværksskoven* (☎65 31 41 40, ⓦwww.teglvaerksskoven .dk; closed Sun–Wed), right in the forest 3km northeast of town at Strandalleen 92, with excellently prepared traditional dishes from a three-course menu (328kr), each paired with wines (208kr). For evening revelry, *Slotscaféen*, just opposite the castle at Slotsgade 5, is as smoky and ratty a bar as you'll find, but a fine place to soak up some local colour.

Kerteminde and around

Some 20km north of Nyborg, past the huge cranes and construction platforms at Munkebo – until recently a tiny fishing hamlet, but now the home of Denmark's biggest shipyard – lies **KERTEMINDE**, itself a place with firm maritime links, with a collection of evocative older residences that still bear the imprints of early warehouses used to store merchandise from Odense's factories. Today, the town is a centre for sailing and beach holidays, and can get oppressively busy in high summer. At any other time of year, though, it makes for a well-spent day, split between the town itself, the Viking-era Ladby Boat just outside, and the verdant Hindsholm peninsula just to the north.

Kerteminde straddles the mouth of the Kerteminde fjord, its harbour – home to Funen's largest fishing fleet – sheltered by two large escarpments to the north and south. The town's centre is ranged around the worn, fifteenth-century **Skt Laurentius Kirke** on Strandgade, whose broad tower and brick nave date to 1350. Inside are a number of Baroque artefacts (the monogrammed pews, for example) and in a vaulted chancel wing, a pair of dangling boots and rapier sword belonging to a local soldier who died fighting off the Swedes in the 1659 Battle of Nyborg. The streets just around the church are the town's oldest: Chr. Jydesvej and Reberbanen, built to avoid transport of night-soil past the homes of the wealthy on Vestergade, and Strandgade and Langegade, which hold a prettily preserved nucleus of shops and houses.

At Langegade 8, in an old trading post dating from 1630, the town museum, **Farvergården** (March–Oct Tues–Sun 10am–4pm; 25kr), sports ten or so rooms that recreate the living and working conditions of townspeople over the years: a middle-class salon, a peasant's living room and a child's playroom, though the only exhibit of real interest centres on the tools of corporal punishment. From here, head south towards the harbour, across the road from the bus station on Margrethes Plads 1, to arrive at the **Fjord&Bælt** (mid-Feb to late June & mid-Aug to Nov Mon–Fri 10am–4pm, Sat & Sun 10am–5pm; late June to mid-Aug daily 10am–6pm; 95kr; ⓦwww.fjord-baelt.dk), an aquarium whose highlight is a fifty-metre-long underwater tunnel that runs 4m beneath the fjord's surface from where you can observe seals and porpoises in their natural environment. The centre also organizes one-hour boat trips (100kr) and two-hour snorkelling excursions (150kr) out to the fjord in summer.

On a grander note, a ten-minute stroll north of the harbour will take you to the one-time house of the "birdman of Funen", the painter Johannes Larsen, which has been opened up as the **Johannes Larsen Museet** (March–May & Sept–Oct Tues–Sun 10am–4pm; June–Aug daily 10am–5pm; Nov–Feb Tues–Sun 11am–4pm; 65kr). The delightful, airy residence, built by Larsen in 1901, has many of its furnishings and knick-knacks still preserved, the walls crammed with studies, sketches and paintings by the artist and his contemporaries. Larsen painted all four walls of the front dining room with a naturalistic winter motif – he intended the mural to be viewed as though looking through bay windows – though the amateurish figures make it clear that his talent lay in his sketches, working on a much smaller scale (see box below). Next door is Larsen's studio, a spacious room containing his most famous work, *Morning Sun* (1936), a study of a faceless, naked maiden wading in the sun-drenched sea. Out back, a large modern building showcases hundreds of Larsen's sketches – most notably his outstanding studies of birds in flight – as well as works by some fifty other Funen artists, including several haunting portraits by Fritz Syberg of his in-laws.

Practicalities

Buses from Nyborg (#890, #891, 37kr) and Odense (#880, #890, 51kr) arrive at a tiny station across from the Fjord&Bælt centre on Hans Schacksvej. Kerteminde's **tourist office**, around the corner at Hans Schacksvej 5 (May to early Sept Mon–Fri 9am–5pm, Sat 9am–4pm; early Sept to April Mon–Fri 9am–4pm, Sat 9.30am–noon; ☎65 32 11 21, ⓦ www.visitkerteminde.dk), has details of local accommodation bargains, which include over a dozen private rooms and B&Bs. A five-minute walk north of here on Hindsholmvej, you can **rent bicycles** (100kr per day) at the Statoil petrol station. Aside from B&Bs, the only truly low-cost **accommodation** option, a ten-minute walk from the town centre at Skovvej 46, is the *Danhostel Kerteminde* **youth hostel** (☎65 32 39 29, ⓦ www.dkhostel.dk), which has dorms (175kr) in simple, chalet-like rooms with four beds, and similarly sized doubles (④). To get there, cross the Kerteminde fjord via the Langesbro road bridge, take the first major road left and then turn almost immediately right. There's also a **campsite**, *Kerteminde Camping* (☎65 32 19 71, ⓦ www.kertemindecamping.dk; early April to late Oct); it's not far from the Larsen museum at Hindsholmvej 80, the main road running along the seafront – a twenty-minute walk from the centre. It has a few A-frame cottages (❸), though in July and early August these are only available by the week. For something more upmarket, try the central three-star *Tornøes Hotel*, right on the water at Strandgade 2 (☎65 32 16 05, ⓦ www.tornoeshotel.dk; ❻); its thirty bright rooms have all mod cons and the ones with lovely sea views only cost a few kroner more.

Inexpensive **eating** in Kerteminde isn't hard to come by, but a meal at *Rudolf Mathis*, Dosseringen 13 (☎65 32 32 33, ⓦ www.rudolf-mathis.dk), is well worth

---

Johannes Larsen

A Kerteminder born and bred, **Johannes Larsen** (1867–1961) is one of the best-known painters of the Funen school, and is remembered for his detailed depictions of wildlife – especially birds – and rural landscapes. Larsen studied in Copenhagen under Kristian Zahrtmann, aligning himself closely with contemporary notables such as Peter Hansen, Fritz Syberg and Poul Christiansen. His fascination with wildlife came to dominate his work throughout the latter part of his life, with many of his days spent at his home at Møllebakken taking in the seascape and making notes and sketches of the numerous birds to visit the grounds. Admiring the work at his museum in Kerteminde, you quickly become aware of his amazingly detailed technique: many of his pencil sketches are virtual anatomical studies of the wings, legs and joints of sea birds, often in full flight. In part, Larsen's intricate knowledge of such **anatomy** came about with the help of local townsfolk, who would often gift him the carcasses of dead birds. In 1921, Larsen set off with explorer and sketch artist **Achton Friis** aboard the *M/S Rylen*, a small wooden sailboat, for a four-year documentary expedition around 132 of Denmark's small islands; both he and Friis were convinced that the islands would soon be overcome by summer homes and plantations – a prediction which has effectively come true. The trip culminated in the book *De Danskes Øer* (Islands of the Danes), a beautiful collection of these sketches and paintings available for sale in the museum shop.

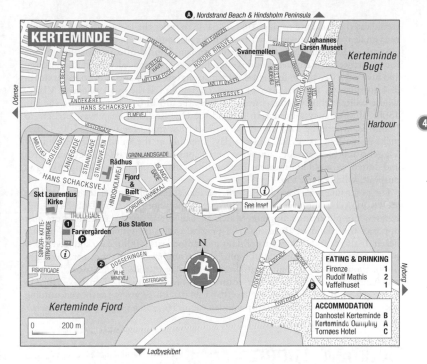

KERTEMINDE

Johannes Larsen Museet
Svanemøllen
Svanevej

Kerteminde Bugt

Harbour

4

FUNEN | The northeast coast

EATING & DRINKING
Firenze 1
Rudolf Mathis 2
Vaffelhuset 1

ACCOMMODATION
Danhostel Kerteminde ... B
Kerteminde Camping ..... A
Tornøes Hotel C

Kerteminde Fjord

0   200 m

▼ Ladbyskibet

a few extra kroner. But just on the harbour across the Langesbro bridge in an old smokehouse – look for the traditional twin white chimneys – it's famous across Funen for its haute cuisine steak and seafood dishes, like fjord lobster with pear chutney and lemongrass marinade (645kr for a four-course meal). In the town centre, *Firenze*, Trollegade 2F (Ⓦwww.rist-firenze.dk), is a small family-run Italian restaurant with sizeable pizzas for around 80kr and specials like steak fillet served with forest mushrooms and brandy cream sauce (199kr), while immediately next door, *Vaffelhuset* is the town's favourite ice-cream joint.

Ladby and the Hindsholm peninsula

An easy trip from Kerteminde is to head 4km southwest to the village of **LADBY** where, along the banks of the fjord at Vikingvej 123, you'll find the **Ladbyskibet** (Ladby Boat; March–May & Sept–Oct Tues–Sun 10am–4pm; June–Aug daily 10am–5pm; Nov–Feb Wed–Sun 11am–3pm; 45kr; Ⓦwww.kertemindemuseer.dk), a chieftain's burial vessel that offers a fascinating glimpse into Viking history. The 22-metre boat was buried, as per Viking tradition, with its owner and all his possessions – weapons, eleven horses and a pack of hunting dogs – and rested peacefully underground for close to a thousand years; it was discovered in 1935 and remains in the original spot where it was buried. Though the wood from the boat has mostly rotted away, its weight over so many centuries has left a perfect impression into the land here – preserved in the small air-cooled, Star Trek-esque subterranean museum – though the chieftain himself, along with any valuables he was interred with, were removed by grave robbers not long after his burial. From the museum's parking lot, it's a short walk along a grassy path to the buried boat. From Kerteminde, bus #482 runs regularly to the museum between Monday and Friday, dropping you 1km away – the route to the museum is well signposted. At weekends, bus travel is more complicated – you have to ring ☎65 32 51 43 to order the *telekørsel* bus, which only runs on demand. In any event, it's much more pleasant to cycle there.

North of Kerteminde is the small and verdant **Hindsholm peninsula**, notable for its picturesque farmsteads and rolling hillocks and especially good for camping and bike rides (see p.166 for rental information; bus #483 also runs to its far north 3–4 times daily). The first place of interest, after 4km, is the small village of **VIBY**, whose whitewashed Gothic church has a few beautiful frescoes dating to the late 1500s. If you fancy a **boat trip** around the Odense fjord, head west of here to Lodshuse, where the *M/S Svanen* (☎20 23 11 88; mid-June to Sept; 100–120kr) picks up passengers several times a day, stopping at the small, scenic islands of Viggelsø and Enebærodde, juniper-covered conservation areas for migratory birds and dotted with old lighthouses. Both of these islands offer some lovely hiking in unspoilt, wild terrain, too.

The peninsula is a great place to pitch a tent and revel in quiet seclusion; there are two good **campsites**: *Camp Hverringe*, Blæsenborgvej 200 (☎65 34 10 52, ⓦwww.camphverringe.dk; late March to late Oct), on the eastern shore just opposite the island of Romsø, has a pristine campsite with a pool and private beach. It also rents bikes (50kr per day) and motorboats (400kr/day) and have a few pricey four-person cabins (500kr plus 200kr surcharge if staying for has night only), though you can only rent these by the day outside high season. Simpler, much more remote and open year-round is *Fyns Hoved Camping*, Fynshovedvej 748 at the peninsula's northernmost tip (☎65 34 10 14, ⓦwww.fynshovedcamping .dk), which has basic two-person wooden cabins (❷) and a gorgeous little beach.

Southern Funen

With its acres of agricultural land interspersed with thick forests, saltmarshes and gorgeous beaches along the coast, Funen's southern shores are the ideal place to get out and explore Denmark's quiet pleasures. The region's two main towns are on the Baltic coast; the larger, **Svendborg**, holds a few interesting sights and a bevy of excellent, while a short bus ride west is the attractive marina town of **Fåborg**, home to one of Funen's most prized art galleries. Both towns offer easy road and ferry access to the islands of the South Funen archipelago (see p.174).

Svendborg

A favourite stop for the Danish yachting fraternity, whose marinas clog the coastline from here to Fåborg, 24km west, **SVENDBORG** exudes a certain gritty charm, with colourful houses lining the cobbled lanes. The town's relatively sizeable population gives it an urban feel – but don't let this put you off. As well as boasting some of the best nightlife in an otherwise very quiet region, Svendborg is a great place to spend a few hours meandering around narrow backstreets, spattered with beautiful bronzes by one of Denmark's best-known sculptors, locally born Kai Nielsen, or heading down to the harbourfront to take in the bustling shipyard, packed with gorgeous old wooden boats from all over Scandinavia and the Baltic.

Arrival, information and accommodation

Svendborg sits at the mouth of the Svendborg Sound, 44km south of Odense, to which it is linked by frequent **trains**. Regular **buses** also run from Odense (#970 or #801), Nyborg (#910) and Fåborg (#930). The #800 long-distance bus originating in Odense also stops at the A9 entrance to town (though not the town centre) before continuing on through to Rudkøbing on Langeland, lumbering onto the ferry to Tårs on Lolland, terminating in Nykøbing on Falster; this scenic ride, which runs up to nine times a day and takes almost four hours, offers a tour of some of the best parts of Funen. Buses arrive at the train station, a quick walk from the ferry terminal at the southern edge of town, where there are luggage **lockers** (10kr per day).

The eager-to-please **tourist office**, at Centrumpladsen 4 (mid-June to Aug Mon–Fri 9.30am–6pm, Sat 9.30am–3pm; Sept to mid-June Mon–Fri 9.30am–5pm, Sat 9.30am–12.30pm; ☎62 23 57 00, Ⓦwww.visitsydfyn.dk), covers the entire southern Funen area and can provide details of private accommodation, up-to-date ferry timetables and free copies of the *South Funen Hikers Guide*, which offers good suggestions for walking tours in and around Svendborg. The office also has a single **internet** terminal (free), though there are many more at Zero (daily 11am–midnight; 22kr per hr), inside the Bycenter shopping mall just across the roundabout.

In terms of **accommodation**, Svendborg's large and very modern *Danhostel Svendborg* (☎62 21 66 99, Ⓦwww.danhostel-svendborg.dk; dorms 250kr July to mid-Sept only, doubles Ⓖ), ten minutes' walk from the centre at Vestergade 45, occupies the Lange company's former foundry and feels more like a simple, mid-range hotel than a hostel. Hotels include the excellent *Ærø*, Brogade 1 (☎62 21 07 60, Ⓦwww.hotel-aeroe.dk; Ⓖ), with classy, modernish rooms and a downstairs restaurant that's regularly packed in summer. If you don't mind staying outside of town, the reasonably priced *Missionshotellet Stella Maris* (☎62 21 38 91, Ⓦwww.stellamaris.dk; Ⓖ), a ten-minute bus ride (#202) along the coast, is an austere

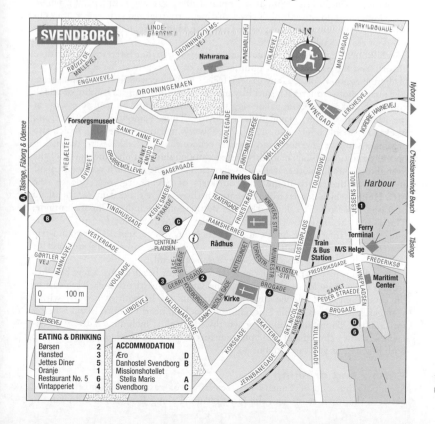

EATING & DRINKING		ACCOMMODATION	
Børsen	2	Ærø	D
Hansted	3	Danhostel Svendborg	B
Jettes Diner	5	Missionshotellet	
Oranje	1	Stella Maris	A
Restaurant No. 5	6	Svendborg	C
Vintapperiet	4		

whitewashed estate overlooking the Svendborg Sound, with a range of rooms and a subtle ecumenical bent. Although none of the area's **campsites** is particularly close to town, Tåsinge, a few kilometres south, has two good choices (see p.175).

The town and around

Svendborg has a few museums whose historical collections could occupy the better part of a day, perhaps before boarding the last evening ferry to one of the islands. All are operated centrally and share the same phone number and website (☎62 21 02 61, ⓦwww.svendborgmuseum.dk). The most interesting is the **Forsorgsmuseet** (Social Welfare Museum; May–Sept Tues–Sun 10am–4pm, Oct–April Tues–Sun 1–4pm; 40kr), Grubbemøllevej 13, a captivating place housed in a former poorhouse with displays detailing how the Danish state has cared for (or ignored) its citizens over the years. The extensive collection includes exhibits on the national health service, with nostalgic recreations of 1950s doctors' and dentists' offices, and a moving section on the experience of orphaned and fostered children in twentieth-century Denmark. From here, head east to the beautiful, half-timbered **Anne Hvides Gård** at Fruenstræde 3 (May to mid-Oct Tues–Sun 11am–4pm; 25kr), Svendborg's oldest secular building, and now a city museum holding displays of local archeological artefacts – the 250-year-old brain of a local woman, for example – as well as changing cultural exhibits on the likes of aristocratic dress and jewellery. If preserved animal life is more your thing, check out the superb **Naturama**, Dronningemaen 30 (Tues–Sun 10am–5pm; 100kr; ⓦwww.naturama.dk), whose three floors of innovative displays cover marine, terrestrial and airborne creatures in eerily lifelike tableaux; the five hundred woodland birds suspended in mid-air on the top floor are especially impressive.

Svendborg's shipbuilding past means there's lots for anyone interested in maritime history, and the harbour, a few minutes south of the centre at the end of Havne-pladsen, is as good a place as any to get a feel of Funen's erstwhile naval importance. The quay is home to several beautifully preserved wooden ships, a handful of which you can board to check out galley riggings and instruments. To gain access, ask at the **Maritimt Center**, Havnepladsen 2 (Mon–Thurs 9am–4pm, Fri 9am–2pm, weekends variable hours; ☎62 23 30 23; ⓦwww.maritimt-center.dk), which also organizes summer afternoon and evening schooner tours (150–250kr, depending on route and time of day) in a dual-masted wooden ship that plies the waters of the Svendborg Sound. Another well-advised option, and one in which you can stop off at some of the sights around the outskirts of Svendborg, is a ride on the **M/S Helge**, which departs from the harbour three to five times daily for the island of Tåsinge (see p.175), calling at several destinations, including Christiansminde, Thurø and the must-see seventeenth-century Valdemars Slot (see p.175). The return sailing time is two hours, and **tickets** (mid-May to Sept; 100kr round-trip from the harbour; information on ☎33 15 15 15, ⓦwww.mshelge.dk) are good for one stop-off along the way, and are purchased on board.

Though this part of Funen isn't exactly a haven for beach bums, a few **beaches** around town draw locals and visitors. The sand at Christiansminde, 1km east of the centre and accessible via a marked path from the harbour, is popular with a younger, partying set, while Smøremosen beach on nearby Thurø island is better for families; Thurø also has a few worthwhile sights, including a lovely seven-teenth-century church and some pleasant forested walks. The Helge ferry runs to both beaches, or you can take bus #201.

Eating and drinking

Svendborg has one of Funen's best selections of **restaurants**, mostly located between the town centre and the ferry terminal along Brogade, and drawing in crowds from all over the island. Accordingly, it's an excellent place to try some of Funen's culinary specialities, but book ahead in the summer to be sure of a table. Similarly, there's no shortage of things to do after-hours.

Børsen Gerritsgade 31 Ⓦ www.borsenbar.dk. This very popular wooden-beamed café-bar is adorned with large exposed copper pipes that deliver fresh draught beer to the bar. Snacks and drinks are served inside or at the tables on the pedestrian walk out front. Along with its adjoined pub, *The Face Inn*, things really get going here at weekends, with all-night dancing.

Hansted Vestergade 2A. A basement music bar with over fifty Danish, Belgian and English beers. On Tuesday evenings, there's live Scandinavian or Celtic folk music, while on the weekends bands play everything from jazz to pop. Hookah pipes (60kr) lend a bit of edge.

Jettes Diner Kullinggade 1 ☎ 62 22 17 48, Ⓦ www.jettesdiner.dk. Period diner offering a variety of scrumptious continental meals, including big salads and over twenty juicy burgers (from

45kr) as well as pricier chilli and steak dishes and large, creamy milkshakes (46kr).

Oranje Jessens Mole ☎ 62 22 82 92, Ⓦ www .oranjen.dk. Set in a ship moored at the harbour, with a yummy catch of the day and unbeatable views out to the Sound. Mains run from 138kr.

Restaurant No.5 Havnepladsen 3A Ⓦ www .restaurant5.dk. This recently expanded harbour-side family restaurant has an edge of swank and a menu filled with tried-and-true Nordic dishes. Also makes some great cocktails in the attached bar: try the *5 Frappa*, with Kahlua, cocoa and cherries.

Vintapperiet Brogade 37 Ⓦ www.vintapperierne .dk. A cosy, friendly wine bar in a courtyard, offering nibbles as well as around a hundred different wines; it's also the only place in town to get that much-needed midday shot of absinthe.

Egeskov Slot

Some 12km north of Svendborg, the Renaissance castle of **Egeskov Slot** (daily: July to mid-Aug 10am–7pm; June & mid- to late Aug 10am–6pm; May & Sept–Oct 10am–5pm; 185kr, grounds only 140kr; Ⓦ www.egeskov.dk) is easily one of the best-preserved in Denmark, with a facade of perfectly kept embrasures, pointy turrets and concealed machicolations (openings in the parapet from which stones or burning objects could be dropped on attackers) plus a five-metre-deep moat, all of which poignantly evoke its importance as a defensive fortification during its heyday. Egeskov was built in 1554 in the middle of a lake by one Frands Brockenhuus, who felled an entire forest (hence the name, "Oak Forest Castle") to underlay its foundations, and its double walls are thick enough to hold hidden staircases and deep wells that ensured ample water supply in the event of a siege. The imposing entrance doors lead to an array of rooms displaying a frightening armoury of daggers and swords, some of which probably felled the myriad lions, tigers and cheetahs whose hides and heads now hang on the walls; other rooms hold pristine examples of Louis XVI chests and secretary desks, while upstairs, there's a music room, assorted galleries with more examples of over-the-top aristocratic wealth, and a lavish guestroom containing two Sumatran busts of slaves brought back from the field as trophies. Less spectacular is the array of smaller museums in other buildings, which include displays on agriculture, horse-drawn vehicles and motorbikes, a grocers' museum and, best of all, the **Egeskov Veteranmuseum**, which has some three hundred antique cars and aircraft.

The castle's grandeur is better appreciated, however, from the beautifully manicured **grounds**, which boast an intricate bamboo maze designed by Danish philosopher-poet Piet Hein as well as award-winning rose and fuchsia gardens, an aviary and a romantic water garden surrounded by azaleas and rhododendrons. It'd be no big chore to spend an entire day lounging around here, but bear in mind that the grounds are packed with visitors during high season. On Wednesdays in July the castle and gardens remain open until 11pm, when the grounds come alive with cannons, open-fire barbecues and fireworks. If you want to stay overnight, there's a free campsite (no facilities) next to the car park. The castle is just twenty minutes from Fåborg by bus #920, or ten minutes by train from Svendborg, then a short walk or ride on bus #920.

Fåborg and around

An alternative base for exploring the south Funen coast, **FÅBORG** is likeably small and sedate, rarely is overwhelmed by holidaymakers as Svendborg and with equally good connections to the archipelago (ferries sail to Søby on Ærø, and to Lyø and Avernakø; see p.183). The town was established in 1229 as a gift from King Valdemar to his daughter-in-law, Eleonore of Portugal, but was later levelled by a succession of fires, in 1672, 1715 and 1728, during which hundreds of the original wooden houses were destroyed. Fortunately, many of them were rebuilt in the same style, accounting for the lovely half-timbered homes which still grace the town's narrow, cobbled roads; of these, the buildings on Grønnegade are in the best condition. Industry thrived around Fåborg in the 1960s, with an active mill and ironworks, but these days the main sources of income are the Danish tourists who come to experience a bit of coastal village life. As such, Fåborg is worth a visit for its aesthetic charm alone, though it also holds an engaging museum of twentieth-century Danish art – and on a clear summer evening, the atmospheric marina is a great place from which to watch the (often breathtaking) sunset.

Arrival, information and accommodation

Buses from Nyborg, Odense and Svendborg arrive at the bus station on Banegård-spladsen, where there's also a friendly and helpful **tourist office** (☎62 61 07 07, ⓦwww.visitfaaborg.dk; June–Aug Mon–Sat 9am–5pm, Sept–May 9am–4pm, Sat 10am–1pm); staff can help find inexpensive private rooms (❸, plus 25kr booking fee), and sell DSB train and bus tickets. **Ferries** to Søby (Ærø), Bjørnø, Lyø and Avernakø leave from a small quay between the tourist office and the central marina. **Accommodation** options in and around town run the gamut.

Accommodation

Fåborg Vandrerhjem Grønnegade 71–73 ☎62 61 12 03, ⓦwww.danhostel.dk/faaborg. Next to the town museum, this is one of the country's most picturesque youth hostels. The simple, modern dorms (150kr) and doubles with shared bath (❷) occupy two old-fashioned wooden buildings that date from the late nineteenth century, but feel much older. April–Sept.

Hotel Fåborg Torvet 13–15 ☎62 61 02 45, ⓦwww.hotelfaaborg.dk. This lovely old brick building has been open as a hotel for nearly a century, and has loads of fin-de-siècle class to prove it. Rooms have firm, comfy beds. ❻

Hotel Mosegård Nabgyden 31 ☎62 61 56 91, ⓦwww.hotelmosegaard.dk. Around 6km southeast of town and 200m from the water, this country-styled mid-range hotel offers simple, bright rooms hung with pretty landscape paintings. To get here, take bus #930 towards Svendborg, get off at Nabgyden, and walk 2km towards the water. ❻

Hvedholm Slot ☎63 60 10 20, ⓦwww.royalclassic.dk. This eighteenth-century estate, 5km out of town in Horne, offers some lavish, castle-style opulence. Each of the rooms will blow your socks off, boasting furnishings like four-poster beds, crystal chandeliers and red silk-upholstered settees. ❼

Svanninge Søgaard Camping ☎62 61 77 94, ⓦwww.svanningecamping.dk. Small cabins (❸) in a medium-sized site splayed out on a verdant nineteenth-century farming estate a half-mile north of town.

The Town

The best place to start exploring is the pedestrianized shopping street of Østergade, which threads west to Torvet, Fåborg's main square, at the centre of which is a bronze reproduction of Kai Nielsen's *Ymerbrønd* **statue** – the sandstone original is housed in the Fåborg Museum. From here, it's a few metres east to the numerous picturesque rows of houses along Adelgade and Tårngade, both of which branch just off Torvet; those at Tårngade 6 and 8 have remained virtually untouched since the 1715 fire, while on Adelgade, nos.19 and 21 are part-built with stones from the church of Skt Nicolai, which was partially dismantled in 1600. At the eastern end of this block, the chunky yellow **Klokketårnet** (mid-June to Aug daily 11am–3pm; 10kr) is all that remains of Skt Nicolai – you can climb the spire for some good views around the town and harbour. Immediately west of the Torvet, **Holkegade** once fed the town from its *holk* ("well"), and the building at no.3 functioned as the local distillery until an explosion in 1728 reduced it to mere cinders, along with nineteen other homes on the block. The building at no.1 has served variously as a trading post, butcher and a telephone exchange, and now holds **Den Gamle Gård** (June–Aug daily 10am–4pm; early April to May & Aug to early Oct Sat & Sun 11am–3pm; early to mid-Dec daily 11am–3pm; 30kr), a largely missable collection of porcelain dishes and nineteenth-century furniture that's notable only for the dainty photo of H.C. Andersen's would-be girlfriend Riborg Voigt.

Folksy housewares aside, the town's main attraction is east of here in the shape of the **Fåborg Museum**, Grønnegade 75 (April–Oct daily 10am–4pm; Nov–March Tues–Sun 11am–3pm; 60kr; ⓦ www.faaborgmuseum.dk), which showcases an impressive collection of richly coloured landscapes by most of the better-known artists of the Funen School (see p.166). The collection is well laid out in small, themed rooms – landscapes, portraits, animals, flowers and so on. From the foyer, which holds Kai Nielsen's larger-than-lifesize marble statue of local patron and museum founder Mads Rasmussen, the first gallery contains nearly all of the School's showcase works: Johannes Larsen's *April Shower*, Peter Hansen's *Ploughman Turns*, and Fritz Syberg's romantic *Evening Games in Svanninge Hills*. All three artists were closely mentored by their teacher, Kristian Zahrtmann, whose vaguely impressionistic *Adam and Eve in the Garden of Eden* (in the same room) is a good example of his characteristic vibrant use of colour juxtaposed with muted fore- and backgrounds, a style which clearly inspired many of his disciples. The rest of the museum is a similar – if less distinguished – collection of

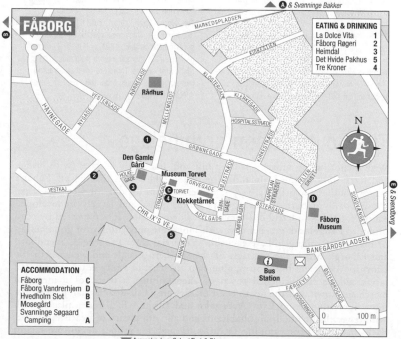

landscapes and portraits, sculptures and sketches, but it's worth heading to the back room to see the original of Kai Nielsen's *Ymerbrønd*, a sandstone likeness of Norse giant Ymer suckling from the udder of a cow, with both animal and human anatomy in full view – legend has it that the milk gave Ymer enough strength to create the world and all of mankind. Though it seems fairly tame these days, the statue caused uproar when it was first unveiled in 1913.

The waters around Fåborg offer a few decent **beaches**, though the sand isn't as alluring as on some of the islands off the coast here. Nearest is the deep-watered Klinten Strand, not terribly big but only 1.5km from the town centre; to get here, follow Langelinie from the harbour or take bus #930 or #962 towards Svendborg and get out at the *Danland Hotel*, from which it's a short walk. North of town, the lovely hilly area of **Svanninge Bakker** offers some of south Funen's best opportunities to get close to nature, with well-marked bicycle and walking paths. The hills begin just 3km north of Fåborg: take bus #360 or #961, or walk along Odensevej, the main road towards Odense.

Eating and drinking

Fåborg's coastal location means there's a good selection of fish **restaurants**, as well as a few places offering solid Italian and continental fare, and a handful of cheaper cafés and late-night kebab and pizza joints.

Fåborg Røgeri Vestkaj 3 ☎62 61 42 32. Great for summer lunches, this harbourside smokehouse serves several dozen inexpensive smoked-fish dishes, which you can enjoy either on wooden picnic tables out front or take with you on the road in vacuum-packed bags.

Heimdal Havnegade 12. A charming bar with lots of interior wood in an excellent setting overlooking the harbour.

Det Hvide Pakhus Christian IX's vej 2 ⓦwww .dethvidepakhus.dk. Set right on the town's harbour, "The White Warehouse" has a solid maritime atmosphere that's also vaguely upscale. The lunch menu has some Scandi standbys, such as herring and shrimp salad, while dinner (3-course meal 325kr) sees more serious steak and fish dishes.

La Dolce Vita Mellemgade 11A ☎62 61 13 99. The laid-back, rustic feel in this inexpensive, Italian-run place makes it an enjoyable departure from the sometimes cloying nature of traditional Danish restaurants. Selections from the sizeable pizza and pasta menu go for under 100kr.

Tre Kroner Strandgade 1 ☎62 61 01 50, ⓦwww .tre-kroner.dk. This corner restaurant has been serving patrons since 1821, and its lively owner and musically themed interior help maintain its rustic atmosphere. There are good smørrebrød plates, but you should order the excellent house speciality, *æggekage* (95kr).

The South Funen archipelago

With quaint fishing villages, rolling hills and fine sandy beaches (with bridge and ferry links to the mainland), the dozen-odd islands that lie off Funen's craggy southern coastline are popular destinations for day- or weekend trips. Closest to Svendborg is **Tåsinge**: peaceful, grassy and largely undeveloped except for the wonderful old estate of Valdemars Slot. It's connected by road bridge to **Langeland**, greener and with a lot more opportunity for good hiking or biking the rolling hills. Reachable via ferries from Langeland, Svendborg and Fåborg, **Ærø** is the prettiest of the southern islands and well worth the effort for its ancient burial sites, abundant stretches of sandy beach, traditional farms and, in the principal town of **Ærøskøbing**, a peach of a medieval merchants' town. Off the north coast of Ærø are a half-dozen small islands, the most interesting being **Lyø**, **Avernakø** and **Drejø** – flat, grassy places, each with fewer than a hundred inhabitants and all with plenty of peace and quiet. Each island has basic camping facilities, though for proper **accommodation** contact the tourist office in Fåborg (see p.172), which arranges stays with local families for around 150kr per person per night.

Tåsinge and Valdemars Slot

Connected to mainland Funen by a bridge over to Svendborg, **TÅSINGE** is peaceful, grassy and largely undeveloped. Aside from the pleasant countryside, the only draw is located just outside the island's main town of **TROENSE**, clustered around a short stretch of road that runs between the seafront and a series of austere but lovable half-timbered thatched houses. Other than admiring these, there's zilch to do, and you'd be well advised to head along the road for a kilometre or so to **Valdemars Slot** (April & early to mid-Oct Sat & Sun 10am–5pm; mid- to late Oct daily 10am–5pm; May–Aug daily 10am–5pm; Sept Tues–Sun 10am–5pm; 80kr *slot*, 125kr for all museums; ⓦwww.valdemarsslot.dk), one of the crown jewels of Denmark's aristocratic landed estates. With twenty-one resplendently furnished rooms, it's the largest private home in Denmark and a must-see on any trip to southern Funen. Built by master architect Hans van Stenwinkel, the castle was commissioned in 1644 by King Christian IV – renowned for his palatial constructions all over Denmark – as a residential estate for his son, Christian Valdemar, but these paternal hopes were dashed when Valdemar died in battle in Poland in 1656. In 1678, the castle and surrounding land were bestowed upon Admiral Niels Juel in payment for his miraculous victory over Sweden in the battle of Køge Bay (see p.119). Valdemars is still owned by his descendants, but it never quite feels like a public museum: display cases, cordoning barrier ropes and in-room guards have pretty much been done away with, allowing you to stroll freely among the living spaces and imagine what it might be like to actually live in such a palatial home. All the rooms are stunning in their own right, though be sure to admire the **Juel Room**, which holds Niels Juel's massive sea chest, in which he stored his most prized military uniforms. The upstairs attic rooms hold a worrying number of stuffed animals, from water buck to wild boar, and a more interesting **ethnographic** collection flaunting the spoils of empire, largely in the form of southern African ritual masks and totems. Outside the main building, two separate wings hold the decent **Museum for Lystsejlads** (Yachting Museum; same hours; 50kr; ⓦwww.lystsejlads.dk), which has a number of finely crafted full-size and scale models of wooden yachts and assorted accoutrements, and the **Legetøjsmuseet** (Toy Museum; same hours; 50kr), which holds a collection of several thousand toys, some dating back to the late nineteenth century. The estate also offers the island's best **eating**: you can snack at the *Æblehaven Kiosk* just outside the castle or go for a full-on meal at the exclusive *Restaurant Valdemars Slot* in the vaulted stone cellars; it's worth timing your trip to coincide with the Sunday lunch buffet (148kr), loaded with Funen delicacies, though the dinner service is also good, if pricey.

Practicalities

Travelling overland from Svendborg, the only public transport is city **bus** #200 (15kr), which runs to Troense, a ten-minute walk to Valdemars Slot; the Helge **ferry** (see p.170) from Svendborg docks at both Troense and Valdemars Slot. As Tåsinge itself has no **tourist office**, the office in Svendborg (see p.169) deals with enquiries concerning the island. Accommodation options are rather scant, though there are four decent **campsites**: the pick is *Vindebyøre Camping* (ⓣ62 22 54 25, ⓦwww.vindebyore.dk), with a smashing location on the north coast offering access to a beautiful beach, and a number of modern two-person cabins (late June to mid-Aug ❹, rest of year ❶). The *M/S Helge* (see p.170) also stops right here. Skip the town's boring **hotel** and make for the tiny thatched home rented out by Erling Larsen, Krogvej 4 (ⓣ62 22 50 03, ⓦwww.ferielejlighed-troense.dk; ❺), with a bright and comfy bedroom, a spacious living area, full kitchen and a picnic table out front. The price includes a small breakfast, and there's also a room (**2**) for singles in a separate house.

Langeland

The largest of Funen's southern islands, long, thin and fertile **Langeland** lies just off Funen's southeast coast, connected by road bridge. Langeland is 60km long but only 10km wide at its broadest point, and islanders have historically established most of their settlements inland, where the climate is more agreeable and the land drier, with coastal forests providing protection from the elements. With several good restaurants, Langeland's capital, **Rudkøbing**, is a good place to visit before exploring the green landscape to the north and south, most easily accessible if you have your own transport. **Cycling** is a perfect way to get around, allowing you to visit the sights – most notably the sculpture gardens of the thirteenth-century **Tranekær Slot** – at your leisure. Southern Langeland holds some interesting out-of-the-way nature spots and archeological finds, but most people come to the island for sun, surf and sand. The **beaches** at the southern tip regularly rank in Denmark's top ten, though the north has its share too, and there are a few excellent camping sites around the island.

Arrival and getting around

Frequent **buses** (#910, 40kr) make the half-hour journey from Svendborg to Rudkøbing, dropping you ten minutes' walk from town at the local school. From here, buses run to all the island's main sites roughly hourly. Fares are priced by zone: a ticket from Rudkøbing to Tranekær, for example, costs 30kr, while a ride from Rudkøbing to Bagenkop, in the far south, costs 48kr. That said, the best way to get around is either private car or bicycle (see below for rental information). Several of the island's harbour towns (primarily Rudkøbing and Spodsbjerg) have **ferry** services to mainland Denmark, including Ærø (see p.179), Lolland (see p.131) and Omø on Zealand; Rudkøbing tourist office can give specific schedule information. If you plan on visiting during the last weekend in July, book accommodation early, as this is when the annual **Langelands Festival** takes place (ⓦ www.llf.dk). Known as Denmark's largest garden party, this music festival draws close to thirty thousand-visitors with primarily Scandinavian groups alongside a few international acts.

Rudkøbing

Diminutive **RUDKØBING** sits on Langeland's western coast, more or less equidistant between the island's southern and northern tips. There's little here save for a laid-back atmosphere, a pleasant fishing harbour and the bulk of the island's restaurants and accommodation – though you might want to take a look at the renovated old buildings pinned up tightly against one another along Smedegade, Vinkældergade and Ramsherred, just north of the town's **church**, or the archeological relics at the **Langelands Museum** (ⓦ www.langelandsmuseum.dk), Jens Winthersvej 12, though the collection is under renovation until 2011; check with the tourist office for details.

The obliging and ever-friendly staff at the **tourist office**, Torvet 5 (mid-June to Aug Mon–Fri 9am–5pm, Sat 9am–3pm; Sept to mid-June Mon–Fri 9.30am–4.30pm, Sat 9.30am–12.30pm; ⓣ 62 51 35 05, ⓦ www.langeland.dk), have a long list of private rooms across the island starting at 125kr per person. They also have details of Langeland's bike rental outlets (best option in town is Lapletten, Engdraget 1, which charges 50kr per day) and sell an English-language cycling map for 30kr. If you're planning to stay on Langeland, your cheapest option is the island's **youth hostel** (ⓣ 62 51 18 30, ⓦ www.danhostel.dk/rudkobing; dorms 150kr, doubles **2**; closed Jan), ten minutes' walk southwest of the centre at Engdraget 11; the grounds are a tad ramshackle but the rooms clean, and you can pitch tents on the grassy lawn for 60kr per person in the summertime. **Hotels** include the super-central *Skandinavien*, Brogade 13

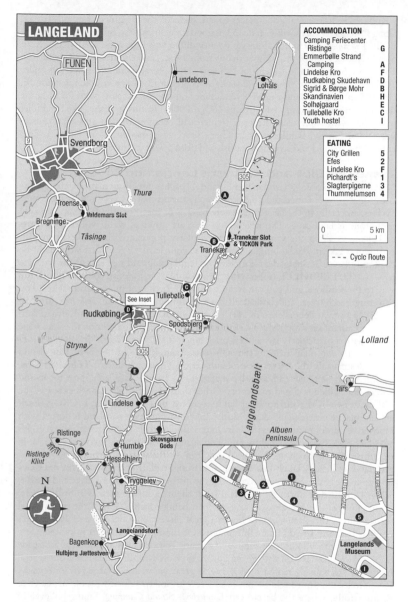

ACCOMMODATION

Camping Feriecenter Ristinge	G
Emmerbølle Strand Camping	A
Lindelse Kro	F
Rudkøbing Skudehavn	D
Sigrid & Børge Mohr	B
Skandinavien	H
Solhøjgaard	E
Tullebølle Kro	C
Youth hostel	I

EATING

City Grillen	5
Efes	2
Lindelse Kro	F
Pichardt's	1
Slagterpigerne	3
Thummelumsen	4

0   5 km

- - - Cycle Route

(☎62 51 14 95, ⊛www.skanhotel.dk; **⑥**), whose agreeable rooms look onto the Gåsetorvet; and the slightly more expensive *Rudkøbing Skudehavn*, Havnegade 21 (☎62 51 46 00, ⊛www.rudkobingskudehavn.dk; **⑦**), with a large indoor pool and spacious apartment-like rooms overlooking the marina. One of the island's best **campsites**, *Færgegårdens Camping*, Spodsbjergvej 335 (☎62 50 11 36, ⊛www .spodsbjerg.dk), is 9km east of town and a few metres from the beach in Spodsbjerg, and has inexpensive cabins (**③**).

Rudkøbing has several good places to **eat**, most of them immediately off Torvet, along Østergade. *City Grillen*, at no. 53, is good for a quick *pølse*, burger or a sandwich, while *Thummelumsen* at no. 15 serves twenty different burgers and sandwiches (from 50kr) with chicken or veal dinner mains from 140kr, and the friendly, Kurdish-run *Efes* at no. 5, serves a full menu of fish and chips, pizza, pasta and salads (all under 100kr). The friendly, homely *Pichardt's* at Bystræde 2 (Ⓦwww.housepichardt.dk; closed Sun) is Langeland's newest restaurant and one of its best, with an in-house delicatessen and a fusion menu (mains 160kr–200kr) featuring dishes like fried fillet of mullet with apple compote or a divine quail breast with foie gras and steamed vegetables. Finally, Rudkøbing's butcher's shop, *Slagterpigerne*, Torvet 6, also does coffee, smørrebrød and scrumptious fish and pork *frikadeller* (meatballs).

Tranekær Slot and northern Langeland

North of Rudkøbing, farmland and sandy beaches are punctuated only by the occasional village. Langeland's flat topography means that it's very popular amongst cyclists, especially in the far north, where patches of forest break up the occasionally monotonous landscape. The beaches up here are good as well, with the sandbars and shallows along the western coast particularly popular with families; best plan is to rent a bike in Rudkøbing and explore at your leisure. Your first stop might be the lovely beach at Stengade, 6km north of Rudkøbing and just east of the roadside town of **TULLEBØLLE** (follow the Stengade Skovvej); dense conifers run all the way to the seashore, and you can swim from thin patches of grassy sand sheltered by towering beech trees. Tullebølle itself has a charming inn, the *Tullebølle Kro* (Ⓣ62 50 13 25; Ⓦwww.tulleboellekro.dk; ❹), offering small, dainty **rooms** with shared bath and a restaurant serving traditional Funen standbys like grilled salmon in white wine sauce, with a particularly large fixed-price lunch for 128kr. North of Tullebølle, it's 10km along the main road to the village of **Tranekær** and northern Langeland's prime destination: the fairytale thirteenth-century manor house of **Tranekær Slot**, a gorgeous fire-engine red house that maintains its original ramparts, spire, moats and stables, but which is closed to visitors. Other than viewing the manor's exterior, the real draw here is the surrounding land, occupied by the beautiful **TICKON Park** art and nature centre (daily dawn–dusk; 25kr), whose open parkland is dotted with innovative outdoor sculptures made by international artists from natural materials. It's a perfect place for a picnic before rambling around to admire the artworks or take in the **museums** (same hours; 25kr each): in front of the manor, there's a collection of thousands of kitschy knick-knacks from tourist sights all over the world; the old water mill opposite has several exhibits covering the history of Tranekær village and the *slot*; while 1km further north on the main road, there's a refurbished **windmill** where, given enough of a breeze, you can see corn being ground. Given the pretty rural surroundings, the Tranekær area is also a great place to try out some of Langeland's popular **bed and breakfast** establishments. Of these, the friendliest is located a few kilometres south, in a former vicarage opposite Tranekær town church at Slotsgade 8: Sigrid and Børge Mohr (Ⓣ58 35 28 02, Ⓦwww.s-mohr.dk; ❹) rent out several first-class, spacious shared-bath rooms with great views and a large terrace outside. If you're looking to rough it a bit, head a few kilometres northwest of Tranekær to **Emmerbølle**, where the beachfront *Emmerbølle Strand Camping*, Emmerbøllevej 24 (Ⓣ62 59 12 26, Ⓦwww.emmerbolle.dk), is easily the island's best **campsite**, sporting a pool, private beach and a dozen or so four-person cabins (from 650kr).

Southern Langeland

Southern Langeland is quite a bit hillier than the north and holds the island's best beaches as well as a few other attractions – though as many of the sights are off the main 305 road, having your own transport is essential if you want to explore. Some

10km south of Rudkøbing, the first reason to turn off the 305 (at the roadside town of Lindelse) is **Skovsgaard Gods**, 3km east of Lindelse at Kågårdsvej 12, agricultural centre (mid-May to Sept Mon–Fri 10am–5pm, Sun 11am–5pm, plus Sat mid-June to early Aug 11am–5pm; museum 540kr). Run by the Danish Nature Conservancy, the grounds of this post-Renaissance estate contain a museum dedicated to horse-drawn carriages, a renovated windmill, a charming café and 10km of well-kept trails that lead through forest and meadow and along the shores of lakes; five pamphlets, available at the entrance, have detailed route maps, though the two-hour guided walks offered (late June to mid-Aug daily 1pm; in Danish only) are equally enjoyable. After working up an appetite on a hike, you might fancy a **meal** at the *Lindelse Kro* (☎ 62 57 24 03, Ⓦ www.lindelsekro.dk), back in Lindelse – its speciality, *æggekage* (149kr), has been made here for over two hundred years, and the classically designed interior and delicious upscale menu make it one of the best restaurants on Langeland; it also has several tidy rooms for rent (Ⓖ). If you want to stay on the coast, head just north to Lindelse Nor, where *Solhøjgaard*, Klæsøvej 9 (☎ 62 51 22 50, Ⓦ www.langeland-a.dk; Ⓢ), is a small farmhouse with several spacious, modern rooms, as well as a private dock and bathing jetty.

A few minutes south, the hamlet of **HUMBLE** is home to a bookshop, bakery, grocery store and the island's largest church, a pretty late-Romantic brick structure with a fancy mid-nineteenth-century altarpiece – making it the largest settlement on southern Langeland, and a good place to stock up on provisions before heading out to the nearby beaches, Langeland's best. Of the numerous sandy beaches here, ideal for sunbathing, paddling and swimming, the finest is just west at **Ristinge**, with a wide expanse of sand; a kiosk sells ice creams and refreshments, and it's also a great point from which to view the island's handsome cliffs, a twenty-minute walk north of the beach. If you want to **stay** in the area, *Camping & Feriecenter Ristinge* (☎ 62 57 13 29, Ⓦ www.ristinge.dk) has tent pitches, a pool, a café and four-person cabins (750kr), though from mid-June to mid-Aug these are only rented by the week.

Another 6km south on the 305, you'll find further respite from beachlife at **BAGENKOP**, a quiet, relatively modern village with a lively harbour great for sampling the catch of the day at the *Fiski* kiosk (Tues–Sat 10am–4pm). Further south along the 305 is **Langelandsfort**, Vognsbjergvej 4b (mid-April to mid-June & mid-Aug to mid-Oct Mon–Fri 10am–4.30pm, Sat & Sun 11am–4.30pm; mid-June to mid-Aug Mon–Fri 10am–5pm, Sun 11am–5pm; early to late Feb Mon–Fri 10am–4pm, Sat & Sun 11am–4pm; 70kr; Ⓦ www.langelandsmuseum. dk), a military compound-turned-museum containing various bunkers, uniforms and military paraphernalia, as well as a wooden minesweeper and a large-scale submarine – both in use by the Danish military until 2004.

Ærø

Reachable by ferries from Fåborg, Svendborg or Rudkøbing, the pretty island of **ÆRØ** (pronounced AIH-ruh) offers a little more variety than Langeland as well as several charming harbourside villages. The radiant **Ærøskøbing** boasts narrow, cobbled streets lined with exquisitely maintained old timbered and tiled buildings, while the quieter **Marstal** holds an impressive maritime museum. To the south, **Rise Mark** and **Store Rise** are the gateway to some lovely Baltic beaches; the latter is also the home of the world's largest collection of solar panels (around four million), and Ærø is nearly entirely energy self-sufficient.

Arrival and getting around

Ærø has three separate ferry terminals in each of the major towns. Ærøfærgerne (☎ 62 52 40 00, Ⓦ www.aeroe-ferry.dk) operates **ferries** five to six times daily from

Svendborg to Ærøskøbing, from Fåborg and Mommark in Jutland to Søby, and from Rudkjøbing in Langeland to Marstal. Tickets for all the routes are sold only on board, and cost 104kr one-way, 166kr return (vehicles 227kr, bikes 24kr, both one-way). Hourly **buses** traverse the island between Søby in the west and Marstal in the east, stopping at Ærøskøbing and passing the outskirts of Store Rise. An unlimited day-pass is available for 72kr, though it's not really necessary unless you plan on trying to cover all the sights on the island in one day – an ill-advised endeavour in any case. Given the more or less linear route of the bus, the best way to see the island is by bike – it's only 35km from the Søby lighthouse on the western tip to Marstal in the east, though you'll need to pedal hard to get up some of the hills. The Ærøskøbing tourist office supplies free bike maps and there's **bike rental** at Pilebækkens Cykler, Pilebækken 11, in the petrol station about 200m west of the main marketplace (☎62 52 11 10; Mon–Fri 9am–4.30pm, Sat 9am–1pm; plus July Sun 10am–1pm; 55kr a day). For a more unusual tour of the island, hop onto one of the **aerial tours** offered by Starling Air (☎62 53 33 94, ⓦwww.starling.dk); from 100kr per person for a short flight, it's unusually affordable.

Ærøskøbing

When passing shipping brought prosperity to Ærø in the nineteenth century, the island split into three divisions: fishermen lived in the windy western tip at Søby; the wealthy shipping magnates and captains resided in Marstal to the east; while

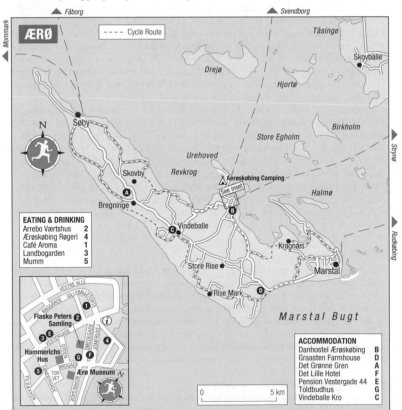

the middle classes collected in **ÆRØSKØBING**, still one of Denmark's most idyllic harbourside towns. The locals have long campaigned for recognition and conservation of the town's fine architectural heritage, and though modernization across Denmark during the 1950s and 1960s radically changed the look and feel of many city centres, remote Ærøskøbing has been preserved. Today, its numerous **preserved** and **restored buildings** – the entire town is protected under Danish law – comprise a virtual open-air museum, illustrating the diversity of the country's architectural traditions. The typical Ærøskøbing half-timbered house sports large front-protruding gables and bays, and an elongated facade that enabled division into individual dwellings, with separate entrances to the street in front and to the courtyard or garden behind.

Information and accommodation

The **Ærø Turistbureau**, Vestergade 1 (mid-June to Aug Mon–Fri 9am–5pm, Sat 9am–2pm, Sun 9.30am–12.30pm; Sept to mid-June Mon–Fri 9am–4pm; ☏62 52 13 00, ⓦ www.arre.dk), is the central point for information about the entire island. Be sure to pick up a copy of the free English-language *Ærø Guide*, which lists summer nature walks (25kr) run by the Ærø Nature and Energy School (☏62 52 25 60). With numerous interesting choices, Ærøskøbing is a perfect place to **spend the night**.

Accommodation

Danhostel Ærøskøbing Smedevejen 15 ☏62 52 10 44, ⓦwww.danhostel.dk/aeroeskoebing. The town youth hostel offers run-of-the-mill rooms (dorms 175kr, shared-bath doubles ❷), but does have ocean views and friendly management. It's 800m south of the ferry dock on the road to Marstal. Open May–Aug.

Det Lille Hotel Smedegade 33 ☏62 52 23 00, ⓦwww.det-lille-hotel.dk. A good, solid option, with homely, bright rooms that share facilities, and a good restaurant. ❻

Pension Vestergade 44 Vestergade 44 ☏62 52 22 98, ⓦwww.vestergade44.com. An exquisite B&B run by a congenial Brit with eight superb, meticulously decorated rooms that share a bathroom; the gardens out back are perfect for high tea. ❻

Toldbodhus Brogade 8 ☏62 52 18 11, ⓦwww.toldbodhus.com. The four charming rooms in this lovely B&B are painstakingly furnished in a unique style each based on a city in which the owners have lived. ❻

Ærøskøbing Camping Sygehusvejen 40 ☏62 52 18 54, ⓦwww.aeroecamp.dk. Appealingly situated next to Vesterstrand beach to the north of town, this pleasant campsite features two dozen cabins (from ❶) in various shapes, sizes and colours. Open May–Sept.

The Town

The town's architectural and social history is beautifully described at the **Ærø Museum**, Brogade 3–5 (mid-June to mid-Sept daily 11am–3pm; late Oct to early April Mon–Fri 10am–1pm, Sat noon–3pm; early April to mid-June daily 10am–3pm; 30kr, joint ticket with the Flaske-Peters Samling and Hammerichs Hus 75kr; ⓦwww.arremus.dk), a simple collection of maps, clothing and housewares culled from island homes. For something a bit more unusual, head to Smedegade 22 for the **Flaske-Peters Samling** (Bottle Peter Museum; mid-June to mid-Aug daily 10am–5pm; mid-Aug to mid-Oct daily 10am–4pm; mid-Oct to early April Tues–Fri 1–3pm, Sat 10am–noon; early April to mid-June 10am–4pm; tickets as for Ærø Museum). The Kalundborg-born "Bottle Peter" made over seventeen hundred tiny ships-in-a-bottle throughout his lifetime, all with amazing attention to detail, and moved here in the 1950s to open a museum to display them. His triumphs include the world's largest bottled ship, elegantly pieced together in front of a tiny, meticulously painted canvas of a Dutch harbour. Another example of the Danes' penchant for amassing various and sundry items is to be found at **Hammerichs Hus** at Gyden 22 (June–Aug daily noon–4pm; tickets as for Ærø Museum), a riot of woodcarvings, furnishings and timepieces from bygone days. This "museum" is really just the home of an inveterate hoarder who travelled the world to bring back ragtag items like stuffed parrots and ceramic tiles. The low-ceilinged house itself is an interesting example of hermit-like pre-modern Danish homes, but its innards serve primarily as a testament to what can happen when you refuse to throw anything out.

Just southeast of the centre lies the town's clean and shallow **beach**, bordered by a public footpath lined with tall poplars and with a dozen or so tiny, brightly painted **beach huts** fronting the dunes, replete with picturesque verandas, balustrades and shutters. Nearby, Ærøskøbing's harbour is the jumping-off point for cruises aboard the dual-masted **schooner** *Mjølnet*, which sails on Tuesdays between July and mid-August on two separate trips: one (departing 10am) heads to nearby Strynø island for a four-hour tour (250kr); the other leaves at 7pm for a two-hour sunset trip (150kr). You can try your skills at the helm or help out raising the mainsail. The same tours sail from Marstal on Wednesdays. To book, ask at the tourist office or at the Maritimt Center in Svendborg (see p.170).

Eating and drinking

Ærøskøbing offers a wide selection of places to eat; though they tend to be quite pricey and are often full in summer, when it's wise to book ahead. There are also a couple of bars, outside of which there is zero to do here at night.

Arrebo Værtshus Vestergade 4 ☎62 52 28 50. This renovated, atmospheric bar, with lots of old maritime photos on the walls and a few chairs and tables out front, is the most popular place in town, with live music – blues, jazz, country and rock – evenings. Summer only.

Café Aroma Gilleballetofte 2A ☎62 52 40 02. A popular burger and fried-fish joint close to the ferry landing, that also serves salads and pricier tapas dishes until 6pm. It's essentially a laid-back café, but in the evenings it fills up with dinner guests who come for the airy atmosphere.

Landbogården Vestergade 54 ☎62 52 10 41. Quiet, casual restaurant offering tasty and affordable *dagens ret* dinner menus like fried fish,

shellfish pasta and smoked salmon (most from 180kr), and also makes a good stop for an early evening or late-night beer.

Mumm Søndergade 12 ☎62 52 12 12. Ærøskøbing's more upscale option, this traditional-looking place is full of character and is popular amongst locals for its tasty American- and Scandinavian-style mains like veal fillet and fried salmon, starting at 160kr. Summer daily; off season Wed–Sat only.

Ærøskøbing Røgeri Havnen 15F. A great place to stop when getting on or off the Svendborg ferry, this harbourside smokehouse offers outstanding fish; the smoked eel fillets (40kr) are highly recommended.

The rest of the island

At the eastern end of the island, modern **MARSTAL** doesn't feel nearly as caught in time as Ærøskøbing, and as there's decidedly less to do here, it's a good place to escape the crowds. During the nineteenth century, Marstal's harbour was among the country's busiest, and continues this naval tradition as home to one of Denmark's top sailing schools. The town's seafaring past is covered in immense detail at the superb **Marstal Søfartsmuseum** (Maritime Museum; May, Sept & Oct daily 10am–4pm; June daily 9am–5pm; July & Aug daily 9am–6pm; Nov–April Mon–Fri 10am–4pm, Sat 11am–3pm; 40kr; ⓦwww.marstal-maritime-museum.dk), Prinsensgade 1, whose three separate buildings detail several hundred years of nautical history via sundry trappings from ships' galleys and over two hundred large-scale model ships. The courtyard out back has a few abandoned ships for kids to climb onto and explore. Aside from the museum, the only thing to do here is visit the local **beach**, Ærøshale, located on a small bit of land jutting out into the sea and lined with colourful beach homes – it's about twenty minutes' walk east of the town centre. Marstal is easily reached by bus from Ærøskøbing (or ferry from Rudkøbing in Langeland; see p.176). The town's **tourist office** (mid-June to mid-Sept daily 10am–3pm; ☎62 52 21 00, ⓦwww.arre.dk) is just across from the museum at Havnegade 4. **Bikes** can be rented at Nørremark Cykelforretning, Møllevejen 77 (☎62 53 14 77; 50kr/day). While there's no real reason to overnight here, there are quite a few good places to **eat**, many located on the cobbled main drag of Kirkestræde – though bear in mind that opening hours are severely reduced outside the tourist season. *Den Gamle Vingård*, Skolegade 15–17 (T 62 53 13 25, W www.gamle-vingaard.com), is the nicest, with walls crammed with memorabilia from Ærø's shipping past, and a menu of sizeable veal, pork, chicken and veg dishes (from 88kr). There is also a pizzeria in the small marina's yacht club (June–Sept only). A good stop for **drinking** is the smoky *Toldbudhus*, Prinsengade 7, with a billiards table and plenty of maritime colour. *Cottage Pub*, Strandstræde 41 (Sun–Thurs 6pm–5am, Fri & Sat 6pm–midnight), is the island's resident Scottish pub, and draws locals from as far away as Søby. Ærø's other towns are somewhat less remarkable than Ærøskøbing and Marstal, with a good deal less bustle as well. In the northwest, **Søby** has little going for it other than the waning fishing industry centred around the small harbour, though if you have a bike you'd do well to head out to the pretty Skjoldnæs **lighthouse** (summer daily 7am–7pm) at the far northwestern tip of the island, 5km from the ferry terminal, which has lovely views. South of Ærøskøbing, via Store Rise, the town of **Rise Mark** offers access to what are far and away Ærø's nicest **beaches**, where deep waters are fronted by vast stretches of chalky sand with windmills towering in the distance. Bus services from Ærøskøbing and Marstal drop you off several kilometres from the sand, so you're much better off coming by bike. The rest of the island is speckled with fine **inns** (*kros*) and working farms, the best of which are *Graasten Farmhouse*, Østermarksvej 20 in Lindsbjerg (T 62 52 24 25, W www.greyfarm.dk; **4**), with classy and colourful rooms let for a minimum of two nights; the handsome, year-round *Vindeballe Kro*, Vindeballevej 1 in Vindeballe (T 62 52 16 13 W www.vindeballekro.dk; **5**), which has quite simple rooms, with and without private bath, and a good restaurant (try the seasoned, pan-fried eel) and bar. In Bregninge, there's *Det Grønne Gren* (T 62 58 20 45, W www .dengronnegren.dk; **5**), Vester Bregninge 17, whose five newly renovated rooms are a bit cramped but adequate.

Avernakø, Lyø and Drejø

Just outside the entrance to the Fåborg and Svendborg sounds splay a half dozen tiny islands that make for some wonderful day-trips – and some even more memorable overnights – while in the south of the country. Crisscrossed by walking paths and offering small, stony beaches, **Lyø** and **Avernakø** are the most westerly of the archipelago's inhabited islands and the most popular to visit, while **Drejø**, further east, remains markedly less touristy but still fairly popular with weekending boaters from Svendborg. All of the islands are small enough to explore on foot, though you might find it more enjoyable to rent a bicycle and bring it with you on the ferry (20kr charge).

Reached from Fåborg, **AVERNAKØ** (W www.avernak.dk) effectively comprises two separate islands connected by a 700-metre causeway. Ferries arrive 1km outside of **Avernak By**, the island's town, where you'll find a well-stocked provisions shop, a café and, just east, the island's small early-sixteenth-century church. East from the town you'll find woods, wild meadows and undulating moors that lead out to the sea, as well as several apartments run by the friendly Lund Jensen (T 62 61 71 21; **4**), Hovedvejen 79, east of Korshavn harbour. Alternatively, you can camp rough at a small site accessible from the path leading northwest out of town. For **food**, there's a small **café** by the ferry landing serving sandwiches and inexpensive Danish dishes (summer only).

Four kilometres west of Avernakø, and roughly half its size, **LYØ** is popular with Danish tourists, who visit the island's unprepossessing town, **Lyø By**, for its small ponds, old church and handful of impressive thatched homes. Paths lead out from town to the rolling green hills in the eastern part of the island, and to the flatter western half, at the end of which is a large *klokkestenen* ("bell stone"), a boulder sitting atop a Stone Age burial chamber which makes a unique bell-like ring when tapped. If you'd like to **stay** overnight, enquire with *Mette Vesterskov* (℡ 62 61 97 39, ⓦ www.lyoe-ferie.dk; ❸), Lyø Bygade 7; there are a few rather dingy rooms, and a **restaurant** serving standard dishes like beef fillet and schnitzel for around 100kr. Rough camping is allowed along the eastern coast: for the best spot, take 1. vej left out of town; once the asphalt ends follow the grassy path which leads to a small waterside bluff. **Ferries** from Fåborg (℡ 62 61 23 07, ⓦ www.oe-faergen.dk; 110kr return) sail daily to Avernakø, and some stop over in Lyø; in the summer, the last return boat from Avernakø is at 9pm.

Sitting just offshore of the mouth of the Svendborg sound, **DREJØ** (ⓦ www .drejo.dk) is smaller than the islands off Fåborg and markedly less touristy, with a landscape primarily of farmsteads and salt marshes. Arriving at the ferry terminal, walk 1km west to the main settlement of **Drejø By**, much of which burned down during a party on Midsummer's Eve in 1942. Your first stop should be **Gammel Elmegaard** (early June to Aug daily 12.30–6pm; 25kr; ⓦ www.gammelelmegaard .dk), an old farmhouse housing a simple museum – look out for the pastel-hued model of the village as it stood before the fire. The town also has a grocery shop and a small inn, *Drejø Kro* (℡ 62 21 47 87, ⓦ www.drejokro-kobmand.dk; ❹), which rents out two small cabins; there's also rough camping just by the ferry dock, with toilet and shower facilities just 50m away, and a few minutes' walk south of here is a small beach. Drejø is reachable via **ferry** from Svendborg (℡ 62 21 02 62; 4–5 daily; 75kr).

Travel details

Trains

Middelfart to: Odense (2–3 hourly; 25–45min).
Nyborg to: Odense (every 30min; 15min).
Odense to: Århus (every 30min; 1hr 35min–2hr 25min); Copenhagen (every 30min; 1hr 15min–1hr 35min); Esbjerg (hourly; 1hr 20min–2hr); Nyborg (every 30min; 15min); Svendborg (every 30min; 40min).
Svendborg to: Odense (every 30min; 45min).

Buses

Ærøskøbing to: Marstal (hourly; 30min); Søby (hourly; 25min).
Fåborg to: Nyborg (hourly; 1hr–1hr 30min); Odense (every 30min; 1hr 20min); Svendborg (Mon–Sat every 30min, Sun hourly; 40min).
Kerteminde to: Nyborg (hourly; 35min); Odense (every 30min; 30min).
Middelfart to: Odense (hourly; 1hr).
Odense to: Fåborg (every 30min; 1hr 20min); Kerteminde (every 30min; 30min); Nyborg (every 30min; 50min); Nykøbing Falster (hourly;

3hr 30min); Svendborg (hourly; 1hr 20min–1hr 40min).
Rudkøbing to: Bagenkop (hourly; 35min); Lohals (hourly; 35min); Spodsbjerg (9 daily; 10min); Svendborg (hourly; 40min).
Svendborg to: Fåborg (Mon–Sat every 30min, Sun hourly; 40min); Odense (hourly; 1hr 20min–1hr 40min); Rudkøbing (hourly; 40min); Nyborg (every 30min; 50min).

Ferries

Some sailings continue all year, others only operate during the summer. Frequencies given below are for weekdays; sailings are often reduced on weekends and public holidays.
Bøjden to: Fynshav (5 daily; 50min).
Fåborg to: Avernakø (6–8 daily via Lyø; 1hr 15min); Søby (2–6 daily; 1hr).
Marstal to: Rudkøbing (3–6 daily; 1hr).
Spodsbjerg to: Tårs (hourly; 45min).
Svendborg to: Ærøskøbing (3–6 daily; 1hr 15min); Drejø (4–5 daily; 1hr 10min–1hr 35min).
Søby to: Mommark (2–5 daily; 1hr).

South Jutland

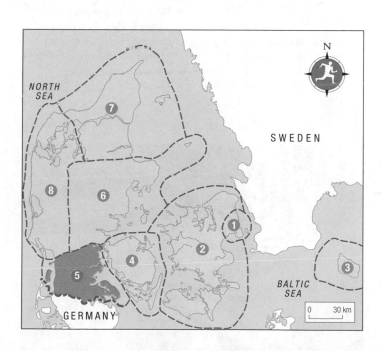

CHAPTER 5

Highlights

✳ **Koldinghus** This thirteenth-century royal castle lay ruined for hundreds of years, and its restoration is nothing short of ingenious. **See p.189**

✳ **Dybbøl Banke** The moats and trenches here serve as an evocative reminder of the 1864 loss of parts of the south – then north Schleswig – to Prussia and Germany. **See p.195**

✳ **Wadden Sea birdwatching** These huge tidal flats offer some of the best birding in the world, with some of the most easy-access opportunities at Magrethe Kog, just west of Tønder. **See p.200**

✳ **Lakolk beach** This fabulous and wide sandy beach on the island of Rømø is excellent for all manner of activities as well as swimming. **See p.201**

✳ **Ribe** The quaint old town centre is ideal for a day's ambling, with beautiful old houses surrounding a grand cathedral. **See p.202**

▲ Lakolk beach on Rømø

5

South Jutland

D enmark's only point of connection with mainland Europe (by way of a shared border with Germany), **south Jutland** is often overlooked by visitors heading straight to Copenhagen on fast intercity trains. This hasn't always been the case, however, as the region's territorially strategic position has long seen it act as a buffer zone between invaders coming from the south and the rest of Denmark. In fact, southern Jutland represents the country's most hotly disputed land, and the constant struggles for control have left the area littered with the castles and fortifications of its would-be rulers. Until the referendum of 1920, which finally ceded the south back to Denmark and away from German control, the area was part of the Danish **Duchy of Schleswig**; controlled by Danish nobles, but with German as the predominant language toward its south, and Danish to its north. With its strong and abiding affiliation to Schleswig, the region has always stood out slightly. Linguistically, the German-influenced local dialect is almost impossible for many Danes to understand – and though the German-speaking population here, who still maintain Teutonic cultural traditions, remain a minority, there's always an unspoken and nagging doubt as to whether things would have turned out better had they voted differently in 1920.

Following reunification, an impressive effort was made to minimize future conflict. The area was in effect designated bilingual, and German-language schools, churches, newspapers and social clubs established. Over the years, the German influence has gradually subsided, and only one German newspaper, *Der Nord Schleswiger*, remains, but while increasing intermarriage between the two language groups is watering down the differences, people here are still very clear about their cultural background.

Most of south Jutland's attractions lie along the two coasts – the interior is primarily agricultural and holds little of interest. The northern metropolis and gateway to the region, **Kolding** boasts an imaginatively restored castle and a good art museum, while to the south **Haderslev** is home to a grand cathedral, while the country's most devastating defeat on home soil is engagingly commemorated in and around **Sønderborg**. Interspersed with scenic fjords, the lush rolling hills on the east coast couldn't be more different to the tidal mud flats and marshes of the west, where the **Wadden Sea** area offers fantastic birdwatching, some lovely beaches on the

---

Mojn

A linguistic quirk that you'll only hear in south Jutland is the word **mojn** (pronounced moin) meaning hello, goodbye or thank you all in one. If you want to fit in, saying *mojn* as you walk into a shop is the way to go about it.

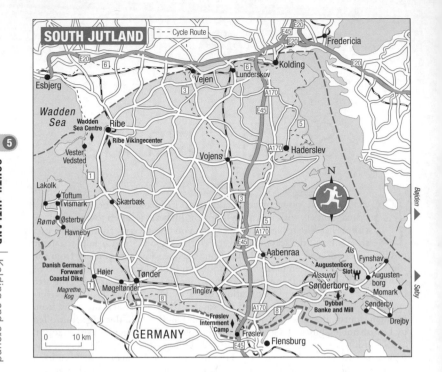

island of **Rømø**, and plenty of possibilities for walking and cycling. Capping the southwest coast, the engaging medieval town of **Ribe** is well worth a day's wander.

Kolding and around

Handsomely positioned on Kolding fjord, **KOLDING** is south Jutland's biggest town. Located within easy reach of the bridge from Funen, and with good road connections to Ribe and Tønder, and motorway and rail links west to Esbjerg and south to German border, it's also the gateway to the region and makes for a convenient base, with a few top-ranking attractions to boot – from **Koldinghus castle** to **Trapholt** art museum, and the nearby medieval town of **Haderslev**. And though the presence of a massive shopping mall on the outskirts has seen the closure of many of the ancient centre's quirkier shops, most of these have been replaced by a string of excellent **eating**, **drinking** and **nightlife** venues.

Arrival and information

Kolding's central **train** and bus **stations** are next to each other on Mazantigade; city buses also stop just outside. Central Kolding is covered by one bus zone, and tickets within this cost 17kr. You can pick up free bus and train timetables and get travel advice at the helpful **tourist office**, on the central square at Akseltorv 8 (July to mid-Aug Mon–Fri 9.30am–6pm, Sat 9.30am–2.30pm; mid-Aug to June Mon–Fri 9.30am–5.30pm, Sat 9.30am–2pm; ⓣ 76 33 21 00, ⓦ www.visitkolding .dk); it also offers free internet access.

Accommodation

Central Kolding has a fairly limited selection of **accommodation** and many of the options are a short bus ride from the centre; the tourist office has an extensive list of **private rooms**, mostly in the suburbs or in the surrounding villages. As most places here are geared toward business travellers, rates can drop significantly during weekends and holidays; check websites for offers.

Best Western Hotel Kolding City Grønningen 2 ⊕75 53 21 22, ⊛www.hotelkoldingcity.dk. Good-value hotel north of the centre and adjacent to the city's park. The spacious but basic rooms are all self-contained with wi-fi and a small balcony. Rates don't vary much throughout the week/year and there's free parking. Bus #1, #2, #3, #5, #6 and #7. **❼**
Comwell Kolding Skovbrynet ⊕76 34 11 00 ⊛www.comwell.com. Large, luxurious hotel next to a small woodland north of the centre, with fab views of the town. The peaceful, modern rooms have all mod cons including wi-fi and big bathtubs, and the complex has a pristine indoor pool, sauna and spa, plus a bar and restaurant, and there are running and bike trails just outside. Bus #5. **❾**
First Hotel Kolding Banegårdspladsen 7 ⊕76 34 54 00 ⊛www.firsthotels.dk/kolding. Across from the train station, this stunning modern new hotel has a whopping 132 rooms over three floors and great views of Kolding Slotsø lake. The tasteful rooms come with free wi-fi, and there's a bar, restaurant and an interior entrance to the city's library which holds a good selection of foreign-language newspapers and magazines. **❽**
Kolding City Camp Vonsildvej 19 ⊕75 52 13 88 ⊛www.koldingcitycamp.dk. Large, modern campsite 3km south of the centre on the main road to Christiansfelt (take bus #3). Packed with facilities (minigolf, tennis, large play area) plus wi-fi throughout, the site also has a range of cabins, from luxurious six-bed

affairs with fully fitted kitchens and private bathrooms (650kr–975kr) to basic cabins sleeping up to four with sofabeds and a sink (395kr–450kr).
Kolding Vandrerhjem Ørnsborgvej 10 ⊕75 50 91 40 ⊛www.danhostelkolding.dk. In a picturesque wooden cabin on a hillside overlooking the city 1.5km northwest of the centre (take bus #3 towards Albuen and get off at Gøhlmannsvej), and with great views of Koldinghus and Kolding Slotsø lake, Kolding's fully modernized hostel has a range of two- to eight-bed rooms, some sharing bathroom facilities. All can be used as dorms (165kr), or rented privately (**❸**).
Koldingfjord Fjordvej 154 ⊕75 51 00 00 ⊛www.koldingfjord.dk. On the wooded banks of Koldingfjord, this majestic hotel was built in 1911 as a sanatorium and offers fresh air and tranquillity. The luxurious rooms, a few with large bathtubs, all have free wi-fi. There's also an indoor pool with sauna and a beautifully positioned restaurant overlooking Koldingfjord. It's convenient for Trapholt art museum (see p.190), and a 20min bus ride from the centre (bus #4). Huge discounts available. **❾**
Saxildhus Hotel Jernbanegade 39 ⊕75 52 12 00 ⊛www.saxildhus.dk. Opposite the train station in a white building from 1910, the character-packed rooms (wi-fi, free minibar stocked with beer and water) come with either antique four-poster beds and wood-beamed ceilings, or with modern Danish furniture. Downstairs, there's a bar and restaurant. **❽**

Koldinghus

Kolding's scenic fjordside setting is not something you immediately notice when arriving at the train or bus station. Instead, it's the castle – and the compact medieval centre crammed behind its hill – that draw your attention, and rightly so. It's not surprising that with such prominence, **Koldinghus castle** (daily 10am–5pm; 70kr; ⊛www.koldinghus.dk) defended both town and country for more than six hundred years. The first structure on this site was a fortress, raised by King Erik Kipling in 1268 to defend the kingdom – then demarcated by the Kolding Å river to the south of Kolding – from incursions by the rebellious Duchy of Schleswig. None of this original structure remains, and Koldinghus was converted to a royal castle in the fifteenth century by Christian I. Its heyday came in the sixteenth century when King Christian III and wife Dorothea set up permanent residence – the oldest elements of the current Koldinghus date back to this period. Their grandson – Christian IV, aka the builder king – spent his childhood here and was later responsible for some of the grandest existing features, including the Giants' Tower. The castle was accidentally burnt down in 1808, and a long period of

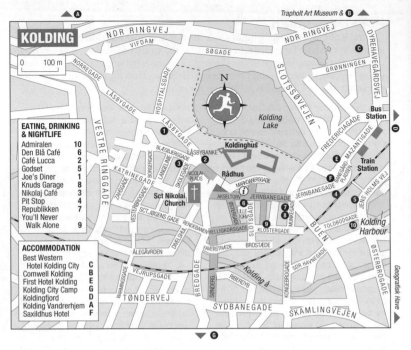

KOLDING

0   100 m

N

Kolding
Lake

Koldinghus

Rådhus

Sct Nikolai
Church

Bus
Station

Train
Station

Kolding
Harbour

Geografisk Have

**EATING, DRINKING
& NIGHTLIFE**

Admiralen	10
Den Blå Café	6
Café Lucca	2
Godset	5
Joe's Diner	1
Knuds Garage	8
Nikolaj Café	3
Pit Stop	4
Republikken	7
You'll Never Walk Alone	9

ACCOMMODATION

Best Western Hotel Kolding City	C
Comwell Kolding	B
First Hotel Kolding	E
Kolding City Camp	G
Koldingfjord	D
Kolding Vandrerhjem	A
Saxildhus Hotel	F

decline followed until restorers finally stepped in in the 1960s and sensitively resurrected it. An important part of the restoration brief was to maintain the building's ruinous look, which is why the original outer walls haven't been rendered and whitewashed, as they were before the fire, and instead retain their raw, weathered, red-brick look. Once inside, a free English-language guide (pick it up at the entrance) will help you find your way around the maze-like **interior**, though if time is short, you might want to concentrate on the highlights described below.

The most dramatic feature is the so-called **Ruin Hall**, where towering modern pillars support the roof and the remaining sections of original brickwork give a clear impression of the magnitude of the rebuild. Today the hall houses changing cultural exhibits. Equally impressive is Christian IV's massive **Giants' Tower**, designed to create as imposing an entry point into southern Denmark as Kronborg (see p.105) in the east and affording sweeping views of the surrounding countryside. During the fire of 1808, half of the tower collapsed, crashing down onto the Great Hall and Christian IV's chapel underneath. Both were completely destroyed, and today, lamps and chandeliers in the reconstructed **chapel** have been imaginatively used to indicate where vaults and nave once were. The **Great Hall**, meanwhile, is most famous for a masked ball held here in 1711 when the 40-year-old, married King Frederik IV openly courted 17-year-old commoner Anna Sophie Reventlow. Soon after, she was abducted from her family home in east Jutland and was the King's consort for ten years, eventually becoming Denmark's queen. On the ground floor of the north wing, the **visitor centre t**akes you through the various phases of the building's history, and the basement **café** serves delicious, if pricey, home-cooked food.

Around Kolding: Trapholt and Haderslev

To get the full benefit of Kolding's stunning fjordside setting, head northeast of the centre on bus #4 from the train station, which also passes the modern **Trapholt** art

museum (Tues & Thurs–Sun 10am–5pm, Wed 10am–8pm; 70kr; Ⓦwww
.trapholt.dk), Æblehaven 23, another of Kolding's highlights. With shrill white
interiors and glass walls that flood it with natural light, the contemporary building
houses outstanding and innovative exhibitions of modern art, craft and furniture
design. The **permanent displays** include a fine selection of chronologically
organized Danish ceramic art – so-called **studio pieces**: funky, oddly shaped pots
– lining the walls of a long central walkway. In **Room 10** you'll find Danish
furniture represented by classic chairs from some of the country's best-known
designers – look for Arne Jacobsen's **myren** ("the ant"), hanging in a rainbow of
colours from the ceiling, and Børge Mogensen's stylish "Spanish" chair, a low,
robust recliner in oak and leather. Check out, too, the Franciska Claussen Collection in **Room 8**, which details the life and art of this forgotten Dane, born in
Aabenraa in 1899 while south Jutland was still under German rule, and best-known
for her surrealist paintings and Art Nouveau advertising posters. Her favourite and
most famous painting, *The Screw*, is strategically positioned so you can study it
sitting comfortably in a so-called Red-Blue chair, designed by Dutch-born Gerrit
Rietveld. The museum's **garden** is also worth a peek, packed with sculptures such
as Bjørn Nørgaard's evocative *Homeless Souls*, made in oak, granite, bronze,
aluminium, steel and lead, as well as **Arne Jacobsen's summerhouse** (Tues–Fri
30min guided tours at 1 & 3pm, Sat–Sun slots at 11am, 1pm & 3pm), accessible
from the exit in front of Room 8; a "Kubeflex" house made in cubic modules that
can be shifted around. The Kubeflex concept was considered an architectural gem
in design circles, but, perhaps too modern for its time, it was never put into production. The central walkway with the ceramic displays culminates in *Café Medina*, a
pricey but beautifully positioned café-restaurant overlooking Kolding fjord.

Haderslev

Some 27km south of Kolding (**bus** #34 or take exit 68 on the E45 motorway),
pretty **HADERSLEV** boasts one of Denmark's best-preserved medieval centres,
its narrow cobbled streets lined by small, wood-beamed townhouses that lean
against each other for support. The obvious place to start your wanderings is the
enormous **Vor Frue Kirke** (daily: June–July 10am–5pm, rest of year 10am–3pm;
free), which towers up over the centre. From its inception in the eleventh century
until the reunification of south Jutland into Denmark in 1920, Vor Frue Kirke was
an adjunct of the main Schleswig cathedral – surprising when you consider its
enormous size – and only became a cathedral in its own right in 1922, when
Haderslev gained Episcopal status. Dating mostly from the fifteenth century, the
red-brick Vor Frue has an almost fairytale aspect, with sixteen-metre-high Gothic
windows and a long, narrow tower next to the main entrance. However, it's the
building's huge scale (especially in comparison to the minute surrounding
townhouses) that provides the wow factor. Inside, look out for the four priest's
robes and other religious garments designed by the current Queen Margrethe II.
Haderslev's medieval centre spreads out from the cathedral, and if you continue
across the square, down Slotsgade, you'll pass some of the town's oldest secular
buildings, dating from the fifteenth and sixteenth centuries. The only ones you can
get inside are the timber-framed buildings at nos. 20 and 22. Built in 1580 no. 20
now houses the **Ehlers Samling** (June–Aug Tues–Fri 10am–5pm, Sat & Sun
1–5pm; Sept–May Tues–Sun 1–5pm; 25kr, joint ticket with Bymuseet i Haderslev
and Arkæologi Haderslev 50kr; Ⓦwww.museum-sonderjylland.dk), a miscellany
of Danish pottery from the Middle Ages until 1940. More interesting, or
intriguing, is the building itself: upstairs, look for the meticulously decorated
original wooden panelling. The building next door, at no. 22, houses **Bymuseet i
Haderslev** (same hours and prices), where you'll find astonishing original frescoes

from the sixteenth century featuring two of the period's biggest warlords – the Assyrian king Ninus and Persian king Cyrus – on horseback. The only other thing to do in Haderslev is look at **Arkæologi Haderslev** (June–Aug Tues–Sun 10am–4pm; Sept–May Tues–Sun 1–4pm; 30kr, joint ticket with Ehler's Collection 50kr; Ⓦ www.museum-sonderjylland.dk), ten minutes' walk east of the centre via Aastrupvej at Dalgade 7; prize processions are two beautifully decorated golden Bronze Age bowls found nearby.

For **food** while you're here, you can't go wrong at the *Haderslev Fiskehus* (Ⓦ www.haderslev-fiskehus.dk; closed Sun) across from the cathedral, where the delightful lunch platter will set you back 62kr.

Eating, drinking and nightlife

Central Kolding has a good selection of **restaurants** and **cafés**, and the city also boasts the region's most active **nightlife** scene, with a wide range of bars, nightclubs and discos. Many of the cafés double as funky clubs at night.

Cafés, restaurants and bars

Admiralen Toldbogade 14 ⓣ75 52 04 21, Ⓦ www.admiralen.dk. Tucked behind the harbour and most easily reached via the railway underpass next to the station, this classy restaurant has a simple menu with a handful of delectable fish dishes, as well as a few meat options. The *pièce de résistance* is the bouillabaisse (285kr), though the traditional steamed cod with mustard sauce (238kr) is also out of this world. Smørrebrød dishes dominate the lunch menu. Closed Sun.

Den Blå Café Lilletorv, Slotsgade 4 ⓣ75 50 65 12, Ⓦ www.denblaacafe.dk. With outdoor seating in a small cosy square, this is Kolding's best option for brunch (108kr), a drink or a light café meal out in the open. In summer, live bands occasionally play in the square, moving into the café during the cold months, when creamy hot chocolate and cake are the perfect accompaniment.

🏃 **Café Lucca** Låsbybanke 4 ⓣ76 33 39 00, Ⓦ www.lucca-kolding.dk. Successful combination of café (with wi-fi), quality restaurant and trendy nightclub, with a largely Spanish/Italian menu. Prices range from 89kr for a delicious classic Caesar salad to 188kr for traditional fried plaice. The popular nightclub (Fri & Sat; free; over-23s only) offers mostly mainstream singalong tunes.

Joe's Diner Låsbygade 27 ⓣ75 50 42 78, Ⓦ www.joesdiner.dk. Modelled on the American small-town diner, with a jovial atmosphere and a predictable menu featuring the usual array of steaks and spare ribs, starting at 120kr for a burger. Portions are enormous. Dinner only.

Knuds Garage Munkegade 5. Busy café-bar, packed with trendy, alternative-type young locals and with lots going on, from backgammon and table-football tournaments to live jam sessions on Thursday nights. The usual array of sandwiches and salads (from 72kr) are supplemented by a huge selection of Danish and foreign beers. Wi-fi, smoking allowed, and an open backyard that gets packed on hot summer days.

Nikolaj Café Skolegade 2, entrance on Blæsbjerggade ⓣ75 50 03 02, Ⓦ www.nicolaicafe.dk. The outstanding café at this arthouse cinema is worth a visit even if you're not seeing a movie. It's not the most intimate of places, but the compensation is the beautifully prepared food, from a hugely popular all-you-can-eat weekend brunch buffet (10am–2pm; 145kr) to salads and sandwiches, a soup (65kr) and pasta of the day (95kr), and the infamous Kolding Steak (185kr) – locally reared beef served with seasonal veg.

Republikken Munkegade 9 ⓣ75 54 14 40, Ⓦ www.republikken.com. A stone's throw from the train station, the laid-back atmosphere at this café makes it a great first stop when arriving in Kolding. Geared towards a mature crowd, with focus on beer and beer tastings, there's also a Sunday-morning indoor flea market, and bluesy live jazz and 1960s rock a couple of evenings a month. Food ranges from sandwiches and salads to steak with all the trimmings (from 109kr) plus an excellent selection of weekend brunch combinations for 109kr (11am–3pm).

You'll Never Walk Alone Klostergade 7A. Ⓦ www .denengelskepub.dk. Popularly known as the "English Pub", and said to have Denmark's largest selection of beers from around the world. The British owners are staunch Liverpool supporters and Premiership football features heavily on the large screen. Often very packed with a separate restaurant section serving basic pub meals. Open from 2pm.

Clubs and live music

🏃 **Godset** Jens Holmsvej 3 ⓣ79 30 10 60, Ⓦ www.godset.net. Unquestionably the region's best music venue, in a characterful, wooden-beamed former freight terminal behind the train station, with live music three to four times a week, from local pop rock to international blues and jazz. Tickets 50–300kr.

Pit Stop Jernbanegade 54. Kolding's best clubbing venue, with a live band one or two nights a week (usually Thurs, sometimes Fri), followed by a DJ playing tunes that lean towards alternative electronica until the early hours. The upstairs lounge, open from 3am onwards, is the only place where the music is subdued enough to have a conversation. Cover 50–70kr, or up to 200kr for gigs.

Sønderborg and Als

With its lush green landscapes subsiding gently into a peaceful coastline, Jutland's southeastern corner is most often seen en route to Funen (covered in Chapter 4) – but with a couple of imposing castles and a string of sheltered sandy beaches, the area holds enough appeal to warrant a couple of days' stay. Laid out along both sides of the Alssund, a narrow but deep channel dividing the island of **Als** from the Jutland mainland, the lively provincial town of **SØNDERBORG**, with its sturdy castle, is a convenient base for exploring the surrounding area, including the nearby line of preserved trenches and moats that point to the town's crucial place in Danish history. Nearby is the haunting **Frøslev Internment Camp**, another significant part of South Jutland's past.

Arrival, information and accommodation

Although the bulk of Sønderborg lies across the Alssund on Als, **trains** go no further than the town's mainland section on the Jutland side of the water, a short walk from the graceful modern road bridge. Long-distance **buses** continue across the bridge to the bus station at the northern fringe of the centre on Jernbanegade. Sønderborg **airport**, 7km north of the centre, has regular **flights** to and from Copenhagen; bus #110 runs from here to the bus station. The **tourist office** (July to mid-Aug Mon–Fri 10am–5.30pm, Sat 10am–1pm; mid-Aug to June Mon–Fri 10am–5pm, Sat 10am–1pm; ☎74 42 35 55, ⓦwww.visitsonderborg.com) is just downhill from the bus station at Rådhustorvet 7 and has a list of private accommodation in the area. Otherwise Sønderborg has a good range of **accommodation** within easy walking distance of the centre; the hostel is a short bus ride away. For **bike rental** head for Jønnes Cykler (☎74 42 63 26, ⓦwww.joennes.dk) at Alsgade 54, while for free **internet** head to the library at Kongevej 19 (book a time slot on ⓦwww.bookingkalender.dk/sonderborg).

Accommodation

Arnkilhus Arnkilgade 13 ☎74 42 23 36, ⓦwww .arnkilhus.dk. A 5min walk north of the centre, this good-value red-brick bungalow looks like a private home – look out for the sign. The fourteen comfortable rooms are all different (some have private bath), and there's free parking and a large terrace at the back. ❻

Comwell Sønderborg Rosengade 2 ☎74 42 19 00, ⓦwww.comwell.com. The grandest hotel in town, a business-oriented place on the seafront around the corner from Sønderborg Slot, with a lovely pool and good restaurant. The spacious rooms all have wi-fi and the pricier ones have a lovely view. Rates are almost half in summer. ❾

Sønderborg Kongevej 96 ☎74 42 34 33, ⓦwww .hotelsoenderborg.dk. Good middle-ground option which looks straight out of the Addams Family. It's close to the centre yet near beautiful woodlands and the south-coast beaches, and the comfortable rooms are all self-contained and have wi-fi. Prices reduce during weekends and holidays. ❼

Sønderborg Camping Ringgade 7 ☎74 42 41 89, ⓦwww.sonderborgcamping.dk. Beautifully located campsite a short walk from Sønderborg marina and 10min from the centre or bus station. Comfortable self-contained cabins available by the week in summer (from 2900kr sleeping three) or by the day the rest of the year (from 400kr). Wi-fi throughout.

Sønderborg City Danhostel Kærvej 70 ☎74 42 31 12, ⓦwww.sonderborgdanhostel.dk. Shiny, modern youth hostel 20min north of the centre, via Perlegade and Kærvej (or take bus #6 from the bus station), which has dorms June to Sept only (160kr) and rooms sleeping up to six all year round, with a few rooms with only two beds ❺. Unusually for a hostel, rates include breakfast.

The town and around

The largest town hereabouts, **Sønderborg** centres around its main attraction of the Sønderborg **Slot**, with its picture-postcard location on the banks of Alssund. It may not be the grandest castle in Denmark, but it's certainly one of the oldest, thought to have been built in 1170 by Valdemar I as a defence against the country's two main threats at the time, Wendish pirates from the Baltic and Germanic forces from the south. Almost four hundred years later it was still one of the strongest fortresses in the kingdom, and was used to imprison the deposed Christian II between 1532 and 1549. The castle's quadrangular shape stems from the era of his successor, Christian III, whose dowager queen Dorothea lived here after his death, and who built the castle chapel. After her departure, Sønderborg fell into disrepair, but was restored in

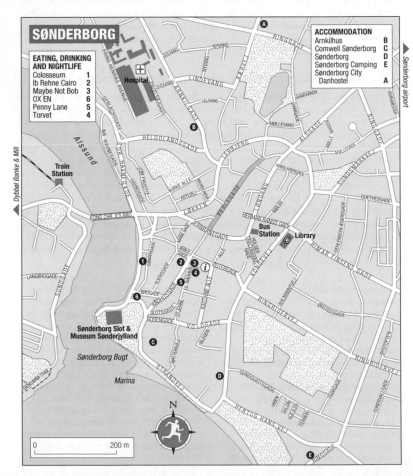

the eighteenth century before being used as a military hospital during the Napoleonic and Danish–German wars. During the latter, it was tossed back and forth between the Danish kings and the dukes of Schleswig, and served as barracks for the Prussian infantry before it was finally handed back to Denmark following the referendum in 1920. A year later it became **Museum Sønderjylland** (Museum of South Jutland: May–Sept daily 10am–5pm; April & Oct daily 10am–4pm; Nov–March Tues–Sun 1–4pm; 40kr; ⓦwww.museum-sonderjylland.dk), and is the most substantial collection of local history in south Jutland. The first floor has detailed displays on the various conflicts during the Schleswig era; look out for the section on the short-lived Als Republic of 1918, born as the German Reich's dissenting northern ports rebelled against the Kaiser and, in emulation of the then-recent Russian revolution, raised a red banner over the town's barracks – the stand lasted only three days. The second floor provides some welcome relief from the battle scenes below, with culturally oriented displays such as a collection of the sought-after silver vinaigrette produced locally; holding a sponge infused with scented water, they were an important status symbol amongst the ladies of Denmark. Accessed via a dark, uninviting guard room from the late 1300s, the ground floor covers the history of the castle itself, with four reconstructed models illustrating its various stages of development.

Dybbøl Banke and Mill

There are a couple of good reasons to cross back over the bridge to the mainland (Jutland) side of Sønderborg: site of the last major battle on Danish soil during the War of 1864 against the Prussians, **Dybbøl Banke** holds the informative Battlefield Centre and the strategically crucial **Dybbøl Mill**, both of which sit amidst a plethora of moats and grassed-over trenches left over from the conflict. Bus #1 from the Sønderborg bus station will take you there in fifteen minutes, but the three-kilometre walk or cycle ride is a much nicer way of arriving; head left on the well-signposted old gendarme trail that runs along the water's edge from the bridge and turn left at the

---

The definitive battle of 1864

Ask any Dane what happened in **1864**, and they'll probably answer that this was the year when Malebrok died in the war, paraphrasing a macabre nursery rhyme in the same vein as England's *Ring-a-ring-a-roses*. Nobody knows who Malebrok was, but the continuing prevalence of the nursery rhyme gives an indication of the enduring effect of the war on the Danish psyche. Although Danes were not unused to defeats, the 1864 trouncing was a major blow: a third of Danish territory was lost to Germany and two-fifths of the population suddenly became German.

Leading up to the war, construction of a new defence line at Dannevirke in south Schleswig to deter attacks from the south had given the Danes a false sense of security – and when well-equipped and highly organized Prussian forces backed by Austria and the new German association of states began to make their way northwards on February 1, they realised that the unfinished Dannevirke line wouldn't hold. Five days later, Danish troops were withdrawn from Dannevirke and marched up to **Dybbøl**, where they were quickly mustered to finish the construction of a new defence line to protect Sønderborg and Als; it was finally completed on March 15. On the same afternoon, the Prussians began their bombardments, using fluted cannons whose range was far greater than anything the Danes had seen before, and slowly worked their way towards the Danish defence line. The final battle at Dybbøl started at 10am on April 18, with Prussian troops attacking the heavily damaged trenches; two hours later, the Danish counterattack collapsed and a truce was called. A final **peace agreement** was reached in August: Holstein and Schleswig became part of the new German federation and remained so up until the referendum of 1920 (see p.292).

stone for lieutenant W.B. Jespersen. During the final clash of the 1864 War (see box, p.195) the remains of medieval Sønderborg were all but destroyed. Most of the trenches and moats you see today are solid German constructions built to protect their newly acquired stronghold against the threat of invading French forces who, in the event, never made it this far. If the trenches have made you curious about what happened here on that fateful day, you can get the lowdown at the **Battlefield Centre** (mid-April to Sept daily 10am–5pm; 55kr, mid-June to mid-Aug 80kr; Ⓦ www.1864 .dk), on the main road from Sønderborg, with military kit, rebuilt trenches and moats, multimedia displays and demonstrations.

Heading back towards Sønderborg look out for the array of beautiful Art Nouveau-style buildings erected between 1864 and 1920 when a large German navy base was set up north of the bridge. The tourist office (see p.193) has a free brochure detailing their locations. On the main road, and strategically located behind the Danish entrenchments, **Dybbøl Mill** (mid-April to Oct daily 10am–4pm; 25kr) gained national importance when it was used by Danish troops (aided by the miller) as a hiding place, lookout point and signalling post in the run-up to the final battle. Some of the most intense fighting took place here, and the mill has since become a national symbol, for both Danes and Germans, in memory of the atrocities of the war and of the bravery of the miller. The story is recounted inside with pictures and maps, though the text is in Danish and German only.

The Frøslev Internment Camp

About 35km west of Sønderborg (bus #10 to Padborg, then bus #263) along cycle route 8 – which hugs the German border – and literally a stone's throw from the border (take the last exit off the E45 motorway, and it's an easy 1km westwards), the **Frøslev Internment Camp**, tucked away in the Frøslev pine plantation, is a thought-provoking reminder of the German occupation of Denmark during World War II. In 1944, a prominent Danish civil servant, Nils Svenningsen, managed to negotiate an agreement with the German occupiers to establish an **internment camp** within the country's borders as a means of stopping deportation of those arrested and detained following the imposition of martial law in 1943 to the dreaded concentration camps in Germany, and to bring home Danish prisoners from the German camps. By the summer of 1944, Frøslev was completed. Over the next nine months, until the end of the war in spring 1945, more than twelve thousand dissidents and political prisoners were incarcerated here. Although under German command, management of the camp was left to the Danes, and conditions were significantly better than those south of the border – inmates were well fed and relatively free to go about their business. However, the German occupiers didn't keep to their end of the deal, and some 1600 prisoners were sent from Frøslev to prison camps in Germany; 220 never returned.

Today the camp is a national memorial and open to visitors. There are a number of museums housed in the camp's various barracks; most interesting is **Frøslevle-jerens Museum** (mid-June to mid-Aug daily 10am–5pm; Feb to mid-June & mid-Aug to Nov Tues–Fri 9am–4pm, Sat & Sun 10am–5pm; free, Ⓦ www .froeslevlejrensmuseum.dk) in bunker H4 and H6 and in the main watchtower, which details living conditions during the camp's nine months of operation.

Eating, drinking and nightlife

Choosing where to eat in Sønderborg is relatively easy as most of the best places are within a small area in the town centre and along the waterfront.

Colosseum Sønder Havnegade 24 ☏74 42 23 06, Ⓦ www.restaurantcolosseum.dk. A family-run

waterfront restaurant serving traditional Danish homecooked food at its best. Try the

Stegt Flæsk special (fried pork served with new potatoes with creamy white parley sauce) for 87kr.

Ib Rehne Cairo Rådhustorvet 4 ⓣ74 42 04 00, ⓦwww.ibrehnecairo.dk. A French-style café named after one of Denmark Radio's most famous foreign correspondents, on the main square. The menu includes a Sunday champagne brunch (119kr), a beautiful smørrebrød lunch platter (119kr), good tapas and burgers, and excellent coffee.

Maybe Not Bob Rådhustorvet 5 ⓣ74 43 08 22, ⓦwww.maybenotbob.dk. A slightly noisy café-pub-nightclub that's hugely popular with young locals as well as foreign students. Closed Sun–Tues and open till 5am Thurs–Sat.

OX EN Brogade 2 ⓣ74 42 27 07, ⓦwww.ox-en.dk. Next door to Sønderborg Slot, this place specializes in sublime Argentinean steaks with all the trimmings from 179kr. During summer, when it's also open for lunch, there's outdoor seating overlooking the harbour, and unmissable herring smørrebrød. Closed Sun.

Penny Lane Rådhusgade 12 ⓣ74 42 70 08, ⓦwww.penny-lane.dk. A good nightlife option with international beers and occasional live jazz. Closed Sun, open till 5am Fri & Sat.

Torvet Rådhustorvet 5 ⓣ74 42 38 80. Next door to the tourist information, this is an excellent spot for outstanding lunchtime smørrebrød and fabulous fresh fish for dinner (195kr). Closed Sun.

Around Als

Five kilometres northeast of Sønderborg (10min by bus #11), and signposted left off the main road to Fynshav (from where a ferry sails to Bøjden on Funen, see p.151), the attractive little village of **Augustenborg** centres around two main streets, lined by picturesque eighteenth-century townhouses that lead up to the ridiculously grand, Rococo-style **Augustenborg palace**, a great pile which looks somewhat misplaced in relation to the size of the village around it. In 1660 Christian III's great-grandson tore down a village here in order to make room for his new manor house on the banks of Alssund, and named it after his wife Augusta. His grandson, August I, also took his turn and created today's painfully symmetrical three-wing Baroque palace. The palace now houses a psychiatric hospital and the only public access is to the gatehouse at the end of Slotsalle, where there's a small exhibit about the palace history; and to the imposing Baroque palace **chapel** (daily 10am–6pm; if locked, pick up a key from the hospital gatehouse), which is built into the palace at the bottom corner of the right wing. Inside, the nave is without benches in order to make room for the wide garments worn by the aristocracy at the time, while the elaborate decoration includes an unusual alabaster baptismal font, a present from Czar Alexander the First.

On the south coast of Als close to a dam linking it with the peninsula of Kegnæs, **Drejby** is a hotspot for wind- and kite-surfing; beginners stay inside the bay, while the more experienced brave the elements on the Baltic side. The long stretch of sand here attracts the crowds during summer, and there's a nudist section to the east of the dam. Good campsites include the well-equipped *Drejby Strand Camping*, right next to the dam at Kegnæsvej 85 (ⓣ74 40 43 05, ⓦwww.drejby.dk), and the more rustic *Sønderkoppel Camping*, past the Kegnæs lighthouse at Piledøppel 2 (ⓣ&ⓕ74 40 51 62). From Sønderborg bus station, bus #19 runs regularly to the dam. Facing east, and reachable via bus #17, the quiet beach at **Momark** is also a pretty place to chill out, especially if you're waiting for the ferry to Søby on Ærø (see p.179).

Tønder and around

Tucked away in the bleak, windswept marshes of Jutland's southeastern corner and just short of the border with Germany, **Tønder** is an intriguing place, its people always managing to prosper despite their inhospitable surroundings. In the thirteenth century, Franciscan monks set up a monastery here and persuaded King Abel to grant a municipal charter to encourage the burgeoning **livestock trade**:

horses and cattle were fattened on the rich grass of the salt marshes and shipped to Holland and beyond. Tønder soon became the richest and most important port in south Jutland, possibly even the country. However, to protect the town and surrounding uplands from the frequent tidal floods, huge dikes were built in the mid-sixteenth century which blocked access to the sea. Facing financial ruin, the people of Tønder determined to find an alternative enterprise and turned to **lace-making**, which became a booming business employing some twelve thousand local women during its mid- to late eighteenth-century heyday. Tønder is still known as a centre of lace-making, with local work widely revered. Today, the town still maintains many links with its German neighbours; the majority of locals voted for the town to remain part of Germany in the 1920 referendum, and you'll hear as much German spoken here as Danish.

The area around Tønder is also worth a couple of days' exploration. The frozen-in-time feel of medieval **Møgeltønder** offers a sense of how the king's outposts might have looked two hundred years ago, while to the east, **Højer** is intrinsically linked to the area's attempts at taming the tidal floods of the marshes, most recently with the magnificent Danish-German Forward Coastal Dike, which marks the beginning of the Danish section of the **Wadden Sea**, known internationally for its prolific birdlife.

Tønder

Central **TØNDER** bears clear evidence of the town's former wealth, its cobbled streets containing many ancient gabled buildings built by wealthy merchants. From the bus and train station on Jernbanegade, head towards the pedestrianized street which transects the compact centre, and whose name changes as you move eastwards from Vestergade, to Storegade and Østergade. Halfway down, at Østergade 1, look out for the former apothecary across from the tourist office (see p.199); dating from 1660, it's a prime example of the lavish houses built on money from the lace trade, with a monumental and beautifully carved sandstone portal that leaves you in little doubt that its owner was very rich indeed. It now houses a jam-packed curio shop with an entire basement section devoted year-round to Christmas decorations. You can wander inside to see the many old features, including a lovely fireplace adorned with Dutch tiles. Continuing down Storegade, the gabled **Drøhses Hus** at no.14 dates from 1672 and boasts a similarly impressive entrance. Home to a branch of **Tønder Museum** (April–Dec Mon–Fri 10am-5pm, Sat 10am–2pm; 25kr), its original features have been fully restored, inside and out. In the basement, changing exhibitions concentrate on various aspects of the lace trade, while the room next door is devoted to beautifully crafted cast-iron stoves; the ground and first floors hold some incredibly intricate and delicate pieces of local lace – the painstaking process of producing it is demonstrated by a working lacemaker during the summer.

The Sort Sol

During spring and autumn, over a million migrating starlings pass through the Wadden Sea marshes on their way north for the summer or south for the winter, and the mesmerizing aerial display that occurs just before sunset as they settle down to roost is known locally as the **Sort Sol** ("Black Sun"). The balletic formation movements of the flocks are a sort of collective stance against predators such as hawks or falcons, and the best places to see them in action are around Tønder, near Ribe or on the island of Rømø. Ask the local tourist offices where the flocks have last been seen, or join one of the excellent organized tours offered by Sort Safari in Møgeltønder (☎73 72 64 00, ⊛www.sortsafari.dk; around 150kr per person including transport).

Heading back towards the train station, passing the Rococo facade of the so-called Dike Baron's house at Vestergade 9, turn left down Kogade and left again down Skibroen to reach the town's two main museums, both located at Kongevejen 51 and accessed via a gatehouse, the only remaining part of the sixteenth-century Tønderhus castle. To the left, **Tønder Museum** (June–Aug daily 10am–5pm; Sept–May Tues–Sun 10am–5pm; 40kr, includes Kunstmuseum; Ⓦwww .museum-sonderjylland.dk) is spread over three floors, its exhibits primarily devoted to trade in this part of south Jutland and the opulent houses built by local livestock and lace merchants; look out for the displays of elaborately decorated wooden furniture and Tønder silverware and lace. The adjoining **Sønderjyllands Kunstmuseum** (same hours and prices) offers changing exhibitions of twentieth-century northern European art, including a significant collection of Danish surrealist works from the 1930s and 1940s. Linked to Tønder Museum by a walkway and run jointly by the two museums (same hours and included in entry fee), the town's former watertower holds – over its seven levels – a collection of chairs by local boy **Hans J. Wegner** (see p.300), whose designs went on to become internationally recognized. It's worth climbing the levels to take in the outstanding view of Tønder and the surrounding marshland from the top. There's also a lift.

Practicalities

As it's only 4km from the German border, Tønder's **transport** network is mainly geared towards north-south travel, with Ribe (see p.202) an easy train ride away. There are no direct transport links from Sønderborg; you have to catch a train to Tinglev and then bus #16 to Tønder. The tourist office on Torvet (July to mid-Aug Mon–Fri 10am–5pm, Sat 10am–2pm; mid-Aug to June Mon–Fri 9am–4pm, Sat 10am–2pm; Ⓣ74 72 12 20, Ⓦwww.visittonder.dk) has reams of information about Tønder and can help find private accommodation.

The only plus side to Tønder's limited range of **accommodation** is that it's varied. The most expensive option is the red-bricked *Tønderhus*, opposite Tønder Museum at Jomfrustien 1 (Ⓣ74 72 22 22, Ⓦwww.hoteltoenderhus.dk; ❼), built during World War I, and, outwardly, little changed since, though there's a smart new section at the back and a popular restaurant. Rooms are clean and comfortable with free wi-fi throughout, and there are good deals in summer. Somewhat cheaper and also in the centre is the *Hostrups*, Søndergade 30 (Ⓣ74 72 21 29, Ⓦwww .hostrupshotel.dk; ❹), overlooking Vidå river and housed in a spacious old villa with creaking floorboards; no two of the tastefully decorated en-suite rooms are the same, although all have free wi-fi; it also has a good restaurant. The best budget option is the **youth hostel**, *Tønder Vandrerhjem*, Sønderport 4 (Ⓣ74 72 35 00, Ⓦwww.danhostel.dk/tonder; closed mid-Dec to Jan), about 1km west of the train station past Tønder Museum and the river, with dorms (July to mid-Sept; 160kr) and doubles (❸). There's also a **campsite** at Holmevej 2A (Ⓣ74 72 18 49, Ⓦwww .tondercamping.dk; April–Oct), with log cabins sleeping four for 2800kr per week.

The best places for **food and drink** include the small and cosy ⚑ *Café Engel*, Gråbrødre Torv (Ⓣ74 72 70 80; closed Sun), open only for breakfast and lunch, with a lovely array of organic sandwiches, salads and cakes from 49kr, and a fantastic Saturday breakfast (11am–1pm; 99kr). Elsewhere, the restaurant at the *Hostrups Hotel* offers good-value traditional Danish food, with beautifully sculpted smørrebrød at lunch (from 32kr a piece) and a daily fish special for 155kr. It's said that Tønder had the world's highest ratio of inhabitants to bars – forty-nine to one – in the eighteenth century. Of the original spots, the atmospheric *Victoria*, Storegade 9 (Ⓣ74 72 00 89, Ⓦwww.victoriatoender.dk), is still going strong and continues to brew its delicious beer as well as offering a good selection of substantial burgers (from 92kr), mouthwatering cakes (32kr), home-made soups (62kr) and more. A bit out of the centre on the road to Ribe, the *Bowler Inn*, Landevej 56 (☎74 72 00 11, Ⓦwww.hotelbowlerinn.dk), is a pub/restaurant renowned for its draught beers and quality steaks (from 129kr), and has a bowling alley.

In the last week of August, the outstanding **Tønder Festival** (see p.31) transforms the town into one big party with live jazz and folk at eight different venues.

West of Tønder

Just 5km west of Tønder and reachable via bus #66 toward Højer, it's well worth taking time to visit the idyllic medieval-era village of **MØGELTØNDER** which – somewhat unbelievably given its diminutive size – was once the region's main town during the area's maritime era; Tønder was merely its harbour. Since then, time seems to have stood still, and the village is ideal for an afternoon of peaceful meandering. The village grew up around **Møgeltønderhus** – the Danish king's most southerly fortified outpost – which was destroyed and rebuilt in the thirteenth, fifteenth and seventeenth centuries. The town and its ruinous fort were eventually given to Field Marshal Hans Schack as a reward for his war victory over the Swedes at the battle of Nyborg in 1661. He tore down the old ruin and built the current **Schackenborg Castle**, which remained within the Schack family for eleven generations until 1979, when it was handed back to the Danish crown; it's now home to the Queen's youngest son, Prince Joachim, and his family. There's no entry to the public, but there are half-hour guided tours of the neatly manicured, moat-enclosed grounds (mid-May to Aug; tickets and times available at Tønder Tourist Office; 30kr) with the possibility, if you're lucky, of a royal sighting; Joachim still farms the land hereabouts. Lined with lime trees, the cobbled Slotsgade is the village's main street; near the castle end at no.42, the *Schackenborg Slotskro* (☎74 73 83 83, Ⓦwww.slotskro.dk) is an outstanding restaurant, with a fabulous selection of dishes made from Schackenborg's home-grown produce; it also has luxurious rooms (❽). At the other end of the street, **Møgeltønder Kirke** (daily 8am–4pm) has some nice frescoes dating back to the twelfth century. For information on guided tours of the Tønder marshes or the Wadden Sea (see box below), visit **Sort Safari** (☎73 72 64 00, Ⓦwww.sortsafari.dk) at no. 22.

Some 7km west of Møgeltønder (and on the route of bus #66), the small, somewhat desolate town of **HØJER** gives an interesting insight into the dramas created by the Tønder coastline. Højer was a seaside town until 1981, when completion of the **Danish–German Forward Coastal Dike** shifted the coastline 2km to the west and reclaimed some twelve hundred hectares of land; the Danish section of this is known as Magrethe Kog. The first dikes were built here as early as the eleventh century, and today's Forward Coastal Dike is the culmination of

---

Wadden Sea aquatic birdlife

A 500-kilometre coastal strip stretching from Den Helder in Holland to Blåvandshug near Esbjerg in Denmark, the **Wadden Sea** is an essential resting and feeding place for **migratory birds** travelling the so-called East Atlantic Flyway, which sees them heading as far north as Greenland in the summer and as far south as southern Africa in the winter. Each year, more than ten million aquatic birds pass through the Wadden Sea, which is one of the world's most important wetland areas, designated as a protected site under the internationally recognized RAMSAR convention. It covers about 900,000 hectares of marsh, tidal flats, sand banks, beaches and dunes and supports over fifty bird species including a number of specimens designated threatened, from the Kentish plover, dunlin and ruff to the gull-billed and little tern, any of which are regular visitors to the saltwater lake in the reclaimed Magrethe Kog near Højer (see above).

the long battle to curb the devastating and powerful west coast storm tides. To learn more head for the **Højer Mill & Marsh Museum** (April–Oct daily 10am–4pm; 25kr), housed in a restored Dutch windmill. It's entirely devoted to the area's unique history with hundreds of photos depicting seasonal life in the marshes before and after the 1925 drainage system was put in place, and some very scary reminders of the destructive and deadly power of storm tides. Although most of the text is in Danish, the photos provide plenty of insight.

If it's not too windy, you might want to check out the Danish-German Forward Coastal Dike and sluice, an easy three-kilometre bike ride west of Højer; the tourist office in Tønder can help with bike rental. Follow the signboards past the old dike and sluice at the outskirts of Højer and it's straight ahead to the very Dutch-looking dike, with the reclaimed Magrethe Kog to the left; it's now a protected nature reserve, a third of it retained as a saltwater lake to provide a home for the area's aquatic birds. The road ends at the dike and the massive Vidå sluice, with its twenty-metre-wide circular tanks and three storm shields; there's an excellent café next to the sluice (May–Sept daily 10am–8pm), serving traditional Danish seafood dishes (from 92kr). Don't leave town without sampling the delicious **Højer sausage** – actually salami, and widely acclaimed as Denmark's best. It's available from the butcher's shop at Søndergade 1, across from the church.

Rømø

Just offshore from and buffering the Wadden Sea tidal marshes, the island of RØMØ is a popular holiday destination for German tourists, offering fantastic beaches and some good examples of the Wadden's classic tidal landscapes.

From Skærbæk, 27km north of Tønder, bus #185 heads across the nine-kilometre causeway over the Wadden Sea tidal flats to the island. Created by the actions of sea, wind and sand over the past two thousand years, Rømø maintains a wild and unkempt appearance, with a duney heathland in its centre, stunning wide beaches along the western side and marshy tidal flats facing mainland Jutland. All of the rocks and stones on Rømø have been transported across. In summer, Rømø is a magnet for **beach** lovers, who flock to the west's sandy shores. The beach is divided into sections for designated activities such as wind riding (☏22 85 50 15, ⓦwww .windtoysdk.com) and kite-buggying (☏50 24 41 92), and there's also a nude bathing section at the southwesternmost corner and a no-go military zone to the north; pick up a free map of the beach sections at the tourist office. **Horseriding** is also very popular on Rømø; Kommandørgården (see p.202) on the east coast has Icelandic ponies and offers guided rides (225kr per 2hr 30min up to 975kr per day), while Thomsens Ridecenter nearby (ⓦwww.Sigurd-Thomsen.com) does guided beach and forest rides on both horses and ponies (210kr per up to 2hr).

If you're interested in Rømø's prolific avian population, head to Tvismark, the first hamlet just south of the causeway. Here, the **Tønnisgård Natur Center** (March–Nov Mon–Fri 10am–4pm; Dec–Feb Mon–Fri 10am–3pm; 15kr; ⓦwww.tonnisgaard.dk), next door to the tourist office at Havnebyvej 30, organizes birdwatching trips to the Stormengene nature reserve at the island's southeastern tip, where there's a high concentration of migrating birds in spring and autumn. The trips are only in German and Danish, though if they're not too busy the guides will do their best to explain things in English, too. The centre also has heaps of material about the island's wildlife and can point you in the right direction if you want to explore on your own.

Although beaches and wildlife are Rømø's two top attractions, the island's cultural history is also fairly absorbing. As a typical Wadden Sea island, Rømø has strong seafaring traditions, and the navigation school that once operated here produced many *kommandører*, whaling-ship captains who built grand residences on their return to the island. Just north of Tvismark in Toftum, the handsome **Kommandørgården**, Jurevej 60 (May–Sept Tues–Sun 10am–6pm; Oct–Nov Tues–Sun 10am–3pm; free), was built in 1749 by one Captain Thacken, and its rich interior and elaborate furnishings are a fine illustration of the wealth brought home from the sea. Further north along Jurevej, on the right-hand side, look out for the fence made of whale jawbones, the only available building material in 1772 when it was made. Heading south, past the tourist office – also housed in an old *kommandør* residence – the **Sct Clemens Church** (Tues–Fri 8am–4pm) is consecrated to the seafaring Sct Clemens and adorned with beautifully crafted wooden model ships hanging from a low wooden ceiling – creating a very cosy unchurchlike space. The southeasterly section of the churchyard is devoted to the graves of foreign war casualties – four German soldiers who died during the battle of Skagerrak during World War I and thirty-two English, Canadian and Australian soldiers who perished during World War II.

Practicalities

Rømø's **tourist office** (daily 9am–5pm; ☎74 75 51 30, ⊛www.romo.dk) is at Havnebyvej 30 in Tvismark, and can help with information about private accommodation (about 250kr per person per day); it's also the island's official holiday letting agency, with a long list of pretty cottages starting at 1300kr per week. The main village of Havneby holds two good-value **hotels**: *Havneby Kro*, at Skansen 3 near the harbour (☎74 75 75 35, ⊛www.havneby-kro.dk; ❻), a traditional inn with sleek modern rooms above a quality restaurant; and the basic *Garni*, Nørre Frankel 15 (take a right just as you enter town; ☎74 75 54 80, ℻74 75 63 80; ❸), with shared facilities. The most child-friendly option is the modern *Kommandørgården* (☎74 75 51 22, ⊛www.kommandoergaarden.dk; ❼), at Havnebyvej 21 in Østerby, 1km north of Havneby. A small holiday village with a large children's play area as well as Icelandic ponies (see p.201) and a host of wellness therapies for adults, it has the usual double rooms as well as self-contained flats (1195kr per day), two-person log cabins (895kr per day) and a **campsite**. Of the island's two other camping options, by far the most popular with the younger beach-loving crowd is *Lakolk* (☎74 75 52 28, ⊛www.lakolkcamping.dk; April to mid-Oct), on the windswept west coast near the Lakolk shopping area which houses restaurants and cafés, and a new popular nightclub. There's also a **youth hostel** (☎74 75 51 88, ⊛www.romo-vandrerhjem.dk; mid-March to mid-Nov) in a beautiful old thatched building at Lyngvejen 7, just north of Havneby (follow the signs off the main road); it has doubles (❷) and four-bed dorms (160kr). The island's only internet café is at the Statoil garage at the main junction. **Public transport** is limited to bus #185, which runs four to six times a day between Skærbæk (on the mainland) and Havneby. Alternatively, the *Garni* hotel rents out bicycles for 60kr per day. It's also possible to **cross the border to Germany** on the ferry that sails from Havneby to List (☎73 75 53 03, ⊛www.romo-sylt.dk; 50min, 70kr).

Ribe

About fifty minutes north of Tønder by train – and twenty minutes from Skærbæk – lies the exquisitely preserved town of **RIBE**. In 856 bishop Ansgar of Hamburg and Bremen built one of Denmark's first churches here as a base for his missionaries arriving from Germany; a hundred years later the town was a major staging post for pilgrims making their way south to Rome. Ribe's proximity to the sea allowed it to evolve into a significant trading port, but continued expansion was thwarted by the dual blows of the Reformation and the sanding-up of the harbour. Since then, not much appears to have changed. The surrounding marshlands, which have prevented the development of any large-scale industry, and a long-standing conservation programme have enabled Ribe to keep the appearance and size of medieval times, and its old town is a delight to wander, not least on a guided tour with the almost authentic night-watchman (see p.205).

Arrival, information and accommodation

From Ribe **train** and **bus stations** on the east side of the river, Dagmarsgade cuts a straight path to the central square, Torvet. Besides the usual services, the **tourist office**, on Torvet to the rear of the cathedral (June & Sept Mon–Fri 9am–5pm, Sat 10am–2pm; July & Aug Mon–Fri 9am–6pm, Sat 10am–5pm, Sun 10am–2pm; Oct–May Mon–Fri 10am–4.30pm, Sat 10am–2pm; ☏75 42 15 00, ⓦwww .visitribe.dk), offers free internet use.

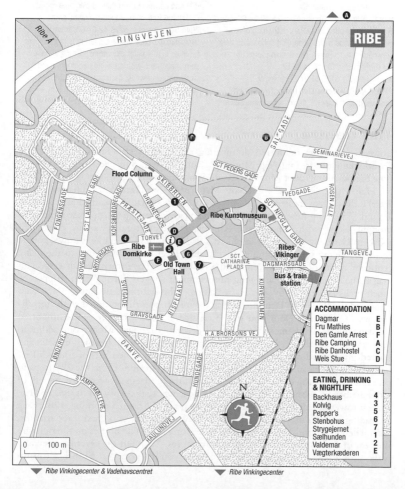

ACCOMMODATION
Dagmar	E
Fru Mathies	B
Den Gamle Arrest	F
Ribe Camping	A
Ribe Danhostel	C
Weis Stue	D

EATING, DRINKING & NIGHTLIFE
Backhaus	4
Kolvig	3
Pepper's	5
Stenbohus	6
Strygejernet	7
Sælhunden	1
Valdemar	2
Vægterkæderen	E

▼ *Ribe Vinkingecenter & Vadehavscentret*   ▼ *Ribe Vinkingecenter*

Accommodation

If you intend to stick around for the nightwatchman's tour, you'll need to **stay overnight**. There's a good range of interesting and affordable accommodation, but book ahead in summer as everything gets packed. The tourist office publishes a list of private rooms that rent for about 200kr per person per night.

Dagmar Torvet ☎75 42 00 33, ⓦwww .hoteldagmar.dk. Wonderful if you can afford it, this beautifully restored place opposite the Domkirke dates from 1581 and claims to be the oldest hotel in Denmark; its gorgeous doubles come with period furniture and loads of character, and there's free wi-fi throughout. **❽**

Fru Mathies Saltgade 15 ☎75 42 34 20, ⓦwww .frumathies.dk. A short walk from the centre across the river down Nederdammen, this bright yellow pub also has a few comfortable rooms, some of which share bathrooms. **❻**

Den Gamle Arrest Torvet 11 ☎75 42 37 00, ⓦwww.dengamlearrest.dk. An intriguing option, originally built as a girls' boarding school and later serving as the town jail. The double rooms are in the former cells. **❺**, en-suite **❻**

Ribe Camping ☎75 41 07 77, ⓦwww .ribecamping.dk. Some 2km north of Ribe along Farupvej (take bus #715), this pleasant campsite is tucked into a woodland area which offers lots of good hiking. As well as pitches the site offers a range of cabins, from basic ones sleeping four (352kr) to lavish, fully equipped luxury huts sleeping six (from 5400kr/week, not available by the day during the high season), which come with and without spa.

Ribe Danhostel Skt Pedersgade 16 ☎75 42 06 20, ⓦwww.danhostel-ribe.dk. An easy walk over the river from the town centre and with views straight out onto the Wadden Sea marshes. Apart from some good-value, pleasant en-suite doubles (**❸**) and dorms (110kr) there's also bike rental (70kr) and free wi-fi around the lobby area.

Weis Stue Torvet 2 ☎75 42 07 00, ⓦwww .weisstue.dk. Cosy doubles sharing bath and toilet facilities in a wonderfully atmospheric teahouse-cum-restaurant, with creaking floorboards and wood-panelled walls; there are only eight rooms, so advance booking is essential year-round. **❻**

The centre

Towering over the town and dominating the wetlands for miles around, **Ribe Domkirke** (July to mid-Aug Mon–Sat 10am–5.30pm, Sun noon–5.30pm; May–June & mid-Aug to Sept Mon–Sat 10am–5pm, Sun noon–5pm; Oct & April Mon–Sat 11am–4pm, Sun noon–4pm; Nov–March Mon–Sat 11am-3pm, Sun noon–3pm; 10kr) is the current incarnation of Ansgar's original church. The cathedral was begun around 1150 using tufa rock, a suitably light material for the marshy base which was brought, along with some of the Rhineland's architectural styles, by river from southern Germany. Originally raised on a slight hill, the Domkirke is now a couple of metres below the surrounding streets, their level having risen due to the many centuries' worth of debris accumulated beneath them. The **interior** is not as spectacular as the cathedral's size and long history might suggest, having been stripped of much of its decoration by one Hans Tausen – the reformist Bishop of Ribe who translated the Bible into Danish – during the mid-sixteenth century. The thirteenth-century "Cat's Head Door" on the south side, a good example of the imported Romanesque design, is one of the few early decorative remains. More recent additions that catch the eye are the butcher's-slab altar and the colourful frescoes, mosaics and stained-glass windows by Carl-Henning Pedersen (a member of the CoBrA movement), added in the mid-1980s. After looking around, climb the 248 steps to peer out from the top of the red-brick **Borgertårn** (Citizens' Tower), so named since it doesn't belong to the church but to the people whose taxes pay for its upkeep. The current tower's predecessor toppled into the nave on Christmas morning, 1283.

Heading away from the cathedral along Overdammen, you cross three streams, channelled in around 1250 to provide water for a mill. The houses on the right are the best of Ribe's many half-timbered structures. Turn left off Overdammen and walk along the riverside Skibbroen and you'll spot the **Flood Column**

The nightwatchman of Ribe

At 10pm every evening between May and mid-September – and also at 8pm from June to August – the **Nightwatchman of Ribe** emerges from the bar of the *Weis Stue* inn, Torvet 2, and makes his rounds. Before the advent of gas lighting, a nightwatchman would patrol every town in Denmark to help keep the sleeping populace safe from fire and flood. The last real nightwatchman of Ribe made his final tour in 1902, but thanks to the early development of tourism in the town, the custom had been reintroduced by 1932.

Dressed in a replica of his predecessor's uniform and carrying an original morningstar pike and lantern (the sharp tip doubled as a weapon), the watchman – a role filled for the last thirty-odd years by octogenarian Aage Gran – walks the narrow alleys of Ribe singing songs written by Thomas Kingo (a local priest who lived in Ribe in the mid-eighteenth century), and talking about the town's history while stopping at points of interest. One song tells people to go to bed and to be careful with lighting fires – sensible advice when most of the town's dwellings are built from wood. It's obviously laid on for the tourists, but the tour is free and good fun.

(*Stormflodssøjlen*), a stout wooden pole showing the levels of the numerous floods that plagued the town before protective dikes were built a century ago.

Continuing along Overdammen, Sct Nicolaj Gade cuts right to the small **Ribe Kunstmuseum** (Tues–Sun 11am–4pm; 30kr; Ⓦ www.ribe-kunstmuseum.dk), housing a reasonable display of works by Danish artists. On the first floor the highlight is *The Christening*, by Skagen painter Michael Ancher (see p.259) depicting a host of fellow Skagen painters – including P.S. Krøyer, wife Anna Ancher and himself – at his child's christening. A handful of accomplished bronze sculptures are supplemented by larger pieces on the back lawn.

Ribe's Viking history – and more – is celebrated at the **Ribes Vikinger** (July & Aug daily 10am–6pm, Wed until 9pm; April–June, Sept & Oct daily 10am–4pm; Nov–March Tues–Sun 10am–4pm; 60kr; Ⓦ www.ribesvikinger.dk), further along Skt Nicolaj Gade opposite the train station. The exhibition is centred around Ribe's history, from its Viking beginnings as Scandinavia's oldest known market place on the banks of Ribe Å river, to the flooding in October 1634 when the floor of Ribe Cathedral was submerged under water and the town all but destroyed. It covers each era succinctly with models, excavated remains and a full-size reconstructed Viking ship.

Ribe Vikingecenter

If you've not yet had your fill on Vikings, head for the **Ribe Vikingecenter** (July & Aug daily 11am–5pm; May, June & Sept Mon–Fri 10am–3.30pm; 80kr; Ⓦ www.ribevikingecenter.dk), 3km south of the centre on Lustrupvej (6min on bus #717). Situated in the grounds of Lustrupholm manor house, it attempts to recreate the Viking lifestyle with costumed attendants demonstrating traditional crafts. It also hosts northern Europe's largest Viking market during the first weekend of May, when "Vikings" from across the globe gather to show off their outfits as well as skills such as archery, fighting and riding. Traditionally prepared food and drink as well as traditional products (leatherwear and jewellery) are sold, and Viking music is played throughout. If the weather's good, it's lots of fun.

Vadehavscentret

A worthwhile day trip out of Ribe, if you want to learn more about the Wadden Sea area's complex ecology and history, is the sleek **Vadehavscentret** (Wadden Sea Centre: daily: April–Sept daily 10am–5pm, mid-Feb to March & Oct 10am–4pm;

60kr; @www.vadehavscentret.dk), 10km southwest of Ribe in the village of Vester Vedsted (bus #711). Storms and tides are explained by way of snazzy, interactive multimedia displays, and there's fascinating film footage of the 1981 floods that left the nearby island of Mandø submerged. It also has an excellent section on bird migration and the global threats to their nesting and feeding habitats. The centre also offers well-organized tours of the area (check the website).

Eating, drinking and nightlife

All of Ribe's best food and drink options are within the town centre. In summer it may be a good idea to book in advance.

Backhaus Grydergade 12 ☎75 42 11 01, @www .backhaus-ribe.dk.Good-value smørrebrød and other traditional Danish dishes for lunch. Dinner is more a meat (or fish) and two-veg affair (from 99kr).

Kolvig Ved Skibroen ☎75 41 04 88, @www.kolvig.dk. This place offers a relaxed riverside setting in the centre of town and a menu made up of delightfully combined, locally sourced, seasonal produce. There are excellent and reasonably priced salads and sandwiches, and in the evening you can choose the set menu (2–4 courses) or go à la carte. Closed Sun.

Pepper's Torvet 9 @www.peppers.dk. Raucous café-bar which turns into a nightclub at midnight. Also featuring a pool table and the occasional live rock band. An in-house photographer snoops around taking incriminating photos which are published on the website the next day. Open Thurs–Sat from 8pm.

Stenbohus Stenbogade 1 @www.stenbohus-ribe .dk. Popular bar-disco across from *Pepper's* with

live blues, folk or rock acts at least once a week. Open Thurs–Sat, live music from midnight.

Strygejernet Dagmarsgade 1 @www.strygejernet .dk. Atmospheric, tiny but distinctive pub, which serves light meals and snacks during the day and delightful draught ales at night. Closed Sun.

Sælhunden Skibroen 13 ☎75 42 09 46, @www .saelhunden.dk. Slightly pricey traditional Danish fare served in a wood-beamed listed building overlooking the harbour.

Valdemar Skt Nicolaj Gade 6 ☎75 42 42 03, @www.cafevaldemar.dk. Next to the art gallery, the relaxing garden setting is a perfect spot for coffee or a cool draught beer during summer. In the evening, there's occasional live music inside. Closed Sun & Mon.

Vægterkælderen Torvet ☎75 42 14 00, @www .hoteldagmar.dk in the basement of the *Dagmar* hotel. A reputable spot to eat, serving two- (259kr) and three-course (298kr) dinners, mostly fishy or meaty Danish specialities. At night, it's a lively bar.

Travel details

Trains

Kolding to: Århus (hourly; 1hr 30min); Copenhagen (hourly; 2hr 15min); Esbjerg (1–2 hourly; 1hr); Fredericia (1–3 hourly; 15min); Tinglev (1–2 hourly; 1hr); Sønderborg (10 daily; 1hr 30min).
Ribe to: Esbjerg (1–2 hourly; 30min); Skærbæk (hourly; 20min); Tønder (hourly; 45min).
Sønderborg to: Kolding (11 daily; 1hr 30min); Tinglev (11 daily; 45min).
Tønder to: Ribe (hourly; 45min); Skærbæk (hourly; 30min).

Buses

Haderslev to: Kolding (1–2 hourly; 45min); Sønderborg (hourly; 1hr), Tønder (10 daily; 1hr 30min).

Kolding to: Haderslev (1–2 hourly; 45min).
Skærbæk to: Rømø (10 daily; 30min).
Sønderborg to: Haderslev (1–2 hourly; 45min).
Tønder to: Haderslev (10 daily; 1hr 30min).

Ferries

Fynshav to: Bøjden (8 daily; 45min).
Mommark to: Søby (2–5 daily; 1hr).

Flights

Sønderborg to: Copenhagen (2–3 daily; 45min).

6

East Jutland

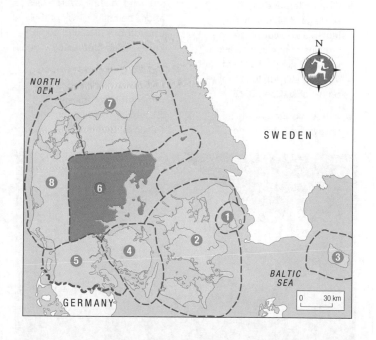

CHAPTER 6 # Highlights

* **Legoland** This brilliant theme park is a must, even if your Lego days ended some years ago. See p.214

* **Canoeing down the Gudenå** Let the gentle current of Denmark's longest river carry you through some of Jutland's prettiest countryside. See p.219

* **Grauballemanden, Moesgård Museum** The remarkable peat-preserved remains of a man who lived in 80 BC are so well kept that you can still see the stubble on his chin. See p.227

* **Århus nightlife** Århus is always lively, with a host

of delightful places to eat, drink or dance the night away. See p.229

* **Djursland beaches** These beautiful sandy beaches are far removed from most people's idea of the unforgiving Scandinavian landscape. See p.232

* **Hiking in Mols Bjerge** These stunning, heath-covered hills afford beautiful views of the Ebeltoft bay area and some lovely walks. See p.232

* **Viborg Cathedral** A grand cathedral, made even more remarkable by Joakim Skovgård's colourful interior frescoes. See p.236

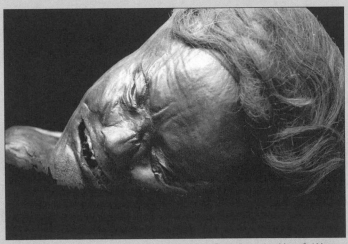

▲ Grauballemanden, Moesgård Museum

East Jutland

The most densely populated part of the peninsula, the **east** is also Jutland's most culturally vibrant region, and the prettiest. Stretching from the Lillebælt bridge (which connects Jutland with Funen and, ultimately, Zealand and Copenhagen) and up past the grandly named **Lake District** to where the **Djursland** peninsula juts out into the Kattegat, the soft, hilly landscapes of the east are largely moraine formations, created in the aftermath of the last Ice Age when the jagged coastline was carved up by melting ice draining into the sea. These strong forces of nature created an unusually pretty landscape that stands out in an otherwise flat country, and with three national cycle routes traversing the area, it's all best seen by bike. The beautiful beaches and meandering rivers are at their most stunning in summer, when they attract holidaymakers in droves, but you'll get a better appreciation of the area's uniqueness during the quieter months of spring and autumn.

The region's main urban draw, **Århus**, is the country's second city, boasting top-notch museums and a heaving nightlife. Among the coastal towns, **Fredericia** has the oddest history, while **Vejle** is home to a few good museums and has an upland packed with historical sights such as the Jelling stone and big-name attractions like Legoland. At the heart of the Lake District, **Silkeborg** is inextricably linked to canoeing on the Gudenå river, while the white-sand beaches of **Djursland** leave little to be desired. North of Djursland, **Randers'** main offering is its recreated rainforests, steaming under massive domes, while **Viborg** boasts a majestic cathedral and countryside suffused with history.

Fredericia and around

Set on the east coast overlooking the nearby island of Funen (covered in Chapter 4), **FREDERICIA** is the rail hub for trains crossing the Lillebælt bridge to Funen, and with its unique military history (and layout), is well worth a quick stop. Envisaged by Christian IV during the Thirty Years' War (1618–47; see p.288) as a strategic reserve capital and a base from which to defend Jutland, Fredericia was eventually founded in 1650 – a year after Christian's death – by his son Frederik III. Three nearby villages were demolished and their inhabitants forced to assist in the building of the new town – and afterwards, they had no choice but to live in it. Military considerations required that Fredericia be built on a strict grid plan, with low buildings enclosed by earthen ramparts reaching up to 15m above street level, and protected further by an encircling moat. More than one million cubic metres of soil were shifted to build the ramparts and nine large bastions. However, seven years after

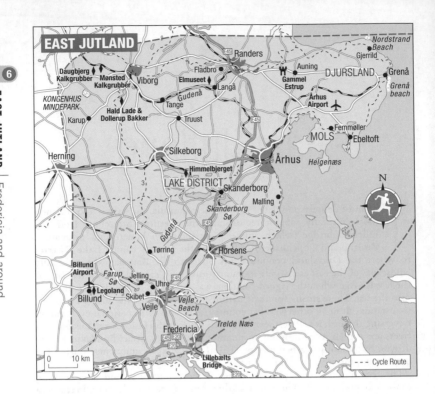

completion, a forceful Swedish army attacked and all but destroyed this supposedly invincible town; most of its citizens fled and Fredericia was left practically deserted. A long and torturous rebuilding process followed, with tax exemptions and promises of religious freedom offered to lure the people back. Catholics, Jews and Huguenots soon arrived from all over Europe, as demonstrated by the town's large Jewish cemetery. The rebuilt fortification was finally completed in 1710, and over the years, until the final defeat in 1864 (see box, p.195), the town played a significant part in the wars over south Jutland. The fortification was decommissioned in 1909, and turned into a public park a few years later. A military feel abides to this day, however; the town centre is dotted with memorials to victorious heroes, and Fredericia is home to the only military tattoo still staged in Denmark.

The twenty-minute walk (or 5min ride on bus #2) along Vesterbrogade from the train station into the town centre takes you through the Danmarks Port, gateway to the most impressive section of the now grassed-over ramparts, which stretch for 4km. A path along the top gives a good perspective on the town's layout, though you'll get an even better view from the top of the **Hvide Vandtårn** (May to mid-June & mid-Aug to mid-Sept Sat & Sun 11am–4.30pm; mid-June to mid-Aug daily 11am–4.30pm; 10kr), a decommissioned water tower at the Prins Georges Bastion, visible from Danmarks Port and a short walk up the rampart. From here, the straight lines and minuscule size of Fredericia's town centre stand out, as do the greenery-covered ramparts that completely encircle the centre. Back down from the ramparts, between the Danmarks and Prinsens Port gateways, the **Den Tapre Landsoldat** ("the brave foot soldier") **statue** by renowned Danish sculptor Bissen epitomizes the local military spirit, its bronze figure holding a rifle in his left hand, a sprig of leaves in his right, and with his foot resting on a captured cannon. The statue commemorates "6 Juli 1849", the day Danish troops secretly assembled in Fredericia to make a momentous (and successful) sortie against the occupying Prussians in the first Napoleonic Wars (see p.290). The downside of the battle was the five hundred Danes killed; they lie in a mass grave in the grounds of the town's church, **Trinitatis Kirke**, on Kongensgade. The anniversary of the battle is still celebrated each year as **Fredericia Day**, with memorial ceremonies on the evening of July 5, and concerts and fireworks on July 6.

The fortifications around the town centre form the core of Fredericia's appeal. A free leaflet about the ramparts can be picked up at the tourist office (see below), itself situated in a beautifully renovated building from 1850 that formerly served as Fredericia's prison, town hall and courthouse. Designed by Ferdinand Meldahl (also renowned for his courthouses in Randers and Aalborg), this unique structure boasts heaps of fine detail, its arches and pillars more redolent of Venice than of Denmark. The only other place worth seeking out within the ramparts, and a short walk away along Jyllandsgade, is the **Jewish cemetery** (mid-June to mid-Aug Wed noon–4pm; outside these hours collect a key at the town museum) on Slesvigsgade 2, holding 550 graves, their tombstones inscribed in meticulous Hebrew writing. The small chapel (same hours; 10kr) houses changing displays on aspects of local Jewish history, though Judaism isn't an active religion here today.

Just outside the ramparts, on the road leading back to the station from Slesvigs Bastion, the **Bymuseet i Fredericia**, Jernbanegade 10 (Fredericia Town Museum; mid-June to mid-Aug daily noon–4pm, Feb to mid-June and mid-Aug to Dec Tues–Sun noon–4pm; 20kr), is, quite predictably, centred around three hundred years of armed conflict via a series of displays in the main building by the entrance. The large, well-presented site also includes typical houses from the seventeenth and eighteenth centuries, moved here from their various locations in town. Keep an eye out for the unusual *soldaterkammeret* (soldier's shack), building 6, an obligatory extension to all townhouses in Fredericia prior to the building of a military barracks in the 1930s, before which all private homes housed soldiers, typically in cold, sparsely furnished shacks at the back. The unusual museum garden is also worth a peek, with crops and flowers that have a historical link with Fredericia. A tobacco section, complete with open drying barn, stems from the Reformed Church members who arrived here from Holland following the promise of religious freedom. Apart from tobacco, they also introduced a range of vegetables to the area including new sorts of potatoes and the Bortfelder turnip.

If it's sunny, you might want to head to the eastern end of Jyllandsgade, where the fine Østerstrand **beach** runs along the entire eastern section of the ramparts, facing Funen on the opposite bank of the Lille Bælt.

Practicalities

Fredericia's **tourist office**, Vendersgade 30D (Mon–Fri 10am–5pm, Sat 10am–1pm; ☎72 11 35 11, ⓦwww.fredericia.dk), has an extensive list of private rooms (20kr booking fee), and cycle maps for sale. **Bicycles** can be rented at Cykel Service, Venusvej 4 (☎75 92 14 09) west of the centre, and there's free **internet** access at Fredericia library at Prinsessegade 27 (Mon–Thurs 10am–7pm, Fri 10am–5pm, Sat 10am–2pm). There are only two **hotels** within Fredericia's ramparts, both near the harbour. The good-value *Postgården*, Oldenborggade 4 (☎75 92 18 55, ⓦwww .postgaarden.dk; ❺, en-suite ❻), has free wi-fi and parking, and a dinner restaurant serving traditional Danish daily specials for 67kr; the smaller, family-run *Sømandshjemmet* on Gothersgade 40 (☎75 92 01 99, ⓦwww.fsh.dk; ❻) has significant weekend reductions, free wi-fi and a good-value restaurant. To the west of the town, outside the ramparts and reachable by bus #2 and #6 from the train station,

a modern **youth hostel**, *Fredericia Vandrerhjem*, Vestre Ringvej 98 (⊕75 92 12 87, ⓦwww.fredericia-danhostel.dk; dorms 225kr, doubles ⑤), has thirty four-bed rooms that can be rented as doubles; while the *Trelde Næs* **campsite** (⊕75 95 71 83, ⓦwww.supercamp.dk; April–Oct) housing cabins sleeping up to six (from 450kr) is beautifully situated at the entry to Vejle fjord, though it's 15km north of town and adjacent to a public beach, so it can get very crowded during fine weather and at holiday times. Take bus #6 from the train station.

For **food**, the restaurants at the two hotels offer good-value dining, while the stylish *Ti Trin Ned*, Norgesgade 3 (closed Sun & Mon; ⊕75 93 33 55, ⓦwww.titrinned.dk), serves high-quality, locally sourced food at fair prices – 395kr for a delicious three-course meal. For something a little different, *Café Carlos*, Sjællandsgade 56 (winter open evenings only; ⊕75 92 04 91, ⓦwww.cafecarlos.dk), has good-value Spanish cuisine including some delightful tapas, while the friendly, family-run *Da Isabella*, Vendersgade 20 (⊕75 95 44 64, ⓦwww.daisabella.dk), does Italian dishes from 59kr, good Danish steaks, and an outstanding all-you-can-eat lunch buffet (59kr). The popular *Det Bruunske Pakhus*, Kirkestræde 3 (⊕72 10 67 10, ⓦwww.bruunske pakhus.dk), hosts live bands every weekend from September to June, while *Café Filmer*, Jyllandsgade 20B, offers music, food and drinks, and is a wi-fi hotspot.

Vejle and around

A twenty-minute train ride north of Fredericia on the mouth of the Vejle fjord, the compact harbour town of **VELJE** is the best base for exploring the contrasting pleasures of the Viking burial mounds at Jelling and – rather more famously – the Legoland complex at Billund, both within easy reach by bus or train.

On Velje's central Kirke Torvet is **Skt Nicolai Kirke** (Mon–Fri 9am–5pm, Sat 9am–noon, Sun 10am–noon) in which a glass-topped coffin holds the peat-preserved body of a woman found in the Haraldskær bog in 1835. Originally, the body was thought to be the corpse of a Viking queen, Gunhilde of Norway, but the claim was disputed and tests carried out in 1977 dated the body to around 450 BC – too old to be a Viking, but nonetheless still the best preserved "bog body" in the country. It's hidden away behind bars in the north transept, but the verger will let you in for a closer look. Another macabre feature, though you can't see it as such, are the 23 skulls – allegedly the heads of thieves executed in 1630 – hidden in the still-visible sealed holes in the outer wall of the northern transept. Not far from the church, and across from the train station at Dæmningen 11, is the less gory and far more contemporary **Økolariet** (Feb–Nov Sat–Thurs 11am–4pm; free; Ⓦ www.okolariet.dk), a state-of-the-art educational centre aimed at children, and focusing on a whole host of different green issues ("økologisk" translates as "organic"). The main themes are climate change, drinking water, waste, energy, and mass consumption, and the facts are presented in easy-to-grasp, interactive ways. Although all of the audio and written text is in Danish, most is pretty self-explanatory. There's a fascinating history of the toilet in the basement.

A short walk west of the centre, on the banks of the partly concealed Vejle Å river, you might also want to check out the outstanding **Vejle Kunstmuseum** at Flegborg 16 (Tues–Sun: April–Oct 11am–5pm; Nov–March Tues–Sun 10am–4pm; 40kr; Ⓦ www.vejlekunstmuseum.dk). It specializes in graphics and drawings, and has an enormous collection, mostly from the fifteenth to nineteenth century, of which a changing selection is on display; look out for the remarkable self-portrait by Rembrandt. Until recently housed in the same building, **Vejle Museum** is slated to reopen at a new location in 2011; check at the tourist office for an update. Operated by the museum, and a fabulous destination on a sunny day, is **Vejle Vindmølle** (May–Oct Tues–Sun 11am–4pm; free), a disused windmill which maintains its full complement of ropes, shafts and pinions, displays a through-the-ages account of milling and affords stupendous views across Vejle and its fjord. The site is a ten-minute walk south of the centre via the steep Kiddesvej, which leads off Søndergade.

Practicalities

Vejle's **train station** is just east of the town centre at Banegårds Pladsen 3. All regional and town **buses** stop at the adjacent Vejle Trafikcenter, as does bus #907 (45min; 65kr) from **Billund Airport** (Ⓦ www.billund-airport.dk), some 30km west of Vejle and served by regular flights from Bornholm and Copenhagen. Across from the train station on Banegårds Pladsen 6, the **tourist office** (July Mon–Fri 9.30am–6pm, Sat 9.30am–2pm; May–June & Aug–Oct Mon–Fri 10am–5pm, Sat 10am–1pm; Nov–April Mon–Fri 10am–4pm, Sat 10am–noon; ☏76 81 19 25, Ⓦ www.visitvejle.com) has a range of free cycle maps. **Bike rental** is available at Buhl Jensen, Gormsgade 14 (☏75 82 15 09) as well as Vejle Cykelservice, Flegmade 11A (☏76 41 00 24). If you've opted for the five-day canoe trip along the Gudenå river to Silkeborg and beyond (see p.219), catch bus #215 from the Trafikcenter for the starting point at Tørring (30min).

Aside from a number of upmarket business hotels, good-value **accommodation** is fairly limited, though the tourist office has a list of private rooms from 175kr per person per night, but charges a steep 40kr booking fee. A short walk west of the centre, halfway between the train station and the art museum, the homely *Park*, Orla Lehmannsgade 5 (☏75 82 24 66, Ⓦ www.park-hotel.dk; ❼, 50kr reduction if you pay in cash), offers spacious rooms with Rococo-style furnishings, and a bountiful breakfast buffet. *Best Western Torvehallerne*, across from the church at

Kirketorvet 10–16 (℡79 42 79 10, ⓌWww.torvehallerne.dk; ⑤), is more upscale, housed in a former printing hall and with luxurious, minimalist rooms that are slightly on the small side; perks include free wi-fi and a popular music venue. Much less convenient, some 5km west of Vejle in the hamlet of Skibet (bus #2), the four-star *Vejle Vandrerhjem* **youth hostel**, Vardevej 485 (℡75 82 51 88, ⓌWww.vejle-danhostel.dk), has en-suite doubles (⑤) and rooms sleeping up to eight. There's also a **campsite** at Helligkildevej 5 (℡75 82 33 35, ⓌWww .vejlecitycamping.dk) with cabins sleeping five, 2km from the centre and close to a popular sandy beach; take bus #4 and get off at the sports grounds.

Central Vejle has plenty of inexpensive **places to eat**. In the courtyard of the wood-beamed Smitskegård, Søndergade 14, *Conrad Café* (℡75 72 01 22, ⓌWww .conradcafe.dk) serves substantial salads and burgers from mid-morning, and drinks with steak or pasta dishes in the evenings – it sometimes has live music, too. For something a little less ordinary head for the large Bryggen shopping mall at Søndertorv 2 where *Nordic Taste* (℡61 27 20 21, ⓌWww.nordictaste.com) serves up delicious Nordic tapas and smørrebrød from a canteen-like counter – eat in or take away. Of the number of English-style **pubs** in town, most popular is the *Tartan* at Dæmningen 40.

Jelling

A twelve-kilometre hop northwest of Vejle, the village of **JELLING** is known to have been the site of pagan festivals and celebrations and, on the right-hand side of the main road to Tørring, has two **burial mounds** thought to have contained King Gorm, Jutland's tenth-century ruler, and his queen, Tyre. The graves were found in the early twentieth century and, although only one coffin was actually recovered, there is evidence to suggest that the body of Gorm was removed by his son, Harald Bluetooth, and placed in the adjacent church – which Bluetooth himself built around 960 after his conversion to Christianity. In the grounds of the present church are two big **runic stones**, one erected by Gorm to the memory of Tyre, the other raised by Harald Bluetooth in honour of Gorm. The texts hewn into the granite record the era when Denmark began the transition to Christianity. They still provide scholars with lots of unanswered questions, however: on his stone to Gorm, for instance, Harald records that it was he who "won" Denmark. Scholars now believe this refers to a battle at Dannevirke (in present-day Schleswig, Germany) where he regained control over southern Jutland, and not, as was the previous thinking, about uniting the country under one ruler. Across the road from the stones on Gormsgade 23, the modern and informative **Kongernes Jelling Exhibition Centre** (Tues–Sun: June–Aug 10am–5pm; Sept–May noon–4pm; free; ⓌWww.kongernesjelling .dk) provides a full breakdown of their history and explores the political as well as religious reasons for Harald's conversion to Christianity.

Train services from Vejle towards Struer and Herning stop at Jelling: both run roughly hourly on weekdays and less frequently at weekends; **bus** #211 runs hourly to Jelling from Vejle bus station. A fun alternative is the **vintage train** between Vejle and Jelling, running every Sunday in July and on the first three Sundays in August (℡75 58 60 60, ⓌWww.klk.dk; 50kr return). By **bike**, it's a scenic ride through the hamlet of Uhre and along the shores of Fårup Sø lake. If you want a bite to **eat**, head for the reliable *Conrad Café* (ⓌWww.conradcafe.dk) at Gormsgade 11.

Legoland and Billund

Twenty kilometres west of Vejle, the village of **BILLUND** has been transformed into a major tourist centre, complete with international airport (see p.213) and rows of pricey hotels. It's all thanks to **Legoland Park** (April–June & mid- to end Aug

Mon–Fri 10am–6pm, Sat & Sun 10am–8pm; July to mid-Aug daily 10am–9pm; Sept & Oct Mon, Tues & Fri 10am–6pm, Sat & Sun 10am–8pm; 259kr; ⓦwww .legoland.dk), a theme park celebrating the tiny plastic bricks that have filled many a Christmas stocking since a Danish carpenter, Ole Kirk Christiansen, started making wooden toys collectively named "Lego", from the Danish phrase "*Leg Godt*", or "play well" (which also, by a happy coincidence, means "I study" and "I assemble" in Latin). In 1949, the Lego company began to manufacture its bricks in plastic, becoming the first company in Denmark to use new plastic moulding-injection techniques; the Lego pieces (or "Automatic Binding Bricks", to be precise) we know today were first created in 1958. The park itself features over fifty fun rides built into a cornucopia of elaborate model buildings, animals, planes and many other weird and wonderful things, such as the new Pirates' Lagoon.

Billund's **tourist office** (same hours as Legoland; ☏76 50 00 55, ⓦwww.visit billund.dk) is located by the main entrance. Most of the nearby accommodation offers all-encompassing package deals. Convenient options include the modern *Legoland Village* **family hostel**, around the corner from Legoland at Ellehammers Allé (☏75 33 27 77, ⓦwww.legoland-village.dk; doubles ❼). It has no dorms, but a good supply of pricey double rooms and other family accommodation. If you've arrived by bus (from Jelling you have to return to Vejle and then take #244), it's best to get off at Legoland and walk the remaining 300m to the hostel. The other option, *Hotel Legoland* (☏75 33 12 44, ⓦwww.hotellegoland.dk; ❾) is within the actual grounds of Legoland but can also be accessed by the Aastvej side entrance, which has Lego-themed rooms and an excellent restaurant with an extensive children's menu. If your only reason to be in Billund is the airport – then the comfy new *Zleep Hotel* (☏75 33 19 00, ⓦwww.zleep.dk; ❼) literally next to the car park at Passagerterminalen 4, has excellent deals if you book more than sixty days in advance; breakfast is not included.

The Lake District: Silkeborg and around

Ensconced in a loose triangle formed by Skanderborg, Århus and **SILKEBORG**, the grandly titled **Lake District** comprises several small lakes amid green, rolling woodlands, and boasts one of the country's highest points, the 147-metre Himmelbjerget. If you've only seen Denmark's larger towns, the region is well worth a couple of days' exploration, preferably by canoe, and there are innumerable campsites in which to stay. The north–south rail route passes first through

The Skanderborg Festival

Although it's difficult to find anything bad to say about the attractive town of Skanderborg, delicately positioned on the banks of Skanderborg Sø, there's no real reason to visit either – unless you're here on the second weekend in August, when the beech woods south of the centre are converted into a visually stunning music festival site. Nicknamed the "country's most beautiful festival", the four-day **Skanderborg Festival** (☏87 93 44 44, ⓦwww.smukfest.dk) is a lot more laid-back than the Roskilde bash (see p.113), and the general idea is more about enjoying the beautiful surroundings and friendly atmosphere than great musical experiences – although they happen as well. Spread over five stages, music acts in 2009 included top Danish names plus The Streets and Kylie Minogue, and DJing by Fat Boy Slim. **Tickets** cost 1700kr for all four days, and all-day day tickets cost 500kr Thursday, 600kr for Friday, 700kr for Saturday, and 605kr for Sunday. They are available at Billetlugen (ⓦwww.billetlugen.dk) and, until they sell out, at the main entrance.

missable **Skanderborg**, notable chiefly for its festival (see box, p.215) but it's the Lake District's other main town, **Silkeborg**, spreading handsomely across several inlets, which serves as the area's lively centre.

Arrival, information and accommodation

Regional buses and trains arrive at the **train station** on Drewsensvej. From here, it's a ten-minute walk along Christian 8 Vej to the Gudenå river lock, which is the most

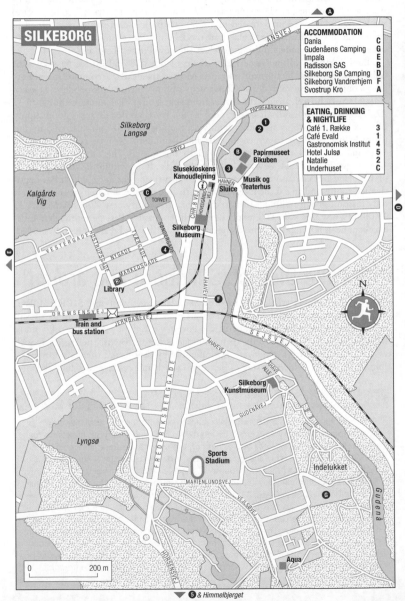

SILKEBORG

ACCOMMODATION
Dania	C
Gudenåens Camping	G
Impala	E
Radisson SAS	B
Silkeborg Sø Camping	D
Silkeborg Vandrerhjem	F
Svostrup Kro	A

EATING, DRINKING & NIGHTLIFE
Café 1. Række	3
Café Evald	1
Gastronomisk Institut	4
Hotel Julsø	5
Natalie	2
Underhuset	C

ANSVEJ

Silkeborg Langsø

PAPIRFABRIKKEN

SØVEJ

Papirmuseet Bikuben

Sluskioskens Kanoudlejning

HAVNEN

Musik og Teaterhus

Sluice

Kalgårds Vig

TORVET

CHR. 8 VEJ

NORDGÅRDS VEJ

ÅRHUSVEJ

Silkeborg Museum

VESTERGADE

HOSTRUPSGADE

TYKEGADE

NYGADE

SØNDERGADE

MARKEDSGADE

Library

AHAVEVEJ

ÅHAVEVEJ

DREWSENSVEJ

JERNBANEVEJ

SEJSVEJ

Train and bus station

FREDERIKSBERGGADE

Silkeborg Kunstmuseum

AHAVE ALLE

GUDENÅVEJ

Lyngsø

Sports Stadium

Indelukket

Gudenå

MARIENLUNDSVEJ

VEJLSØVEJ

HORSENSVEJ

N

0   200 m

Aqua

& Himmelbjerget

central point from which to get to grips with the town's offerings. Silkeborg's layout is somewhat complicated: the Gudenå river delineates the edge of the town centre to the east while the Silkeborg lakes separate the residential and industrial suburbs in the north from the old town centre, which has a line of classy patrician villas along the Gudenå riverbank to the south. The helpful **tourist office**, across from the sluice at Åhavevej 2A (April to mid-June and Sept–Oct Mon–Fri 9.30am–4pm, Sat 10am–1pm; mid-June to Aug Mon–Fri 9.30am–5.30pm, Sat & Sun 10am–2pm; Nov–March Mon–Fri 10am–3pm, Sat 10am–1pm; T86 82 19 11, W www.silkeborg.com) has a lengthy list of affordable rooms, charging only a 10kr fee. Although **hotels** are plentiful, the region's popularity makes them relatively expensive. We've listed some of the best options below, as well as a hostel and two campsites. There's free **internet** access at the library, Hostrupsgade 41.

Hotels and hostels

Dania Torvet 5 T00 02 01 11, W www.hoteldania
.dk. Silkeborg's grand old hotel prides itself in having housed H.C. Andersen for a number of years as well as a number of royals. The plush, atmospheric rooms come at a price but are reduced by almost a third at weekends. **9**

Impala Vestre Ringvej 53 T86 82 03 00, W www.impala.dk. With a picture-perfect location on the northern bank of Silkeborg Langesø lake and a 20min walk from the train station (10min on bus #3 from the bus station), Impala has a range of good-value, if characterless en-suite rooms. **7**

Radisson SAS Papirfabrikken 12 T88 82 22 22, W www.radisson.com. Modern, central hotel in a section of the refurbished paper mill which overlooks the Gudenå river and lock. The en-suite rooms are simple and stylish with free wi-fi, but a tad on the small side. **9**

Silkeborg Vandrerhjem Åhavevej 55 T86 82 36 42, W www.danhostel -silkeborg.dk. Beautifully situated hostel on the banks of the Gudenå, with dorms (July to mid-Sept only; 250kr), affordable quads (650kr) and six-bed rooms (850kr), but no doubles.

Svostrup Kro Svostrupvej 58 T86 87 70 04, W www.svostrup-kro.dk. A traditional Danish inn, next to the Gudenå river 8km northeast of the centre off the road to Randers. With creaking floorboards and wood-beamed ceilings, this place oozes character and cosiness. **8**

Campsites

Gudenåens Camping Silkeborg Vejlsøvej 7 T86 82 22 01, W www.gudenaaenscamping.dk. Scenically located campsite 2km south of the centre in a wooded area on the banks of the Gudenå river and near Silkeborg Kunstmuseum and Silkeborg Vandrerhjem. The site also encompasses a number of comfortable cabins sleeping six, some self contained (5500kr per week), others sharing bathroom facilities (4200kr per week).

Silkeborg Sø Camping Århusvej 51 T86 82 28 24, W www.seacamp.dk. Some 2km from the centre, just off the main road to Århus on the banks of Silkeborg Langesø lake, and most easily reached via the regional buses to and from Århus. Bicycle and canoe rental are ample compensation for its isolation from town, as are the dorm bunks (125kr) and pretty cabins sleeping four (from 2900kr per week). Wi-fi throughout. Mid-April to mid-Oct.

The Town

Silkeborg has little history of its own – it was still a small village in 1845 when the local river was harnessed to power a paper mill that brought a measure of growth and prosperity, something you can learn more about at the **Papirmuseet Bikuben** (Paper Museum; June–Aug daily noon–5pm, May & Sept Mon–Fri noon–5pm; 30kr; W www.papirmuseet.dk), Papirfabrikken 78, housed in the old paper mill by the Gudenå lock, which also holds the town's theatre; entry is through the back. The Silkeborg mill was one of the few in the world making paper of high enough quality to be used to print banknotes, and there's an intriguing section about money-making and the various countries' bills that have been produced here. The exhibit also explains the process of paper-making, from papyrus to modern methods.

Following the Gudenå river southwards, sticking to the western bank, takes you past another three interesting attractions. First up, behind the tourist office at Hovedgårdsvej 7, is the **Silkeborg Museum** (May to mid-Oct daily 10am–5pm;

mid-Oct to April Sat & Sun noon–4pm; 50kr; Ⓦ www.silkeborgmuseum.dk). In 1938, the discovery of the well-preserved body of an Iron Age woman – the so-called **Elling Girl** – in a bog 15km west of Silkeborg added greatly to the appeal of the town's budding museum. As preserved bodies go, however, it has since been overshadowed by the discovery of the **Tollund Man** in 1950 in the same bog, a corpse of similar vintage whose head – gruesome as it may sound – is in such good condition that it's been deemed the world's best preserved prehistoric body. Housed in a dark, tomb-like room in the museum's new section at the back, Tollund Man lies with stubble still visible on the chin and, according to researchers, the remains of his last meal in his belly, a gruel made of thirty different types of grain and seed, including flax, barley and willow herb. All of this, and much more about how he was discovered is thoroughly described on placards in his "room". The rest of the museum's local history exhibits are bit of a mish-mash, and are imminently due for refurbishment.

An equally worthwhile call is the excellent collection of abstract works by Asger Jorn and others in the beautifully situated **Silkeborg Kunstmuseum** (April–Oct Tues–Sun 10am–5pm; Nov–March Tues–Fri noon–4pm, Sat & Sun 10am–5pm; 60kr; Ⓦ www.silkeborgkunstmuseum.dk), further along the Gudenå river's west bank, bordering the Indelukket park at Gudenåvej 7. It was to Silkeborg that Jorn, Denmark's leading modern painter and founder member of the influential CoBrA (Copenhagen-Brussels-Amsterdam) group, came to recuperate from tuberculosis. From the 1950s until his death in 1973, Jorn donated an enormous amount of his own and other artists' work to the town, which displays them proudly in this purpose-built museum. Pieces to look out for include the enormously long and colourful *The Long Voyage* tapestry in Room 13, which Jorn made together with Dutch artist Pierre Wemaëre, and the powerful sketches given to Jorn by his teacher Fernand Legér in Atelier 1. An informative fifteen-minute film about Jorn is shown on request in the small auditorium just as you enter. The beautiful grounds around the museum are littered with sculptural and ceramic works by Jorn and his contemporaries.

For something less cultural, head for the **Aqua** freshwater aquarium (mid-June to mid-Aug daily 10am–6pm; mid-Aug to mid-June Mon–Fri 10am–4pm, Sat & Sun 10am–5pm; 110kr; Ⓦ www.aqua-ferskvandsakvarium.dk), set in the beautiful former tuberculosis sanatorium at Vejlsøvej 15, a fifteen-minute walk south of the art museum through Indelukket park (10min on bus #10). It has a variety of huge tanks with freshwater fish alongside numerous water birds and mammals, including some cute otters. You can also get here by taking the *Hjejle* steamer (Ⓦ www.hjejlen.com; May–Sept 4–6 trips daily; 70kr return to Aqua, 110kr return to Himmelbjerget), the world's oldest coal-burning paddle steamer, which departs from the lock by Silkeborg Museum. After the aquarium, the steamer carries on along the Gudenå river into Brassø, Borresø and Julsø lakes before reaching the foot of **Himmelbjerget** ("Sky Mountain"), one of Denmark's highest hills; from here the 147-metre trek to the top takes about thirty minutes, and your reward is some magnificent views.

Eating, drinking and nightlife

Most of Silkeborg's best places to **eat**, **drink** and be merry are around the lock area and nearby along pedestrianized Søndergade. The **Riverboat Jazz Festival** (Ⓣ 86 80 16 17, Ⓦ www.riverboat.dk), staged during the last week of June, draws musicians from all over the globe for a four-day session of New Orleans and Dixieland jazz as well as more experimental stuff. It's mostly free, with bands playing on squares and stages placed strategically throughout the town (including one by the lock).

Restaurants and bars

Café 1.Række Papirfabrikken 80 Ⓣ 86 80 59 00, Ⓦ www.cafe1raekke.dk. With its open terrace facing

the Gudenå river lock, this is Silkeborg's trendiest daytime hangout. The heavily laden smørrebrød (28kr a piece) and daily special (48kr) are two sure-fire

winners, but nothing beats the freshly made cake of the day served with coffee (free refills) for 48kr. Linked to the theatre, the café stays open late on performance nights, otherwise it closes at 5pm.
Café Evald Papirfabrikken 10B ☎86 80 33 66, Ⓦwww.cafe-evald.dk. Brasserie-style café that does great brunch (10am–2pm) and the usual array of burgers, pastas and salads at very reasonable prices, while in the evenings, the large selection of imported draught beer draws in the crowds. The balcony overlooking the Gudenå river gets packed in summer. Open till late Fri & Sat.
Gastronomisk Institut Søndergade 20 ☎86 82 40 97, Ⓦwww.gastronomiske.dk. A French-style café by day and a gourmet restaurant by night, with the focus on fresh, local produce and careful preparation. Portions aren't huge but quality is high and prices very reasonable for what you get – a four-course set menu costs 320kr. Closed Sun, and Mon for dinner.
Hotel Julsø Julsøvej 14 ☎86 89 80 40, Ⓦwww.hotel-julso.dk. At the foot of Himmelbjerget, this picturesque place does a fabulous lunch platter of traditional smørrebrød (169kr) and a range of mostly Italian-inspired meals, such as the escalope caprese with mozzarella and fresh basil (also 169kr). Best way to get here is by canoe or the *Hjejle* steamer (see opposite). Booking recommended. Closed Nov–March.
Natalie Papirfabrikken 10E ☎86 86 10 14, Ⓦwww.natalie-silkeborg.dk. Mexican/Italian restaurant offering well-made tacos and burritos or pasta and pizzas as the main staples. The 79kr lunch (Sat & Sun only) and the three-course evening meals (choose between Mexican or Italian) for 199kr are extremely good value.
Underhuset Torvet 7 ☎86 82 37 36, Ⓦwww.underhuset.dk. Popular gastropub specializing in seafood and its trademark plate of oysters. Mains in the restaurant section start at 200kr, while many of the same dishes are available in the pub section for much less. Lunch comprises traditional Danish fare such as *flæskesteg med rødkål*, while dinner is primarily seafood, such as lobster and fried plaice.

Canoe trips along the Gudenå

The highlight of a trip to Silkeborg, and the town's main claim to fame among Danish holidaymakers, is a **canoe trip** on the 162-kilometre **Gudenå river**, Denmark's

Canoe rental

The Silkeborg tourist office (see p.217) organizes a range of **canoe package trips**. The most popular is the Family Tour, which costs 3095kr per canoe for five days, and includes canoe and tent rental as well as campsite fees along the way. The so-called "luxury tours" include overnight stops at traditional inns along the way, and start at 3750kr for three days (two nights). If you'd rather have the flexibility **going independently**, we've listed some of the most convenient canoe rental outlets below. All the operators' prices include a two-person canoe, lifejackets, and oars. Transport of the canoe to and/or from starting and end points usually costs 100kr. You can also rent tents, or have pre-pitched tents waiting for you at the campsites. The tourist office in Silkeborg can store luggage for you while you are away. Note that from Silkeborg, you can rent canoes by the hour year-round.

Slusekioskens Kanoudlejning Havnen, Silkeborg ☎86 80 08 93 Ⓦwww.kano4you .dk. From Silkeborg, low-season prices (May to mid-June & mid-Aug to Sept) are 360kr for one day and 1050kr for five days; in high season (mid-June to mid-Aug) it's 360kr for one day or 1250kr for five. From Tørring, five days costs 1650kr, ten days 2400kr. Renting a canoe by the hour costs 90kr.

Gudenåens Camping Silkeborg (see p.217 for contact details). Canoe rental by the hour costs 75kr, 270kr by the day. In low season they're open for negotiation.

Søhøjlandets Kanoudlejning Trust Camping, Sørkelvej 12, Truust ☎86 87 11 41, Ⓦwww.kanogudenaa.dk. In low season (April–June & Aug to mid-Oct), costs are 200kr per day. In high season (July), it's 350kr for one day, 1350kr for five days, including transport of canoe.

Tørring Kanoudlejning og Kanofart Aagade 31, Tørring ☎75 80 13 01, Ⓦwww.kano-udlejning.dk. Three days for 1300kr, five days for 1650kr, ten days for 2400kr. Minimum rental period is three days.

best plan is to sign up for one of the many all-in packages offered by the board (see box, p.219). At most points, the water is no more than wading while at others it deepens and is perfect for swimming, and it's hard to imagine g more peaceful than letting the current gently pull you along while passing through stunning, virtually undisturbed countryside, punctuating your journey at the campsites which are located at regular intervals along the river's course. **From Silkeborg**, there are a range of options, including day-trips from town – the paddle to Himmelbjerget and back, including a hike up the mountain is very popular – or longer, five-day jaunts downstream to Fladbro by Randers (see p.235), overnighting at campsites or inns along the way. Alternatively, you can start at the source of the Gudenå, just outside **Tørring** by Vejle, and do the five-day journey downstream to Silkeborg, though this is only possible after mid-June due to the low water levels at Tørring. You can also do the entire river in ten days, or any combination of the above routes. (Note, however, that apart from the stretch to Himmelbjerget from Silkeborg, going upstream is illegal.) During school holidays the river can become a virtual canoe motorway, with only one-way traffic, and this period is probably best avoided.

As well as taking you through some beautiful scenery, the river also passes a number of museums and attractions that warrant a longer stop. One of the best is the hugely popular **Elmuseet** (April–Oct daily 10am–5pm; 80kr; Ⓦ www .elmuseet.dk), on the banks of Tange Sø lake, 20km southeast of Viborg. Housed in ten buildings on the spectacular grounds of the Gudenå hydroelectric power station, the museum deals with all things electric.

Århus

Right at the heart of the country geographically, and often regarded as Denmark's cultural capital, **ÅRHUS** typifies all that's good about Danish cities. It's small enough to get to know in a few hours, yet big and lively enough to have plenty to fill both days and nights, and the combination of laid-back atmosphere and a surprising number of sights might keep you around longer than planned. Århus is also something of an architectural showcase, with several notable structures spanning a century of Danish and international design. A number of these buildings form the campus of Århus's **university**, whose students contribute to a nightlife scene that's on a par with that of Copenhagen.

Despite Viking-era origins, the city's present prosperity is due to its long, sheltered bay (on which a harbour was first constructed during the fifteenth century) and the more recent advent of railways, which made Århus a nationally important trade and transport centre. It's easily reached by train from all the country's bigger towns, is linked by sea with Zealand (a fast catamaran service linking Århus with Odden, and a slower ferry linking it with Kalundborg), and also has an international airport with regular connections to Copenhagen.

Arrival, information and city transport

Whichever form of public transport brings you to Århus, you'll be deposited within easy reach of the hotels and main points of interest. **Trains** and **buses** stop at their respective stations on Banegårds Pladsen and Ny Banegårds Gade, both on the southern edge of the city centre. The **tourist office** (July–Aug Mon–Fri 10am–5.30pm, Sat 10am–3pm; Sept–June Mon–Fri 10am–4.30pm; ☎87 31 50 10, Ⓦ www.visitaarhus.com) is at Banegårds Pladsen 20. **Ferries** from Zealand dock just east of the centre at the end of Nørreport, a short distance from the heart of old Århus. Buses from the **airport** (Ⓦ www.aar.dk), some 45km northeast of

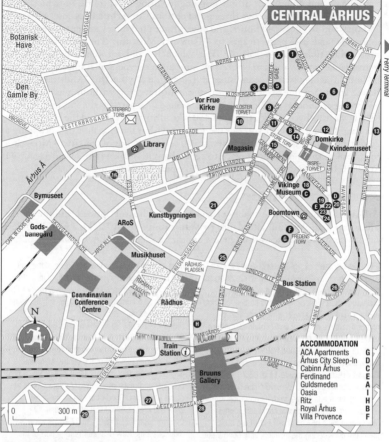

CENTRAL ÅRHUS

EATING, DRINKING & NIGHTLIFE

Billabong Bar	19	Gaucho	23	Pinden	20	Tir na noq	21
Bridgewater Pub	24	Globen Flakket	24	Raadhuus Kafeen	25	Train	26
Broen	13	Gourmet Garagen	6	Ris Ras Filliongongong	8	Under Masken	14
Bryggeriet Sct Clemens	18	Gyngen & Musikcaféen	2	Royal Århus	B	Voxhall	16
Carlton	11	Herr Bartels	17	Den Sidste	1		
Casablanca	12	Jorden	9	Simoncini	29		
The Cockney Pub	15	Karls Sandwichbar	3	Smagløs	10		
Le Coq	7	Klassisk 65	27	Social Club	4		
Emmerys	5	Ministeriet	10	Svej	23		
Fatter Eskild	22	Nordisk Spisehus	28	Svineriet	6		

the city, arrive at (and leave from) the train station; the one-way fare for the forty-five-minute journey is 90kr.

Getting around is best done on foot: the city centre is compact and you'll need to use **buses** only if you're venturing out to the University and Moesgård Museum, or the beaches or the woods on the city's outskirts. If you do, note that the transport system divides into four zones: one and two cover the whole central area; three and four reach into the countryside. The basic ticket is the "**billet**", which costs 18kr from machines at the rear of buses and is valid for any number of journeys for up two hours from the time stamped on it. If you're around for several days and doing a lot of bus hopping (or using local trains, on which these tickets are also valid), you have three good options. An **Århus Pass** costs 119kr for 24 hours and 149kr for 48 hours, and covers unlimited travel and entrance to most museums, and half-price tickets to ARoS Art Museum. The third option is a **multi-ride ticket** (*Klippekort*: 115kr), which is valid for ten trips within the immediate city area and can be used by more than one person at once. Tickets can be bought at newsstands, campsites and shops displaying the "Midttrafik" sign; there's an instant fine of 500kr if you're caught travelling without one.

Cycling is another viable way to get around. As part of the citybike scheme (Ⓦwww.aarhusbycykel.dk), there are 450 bikes distributed around the city between May and October, which you can use for free within the city limits by dropping a 20kr deposit into the slot on the bikes. If you're heading out of the city to Moesgård, for instance, the most central place to rent a bicycle is Bikes4rent, Vendersgade 41 (Ⓣ20 26 10 20, Ⓦwww.bikes4rent.dk; 75kr per day, 245kr per week).

Accommodation

Århus has some fairly reasonably priced **hotel** and **hostel** options, and the tourist office can help you find affordable **private rooms** (from 400kr a night). Unless otherwise stated, all the options below appear on the Central Århus map on p.221.

Hotels and guesthouses

ACA Apartments Fredensgade 18 Ⓣ40 27 90 30 Ⓦwww.hotelaca.dk. Refurbished apartment building a short walk from the bus station, offering about a third off if you're staying more than two nights. There's a range of self-contained, modernized rooms and apartments with fully fitted kitchens or kitchenettes and free internet. Breakfast is not included in the price. Ⓞ

Cabinn Århus Kannikegade 14 Ⓣ86 75 70 00, Ⓦwww.cabinn.com. Inexpensive chain hotel on the banks of the Århus Å river, with its entrance in front of the theatre. The functional cabin-like rooms (everything folds up and packs away) are a bit small but considering the location, very good value. Free internet. Breakfast buffet is 60kr. Ⓞ

Ferdinand Åboulevarden 28 Ⓣ87 32 14 44, Ⓦwww.hotelferdinand.dk. Exclusive hotel on the banks of Århus Å river, with only eight luxurious suites, a trendy riverside café and a classy restaurant. The tastefully decorated suites are French/ Italian-inspired and come with separate living room and a small kitchenette. Breakfast is not included. Ⓞ

🏃 **Guldsmeden** Guldsmedegade 40 Ⓣ86 13 45 56, Ⓦwww.hotelguldsmeden.dk. Boutique hotel in the centre, a 10min walk from the station. Rooms are delicately decorated in French colonial style, and no two are the same. Rooms in the annexe, at the foot of a tranquil garden, all share bath. Scrummy organic breakfast buffet included. Ⓞ

Havnehotellet Marselisborg Havnevej 20 Ⓦwww .havnehotellet.dk (see Around Århus map, p.227). Unmanned hotel – hence no phone number – on the Århus marina quay (10min on bus #6 or #19

from the centre), with stunning views of the bay and good restaurants nearby. Checking in to the bright and breezy en-suite rooms, with free wi-fi, happens on a computer in the foyer, and booking is only possible online. Ⓞ

Helnan Marselis Strandvejen 25 Ⓣ86 14 44 11, Ⓦwww.marselis.dk (see Around Århus map, p.227). Bus #6 or #19. Stunningly located beachfront hotel a few kilometres south of the centre. All rooms overlook Århus Bay, and facilities include swimming pool, bar and restaurant, while Marselis woods are at the back door. Good offers on all-inclusive weekend breaks. Breakfast not included. Ⓞ

Oasia Kriegersvej 7 Ⓣ87 32 37 15, Ⓦwww .hoteloasia.dk. New designer hotel – part of the Best Western chain – in a historic building a short walk from the train station. The stylish rooms feature Thorsen furniture, the famously comfortable Hästens beds, and free wi-fi. Ⓞ

Ritz Banegårds Pladsen 12 Ⓣ86 13 44 44, Ⓦwww.hotelritz.dk. As the name implies, this Art Nouveau-style Best Western hotel in front of the train station is both pricey (though with discounts at weekends) and elegant. Free wi-fi. Ⓞ

Royal Århus Store Torv 4 Ⓣ86 12 00 11, Ⓦwww .hotelroyal.dk. The city's grand old four-star hotel, right on the main square and with a beautiful winter garden and the city's only casino (see p.230). The spacious rooms are elaborately furnished with ornately carved dark mahogany furniture, and the marbled bathrooms are downright luxurious. Ⓞ

Villa Provence Fredens Torv 12 Ⓣ86 18 24 00, Ⓦwww.villaprovence.dk. Classy, small boutique hotel a stone's throw from the bus station centred around a charming Mediterranean courtyard. The individualized rooms are all beautifully decorated in light Provencal style, featuring old French-Belgian film posters. Children under 10 not allowed. ⑧

Sleep-ins and youth hostels

Århus City Sleep-In Havnegade 20 ⓣ 86 19 20 55, ⓦ www.citysleep-in.dk. Bus #3. Near both the city centre and harbour, offering dorm beds (140kr), and doubles with shared or private bath (both ④). Guests without sleeping bags have to rent sheets and blankets (50kr); facilities include a games room, café and internet (20kr per hr)

Århus Vandrerhjem Marienlundsvej 10 (see Around Århus map, p.227) ⓣ 86 16 72 98, ⓦ www .aarhus-danhostel.dk. Bus #1, #6 #8, #9, #16, #56 or #58. Much more peaceful than the central *Sleep-In*, this is 4km northeast of town in the middle of Risskov wood, close to the popular Den Permanente beach. As well as dorms (160kr), it has

a hotel-style wing with en-suite doubles (⑥) and, for a bit less, doubles with shared bath.

Campsites

Blommehaven Ørneredevej 35, Højbjerg (see Around Århus map, p.227) ⓣ 86 27 02 07, ⓦ www .camping-blommehaven.dk. Bus #6 or #19. Some 5km south of the city centre, overlooking the bay and with access to a beautiful beach. The site holds a number of self-contained cabins sleeping four (525kr) and six (600kr). Open April–Aug.

Århus Camping Randersvej 400, Lisbjerg (see Around Århus map, p.227) ⓣ 86 23 11 33, ⓦ www .aarhuscamping.dk. Bus #117 or #118 (three zones from the centre). Around 8km north of the city centre and convenient for the E45 motorway, this campsite is not nearly as well situated as *Blomme-haven* but the comfortable new cabins (from 315kr per day for cabins sleeping two) and on-site cafeteria tick all the right boxes and are excellent value. The nearby ancient woodland is well worth exploring. Open all year.

The City

For reasons of simple chronology, Århus divides into two clearly defined, easily walkable parts. The **old section**, close to the Domkirke, is a tight cluster of medieval streets with several interesting churches and a couple of museums, as well as the bulk of the city's nightlife. The (relatively) **new sections** of Århus form a collar around the old centre, inevitably with less character, but nonetheless holding plenty that's worth seeing, not least the city's major architectural works.

Århus Domkirke and around

Århus's main street, **Søndergade**, is a pedestrianized strip lined with shops and overpriced snack bars that leads from the train station (where it's initially called Ryesgade), through Skt Clemens Torv and across Århus Å river into the main town square, Bispetorvet. From here, the streets of the old centre form a web around the **Domkirke** (May–Sept Mon–Sat 9.30am–4pm; Oct–April Mon–Sat 10am–3pm). Take the trouble to push open the cathedral's sturdy doors, not just to appreciate the soccer-pitch length – this is easily the longest church in Scandinavia – but to take in a couple of features that spruce up the plain Gothic interior, which is mostly a fifteenth-century rebuilding after the original twelfth-century structure was destroyed by fire. At the eastern end, a grand tripartite altarpiece by the noted Bernt Notke is one of few pre-Reformation survivors (you can see all the sections of the altarpiece on a model behind the pulpit). Look also for the painted – as opposed to stained-glass window behind the altar, the work of Norwegian Emmanuel Vigeland (brother of Gustav); it's most effective when the sunlight falls directly on it.

From the time of the first settlement here, in the tenth century, the area around the cathedral has been at the core of Århus life. A number of Viking remains have been excavated on Skt Clemens Torv, across the road from the cathedral, and some are now displayed as part of the **Vikinge Museum** (Mon–Fri 10am–4pm, Thurs until 5.30pm; free; ⓦ www.vikingemuseet.dk) in the basement of the Nordea bank at Skt Clemens Torv 6 (entrance inside the bank on the left). Also on display are sections of the original ramparts around the settlement which was then known as

Aros (as explained in the museum's accounts of early Århus). Also close to the cathedral, in a former police station on Bispetorvet, the **Kvindemuseet** (Women's Museum; daily: June–Aug 10am–5pm; Sept–May Tues & Thurs–Sun 10am–4pm, Wed 10am–8pm; 40kr; Ⓦ www.kvindemuseet.dk) is one of Denmark's most innovative, with a detailed exhibition of diverse aspects of mostly Danish women's lives past and present. A new section – Boys' and Girls' Stories – is especially fun for kids. After visiting the museums here, you might want to venture into the narrow and enjoyable surrounding streets, lined by innumerable old and well-preserved buildings, many of which now house browseable antique shops, chic boutiques and French-style cafés, the latter some of the city's best drinking spots (see p.230).

West along Vestergade from the Domkirke, behind the Frue Kirke Plads square, the thirteenth-century **Vor Frue Kirke** (May–Aug Mon–Fri 10am–4pm, Sat 10am–2pm; Sept–April Mon–Fri 10am–2pm, Sat 10am–noon) is actually the site of three churches, the most notable of which is the eleventh-century **crypt** (go in through the main church entrance and walk straight ahead), which was discovered, buried beneath several centuries' worth of rubbish, during restoration work on the main building in the 1950s. There's not a lot to see, but the tiny, rough-stone building, resembling a hollowed-out cave, is strong on atmosphere, especially during the candlelit Sunday services. Except for Claus Berg's fine altarpiece, there's not much to warrant a look in the main church. However, you can make your way through the cloister that remains from the pre-Reformation monastery – now an old folks' home – to see the medieval frescoes inside the third church, which depict local working people rather than the more commonly found biblical scenes.

The Rådhus and around

Modern Århus begins as soon as you arrive at the train station which, although from 1927 and not modern in itself, has been integrated into the Bruuns Gallery multi-storey state-of-the-art shopping mall and cinema. From here it's a short walk along Park Allé to one of the modern city's major sights: the functional **Rådhus** on Rådhuspladsen, completed in 1941 and as capable of inciting high passions today – for and against – as it was when it opened. From the outside, it's easy to see why opinions should be so polarized, as the coating of grey Norwegian marble lends a sickly pallor to the facade. But on the inside (enter from Rådhuspladsen), the finer points of architects Arne Jacobsen and Erik Møller's vision make themselves apparent, amid the harmonious open-plan corridors and extravagant quantities of glass. You're free to walk in and look for yourself (Mon–Fri 9am–4pm). Inside, above the entrance, hangs Hagedorn Olsen's huge mural, *A Human Society*, symbolically depicting the city emerging from the last war to face the future with optimism. Perhaps most interesting of all, however, if only for the background story, are the walls of the small Civic Room, covered by intricate floral designs in which artist Albert Naur, working during the Nazi occupation, concealed various Allied insignia. You can also tour the bell tower on Tuesdays and Thursdays at 2pm (June–Aug; 35kr); advance tickets are sold at the tourist office (p.220).

More recent examples of Århus's municipal architecture include the glass-fronted **Musikhuset** (concert hall: daily 11am–9pm; Ⓦ www.musikhusetaarhus .dk), a short walk from the Rådhus along Frederiks Allé, which has been the city's main venue for opera and classical music since it opened in 1982. It's worth dropping into, if only for the small café where you might be entertained for free by a string quartet or a lone fiddler. A monthly list of forthcoming concerts and events is available from the box office or the tourist office.

Just next door, the most recent addition to the cityscape is the large red-brick **ARoS** art museum (Tues–Sun 10am–5pm, Wed till 10pm; 90kr; Ⓦ www.aros .dk), a remarkable building designed by the same architects as the Black Diamond extension to the Royal Library in Copenhagen (see p.63). Built on a slope, the main entrance is confusingly on the fourth floor, spreading the seven floors of the exhibition over the three floors above and the three below, all connected by a massive white spiralling staircase and a sleek glass lift. The collection gives a good overview of the main national trends, from late eighteenth-century formal portraits and landscapes by Jens Juel and finely etched scenes of domestic tension by Jørgen Sonne, through to more internationally renowned names, particularly Vilhelm Hammershoi, represented here by some of his moody interiors. There are lots of worthwhile modern pieces, too. Besides the radiant canvases of Asger Jorn and Richard Mortensen, don't miss Bjørn Nørgård's sculpted version of Christian IV's tomb: the original, in Roskilde Cathedral, is stacked with riches; this one features a coffee cup, an egg and a ballpoint pen. Other highlights include the spookily lifelike five-metre-high sculpture, *Boy*, by Ron Mueck. There's also a good café with free wi-fi and a very browseable museum shop, plus magnificent views of the city's skyline from the rooftop terrace.

From ARoS's back ground-floor exit, Aros Allé leads past the new Musikhus extension and the grand, slimline *SAS Radisson* hotel and Conference Centre next door. Turn right down Skovgaardsgade for the **Bymuseet** (City Museum; daily 10am–5pm, Wed until 8pm; 30kr; ⓦwww.bymuseet.dk; bus #18), Carl Blochs Gade 28, housed in the disused Hammel railway station and a modern extension from 2005. The latest addition to Århus's array of museums, the Bymuseet approaches the history of the city from a thematic rather than chronological perspective. Topics like Århus's role in the Danish film industry and Århus as a city of education are imaginatively tackled with old film clips, models, photos and diagrams, as well as in-depth background narratives. There's also a small café, where you're allowed to bring your own food.

Den Gamle By and Botanisk Have

It's just a few minutes' walk from Bymuseet to Viborgvej and the city's best-known attraction, **Den Gamle By** (The Old Town; Jan 11am–3pm; Feb & March 10am–4pm; April–June & Sept–Nov 10am–5pm; July–Aug 9am–6pm; Dec 10am–7pm; 100kr; ⓦwww.dengamleby.dk). An open-air museum of traditional Danish life, it consists of around 75 half-timbered townhouses (including a popular Mayor's House of 1597) from all over the country, which have been moved here since the museum's inception in 1914. With many of the buildings used for their original purpose, the overall aim is to give an impression of an old Danish market town, complete with bakers, craftsmen and the like. This is done very convincingly, although the period flavour is strongest outside high season, when visitors are fewer.

Once you're inside Den Gamle By you're effectively also inside the **Botanisk Have** (Botanical Garden; unrestricted access; free). The largest and oldest park in Århus, a trip to the botanical garden has been one of the most popular outings for local Århusianere (people from Århus) for generations. Its undulating hills give a great sense of space, while the small, intimate dips provide ideal cover for an afternoon's lazing in the sun (or studying for exams – the gardens' primary use during spring). For the botanically interested, the thousands of plants and trees are all labelled with their Danish and Latin names. Buses #3, #14, #15, #25, #51 and #55 come here from the centre.

Universitetsparken

A fifteen-minute walk from Den Gamle By along Langelandsgade (or 5min on bus #17 from Vesterbrogade), the **Universitetsparken** (university campus) is a prime example of modern Danish architectural style. Sprawled across a green hillside overlooking the city, the distinctive yellow-brick buildings, mostly designed by C.F. Møller and completed just after World War II, feature white-framed rectangular windows and no decorative touches whatsoever. There are two museums on campus that are worth looking out for. The **Naturhistorisk Museum** (Mon–Thurs 10am–4pm, Fri 10am–2pm; 50kr; Ⓦwww.naturhistoriskmuseum.dk) has an interesting and well-presented exhibition on Danish natural history (sadly only in Danish), with displays showing bone fragments and sketches of animals that used to inhabit these shores in the time gaps between the ice ages – four in total – such as the woolly rhinoceros and the forest elephant. The much grander **Steno Museum** (Tues–Fri 9am–4pm, Sat & Sun 11am–4pm; 45kr; Ⓦwww.stenomuseet.dk) could easily swallow up an entire afternoon. Divided into two distinct sections on two sides of a staircase – Medical History and the History of Science – the museum manages to balance itself perfectly between educating and displaying the curious. The **Medical History** section starts downstairs with an insight into hospital wards and operating theatres in the eighteenth century, with some gruesome tools of the trade such as a dentist's foot-operated drill. Upstairs, focus is on the development of medicine over the ages. A plague-doctor's outfit with its hawk-nosed mask – providing room for medicinal herbs to overpower the smell of rot – and Marie Curie's research on radiology are among the exhibits given meticulous attention. Across the staircase landing, you step into a cartographer's paradise, with the **History of Science** section kicking off with maps through the ages, including the astounding upside-down world map by Al-Idrissi from 1154. This is followed, on the first floor, with the history of astrology from the Stone Age via Stonehenge and the Egyptian pyramids through to today. There's also a mind-boggling section on Babylonian sexagisimal maths. The museum also houses a small planetarium (shows only in Danish) and has a herb garden with over three hundred medicinal herbs. To get to the campus from the centre, take bus #2, #3, #11, #14, #54, #56 or #58.

Out from the city

On Sundays, post-brunch Århus resembles a ghost town, with most locals spending the day in the parks, woodlands or beaches on the city's outskirts. The closest beach (Den Permanente) and woods (Risskov) are just **north of the city** at Risskov, near the *Århus Vandrerhjem* hostel, easily reached on buses #6 or #16, or on any local trains headed for Grenå or Hornslets, some of which halt at the tiny Den Permanente train platform by the beach (but check before boarding, as not all trains stop here). Den Permanente beach is narrow but scenic, with an old-fashioned public bathhouse and, as it's a Blue Flag beach, the water is sparkling clean. The thick forest behind is crisscrossed with walking and cycling trails.

For a more varied day, head **south** through the thick Marselisborg Skov forest via the prehistoric museum at Moesgård and on to the hugely popular Blue Flag Moesgård beach (or take bus #19 from the centre). This is also ideal territory for cycling or hiking – see p.222 for details of bicycle rental, and contact the tourist office for maps and suggestions on routes.

Marselisborg Skov and Slot

Marselisborg Skov, 4km south of the city centre, is a large park that contains the city's sports and horse-trotting stadiums and sees a regular procession of people exercising their dogs. Further south, across Carl Nielsen Vej, is the diminutive **Marselisborg Slot**, summer home of the Danish royals, whose landscaped grounds can be visited during daylight hours (free) when they're not in residence (usually at all times outside Easter, Christmas and late June to early Aug); if guards are posted by the gate, they're in and there's a changing of guards at noon. Around the *slot*, the park turns into a dense forest, crisscrossed with footpaths but still easy to get lost in.

A simpler route to navigate, and one with better views, is along Strandvejen, which runs between the eastern side of the forest and the shore.

Moesgård Museum

Occupying the buildings and grounds of an old manor house 10km south of Århus city centre, **Moesgård Museum** (April–Sept daily 10am–5pm; Oct–March Tues–Sun 10am–4pm; 60kr; Ⓦ www .moesmus.dk) traces the story of Danish civilizations from the Stone Age onwards via copious finds and easy-to-follow illustrations. It's the Iron Age which is most comprehensively covered and produces the most dramatic single exhibit: the **Grauballe Man**, the remains of a body, dated to 80 BC, which was discovered in a peat bog west of Århus in a state of such excellent preservation that it was possible to discover what the deceased had eaten for breakfast (burnt porridge made from rye and barley) on the day of his death. Also remarkable is the extensive **Illerup Ådal** collection of weapons and military paraphernalia, dating from around 200 BC and recovered, in relatively good condition, from the Ådal bog. Only a roomful of imposing runic stones captures the imagination as powerfully. Bus #6 runs here direct from the city, while bus #19 takes a more scenic route along the edge of Århus Bay, leaving you with a walk of just over 2km.

Outside the museum, the **prehistoric trail** runs from the far corner of the courtyard to the sea and back again (follow the red dots), a distance of about 3km each way, heading past a scattering of reassembled prehistoric dwellings, monuments and burial places – a trail guide is available in English (15kr), and there's a map on the back of your entry ticket. On a fine day, the walk itself is as enjoyable as the actual sights, and you could easily linger for a picnic when you reach the coast, or stop for a coffee and a snack at the *Skovmøllen* restaurant en route. Bus #19 goes back to the city from a stop about a hundred metres back to the north of the trail's end at the beach.

Eating

Central Århus is loaded with **eating** possibilities, though nothing is particularly cheap. In general, it's wise to follow locals and students away from the heavily touristed Domkirke and Store Torv to streets such as Mejlgade, Nørre Allé, Vestergade or Skolegade. If you're prepared to pay a bit more, Åboulevarden – the northern bank of the uncovered section of the Århus Å river – offers a string of trendy eating and drinking venues, and is a good place to head throughout the day for brunch, as well as for lunch or dinner. You'll also find a host of popular fine dining restaurants in the residential area of Frederiksbjerg just south of the centre, predominantly along Jægergårdsgade.

If money is tight, or you just want to stock up with delicious smørrebrød for a picnic, try *Frokostspecialisten* at Frederiks Allé 105. For more general food shopping, there's a late-opening DSB **supermarket** (8am–midnight) at the train station, and several other downtown supermarkets of varying quality.

Unless otherwise stated, the places below are on the Central Århus map, p.221.

Cafés and restaurants

Bryggeriet Sct Clemens Kannikegade 10–12 ☎86 13 80 00, ⓦ www.bryggeriet.dk. A popular modern brewery-cum-restaurant which does delicious spare ribs for 171kr, best washed down with freshly tapped unfiltered beer; the steaks aren't bad, either. Lunch ranges from 65kr for dish of the day to a filling smørrebrød platter for 115kr. Closed Sun.
Crêperiet Marselisborg Havnevej 24 ☎86 12 13 00, ⓦ www.creperiet.dk (see Around Århus map, p.227). Rustic, glass-fronted restaurant on the habourfront with both indoor and outdoor seating, serving crêpes with over 25 mouthwatering fillings (41–149kr), sweet and savoury. The beautiful fish soup (125kr) is also worth trying, and there's a good range of wine. Bus #6 from the station. April–Aug open daily, rest of year closed Mon & Tues.
Emmerys Guldsmedegade 24–26 ☎86 13 04 00, ⓦ www.emmerys.dk. Housed in the city's oldest patisserie, this modern bakery outlet offers wonderful freshly ground coffee and delicious home-made bread and cakes, as well as simple, flavour-packed wholemeal breakfasts and sandwiches – but it's the gorgeous pastries that make a permanent imprint in the memory. Open daily from 7am until early evening.
Gaucho-Argentisk Bøfhus Åboulevarden 20 ☎86 13 70 65, ⓦ www.gaucho.dk. Excellent choice if you're longing for a big, juicy steak, and despite the riverside location, prices aren't too bad – a 200g sirloin served with veg and chips goes for only 199kr. Some of the steak menus are half-price between 4pm and 5.45pm.
Globen Flakket Åboulevarden 18 ☎87 31 03 33, ⓦ www.globen-flakket.dk. This large riverside café, with outdoor seating and a posh restaurant downstairs, is one of the town's most popular places for brunch (9am–1pm), which starts at 92kr for the veggie version; don't be surprised if

you have to wait for a table during weekends. There's also a weekday breakfast (25kr) and lunch buffets (both 88kr) and the usual array of salads and sandwiches.
Gourmet Garagen Mejlgade 35 ☎86 12 30 24, ⓦ www.gourmetgaragen.dk. Tasty Italian country cuisine that won't break the bank, served in a rustic back building in the city's medieval centre. The limited menu changes daily depending on seasonal variation; prices start at 145kr for mains. Dinner only, Tues–Sat.
Gyngen Mejlgade 53 ☎86 19 22 55, ⓦ www .gyngen.dk. Good-value organic meat and veggie dishes served up within the Fronthuset culture centre. The daily seasonal salad costs 65kr, full-on veggie or meat burgers with chips and salsa and relish cost 120kr, while main courses at dinner start at 130kr; local bands sometimes play after dinner (check for listings). Closed Sun & Mon.
Karls Sandwichbar Klostergade 32 ☎86 12 98 11, ⓦ www.karlssandwich.dk. The best burgers in town: huge and home-made, served with large portions of fries (from 50kr). Can't beat it. Open till 6am Thurs–Sat.
Klassisk 65 Jægergårdsgade 65 ☎86 13 12 21, ⓦ www.klassiskbistro.dk. One of the string of new restaurants along Jægergårdsgade, this one is also a wine bar with an immense stock of wines that beautifully complement the well-prepared, flavour-some dishes, such as home-made gravad lax (98kr) and juicy steak (295kr). The knowledgeable waiters will recommend suitable wines for each dish. Also a hit for the Sunday brunch (165kr), served in two seatings (10am & 12.15pm) – booking recommended.
Le Coq Graven 16 ☎86 19 50 74, ⓦ www .cafe-lecoq.dk. Romantic little restaurant serving authentic French food such as the mouthwatering *coquelet au vin blanc* for 185kr. To work up an

appetite, there's table football at the café-bar at the front. Dinner only.

Ministeriet Kloster Torvet 5 ☎86 17 11 88, ⓦwww .ministeriet.org. Popular café with outdoor seating on the square, serving good food ranging from breakfast (55kr; 9.30am–noon) and brunch (from 90kr; until 3pm), to sandwiches and salads until 5pm, as well as burgers (chicken or meat). Great tapas too.

Nordisk Spisehus MP Bruunsgade 31 ☎86 17 70 99, ⓦwww.nordiskspisehus.dk. Refreshingly unpretentious gourmet place serving a small but delectable range of high-quality Nordic dishes using seasonal and innovative ingredients such as haws and cloudberries. A two-course meal will set you back 200kr. Also takeout (order online).

Pinden Skolegade 29 ☎86 12 11 02, ⓦwww .pinden.dk. Traditional Danish eatery known for its *stegt flæsk med persille sovs*; six pieces of *flæsk* with potatoes go for 92kr, all-you-can-eat 125kr; there's also good smørrebrød. Closed Sun.

Raadhuus Kaféen Sønder Allé 3 ☎86 12 37 74, ⓦwww.raadhuus-kafeen.dk. Traditional eatery with dark furnishings and wood-panelled walls, offering all-day Danish specials such as *frikadeller* or *flæskeæggekage* for 88kr, and which claims to have the city's longest list of smørrebrød toppings.

Seafood Marselisborg Havnevej (see Around Århus map, p.227) 44 ☎86 18 56 55, ⓦwww.seafood -aarhus.dk. A great choice if you're prepared to splash out, with fantastic views of the Århus Bay area and a delectable range of seafood, from Brittany oysters to hake steamed in white wine. Main courses from 235kr. Closed Sun & Mon Sept–March.

Simoncini Jægergårdsgade 6 ☎86 23 20 84, ⓦwww.simoncini.dk. Authentic Italian gourmet restaurant, at the Frederiks Allé end of Jægergårdsgade serving delightful meals such as *spaghetti alle vongole* (115kr) and fish of the day (195kr) plus a mouthwatering array of Italian cheeses. Also does takeout. Tues–Sat, dinner only.

🏃 **Svineriet** Mejlgade 35 ☎86 12 30 00, ⓦwww.svineriet.dk. Excellent, laid-back place in a back yard, serving superb seasonal three- and six-course meals for 295kr and 895kr respectively, the latter – nicknamed "The whole hog" (in Danish *Svineriet*) – includes a glass of fine wine with each course. Tues–Sat, dinner only.

Drinking and nightlife

Århus is the only place in Denmark with a **nightlife** scene to match that of Copenhagen, offering a diverse assortment of ways to be entertained, enlightened or just inebriated almost every night of the week. And while things sparkle socially year-round, if you visit during the annual **Århus Festival** (*Århus Festuge*), an orgy of arts events held over the first week in September (check what's on with the tourist office or visit ⓦwww.aarhusfestuge.dk), you'll find even more to occupy your time. Equally, during the third week of July, **Århus Jazz Festival** (ⓦwww.jazzfest.dk), transforms the city to a jazz lover's paradise, with groovy tunes oozing from every street corner.

The city has a wonderful endowment of cafés, and the ones in the medieval streets close to the cathedral are among the most popular places to go for a **drink**. There's little to choose between them – each pulls a lively, cosmopolitan crowd and the best plan is simply to wander around and try a few – but we've listed the most enduring options below.

Home to a music school that's produced some of the country's most successful performers, Århus boasts a music scene that's well known throughout Denmark – so if you're looking for **live music**, you won't have to look far. Basic details of all events are available from the tourist office, where you can pick up flyers and free local magazines. Århus's **clubbing** scene is equally lively, with both *Voxhall* and *Train* staging club nights when they aren't hosting live bands, and plenty of more mainstream venues providing less achingly cool places to dance. Early in the week, admission to any club is likely to be free; on Thursday, Friday or Saturday, you'll pay 20–60kr.

Cafés and bars

Billabong Bar Skolegade 26 ⓦwww.billabongbar .dk. The city's only Aussie bar, full of hardy outback types and serving local and foreign ales. There's a happy hour on weekdays until 6pm.

The Bridgewater Pub Åboulevarden 22 ⓦwww .bridgewater.dk. This riverbank English pub with real ales on tap is the place to go for your football fix, with three large screens and live NFL on Sundays.

Carlton Rosengade 23 ⓦ www.carlton.dk. Right in the centre of this quaint, café-heavy medieval quarter, and always buzzing at night. The food is pricey, so most people only come to drink. Closed Sun.

Casablanca Rosengade 12 ⓦ www.cafe -casablanca.dk. A good place to start the evening, this is Århus's oldest café, with movie-themed decorations and live jazz on Wednesday evenings. Closed Sun.

The Cockney Pub Maren Smeds Gyde 8 ⓦ www .cockneypub.dk. Down a tiny alleyway from Skt Clemens Stræde, this popular real-ale pub features haggis nights and whisky-tasting sessions – and they pride themselves on making a proper cup of tea. Closes early Sun.

Jorden Badstuegade 3 ⓦ www.cafejorden.dk. Cosy café in the medieval cathedral area, which serves quality brunch until mid-afternoon, and gets very lively at night when the drinkers arrive.

Pinds Café Skolegade 11 ⓦ www.pindscafe.dk. Fun place to meet the locals, where dancing on the tables isn't uncommon. Closed Sun.

Ris Ras Filliongongong Mejlgade 24 ⓦ www .risras.dk. Named after a well-known Danish children's rhyme, this is a popular student hangout that excels in a huge range of good beer and cigars (smoking is still allowed, here); there's an art gallery in the basement too.

Smagløs Kloster Torvet 7 ⓦ www .smagloes.dk. Old-timer on the café scene that's packed with lunchers by day and students by night; it's especially busy when there's live music a couple of nights a week.

Svej Åboulevarden 22 ⓦ www.svej.dk. Tucked in among the thick row of cafés and bars lining Århus Å river, with chairs spilling out onto the pavement, this is *the* place to be seen on sunny summer evenings. The long drinks menu includes a host of delicious wine – all sold by the glass as well as the bottle – and a huge array of flavoured snaps.

Tir na nog Frederiksgade 40 ⓦ www.tirnanog.dk. The city's one and only Irish pub, with live Irish folk a couple of nights a week, Champions League football – and Guinness, of course.

Under Masken Bispegade 3. Cosy yet quirky bar, with masks from around the globe decorating the walls and a wide selection of foreign beers. One of the few places in town where smoking is still allowed.

Universitets Baren Nordre Ringgade 3 ⓦ www .universitetsbaren.dk (see Around Århus map, p.227). Found in building no. 1422 at the city's university campus, this student bar is now so popular that non-students also turn up in

droves – possibly due to the extensive beer menu. Closed Sun.

Clubs

Broen Nordhavnsgade 20 ⓦ www.mf-broen.dk. Set in a boat moored in the harbour and divided into five separate sections with different decor and styles of music, from mainstream hip-hop to Frank Sinatra. Fri & Sat only.

Herr Bartels Åboulevarden 46 ⓦ www.herrbartels .dk. Sleek bar/nightclub with a cool metallic interior and a long list of cocktails, including a tasty selection of alcoholic iced teas. The dance-floor is always packed. Thurs over 18s only, Fri & Sat over 23s.

Royal Århus Store Torv 4 ⓦ www.royal-casino.dk. Flash hotel basement housing a combined casino/ nightclub that's liveliest early in the week. Smart dress code applies.

Den Sidste Paradisgade 9 ⓦ www.cafeparadis.dk. *Den sidste* ("the last") is a lively final stop for all-night partygoers, who fill the dance floor until the wee hours. Fri & Sat.

Social Club Klostergade 34 ⓦ www.socialclub.dk. The city's coolest club, playing the newest, hottest dance tunes. Massive discounts for students. Thurs over 18s only, Fri & Sat over 20s.

Live music venues

Fatter Eskild Skolegade 25 ☏ 86 19 44 11, ⓦ www.fattereskild.dk. Piano bar hosting Danish bar-bands and R&B acts five nights a week. Closed Sun & Mon.

Musikcafeen Mejlgade 53 ☏ 86 76 03 44, ⓦ www.musikcafeen.dk. On the first floor of the Fronthuset cultural centre, this is Århus's main venue for up-and-coming Danish and international bands, as well as live jazz, rock and the odd techno act. Entrance fee 20–150kr. Closed Sun.

Musikhuset Thomas Jensens Allé ☏ 86 40 90 50, ⓦ www.musikhusetaarhus.dk. City-centre concert hall which plays host to classical music, opera and, occasionally, mainstream pop bands.

Train Toldbogade 6 ☏ 86 13 47 22, ⓦ www.train .dk. Attracting an older crowd and slightly more well-established bands than rival *Voxhall* (see below). Gigs take place three or four nights a week; admission runs 100– 600kr, with doors opening at 9pm and the main band on a couple of hours later.

Voxhall Vester Allé 15 ☏ 87 30 97 97, ⓦ www .voxhall.dk. Århus's premier venue, hosting the cream of Danish and international independent acts from hip hop to world music. Tickets cost 100–400kr.

Listings

Airport Tirstrup Airport: information
☎87 75 70 00; arrivals and departures board
at 🌐www.aar.dk.

Bookshops English Books and Secondhand
Things, Frederiks Allé 53 (☎52 90 28 35, Mon–Fri
11.30am–5.30pm, Sat 11am–2pm), fully lives up
to its name.

Bus enquiries Local buses ☎86 12 86 22,
🌐www.midttrafik.dk; Abildskou's Århus–Copenhagen coach reservations ☎70 21 08 88, 🌐www
.abildskou.dk.

Car rental Avis, Spanien 63 ☎86 19 23 99,
Jens Baggesens Vej 27 ☎86 16 10 99 and
Tirstrup Airport ☎86 36 36 00, 🌐www.avis.dk,
Europcar, Sønder Allé 35 ☎89 33 11 11 and
Tirstrup Airport ☎86 36 37 44, 🌐www
.europcar.dk.

Doctors Between 4pm and 8pm, call ☎86 20
10 22. Outside these hours, contact the Kommune-
hospital (see above).

Ferries and catamarans Mols Linien to either
Odden or Kalundborg on Zealand ☎70 10 14 18,
🌐www.mols-linien.dk.

Hospitals There's a 24hr emergency department
at Århus Universitetshospital, Nørrebrogade 44
(☎89 49 44 44).

Internet cafés Boomtown, Åboulevarden 21
(🌐www.boomtown.dk; Mon–Thurs & Sun 11am–
midnight, Fri & Sat 11am–8am, gates shut at
midnight; 30kr per hr); Gate 58, Vestergade 58B
(🌐www.gate58.dk; Mon–Fri 10am–midnight, Sat &
Sun noon–midnight; 18kr per hr until 2pm then
28kr per hr;) and free internet access at Århus
Library, Møllegade 1 (Mon–Thurs 10am–8pm, Fri
10am–6pm, Sat 10am–3pm).

Markets There's a fruit, veg and flower market
every Wednesday and Saturday on Bispetorvet,
beside the cathedral (early morning till noon), though
the one on Saturday mornings (10am–2pm) along
Ingerslevs Boulevard, south of the centre, is livelier.

Pharmacy Løve Apoteket, Store Torv 5 ☎86 12
00 22, is open 24hr.

Police Århus Politisation, Ridderstræde 1
☎87 31 14 48.

Post office Banegårds Pladsen, by the train station
(Mon–Fri 9.30am–6pm, Sat 10am–1pm),

Djursland and north to Randers

East of Århus, the Djursland peninsula – known lovingly as Jutland's nose – boasts some of the prettiest landscapes in Denmark, its rolling hills and sandy beaches providing sufficient ingredients for a couple of days' pleasurable exploration. The southern coastal stretch, known as **Mols**, is especially delightful and attracts huge numbers of (mostly German) tourists every year, its heath-covered hills affording some superb views of the Ebeltoft and Kalø bay areas. **Ebeltoft**, the area's pretty urban centre, has a laid-back holiday feel year-round, and has a few interesting attractions should the weather warrant indoor activities. Right on the other side of the peninsula, the white sandy beaches of the north coast are less protected and a little wilder. Heading back inland, **Gammel Estrup Slot** provides an enlight-ening insight into the country's long agricultural history and life of the landed gentry in times gone by. The large town of **Randers** isn't all that appealing, though it does have its recreated "rainforest" domes and an Elvis museum; and if you're canoeing down the Gudenå from Silkeborg (see p.219), you'll end up at Tørring, just outside town.

Ebeltoft

Easily reached by regular buses from Århus (#123) and Randers (#212), and by the frequent Mols-Linien ferry services from Odden in Zealand (see p.99), **EBELTOFT** is a cute little town, with pretty timber-framed houses lining its cobbled streets. A thriving market centre in medieval times, it was sacked by the invading Swedes in 1659 and has only emerged from economic decline thanks to tourism: try to arrive in early summer, before the streets are overrun. Ebeltoft's main appeal is its proximity to a string of outstanding beaches, which run from its western outskirts along the Ebeltoft Vig bay coastline to Mols Bjerge (see p.232). There are also a few good sights in the town itself, and the pretty centre is postcard-perfect enough to deserve a stroll.

Ebeltoft's two best attractions are by the harbour, a short walk downhill from the bus station. The **Fregatten Jylland** (daily: April–Aug 10am–5pm; Sept–Oct 11am–4pm; Nov–March 11am–3pm; 95kr; Ⓦ www.fregatten-jylland.dk) is a beautifully restored nineteenth-century frigate kitted out with an array of guns and cannons. The last wooden ship to be built in Denmark before the advance of iron (at a time when Denmark was a naval power to be reckoned with), it saw plenty of action, most famously at the 1864 battle of Helgoland, when the Prussian fleet was completely out-manoeuvred and forced to retreat (the victory was short-lived, though, as the Prussians won the war on the ground shortly after). Miniature recreations of famous sea battles are displayed in the frigate's exhibition hall, alongside a breakdown of its colourful history – it served as the king's royal yacht at one point – and descriptions of life on board. Nearby at Strandvejen 8, the **Glas Museet** (April–June & Sept–Oct daily 10am–5pm; July–Aug daily 10am–6pm; Nov–March Tues–Sun 10am–4pm; 75kr; Ⓦ www.glasmuseet.dk) is a stunning showcase of artworks in glass from all over the world, many housed in a spectacular new waterfront extension. Pieces to look out for include an unusual crystal-shaped blue glass table and a collection of gold-covered Japanese jewellery boxes. If you're feeling flush, there's also a gallery and shop selling some of the items. From April until October (daily 10am–5pm), local artisans demonstrate the art of glass blowing on-site.

Ebeltoft's main appeal, its **beaches**, begin on the town's outskirts and continue towards Mols Bjerge, and the sheltered setting on the bay means the shallow water is usually a degree or two higher than elsewhere in Denmark. Unlike the pristine shores of north Jutland and the west coast of Jutland, the beaches here are left relatively unkempt, with seaweed and jellyfish sometimes abundant – but this doesn't seem to deter the beachgoers. The calm waters here are an ideal place to learn to windsurf or sail a dinghy; get information about lessons and kit rental at the **tourist office** by the harbour at S.A. Jensensvej 3 (July to mid-Aug Mon–Fri 9am–5pm, Sat & Sun 10am–4pm; mid-Aug to June Mon–Fri 9am–4.30pm, Sat 10am–1pm; Ⓣ86 34 05 28, Ⓦ www.visitdjursland.com).

The two best **accommodation** options are the sleek *Hotel Ebeltoft Strand*, overlooking Ebeltoft Bay and a stone's throw from Fregatten Jylland, on Ndr. Strandvej 3 (Ⓣ86 34 33 00, Ⓦ www.ebeltoftstrand.dk; ⓿) with a slightly cheaper section on a hillside overlooking the bay ten minutes' walk away (❼), and the *Ebeltoft Vandrerhjem* **youth hostel**, behind the harbour at Søndergade 43 (Ⓣ86 34 20 53, Ⓦ www.danhostel.dk/ebeltoft; dorms 160kr, doubles ❸, all with shared facilities). *Hotel Ebeltoft Strand* is also the town's premier live music venue and houses a couple of good restaurants. Of the several **campsites** along the bay, the closest to Ebeltoft is *Ebeltoft Strand Camping* (Ⓣ86 34 55 33, Ⓦ www.publiccamp .dk), on Nordre Strandvej. It has cabins sleeping four (550kr) and six (800kr) and rents out bikes (25kr per hr and 100kr per day).

Mols Bjerge

Djursland's beautiful stretch of southern coastline, **MOLS** has been endowed with a bountiful supply of outstanding natural scenery that encompasses pretty highland landscapes, sandy beaches and small, cute villages. The rolling hills here – roughly between Femmøller (7km west of Ebeltoft) and the Helgenæs peninsula – are known collectively as **MOLS BJERGE**, a stunning mosaic of open woodland and heath, carpeted with an explosion of wild flowers in spring and summer supporting rare butterflies and other insects, and with a smattering of Bronze Age burial mounds adorning the highest points. This beautiful highland landscape has recently been designated a national park, protected by the Danish nature conservancy agency and with a wide network of trails and tracks. The best way to explore is on foot or by bike (for rental outlets, see p.232). National cycle routes #2 and #5 run along the northern edge, but the gravel tracks within the protected area are also ideal for cycling (note that the trails are for hikers only). Turn off at **Femmøller**, just after the roadside mill, and the track will take you straight into Mols Bjerge proper. Bus #123, linking Ebeltoft and Århus, stops at Femmøller, from where the marked **Den Italienske Sti** trail takes you to the heart of the area and to the unmanned **Molbolaboratiorie visitor centre** (open 24/7), where you can pick up free walking maps of the area. At the foot of Mols' so-called mountains, along the heath-covered coastal strip, the tightly packed holiday homes form a buffer between the mountains and the sandy beaches. Unfortunately, if you want easy access to both beaches and the mountains, you'll find that there are very few **accommodation** options. Your best bet is to stay in Ebeltoft, or at the outrageously luxurious *Mols Kroen* inn (℡86 36 22 00, 🅦www.molskroen.dk; ❾) at Hovedgaden 16, 2km before Femmøller on the main road from Ebeltoft and right on Femmøller Strand beach. If you want to splash out, the inn's gourmet **restaurant** is worth a visit; main courses mix weird and wonderful ingredients – such as pickled oxtail, lobster and creamy Jerusalem artichoke mash in the same dish, for example – and start at 165kr.

The north coast

If it's only beaches you're after, head 10km north of the town of Grenå (Djursland's missable main town on the peninsula's east coast) by local bus #352 to **GJERRILD**, a small and quiet village with an inn, bakery, grocery and a small castle, Sostrup Slot, now a religious retreat run by Cistercian sisters and with a pleasant park open to the public. Continuing 4km north of Gjerrild along Langholmvej (no public transport) will take you to the Blue-Flag **Nordstranden beach**, among the best in the country, with miles of soft sand and basic facilities. **Accommodation** is limited to the excellent *Gjerrild Nordstrand Camping* (℡86 38 42 00, 🅦www.gnc.dk; April to mid-Sept), 500m from the beach, which also has a small shop. Back in Gjerrild, there's also the atmospheric *Gjerrild Vandrerhjem* **youth hostel**, Dyrehavevej 9 (℡86 38 41 99, 🅦www.danhostel-gjerrild.dk), set on the fringes of a woodland in an old railway station with en-suite doubles (❹) and bunk rooms sleeping up to eight.

Gammel Estrup Slot

An interesting stop en route from Grenå to Randers, a few kilometres after the village of Auning and reachable by bus #214, **Gammel Estrup Slot** is an imposing sixteenth-century pile in Gothic renaissance style. Exactly as you'd imagine a castle to look, it's a commanding three-winged, red-brick building with a tower in each corner with a cobbled courtyard, surrounded by a moat and a bridge leading to the farm building outside. The castle complex holds two unusual museums; a joint 85kr ticket covers entry to both. Inside the castle, to the right as you enter the courtyard, the **Jyllands Herregårdsmuseum** (Manor House Museum: April–June & mid-Aug to Oct daily 10am–5pm; July to mid-Aug daily 10am–6pm; Nov–March Tues–Sun 10am–3pm; 🅦www.gammelestrup.dk) serves to illustrate the lives of the landed gentry in the eighteenth century. Richly furnished rooms are bedecked with family portraits, while the grand great hall and enormous castle kitchen, with its beautiful vaulted ceiling, give a sense of the size and splendour of the dinner parties held here. Throughout the castle offers lovely views of the **grounds**, with beautiful parkland, an orangery and rows of carp ponds. Across the stream feeding the carp ponds, the immense **Dansk Landbrugsmuseum** (Danish Agriculture Museum: same hours; ⓦ www.gl-estrup.dk) could easily take up an entire afternoon. Occupying old farm buildings and the surrounding grounds, its exhibits trace agricultural development in Denmark from the Stone Age until the present. Two particularly fascinating new sections focus on the cultural history of food, and how meat and dairy production have played a part in the development of the traditional Danish meal. Outdoors, there's a botanic garden with beehives, where native species of grain and fruit are grown, including the organic barley used in the small on-site brewery; you can buy the beer in the museum shop.

Randers

Strategically located at the point where the Gudenå river narrows and runs into Randers fjord, the town of **RANDERS** came into existence as a place where Vikings crossed the river in the tenth century. A trading and manufacturing base since the thirteenth century, its growth has continued apace over the years, leaving a tiny medieval centre miserably corralled by a bleak new industrial zone. The town's main historical sight is the house at **Storegade 13**, said to be the place where Danish nobleman Niels Ebbesen killed the German count, Gerd of Holstein, in 1340; a shutter on the upper storey is always left open to allow the count's ghost to escape lest the malevolent spirit should cause the building to burn down. However, Randers' biggest tourist attractions – and one of the most popular in Jutland – is the **Randers Regnskov** (Randers Rainforest; mid-June to mid-Aug daily 10am–6pm; mid-Aug to mid-June Mon–Fri 10am–4pm, Sat & Sun 10am–5pm; 150kr; ⓦ www .regnskoven.dk), a recreation of tropical rainforests – African, Asian and South American – set alongside the river Gudenå. Enclosed within three giant domes, you wander through the dense, damp foliage, watching out for the birds, animals and amphibians, which include a number of rare turtles and a flying fox, for the most part left to run about freely. One of the most terrifying bits is the Asian temple where a formidable assortment of vipers, boas and pythons lounge about. Also fascinating are the busy leaf-cutter ants whose trails you can follow through glass tubing to and from their glass-fronted nest.

Otherwise, Randers holds a few decent museums. The Culture Centre, near the bus station on Stenmannsgade 2, holds the imaginatively presented **Kulturhistorisk Museum Randers** (Tues–Sun 11am–5pm; free; ⓦ www.khm.dk) on the first floor and **Museet for Dansk Kunst** (same hours; free; ⓦ www.randerskunstmuseum.dk) on the second. With a permanent collection of over two thousand pieces, mostly by Danish artists, you could easily kill a couple of hours here, not least for the wacky glass and mirror installation *Cosmic Space* by the Faroese artist Trondur Patursson. A little further down the road, at no. 9C, the **Elvis Unlimited Museum** (Mon–Fri 10am–5.30pm, Sat 10am–2pm; 50kr; ⓦ www.elvispresley.dk) has tons of paraphernalia, including the King's personal record collection, two of his guitars, clothes and the Presley archives as collated by the FBI.

Practicalities

Randers' **bus station** is right in the centre at Dytmærsken 12; the **train station** is on the outskirts, ten minutes' walk west of the centre at Jernbanegade 29. The two best **hotels** in town are the classic old grand Art Deco *Hotel Randers*, in the centre on Torvegade 11 (ⓣ 86 42 34 22, ⓦ www.hotel-randers.dk; ❽) with significant reductions at weekends, and the cheaper and cosier *Stephansen* (ⓣ 86 44 27 77, ⓦ www .stephansenhotel; ❼) housed in a beautifully restored old wood-beamed building next to the courthouse at Møllestræde 4. The *Randers Vandrerhjem* **youth hostel** (ⓣ 86 42 50 44, ⓦ www.danhostelranders.dk; mid-Feb to Nov; dorms 285kr, doubles ❺) is five minutes' walk north of the centre at Gethersvej 1; town bus #6 stops 200m from the front door on Hobrovej. The nearest **campsite**, *Randers City Camp* (℡86 42 93 61, ⓦwww.randerscitycamp.dk), with cabins sleeping four and six (from 175kr) and a swimming pool, is 6km west of Randers at Fladbro, which is also the final staging point for canoe trips down the Gudenå river (see p.166). To get there, take bus #10 to the golf course, from where it's a ten-minute signposted walk. Note that some #10 buses do go all the way to the campsite stop, so ask the driver.

Randers has plenty of relatively inexpensive **restaurants**, the best being the traditional *Niels Ebbesens Spisehus* (℡86 43 32 26, ⓦwww.nielsebbesens.dk), Storegade 12 (see p.234). Downstairs in *Hotel Randers* there's also the stylish *Café Mathisen* (closed Sun) which does a good range of salads and sandwiches as well as the popular Mathisen burger (118kr). As for **nightlife**, Storegade holds a good selection of bars where you can sample the local Thor beer; try the popular *Tante Olga*, Søndergade 6 (ⓦwww.tanteolga.dk), which has something going on every weekend (Thurs–Sat), or the laid-back *Maren Knudsen Øl & Vinkælder* in the basement of no.5. In early August the town celebrates **Randers Ugen**, a week packed with all sorts of cultural events; the rest of the year, major live concerts and theatre performances are regularly staged at *Værket* (ⓦwww.vaerket.dk), a converted power station on Mariagervej.

The best way to see the countryside around Randers is by **bike**, rentable at Schmidt Cykler, Kirkegade 7 (℡86 41 29 03) and at Fladbro camping (see above). For free **internet** access, head for Randers library at the Culture Centre (see p.234).

Viborg and around

Some 40km west of Randers and historically at the junction of all major roads in Jutland, **VIBORG** was one of the most important communities in the country until the mid-eighteenth century. From Knud in 1027 to Christian V in 1655, every Danish king was crowned here in Viborg; Hans Tausen's Lutheran preaching began in here in 1528, eight years before Denmark's official conversion from Catholicism; and until the early nineteenth century the town was the seat of a provincial assembly. As the national administrative axis shifted towards Zealand, however, Viborg's importance waned, and although it's still home to the high court of West Denmark, it's now primarily a market town, with only its majestic cathedral giving a hint of its past glory days. With its picturesque lakeside setting and a quaint compact centre housing two good museums, Viborg is a good base from which to explore the surrounding countryside. To the south, the tranquil hills of **Dollerup** are rich in history, while the **limestone mines** to the east serve as a spooky reminder of the harsh lives of miners in times past. Last but not least, the bleak moorlands of **Kongenshus**, smothered in heather during the autumn, offer some great hikes.

Arrival, information and accommodation

Trains and **long-distance buses** arrive at their respective stations on Viborg's western side at Banegårds Pladsen 2 and 4, roughly 1km from the centre. If coming from Randers by train, note that you'll need to change at Langå. The **tourist office** (June–Aug Mon–Fri 9am–5pm, Sat 9am–2pm; Sept–May Mon–Fri 9am–4pm, Sat 10am–1pm; ℡87 87 88 88, ⓦwww.visitviborg.dk) is close to the cathedral at Nytorv 9; it has a long list of reasonably priced **private rooms** starting at about 150kr per person and also rents out **bikes** (100kr per day). For free **internet** access head for Viborg library at Vesterbrogade 15 (Mon–Thurs 10am–7pm, Fri 10am–6pm, Sat 9.30am–2pm). Viborg's few **hotels** are all fairly pricey. Most central is the grand old *Palads*, Sct Mathias Gade 5 (℡86 62 37 00, ⓦwww.hotelpalads.dk; ➐), a short walk from the train station with free internet. More expensive is the modern *Golf*

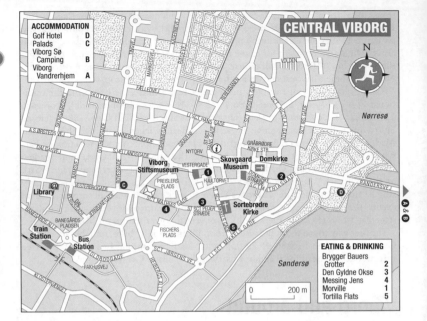

Hotel Viborg, Randersvej 2 (☎86 61 02 22, ⓦ www.golf-hotel-viborg.dk; ⑤), next to a golf course and with a fabulous lake view and free wi-fi. Also close to the lake, but on the opposite side to the town centre (a 2km walk, or local bus #707), are the *Viborg Vandrerhjem* **youth hostel**, Vinkelvej 36 (☎86 67 17 81, ⓦ www.danhostel .dk/viborg; dorms 150kr, doubles ④; Feb–Nov); and the *Viborg Sø Camping* **campsite** (☎86 67 13 11, ⓦ www.camping-viborg.dk; April to mid-Oct) with comfortable cabins sleeping four (525kr).

The Town

Viborg is cut in half by a lake named Nørresø in its northern reach, Søndersø to the south, and spanned by the Randersvej bridge. Central Viborg is concentrated in a small area, though, and most parts of the old town are within a few minutes' walk of each other. The logical place to start exploring is the **Domkirke** (April–Sept Mon–Sat 11am–4pm, Sun noon–4pm; Oct–March Mon–Sat 11am–3pm, Sun noon–3pm), whose twin towers are the town's most visible feature. Built by Bishop Eskil in 1130, the original cathedral was destroyed by fire in 1726 and rebuilt in today's Baroque style in 1860 by one Claus Stallknecht – though he did the job so badly that it had to be closed for two years and refinished. The **interior** is dominated by the brilliant frescoes of **Joakim Skovgaard**, who took twelve years to cover the walls and arches with the entire story of the Bible in an unusually dramatic and colourful style. Look out especially for the angels opening the gates to heaven. Skovgaard is commemorated at the **Skovgaard Museum** (Tues–Sun: June–Aug 10am–5pm; Sept–May 11am–4pm; 35kr; ⓦ www.skovgaardmuseet.dk), inside the former Rådhus across from the cathedral – a neat building with which Claus Stallknecht made amends for his botched job over the road. There's a good selection of Skovgaard's paintings on display – although they're a little anticlimactic after his splendid work in the cathedral – plus some works by other members of his family.

Two minutes' walk away on Store Sct Mikkels Gade, there's another interesting church in the form of the late-Romanesque **Sortebrødre Kirke**, the sole remains of the cloisters built by Dominican Black Friars, one of four monastic orders in Viborg abolished during the Reformation; ask at the sacristan office next door for the key. Inside the church, the sixteenth-century Belgian altarpiece is the star turn, with 89 gilded oak figures in high relief around the central Crucifixion scene. For a broader perspective on Viborg's past, visit **Viborg Stiftsmuseum** (Viborg District Museum: mid-June to Aug Tues–Sun 11am–5pm; Sept to mid-June Tues–Fri 1–4pm, Sat & Sun 11am–5pm; 40kr; Ⓦwww.viborgstiftsmuseum.dk), on the northern side of Hjultorvet between Vestergade and Store Sct Hans Gade. The three well-stocked floors hold everything from prehistoric and archeological artefacts to clothes, furniture and household appliances.

Eating, drinking and nightlife

During the day, you could do worse than pick up some smørrebrød (the best outlet is the *Stjerneskuddet* deli at Jernbanegade 14), and **eat** alfresco in one of the numerous parks or on the banks of the lake. Plenty of reasonably priced eating places can also be found on and around Sct Mathias Gade.

Restaurants and bars

🏃 **Brygger Bauers Grotter** Sct Mathias Gade 61 ☎86 61 44 88 Ⓦwww .bryggerbauersgrotter.dk. Romantic, candlelit cellar restaurant serving delicacies such as quail baked in orange and port (188kr) for dinner. The lunchtime herring platter (77kr) and salad of the day with fresh bread (66kr) are also recommended.
Den Gyldne Okse Store Sct Peder Stræde 11 ☎86 62 27 44, Ⓦwww.gyldneokse.dk. Small, modern place serving juicy steaks from around 248kr (208kr at lunch) and burgers starting at 92kr. Closed Sun.
Messing Jens Sct Mathias Gade 48 ☎86 62 02 73, Ⓦwww.messingjens.dk. A café-cum-cocktail

bar and nightclub, offering the usual café-style meals (from 62kr) and funky tunes from the DJ until the early hours. Closed Sun.
Morville Hjultorvet 2 ☎86 60 22 11, Ⓦwww .cafemorville.dk A glitzy café-restaurant, with DJs at night. You can just have a coffee or cool beer, or mouthwatering main meals such as fillet of lamb with new potatoes and veg (175kr). It's also the town's main brunch spot (10am–1pm; 115kr).
Tortilla Flats Store Sct Mikkelsgade 2 ☎86 62 79 97, Ⓦwww.tortillaflats-viborg.dk. Lively Mexican restaurant with authentic and affordable Mexican dishes such as a tasty chicken enchilada with green chilli sauce for 99kr. Dinner only, closed Mon.

Around Viborg

The area **around Viborg** is excellent for cycling, with plenty of pleasant spots within easy reach; there's also a decent local bus service. Leaving Viborg, heading south on Koldingvej and turning west towards Herning brings you into **Dollerup Bakker**, a beautiful area of soft hills and meadows on the shores of **Hald Sø** lake. For all its peace, the district's history is a violent one. This is where Niels Bugge led a rebellion of Jutland squires against the king in 1351, and where the Catholic bishop, Jorgen Friis, was besieged by Viborgers at the time of the Reformation. Much of the action took place around the manor houses that once stood here, such as Hald Slot, the ruin which can be reached by following the **footpath** along Hald Sø's western shore. From June to August, rowing boats are available for rent from the historic lakeside inn *Niels Bugges Kro*, which also does good meals and has three comfortable rooms (☎86 63 80 11, Ⓦwww.niels-bugges-kro.dk; Ⓞ).

The limestone mines and Kongenshus Mindepark

About 11km west of Viborg are the **Mønsted Kalkgruber** (Mønsted Limestone Mines: April–Oct daily 10am–5pm; 60kr; Ⓦwww.monsted-kalkgruber.dk), which wind underground for some 60km and stay at a constant temperature, regardless of external weather. Wandering around their cool, damp innards can be magically atmospheric – although a century ago, conditions for the workers here were so horrific that when Frederik IV visited he was sufficiently appalled to bring about reforms; the mines were subsequently known as "Frederik's Quarries" or, more venomously, "The King's Graves". The site closes in winter, when the mines are taken over by an enormous colony of hibernating bats. Bus #28 runs here from Viborg. En route – some 9km from Viborg, between Mønsted and Raunstrup – a lay-by to the left holds the **Jutlands Stone**, an inscribed rock surrounded by lots of cigarette ends, which marks the precise geographical centre of Jutland.

Just beyond Mønsted (and also served by bus #28) is another set of limestone mines, **Daugbjerg Kalkgruber** (daily: June 10am–4pm; July to mid-Aug 10am–6pm; mid-Aug to Oct & end March to May 11am–4pm; 50kr; ⓦwww.daugbjerg-kalkgruber.dk), unlit and much narrower than those at Mønsted, and therefore quite spooky. The entrance was found by chance fifty years ago and no one has yet charted the full extent of the passages.

A marked contrast to the rugged landscape around the limestone mines and the rolling hills of Dollerup Bakker, **Kongenshus Mindepark** (15kr, cars 30kr excluding passengers; ⓦwww.kongenshus.dk) is a vast, open and windswept moorland which serves as a memorial to the desperate lives of the heath farmers who have attempted to cultivate this area since the mid-eighteenth century. Given the desperately poor soil here, all attempts failed, and as the wind howls around this stark, inhospitable heath, you can only marvel at their determination. But while the area isn't well placed for farming, it does offer some great **walking**, especially in autumn, when purple heather carpets the landscape; pick up a free trail map at the car park. The grand former home of one of the settlers, who tried to keep sheep here and was rewarded for his efforts by a grant from Frederik V, has now been opened up as the *Kongenshus* **hotel** (☎97 54 81 25, ⓦwww.kongenshushotel.dk; ❼); its delightful restaurant does fine Danish food. There's no public transport to the park.

Travel details

Trains

Århus to: Aalborg (2 hourly; 1hr 30min); Copenhagen (2–3 hourly; 3hr); Fredericia (4 hourly; 1hr); Randers (2 hourly; 30min); Silkeborg (2 hourly; 50min); Vejle (4 hourly; 45min); Viborg (2 hourly; 1hr 15min).
Fredericia to: Århus (4 hourly; 1hr); Copenhagen (2 hourly; 2hrs); Vejle (3 hourly; 15min).
Randers to: Aalborg (2 hourly; 45min); Århus (2 hourly; 30min); Copenhagen (2 hourly; 3hr 30 min); Viborg via Langå (hourly; 1hr).
Silkeborg to: Århus (2 hourly; 50min).
Vejle to: Århus (4 hourly; 45min); Copenhagen (1–2 hourly; 2hr 15min); Fredericia (3 hourly; 15min).
Viborg to: Århus (2 hourly; 1hr 15min); Copenhagen via Langå (1–2 hourly; 5hr); Randers via Langå (hourly; 1hr).

Buses

Århus to: Copenhagen (4–6 daily; 3hr); Ebeltoft (hourly; 1hr 30min); Randers (3 hourly; 1hr); Silkeborg (3 hourly; 1hr); Viborg (9 daily; 1hr 30min).

Ebeltoft to: Århus (hourly; 1hr 30min); Copenhagen (2–4 daily; 3hr)
Randers to: Århus (3 hourly; 1hr); Copenhagen (3–4 daily; 4hr); Silkeborg (hourly; 1hr 30min); Viborg (1–2 hourly; 1hr).
Silkeborg to: Århus (3 hourly; 1hr); Copenhagen (2 daily; 4hr); Randers (hourly; 1hr 30min); Viborg (hourly; 1hr).
Viborg to: Århus (9 daily; 1hr 30min); Randers (1–2 hourly; 1hr); Silkeborg (hourly; 1hr).

Ferries

Århus to: Kalundborg (1–6 daily; 2hr 40min); Sjællands Odde (5–10 daily; 1hr).
Ebeltoft to: Sjællands Odde (5–7 daily; 45min).

Flights

Århus to: Copenhagen (5-10 daily; 40min).
Billund to: Copenhagen (3–6 daily; 45min); Rønne (June–Sept & Christmas holidays 2 weekly; 1hr).

7

North Jutland

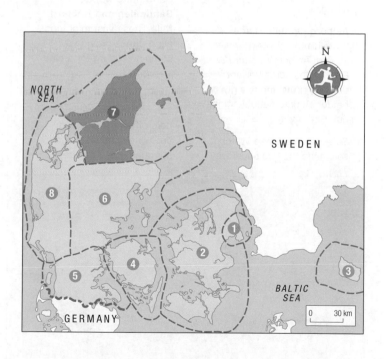

CHAPTER 7 # Highlights

✳ **Fyrkat** Impressive, perfectly symmetrical Viking fortification, with beautiful tribute to Viking craftsmanship in the reconstructed longhouse nearby. See p.242

✳ **Rold Skov** The country's largest forest, the beech and conifer woodlands here are ideal for hiking or mountain biking. See p.244

✳ **Aalborg nightlife** Home of the wildest nightlife for miles around, Aalborg's Jomfru Ane Gade holds some brilliant drinking spots and is a great bet for an unforgettable night out. See p.250

✳ **Salt-making, Læsø** Watch salt made the traditional way on this isolated island with its scenic saline marshes. See p.257

✳ **Meeting of the seas, Grenen** Stand with one foot in the Kattegat and another in the Skagerrak, and watch the waves clashing over your toes. See p.260

✳ **Sand dune walks, Sandmilen and Råbjerg Mile** These vast migrating sand dunes provide a stunning setting for a hike. See p.261

✳ **Harbourside dining, Skagen** The outstanding restaurants here offer fresh fish and fine wine in atmospheric surroundings. See p.262

▲ Råbjerg Mile

North Jutland

North Jutland is the furthest you'll get from the bright lights of Copenhagen, both geographically and in terms of the area's remote feel. Though it does have a few bright lights of its own in the shape of **Aalborg**, the country's fourth largest city, north Jutland has a distinctly no-nonsense, rural flavour; its population, meanwhile, are known for keeping themselves to themselves – understatement is the prevailing philosophy, and a modest smile here equates to what would be a raucous laugh in other parts of the country. The area is bisected by the **Limfjorden**, the body of water which connects the Skagerrak and Kattegat seas, and which served as the region's main transport artery for centuries until the western outlet (for more on which, see Chapter 8) was blocked off by sand drifts in 1100 (it reopened again in 1825). To the south of the Limfjorden and north of the much smaller Mariager fjord, the **Himmerland** area holds some remarkable remnants of the Viking era, most notably the fortification at Fyrkat. More contemporary history comes to the fore at the country's largest forest, Rold Skov, where the tree-smothered hills of **Rebild Bakker** play host to the largest American Independence celebrations outside of the US each July; at other (quieter) times, Rold Skov – and specifically Rebild Bakker – offers some superb hiking and mountain-biking. Sitting snugly on the banks of Limfjorden, **Aalborg** makes a convenient base while exploring the region, with some great places to eat and party, and a few outstanding museums, too. To the north of the Limfjorden, the highlight of the **Vendsyssel** region is **Skagen**, a uniquely atmospheric town on the northern tip of Denmark, whose unusual natural light has long attracted artists. To the south, ferries from the east-coast port of **Frederikshavn** head out to the windswept island of **Læsø**, which offers an unusual history and an intriguing landscape. Southwest of Skagen, the **Jammerbugt** bay is graced with a string of excellent beaches and their accompanying holiday towns, the Danes' top vacation spots for decades – most popular among these is the town of **Løkken**.

Himmerland

North of Randers (covered in Chapter 6), you enter into Himmerland through **Hobro**, the only town of any size in a region largely devoid of major urban settlements. Himmerland's main asset is the **Rold Skov** forest, laced with some excellent hiking and mountain-biking trails. In the middle of the woodlands, the **Rebild Bakker** park is characterized by the museums and souvenir shops by its main entrance. The park was donated to the government by Danish Americans,

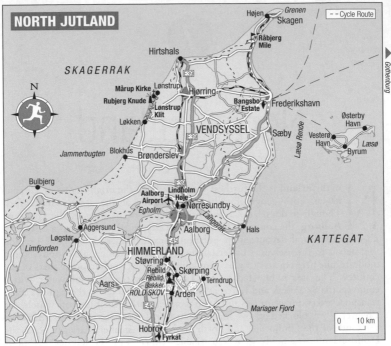

and today, US-based "pilgrims" flock in to get close to their Danish roots and, on July 4, descend en masse to celebrate American Independence. The other main draw hereabouts is the unique Viking fortifications of Fyrkat, on the outskirts of Hobro; an amazing structure that gives an insight into Viking era politics.

Hobro and Fyrkat

Attractively positioned at the mouth of the Mariager fjord, **HOBRO** is an appealing place for an idle wander, but the main reason to visit is the **Fyrkat Viking fortification** (daily: May 10am–4pm; June–Aug 10am–5pm; Sept 10am–3pm; 60kr for joint ticket with Vikingecenter Fyrkat; Ⓦwww .sydhimmerlandsmuseum.dk), some 3km southwest of the centre. What makes Fyrkat remarkable is the astounding symmetry of its perfectly round rampart, some 120m in diameter and with access points set precisely at each corner of the "compass". The construction has been carbon dated to 980–81, the same date as three similar fortifications at Aggersborg on Limfjorden's northern bank, Trelleborg on Zealand (see p.121) and Nonnebakken on Funen. This coincidence – together with the fact that they were all of an unusually high standard and were in use for a maximum of just twenty years – has left researchers baffled. At the time of construction, Denmark was ruled by **Harald Bluetooth** (for more on whom, see p.214) who, ten years prior, had lost control of the country's main southern stronghold, Dannevirke (now in Schleswig) to the Germans. The prevailing theory is that Harald built the four fortifications as tax collection points to fund the recapture of Dannevirke; the attached longhouses would have been used to store the citizens' contributions (in those days, livestock, crops and the like rather than money). If this is true, then his tactic seems to have worked, as Dannevirke was again under Danish rule by 983. All four fortifications were abandoned not long after Harald's death in 986 or 987 – possibly because then, as now, nobody likes the tax man, and Harald's successor (and son) Sven needed the people behind him.

From the entrance by the main road a small track leads to the grass-covered rampart, which at first glance looks like the outer wall of a dike. You can go inside the fortification through any of four access points, each of which has steps leading to the path along the rampart's rim, which provides an awe-inspiring overview of the site. Marks on the ground indicate the strict symmetrical positioning – in four groups of four – of the solid longhouses that once stood within the rampart. On a hill outside, an exact copy of a **longhouse** has been erected; it's a remarkably sturdy building that would have required a huge amount of materials and labour – the timber for this and the ramparts is thought to have been shipped in from Norway.

There's no public transport from Hobro to Fyrkat, though the fairly lengthy walk from the centre is pleasant enough. From the bus station, head south down Brogade and after about 200m turn left into Sønder Allé; this leads into Fyrkatvej and becomes a rural road. Continue past Vikingecentret Fyrkat (see p.242) and into a river valley, where Fyrkat sits on the banks of the Onsild stream. Alternatively, there's a path leading straight to Fyrkat from the town campsite (see below). On your way back from the site, pop into the **Vikinge-center Fyrkat** (same hours; 60kr for joint ticket with Fyrkat; ⓦwww.fyrkat .dk), a replica of a wealthy Viking farmstead from the same era which provides a good contrast to the sterility and magnificence of Fyrkat itself. It consists of nine ramshackle structures, each with separate functions and all much smaller than the Fyrkat longhouses. Most evocative is the thirty-metre furnished longhouse, with separate sections for livestock, sleeping and food preparation. In summer, this is an excellent place to get an impression of life during Bluetooth's era via the demonstrations of traditional Viking activities like bronze casting, spinning and dyeing; at other times, you can wander in and out of houses freely.

To get some background on what you've seen at the sites, head back into town to the **Hobro Museum**, Vestergade 21 (May–Sept daily noon–5pm; 30kr, or free with Fyrkat/Vikingecenter tickets; ⓦwww.sydhimmerlandsmuseum.dk). There are displays of the best finds from the many archeological excavations at Fyrkat, including knives, forks and some funky little keys which may have opened chests containing tax contributions. Artefacts from a burial ground next to the fortifica-tion include gifts and treasures that the dead were to take with them on their final journeys, and indicate that although the Jelling Stone inscriptions (see p.214) suggest that Danes had already been converted to Christianity during Fyrkat's era, the people who died here were all still heathen. This discovery has led to much speculation about how – and from which direction – Christianity was introduced to Denmark (for more, see Contexts, p.285).

Seeing the Fyrkat sites and the museum will easily take up a day, so you might want to spend a night in Hobro. The only **hotel** is the four-star *Amerika*, Ameri-kavej 48 (☎98 54 42 00, ⓦwww.hotelamerika.dk; ❼), a fifteen-minute walk from Hobro harbour, with a scenic path leading down to the Mariager fjord. The nearby *Hobro Vandrerhjem* **hostel**, at no.24 (☎98 52 18 47, ⓦwww.danhostelnord .dk/hobro; dorms 200kr, doubles ❹), is a much cheaper option. Reached via a two-kilometre path from Fyrkat, *Hobro Camping*, Skivevej 35 (☎98 52 32 88, ⓦwww.hobrocamping.dk-camp.dk), has eight fully equipped four-person cabins from 350kr per day.

Rold Skov and Rebild Bakker

Some 15km north of Hobro, bands of conifer and beech spreading over the rolling hills mark the beginning of **ROLD SKOV**, a lovely place to spend a leisurely day taking in fresh air and beautiful scenery. Covering some eighty square kilometres, the forest stretches from Arden in the south to the small town of Støvring in the north, and from Terndrup in the east to the E45 motorway in the west – a huge woodland in Danish terms, and one that's associated with innumerable myths and stories such as that of the infamous highway robbers of Rold, who would graciously serve their victims a shot of snaps before robbing them bare. Seventy-five percent of the forest is in private hands, with limited public access, but the remaining state-owned area is open to the public, with some outstanding hiking trails as well as a circular 23-kilometre mountain-bike route around the perimeter.

In the middle of Rold Skov and 20km north of Hobro, the small settlement of **REBILD** makes a convenient base for exploring the area; to get here from Aalborg or Hobro, catch the train to Skørping, then take bus #104. Rebild sits at the edge of the pretty, heath-covered **Rebild Bakker** hills, a part of Rold Skov that was bought in 1912 by a group of Danish emigrés living in America who presented it as a gift to the Danish government on three conditions: that it remain wild; that it remain open to the public; and that Danish Americans be allowed to celebrate American holidays here. Today it's best known as the venue for massive **American Independence Day** celebrations. Every July 4, festivities are staged at the *Gryden* ("cooking pot") natural amphitheatre – a short walk from the entrance – where a number of valleys run together. Many well-known names have appeared as keynote speakers, from Walt Disney and Danny Kaye (who played Hans Christian Andersen in the 1952 film of the same name) to Richard Nixon, Walter Cronkite and Danish-American comedian Viktor Borge. Because of the event's high profile, the area around the entrance to Rebild Bakker has become something of a tourist trap year-round, heaving with elderly Danish-American tourists and awash with souvenir shops and overpriced restaurants. Most interesting of the museums here is the **Spillemands Jagt og Skovbrugs Museet** (Fiddlers, Hunting and Forestry Museum: May–Aug daily 10am–5pm; Sept daily 11am–4pm; Oct–April Sun 1–5pm; 25kr; Ⓦwww.roldskovmuseerne.dk) which gives an insight into the tough life of loggers and the region's infamous poachers, also known for their prowess as fiddle players. Although all of the labelling is in Danish, the displays give a good impression of the difficult living conditions, and the region's isolation from the rest of Denmark. There's also a good-value café and, should you fancy a bit of folk dancing, fiddle-accompanied sessions in summer (July & Aug Wed 7–10.30pm; free).

Thanks to the Independence festivities, there's a surprising number of **places to stay** in diminutive Rebild. Needless to say, booking on or near July 4 must be done years in advance – at other times there are good discounts to be had. Most luxurious is the four-star *Comwell Rebild Bakker*, Rebildvej 36 (Ⓣ98 39 12 22, Ⓦwww.comwell.com; Ⓑ), which has a fitness spa, swimming pool and a fancy restaurant. Nearby at Rebildvej 23, the picturesque, thatch-roofed **youth hostel**, *Rebild Vandrerhjem* (Ⓣ98 39 13 40, Ⓦwww.danhostel.dk/rebild; mid-Feb to mid-Dec) has dorm beds (225kr) in en-suite rooms sleeping up to six, also sold as doubles (Ⓞ). The adjacent **campsite** (Ⓣ98 39 11 10, Ⓦwww.safari.dk-camp.dk) has four- and six-person cabins (from 450kr per day), and is open year-round. However, by far the most atmospheric place to stay is ⚑*Rold Storkro*, Vælderskoven 13 (Ⓣ98 37 51 00, Ⓦwww.roldstorkro.dk; Ⓞ), a traditional inn a few kilometres down the road towards Hobrovej; its **restaurant** is also especially good, with game in some guise on the menu daily.

Aalborg and around

Hugging the south bank of the Limfjorden, **AALBORG** is the obvious place to spend a few days before venturing out to the wild countryside and stunning beaches of the far north. The profits from the seventeenth-century herring boom briefly made Aalborg the biggest and wealthiest Danish town outside Copenhagen, and much of what remains of the well-preserved **old Aalborg** – chiefly the area within Østerågade (commonly abbreviated to Østerå), Bispensgade, Gravensgade and Algade – dates from that era, standing in stark contrast to the new roads that slice through it to accommodate the traffic using the Limfjorden bridge, which links the old town to the northern suburbs and a couple of notable sights. Today, Aalborg is the main transport terminus for northern Jutland and thanks to the presence of Aalborg University in its outskirts, boasts the liveliest nightlife for miles around.

Arrival, information and city transport

Both long-distance and local buses stop at the modern **bus terminal**, near the **train station** at J.F. Kennedys Plads, ten minutes' walk southwest of the centre and within easy reach of Aalborg's hotels and main attractions. **Aalborg Airport** (Ⓦ www.aal.dk) is 6km northwest, and connected to the centre by metro bus #2 (every 15–30min). Although most of Aalborg is easy to explore on foot, you may find a **bus** easier for some of the outlying sights. Aalborg town buses come in two categories: "metro" (with fast direct links to the suburbs) and "by" (operating within the town centre). The local bus company Nordjyllands Trafikselskab operates a zonal system, with all of Aalborg encompassed within one zone (only the airport is in the next). A single ticket (*billet*; 16kr) is valid for one hour's travel within two zones; a multi-ride ticket (*klippekort*; 116kr) is valid for ten trips in any two zones, and can be used by more than one person at once. A more enjoyable option is to get around by **bike**; the most central rental outlet is Munk's Efterfølger, Løkkegade 25 (Ⓣ 98 12 19 46, Ⓦ www.cuh.dk). The helpful **tourist office** is centrally located at Østerågade 8 (mid- to end June & Aug Mon–Fri 9am–5.30pm, Sat 10am–1pm; July Mon–Fri 9am–5.30pm, Sat 10am–4pm; Sept to mid-June Mon–Fri 9am–4.30pm, Sat 10am–1pm; Ⓣ 99 31 75 00, Ⓦ www.visitaalborg .com), and has information about the entire north Jutland region including bus and ferry timetables, plus excellent free cycling maps.

Accommodation

Bargain-priced **hotels** are hard to find in Aalborg. The tourist office has a list of private rooms in the area that go for a fixed rate of 350kr per night (plus a 25kr fee if you want the tourist office to make the booking). For a little more adventure, catch the half-hourly, five-minute ferry (Ⓣ 99 31 23 59; 6.30am–11.15pm; 16kr) from near the campsite (bus #13 from the centre) to the small island of **Egholm**, where there's free camping under open-sided shelters. In the twelfth century, the island was King Valdemar's hunting ground; today, it's largely farmed but still virtually uninhabited and crisscrossed by hiking trails. In summer, there's a good restaurant (see p.251) by the small ferry harbour.

> Some years ago, it was officially decreed that the Danish double "Aa" would be written as "Å". The mayor of Aalborg and many locals resisted this change, and eventually forced a return to the previous spelling of their city's name – though you may still see some maps and a few road signs using the "Å" form.

Central Aalborg

Hotel Chagall Vesterbro 36–38 ☎ 98 12 69 33, ⓦ www.hotel-chagall.dk. On a busy thoroughfare leading onto the bridge crossing Limfjorden, this modern hotel is within easy reach of the train station and centre. Inevitably the comfortable, colourful rooms have plenty of Chagall reproductions on the walls. ❼

First Slotshotel Aalborg Rendsburggade 5 ☎ 98 10 14 00, ⓦ www.firsthotels.com. Brand-new, stylish waterfront hotel a short walk from the equally new Utzon Centre. Rooms are light and airy with free wi-fi. Ask for a room facing Limfjorden, as these have private balconies. ❼

Park Hotel J.F. Kennedys Plads 41 ☎ 98 12 31 33, ⓦ www.park-hotel-aalborg.dk. Beautifully renovated old railway hotel across from the bus terminal, with dark wood panelling and soft carpets. Rooms are a little small and come with either a shower or, for 50kr more, a bathtub. There's a popular streetside café out front in summer. ❼

Prinsen Prinsensgade 14–16 ☎ 98 13 37 33, ⓦ www.prinsen-hotel.dk. Comfortable (albeit basic) hotel across from the train station, with a range of rooms, a cosy in-house bar plus free parking and wi-fi. Guests get reduced rates for the fitness centre across the street. ❻

Radisson SAS Limfjord Ved Stranden 14–16 ☎ 98 16 43 33, ⓦ www.radissonblu.com/hotel-aalborg. A stone's throw from the centre and overlooking Limfjorden, this is one of the city's most upmarket hotels, with its own casino, two restaurants (one rooftop with fabulous views) and free wi-fi. As you'd expect in this price range, rooms are stylishly decorated, with the emphasis on modern Scandinavian design. ❾

Greater Aalborg

Aalborg Sømandshjem Østerbro 27 ☎ 98 12 19 00, ⓦ www.hotel-aalborg.com. This family-oriented seaman's home is among the city's cheapest year-round options. It's rather plain-looking inside and out, but the rooms – from one- to four-bed – are tidy, fully modernized and clean. There's also wi-fi throughout (30kr per hr) and a good-value restaurant (daily 6–7pm; daily specials 65kr). A stone's throw from the new harbourfront promenade and a 15min walk east of the centre, or take bus #12, #17 or #18. ❻

Aalborg Vandrerhjem, Camping og Hytteø Skydebanevej 50 ☎ 98 11 60 44, ⓦ www.bbbb.dk. Large Danhostel to the west of the town, beside a marina on the banks of the Limfjorden, with dorms (285kr/190kr for under 26s who book and pay online) in rustic cabins sleeping five (428kr–650kr), en-suite doubles (528kr), and hostel rooms sleeping up to five. There's also a campsite and free wi-fi throughout. Take bus #13 from the centre to Skydebanevej, from where it's a 10min walk.

Krogen Skibstedvej 4 ☎ 98 12 17 05, ⓦ www.krogen.dk. Homely place, some 2km west of the city centre, with a large leafy garden; rooms costing 650kr have shared facilities. Buses #15 and #38 run closest to the hotel; get off at Constancevej and continue along it for 5min. ❻

Strand Parken Skydebanevej 20 ☎ 98 12 76 29, ⓦ www.strandparken.dk. About 1.5km from the centre and 800m from the hostel, and next door to Aalborg's open-air swimming pool, this appealing campsite stretches down to the banks of Limfjorden. It features a range of cabins sleeping up to six people (from 350kr per day for two). Mid-April to mid-Sept; open on demand in winter.

Zleep Hadsundvej 182 ☎ 98 10 97 00, ⓦ www.zleep.dk/hotel_aalborg. In the corner of an office block, this is the newest shoot on the Zleep chain of budget hotels offering clean, no-frills rooms, with wi-fi throughout, and lots of vending machines selling snacks and drinks. Outstanding offers if you book in advance online. Buses #2 and #12 stop a 5min walk away. ❺

The old town

The tourist office on Østerågade is as good a place as any to start exploring Aalborg, with one of the town's handsome seventeenth-century structures standing directly opposite. The **Jens Bangs Stenhus** is a grandiose five storeys of Dutch Renaissance style and, incredibly, has functioned as a pharmacy ever since it was built. Jens Bang himself was Aalborg's wealthiest merchant but was not popular with the governing elite, who conspired to keep him off the local council. The host of goblin-like figures carved on the walls allegedly represent the councillors of the time, while another figure, said to be Bang himself, pokes out his tongue towards the former Rådhus, next door, the predecessor to the present eighteenth-century building further down Østerågade.

The commercial roots of the city are further evidenced within **Budolfi Domkirke** (June–Aug Mon–Fri 9am–4pm, Sat 9am–2pm; Sept–May Mon–Fri

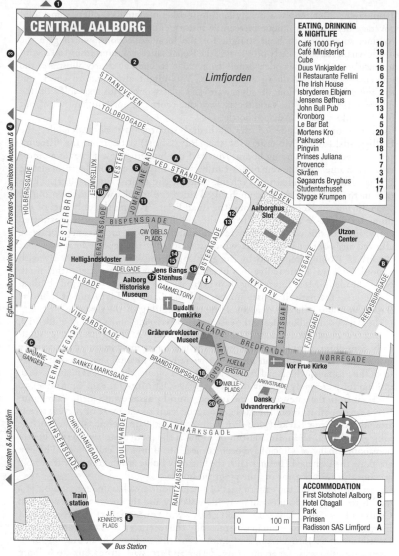

CENTRAL AALBORG

EATING, DRINKING & NIGHTLIFE

Café 1000 Fryd	10
Café Ministeriet	19
Cube	11
Duus Vinkjælder	16
Il Restaurante Fellini	6
The Irish House	12
Isbryderen Elbjørn	2
Jensens Bøfhus	15
John Bull Pub	13
Kronborg	4
Le Bar Bat	5
Mortens Kro	20
Pakhuset	8
Pingvin	18
Prinses Juliana	1
Provence	7
Skråen	3
Søgaards Bryghus	14
Studenterhuset	17
Stygge Krumpen	9

Limfjorden

Aalborghus Slot

Utzon Center

ACCOMMODATION

First Slotshotel Aalborg	B
Hotel Chagall	C
Park	E
Prinsen	D
Radisson SAS Limfjord	A

0   100 m

Train station

Bus Station

9am–3pm, Sat 9am–noon; Ⓦ www.aalborgdomkirke.dk), just a few steps behind the Jens Bangs Stenhus and easily located by its bulbous spire. Inside, there's a list (rather than the more customary portraits of nobles) of the town's merchants during the 1660s. A small but elegant specimen of sixteenth-century Gothic, the cathedral itself is built on the site of an eleventh-century wooden church; only a few tombs from the original remain, embedded in the walls close to the altar. Apart from these and the aforementioned list, there's little to see inside, but plenty to hear when the electronically driven bells ring out each hour, sending a cacophonous racket across the old square of **Gammeltorv**, on which the cathedral stands. Across the square from the cathedral, the **Aalborg Historiske Museum**, Algade 48 (Tues–Sun

10am–5pm; 20kr; Ⓦwww.nordjyllandshistoriskemuseum.dk), offers some solid coverage of Aalborg's unique mercantile history. The prehistoric section is fairly routine, so it's best to head straight for the local collections, which give the lowdown on Aalborg's early prosperity; the Renaissance-era room from 1602, with immaculately carved wooden panels from floor to ceiling, clearly illustrates the immense wealth in Aalborg at the time. You might also want to check out the impressive collection of silverware and glasswork, with examples of the different designs from the various glass-working centres in north Jutland – look out for the funky armadillo-shaped bottle.

On the opposite side of the cathedral square, just off Adelgade, the **Helligåndskloster** (Monastery of the Holy Ghost) dates from the fifteenth century, before the herring boom. Much of the building now serves as a senior citizens' home, and the remainder can be seen only on one of the informative English-language guided tours (check times at the tourist office; 40kr). These take in the refectory, largely unchanged since the monks were thrown out in 1536 during the Reformation, and the small Friars' Room, the only part of the monastery into which nuns (from the adjoining nunnery) were permitted entry. Indeed, this was one of the few monasteries where monks and nuns were allowed any contact at all, a fact which accounts for the reported hauntings of the Friars' Room – reputedly by the ghost of a nun who got too friendly with a monk, and was buried alive in a basement column as punishment (the monk was beheaded). Most interesting, however, are the **frescoes** of various biblical characters – dramatically posed images of Jesus, Samson, Mary and St John the Baptist amongst others – that cover the entire ceiling of the chapel.

The rest of old Aalborg lies to the east across Østerågade, and is mainly residential, with a few notable exceptions. The sixteenth-century **Aalborghus Slot** (grounds daily 8am–9pm; free) is technically a castle but looks much more like a country manor, and has always had an administrative rather than a military function. Aside from the grounds, which make a scenic spot for a picnic, the castle is mainly worth visiting for its severely gloomy **dungeon** (May–Oct Mon–Fri 8am–3pm; free), to the right from the gateway, and the **underground passageways** (daily 8am–9pm; free) that run off it. From the castle, Slotsgade leads to the maze of narrow streets around **Vor Frue Kirke** (Mon–Fri 9am–2pm, Sat 9am–noon; Ⓦwww.vorfrue .dk); give the church a miss in favour of a look at the meticulously preserved houses hereabouts, many of which have been turned into upmarket craft shops. The best are along the L-shaped Hjelmerstald: the ungainly bulge around the midriff of no.2 accounts for its nickname of "the pregnant house".

North of the castle, the eastern part of the harbour area has undergone a bit of a facelift recently, with a pleasant quayside walkway and the spectacular new **Utzon Center** (Tues–Sun 10am–5pm; 60kr; Ⓦwww.utzoncenter.dk) at the corner of Fjordgade. Devoted to – and in the spirit of – the recently deceased, world-famous Danish architect Jørn Utzon, best-known for the Sydney Opera House, this is essentially a showcase for architecture, design and art, with strong links to Aalborg University. The building is inspired by Utzon's childhood in Aalborg, the shape of the roof – most noticeable in the main hall, which houses a Spidsgatter boat designed by Utzon's father – reminiscent of the nearby dry dock, and its high-ceilinged rooms are linked by a central courtyard. In typical Utzon style it's a raw building in natural colours that openly reveals all the construction elements. As well as the changing exhibits, there's a section of the university library (including the Utzon collection) and a good café.

If you're here for the Rebild fest (p.244) and of Danish descent, or particularly interested in Danish social history, you might want to visit the **Dansk Udvand-rerarkiv** (Danish Emigration Archives: Mon–Wed 9am–4pm, Thurs 9am–5pm,

Fri 9am–2pm; Ⓦwww.emiarch.dk; free), nearby at Arkivstræde 1. The story of Danish migration overseas is recorded through immense stacks of files and books; given enough background facts, details of individual migrants can be traced. There is one last point of interest in this part of town. East of Østerågade, at Algade 19, the **Gråbrødrekloster Museet** (Franciscan Friary Museum: Tues–Sun 10am–5pm; 20kr) gives some insight into Aalborg's early history; set below ground, it's entered by way of an elevator where you pay your entrance by inserting a coin into the slot. The remains of the friary were discovered during archeological excavations in the 1990s, and the foundations and walls that were unearthed, alongside skeletons from nearby graveyards, form the bulk of the display. Models and information panels give an excellent introduction to Aalborg in the Viking and Middle Ages.

Out from the centre

There's a lot more to Aalborg than its old town, with several interesting options reachable by short bus rides from the centre. Among the highlights is **KUNSTEN** (North Jutland Art Museum; Tues–Sun 10am–5pm; 60kr; Ⓦwww.nordjyllands kunstmuseum.dk), south of the centre on Kong Christians Allé and housed in a stunning white marble building designed by the celebrated Finnish architect Alvar Aalto which is worth a look in its own right, with every tiny detail, from door handles to window panes, meticulously chosen to best accentuate the building's pristine lines. Perfectly illuminated with natural light from all sides, the works on show comprise one of the country's better modern art collections, strikingly contemporary in both form and content. Alongside numerous Danish pieces, it features works by Max Ernst, Andy Warhol, Le Corbusier and, imposingly stationed next to the entrance, Claes Oldenburg's wonderful *Fag-ends in a Colossal Ashtray*. After leaving the museum, you can get a Danish pastry and coffee, plus a grand view over the city and the Limfjorden, by hopping in the lift to the top of the 103-metre **Aalborgtårn** (Aalborg Tower; daily: July 10am–5pm; April–June & Aug to late Oct 11am–5pm; 30kr; Ⓦwww.aalborgtaarnet.com), on the hill just behind. Built for the Industry Exhibition of 1932, it was meant to have been torn down immediately afterwards, but proved so popular that it stayed. A small exhibit inside tells its story. To get here, take bus #15, or head out on foot along Vesterbro (15min).

From the tower, you can see what looks like a set of large concrete bunkers on a hill to the southeast of the city. This is the **Gug Kirke** (Mon–Fri 9am–4pm; Ⓦwww.gugkirke.dk) on Nøhr Sørensens Vej 7, designed by Inger and Johannes Exner and completed in the early 1970s. It's one of the most unusual churches in the country: except for the iron crucifix and the wooden bell tower, the whole thing, including the font, pulpit and altar (decorated with a collage of newspapers from the days when porn was legalized in Denmark) is made of concrete. The idea was to blend the church into the mostly high-rise parish it serves, and for it to function as a community centre: the perfectly square interior can be turned into a theatre, while the crypt doubles as a café and youth club. It's unique enough to merit a closer look; take bus #13 from the city centre, or catch #14 from the art museum and change onto #13 at Jyllandsgade.

Aalborg Marine Museum and Forsvars-og Garnisons-Museum

West of the centre, en route to the campsite and hostel, are two museums primarily aimed at kids and military buffs. Closest to town, on the banks of the Limfjorden next to a picturesque marina at Vestre Fjordvej 81, the **Aalborg**

Marine Museum (daily: May–Aug 10am–6pm, Sept–April 10am–4pm; 75kr; ⓦ www.aalborgmarinemuseum.dk) is a collection of top-notch naval paraphernalia put together by a group of enthusiasts. Initially only centred around the last Danish-built submarine, the *Springeren*, it has since expanded to house the world's fastest torpedo boat, the *Søbjørn*, as well as interesting exhibits on the history of Aalborg's boatyard and harbour. You can clamber into both vessels and get a real feel for the claustrophobic conditions on board. Further west, next to the campsite and on the corner of Egeholm Færgevej – the road leading to the Egholm ferry (see p.245) – the **Forsvars-og Garnisons-Museum** (Defence and Garrison Museum; daily: April–June & Sept–Oct 11am–4pm; July & Aug 10am–5pm; 50kr; ⓦ www.forsvarsmuseum.dk) has more of a hardcore military flavour, with guns, uniforms, tanks and medals galore. Again, it's all very touchy-feely – you get to crawl inside tanks and jets – and is a real hit with children, while the displays give some interesting insight into the town's military past. Aalborg has been a garrison town for over two hundred years and, since World War II, has housed the country's largest garrison. During the German occupation of Denmark, Aalborg also had crucial strategic importance, with the Germans constructing three airstrips and the enormous hydroplane hanger that today houses the collection.

Both museums are a good twenty-minute walk from the centre; bus #13 passes nearby.

Lindholm Høje

A few kilometres north of Aalborg on the Nørresundby side of the Limfjorden, **Lindholm Høje** (unrestricted access) is one of the country's most important late Viking and Iron Age burial grounds; it's a captivating place, especially at dawn or dusk when the magical light on the south-facing hillside gives the site an almost surreal appearance. There are a number of very rare Viking ship monuments here – cremation graves demarcated with stones arranged in the outline of a ship – as well as more than six hundred burial sites marked with stones or mounds, the oldest at the top of the hill, the newest at the foot. A number of these burial sites and dwellings are reconstructed in the adjacent **Lindholm Høje Museum** (April–Oct daily 10am–5pm; Nov–March Tues–Sun 10am–4pm; 40kr), which also gives some far-reaching insights into life in the site's settlements during the Viking era. From Aalborg, you can get here by metro bus #2 (every 15–30min), or walk in under an hour: go over the Limfjorden bridge, take Vesterbrogade into Thistedvej, turn right into Viaduktvej, and carry straight on until Vikingvej, which leads to the museum, appears on the left.

Eating, drinking and nightlife

Aalborg comes alive at night, when partygoers from all over northern Jutland (and from near-teetotal Sweden) descend on the city. The **eating**, **drinking** and **nightlife** scene centres on Jomfru Ane Gade, a small street close to the harbour between Bispensgade and Ved Stranden. Jomfru Ane was a noblewoman and reputed witch who, because of her social standing, was beheaded rather than burnt at the stake – though nowadays, the street is more synonymous with getting legless than headless. Several of the Jomfru Ane Gade bars host live music; just walk along, listen, and decide which appeals. An excellent alternative, for something grander and less alcohol-oriented, are the international rock, pop, dance, musical and theatre performances at **Aalborg Kongres & Kultur Center**, Europa Plads 4 (ⓣ 99 35 55 65, ⓦ www.akkc.dk), the city's main theatre and concert venue.

Cafés and restaurants

Café Ministeriet Mølleplads 19 ☎98 19 40 50, ⓦwww.cafeministeriet.dk. Cool, busy café with a large terrace on Mølleplads, and DJs playing on the square on summer evenings (Fri & Sat). Food starts with filling breakfast (79kr) and brunch (114kr) from 10am until 2pm, and continues with the usual array of salads, sandwiches, burgers and snacks, as well as excellent hot meals such as mozzarella-stuffed chicken for 89kr, and baked salmon for 89kr. Also a good place for delicious cocktails.

Il Restorante Fellini Vesterå 13 ☎98 11 34 55, ⓦwww.fellini.dk. Genuine Italian restaurant with fabulous pasta and soups; the novel Italian brunch (Mon–Sat 11.30am–3pm) is a delightful alternative, more of a lunch platter with a selection of Italian cheeses, ham, fresh bread, fruit and cake (138kr including coffee).

Isbryderen Elbjørn Strandvejen 6B ☎43 42 34 34, ⓦwww.isbryderen-elbjoern.dk. Docked across from the *Radisson SAS Limfjorden* hotel, this converted icebreaking ship is fun if you're looking for something different or travelling with kids. With good-quality meat and fish dishes that don't break the bank (from 148kr), it's also great for traditional lunch classics such as *Stjerneskud* and fish balls with rémoulade. There's a small exhibit on board telling the ship's icy history. Closed Sun & Mon.

Jensens Bøfhus C.W. Obels Plads 3 ☎98 16 63 33, ⓦwww.jensens.com. Chain restaurant serving the usual good steaks and salads, but unusually housed in a beautiful half-timbered former merchant's house dating from 1585, and full of charm.

Kronborg Egholm 1, Egholm ☎98 17 27 75, ⓦwww.kronborg-egholm.dk. This quintessentially Danish restaurant on the small island of Egholm serves tasty traditional fare like all-you-can-eat *stegt flæsk* (102kr) at lunch and the speciality fried eel (218kr) at dinner. May–Sept only.

Mortens Kro Mølleå Arkaden, Mølleå 4–6 ☎98 12 48 60, ⓦwww.mortenskro.com. Despite the "kro" in the name, this isn't a traditional inn, but rather a gourmet restaurant set in a temple to modern Scandinavian design. Food comes at a price, starting at 248kr for a dish of fried lemon sole served with shellfish and a veggie gratin, but it's worth every øre. Dinner only, closed Sun.

Pingvin Brandstrupsgade 11 ☎98 11 11 66, ⓦwww.cafepingvin.dk. Across the square from *Café Ministeriet*, this is a top-of-the-range tapas and wine bar, with over thirty scrumptious tapas, and a host of fine international wines all sold by the glass (from 50kr). Reservations necessary. Closed Sun

Prinses Juliana Vestre Havnepromenade 2 ☎98 11 55 66, ⓦwww.prinsesjuliana.dk. On the western side of the bridge across Limfjorden, this floating gourmet restaurant is onboard a beautiful old wooden Dutch school ship. Food isn't cheap but once you taste the delicious braised lamb with toasted morels and petit pommes (270kr) or the veal roast with baked potato mash and fresh veg (290kr) you'll see why.

Provence Ved Stranden 11 ☎98 13 51 33, ⓦwww.restaurant-provence.dk. Around the corner from Jomfru Ane Gade, the tightly packed tables at this romantic French restaurant overlook the Limfjorden. Serving only food from Provence – even the bread is imported – there's an excellent selection of seafood, including a mouthwatering platter for two at 288kr. Book ahead.

Stygge Krumpen Vesterå 1 ☎98 16 87 87 ⓦwww.styggekrumpen.dk. Three French-style eateries in one: at the front a café serving not-so-French brunch (from 10.30am) featuring American pancakes and a selection of European salamis, plus a host of delicious sandwiches; upstairs a new seafood restaurant with an elaborate buffet at lunch (128kr) and dinner (248kr); and at the back, fine dining at its best – duck à l'orange (198kr) and chateaubriand (288kr) among the French delicacies on the menu.

Søgaards Bryghus O.W. Obels Plads 1A ☎90 10 11 14, ⓦwww.soegaardsbryghus.dk. Excellent combination of microbrewery, restaurant and butcher's shop, offering juicy steaks (from 225kr) and an extensive range of home-made beer; you can also stock up on cold cuts for the picnic basket. Closed Sun.

Bars, clubs and live music venues

Café 1000 Fryd Kattesundet 10 ☎98 13 22 21, ⓦwww.1000fryd.dk. Cultural centre hosting alternative-type international live bands two to three nights a week; also a popular café/bar with a twice-daily happy hour (3–4.30pm & 10–11pm).

Cube Jomfru Ane Gade 10 ☎98 10 33 10, ⓦwww.cubeonline.dk. The music at this fun if run-of-the-mill disco is predominantly R&B and house classics, and the dancefloor is packed throughout the night. Not a hangout for sober types. Fri & Sat only.

Duus Vinkjælder Østerågade 9 ☎98 12 50 56. This atmospheric wine bar in the cellar of the Jens Bangs Stenhus from 1624 is the perfect place for a quiet evening drink. Closed Sun.

The Irish House Østerågade 25 ☎98 14 18 17, ⓦwww.theirishhouse.dk. Fun Irish pub housed in the former mayoral residence from 1616, with live music (Thurs–Sat; mostly Irish folk) and a wide range of beers and whiskies. Traditional Irish stew is served until 6pm.

John Bull Pub Østerågade 20 ☏ 98 19 45 05 ⓦ www.john-bull.dk. Proper English pub with live folksy music on the menu every Thursday and Saturday. Also a large widescreen TV for the obligatory football viewing, and outdoor seating in the summer.

Le Bar Bat Jomfru Ane Gade 27 ☏ 98 13 32 41. Small, cosy, live music venue with gigs every Wednesday to Saturday and stand-up comedy (mostly in Danish) a couple of times a month. Good cocktails, too. Closed Sun–Tues.

Pakhuset Ved Stranden 9 ☏ 98 11 60 22, ⓦ www.pakhusetaalborg.dk. Hugely popular,

old-fashioned nightclub in a wood-beamed, red-brick old warehouse playing singalong hits from the 1960s and onwards. Fri & Sat only, open until 5am.

Skråen Strandvejen 19 ☏ 98 12 21 89, ⓦ www .skraaen.dk. A short walk from the centre, next to university buildings, this former tobacco factory is a good place to catch gigs by better-known Danish rock acts on two stages, the larger hall and the smaller, more intimate café.

Studenterhuset Gammeltorv 11 ☏ 98 11 05 22, ⓦ www.studenterhuset.dk. The country's largest student-run music venue, with a café (shut during student holidays) and live up-and-coming, mostly Danish bands and DJs playing three to four nights a week. Music starts after 9pm. Closed Sun.

Listings

Airport Aalborg lufthavn is 6km northwest of the centre. For information contact ☏ 98 17 11 44, ⓦ www.aal.dk.

Bus enquiries Local buses and regional buses ☏ 98 11 11 11, ⓦ www.nordjyllandstrafikselskab .dk; Abildskou's Aalborg–Copenhagen coach reservations ☏ 70 21 08 88, ⓦ www.abildskou .dk; Thingaard Express bus connecting Frederikshavn and Esbjerg via Aalborg: reservations ☏ 98 11 66 00, ⓦ www.ekspresbus.dk; X-bus long-distance coaches crisscrossing Jutland: reservations ☏ 98 90 09 00, ⓦ www .xbus.dk.

Car rental Avis, J.F. Kennedys Plads 3 ☏ 98 13 3 0 99, and at Aalborg Airport ☏ 98 17 72 77; Europcar, Jyllandsgade 6 ☏ 98 13 23 55 and at Aalborg Airport ☏ 98 17 53 55; Hertz, Jyllandsgade 28 ☏ 98 17 15 99 and at Aalborg Airport ☏ 98 17 15 99.

Dentist Lille Borgergade 21, Nørresundby ☏ 25 20 29 00 (Mon–Fri 8am–3pm); outside these hours ring ☏ 70 20 02 55 or go to the emergency department at Aalborg Sygehus (see below).

Hospitals There's a 24hr emergency department at Aalborg Sygehus, Hobrovej 18–22 ☏ 99 32 26 92.

Internet cafés In the Matrix, J.F. Kennedyarkaden 1F (daily noon–7am; 17kr per hr). There's free wi-fi at Aalborg's libraries, most central is the main one at Rendsburggade 2 (Mon–Thurs 10am–7pm, Fri 10am–6pm, Sat 10am–3pm).

Markets There's a lively fruit, veg and flower market every Wed and Sat on Ågade (7am–2pm).

Pharmacy Aalborg Budolfi Apoteket, Algade 60 ☏ 98 12 06 77, is open 24hr.

Police Politigården i Aalborg, Jyllandsgade 27 ☏ 96 30 14 48.

Post office Algade 42 (Mon–Fri 9.30am–6pm, Sat 9.30am–1pm).

Vendsyssel

North of Aalborg, the windblown, triangular-shaped **Vendsyssel** region is roughly delineated by Limfjorden to the south and, to the northeast and northwest, the two seas connected by the Limfjorden, the Kattegat and Skagerrak. The area is renowned for its unique **Vendelbo** humour – quietly and succinctly, without the faintest hint of a smile, you will find your leg pulled when you least expect it. **Frederikshavn** on the east coast is a major transport hub, with ferries to Norway, Sweden and the scenic island of **Læsø**, and difficult to avoid. The highlight of the area is **Skagen**, right at the northern tip, with a magical light reflecting from the two open seas. It's this light that made Skagen the haunt of Danish artists in the late nineteenth century, and today it holds a number of outstanding museums in their memory. To the southwest of Skagen, the **Jammerbugten bay** area offers strangely compelling views of bleak moorland and windswept dunes. The biggest town along the bay is **Løkken**, a good base from which to explore the excellent beaches. Thanks to its good ferry links with Norway and Sweden, Vendsyssel is trisected by two fast motorways, making travel by car or bus between Aalborg and the major towns here quick and easy. The rail network, on the other hand, has lagged far behind the rest of the country, with the only rail link to Skagen zigzagging via Hjørring and Frederikshavn.

Frederikshavn and Læsø

Some 65km northeast of Aalborg, **FREDERIKSHAVN** is a major international ferry port, with connections to Oslo in Norway and Göteborg in Sweden, and as such is usually full of Swedes and Norwegians taking advantage of Denmark's liberal drinking laws. Though it's not the most captivating of places, Frederikshavn is the region's transport hub; buses and trains to and from Skagen pass through, and it's also the departure point for ferries to the pretty island of **Læsø**, so you're likely to find yourself here at some point during your travels in north Jutland.

Arrival, information and accommodation

Buses and **trains** terminate at the train station, on the eastern side of town on Skippergade; private trains to Skagen leave from here, too. Crossing Skippergade and walking along Kirkepladsen brings you to the town centre in a couple of minutes. The **ferry** docks, off Havnepladsen, are equally central. The modern, glass-fronted **tourist office**, nearby on the corner of Havnegade and Havnepladsen (July to mid-Aug Mon–Sat 9am–6pm, Sun 9am–2pm; mid-Aug to June Mon–Fri 9am–4pm, Sat 11am–2pm; ☏98 42 32 66, Ⓦwww.frederikshavn-tourist.dk) has **bicycles** you can use for free, and can help with **private accommodation** (from 300kr per room per night, plus a 25kr booking fee). There's free **wi-fi** at Frederikshavn library at Parallelvej 16 (Mon–Fri 10am–6pm, Sat 10am–1pm; ☏98 43 91 00). With a steady stream of international travellers passing through Frederikshavn there's a wide and surprisingly affordable range of places to stay.

Accommodation

Frederikshavn Sømandshjem Tordenskjoldsgade 15B ☏98 42 09 77, Ⓦwww.fshotel.dk. Excellent value close to the centre, this spotless four-storey seaman's home offers comfortable rooms with free wi-fi and significant discounts at restaurant *Vægteren* (see p.255). **7**

Frederikshavn Vandrerhjem Buhlsvej 6 ☏98 42 14 75, Ⓦwww.danhostel.dk/frederikshavn. About 1km north of the centre, this slightly uninspiring hostel has dorms (100kr) and doubles (❸), some en suite. It's 2min by bus #2 from the station. Closed Dec & Jan.

Herman Bang Tordenskjoldsgade 3 ☏98 42 21 66, Ⓦwww.hermanbang.dk. Atmospheric old hotel a short walk from the ferry dock, with an array of

light and breezy rooms with free wi-fi. The in-house wellness centre, with spa, stone massage and much more, makes it an ideal place to regroup, and there's a popular Italian-American restaurant. **7**

Nordstrand Camping Apholmenvej 40 ☏98 42 93 50, Ⓦwww.nordstrandcamping.dk. Luxurious campsite 3km north of the centre (bus #4) near the marina and Palmestrand beach with self-contained cabins sleeping six only available by the week (5350kr) and more rustic ones sharing kitchen and bathroom facilities with the campsite, sleeping four and available by the day (275kr). April to mid-Oct.

Turisthotellet Margrethesvej 5 ☏98 42 90 55, Ⓦwww.turisthotellet.dk. Small family-run hotel near the ferry harbour in a quiet part of town, with no-frills, comfortable, en-suite rooms. **6**

The town and around

If you only have half an hour to spare in Frederikshavn, make for the squat, white **Krudttårn** tower (June–Aug Tues–Sun 10am–5pm; 15kr), on Havnepladen near the train station, which has maps detailing the harbour's (now ruined) seventeenth-century fortifications, of which the tower was a part, and a collection of weaponry,

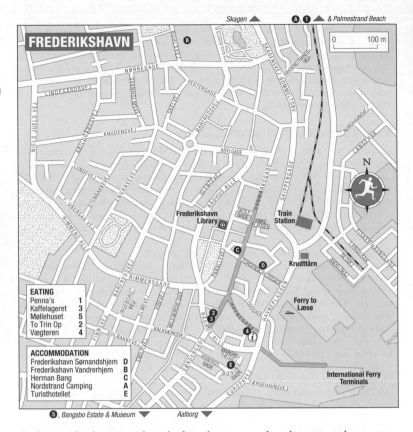

uniforms and military paraphernalia from the seventeenth to the nineteenth centuries. With more time on your hands, take the fifteen-minute ride on bus #3 to Møllehuset at the edge of the **Bangsbo Estate** and walk on through the beautifully groomed botanic gardens to the **Bangsbo Museum** (Tues–Sun 10am–5pm; 40kr; Wwww .bangsbo-museum.dk), set in the manor building on the southern fringe of the estate. Here, comprehensive displays chart the development of Frederikshavn from the 1600s alongside a slightly grotesque, but very engrossing, collection of pictures, bracelets, rings and necklaces made of human hair. The barns and outbuildings store an assortment of maritime articles distinguished only by the twelfth-century *Ellingåskibet*, a ship found north of Frederikshavn, plus a worthwhile exhibition covering the German occupation during World War II and the rise of the Danish resistance movement. The estate also encompasses a large **deer park** and **rock garden** (daily dawn–dusk; free) with various viewpoints and picnic spots. **Bangsbo Fort** at the northern perimeter has cannon and concrete gun emplacements built by the German occupiers during World War II – they never actually hit anything, however. You can experience the claustrophobic living conditions inside the German bunkers at the **Bunker Museum** (June–Aug Tues–Sun 10am–5pm; 30kr; tours at 1pm included in the price) inside the fort. Otherwise, on sunny days, you could do worse than join the rest of Frederikshavn at one of its many child-friendly **beaches**. Most popular is the lush palm tree-endowed Palmestrand, just north of the centre (10min on bus #4), with beach volleyball courts and soft, powdery white sand.

Eating, drinking and nightlife

There are a number of good places to **eat out** in Frederikshavn. Hands down, the town's best coffee is served at *Kaffelageret* (T98 43 94 94, Wwww.kaffelageret.dk) which also does magnificent sandwiches and burgers. There's more traditional Danish fare – with an emphasis on game from the nearby Bangsbo Estate – at the picturesque wood-beamed *Møllehuset Inn* at Skovalléen 45 (T98 43 44 00, Wwww.mollehuset.dk; take bus #3). For fresh fish, marinated herring and the occasional lunchtime jazz session, head for *Penna's* (T98 43 82 98, Wwww.pennas.dk), overlooking the marina and just north of the centre at Nordre Strandvej 48. In the centre, the best dinner option is *Vægteren*, Havnegade 8 (T98 42 17 34, Wwww.vaegteren.dk; closed Mon), with Danish/French-inspired cuisine; it's also a good bet for a quiet evening **drink**. For a more raucous night out follow the hordes of Norwegians and Swedes usually drinking their way across town, often ending at the *To Trin Op* nightclub at Søndergade 15 (Thurs–Sat only).

Læsø

With a total land area of just eighteen square kilometres, **LÆSØ** is the place to head if you're seeking rural calm in a beautiful setting. Although its livelihood is almost entirely based on tourism, the majority of the islanders (some eight hundred in total) would much rather keep the peace and quiet of their beautiful island to themselves. There's no special treatment for tourists here – what you see is what you get – but if you can accept that, the outstanding beaches, low-key attractions and distinctly rural Vendelbo vibe make for a memorable experience.

Arrival and information

The only way of getting to Læsø is by **ferry** from Frederikshavn (T98 49 90 22, Wwww.laesoe-line.dk; 3–6 daily; 1.5hr; only return tickets 150kr). Læsø's **tourist office** (mid-June to Aug Mon–Fri 9am–4pm, Sat & Sun 9am–3pm; May to mid-June Mon–Fri 9am–4pm, Sat 10am–noon; Sept–April Mon–Fri 9am–2pm, Sat 10am–noon; T98 49 92 42, Wwww.laesoe-tourist.dk) is close to the Vesterø Havn ferry terminal at Vesterø Havngade 17, and has useful free maps of the island. All bus transport on Læsø is free; the sole bus route (#840) linking the three main towns departs roughly once an hour from Vesterø Havn, less frequently during weekends and school holidays. Bikes are easily the best way of **getting around**; you can rent them at Jarvis Ny Cykelservice, Vesterø Havnegade 29 (T98 49 94 44, Wwww.jarvis-laesoe.dk), a short walk from the ferry terminal and tourist office on the main road to Byrum. Should the idea of **horseriding** on the beach or through Rønnerne grab your fancy, head for Rønnergården, Egegårdsvej 4 (T98 49 14 39, Wwww.naturridning.dk), or Krogbæksgård, Storhavevej 8 (T98 49 15 05, Wwww.rideferie.dk); both are close to Byrum, and offer holiday packages as well as straight rides.

Accommodation

There is a relative abundance of **accommodation** on Læsø, although places are generally small and, thanks to the influx of visitors in the tourist season, often fully booked – it's a good idea to reserve in advance. The tourist office has a list of **private rooms** and **holiday-home rentals**.

Carlsens Havnebakken 8, Vesterø Havn T98 49 90 13, Wwww.carlsens-hotel.dk. Small hotel, overlooking the harbour and within spitting distance of the ferry terminal; all rooms have free wi-fi and shared facilities. ⑥

Havnebakken Havnebakken 12, Vesterø Havn T98 49 90 09, Wwww.havnebakken.dk.

Atmospheric former seaman's home next door to *Carlsens*, with a range of different rooms (some sharing bathroom facilities); the more expensive ones overlook the harbour. ⑥–⑦

Læsø Camping og Hytteby Agersigen 18, Vesterø Havn T98 49 94 95, Wwww.laesoe.dk-camp.dk. Appealing campsite, a 20min walk

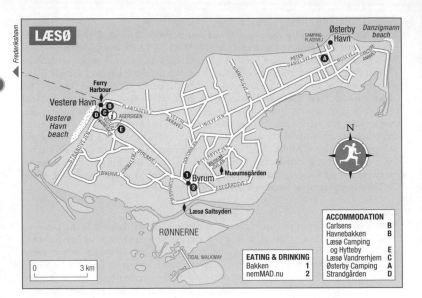

LÆSØ

Østerby *Danzigmann*
Havn *beach*

CAMPING-
PLADSVEJ

PETER
DANIELSVEJ

Ferry
Harbour

Vesterø Havn

*Vesterø
Havn
beach*

PLANTAGEVEJ
AGERSIGEN

VESTRE
SKRAVEJ

LINJEVEJEN

HIMMERIGE JEN

MOSEVEJEN

DANZIG
ANNEX

N

Byrum

Mueumsgården

ØSTERBYVEJEN

MUSEUM
SVEJ

STRANDVEJEN

TØRKERIVEJ

STARBAELSVEJ

BYRUMVEJ

DOKTORVEJEN

EGEGÅRDSVEJ

STORVEJEN

Læsø Saltsyderi

RØNNERNE

TIDAL WALKWAY

0   3 km

ACCOMMODATION	
Carlsens	B
Havnebakken	B
Læsø Camping	
og Hytteby	E
Læsø Vandrerhjem	C
Østerby Camping	A
Strandgården	D

EATING & DRINKING	
Bakken	1
nemMAD.nu	2

from the ferry terminal, housing a small village of four-person log cabins with cabins sharing facilities with the campsite (395kr per day, 2295kr per week), and others self-contained (495kr per day, 3250kr week). May–Sept.

Læsø Vandrerhjem Lærkevej 6, Vesterø Havn ☎98 49 91 95; ⓦwww.laesoe-vandrerhjem.dk. Lovely hostel a 10min walk from the harbour (signed) with dorm beds (200kr) and doubles (④). May–Sept.

Strandgården Strandvejen 8, Vesterø Havn ☎98 49 90 35, ⓦwww.hotel-strandgaarden.dk.

Quaint thatch-roofed hotel near a stunning beach, with a range of rooms, the cheapest sharing facilities. Room and dinner packages are available. April to mid-Oct. ⑥–⑧

Østerby Camping Campingpladsvej 8, Østerby Havn ☎98 49 80 74, ⓦwww.oesterbycamping.dk. Just 200m from a gorgeous beach, with log cabins sleeping six (350kr per day, 2100kr per week), and bike rental for residents. Mid-May to Aug.

The island

The ferry from Frederikshavn docks at the town of **VESTERØ HAVN**, little more than an enlarged village spread around the harbour, which was built in 1872 with the compensation islanders received when Læsø lost its status as the last place in Denmark where home distillation of alcohol was legal. Vesterø Havn is home to Læsø's tourist office (see p.255), and its bike-rental outlet (see p.255) comes in handy if you opt to explore the island by bike in a day and catch the last ferry back. From Vesterø Havn, bus #840 makes the ten-minute journey along Byrumvej to the island's main town, **BYRUM**, which has nothing much to distinguish it other than a few shops and places to eat. It is, however, just north of **Rønnerne**, a mosaic of tidal mudflats, salt marshes and coastal heathland which supports significant bird populations, and is perfect for hiking, cycling or horseriding – keep an eye on the tide, though, as it comes in fast and floods the mudflats. You can also explore Rønnerne by way of an excellent four-hour tractor-bus tour (mid-June to Aug at 1pm; 150kr; ☎98 49 91 56, ⓦwww.roennerbussen.dk), which departs from the main square in Byrum – guides point out all the sights.

Thanks to the high salinity of the marshes, the Rønnerne area was also where the island's **salt manufacturing** industry was established in the early Middle Ages, while

Læsø was still the property of the cathedral of Viborg. Within the hundreds of small shacks built here, a large basin of marsh-water was kept under a constant boil, evaporating the water to leave crystallized salt. Unfortunately, the amount of firewood required to keep all the basins bubbling meant that Læsø was soon stripped of all its trees, and by 1652, salt manufacturing had been banned. Today, the area bears clear evidence of its past, with small squares of land sunk into the marshes where the salt shacks once stood. For the sake of tourism, and to keep local history alive, traditional methods have been revived on the edge of Rønnerne at **Læsø Saltsyderi** (daily: July 10am–5pm; Aug–June 10am–4pm; free; ⓦ www.sydesalt.dk). With three basins on the constant go, the experience is enhanced by a mix of smoky fumes and damp swampy air. The salt produced here is of extremely high quality, and all of Denmark's top restaurants swear by it; you can buy a sample at the small shop on site.

Back in Byrum, a ten-minute bike ride along the road out of town in the opposite (northeast) direction toward Østerby Havn will take you to the **Museumsgården**, Museumsvejen 3 (mid–April to mid–June & Sept–Oct Tues–Sun 11am–3pm; mid-June to Aug daily 10am–4.30pm; 50kr; ⓦ www.laesoe-museum.dk), a highlight amongst Læsø's clutch of minor museums. An old seaweed-thatched farmstead, it has been left exactly as it was when the last inhabitant moved out some sixty years ago – and she didn't change it much during her lifetime either. With no electricity and displaying the astounding assortment of gadgets necessary to make absolutely everything from scratch, stepping inside feels like walking into a time capsule – you can almost sense the constant struggle that dominated life here.

On a more positive note, Læsø is also home to a string of stunning sandy beaches, of which **Danzigmann** on the northeastern tip, 4km east of **ØSTERBY HAVN** – the smallest of the island's three towns – is one of the best. But as the entire north coast is one long strip of sand, there's nothing to stop you from picking your own private spot. All the beaches on Læsø are sandy and shallow, and, after stormy days, sprinkled with lumps of amber that make for wonderful beachcombing.

Eating

All of Læsø's hotels double as **restaurants**. Other good options – both on the main street in Byrum – are *Bakken* at no. 89 (ⓣ 98 49 11 20, ⓦ www.restaurant-bakken .dk), an old-fashioned inn specializing in traditional smørrebrød, and the modern *nemMad.nu* at no. 62 (ⓣ 98 49 98 60, ⓦ www.nemmad.nu), serving crispy Læsø-style pizza from a wood-fired oven.

Skagen and around

Forty kilometres north of Frederikshavn, perched on a narrow peninsula at the very tip of Jutland (and Denmark) **SKAGEN** sits amid a desolate landscape of heather-topped, windswept sand dunes, its houses painted a distinctive bright yellow. Sunlight seems to gain extra brightness as it bounces off the two seas that collide just offshore, a phenomenon that attracted the renowned **Skagen artists** to the area in the late nineteenth century. Their time here, and the work they produced, is the focus of most of Skagen's cultural attractions. The town's tranquil setting, meanwhile, highlighted by the imposing landscapes that surround it, has made it a popular holiday destination in the summer, when hotels and restaurants are packed and pre-booking accommodation is essential. Visiting outside the peak period gives you a much better chance of experiencing the area's unique scenery and atmosphere.

Arrival and information

Privately operated **trains** to Skagen leave from Frederikshavn roughly once an hour. **Buses** stop at Skagen's **train station** on Sct Laurentii Vej, which also

AROUND SKAGEN

N

Skagerrak

Gamle Skagen

Skagen Odde
Naturcenter

Grenen
Kunstmuseum

Frederikshavnvej
Station

Grenen

Skagen Station

Skagen
Klitplantage

Den
Tilsandede
Kirke

Skagen

Sandmilen

Kattegat

Kandestederne

Hulsig
Station

0   3 km

--- Cycle Route

EATING
De 2 Have   1

Råbjerg
Mile

Bunken
Klitplantage

Bunken Station

ACCOMMODATION
Grenen Camping   B
Poul Eeg Camping   A
Skagen Vandrerhjem   C

houses the **tourist office** (April to mid-June & Sept–Oct Mon–Fri 9am–4pm,
Sat 10am–2pm; mid- to end-June & Aug Mon–Fri 9am–5pm, Sat 10am–4pm;
July Mon–Sat 9am–6pm, Sun 10am–4pm; Nov–March Mon–Fri 10am–4pm,
Sat 10am–1pm; ☎98 44 13 77, ⊛www.skagen-tourist.dk). There's **bicycle**
rental next door at Skagen Cykeludlegning (☎98 44 10 70, ⊛www.skagen
-cykeludlejning.dk), and the Skagen Bybus town bus stops outside. There's free
internet access across the road at the library at no. 23 (☎98 45 92 00; Mon &
Thurs 10am–6pm, Tues, Wed & Fri 1–6pm, Sat 10am–1pm).

Accommodation

Staying overnight in Skagen is infinitely preferable to going back to Frederikshavn, and there are a number of options, though none is particularly cheap.
Private accommodation (from 325kr upwards) can be arranged through the
tourist office for a steep 75kr booking fee; all rooms are within 3km of the centre
and come without breakfast.

Unless otherwise stated, all of the places below are marked on the map on p.260.

Badepension Marienlund Fabriciusvej 8, Skagen
☎98 44 13 20, ⊛www.marienlund.dk. Rustic
farmhouse a short walk from the centre and near a
pretty sandy beach, with fourteen tidy rooms, all en
suite and with wi-fi. Closed mid-Nov to Feb. **❼**

🎿 **Brøndum** Anchervej 3, Skagen ☎98 44 15
55, ⊛www.broendums-hotel.dk. Well known
for its association with the Skagen artists, this is by
far the most atmospheric spot around; the fact that
few of the rooms have their own bathrooms and all
are far from luxurious keeps the price down, but
book well ahead in summer. Good food, too. **❼**
Clausens Sct Laurentii Vej, Skagen 35 ☎98 45 01
66, ⊛www.clausenshotel.dk. A traditional
yellow-painted Skagen building dating from the
nineteenth century, with a range of colourful

rooms, some en suite. The rooms are nothing to
write home about, but it is centrally located. **❼–❾**
Finns Hotel Pension Østre Strandvej 63, Skagen
☎98 45 01 55, ⊛www.finnshotelpension.dk. Just
east of the centre, this unusual log cabin used to be
a count's holiday home. It now houses five double
rooms (and one single), all packed with character;
the cheapest has a shared bathroom in the hallway.
No children. Closed mid-Oct to March. **❻**
Foldens Sct Laurentii Vej 41, Skagen ☎98 44 11
66, ⊛www.foldens-hotel.dk. Yellow townhouse a
stone's throw from the train station and tourist
office, with a range of comfortable en-suite rooms
– though as there's often live music in the café
downstairs, it's not the best choice if you're after
peace and quiet. **❼**

Grenen Camping Fyrvej (see Around Skagen map, p.258) ☏ 98 44 25 46, ⓦ www.grenencamping.dk. Right on the beach, on the road to Grenen, with cabins sleeping four at 375kr per day (July to mid-Aug week only at 3000kr). May to mid-Sept.

Hotel Lille Nord Vestre Strandvej 28, Skagen ☏ 98 44 67 16, ⓦ www.lille-nord .dk. Set in the old ships' smithy near the harbour, this pretty place is a quieter alternative to the hotels in the town centre. The pleasant, spacious rooms are all en suite. April–Oct. ❾

Poul Eeg Camping Batterivej 21 (see Around Skagen map, p.258) ☏ 98 44 14 70, ⓦ www .pouleegcamping.dk. Pretty campsite on the road

leading to Skagen Odde Naturcentre, encircled by pine forest. May to mid-Sept.

Skagen Sømandshjem Østre Strandvej 2, Skagen ☏ 98 44 25 88, ⓦ www.skagenhjem.dk. Large yellow building next to the harbour, this former seaman's home has a large range of basic rooms, some with shared bathrooms, and a good-value restaurant (see p.262). ❻–❼

Skagen Vandrerhjem Rolighedsvej 2 (see Around Skagen map, p.258) ☏ 98 44 22 00, ⓦ www .skagenvandrerhjem.dk. West of the town centre, a short walk from Frederikshavnvej train station (the last before Skagen) with dorms (150kr) and doubles (❺), some en suite. Mid-Feb to Nov.

The town and around

Skagen was transformed from a small fishing community to the fashionable and popular holiday destination of today by the arrival – and subsequent success – of painters Michael Ancher and P.S. Krøyer, and writer Holger Drachmann during 1873 and 1874. These early pioneers were later joined by Lauritz Tuxen, Carl Locher, Viggo Johansen, Christian Krogh and Oskar Björck, and the group became known as the **Skagen Artists**. They often met in the bar of *Brøndum's Hotel*, off Brøndumsvej, and the then-owner's stepsister, Anna, herself a skilful painter, soon married Michael Ancher. The grounds of the hotel now house the **Skagens Museum** (May–Aug daily 10am–5pm; Wed until 9pm; Sept–April Tues–Sun 10am–5pm; 80kr; ⓦ www .skagensmuseum.dk), which contains the most comprehensive collection of the Skagen artists' work anywhere in the world. The majority of the canvases depict local coastal scenes, capturing subtleties of colour enhanced by the area's strong natural light. Many of the paintings, particularly those of Michael Ancher and Krøyer, are outstanding, but it's the work of Anna Ancher, perhaps the least technically accomplished, which often comes closest to achieving the naturalism that these artists sought. Paintings such as her *Pigen i Køkkenet* ("The Girl in the Kitchen") stand out, with the bright Skagen light shining through yellow curtains onto the central figure.

There's more on the Skagen artists a few strides away at Markvej 2–4, where **Michael & Anna Anchers Hus** (May–Sept daily 10am–5pm; April & Oct Mon– Thurs & Sat–Sun 11am–3pm; Nov & Feb–March Sat 11am–3pm; 70kr; ⓦ www .anchershus.dk), the Anchers' former home, has been restored with the intention of evoking the atmosphere of their time through an assortment of squeezed tubes of paint, sketches, paintings, books, ornaments and piles of canvases. There's more from this period at **Drachmanns Hus** (May Sat & Sun 11am–3pm; June–Sept daily 11am–3pm; 30kr; ⓦ www.drachmannshus.dk) on the other side of town, ten minutes' walk from the centre at Hans Baghs Vej 21, where writer Holger Drachmann lived from 1902. A large collection of Drachmann's paintings and sketchbooks are on display, although he was best known for his lyrical poems – at the forefront of the early twentieth-century Danish Neo-Romantic movement. Such was Drachmann's cultural importance that, on his death, the major Danish newspaper *Politiken* devoted most of its front page to him; facsimiles are on display.

Skagen does have more to it than its artistic associations, however, and its prior incarnation as a remote rural fishing community is well documented at the **Skagens By og Egnsmuseum** (Skagen Town and Regional Museum; March– April & Oct Mon–Fri 10am–4pm; May–June & Aug–Sept Mon–Fri 10am–4pm, Sat & Sun 11am–4pm; July Mon–Fri 10am–5pm, Sat & Sun 11am–4pm; Nov– Feb Mon–Fri 11am–3pm; 40kr; ⓦ www.skagen-bymus.dk), at P.K. Nielsensvej 8–10, a fifteen-minute walk south of the centre along Sct Laurentii Vej (or the

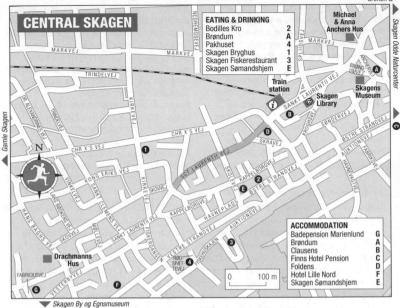

CENTRAL SKAGEN

EATING & DRINKING	
Bodilles Kro	2
Brøndum	A
Pakhuset	4
Skagen Bryghus	1
Skagen Fiskerestaurant	3
Skagen Sømandshjem	E

Michael & Anna Anchers Hus

Train station

Skagen Library

Skagens Museum

Drachmanns Hus

ACCOMMODATION	
Badepension Marienlund	G
Brøndum	A
Clausens	B
Finns Hotel Pension	C
Foldens	D
Hotel Lille Nord	F
Skagen Sømandshjem	E

0   100 m

Skagen By og Egnsmuseum

prettier Vesterbyvej). Built on the now-stabilized sand dune from which local women would watch for their husbands returning from sea during storms, the displays on local fishing techniques are reinforced with photos showing huge numbers of fish strewn along the quay prior to being auctioned. The most interesting displays are set in the auxiliary buildings, where rich and poor fishermen's houses have been reconstructed: the rich house includes a macabre guest room, kept cool to facilitate the storage of bodies washed ashore from wrecks, while the poor man's dwelling makes plain the contrast in lifestyles: it possesses just two rooms to accommodate the fisherman, his wife and fourteen children.

Skagen Odde Naturcenter and Grenen

There are a few more attractions outside Skagen town proper, all anchored around the region's stunning and wild landscape, and well worth seeking out. At the northern outskirts of Skagen, via a half-hour walk along Sct Laurentii Vej or by Skagen Bybus bus from the station during summer, you'll reach Batterivej and the **Skagen Odde Naturcenter** (May–Oct Mon–Fri 10am–4pm, Sat & Sun 11am–4pm; 65kr; Ⓦ www.skagen-natur.dk), set in a serene building designed by Jørn Utzon (see p.248). The flat concrete structures with black-capped roofs blend beautifully into the surrounding heath-covered dunes, and you quickly get the impression that the exhibit inside is just an excuse to show off the unusual building itself. The displays explore how the natural forces around Skagen – sand, water, wind and light – interact with each other, something that's very evident just outside the centre's concrete walls.

The forces of nature can be further appreciated some 4km north of Skagen (reachable via hourly Skagen Bybus bus in summer) at **Grenen**, the northernmost tip of Denmark and the meeting point of two seas – the Kattegat and Skagerrak. From the bus stop and car park at the end of Fyrvej, the Sandormen tractor-drawn bus (April–Oct; 20kr return) runs regularly along the beach to the tip, though it's nicer to walk the half-kilometre. The spectacle of their clashing waves (the seas flow in opposing directions) is a powerful draw, although only truly dramatic when the winds are strong. At other times, the magical light reflecting off the two seas is beautiful. On your way back, spare a thought for Holger Drachmann (see p.259), a man so enchanted by the seas here that he chose to be buried in a dune close to them. His tomb is signposted from the car park. There's a further reference to arts in the adjacent car park, where the **Grenen Kunstmuseum** (daily: May to mid-Sept 11am–3pm; 50kr; Ⓦ www.grenenkunstmuseum.dk) is devoted to more recent Skagen artists such as Axel and Eva Lind, best known for their clunky, almost African-looking sculptures. At the main entrance look out for Carl Milles' elegant bronze sculpture, a preliminary work for the UN building in New York.

The sand dunes and around

Down the peninsula from Skagen, and stretching from coast to coast, the **Skagen Klitplantage** is a pine plantation established on the area's dunes at the beginning of the last century to stop the sand from drifting into the sea. Crisscrossed by signposted paths, the rolling, tree-covered dunes are popular for hiking and cycling. Off to the right as you enter the area from Skagen (follow the red-signposted path), is **Den Tilsandede Kirke**, the "Buried Church" (June–Aug daily 11am–5pm; 10kr), a perfect illustration of why the dunes need stabilizing. Its name is somewhat misleading, since all that's left here is the tower of a fourteenth-century church, built in what was then a minor agricultural area. From the beginning of the sixteenth century, the church was assaulted by vicious sandstorms; by 1775 the congregation could only reach the building with the aid of shovels. In 1810 the nave and most of the fittings were sold, leaving just the tower as a marker to shipping – while not especially tall, its white walls and red roof are easily visible from the sea. The original church floor and cemetery lie buried beneath the sands, though you can go into the unfurnished interior.

The incredible severity of the storms becomes even more obvious 2km south of the church (follow the green path), where the huge **Sandmilen** migratory dune is on the last leg of its travels across the peninsula, blowing sand straight into the Kattegat. There's a much larger migratory dune, **Råbjerg Mile**, about 17km south of Skagen, midway between the east and west coasts and two stops from Skagen on the Frederikshavn train; a signposted path from the station leads to it through **Bunken Klitplantage** plantation. Covering one square kilometre, it's the largest dune in the country and harbours an enormous destructive force, with its four million cubic metres of sand moving at approximately fifteen metres per year. Råbjerg Mile is at the infancy of its journey across the peninsula – it's estimated that it will reach the Frederikshavn road by 2020, and the Kattegat by 2050, where

Skagen Festival

During the last weekend of June or the first weekend of July – generally on the same weekend as Zealand's Roskilde Festival (see p.113) – the entire town of Skagen becomes one big festival site. Although the dates of the two festivals coincide, there's never much competition between the two, as the **Skagen Festival** caters for a completely different audience. Since its inauguration in 1971, the event has drawn folk-music lovers of all ages and, in the genre's tradition, it's a laid-back affair with the emphasis on good music and good beer. Unlike most other festivals, tickets are sold for an evening at a venue, although concerts at the two large stages at the harbour and the town square are free. Musicians are mostly Danish, with a sprinkling of northern European and North American folk bands. Tickets cost 75–300kr – check Ⓦ www.skagenfestival.dk for more details. Accommodation in Skagen during the festival is booked solid, so you'll need to reserve well in advance.

it will blow out to sea as Sandmilen is doing today. Both dunes are stunning places to go for a walk – though for obvious reasons, there are no trails on either of them.

Eating, drinking and nightlife

There are plenty of **eating** options in Skagen – all of the hotels have good restaurants, though most of them are expensive. We've listed some of the best options. For **music** and **drinking**, the two quayside restaurants form the core of Skagen's relatively sedate nightlife. Unless otherwise stated, all of the places below are marked on the Central Skagen map, p.260.

De 2 Have Fyrvej 42, Grenen (see Around Skagen map, p.258) ☎98 44 24 35, ⓦwww .restaurantde2have.dk. In the same building as Grenen Kunstmuseum, with stunning views of both Skagerrak and Kattegat, this is a fine place to lunch, not least for the good selection of heavily laden traditional smørrebrød (from 78kr). May–Sept only.

Bodilles Kro Østre Strandvej 11 ☎98 44 33 00, ⓦwww.bodilleskro.dk. Cosy inn serving traditional Danish fare including outstanding lunchtime smørrebrød platter (129kr). Other specialities include a mean *bøf med løg*.

Brøndum Anchervej 3 ☎98 44 15 55, ⓦwww .broendums-hotel.dk. A legendary lunchtime herring platter (140kr), a good selection of elaborately decorated smørrebrød (from 65kr a piece), and fresh fish on the evening menu (from 180kr), with seating inside or in the beautiful hotel garden.

Pakhuset Rødspættevej 6 ☎98 44 20 00, ⓦwww .pakhuset-skagen.dk. Set in a former frozen-fish warehouse, this seafood-oriented place has an upstairs restaurant offering great harbour views, and a downstairs café with outdoor seating. Fish at both is always fresh and the menu upstairs changes daily. Speciality in the café is *fiskefrikadeller* with remoulade (85kr), and there's live music most weekends. Closed Jan.

Skagen Bryghus Kirkevej 10 ☎98 45 00 50, ⓦwww.skagenbryghus.dk. Brewery pub housed in Skagen's former power station with an excellent selection of home-brewed beer and good-quality pub grub such as burger and chips (110kr) and meatballs on rye (85kr). Open daily July & Aug, Wed–Sat April–June & Sept–Dec.

Skagen Fiskerestaurant Fiskehuskajen 13, Skagen ☎98 44 35 44, ⓦwww .skagen-fiskerestaurant.dk. The superb fish dishes served up at this red wooden shack by the harbour are probably the best in Skagen, if not the entire country. The upstairs restaurant does oysters, lobster, bouillabaisse and the like, all freshly caught, starting at 275kr. Equally delicious are the fishy delights in the less formal, sand-floored *barstue* downstairs, with herring platters (92kr) and an array of other traditional fish dishes served on the quayside. The *barstue* is also a fine place for evening drinks, with live music nightly in summer. Open Easter–Sept.

Skagen Sømandshjem Østre Strandvej 2, Skagen ☎98 44 25 88, ⓦwww.skagenhjem.dk. Good-value cafeteria in the downstairs section of *Skagens Sømandshjem*, which does a filling breakfast buffet (78kr) and bargain meals throughout the day, including a daily special for 64kr.

The Jammerbugt coast and Hjørring

From Skagen, a minor road leads for about 25km from the east-coast town of Ålbæk and across to the otherwise missable **Hirtshals**, which marks the beginning of the windswept, west-coast **Jammerbugt bay** area. Stretching down to Bulbjerg point, the bay's wide, sandy beaches attract droves of holidaymakers. Thanks to centuries of sand drifts and migratory dunes blowing inland from the west, no roads run along the coastline here, so the best way of exploring is to hop on a bike – the relatively flat national cycle route #1 hugs the coastline.

Along the Jammerbugt coastline

The desolate harbour town of Hirtshals marks the beginning of the **JAMMER-BUGT** coastline, endowed with a succession of holiday towns and beautiful sandy **beaches** – though note that the prevailing westerly winds and strong currents can mean that swimming is dangerous – ask around before you venture in. One long strip of sand, mirrored by national cycle route #1, lines the coast for about 15km before reaching the small fishing village of **Lønstrup** which gained some uneasy notoriety in 1877 when, following an unusually heavy downpour, a mudslide washed six houses into the sea, to the great surprise of homeward-bound local fishermen who spotted the wooden buildings bobbing up and down in the water – fortunately, there were no fatalities. You'll find further evidence of just how strong the forces of nature are in these parts if you head south of the village to the imposing **Lønstrup Klit** cliffs, which line the coast for another 15km as far as the town of Løkken (see below). Between twenty and a hundred metres high, they provide a scenic backdrop to the popular sandy beaches below, and the cycle route that runs parallel to the cliff edge offers some lovely perspectives over the bay. Driven by the unrelenting westerly winds, the crashing sea eats away a couple of metres of cliff each year, something that's very obvious just south of Lønstrup, where the pretty medieval church of **Mårup Kirke** is balanced delicately on the cliff's edge, having been built in the thirteenth century in the centre of a settlement which has long since dispersed. There's little of interest in the church itself, but among the tombstones in the churchyard are the graves of 33 of the 226 British sailors who perished when their frigate, *The Crescent*, was shipwrecked just offshore during a storm in 1808. Some 2km further south along the cliffs, the **Rubjerg Knude** lighthouse provides yet more proof of the destructive force of the westerly winds. When first built in 1900, it was 60m above sea level and 200m inland; by 1968, the wind-whipped sand drift had become so high that it was no longer visible from the sea, and it was decommissioned. It was then opened up as a museum on the dunes but, by 2002, even this had to be closed, as the drifting sand had blocked the door and made it impossible to get in and out. Today, it offers a superb photo opportunity, with the force of the wind incessantly changing the shape of the massive dunes in front.

At the southern end of Lønstrup Klit, where the cliffs melt into the beach, the small seaside resort town of **LØKKEN** hosts a plethora of **activities** on its wide sandy beaches – including kite flying, windsurfing, paragliding, beach volleyball and surfing. Lots of places in town and at the campsites offer lessons and rent out kit.

South of Løkken, the white sandy beaches continue in an uninterrupted strip to **BLOKHUS**, made up almost entirely of holiday homes, which mean that the sand gets a bit overrun during the summer, though it feels impossibly desolate and remote during the rest of the year. It's some 40km from Blokhus down to the limestone hillock at **Bulbjerg**, which marks the end of the Jammerbugt coast and is home to vast colonies of birds. National cycle route #1 runs inland slightly along this stretch, through numerous pine plantations established on the dunes to hold on to the shifting sands.

Practicalities

There are no direct **bus** connections between Jammerbugten's coastal towns, so unless you have a car or are riding along national cycle route #1, you'll inevitably have to go inland in order to catch a bus along the coast. To get from Skagen to Lønstrup by public transport, catch the train to Hjørring via Frederikshavn, and then bus #740 to Lønstrup. From Lønstrup to Løkken, it's bus #740 back to Hjørring, and then the #71 towards Aalborg. From Løkken to Blokhus, catch bus #71 to Pandrup, and then bus #200 from Aalborg to Blokhus. The only way to reach Bulbjerg is under your own steam, via cycle route #1 or the main road from Fjerritslev.

There's a good range of **accommodation** along the coast between Hirtshals and Løkken, and we've listed some of the better options below. The entire coastline is **holiday home** territory (see Basics, p.27 for more), rented by the week. In terms of standard accommodation, there's a range of bright rooms in Lønstrup at the former merchant's house, *Hotel Marielle*, Strandvejen 94 (☎ 98 96 07 00, ⓦwww .hotel-marinelle.dk; ⑥), near the town centre and a short walk from the cliffs and beach. Otherwise, Løkken is probably the most convenient base for exploring the Jammerbugt coast. In the centre, the *Klitbakken*, Nørregade 3 (☎98 99 11 66, ⓔhotel.klitbakken@privat.dk; ⑥), has balconied rooms and a popular café/bar downstairs. There's also the cheaper and more atmospheric *Villa Vendel* (☎98 99 14 56, ⓦwww.villavendel.dk; ④) a charming old townhouse at Harald Fischersvej 12, with five rustic rooms. However, if you want to be close to the beach, your best bet is one of the town's **campsites**. *Løkken Campingcenter & Hytteby* (☎98 99 17 67, ⓦwww.loekken-hytteby.dk; June to mid-Sept) is a short walk from both the beach and town centre at Søndergade 69; ask to be dropped at Junivej if you're arriving on bus #71. It has modern cabins sleeping four (from 1550kr per week). If you'd rather be right on the beach, *Løkken Strand Camping* (☎98 99 18 04, ⓦwww.loekkencamping.dk; May to mid-Sept), 1km north of the centre at Furreby Kirkevej 97, has cabins sleeping five (from 3450kr per week); from May to June they're rented out on a daily basis for 175kr, plus a 70kr fee per person.

There are plenty of **eating options** in the towns along the coast. In Lønstrup, the best is *Caféen Lønstrup* (☎98 96 08 84, ⓦwww.cafeenloenstrup.dk; closed Mon) offering a range of well-prepared seafood dishes such as fresh crab-claw salad and fried plaice (from 88kr) and a seafood and steak grill buffet that's fantastic on hot summer nights. The café also hosts live bands most evenings in the holiday season, and has a good selection of foreign and local beers. *Restaurant Løkken Badehotel* (☎ 98 99 22 00, ⓦwww.restaurantlb.dk), on Løkken's central square at Torvet 8, has outdoor seating in the summer, and is a good bet for delicious lunchtime salads and sandwiches (from 75kr), and a full-on three-course gourmet menu for 269kr at dinner.

Travel details

Trains

Aalborg to: Århus (2 hourly; 1hr 30min); Copenhagen (2 hourly; 4hr 30min–5hr); Frederikshavn (hourly; 1hr 15min); Hjørring (1–2 hourly; 45min); Hobro (2 hourly; 30min); Randers (2 hourly; 45min); Skørping (2 hourly; 20min).

Frederikshavn to: Aalborg (hourly; 1hr 15min); Copenhagen (9 daily; 5hr 45min); Hjørring (1–2 hourly; 30min); Skagen (1–2 hourly; 40min); Århus (hourly; 3hr).

Hobro to: Aalborg (2 hourly; 45min); Randers (2 hourly; 15min); Skørping (2 hourly; 10min); Århus (2 hourly; 45min).

Skagen to: Frederikshavn (1–2 hourly; 40min).

Skørping to: Aalborg (2 hourly; 20min); Hobro (2 hourly; 10min); Randers (2 hourly; 30min); Århus (hourly; 1hr 15min).

Buses

Aalborg to: Blokhus (hourly; 1hr); Copenhagen via Randers (3 daily; 4hr 45min); Løkken (1–2 hourly; 1hr); Thisted (1–2 hourly; 1hr 40min).

Frederikshavn to: Esbjerg via Aalborg and Viborg (2–3 daily; 5hr).

Hjørring to: Lønstrup (hourly; 30min); Løkken (1–2 hourly; 30min).

Skørping to: Rebild (hourly; 5min).

Ferries

Aalborg to: Egholm (2 hourly; 5min).

Frederikshavn to: Læsø (2–5 daily; 1hr 30min).

Læsø to: Frederikshavn (2–5 daily; 1hr 30min).

Flights

Aalborg to: Copenhagen (14–21 daily; 45min).

8

West Jutland

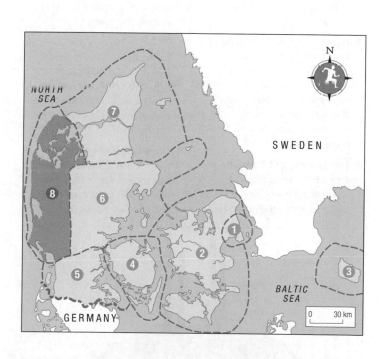

CHAPTER 8

Highlights

✳ **Stone Age collection, Thisted Museum** The outstanding displays here include an elaborate collection of flint tools and worked-up amber found within the region. See p.269

✳ **Local beers** Please your palate by sampling some of the local brews from the Thisted, Skive or Fur breweries. See p.269, p.273 & p.274

✳ **Hanstholm II battery** This enormous German-built battery from World War II offers a fascinating labyrinth of ammunition stores, crew's quarters and technical sections centred around four huge guns. See p.270

✳ **Windsurfing at Klitmøller** One of the world's top windsurfing spots, and a great place to watch the daredevil

antics of the experts or have a go yourself. See p.271

✳ **Moler cliff hikes** The dramatic moler cliffs lining the northern coastlines of Mors and Fur offer some extremely picturesque hiking. See p.272 & p.274

✳ **Elia sculpture, Herning** This enormous, fire-spurting cast-iron sculpture is a truly magnificent piece of art. See p.276

✳ **Birdwatching at Tipperne** Designated a bird sanctuary in its entirety, this marshy peninsula offers great opportunities for spotting local birdlife. See p.277

✳ **Ringkøbing town centre** Sample the great selection of restaurants and cafés lining Ringkøbing's cobbled town square. See p.277

▲ Elia sculpture, Herning

West Jutland

B
attered relentlessly by the thundering waves of the North Sea, Jutland's
long western strip, from Hanstholm in the north to Esbjerg in the south,
is as windswept and wild as it is desolately beautiful. With its almost
unbroken line of sandy beaches and windswept dunes overlooked by an
array of pretty summer cottages, the beautiful coastline rightly attracts German
tourists in their thousands, but it's the unforgiving westerly winds that characterize the region, and can make it challenging to explore. To the north is the
Limfjordslandet, the western portion of the Limfjorden, which wriggles inland
from the Skagerrak past islands and peninsulas that were carved out during the
last Ice Age. On its western shores, the **Thy** region holds the country's first
national park with its host of stunning beaches and outstanding windsurfing
opportunities, all accessible from the park's main town of **Hanstholm**. Further
inland **Thisted** – Thy's atmospheric administrative and historical capital boasts
pretty fjordside beaches and an excellent museum. The mid-fjord island of **Mors**
and the adjacent **Salling** peninsula offer more bucolic charm and stunning cliffs
ideal for hiking. The area south of Limfjordslandet is more desolate, with large
expanses of heathland and forest. To the southeast, **Herning** is best known for its
textile industry, while to the north, **Struer**, home of renowned hi-fi manufac-
turers Bang & Olufsen, is one of the country's most important industrial centres.
Following the coastline southwards, the ancient harbour town of **Ringkøbing**,
strikingly set on the banks of the Ringkøbing fjord, is an ideal base for exploring
the area. There are plenty of birdwatching possibilities on the Ringkøbing fjord,
as well as some gorgeous beaches here and in the far south around **Blåvands Huk**,
within easy distance of the relatively sizeable town of **Esbjerg**. National cycle
route #1 hugs the western coastline, and with fairly scatty public transport
connections, a **bike** is by far the best way to explore – though you'll need sturdy
legs to cope with the winds.

Limfjordslandet

LIMFJORDSLANDET comprises the area around the western portion of the
Limfjorden, the body of water that separates northern Jutland from the rest of the
peninsula. In around 1100, just as the Viking era was coming to a close, the waters
of Limfjorden stopped flowing when the outlet to the Skaggerak was shut off by
sand drifts. The fjord became a brackish lake and its reign as the region's main
transport artery ended, destroying its trade and isolating it financially and
geographically for over eight hundred years. In 1825, a storm reopened the outlet

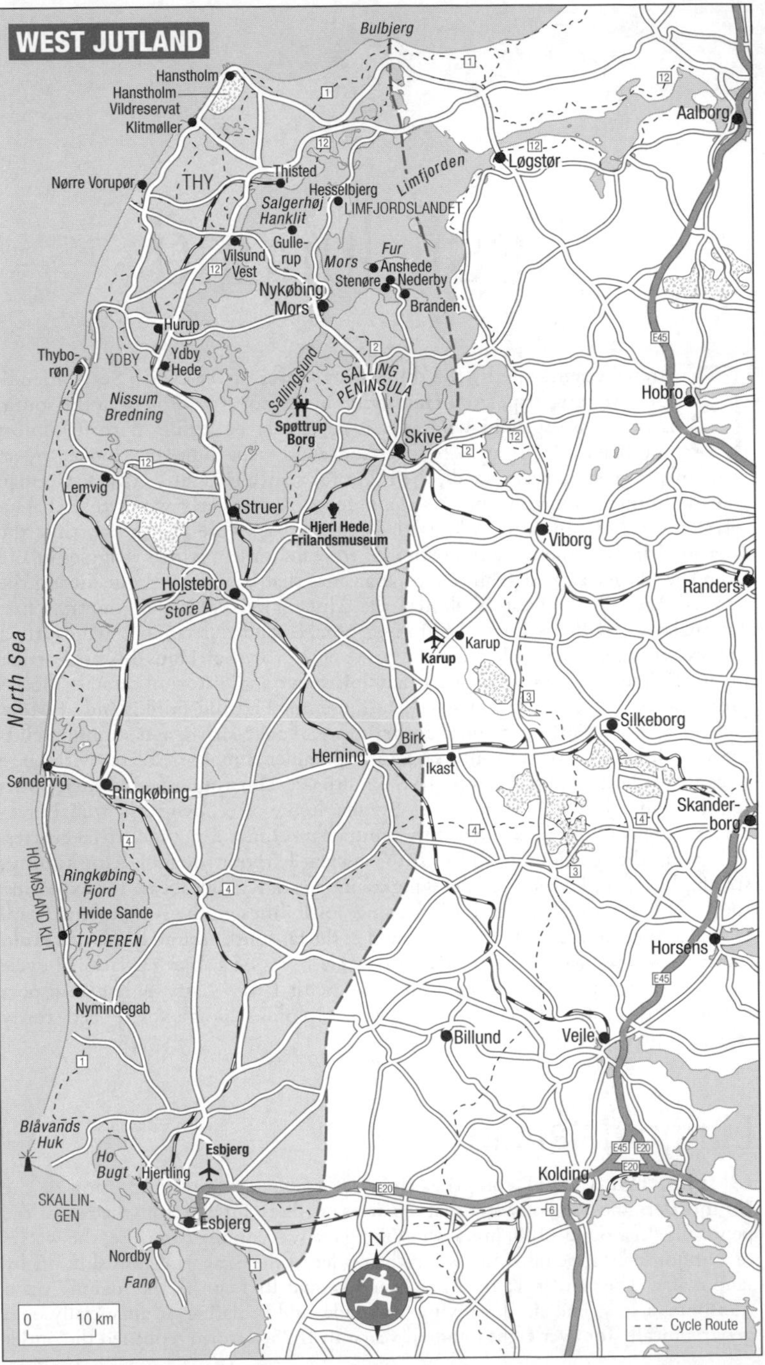

WEST JUTLAND

Bulbjerg

Hanstholm
Hanstholm
Vildreservat
Klitmøller
Nørre Vorupør
THY
Thisted
Hesselbjerg
Limfjorden
Løgstør
Aalborg

Salgerhøj
Hanklit
LIMFJORDSLANDET
Gulle-
rup
Fur
Vilsund
Vest
Mors
Anshede
Stenøre
Nederby
Hurup
Nykøbing
Mors
Branden

Thybo-
røn
YDBY
Ydby
Hede
Sallingsund
SALLING
PENINSULA
Hobro

Nissum
Bredning
Spøttrup
Borg
Skive

Lemvig
Struer
Hjerl Hede
Frilandsmuseum
Viborg
Randers

Holstebro
Store Å
Karup
Karup
Silkeborg

North Sea
Birk
Herning
Ikast
Skander-
borg

Søndervig
Ringkøbing
Ringkøbing
Fjord
Hvide Sande
TIPPEREN
Horsens

HOLMSLAND KLIT
Nymindegab
Billund
Vejle

Blåvands
Huk
Ho
Bugt
Hjertling
Esbjerg
Kolding

SKALLIN-
GEN
Esbjerg

Nordby
Fanø
N

Horns Rev

0   10 km

- - - Cycle Route

and the waters once more started flowing from west to east. Harbours soon sprung up in Limfjordslandet's shore towns and the region's economy flourished, again centred on trade and fishing.

The region's long period of isolation goes some way to explaining why it still feels remote and somewhat disconnected from the rest of Denmark. The most visited part of Limfjordslandet is the **Thy** region, which occupies the northwestern corner and boasts both a wild Skagerrak coastline – now the Thy National Park – and the more tranquil shores of the Limfjorden itself, a varied landscape encircled by beautiful beaches. There are some interesting and very different sights and museums in Thy's two main towns, **Thisted** and **Hanstholm**, while the Limfjord island of **Mors** and the **Salling** peninsula are both idyllic, their main attraction being the dramatic cliffs lining their northern coastlines. Sections of Thy's Skagerrak coast attracts legions of northern European tourists in the summer, when it's best to arrange accommodation in advance. At other times, this is a rarely visited part of the country, and it can sometimes feel as if you have the entire place to yourself. Bear in mind, though, that the weather here is unpredictable, and that getting around is difficult: trains only reach to the fringes at Thisted and Skive, so you'll need to rely on buses if you're without your own transport.

Thy

Encircled by water on three sides, with a small sliver of land in the north its only natural connection with the rest of Jutland, the landscape of the **Thy** region ranges from windswept sand dunes on the west coast to heathland and, in the east, fertile farmlands. This gorgeous variation means that Thy has a lot to offer in terms of the great outdoors, and its few towns hold some interesting attractions, too.

Thisted

Thy's administrative centre and the terminus of the local rail line from Struer, the pleasant market town of **THISTED** is delicately positioned on the banks of Limfjorden, and boasts a large marina and a harbour that fills to capacity each September for the **Limfjorden Rundt regatta** (Ⓦ www.limfjordenrundt.dk), when some fifty traditional wooden sailing ships dock here on their way around the fjord. Even if your visit doesn't coincide with the regatta, it's worth heading down to the waterfront to take in Thisted's magnificent fjordside setting, its entire shoreline blessed with fine **beaches**. You'll find changing facilities and a bathing pier at Søbadet, west of the centre in front of the large Thisted Bryghus brewery, where Henning Wienberg Jensen's *Thisted Pigen* statue of a young girl stares pensively out over the water. (It was this statue that stood in when Copenhagen's *Little Mermaid* went on tour in the Far East in 2009.) Incidentally, Thisted Bryghus produces the delicious, prize-winning Thy Pilsner – among the country's best lagers and definitely worth tasting before you leave. The only other thing worth sticking around for is the outstanding **Thisted Museum**, right in the centre at Jernbanegade 4 (daily Mon–Fri 10am–4pm, Sat & Sun 1–4pm, Sept–May closed Mon; 30kr; Ⓦ www.thistedmuseum.dk). The collection includes an elaborate display of flint tools and worked-up amber found within the region, which suggest an usually high population density during the Stone Age. The flint was mined around what's now the town of Hov, 10km east of Thisted, and it was even exported to Norway, indicating a high degree of social organization at the time. Other ground-floor displays include an exhibit illustrating how the region's numerous Bronze Age burial mounds were constructed, alongside glamorous gold and bronze items found inside them. Upstairs, displays are devoted to two of Thisted's famous townsmen: **Christian Kold**, heavily involved in the establishment of the uniquely Danish Folkehøjskole (People's High Schools); and

I.P. Jakobsen, a poet and naturalist who translated Darwin's *Origin of Species* into Danish. Both exhibits are a step back in time, with desks and working paraphernalia on display as though Kold and Jakobsen had simply just left the room.

Practicalities

It's an easy **train** journey to Thisted from Struer (see p.274), embarkation point of the regional train service; if you're travelling from northern Jutland, you'll have to catch **bus** #70 or the faster #970X from Aalborg. Thisted's bus and train stations are next to each other on Jernbanegade, close to the marina and behind Thisted Museum. Set in the downstairs section of the old town hall at Store Torv 6, the helpful **tourist office** (mid-June to Aug Mon–Fri 9am–5pm, Sat 9am–1pm; Sept to mid-June Mon–Fri 9am–4pm; T 97 92 19 00, W www.visitthy.dk) rents out bicycles (70kr/day) – you pick them up at Statoil on Østerbakken 63, five minutes' walk up Østerbakken hill from the marina.

With some good places to **eat** and **sleep** – not to mention its beaches – Thisted is an appealing place to stay for a couple of nights. Options include ⚡ *Basses Kro*, Vestergade 28A (T 97 92 16 97; ⑤), a small inn on the pedestrianized street with four cosy rooms sharing facilities and with access to a small kitchen; its restaurant serves good-value traditional Danish lunches and dinners. Across from the train and bus stations at Frederiksgade 16, the plush *Hotel Thisted* (T 97 92 52 00, W www .hotelthisted.dk; ⑦) has stylish en-suite rooms, and a restaurant serving delicious, heavily laden smørrebrød for lunch (from 36kr a piece) and a good array of French-inspired options for dinner. The *Thisted Vandrerhjem* **hostel**, Kongemøllevej 8 (T 97 92 50 42, W www.danhostelnord.dk/thisted; dorms 150kr, doubles ④), is 3km north of Thisted in the village of Skinnerup (bus #96 or #322 towards Hanstholm); *Thisted Camping*, Iversensvej 3 (T 97 92 16 35, W www.thisted-camping.dk; April–Oct), a ten-minute walk east of the centre on the banks of Limfjorden, has ten new log cabins sleeping four (500kr), six (700kr) and eight (900kr).

Hanstholm

Thy's only other sizeable settlement, the relatively new harbour town of **HANSTHOLM** perches on Jutland's most northwesterly point – known as Jutland's shoulder – with the unruly Skagerrak surrounding it on three sides. This strategic position wasn't lost on the Germans during World War II, when the Third Reich constructed a huge fortification here as part of the 5000-kilometre **Atlantic Wall** coastal defence, which ran from the French–Spanish border all the way up to Norway via the entire west coast of Denmark, and was designed to destroy Allied craft before they had a chance to drop their bombs or land. The entire Danish west-coast coastline is still littered with the remains of the Wall's pillboxes, batteries and bunkers, and the largest of these – in fact the most extensive in northern Europe – is the **Hanstholm II battery**, set on a cliff overlooking the harbour. It covers a total of nine square kilometres and, while in operation, was manned by more than three thousand soldiers. Today, an enormous bunker centred around one of the four huge guns has been opened up as the **Museumscenter Hanstholm** (daily: Feb–May & Sept–Oct 10am–4pm; June–Aug 10am–5pm; 60kr; W www.museums centerhanstholm.dk). It comprises a labyrinth of small rooms (the map handed out by the entrance is crucial in order not to get lost) from ammunition stores to the crew's quarters and a technical section all restored to look as they would have when the battery was in operation. The gun pit in the centre once held a 38-centimetre cannon-gun which was used to police shipping traffic on the Skaggerak and access to the Baltic – there's a similar cannon-gun by the main entrance. Adjoining the bunker is an exhibition centre displaying German and Italian weaponry and uniforms, as well as the remains of Allied planes shot down here. Sadly, all the labelling in this section is in Danish and German only, though there is some English in the bunker itself. Despite this, the museum is immensely absorbing, not least because of the sheer scale of the place. The hordes of excited Germans who come to see where their parents and grandparents were based during the war also adds to the sense of authenticity.

Apart from the Museumscenter, there's nothing in Hanstholm worth hanging around for, especially since there's no town centre to speak of (most of the action is centred on the harbour), though you may want to stay over while exploring the national park. The best-value option – and a great spot for lunch after you've visited the museum – is 本 *Hanstholm Sømandshjem* (☎97 96 11 45, Ⓦwww.hshh.dk; ❻), in the harbour area at Kai Lindbergs Gade 71, which has basic en-suite rooms plus a couple of four- and six-bed dorms (150kr) sharing facilities, and a **cafeteria** serving proper home-cooked daily specials such as fried plaice, *hamborgerryg* or *medisterpølser med rødkål*, always accompanied by a salad buffet, and a three-slice smørrebrød packed lunch for 40kr.

Bus #322 plies the road between Thisted and Hanstholm, stopping at Klitmøller on the way. There's an ever-increasing number of demarcated **bike** routes throughout the park, and you can rent mountain bikes at Hanstholm Naturskole (☎99 17 30 53, Ⓦwww.hanstholm-naturskole.dk), housed in the historic lighthouse overlooking the harbour at Tårnvej 23.

Along the coast

South of Hanstholm, the spectacular **Thy National Park** follows the coast south until Limfjorden's inlet. Hiking trails go off into the park from both sides of the main road, and offer a superb way to take in the gorgeous scenery. Just after entering the park, have a quick peek inside the German-built **Hanstholm I** fortification (no set hours; free) just outside Hanstholm and signposted to the left from the main coast road. It's one of the country's best-preserved coastal batteries, with German graffiti slogans still clearly visible on the inside walls. In a bizarre sort of way, it blends in beautifully with the surrounding coastal heathland and, as the battery saw no action, the Germans keeping watch must have considered themselves very lucky given the breathtaking scenery. Past Hanstholm I, the main road to Klitmøller gives a great impression of the vast, windblown open expanse that makes up the national park. Most of this section is treeless, with coastal dunes to the right of the road, and open heathland to the left. The section of heathland between Hanstholm I and Klitmøller is closed to the public from April to mid-June during the breeding season, when up to forty different bird species visit, including the endangered golden plover. Just before you reach Klitmøller, a marshy area to the southeast is inhabited by rare plants such as water crowfoot and bur reed, and supports a significant aquatic bird and otter population; due to its ecological sensitivity, this part is permanently closed to the public.

After about 10km, the road branches off to the right to the small beachside town of **KLITMØLLER**, aka Hawaii II in recognition of its optimal windsurfing conditions, with a "wave spot" ideal for jumps and other acrobatics, and less demanding stretches suitable for beginners. If you want to give it a try, Westwind Klitmøller (☎97 97 56 56, Ⓦwww.westwind-klitmoller.dk), a short walk from the beach at Ørhagevej 150, offers lessons in windsurfing, surf-riding and kite-surfing, and rents out kit too. If you want to linger and soak up the surf-dude scene, the two best places to **stay** are campsites. Near the town centre, *Klitmøller Camping* at Vangvej 16 (☎97 97 50 20, Ⓦwww.klitmoller-camping.dk) is slightly worn, but has five cabins sleeping three, four and six (from 275kr) and self-contained apartments, (❹), while *Nystrup Camping* at Trøjborgvej 22, just outside town in a dramatic national park landscape of heath-covered dunes (☎97 97 52 49, Ⓦwww.nystrupcampingklitmoller.dk), has cabins sleeping two, four and six (from 250kr) and also rents out bikes (50kr per day) and organizes surfing lessons through West Wind (see p.277). **Bus** #322 from Hanstholm passes Klitmøller en route to Thisted.

Mors and the Salling peninsula

Though **Mors** is an island and **Salling** a peninsula, they share many similarities, most obviously their outstandingly beautiful landscapes and unique geology. The northern fringes of both, including the tiny island of **Fur** just north of Salling, bear witness to the enormously powerful forces of nature that shaped them some sixty million years ago. Their coastlines are lined by dramatic, steep **moler cliffs** – unique to this part of Denmark and characterized by decorative seams of volcanic ash, and chalk-like rock that holds numerous fossils and giant crystal formations. Away from the north coasts lies a more sedate landscape of fertile farmland and gentle rolling hills, which holds a few rural sights and an imposing medieval castle.

Mors

Tucked snugly between Thy and the Salling peninsula, **MORS** (also known as Morsø) is the largest of Limfjorden's islands, with a land area of 368 square kilometres. It's connected to the wider world via bridges to Thy and Salling, and by two rickety wooden ferries that run across Nessund to southern Thy, and across Feggesund to north Jutland, just south of Bulbjerg. Aside from transport to and from the ferry docks to the island's agreeable main town of **NYKØBING MORS**, public transport here is pretty dire, and the best way to explore is on foot or by bike (see below for bike-rental outlets).

Mors' main attraction are the **moler cliffs** that run along its northern coast, stretching for some 20km between the Vilsund Vest bridge and the Feggesund ferry dock. The coastal path along the clifftop offers outstanding views across to Thisted, but to get the full moler experience it's best to clamber down onto the beach, via one of the many tracks, and take in the spectacular formations from the beach. Some 500m north of the town of Gullerup, the most impressive section, known as **Hanklit**, has a forty-metre moler band with stripes of dark volcanic ash making beautiful patterns. Mors' highest point is nearby at **Salgerhøj**, an 89-metre moler cliff that affords spectacular views. To learn more about moler and the geology of Mors, head to **Móler Museet**, Skarrehagevej 8 (May–June & mid-Aug to Oct Mon–Fri 10am–4pm, Sat & Sun noon to 4pm; July to mid-Aug daily 10am–5pm; 50kr; Ⓦwww.dueholmkloster.dk), signposted off the main road just before Feggesund at Hesslebjerg, and reached via bus #701 from Nykøbing Mors to Feggesund. You can dig up fossils at the bottom of a moler pit and museum staff will try to date your finds for you.

Practicalities

Getting to Mors is straightforward. The main road connecting Viborg and Thy bisects the island, with a state-of-the-art modern bridge linking it to the Salling peninsula in the east, and the older Vildsund bridge connects it to Thy in the west; the fast #92 Ⓢ Viborg to Thisted bus plies this route every hour. Mors' **tourist office**, Havnen 4 (July Mon–Fri 9am–6pm, Sat 9am–3pm; June & Aug Mon–Fri 9am–5pm, Sat 9am–2pm; Sept–May Mon–Fri 9am–5pm, Sat 9am–noon; Ⓣ97 72 04 88; Ⓦwww.visitmors.dk), is at the harbour in Nykøbing Mors. It rents out bicycles (60kr per day) and sells excellent cycling and hiking maps of Mors.

Although **accommodation** on Mors is limited, there are a few good options. In Nykøbing Mors, best choices are *Pakhuset* on Havnen (Ⓣ97 72 33 00, Ⓦwww .phr.dk; Ⓐ), a charming harbourside converted warehouse with a classy French restaurant and free wi-fi; and the ⚐ *Nykøbing Mors Vandrerhjem*, Øroddevej 15

Denmark's great outdoors

Although hibernation mode tends to take over during the winter, when most people stay indoors and fend off the cold with hearty food and plenty of warming *gløgg* wine, the mass exodus to the countryside at the first signs of snowmelt is proof that Danes are some of Europe's most enthusiastic lovers of outdoor pursuits. With endless possibilities for hiking, cycling, canoeing and, perhaps surprisingly, long days at the beach, Denmark is a fantastic place to get out and luxuriate in the great outdoors.

Trekking path on the island of Møn ▲

Møns Klint chalk cliff ▼

Hiking

Rambling through open fields, along the coast or up into the undulating, heathy hills is one of the most invigorating ways to explore Denmark, and with a network of waymarked **trails** crisscrossing the most visually striking parts of the country, **hiking** here couldn't be easier – you can pick up detailed (free) trail guides in all the tourist offices. Many trails can be walked in half a day, but to really get the flavour of the Danish countryside, you'll need to plan a longer route, overnighting along the way. As most of the trails are in rural parts, it's a good idea to bring your own food, and it's also fun to add to your meal by sampling the abundant berries that grow in Denmark's state forests.

Some of the best walks include the long-distance former army road **Hærvejen** which extends 250km from Viborg in Jutland to the German border, passing historical sites such as the Jelling runic stone (p.214); the crags, bluffs and hummocks of **Bornholm**'s northwestern corner, loomed over by the ruins of the thirteenth-century Hammershus citadel; and, in Zealand's southeast, the well-manicured, signposted walk along the cliffs and seashore at **Møns Klint**.

Canoeing

One of the best ways to see the Danish countryside is by canoe. Denmark has forty navigable rivers perfect for spending a day out on the water – the Gudenå, Suså and Skjern Å have the best facilities – as well as countless lakes, canals and sheltered fjords, including North Jutland's Limfjorden and Zealand's Roskilde Fjord, Holbæk Fjord and Isefjord. You'll find canoe- and kayak-rental shops and campsites for overnighting along many of the waterways.

Cycling

Bikes are ubiquitous in Denmark. Danes tend to cycle almost as often as they walk, and the cycling paths that navigate the country's scenic lanes, coastal roads and dense forests (as well as most towns and cities) make Denmark one of Europe's most cycle-friendly countries. The network of eleven long-distance national cycle routes (indicated with large blue signs and marked on the relevant maps within the Guide) cover 4325km, and pass by the deep fjords of western Jutland, the flat plains of northern Funen and as far afield as the wide open grassy pastures of Lolland and Falster. One of the most popular is the Hærvejen route, from Viborg all the way north to Skagen, passing ancient burial cairns and medieval churches en route. If you're after some coastal riding, head for the southern Funen archipelago, whose hundred-odd islands, islets and skerries are wonderfully far-flung, tranquil places to ride. By far the most popular destination for cyclists is the island of Bornholm, where a web of well-maintained, secluded routes runs along the crisp, clean Baltic shoreline and through coniferous forests.

Beaches

Few people associate Denmark with beaches, so it might come as a surprise to learn that the country's 7300km of coastline boasts scores of top-notch shores of white sand perfect for summer sunning, swimming and – in a few places – surfing. And thanks in part to the Danes' staunch respect for the environment, over two hundred of the county's beaches have been given blue flag status – the water is pristine and unpolluted almost

▲ Red deer

▼ Cycling – and canoeing – in Copenhagen

everywhere, and it's warmer than you might think: around 15° C (59°F) in July and August.

Kite-surfing ▲

Amager Strandpark, Copenhagen ▼

Denmark's top beaches

▸▸ **Tisvildeleje, Zealand** With a decidedly upmarket feel, this sandy beach boasts ample facilities, family-friendly sandbars and shallows and a host of superb restaurants and cafés. See p.109

▸▸ **Hvide Sande, Jutland** This popular beach boasts excellent facilities, and is one of the best places in the country for windsurfing, with plenty of places from which to rent watersports gear. See p.277

▸▸ **Dueodde, Bornholm** Easily accessible, with lengthy shallows and the warmest water off Bornholm, the powdery sand at this mid-Baltic gem is said to be some of the finest in Europe. See p.149

▸▸ **Ristinge, Langeland** Sheltered to the north by towering cliffs and dunes, this handsome beachfront is just minutes' walk from a well-placed campsite. See p.179

▸▸ **Klitmøller, Jutland** Denmark's largest concentration of beaches lie along Jutland's west coast, and the winds that blow in off the sea here make Klitmøller the perfect spot for a lesson in windsurfing or kitesurfing. See p.271

▸▸ **Amager Strandpark, Zealand** Set just south of the capital, this unpretentious beach offers clean water and great views of the Øresund bridge to Sweden. See p.78

▸▸ **Charlottenlund Strand, Copenhagen** Just north of the city centre, this small, secluded beach is very popular and offers great facilities and a designated nude bathing area. See p.96

(T 97 72 06 17, W www.danhostelnord.dk/mors; dorms 150kr; doubles ⑤), a fabulously located hostel on a finger of land jutting out into the Sallingsund sound. Five kilometres south of Nykøbing Mors, next to the bridge to Salling, there's the *Sallingsund Færgekro*, Sallingsundvej 106 (T 97 72 00 88, W www .sallingsund-faergekro.dk; ⑦) a traditional ferry inn with forty-odd en-suite rooms, some with balconies overlooking Sallingsund; it also has a basic campsite.

The Salling peninsula

Extending northwards up into the Limfjorden, the **Salling peninsula** offers complete rural idyll: field after field, and not much else, all well suited to gentle hiking and biking. On the eastern coast at the foot of the peninsula (and on the rail line between Viborg and Struer), the principal settlement of **SKIVE** is a typical Jutland market town serving a large rural catchment area. Its host of shopping malls and supermarkets makes it a good place to stock up and, as the region's transport hub, it makes a convenient base. If you're here in August, you'll find the town overtaken by the Limfjorden Rundt **regatta** (W www.limfjordenrundt.dk), which finishes here and sees the scenic harbour filled to capacity with old wooden sailing ships – one of which, the two-masted schooner *Lovise-Moland*, offers cruises up and down the Limfjorden; book via the tourist office (see below). Otherwise, there's not much to do in the town itself, but head 20km or so southwest of Skive and you'll find the **Hjerl Hedes Frilandsmuseum** (daily: July to mid-Aug 10am–6pm, May–June & mid-Aug to Sept 10am–5pm, April & Oct 10am–4pm; July to mid-Aug 105kr, rest of year 60kr; W www.hjerlhede.dk). One of Denmark's most successful heritage tourism projects, this open-air museum attempts to recreate the development of a local village from the years 1500 to 1900, with a forge, inn, school, mills, a vicarage, a dairy, a grocer's shop and farms, all relocated here from their original sites around Jutland. By far the best time to come is during summer (mid-June to mid-Aug), when the place is brought to life by a hundred or so men, women and children dressed in traditional costumes, who provide demonstrations of the old crafts and farming methods. To get here from Skive, take the train to Vinderup (5–10 daily; 11min; bicycles allowed), from where it's an eight-kilometre walk, taxi- or cycle ride.

Practicalities

Salling is best explored by bike, and you can rent one (60kr per day) at Skive's **tourist office**, Østerbro 7 (mid-June to Aug Mon–Fri 9.30am–4pm, Sat 9.30am–1pm; Sept to mid-June Mon–Fri 10am–4pm, Sat 9.30am to noon, T 97 52 32 66, W www.visitskive.dk). Although Skive's **accommodation** is a bit thin on the ground, there is one good option ten minutes' walk from the bus and train stations (themselves south of the centre by the Skive Å river), but near a busy junction at Søndre Blvd 1: the grand old Best Western *Hotel Gl Skivehus* (T 97 52 11 44, W www.skivehus.dk; ⑧) with free wi-fi; it also houses the popular ⅄ *Barbara's* restaurant (T 97 52 16 32, W www.barbaras.dk), and a pub serving beer from the local Hancock Bryggerierne brewery.

Around Salling

Salling's west coast is endowed with some nice pebbly fjord beaches, but the real attraction is the medieval castle of **Spøttrup Borg** (April Tues, Wed & Sun 11am–5pm; May–Aug daily 10am–6pm; Sept daily 10am–5pm; Oct daily 10am–4pm; 50kr; W www.spottrupborg.dk), Borgen 6A, 2km west of the village of Rødding and reachable via bus #43 from Skive. An imposing four-winged structure surrounded by a double moat, with an adjacent herb garden and wildlife lake, it was restored in 1941 and remains one of the best-preserved medieval castles in Denmark, with sparsely furnished rooms that beautifully highlight its many architectural quirks.

Just off Salling's northern tip, yet still considered part of the peninsula, is the tiny island of **Fur**, connected by a ferry between Branden and the main settlement of **STENØRE**. Fur's entire north coast is taken up with dramatic **moler** cliffs, with pebbly fjord beaches at the bottom strewn with mussel shells. The cliffs are best explored on foot, and the **tourist office** in Stenøre (June to mid-Sept Mon–Fri & Sun 10am–4pm, Sat 9am–5pm; mid-Sept to May closed Sun; ☎97 59 30 53, ⓦwww.fursund.dk) hands out free pamphlets detailing the demarcated hiking trails. It also rents out bikes (60kr per day) which, if you don't have your own transport, will come in handy, as the only bus on Fur (no #42 from Skive) merely does a small circuit of the island's southern half. On your ride or hike, be sure to make your way toward **Anshede** on the western tip where, just outside the settlement, the Fur Bryghus **microbrewery**, Knudevej 3, offers beer made with water filtered through the volcanic ash and moler, giving it a special and very moreish taste. You can sample the beer in the brewery restaurant (☎97 59 30 60, ⓦwww.furbryghus.dk; closed Jan–March), which does a delicious Sunday buffet lunch (169kr) using mainly local produce, and à la carte lunch the rest of the week. If the cliffs have sparked an interest in moler and Fur's unique geology, you might want to head over to the east coast to **NEDERBY**, where the **Fur Museum**, Nederby 28 (daily: April to mid-June & Sept–Oct noon to 4pm; mid-June to Aug 10am–5pm; 35kr; ⓦwww.furmuseum.dk), has a vast collection of rare fossils – plants, fish, birds and insects – and a small exhibit about Fur.

If you want to **stay** here, try the atmospheric *Fur Strand Hotel* (☎97 57 85 00, ⓦwww.furstrandhotel.dk; ⓺) in Stenøre, which has eight beautiful en-suite rooms, and an excellent restaurant (closed Oct–Easter) featuring live folk-music evenings now and again.

Struer and Herning

Thanks to the presence of hi-fi giant Bang & Olufsen in **Struer** and the country's textile industry in **Herning**, the central portion of western Jutland comprises the island's industrial heartland, but commerce aside, its vast open heathland and pine forests are hardly overrun by development with the main towns well spread out. Transport in this region is fairly easy. Fast intercity and slower regional trains (from Vejle and Fredericia respectively) connect the two towns, and there are also regional trains from Thy to Struer.

Struer

Before the arrival of Bang & Olufsen in 1925 (see box opposite), **STRUER** was just another fjord town with a working harbour. Today, it's a modern, thriving place with a host of sleek buildings – not least Bang & Olufsen's eye-catching glass-fronted centre on Hjermvej. That said, the only real reason to visit is to see the snazzy underground glass pyramid extension of the **Struer Museum**, Søndergade 23 (March–Oct daily 10am–4pm; 60kr; ⓦwww.struermuseum.dk), entirely devoted to Bang & Olufsen and using lots of fabulous B&O products to detail the company's history and its effect on the town's – and the region's – development. The **tourist office** at Smedegade 7 (June–Aug Mon–Fri 10am–5pm, Sat 10am–1pm; Sept–May Mon–Fri 10am–4pm; ☎96 84 85 01, ⓦwww.visitnordvestjylland.dk) organizes four hugely popular, free, three-hour tours of the Bang & Olufsen factory during summer, which include the "BeoLiving" areas, where luxurious new designs are trialled. Tour dates are decided in the spring so you'll need to contact the tourist office in advance to secure a place. If all of this

Bang & Olufsen

The fantastic audiovisual systems made by **Bang & Olufsen** (B&O; ⓦ www.bang -olufsen.com) are the epitome of Denmark's tradition of excellence in design, and are world renowned both in terms of their stylistic excellence and their high quality – and, of course, their top-drawer prices. The company has its roots in Struer, first established here in the attic of **Svend Olufsen**'s family home where, in 1925, he and fellow engineer **Peter Bang** designed their first radio, which ran on mains rather than battery power (as was then the norm). From the very beginning the driving force behind their technological innovations was consumer convenience, and the radio was soon followed by the first-ever radio-gramophone, a button-operated mains radio, a radio with pre-set tuning buttons and the world's first stereo record player. All these products were huge commercial successes, and the company went from strength to strength; today Bang & Olufsen is a weighty international player with outlets in more than eighty countries. But unlike most other hi-tech industries, B&O has opted to keep the major part of its operations in Struer and the company is by far the town's biggest employer.

has left you hankering for your own B&O system – but you don't want to blow your savings – Bremdal Radio og TV at Bremdalvej 8 (ⓣ 97 85 33 66, ⓦ www .bremdal-radio.dk) sells fully refurbished second-hand kit, all perusable on its website. For a bite to **eat**, *Café Petit* at Fiskergade 2 (ⓣ 97 46 40 41, ⓦ www .cafepetit.dk; closed Sun) does delightful club sandwiches, bagels, omelettes and wraps for lunch. And should you want a **bed** for the night, the modern *Grand Hotel*, right in the centre at Østergade 24 (ⓣ 97 85 04 00, ⓦ www .struergrandhotel.dk; ❼), has stylish rooms fully kitted out with B&O gear plus free wi-fi. Much cheaper is *Struer Vandrerhjem*, Fjordvej 12 (ⓣ 97 85 53 13, ⓦ www.struer-vandrerhjem.dk; doubles ❸), just off the bridge to Thy and near a child-friendly fjord beach. *Bremdal Camping* (ⓣ 97 85 16 50, ⓦ www .bremdal-camping.dk) is just next door. There's free **internet** access at Struer library at Smedegade 1.

Herning

About 50km southeast of Struer, and 38km west of Silkeborg (see p.215), the modern conference town of **HERNING** grew to its present size mainly because of its status as epicentre of the Danish textile industry, though the trappings of this – and, consequently, the town's attractions – are pretty much restricted to its outskirts rather than the thriving and compact commercial centre. In the industrial suburb of Birk (bus #19 or one stop on the train to Århus), **Birk Centerpark**, is an eldorado for the artistically and architecturally inclined. A long narrow green industrial estate, spanning from the railway tracks in the south to the old Silkeborg highway in the north, it's peppered with sculptures and holds some unusual and innovative buildings, some housing museums. Arriving from the Silkeborg road end in the north, the first of these is the **Carl-Henning Pedersen & Else Alfelts Museum** art museum, Birk Centerpark 1 (May–Oct Tues–Sun 10am–5pm; Nov–April Tues–Fri 10am–5pm, Sat & Sun noon–5pm; 50kr for joint ticket with HEART; ⓦ www.chpeamuseum.dk), dedicated to two founding members of the CoBrA art movement (see p.97) and with a permanent exhibit displaying only their work. The colourful ceramic tiles by Carl-Henning Pedersen that cover the circular museum building – and the circular wall of the large round inner courtyard next door – are a good prelude to what is shown inside. The building is from 1965, and was designed by C.F. Møller for the Angli shirt factory. The factory's founder, Aage Damgaard, was a patron of the arts and invested heavily in local art during the factory's existence. Behind the building, the shrub-encircled **sculpture park** was originally designed as a recreational area for the factory workers at Angli, and holds a host of modern pieces. Aage Damgaard's extensive collection was eventually merged with that of the local art council to form the collection now displayed in the spectacular new **HEART** (Art Museum; May–Oct Tues–Sun 10am–5pm; Nov–April Tues–Fri 10am–5pm, Sat & Sun noon–5pm; 50kr for joint ticket with Carl-Henning Pedersen & Else Alfelts Museum; Ⓦ www.herningkunstmuseum.dk) across the street. Opened in 2009, the unusual building was designed in Damgaard's spirit with textured white fabric walls and flapping shirtsleeve-shaped wings. Inside, the contemporary collection includes an especially good section on the CoBrA movement. Next door, the unusual concrete building that looks like a collection of old-fashioned air-conditioning units was designed by Jørn Utzon (see p.248) as a prototype unit for a larger school complex in the area; it is now a private home so you can't go inside. Heading southwards through the park, you'll pass many more beautiful buildings housing educational facilities and innovative industry, and eventually reach the enormous, awe-inspiring cast-iron sculpture, *Elia*, which spurts fire roughly every nineteen days, and has pillars that attract lightning and resonate it back out into the sky – a truly mind-boggling piece. Check Ⓦ www.elia.dk to see when it last went off.

Thanks to Herning's status as a conference town there are plenty of places **to stay**, though none comes cheap. You'll get most for your money at the small, family-run *Hotel Vester*, Engdahlsvej 7B (Ⓣ 97 22 14 22, Ⓦ www.hotel-vester .dk; ❻), within easy access of Birk Centerpark (bus #19). **Trains** from Århus, Vejle, Skjern and Struer stop at Herning station, south of the centre on Banegårdspladsen, and there's a fast motorway linking it with Ikast en route from Silkeborg. Herning's **tourist office**, Torvet 8 (Mon–Fri 10am–5pm, Sat 10am–1pm; Ⓣ 96 27 22 22, Ⓦ www.visitherning.com), can help with canoe rental (300kr per day, plus 100kr to transport it back to Herning), should you be tempted by a trip down Store Å towards Nissum Fjord.

Ringkøbing and around

The ancient fjord town of **Ringkøbing**, on the inner banks of Ringkøbing Fjord, can thank the weather for its somewhat turbulent history. Its first major growth spurt occurred in 1100, when sand drifts closed off Limfjorden's outlet in the north, halting all transport into Limfjordslandet via the fjord (see p.267) and allowing Ringkøbing (with its narrow outlet from the fjord to the open sea at Nymindegab) a piece of the trade action. The town soon became one of west Jutland's most important harbours, serving uplands as far afield as Holstebro, Lemvig and Viborg, but with wind and weather constantly changing the shape of the coastline, the gap at Nymindegab gradually narrowed and trade moved to Ribe and Hjertling. By 1825, Ringkøbing's role as an export harbour came to a complete halt when the Limfjorden outlet reopened after a bad storm, and even though a new access point was opened up at Hvide Sande in the early nineteenth century (and protected and regulated with a sluice), Ringkøbing morphed into a market town and hub for the region's tourism. Ringkøbing's narrow **Holmsland Klit** strip of sand attracts visitors – mostly Germans – in their thousands, while the area around **Hvide Sande** is equally popular and a prime territory for water sports. There's also plenty on offer away from the beach, with a lovely bird sanctuary to the south of Ringkøbing, Tipperne Nature Reserve.

Ringkøbing

A pretty town with a compact walkable centre and a small harbour, **RINGKØ-BING** is notable for its amazing views of the fjord, which looks so vast from here it's hard not to assume that you're looking out to sea. Despite its long history, it's not a particularly sizeable place, and apart from enjoying the view, there's not much to detain you, though it's a good base for exploring this part of the coast, with most public transport hereabouts passing through town. You might want to have a quick look at the **Ringkøbing Museum**, near the harbour at Herningvej 4 (Jan–June & Sept–Oct Mon–Thurs noon–4pm, Sat 10am–2pm; July–Aug Mon–Sat 11am–5pm; Nov & Dec Mon–Sat noon–5pm; 40kr; ⓦwww.riskmus.dk), where, alongside an informative section on Ringkøbing's turbulent history, there's a small, quirky collection of knick-knacks dating back to the early days of Greenland explorations, and a genuine cast-iron chastity belt.

There is not a huge choice when it comes to **accommodation** in Ringkøbing itself; most visitors either rent holiday homes or stay at one of the beach hotels. The two best places in town, at different ends of the scale, are the romantic *Hotel Ringkøbing*, Torvet 18 (☎97 32 00 11, ⓦwww.hotelringkobing.dk; ❼), an old wood-beamed affair on the central town square with a range of atmospheric rooms with free internet access; and the *Ringkøbing Vandrerhjem* **hostel**, Kirkevej 28 (☎97 32 24 55, ⓦwww.rofi.dk; dorms 150kr, doubles ❹), set within Rofi Centret, a modern sports and training centre on the northern outskirts, off the road to Holstebro (bus #15 then a short walk from Rindum Gymnasium). The **tourist office** on Torvet (Mon–Fri 9.30am–4pm, Sat 10am–1pm; ☎70 22 70 01, ⓦwww.visitvest.dk) has a long list of agents renting holiday homes. What Ringkøbing lacks in accommodation, it makes up for in good **places to eat**. The harbour is lined by a number of informal and excellent seafood shacks, including the slightly upmarket *Café Kræs*, Ved Fjorden 2B (☎97 32 42 88), which offers delicious fish balls with rémoulade (65kr) on the lunch menu and mains such as fish of the day fried in butter with all the trimmings (185kr) for dinner. Of the more formal cafés and restaurants near Torvet, *Restaurant Torvestuen* at *Hotel Ringkøbing* does a beautiful herring platter for lunch (89kr) and the likes of fried plaice (159kr) and traditional apple tart (35kr) for dinner. **Trains** from Esbjerg, Århus and Struer stop at the train station, just northeast of the centre; the regional bus station is further along on the same street.

South of Ringkøbing

South of Søndervig and lining the coast for some 35km, the **Holmsland klit** dunes separating Ringkøbing Fjord from the North Sea have a magical, almost surreal feel as you travel along the narrow road on top of them. The holiday feel proper doesn't start until you reach the town of **Hvide Sande**, built up around the lock that controls the gap into the fjord. **Watersports** are the order of the day here, from windsurfing and kite-surfing to waterskiing and wave-riding, and you can have a go either in the calm, shallow waters of the fjord or along the wild west coast. West Wind (ⓦwww.westwind.dk) is the best bet for lessons and kit rental (175kr per 3hr); it has two outlets on the banks of Ringkøbing Fjord, south of the sluice at Sønder Klitvej 1 (☎97 31 28 99) and north of it at Gytjevej 15 (☎97 31 25 99).

South of Hvide Sande, the coast road takes you past the southern end of the marshy **Tipperne** peninsula, which pokes up into Ringkøbing Fjord and has been designated a bird sanctuary in its entirety. To cause the least possible disturbance to the birds, it's open to the public only for a few hours on Sundays outside the breeding season (Feb–March & Sept–Nov 10am–noon; April–Aug 8–10am; free), and you're not allowed to stop on the road leading to the large birdwatchers' observation tower by the fjord. From here, there's a two-kilometre signposted circular hiking trail through the marshes. Although the hours are awkward, it's well worth visiting, as the birdlife within the reserve is incredibly varied, with ruff and dunlin the two most important species.

Hvide Sand makes a great base if you want to spend time on the beach. The basic *Hvide Sande Sømandshjem*, Bredgade 5 (℡ 97 31 10 33, Ⓦ www.hssh.dk; ❻) is the best-value place to **stay**, with sparkling en-suite rooms and an excellent **restaurant** serving smørrebrød at lunch, and a daily special (95kr) plus a range of filling mains at dinner. Otherwise, for beautifully prepared fresh fish, head north of the sluice to ⚒ *Restaurant Lygten*, Nørregade 53 (℡ 97 31 63 03), which doubles as a fishmonger and chandler. **Bus** #58 runs from Ringkøbing to Hvide Sande and Tipperne along Holmsland klit.

Esbjerg and around

With a ferry connection to **ESBJERG** from Harwich in the UK and budget flights from Aberdeen, west Jutland's only city has gained something of a reputation as a weekend-break destination. If this is your first view of the country, bear in mind it's an entirely untypical one. Esbjerg is a baby by Danish standards: purpose-built as a deep-water harbour during the nineteenth century, it went on to become one of the world's biggest fishing ports. Nowadays, it's used as a supply point for the North Sea oil industry and holds a large fish-oil factory, though it does maintain some of its original Victorian-era charm, and handsome townhouses abound. There's plenty to fill your time should you find yourself staying here a few days, most notably the **Esbjerg Kunstmuseum** and the **Fiskeri og Søfartsmuseet**. The city also makes a great base from which to explore the surrounding area, particularly the superb beaches on the island of **Fanø**, a short ferry ride away, and the vast open landscapes around **Blåvands Huk**, Denmark's most westerly point.

Arrival, information and accommodation

The Esbjerg **tourist office**, at Skolegade 33 (mid-June to Aug Mon–Fri 10am–5pm, Sat 10am–2.30pm; Sept to mid-June Mon–Fri 10am–5pm, Sat 10am–1pm; ℡ 75 12 55 99, Ⓦ www.visitesbjerg.dk), on a corner of the main square, Torvet, can give you all the practical information you might need, as well as leaflets describing a short self-guided walking tour of the city's early twentieth-century buildings, and three longer round-trip cycling routes around the area. The **passenger harbour** is a well-signposted fifteen-minute walk from the centre (bus #5), and trains depart to and from Copenhagen, Århus, Fredericia and Struer via Ringkøbing from the **train station** on Jernbanegade. Long-distance buses arrive at the **bus terminal** further up the road. Esbjerg **airport** (Ⓦ www.esbjerg-lufthavn.dk) is 9km northeast of the city centre. Bus #8 leaves hourly from the bus terminal and costs 24kr one-way. There's free **internet** access at the library at Nørregade 19.

If you're staying, the tourist office has a list of private **accommodation**; otherwise the following options are the best of the bunch.

Ansgar Skolegade 36 ℡ 75 12 82 44, Ⓦ www
.hotelansgar.dk. Central mid-range hotel with 52
comfortable rooms – each one slightly different to
the next – a homely atmosphere and free wi-fi. ❼
Hotel Bell-In Skolegade 45 ℡ 75 12 01 22,
Ⓦ www.bell-in.dk. Above a Chinese restaurant, this
is a good, central, low-priced option with some

rooms sharing bathrooms. ❺
Britannia Torvet ℡ 75 13 01 11, Ⓦ www.britannia
.dk. Plush, modern place on the central square,
with furniture created by Danish design legend
Arne Jacobsen – stylish Swan chairs and sofas –
as well as free parking and serious reductions at
weekends. ❽

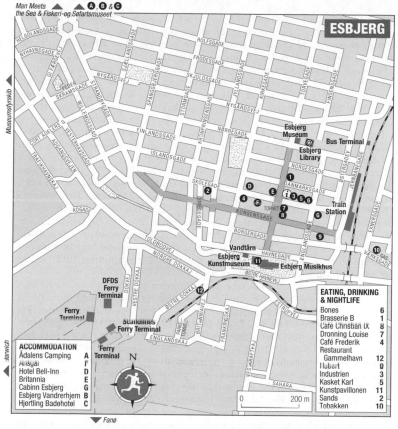

Man Meets ▲ ▲ **Ⓐ,Ⓑ & Ⓒ**
the Sea & Fiskeri-og Søfartsmuseet

ESBJERG

Museumsfyrskib ◄

◄ Harwich

ACCOMMODATION
Ådalens Camping	A
Ansgar	F
Hotel Bell-Inn	D
Britannia	E
Cabinn Esbjerg	G
Esbjerg Vandrerhjem	B
Hjertling Badehotel	C

EATING, DRINKING & NIGHTLIFE
Bones	6
Brasserie B	1
Café Christian IX	8
Dronning Louise	7
Café Frederik	4
Restaurant Gammelhavn	12
Hubert	9
Industrien	3
Kasket Karl	5
Kunstpavillonen	11
Sands	2
Tobakken	10

▼ Fanø

0   200 m

Cabinn Skolegade 14 ☎75 18 16 00,
ⓦwww.cabinn.com. Twin-towered hotel,
with a mixture of simple, inexpensive cabin-style
rooms and more pricey traditional hotel accommodation, all with free wi-fi. ❸
Danhostel Esbjerg Gammel Vardevej 80 ☎75
12 42 58, ⓦwww.esbjerg-danhostel.dk. The
town's former Maritime School and now a comfy
hostel, a 25min walk north of the centre (or bus
#4 from the train station) with dorms (180kr) and
some doubles ❹. Closed mid-Dec to mid-Jan.

Hjerting Badehotel ☎75 11 70 00, ⓦwww
.hotelhjerting.dk. If the beach is the draw, this
recently reopened traditional beach hotel 20min
north of the centre on bus #3 offers luxury galore
as well as fabulous sea views. ❽
Ådalens Camping Gudenåvej 20 ☎75 15 88 22,
ⓦwww.adal.dk. A well-equipped campsite with
cabins sleeping two (396kr) and four (486kr), 6km
north of Esbjerg along the Sædding Strandvej
coast road, and reached by bus #1 from the train
station.

The City

The best place to get your bearings – and appreciate how small a city Esbjerg is
– is from the top of the **Vandtårn** (Water Tower; June to mid-Sept daily
10am–4pm; April–May & mid-Sept to Oct Sat & Sun 10am–4pm; 15kr), a short
walk from the harbour towards the centre at Havnegade 22. There are sweeping
views of the harbour and surrounding marshes, and on a good day you can see as
far as Fanø. A small exhibit inside details the tower's history. Next door at
Havnegade 18–20, **Esbjerg Musikhus** (☎76 10 90 00, ⓦwww.mhe.dk) shares a

grand entrance and foyer with the town's art museum. The latter houses two concert halls where a wide range of music is performed – from classical to contemporary – and the fascinating modern building is an attraction in itself, designed under the direction of Jørn Utzon (see p.248) and an enthralling piece of modern architecture, resembling a giant concrete tomb surrounded by massive white flowers. The **Esbjerg Kunstmuseum** next door (daily 10am–4pm; 40kr) includes a modest collection of contemporary pieces, its highlight being some huge steel plates splattered in the blood of their creator, Danish *enfant terrible* Christian Lemmerz. In recent times it also exhibited – to much hand-wringing – Lemmerz's gory collection of dead pigs, and a forum on sex and pornography. As an unusual feature, the museum stores in the basement are open to the public. Filed away in order of purchase (with two boxes of index cards listing what's there) are paintings by Danish modern artists such as Asgar Jorn and Richard Mortensen, which you're free to pull out and study. To get a sense of the city's newness, you might want to drop into the **Esbjerg Museum**, Torvegade 45 (June–Aug daily 10am–4pm; Sept–May Tues–Sun 10am–4pm; 30kr, free Wed; ⓦ www.esbjergmuseum.dk), where the meatiest of the few displays recalls the so-called "American period" of the 1890s, when Esbjerg's rapid growth matched that of the US goldrush towns – albeit that the masses came here in search of herring rather than gold. The museum also houses an impressive collection of amber that includes some ancient jewellery.

If the Musikhus has left you in the mood for more aesthetic appreciation, take a bus (#3 or #8 from the train station) out along the coastal road until you arrive at the four nine-metre-high ghostly, chalk-white figures known as the **Mennesket ved Havet** (*Man Meets the Sea*). Put in place in 1995 by artist Sven Wiig Hansen, this grand piece of public art reflects on Esbjerg's relationship to the sea, with four temple-like rigid figures sitting in a line looking out over the waves. With the beach in the foreground and reflected light from the water making the figures look almost luminous, it provides an excellent photo opportunity. Just around the corner on Tarphagevej is the wonderful **Fiskeri og Søfartsmuseet** (Fisheries and Maritime Museum; daily: July–Aug 10am–6pm; Sept–May 10am–5pm; 85kr; ⓦ www.fimus.dk), where you can cast an eye over the old boats and other vestiges of the early Esbjerg fishing fleet. This is an excellent place to take the kids, not least because of the adjoining Sealarium, part of a seal research centre (feeding times 11am and 2.30pm). Some dark and spooky German wartime bunkers and an old working port – rebuilt brick by brick – make up the rest of this engaging museum.

With an hour to kill before your boat leaves, nip around the harbour to the **Museumsfyrskib** (Lightship Museum: May–Sept daily 10am–4pm; 20kr), which gives a vivid impression of the North Sea lightshipman's lot.

Eating, drinking and nightlife

Esbjerg's **eating** options are fairly limited for those on a tight budget, though the usual run of hot-dog grills and bakeries is scattered throughout the city. In terms of **nightlife**, the city is geared to the thousands of sailors – many of them English – who pass through this busy port. There are strip bars on Skolegade, but these can get quite rowdy and aren't recommended for the fainthearted. If you've just arrived from Britain and want to make a more gentle transition to Danish culture (and prices), sip a beer or two at one of the city's pubs such as *Kasket Karl* at Skolegade 29, or the popular *Hubert* at Kongensgade 10 which features over seventy varieties of beer plus live blues and jazz. For more live music, check out what's on at *Tobakken* (ⓣ75 18 00 00, ⓦ www.tobakken.dk), the city's large multifaceted concert venue at Gasværksgade 2, or head for *Industrien* (ⓣ75 13 61 66, ⓦ www.cafeindustrien.dk), Skolegade 27, which has DJs and live music as well as a bar and café.

Cafés and restaurants

Bones Skolegade 17 ⊤75 13 61 18, Ⓦwww
.bones.dk. This dependable chain offers decent
value, with dishes such as mouthwatering
barbecue ribs for 129kr, burgers for 119kr and
steak with all the trimmings from 139kr. Lunchtime
prices are substantially cheaper.

Brasserie B Torvegade 14 ⊤75 13 01 11,
Ⓦwww.britannia.dk. On the ground floor of *Hotel
Britannia*, this brasserie, bar and café has a large
terrace with a popular grill buffet on sunny summer
days. Otherwise, a good range of excellent seafood
dishes (from 195kr) and the 99kr herring lunch
platter are also worth sticking around for.

Café Christian IX Torvet 17 ⊤75 12 94 00,
Ⓦwww.chr9.dk. Popular café on Esbjerg's main
square, good for brunch, lunch, salads and
sandwiches, or just a coffee. In the evening beer
and cocktails takes centre stage, with the
occasional fun cabaret or live music act playing in
the basement.

Café Frederik Skolegade 46 ⊤75 12 02 33,
Ⓦwww.cafefrederik.dk. Small, French-style café
which starts with brunch from 11am (10.30 at
weekends) and continues with well prepared
omelettes, soups, sandwiches and salads (from
89kr) throughout the day, culminating in an
evening grill menu (from 179kr) Also the venue for
regular and hugely popular drag shows costing
289kr including dinner.

Dronning Louise Torvet 19 ⊤75 13 13 44,
Ⓦwww.dr-louise.dk. A large, glitzy place with
outdoor seating on the city's main square, with a
good selection of local and imported beers and an
extensive café menu that includes a proper English
fried breakfast for 79kr; salads and sandwiches
and a range of more substantial evening meals
(from 149kr) are also available. Live music every
Thurs, and DJs Fri and Sat.

🎿 **Kunstpavillonen** Havnegade 20 ⊤75 12
64 95 Ⓦwww.josef-kunsten.dk. Set upstairs
in the Esbjerg Kunstmuseum building with great
views of Esbjerg harbour, specialities here include
the excellent lunchtime herring and cheese platter
(148kr); the French-style three-course dinner
(300kr) draws in a well-heeled crowd. Closed Sat,
and Sun for dinner.

Restaurant Gammelhavn Britanniavej 5 ⊤76 11
90 00, Ⓦwww.gammelhavn.dk. Set in the old dock
area, this outstanding restaurant does a five-course
gourmet menu (595kr) featuring unusual combinations such as braised sweetbreads served with
smoked potatoes and mocha sauce. There's a
more run-of-the-mill à la carte menu at lunch.

🎿 **Sands** Skolegade 60 ⊤75 12 02 07,
Ⓦwww.sands.dk. Excellent for traditional
Danish food and service – try the daily special for
99kr, or the lunchtime smørrebrød platter for 159kr.
Closed Sun.

Around Esbjerg: Fanø and Blåvands Huk

From Esbjerg it's a straightforward ferry trip to **Fanø**, a long, flat island at the
northern end of the Wadden Sea (see p.200) with superb beaches that draw
German holidaymakers in droves. Fanøtrafikken ferries (⊤33 15 15 15, Ⓦwww
.fanoetrafikken.dk; 35kr return) run frequently between Esbjerg and the island's
main village, **Nordby**, where the **tourist office** at the harbour (July–Aug Mon–
Fri 9am–5pm, Sat & Sun 10am–4pm; Sept–June Mon–Fri 10am–5pm, Sat
10am–1pm; ⊤75 16 26 00, Ⓦwww.visitfanoe.dk) has information on accommodation and the few sights (a couple of fairly ordinary local museums and a
windmill). Of the island's eight **campsites**, the best is *Feldberg Strand Camping*
(⊤75 16 36 80, Ⓦwww.feldbergcamping.dk), Kirkevej 39, on the west-coast
Rindby Strand beach.

The other worthwhile trip out of town is a visit to Denmark's most westerly
point and the northern tip of the Wadden Sea (see p.200), **Blåvands Huk**, some
40km northwest of Esbjerg and reachable by bus #40. The road curves around the
Ho Bugt bay area and ends abruptly at the 39-metre-high Blåvands Huk **lighthouse** (daily May–Oct 10am–5pm, Nov–April 10am–3pm; 20kr). From the top
of the lighthouse, you get a stunning view of the desolate surrounding landscape
and the unusually wide sandy **beaches** below. To the north are wild windswept
west-coast beaches and to the southeast, tucked under a finger of land known as
Skallingen, are more sedate and shallow child-friendly beaches, protected by the
world's largest sea wind turbine park at Horns Rev. Blåvands Huk and Skallingen
mark the northernmost reaches of the Wadden Sea tidal flat area stretching down

via Germany to Holland and providing essential breeding and nesting ground for birds; on the Ho Bugt side of Skallingen, there's a good chance of spotting dunlin and bartailed godwit, especially during spring and autumn. If you want to **stay** by one of the country's best beaches, the best option is *Hvidbjerg Strand Camping*, Hvidbjerg Strandvej (☎75 27 90 40, ⓦ www.hvidbjerg.dk), on the Skallingen side of the lighthouse.

Travel details

Trains

Esbjerg to: Copenhagen (9 daily; 3hr 15min); Herning (5 daily; 2hrs); Kolding (1–3 hourly; 1hr); Ribe (1–3 hourly; 30min); Ringkøbing (hourly; 1hr 20min); Struer (hourly; 2hr 15); Århus (10 daily; 4hr).
Herning to: Copenhagen (9 daily; 3hr 45min); Esbjerg (5 daily; 2hr); Fredericia (hourly; 1hr 15min); Ringkøbing (7 daily; 1hr); Silkeborg (2 hourly; 45min); Struer (1–2 hourly; 45min); Vejle (hourly; 1hr); Århus (1–2 hourly; 1hr 30min).
Ringkøbing to: Esbjerg (hourly; 1hr 20min); Herning (7 daily; 1hr); Struer (hourly; 1hr); Århus (8 daily; 3hr 15min).
Struer to: Copenhagen (9 daily; 4hr 30min); Esbjerg (hourly; 2hr 15min); Herning (1–2 hourly; 45min); Ringkøbing (hourly; 1hr); Skive (1–2 hourly; 30min); Thisted (12 daily; 1hr 30min); Århus (hourly; 2hr).
Skive to: Copenhagen (2 daily; 5hr); Struer (1–2 hourly; 30min); Viborg (1–2 hourly; 30min); Århus (1–2 hourly; 1hr 45min).
Thisted to: Struer (12 daily; 1hr 30min).

Buses

Esbjerg to: Frederikshavn via Aalborg and Viborg (2–3 daily; 5 hr); Ribe (11 daily; 45min).
Hanstholm to: Klitmøller (8 daily; 15min); Thisted (1–2 hourly; 45min).
Klitmøller to: Hanstholm (8 daily; 15min); Thisted (8 daily; 30min).
Nykøbing Mors to: Skive (1–2 hourly; 45min); Thisted (hourly; 30min).
Ringkøbing to: Hvide Sande (hourly; 30min).
Skive to: Stenøre, Fur (hourly; 1hr); Nykøbing Mors (1–2 hourly; 45min).
Thisted to: Aalborg (hourly; 1hr 45); Hanstholm (1–2 hourly; 45min); Klitmøller (8 daily; 30min); Nykøbing Mors (hourly; 30min).

Ferries

Esbjerg to: Nordby, Fanø (12–24 daily; 12min).
Salling to: Stenøre, Fur (20–24 daily; 5min).

Contexts

Contexts

History

S pend any significant time in Denmark and it'll soon strike you that the country's history is entirely disproportionate to its size. Nowadays a small nation, Denmark ("Danmark") and the many monarchs who have ruled it have nonetheless played a central role in key periods of European history, firstly as the home of the Vikings, later as a medieval superpower and, most recently, as one of the wealthiest members of the EU.

Early days to the Vikings

The earliest reliable archeological evidence of **human habitation** on the land that currently comprises Denmark dates to a period some 50,000 years ago – though it's unlikely that any settlements of this time were permanent, as much of the land was still covered by ice. Arguably the most significant change in early Danish history occurred during the Neolithic period (3000–1500 BC), when forests were cleared, land cultivation and livestock-herding became a staple of human life and locals instituted a series of rituals and religious practices to temper their hard lives.

By the advent of the Iron Age in 500 BC, conflicts between neighbouring communities to secure land had become common, and when the Roman Empire began its advances into northern Germany in 5 AD, hitherto ad-hoc fighting units were effectively organized into small armies, equipped with horsemen, archers, soldiers and sophisticated weaponry.

Around 500 AD, a tribe from Sweden calling themselves *Dani* ("**Danes**") migrated southwards and took control of what became known as **Danmark**, an area of land that at that time included Jutland, Funen and Zealand, as well as Skåne in southern Sweden and the region surrounding the Oslofjord in Norway. The majority of people who lived on this land were farmers, though there was a growing class of merchants and skilled peasant sailors in and around Viken, a small bit of land flanking the Oslofjord and a provenance that led these hearty men to become known as Víkingar ("Vikings"). They began leading raids to the coasts of the Hebrides, Brittany and Frisia, and further afield to Iceland, Greenland and even the Caspian Sea. Disgruntled when Scandinavian rulers began exacting large tariffs on the sales and purchases of goods to arrive through Danish waters, they opted to follow the trading routes to the source of the wealth entering the country. Their contact with Western European traders had familiarized them with ship-building techniques and given them glimpses of the many internal conflicts plaguing numerous European kingdoms – political feuds and schisms that they were later able to exploit and profit from. While the common mythology of the Vikings locates them as burly, helmeted barbarians ruthlessly engaging in bloody battle, raiding churches, kidnapping local women and generally wreaking havoc, such depictions tend to disregard the **enduring influence** they had on trade, language, and the political and cultural institutions of the countries and peoples with whom they came into contact.

Back on the home front, the **first Danish state** had been established by King Godfred around 800, though a century later the Norwegian chieftain **Harthacnut** conquered Jutland and began to expand eastwards over the rest of Denmark, establishing the foundations of the modern Danish nation – the oldest in Europe. It wasn't until the baptism of **Harald Blåtand**, commonly known to the rest of the world as **Bluetooth,** that Christianity became the state religion, even if his reasons for doing so (to stave off imminent invasion by French and Germans) weren't entirely spiritual. In 990, Harald's son **Sweyn I** ("Forkbeard") joined the Norwegians in attacks on Britain, whose puppet king at the time was the aptly named Ethelred "the Unready"; by then England was seen as a potential source of income through the exaction of silver tribute. By the time of Sweyn's death in 1014, England was all but under Danish rule, though it took a further two years of warring on the part of Sweyn's son, **Knud** (Canute), before he was installed as King of England, marrying Ethelred's widow into the bargain. By 1033, the Danes thus controlled a sizeable empire around the North Sea, including all of England and Normandy, most of southern Sweden and, of course, Denmark itself, dominating trade in the Baltic. This was the zenith of Viking power, and it's from this period that we get the first historical record of the small fishing village of Havn (literally "Haven" or "Harbour"), later to become København or **Copenhagen**, when it was mentioned in 1043 after King Magnus sought refuge there following his defeat in a sea battle in the Øresund. The last major Viking expedition took place in 1066, with Harald Harðráði losing to the king of England at the battle of Stamford Bridge.

The rise of the Church and the Valdemar era

During the eleventh and twelfth centuries, Denmark was weakened by violent **internal struggles**, not only between different would-be rulers but also among the Church, nobility and monarchy. Following the death of Sweyn II in 1074, two of his four sons, Knud and Harald, fought for the throne, with Harald (supported by the peasantry and the Church) emerging victorious. A mild and introspective individual, Harald III was nonetheless a competent monarch, his crowning achievement being the introduction of the first real Danish currency. He was constantly derided by Knud and his allies, however, and after his death in 1080 his brother became King Knud II. He made generous donations to the Church, but his introduction of higher taxes and the absorption of all unclaimed land into the realm enraged the nobility. The farmers of north Jutland revolted in 1086, forcing Knud to flee to Odense, where he was slain on the high altar of Skt Albani Kirke. The ten-year period of poor harvests that ensued was taken by many to be divine wrath, and there were reports of miracles occurring in Knud's tomb, leading to the murdered king's canonization in 1101.

It wasn't until the accession of Knud's right-hand man, **Valdemar I** (the Great), in 1157 that the country was once again united and freed of factional bickering. Valdemar strengthened the crown by ending the elective function of the *ting*, or local council, and shifting the power of election of the monarch to the Church. Technically, the *ting* still influenced the choice of king, but in practice hereditary succession became the rule. After Bishop Eskil's retirement, **Bishop Absalon** became Archbishop of Denmark, erecting a fortress at the fishing village of Havn (in 1254, it would become København, or "merchants' harbour") to counter the Wendish pirates, German-based groups that had previously raided the coast with impunity. Besides being a zealous churchman, Absalon possessed a sharp military mind and came to greatly influence Valdemar I and his successor, Knud IV. During this period, Denmark saw some of its best years, expanding to the south and east, and taking advantage of internal strife within Germany, with Havn seeing rapid economic and social development. In time, after Absalon's death and the succession of **Valdemar II**, Denmark controlled all trade along the south coast of the Baltic and in the North Sea west of the Ejder. Valdemar II was also responsible for subjugating Norway, and in 1219 he set out to conquer Estonia and take charge of Russian trade routes through the Gulf of Finland. (According to Danish legend, the red-and-white crossed *Dannebrog* – the world's oldest state flag – fell down from heaven during a battle in Estonia in that same year.)

Those years of expansion brought Denmark great prosperity, and the rule of law was concentrated in the monarch, rather than the more disparate *ting*. The king could still easily be brought to account, though: **Erik V**'s powers were limited by a *håndfæstning*, or charter, that included an undertaking for annual consultation with the **Danehof**, or Council of the Danish Realm – an institutional forum that assured the nobility a deciding voice in government, and one that was to survive as a major influence in the Danish government until 1660. In 1319, **Christoffer II** became king only after agreeing to an even sterner charter, which allowed for daily consultations with a *råd* – a council of nobles.

In 1332, Skåne, the richest Danish province, inflicted a final insult on Christoffer when its inhabitants revolted and transferred their allegiance to the Swedish king Magnus – though this was reclaimed within twenty years. In 1361, King **Valdemar IV** attacked and conquered Gotland, much to the annoyance of the Hanseatic League, a powerful Lübeck-based group of tradesmen who were using it as a Baltic trading base; they, in turn, took Copenhagen in 1369, dismantling Absalon's castle brick by brick, with the intention of ending Danish control of the Øresund once and for all. A number of anti-Danish alliances sprang up and the rest of the country was slowly plundered until peace was agreed in 1370 under the **Treaty of Stralsund**, guaranteeing trade for the Hanseatic partners by granting them control of castles along the west coast of Skåne for fifteen years and stipulating that the election of the Danish monarch had to be approved by the Hanseatic League – the peak of their power.

The Kalmar Union

Despite these temporary losses, Denmark's fortunes continued to prosper, aided and abetted by the creation in 1397 of the **Kalmar Union**, an alliance between the three nations aimed at countering the Hanseatic League's influence on regional trade which allowed for a Scandinavian federation sharing the same monarch and foreign policy, while allotting each country its own domestic legislation. Unhappy with the Holstein privateers who were interfering with their trade, the Hanseatic League initially supported King **Erik VII** ("of Pomerania"), though his harsh trade policies favouring Danish merchants over Hanseatic traders soon led to a war with the League, resulting in Erik imposing the **Sound Toll** (*Øresundstolden*) on shipping passing through the narrow strip of sea off the coast of Helsingør in 1429. The toll became an endless source of revenue that would underpin Denmark's fortunes for the next four centuries.

For the time being, however, the conflicts with the Holsteiners and the Hanseatic League had badly drained financial resources, resulting in the election of **Christoffer III**, a judicious king who granted the Hanseatic League exemption from the Sound Toll and moved the Danish capital from ecclesiastical Roskilde to commercial Copenhagen in 1443; revenues from the toll allowed the city's merchants and taxmen to seize growing amounts of trade from the declining ports of the Hanseatic League and to establish itself as the principal harbour in the Baltic. The construction of Scandinavia's first **university** helped to establish the city as a cultural as well as administrative hub. Around the same time, the **Kronborg Slot**, just north at Helsingør, was built to control the Øresund and enforce payment of the toll, further entrenching Copenhagen's pre-eminence in the region.

The Reformation and Danish–Swedish conflicts

Frederik of Holstein-Gottorp (heir to half of Schleswig-Holstein) became King **Frederik I** in 1523, at which time there was a growing unease with the role of the Church in Denmark, especially with the power – and wealth – of its bishops. Frederik, while decidedly a Catholic, refused to take sides in religious disputes and did nothing to prevent the destruction of churches, well aware as he was of the groundswell of peasant support for Lutheranism. When he died in 1533, the fate of the **Reformation** hinged on which of his two sons would succeed him. The elder and more obvious choice was Christian, but his open support for Lutheranism set the bishops and nobles against him, while the younger son Hans, just 12 years old, was favoured by the Church and the aristocracy. The three-year **civil war** that thus ensued saw peasant uprisings across the country and a year-long siege of Copenhagen. Though the city's defensive ramparts held firm, many of its citizens starved to death or died of disease. The war ended in 1536 with Christian III on the throne, presiding over the new **Danish Lutheran Church**, with a constitution locating the king at its head and Lutheranism installed as the official state religion.

New trading routes across the Atlantic had reduced the power of the Hanseatic League, and Christian's young and ambitious successor, **Frederik II**, saw this as a chance to extend the borders of the Danish kingdom. Sweden, however, had its own expansionist designs, and the resulting **Seven Years' War** (1563–70) between the two countries caused widespread devastation and plunged the Danish economy into crisis. The predicament turned out to be short-lived: price rises in the south of Europe led to increasing Danish affluence, reflected in the rebuilding of Krogen fortress in Helsingør as the magnificent renaissance castle of Kronborg. By the time a 10-year-old **Christian IV** came to the throne in 1596, Denmark was a solvent and powerful nation, its capital now home to the largest naval force in Europe, with Sound Toll revenue providing a consistent source of income for royal purses. Known as the "Great Builder", Christian characterized his sixty-year reign with bold new town layouts and great architectural works, nearly doubling the size of Copenhagen by expanding the defensive fortifications to the north and reclaiming the island of Christianshavn to the east, helping the city to become a major European capital.

But the architectural vision of Christian was not matched by his political astuteness. As arch-rival Sweden's military strength grew, the Danes' steadily weakened, and in 1625 Christian IV took Denmark into the unsuccessful **Thirty Years' War**, defeat leading to increased taxes and rampant inflation. A worse fate awaited though: in 1657, during the reign of **Frederik III**, Denmark lost all its Swedish provinces in a short war ended at the **Treaty of Roskilde**, though monopolization of Baltic trade was, for the time being, thwarted for both countries.

Absolute monarchy

The conflict with Sweden and the loss of former territory left Denmark heavily in **debt**, and, with the financial and political power of the nobles of the *Danehof* slowly fading, the city's burghers decided that everyone, including the nobility, should pay the taxes needed. Frederik III reinstated the king as absolute monarch, removed all powers from the *Danehof*, and heralded a **new constitution** that bound him merely to uphold the Lutheran faith and ensure the unity of the kingdom. With noble influence on royal decision-making drastically reduced, Copenhagen

Danish colonies

As with many European nations, the discovery and development of trade routes with Asia, and the European settling of the Americas in the fifteenth century, inspired Denmark to establish and maintain a number of foreign **colonies**. These included settlements in South **India,** the Nicobar Islands in the eastern Indian Ocean, the **West African Gold Coast** (at Accra) as well as St Thomas, St John and St Croix in the **Caribbean**. The United States purchased these latter islands from Denmark in 1917 for $25 million after the abolition of slavery had sent many of them into economic ruin.

Closer to home, Denmark had been in control of the Faroe Islands, Greenland and Iceland after the **Treaty of Kiel** in 1814. Iceland won its soverignty from Danish rule in 1944; the eighteen **Faroe Islands** still maintain the status of autonomous region under the Danish Crown, while **Greenland** (*Kalaallit Nunaat*, or "land of men" in Greenlandic), meanwhile, was granted home rule in 1978, and in 2009 ushered in a new series of reforms designed to eventually secure independence from Denmark, including making an Inuit tongue the country's official language, and recognizing Greenlanders as a separate people from the Danes.

Both the Faroes and Greenland can be visited via regular **flights** from Copenhagen; for more information, visit ⓦ www.faroeislands.com and ⓦ www.greenland.com.

was made a free city, with commoners accorded the same privileges as nobles. Frederik III began a rebuild of the military forces and, following three minor wars with Sweden, managed to bring a more or less peaceful coexistence to Denmark.

In 1699, **Frederik IV** set about creating a Danish militia to make the country less dependent on foreign mercenaries – a force whose abilities were tested in the **Great Northern War** (1709–20). The two decades of peace that followed saw the arrival of **Pietism**, a form of Lutheranism that strove to renew the devotional ideal. Frederik embraced the doctrine towards the end of his life, and it was adopted in full by his son, **Christian VI**, who took the throne in 1730. He prohibited entertainment on Sunday, closed down Det Kongelige Teater, and made court life a sombre affair: attendance at church on Sundays became compulsory and confirmation obligatory. Meanwhile, in 1711, bubonic plague wiped out a third of Copenhagen's population, while two devastating **fires** in 1728 and 1795 forced the reconstruction of most of the city, during which the basis of the present-day street plan was established.

The Enlightenment

Despite the orthodox beliefs of Christian VI, Pietism was never widely popular, and by the 1740s its influence had waned considerably. The reign of his successor **Frederik V**, who took the throne in 1746, saw a great cultural awakening: grand buildings such as Amalienborg and Frederikskirke were erected in Copenhagen, and there was a new flourishing of the arts, noted in part by the founding of Det Kongelige Danske Kunstakademi ("The Royal Danish Academy of Art") in 1754. The king, perhaps as a reaction to the puritanism of his father, devoted himself to a life of pleasure and allowed control of the nation effectively to pass to the civil service. Political life enjoyed a period of relative stability, and, with their international influence significantly reduced by the ravages of the Great Northern War, the Danes adopted a position of **neutrality** – a position that saw the economy benefit as a consequence.

In 1766, **Christian VII** took the crown, but his unpredictable mental state and moods soon prevented him from carrying out even the bare minimum of official duties. Decision-making became dominated by a young German court physician close to the king, **Johann Friedrich Struensee** (see p.305), who arrogantly introduced a number of sweeping **reforms**: the Privy Council was stamped out, the Treasury became the supreme administrative organ, the death penalty was abolished and the press was freed from censorship.

Progressive though such moves may have seemed compared to other parts of Western Europe at the time, there was opposition from several quarters: merchants complained about the freeing of trade, and the burghers of Copenhagen were unhappy with their city losing its autonomy. Following well-founded rumours about a relationship between Struensee and the queen and multiple claims by the press that he was holding the monarch prisoner, a 1772 **coup** led by Frederik V's second wife, Juliane Marie of Brunswick, and her son Frederik, resulted in Struensee being arrested, tried and executed, while the dazed king was paraded before his cheering subjects. All those who had been appointed to office by Struensee were dismissed, and with anti-German sentiment rampant among many in the country, Danish was instituted as the language of the court and army, and in 1776 it was declared that no foreigner should be given a position in royal office.

The Napoleonic Wars and the Age of Liberalism

In the wider sphere, the country prospered through its dealings in the Far East, with Copenhagen consolidating its role as the new centre of Baltic trade, and the outbreak of the American War of Independence provided neutral Denmark with fresh commercial opportunities. But despite its improving domestic position, the country found itself once again embroiled in the mire of international power struggles with the outbreak of the **Napoleonic Wars** (1796–1815), reluctantly siding at first with the **League of Armed Neutrality** (Russia, Prussia and Sweden) in an attempt to stay out of the conflict between expansionist Britain and revolutionary France. Although this move initially had the effect of maintaining trading links across the Atlantic until the end of the war, the British, considering the league potentially hostile and fearing Danish sympathy with Napoleon's continental blockade, sent a fleet under Admiral Nelson to Copenhagen in 1801, damaging the powerful Danish navy and obliging them to withdraw from the agreement. The pact between France and Russia left Denmark in a difficult situation: to oppose this alliance would leave them exposed to a French invasion of Jutland, but to oppose the British and join with the French would adversely affect trade. In 1807, the British returned, worried that Napoleon's advancing armies would take over the newly rebuilt Danish fleet if they didn't, occupying Zealand and commencing a murderous three-day bombardment of Copenhagen that saw many of its finest buildings heavily damaged, before towing away what was left of the Danish fleet. Sweden had aligned with the British and was demanding the ceding of Norway if Denmark were to be defeated – which, under the **Treaty of Kiel**, was exactly what happened. With the loss of the Norwegian minority, the Danes had for the first time in several hundred years become a majority in their own country.

The Napoleonic Wars had destroyed Denmark's international prestige and left the country bankrupt, and the period up until 1830 was spent in recovery. Yet despite such an inauspicious beginning to the new century, Denmark managed to pull itself up quickly, nowhere more noticeably than in areas of cultural production, where a **national Romantic movement** had gained pace, under which for two decades the Danish arts flourished as they never had before (or since). **Hans Christian Andersen** (see p.159) charmed the children (and adults) of the world with his colourful fairytales about unfortunate and forgotten characters, while **Søren Kierkegaard** (see p.74) scandalized it with his philosophical works. At the same time, the nation's visual media reached new heights under the auspices of sculptor **Bertel Thorvaldsen** (see p.63), and C.W. Eckersberg, who led the emergence of the first entirely Danish school of painting. Social changes were in the air, too: in 1810, the theologian **N.F.S. Grundtvig** developed a new form of Christianity that was free of dogma and drew on the virtues espoused by the heroes of Norse mythology. In 1825, he left the intellectual circles of Copenhagen and travelled the rural areas to guide a religious revival, eventually modifying his earlier ideas in favour of a new faith in the wisdom of "the people" – something that was to colour the future liberal movement.

On the political front, there was trouble brewing in Danish-speaking **Schleswig** and German-speaking **Holstein**, which, in response to the wave of nationalism in France and Germany, were demanding their independence. A liberal movement grew among a group of Copenhagen scholars and its **first newspaper**, *Fædrelandet* ("The Fatherland"), appeared in 1834. By 1848, when **Frederik VII** took the throne, the liberals had organized themselves into the **National Liberal Party**, and the king signed a **new constitution** that made Denmark the most democratic country in Europe, guaranteeing freedom of speech, freedom of religious worship, and many other civil liberties. The king gave up the powers of an absolute monarch, and legislation was put in the hands of a *Rigsdag* (parliament), elected by popular vote and consisting of two chambers: the lower *Folketing* and upper *Landsting*.

Within Schleswig-Holstein, however, there was little faith that the equality granted to the people in the constitution would be upheld. The bickering between the disgruntled Danish royals who ruled the region and the Danish rulers in power in Copenhagen, meanwhile, had become emblematic of such conflicts between centre and periphery. The treaty ending a series of disastrous wars in 1864 resulted in Denmark ceding both Schleswig and Holstein to Germany, leaving the country smaller than it had been for centuries and dealing a substantial blow to Danish morale, with a third of its territory and two-fifths of its population lost. The ramifications of this historical moment should not be underestimated: with the loss of such territory, Denmark became for the first time in its history an **ethnically homogenous country**, and the nation began to assuage its sense of defeat by developing the ethos of being a proudly close-knit socio-cultural community.

A new constitution following the election of 1866 retained the procedure for election to the *Folketing*, but made the *Landsting* franchise dependent on land and money and allowed twelve of the 64 members to be selected by the king – a group affiliated with a more conservative Centre Party. The opposition was shortly combined into the **United Left**, which called for equal taxation, universal suffrage in local elections and more freedom for the farmers. The United Left became the majority within the *Folketing* in 1872.

The ideas of **revolutionary socialism** had begun percolating through the country in 1871 via a series of pamphlets edited by Louis Pio, and workers quickly began banding together, forming trade unions and workers' associations, while the intellectual Left also began to mobilize. A series of lectures delivered by Georg Brandes in Copenhagen cited Danish culture, in particular its literature, as dull and lifeless compared to that of other countries and called for fresh works that questioned and examined society, instigating a bout of literary attacks on institutions such as marriage, chastity and the family, and sparking a conservative backlash as factioned groups in the government formed themselves into the **United Right**.

The Danish capital, meanwhile, had been undergoing a massive transformation. In 1851, Copenhagen's external fortifications were demolished, finally allowing the cramped city to expand beyond its medieval limits and sowing the seeds for the new industrial era. Railways, factories and shipyards began to change the face of the city, which was gradually developing into a thriving **manufacturing centre**, while the new working-class districts of Nørrebro and Vesterbro were flung up, with Copenhagen's workers packed into slum tenements that would subsequently become hotbeds of left-wing political activity. The second half of the nineteenth century also saw the establishment of the Carlsberg Brewery, the rapid growth of the Royal Danish Porcelain factory and the founding of several recreational possibilities for the city's aspiring bourgeoisie, from the two main department stores, Magasin du Nord and Illums Bolighus, to Det Kongelige Teater and the City Zoo.

World War I and Parliamentary democracy

By the end of the nineteenth century the power of the right was in severe decline. The elections of 1901, under the new conditions of a secret ballot, saw the United Right reduced to the smallest group within the *Folketing* and heralded the beginning of **parliamentary democracy**, the government quickly ushering in a number of reforms, most notably a sliding-scale income tax and free schooling beyond the primary level. As the years went by, Social Democrat support increased, while the left, such as it was, became increasingly conservative. In 1905, a breakaway group formed the **Radical Left** (*Det Radikale Venstre*), politically similar to the English Liberals, whose alliance with the Social Democrats enabled the two parties to gain a large majority in the *Folketing* in the election of 1913, and a year later conservative control of the *Landsting* was ended. Social advances were made, but further domestic progress was halted by international events as Europe prepared for war.

Denmark had enjoyed good trading relations with both Germany and Britain in the years preceding **World War I**, and was keen not to be seen to favour either side in the hostilities. On the announcement of German mobilization, the now Radical-led cabinet, with the support of all the other parties, issued a **statement of neutrality** and was able to remain clear of direct involvement in the conflict. At the conclusion of the war, attention was turned again towards Schleswig-Holstein, and under the **Treaty of Versailles** it was decided that Schleswig should be divided into two zones for a referendum – in the northern zone a return to unification with Denmark was favoured by a large percentage, while the southern zone elected to remain part of Germany – and a new German–Danish border was drawn up just north of Flensburg. As many of the towns that remained in Denmark kept their large bilingual, pro-German minority – especially places such as Tønder and Åbenrå – strong German identities persisted, resulting in the growth of German-language schools and newspapers in the region.

High rates of unemployment and the success of the Russian Bolsheviks led to a series of strikes and demonstrations, the unrest coming to a head with the **Easter Crisis** of 1920. During March of that year, a change in the electoral system towards greater proportional representation was agreed in the *Folketing* but the prime minister, **Carl Theodore Zahle**, whose Radicals stood to lose support through the change, refused to implement it. The king, Christian X, responded by dismissing him and asking **Otto Liebe** to form a caretaker government to oversee the changes. The royal intervention, while technically legal, incensed the Social Democrats and the trade unions; the latter were already facing a national lockout by employers in response to demands for improved pay rates, and saw the king's act as an affront to the idea of a democratic parliamentary system. Perceiving the threat of a right-wing coup, the unions began organizing a general strike to begin after the Easter holiday, with a large republican demonstration held outside Amalienborg. On Easter Saturday, urgent negotiations between the king and the existing government concluded with an agreement that a mutually acceptable caretaker government would oversee the electoral change and a fresh election would immediately follow. Employers, fearful of the power the workers had shown, met many of the demands for higher wages.

The next government, dominated by the Radical Left, fortified existing social policies, and increased state contributions to union unemployment funds, and despite a general economic depression, major public works were funded over the coming years, such as the bridge between Funen and Jutland over the Lille Bælt, and the Stormstrømsbro, linking Zealand to Falster.

The Nazi occupation and World War II

When **World War II** broke out, Denmark again made efforts to remain neutral, this time in vain. While the country itself had little military significance for the Nazis, the sea off Norway was being used to transport iron ore from Sweden to Britain, and the fjords offered good shelter for a fleet engaged in a naval war in the Atlantic. To gain access to Norway, the Nazis planned an **invasion of Denmark**. At 4am on April 9, 1940, the German ambassador in Copenhagen informed Prime Minister Stauning that German troops were preparing to cross the Danish border and issued the ultimatum that unless Denmark agreed that the country could be used as a German military base – keeping control of its own affairs – Copenhagen would be bombed. To reject the demand was considered a postponement of the inevitable, and to save Danish bloodshed the government acquiesced at 6am. "They took us by telephone," lamented one Danish minister.

A national coalition government was formed that behaved according to protocol but gave no unnecessary concessions to the Germans. Censorship of the press and a ban on demonstrations were imposed, ostensibly intended to prevent the Nazis spreading propaganda. But these measures, like the swiftness of the initial agreement, were viewed by some Danes as capitulation and were to be a thorn in the side of the Social Democrats for years to come.

The government was reshuffled to include various non-parliamentary experts, but the German upped their demands, and within a matter of weeks, the krone was to be phased out and German currency made legal tender. Public reaction was naturally hostile, and groups of Danes began a systematic display of **antipathy to the Germans**. Children wore red, white and blue "RAF caps", Danish customers walked out of cafés when Germans entered, and the ban on demonstrations was flouted by groups who gathered to sing patriotic songs. On September 1, 1940, an estimated 740,000 Danes around the country gathered to sing the same song simultaneously. The king demonstrated his continued presence by riding on horseback each morning through Copenhagen. For its part, the Danish government continued its balancing act, knowing that failure to co-operate at least to some degree would lead to a complete Nazi takeover; it was with this in mind that Denmark signed the Anti-Comintern Pact, which made Communism illegal but allowed only Danish police to arrest Danish Communists. **Vilhelm Buhl**, who was appointed prime minister on May 3, 1942, had been an outspoken opponent of the signing of the

Anti-Comintern Pact and it was thought he might end the apparent appeasement. Instead, the tension between occupiers and occupied was to climax with Hitler's anger at the curt note received from Christian X in response to the Führer's birthday telegram. Although it was the king's standard reply, Hitler took the mere "thank you" as an insult and immediately replaced his functionaries in Denmark with hardliners who demanded a new pro-German government. In 1943, elections were called in an attempt to show that freedom of political expression could exist under German occupation. The government asked the public to demonstrate faith in national unity by voting for any one of the four parties in the coalition, and received overwhelming support in the largest-ever turnout for a Danish election.

Awareness that German defeat was becoming inevitable stimulated a wave of strikes throughout the country. Berlin declared a state of emergency in Denmark, and demanded that the Danish government comply – which it refused to do. Germany took over administration of the country, interning many politicians and requiring the king to appoint a cabinet from outside the *Folketing*. For the first time in Denmark, Germans were free to round up Danish Jews. A resistance movement was organized under the leadership of the **Danish Freedom Council**. Sabotage was carefully co-ordinated, and an underground army, soon comprising over 43,000 patriots, prepared to assist in the Allied invasion. In June 1944, rising anti-Nazi violence led to a curfew being imposed in Copenhagen and assemblies of more than five people being banned, to which workers responded with a spontaneous general strike. German plans to starve the city's inhabitants had to be abandoned after five days, and Copenhagen itself largely escaped the devastation suffered by other European cities. Denmark's two moments of glory during the war came with the **smuggling of seven thousand Jews to Sweden** to avoid their deportation to concentration camps, and later, during a British air raid on the Nazi headquarters at Rådhuspladsen, when many of the captured members of the Danish resistance were momentarily able to escape. Only 481 Danish Jews were sent to the prison camp at Theresienstadt, many of whom actually survived due to action on the part of both the Danish government and Church organizations. Moreover, unlike in other European countries, when the Jews returned to Denmark, they found their homes, pets, gardens and personal belongings had been cared for by their neighbours.

The postwar period

After the German surrender in May 1945, a **liberation government** was created, composed equally of pre-war politicians and members of the Danish Freedom Council, with Vilhelm Buhl as prime minister. While Denmark had been spared much of the infrastructural damage and devastation seen elsewhere in Europe, it did find itself besieged with massive economic problems and it soon became apparent that the liberation government, whose internal differences earned it the nickname "the debating club", could not function as such. In the ensuing election there was a swing to the Communists, and a minority Venstre government was formed.

Domestic issues soon came to be overshadowed by the international situation as the **Cold War** began. Denmark had unreservedly joined the United Nations in 1945, and had joined the IMF and World Bank to gain financial help in restoring its economy, with Marshall Plan aid bringing further assistance in 1947. As world power became polarized between East and West, the Danish government at first tried to remain impartial, but in 1947 agreed to join NATO – a total break with the established concept of Danish neutrality (though to this day, Danes remain largely opposed to nuclear weapons).

The years after the war were marked by much political manoeuvring among the Radicals, Social Democrats and Conservatives, resulting in many hastily called elections and a number of ineffectual compromise coalitions distinguished mainly by the level of their infighting. Working-class support for the Social Democrats steadily eroded, and support for the Communists was largely transferred to the new, more revisionist, **Socialist People's Party**. In spite of political wrangling, Denmark succeeded in creating one of the world's most successful **welfare states**, with a comprehensive programme of cradle-to-grave benefits, and a quality of life that soon ranked among the highest in the world. Social reforms, meanwhile, continued apace, not least in the 1960s, with the abandoning of all forms of censorship and the institution of cost-free abortion. Such measures are typical of more recent social policy, though Denmark's odd position between Scandinavia and the rest of mainland Europe still remains a niggling concern. In 1972, Denmark became the first Scandinavian member of the EC – Sweden, the second, didn't join until 1995 – though public enthusiasm remained lukewarm.

The fin de siècle

Copenhagen itself became the centre of attention when, in 1971, the old military base on the eastern side of Christianshavn was taken over by squatters, who created the "Free City" of **Christiania**. Initial, unsuccessful attempts by the police to clear the squatters were followed by a twelve-year trial period, after which the city was legally recognized, even to the point where "Pusherstreet" is now marked on official maps. Perhaps the biggest change in the 1970s, however, was the foundation – and subsequent influence – of the new **Progress Party** (*Fremskridt-spartiet*), headed by Mogens Glistrup, who claimed to have an income of over a million kroner but to be paying no income tax through manipulation of the tax laws. The Progress Party stood on a ticket of immigration curbs and drastic tax cuts, and Glistrup went on to compare tax avoidance with the sabotaging of Nazi railway lines during the war. He also announced that if elected he would replace the Danish defence force with an answering machine saying "we surrender" in Russian. He was eventually imprisoned after an investigation by the Danish tax office; released in 1985, he set himself up as a tax consultant.

The success of the Progress Party pointed to dissatisfaction with both the economy and the established parties' strategies for dealing with its problems. In September 1982, **Poul Schlüter** became the country's first Conservative prime minister of the twentieth century, leading the widest-ranging coalition yet seen – including Conservatives, the Venstre, Centre Democrats and Christian People's Party. In keeping with the prevailing political climate in the rest of Europe, the prescription for Denmark's economic malaise was seen to be spending cuts, not sparing the social services, and with an extension of taxation into areas such as pension funds. These policies continued until the snap election of 1987, which resulted in a significant swing to the left. Nevertheless, Schlüter was asked to form a new government, which he did in conjunction with the Progress Party in order to gain a single-seat working majority. A further election, in May 1988, largely served to affirm the new Schlüter-led government, if only because of the apparent lack of any workable alternative.

The urban landscape of the capital also began to experience significant change during the 1980s, when the city government initiated attempts at cleaning up the run-down neighbourhoods of Nørrebro and Vesterbro. First came the disastrous demolition of a number of ramshackle but character-rich buildings in Nørrebro and their replacement with ugly modernist concrete housing estates. The city's population protested, and the remaining buildings there and in Vesterbro were spared demolition and restored, after which the value of the buildings soared and the former working-class inhabitants were pushed out into the suburbs. At the same time, concerns arose about the culture and character of Denmark – the very face of Danish citizens, in fact. The arrival since the 1960s of substantial numbers of immigrants – the so-called **new Danes** – began to raise questions about the future of the country. Guest workers, mostly from Yugoslavia and Turkey, brought in during the boom years of the 1960s to fill lower-paid jobs, became suddenly less welcome in the 1970s, as unemployment rates began to rise and the ugly face of racism reared its head.

Since the 1970s the major barometer of national sentiment in Denmark has been how people have perceived the country's role in Europe. In January 1993, Schlüter's government was forced to resign over a political scandal (it was revealed that asylum had been denied to Sri Lankan Tamil refugees in the late 1980s and early 1990s, in contravention of Danish law). The Social Democrats, led by **Poul Nyrup Rasmussen**, took power in 1994 and formed a four-party coalition. For the first time in ten years Denmark was ruled by a majority government – a centre-left majority coalition that came under attack for its weak policies on tax reform, the welfare state and the thorny issue of **European union**. Though traditionally a reluctant member of the EC, Denmark was carried into the European **Exchange Rate Mechanism** (or ERM, then viewed as the first step towards a single European currency) by Schlüter at the start of the 1990s, a move that transformed the Danish economy into one of the strongest in Europe and made its inflation rate the lowest of any EC member. The price for this, however, was soaring unemployment and further cuts in public spending.

The outcome of the referendum on the **Maastricht Treaty** (the blueprint for European political and monetary union) in June 1992, however, provided an unexpected upset to the Schlüter applecart. Despite calls for a "yes" vote not only from the government but also from the opposition Social Democrats, over fifty percent of Danes rejected the treaty – severely embarrassing the prime minister and sending shivers down the spine of every western European government. After a revised treaty went to a **second referendum** in May 1993, nearly 57 percent of the Danish population voted in favour, but anti-European feelings boiled over during the vote, and the night after the referendum young left-wingers and anarchists came together in central Copenhagen to declare the area an "EU-free zone". The police moved in to break up the demonstration, battles with the demonstrators ensued, and, for the first time in history, the Danish police opened fire against a crowd of civilians. While nobody was killed, the incident sparked off a major investigation into the actions of the police, and while Denmark avoided the risk of economic isolation in an increasingly integrated European community, doubts among the Danish people remain, along with a continuing dissatisfaction at the way the "yes" vote was achieved.

Rasmussen and the Social Democrats retained the largest share of the vote in subsequent elections in 1998 and, as the millennium dawned, the country was well placed for life in a new Europe. Danes were ranked at the top of the newly created "European Future Readiness Index", which measures social costs and problems such as environmental quality, healthcare costs, poverty and unemployment, while the organization Transparency International revealed that Denmark had been chosen as the world's **least corrupt nation**: of 99 countries surveyed, only Denmark received a perfect score on its "Anti-Corruption Index". All was not absolutely well, however. In 1999, crime and poverty in Copenhagen were becoming a serious worry for the first time in many years, and decade-long tensions about the growing number of immigrants in the city finally reaching boiling point in November 1999 when **riots** in Nørrebro protested the extradition of a second-generation Turkish immigrant, with police using tear gas to quell more than one hundred protesters – the first such disturbance since the 1993 anti-Maastricht demonstrations.

The new millennium

In September 2000, the Danish people returned an unexpected "no" vote in the referendum held to decide if the country should finally enter the **Eurozone**. In spite of strong governmental support and many sound economic arguments for membership, 47 percent of the population voted against adopting the euro, leaving Denmark and the UK as the only two EU countries retaining a national currency. Support for the rejection came from the two political extremes, with the nationalist right wanting to retain "Danishness" in all its forms, and the far Left seeking a less centralized government away from Brussels. Although financial doom was predicted as a consequence of the "no" vote, no major negative implications materialized and the Danish economy remained solid, even growing. That same year, the landscape of Copenhagen and its environs changed forever with the opening of the **Øresund Bridge**, a road-and-rail link connecting the capital with southwest Sweden. In addition to significantly enhancing the city's connections with the rest of Scandinavia, it has brought the nearby Swedish city of Malmö within thirty minutes of central Copenhagen. While as an economic initiative the bridge itself may have proved something of a flop – steep tolls have kept the number of cars using the bridge far below expected figures – the Øresund region as a whole is booming, with a network of Danish and Swedish universities, cross-border migration and an influx of biotech, medical and food companies employing tens of thousands of people.

In November 2001, the political tide changed once again when Poul Nyrup Rasmussen and the centre-left coalition lost the election to a right-wing coalition led by **Anders Fogh Rasmussen**, which immediately passed strict laws curbing immigration. This radical shift reflected the global move to the political right that followed the September 11 attack in America; a feeling of growing resentment against refugees and second-generation Danes (mainly from Turkey) had already been nurtured by the right-wing, anti-elitist Pia Kærsgård, and after the World Trade Center tragedy, people started listening. As well as taking a hostile position toward "foreigners", the new government marked itself as anti-environment (by way of massive scaling down of energy-saving initiatives); anti-development (through cuts in overseas aid) and anti-culture (via the slashing of financial support to alternative types of entertainment). Fogh Rasmussen also upped the military budget and supported the invasion of Iraq, sending troops (and a much-ridiculed submarine) to the Gulf. Though significant anti-war demonstrations ensued, the election of February 2005 gave a second term to Fogh Rasmussen's conservative coalition, with the Folkeparti, the Danish People's Party, taking 24 seats out of 179; the victory, however, was seen more as a reaction against Social Democrat leader **Mogens Lykketoft**'s lack of charisma than as a mark of support for Rasmussen's political platform, and the failure to engage the electorate has left the average Dane feeling increasingly disconnected from politics.

Denmark today

In recent years, Denmark has repeatedly found itself in the international headlines, a testament to its ability to still wield a disproportionately large amount of influence. The modicum of national joy that came from the birth of the new crown prince to Crown Prince Frederik and his Australian-born wife Mary in October 2005 was quickly tempered by the global uproar over what many saw to be **anti-Muslim cartoons** printed in Danish newspapers that soon followed, a dark episode in modern Danish history that tested political allegiances, challenged tenets of freedom of speech and heightened tensions over Denmark's treatment of its immigrant population, approximately 150,000 of which are Muslim. The incident, incidentally, saw a 1700-percent rise in applications for the conservative party, the Folkeparti, and a fall in asylum applications by some sixty percent.

Denmark also has a large number of interim **asylum seekers**, many whose applications have been rejected but who cannot be repatriated due to fear for their safety. Until officially admitted, refugees are banned from working or pursuing an education and must survive on government handouts. The coalition government has scrapped the right to asylum on humanitarian grounds, cut social benefits for refugees and imposed strict family reunification laws. Critics say that the government has failed to abide by the UNHCR's definition of a refugee; supporters counter that Denmark long left its borders open for people to come in and take advantage of the Danish welfare system. In the meantime, many of those hoping to settle permanently in the country are held in Sandholm, a former army base half an hour from Copenhagen that is Denmark's largest asylum centre, a legal no-mans-land with some six hundred asylum seekers living in limbo. Some interim refugees have been kept at Sandholm for nearly a decade, with no real rights – including a bar on working and officially studying the Danish language – or, for that matter, knowledge of when things might change for the better.

To make matters worse, one of the social experiments that had proven emblematic of Danish liberalism and tolerance has begun to go sour. In 2002, as part of a crackdown on drug dealers, 53 arrests were made in **Christiania**, home to over a thousand artists, activists, hippies and misfits – two-thirds of whom either live on social welfare or have no reported income – and a locale that once attracted up to half a million tourists annually (although admittedly many of them came to buy cheap marijuana). Residents who had previously been granted free use of the land were now required to negotiate with the state and to pay a fixed monthly fee upwards of 1000kr for utilities and services. Christiania has since lost its special status, many have prognosticated that it's only a matter of time before the city kicks out the current residents and begins to develop on the land – eighty acres of prime waterfront real estate.

On the positive side, Denmark was rated the happiest country in the world by several sociological studies in 2006, and Copenhagen deemed the most livable city in the world by *Monocle* magazine two years later. These accolades serve as reminders that Denmark has evolved as a tenuous, **modern–day dichotomy**: a successful, socially progressive liberal democracy with cradle-to-grave care that observes a liberal outlook towards gay matrimony – it was the first country in the world to legalize gay and lesbian partnerships – and yet has policies often perceived as xenophobic, such as its draconian regulations on marriages between Danes and foreigners, in which both partners are required to be at least 24 years old (causing many young Danes to relocate to Sweden with their non-Danish partners).

The Folkeparti has made its intentions clear with a manifesto proclaiming that "Denmark belongs to the Danes and its citizens must be able to live in a secure community…developing only along the lines of Danish culture" – and though these somewhat brazen statements only reflect the views of a small percentage of the population, support does not seem to be waning.

The economy, furthermore, is in a bit of a state on the heels of the global economic crisis, with plummeting house prices, many people with once-secure jobs out looking for work and a general state of insecurity all around. This is compounded by a general unease about the consequences of European expansion, the ramifications of the state's increasingly conservative leanings and a falling investment in the public sector. While the situation in Denmark on the surface appears better than in many neighbouring nations, many underlying factors suggest that the country's future prosperity will remain increasingly fragile, at least for the short term.

Danish design

The earliest of Danish designers – Stone Age hunters and carvers and, later, Viking shipbuilders – relied upon an intimate **relationship with their environment** and the skill to make efficient use of available materials such as clay, wood and leather. Utility and durability were championed over frill and embellishment – an approach that led to the trademark simplicity and prioritizing of function over form that characterizes Danish design.

As early as the 1820s, Empire-style architect-designer **Gustav Friedrich Hetsch** remarked that "the object of everything relating to interior design and architecture, large or small, must be that it answers its purpose and meets two main conditions: usability and suitability…beauty must always depend on usefulness because without this no satisfaction can be gained for the eye or the spirit." Such a call for **functional design** in household objects and public spaces thereafter became an inherent property of Danish (and Nordic) design.

Following the ornate, elaborate constructions of Renaissance and Baroque castles that typified Denmark's rural landscape before the eighteenth century, **Rococo** came into fashion in many upper-class households, with light-hearted motifs such as the elaborate Chinoiserie borrowed from the French court. At the beginning of the nineteenth century, **Neoclassicism** was adopted by many architects and designers, with sophisticated urban interiors that looked away from grandeur and opulence and towards simple and clean geometric lines in details such as cornice mouldings, plaster relief and slender, hanging lamps. In the 1860s, the Neoclassical style was dethroned by **Romanticism**, which culled its properties from a variety of heterogeneous sources. Most notable among such works were those of skilled Danish cabinet-makers, prized for their sophisticated detail in fine, untreated wood surfaces.

Towards Modernism

In the 1920s and 1930s, the work of designer **Kaare Klint** marked a critical turn for Denmark's design tradition. In contrast to the Bauhaus designers, who had rejected **Modernism** by creating objects that had little relation to the everyday lives of people, Klint embraced it, tirelessly researching the human form to design comfortable and pragmatic shapes that respected the tradition of classical furniture-making, and becoming the forefather of modern ergonomic design in the process. Klint's productions range from the classical, woven *Faaborg* chair (1914) and the *Red* chair (1927) to more exotic *Safari* and *Deck* chairs (1933, 1936). But his concepts were never mass-produced, since they relied on careful precision techniques at the time unavailable in furniture production, as well as the designer's time and money – commodities which, in the new industrial age, were becoming increasingly scarce.

As modernization arrived comparatively late to Denmark, appreciation of traditional handmade craft and building methods remained stronger domestically than in other European nations. When industrialization overtook the largely agricultural Danish economy in the 1950s, those notions of superior-quality craftsmanship and attention to detail were implemented in industrial manufacturing and design – most memorably in the work of designers such as **Poul Henningsen** (known sometimes simply as **PH**), the best-known innovator of early Danish lighting design, whose constructions, including the *PH Lamp* (1926), employed different shades of coloured glass with frosted surfaces that radiated golden hues. Contemporaries of Henningsen continued his tradition of user-friendly simplicity, like **Kay Bojesen** and his *Bastik* cutlery for Faadvad (1938) and streamlined teak salad bowl and servers; teak became one of the most fashionable hardwoods, with the work of **Finn Juhl** and **Peter Hvidt** helping to codify the popular "Teak Style".

Later mid-century furniture makers such as **Børge Mogensen** and **Hans Wegner** advocated the ideas of Klint through their modern interpretations of classic furniture pieces, with works like Mogensen's *Shaker* chair (1944), featuring a simple, curved back, beech-frame construction and paper-cord seat, and Wegner's more eccentric *Chinese* chair (1943) and the supremely comfortable and elegant *Peacock* chair (1947). With more than five hundred single chair designs to his name, Wegner, in particular, has done more – bar possibly Arne Jakobsen – for the international image of Danish design than anyone else. His big breakthrough came in 1949, when his *Round* chair was hailed by critics as "the world's most beautiful chair", and it rose to even further stardom when it was used in the televised debates between Kennedy and Nixon in the 1960s, after which it became referred to, quite matter-of-factly, as "*The Chair*". Wegner's designs went on to win worldwide critical acclaim during the 1950s and 1960s, and his pieces are now found in museums all over the world.

Postwar to the present

During the 1950s, the earliest of Denmark's "modern" designers sought influence from as far afield as the traditions of the Japanese and the American Shakers, builders who paid homage to their natural environment through simple designs. Such organic construction is most visible in the work of **Arne Jacobsen**, who easily ousts Wegner as Denmark's most renowned designer. Equally adept as both architect and interior designer, among his works of note are the *Ant* chair (1951), an elegant three-legged piece with a narrow waist whose minimalist artistic design marked a distinctive break from traditional approaches to designing furniture, and his *Model No. 3107* chair (1955), which went on to become one of the best-selling chairs ever. Jacobsen's finest and most elegant work is the *SAS Royal Hotel* in Copenhagen (1960), in which he designed everything from the elegant curtained structure itself all the way down to the silverware for the hotel's restaurant. The hotel also became a showcase for his iconic fibre-and-leather *Swan* and *Egg* chairs (1957).

After the early success of Jacobsen, Danish designers began to make use of the shapes afforded by new synthetic materials like fibreglass and foam, a development evident nowhere more than in the work of **Verner Panton**, the eccentric *enfant terrible* of Danish furniture, known for playful shapes in bold colours and new materials. His best-known piece is the iconic *Panton* chair, or *Stacking* chair (1959), a durable, canti-levered one-piece that has been regularly produced by Vitra for several decades.

Though a global recession in the early 1970s effected a drop in interest in pricier, design-heavy furniture, Danish design firms like **Bang & Olufsen** (see p.275), **Stelton** and **Georg Jensen** countered this by reaffirming the production of very pragmatic household objects. The hi-tech stereos of Bang & Olufsen are found in households across the country, and their streamlined, futuristic design is known the world over. This style has since been co-opted by furniture makers such as **Niels Jørgen Haugesen**, whose *X-line* chair (1977) employs similar lines.

Since then, Denmark has witnessed a merger of product and graphic design, ranging from the modern industrial design of groups such as **Danfoss** and **Louis Poulsen** to the more consumer-focused **Jacob Jensen** and **Dissing+Weitling**, and recent innovators in furniture and housewares such as **Hay** and **Normann Copenhagen**. Still, the hallmarks of traditional Danish design – attention to detail, user-friendly functionality and the utilization of natural, organic forms – are as much in evidence today as they were half a century ago.

Cinema

D anish cinema has played several key roles in the history of film – in the early days with innovator Carl Dreyer and more recently with anti-establishment Lars von Trier, two artistic masterminds who have inspired generations of Danes to aspire to filmic greatness. These days, Danish film is a burgeoning industry, with a half-dozen or so very accomplished directors producing several exportable hits each year, making it one of the most successful (and well-known) of all "minor" European cinemas.

The first century

The first Danish film, *Travel with Greenlandic Dogs* (1897), was a documentary on life in the colonies by photographer Peter Elfelt, and from early on the Danish film industry exported many of its earliest productions of silent fictional and documentary films abroad. After the growing pains of early newsreel-length documentaries and short erotic melodramas Danish cinema produced its first prominent international wunderkind, **Carl Theodore Dreyer**. Dreyer honed his skills in Germany and France before achieving international renown with his most famous film, *The Passion of Joan of Arc* (1928), a stark and barren picture of emotional intensity about the trial and death of the French saint; the lead role, played by Maria Falconetti, is often considered to be one of the single greatest film performances ever. Dreyer went on to direct nine silent films and six spoken features – slow-paced, passionate studies of human psychology that explore the lives of people experiencing severe personal or religious crises. "*Joan*" aside, Dreyer is best known for his later productions *The Word* (1955), a penetrating story about power and love in a Jutland parish and *Gertrud* (1964), his last film, an exploration into the tragedy of a woman who leaves her flaccid marriage in search of ideal love. His once hard-to-find films have recently been restored, resubtitled and re-released on DVD by Criterion (@www.criterion.com) and BFI (@www.bfi.org.uk).

While Dreyer proved a hard act to follow, the **German occupation** was a boon to the Danish film industry since a ban on film imports from the Allied countries created a new appetite for domestic films. Several films from that period stand out, most notably *The Red Horses* (1950), an adaptation of one of Danish writer Morten Korch's novels, a huge success that was followed by adaptations of eighteen other Korch works. Around this same time the genre of popular comedy gained new ground among Danish filmmakers, who also emerged with an increased number of art-house films, stimulated further by the New Wave cinema in Europe in the 1960s. Directors like **Astrid Henning-Jensen**, **Palle Kjærulff-Schmidt** and **Henning Carlsen** explored the new language of realism in film, with productions such as *Weekend* (1962) and *Once There Was a War* (1966), both based on scripts by famed Danish writer Klaus Rifbjerg. In the 1970s, amidst an increase in interest in film production among younger generations, the **Danish Film Institute** was established to provide grants and subsidies for up-and-coming filmmakers, since when nearly all Danish films have been made with at least some state support.

Dogme and the New Danish Cinema

The films of several prominent directors since the late 1980s have managed to transform Danish filmmaking into one of the more vibrant in European cinema. During the late 1980s, two screenplays adapted from popular Danish novels provided renewed recognition abroad when, in a feat of near statistical impossibility, Denmark won the Academy Award for Best Foreign Film two years in a row, first in 1987 with **Gabriel Axel**'s interpretation of Karen Blixen's *Babette's Feast*, and the following year with **Bille August**'s *Pelle the Conqueror*, a haunting film based on the first part of a trilogy of novels by Martin Andersen Nexø.

Dreyer's legacy as Denmark's most famous filmmaker was challenged at the end of the twentieth century with the advent of writer-director **Lars von Trier**. Born in Copenhagen in 1956, this ambitious and stylistically unique Danish filmmaker has held close the mantra that film should be "like a stone in your shoe", and his array of regular international public and critical successes often tackle themes of mercy and ethics. In the late 1990s, von Trier became known for **Dogme 95** (ⓦwww.dogme95.dk), a distinctive European film movement he founded with Thomas Vinterberg in protest at big-budget Hollywood studio productions and their reliance on computer and film technology. *Dogme* ("Dogma") created a manifesto of strict rules for its filmmakers – the so-called "**Vow of Chastity**" – which intended to purify the filmmaking experience so as to enable story and acting to dictate how films are created. Dogme films are generally technically simple – and occasionally even employ non-actors – with storylines that are often complex, in-depth explorations into the human condition.

Von Trier's films are testaments to how much can be accomplished by simply relying on a strong storyline, talented actors and expert direction. In 1998, he released *The Idiots* (1998), possibly his most disturbing film, a mockumentary about a group of friends who feign mental retardation in public, inciting unrest wherever they roam. A handful of successful slow-paced, emotionally charged character studies of women followed, including the dark melodramatic *Breaking the Waves* which starred Emily Watson and won the jury prize at Cannes, and *Dancer in the Dark* (2000), a beautiful and penetrating musical portrayal of a factory worker in small-town America who sacrifices herself for her son's benefit, starring Bjork and Catherine Deneuve. Von Trier had a string of moderate successes after the millennium until 2009's *Antichrist*, a dark, graphic and highly controversial horror story of marriage and depression starring Willem Dafoe and Charlotte Gainsbourg.

As the driving force behind what's been hailed as the **New Danish Cinema**, von Trier regularly steals the spotlight from other contemporary Danish directors, but a number of his colleagues' films have experienced notable success both domestically and abroad. Most memorable are **Thomas Vinterberg**'s *The Celebration* (1998), a family drama about suicide that plays out over a weekend reunion, and two romantic comedies: **Søren Kragh-Jacobsen**'s *Mifune* (1999) and **Lone Scherfig**'s *Italian for Beginners* (2000) – both offering humorous insights into Danish society and making a splash on screens abroad. Scherfig's quirky English-language *Wilbur Wants to Kill Himself* (2002) was a superb amalgam of dark humour and deep sadness. Recent years have seen such box-office successes as *Dear Wendy* (2005), a collaboration between von Trier as screenwriter and Vinterberg as director; Susanna Bier's *After the Wedding* (2007), and *Flammen og Citronen* (2008).

Books

A lthough the number of English-language books on Denmark is nowhere near that of many other European countries, we've compiled some of the better titles out there. In terms of **history** and **society**, the sheer volume of books on the Vikings leaves you with the impression that historians consider it the only period worth writing about. The outlook for **literary fiction** is a bit more promising, as the past few years have seen a marked rise in North American and British public appreciation of contemporary Danish authors – due in no small part to the phenomenal international success of novelist **Peter Høeg** – and a resultant increase in the number of English-language translations of their better known works, as well as reissues of some of the classics. The most recent information on who's been published where in English translation can be found at ⓦ www.literaturenet.dk. The majority of books listed here are currently in print, while most of those that aren't should be easy to find in secondhand bookstores. Those marked with a ⚘ indicate titles that are particularly recommended.

History, politics and philosophy

W.H.Auden (ed) *The Living Thoughts of Kierkegaard*. In this bold new anthology of the Danish philosopher's work, the celebrated poet Auden has selected his favourite Kierkegaard essays and written a sparkling introductory essay contextualizing his writings and ideas.

John Robert Christianson *On Tycho's Island: Tycho Brahe, Science, and Culture in the Sixteenth Century*. This pioneering study chronicles how Danish-born Brahe – chemist, philosopher and poet – used his charismatic personality to influence a number of contemporaries, reforming European thought ultimately to usher in the Scientific Revolution, marking the birth of modern science.

Kevin Crossley-Holland *Penguin Book of Norse Myths: Gods of the Vikings*. A superb collection of over thirty separate prose translations of the seminal Scandinavian myths, filled with fighting gods, mystical magicians and tales of love, deceit and destruction.

Tom Cunliffe *Topsail and Battleaxe*. The intertwined stories of the tenth-century Vikings who sailed from Norway, past the Faroes and Iceland to North America, and the author's parallel trip in 1983 – made in a 75-year-old pilot cutter. Enthusiastically written, and illustrated with terrific photos.

Tony Griffiths *Scandinavia: At War With Trolls*. A concise and witty cultural history of modern Scandinavia and the contributions of its great thinkers, artists and musicians from the eighteenth century to today, this short book provides insight into the people and ideas that have helped shape the Scandinavian psyche.

Knud Jespersen *A History of Denmark*. The only modern history of Denmark available in English, this short book provides a wealth of information on royalty, the Church, economics and politics, as well as some interesting insights into what has created a specific Danish cultural identity. The clipped style makes it a very quick read.

⚘ **Gwyn Jones** *A History of the Vikings*. The most thorough of any of the Viking histories, this well-written, painstakingly-documented chronological account includes a number of drawings, maps and photographs that complement the pop-academic tone of the book.

Søren Kierkegaard *Either/Or.*
Kierkegaard's most important
(and most approachable) work, a
monumental philosophical tract
packed with wry and wise musings on
love, life and death in nineteenth-
century Danish society.

Emmy E. Werner *A Conspiracy of
Decency.* A short, well-written account
detailing how the Danish people were
able to rescue nearly all of the
country's Jews from deportation – and
death – by hiding them and granting
them asylum. Eyewitness accounts
make for quite compelling reading.

Biography

Jens Andersen *Hans Christian
Andersen: A New Life.* This biography
by Andersen (no relation) leaves out
HC's earliest days to focus on the parts
of his life that most affected him, and
like many such bios, explore his sex
life (or lack thereof) in great detail.
Packed with facts and footnotes, it's a
rewarding read.

Joakim Garff *Søren Kierkegaard: A
Biography.* The most comprehensive
book on Kierkegaard's life to date, this
800-page tome is surprisingly readable,

due in part to its masterful translation
into English.

Jack Stevenson *Lars Von Trier.* The
biographical aspects of this compact
tome focus on Von Trier's formation
as a cutting-edge director and
emphasizes exactly who and what has
influenced his work.

Judith Thurman *Isak Dinesen:
The Life of Karen Blixen.* The most
penetrating biography of Blixen,
elucidating details of the farm period
not found in the two "Africa" books.

Literature

Hans Christian Andersen *Hans
Andersen's Fairy Tales.* Still the
most internationally prominent figure
of Danish literature, Andersen's fairy
tales are so widely translated and read
that the full clout of their allegorical
content is often overlooked: interest-
ingly, his first collection of such tales
(published in 1835) was condemned
by many critics for its "violence and
questionable morals". *Travels* is a
small collection of his accounts while
travelling in Europe and the Mediterranean, offering a unique insight into
Andersen's powers of observation and
social critique. His autobiography,
The Fairy Tale of My Life, makes a fine
alternative to the modern biographical portraits now available – though
don't expect too much exploration
into the author's darker sides.

Mikkel Birkegaard *The Library of
Shadows.* This bestselling thriller is

about a man who inherits a secondhand bookshop from his father and is
then forced to explore a dark family
secret hidden in the depths of the
shop. Great if you're interested in the
transformative power of reading.

Karen Blixen (Isak Dinesen) *Out of
Africa.* This account of Blixen's
attempts to run a coffee farm in
Kenya after her divorce is a lyrical
and moving tale, and was turned
into an Oscar winner by Sydney
Pollack. But it's in *Seven Gothic Tales*
that Blixen's fiction was at its zenith:
a flawlessly executed, weird, emotive
work, full of twists in plot and
strange, ambiguous characterization.

Tove Ditlevsen *Complete Freedom.*
A selection of short stories by one of
Denmark's first feminist writers that
explores themes of greed, family
relationships and anti-Semitism.

A second work, *Early Spring*, is a captivating autobiographical novel of growing up in Copenhagen's working-class Vesterbro district during the 1930s.

Jakob Ejersbo *Nordkraft*. Journalist Ejersbo's first novel is a story about three going-nowhere, hash-smoking youths struggling to survive in the city of Aalborg, and an exploration into Danes' perception of ethnic and cultural difference. The author's raw style has been compared to early Irvine Welsh.

Per Olov Enquist *The Visit of the Royal Physician*. A gripping, racy and witty historical novel by one of Sweden's best-loved novelists, set in King Christian VII's Danish court in the 1760s: the king is a halfwit, the queen is duplicitous and the forces of the Enlightenment are arranged against the reactionaries. The narrative charts the power struggles of the various weasly courtiers who manipulate the young and mentally unstable king, including his German doctor, the charismatic Johann Struensee. Great stuff.

Michael Frayn *Copenhagen*. Frayn's devastating, beautifully written play re-examines the reasons and tensions behind the mysterious 1941 visit to Nazi-occupied Copenhagen by the German atomic physicist, Werner Heisenberg, to see his former close colleague and friend Niels Bohr, now working for the opposite side in the race to develop the atomic bomb.

Jens Christian Grøndahl *Silence in October*. One of Europe's most widely read contemporary authors, Grøndahl has written over a dozen novels, several now in English translation. *Silence*, his ninth, is a stream-of-consciousness tale in which an art critic tries to come to terms with the unexpected death of his wife. The author delicately weaves the relationships between time, space and form as a metaphor for comprehending human emotion.

Peter Høeg *Miss Smilla's Feeling for Snow*. Høeg is easily Denmark's most famous modern author. A worldwide bestseller and Høeg's best-known work, this compelling thriller deals with Danish colonialism in Greenland and the issue of cultural identity. Other acclaimed books include *Borderliners* and his most recent novel, *The Silent Girl*.

Johannes V. Jensen *The Fall of the King*. 1944 Nobel Prize-winner Jensen's masterpiece vividly depicts an overlooked period of Danish history covering the tumultuous reign of Christian II (1513–23) and his many years in captivity at Sønderborg Slot, superbly described through the eyes of his servant and friend, Mikkel Thøgersen.

Thomas E. Kennedy *Kerrigan's Copenhagen: A Love Story*. The Danish capital co-stars in this witty, erudite, Joycean tale of an American writer attempting to come to terms with his past in Copenhagen's many bars. Each chapter is devoted to a different watering hole, with the loveable if frustrating hero encountering a host of characters, and musing on topics like city life, beer, books, jazz, sex, cigars and architecture.

Martin Andersen Nexø *Pelle the Conqueror*. Though the novel became more popular abroad after it was made into an Oscar-winning film by Bille August in 1989, this moving tale about life as an immigrant has been a classic in Denmark for years. Nexø, one of eleven children born in the slums of Copenhagen in the late nineteenth century, was himself no foreigner to poverty, accounting for his poignant, unsentimentalized character descriptions.

Morten Ramsland *Dog's Head*. Ramsland, a self-described "anarchist writer" once declared unfit for grammar school, won the prestigious Golden Laurel prize in 2006, and is just now beginning to achieve acclaim in Denmark and reach European audiences. This quirky debut novel follows a Danish expat who returns home to deal with ghosts from his family's past.

🏃 **Hans Scherfig** *Stolen Spring*. A group of Copenhagen youths studying for their high-school exams feel they're missing out on the most important spring of their lives. A classic novel, mandatory reading for all Danish school students.

Snorri Sturluson *Prose Edda, King Harald's Saga*. Classics of Norse mythology, these historical tales were composed in the early thirteenth century and are the most extensive source for modern knowledge about the period. Newly translated by an American scholar of archeology, this is exceptional, invigorating reading.

🏃 **Rose Tremain** *Music and Silence*. Captivating historical novel that follows the lives of Christian IV, his consort, his English lutenist and their lovers. Life in the many castles around Denmark is brilliantly described, and the novel provides a fascinating insight into Danish aspirations and superstitions during the period.

Anthropology, culture and design

Christer Elfving & Petra de Hamer *New Scandinavian Cooking*. A cook's tour through Scandinavia's capital cities, mixing history, culinary trends and tips on the hottest chefs and restaurants with delicious modern recipes.

🏃 **Charlotte and Peter Fiell** *Scandinavian Design*. This Taschen classic is a massive reference tome covering every major Scandinavian designer of the twentieth century – from Aalto to Wirkkala.

Mette Hjort *Small Nation, Global Cinema*. A must for anyone interested in modern Danish cinema, this book looks at the emerging success of the New Danish Cinema, focusing on themes of nationalism, cultural diffusion and representation of ethnic minorities, with emphasis on the Dogme 95 movement. Though it's a decidedly academic publication, the language still makes it very accessible to most readers.

🏃 **Bradley Quinn** *Scandinavian Style*. There's lots of eye candy in this bright coffee-table book, which highlights contemporary interior and furniture design as much as the influential Baroque, Gustavian and Nordic Classicist styles that still figure prominently in many of the region's older homes.

Jørgen Sestoft, Jørgen Hegner Christiansen & Kim Dirkinck-Holmfeld *Guide to Danish Architecture*. Great for architecture buffs, this compact, two-volume set provides a solid overview of all of Denmark's major constructions of the last millennium. A large fold-out country map helps you find the mentioned works.

Carsten Thau & Kjeld Vindum *Arne Jacobsen*. A gargantuan, descriptive compendium featuring loads of full-page colour photographs and detailed commentaries on the works of Jacobsen, Denmark's most famous designer, from his iconic Ant and Swan chairs to lesser-known works.

Language

Language

Danish

T hough similar to German in some respects, **Danish** has significant differences in pronunciation, with Danes tending to swallow the ending of many words and leaving certain letters silent. In general, English is widely understood throughout Denmark, as is German, and young people especially often speak both fluently. However, even with little need to resort to Danish, learning a few phrases will surprise and delight any Danes you meet. If you can speak Swedish or Norwegian, then you should have little problem making yourself understood – all three languages share the same root.

The language section below will equip you with the bare essentials, but if you want something more comprehensive, the *Berlitz Danish–English Dictionary* and *Berlitz Danish Phrase Book* are good reference guides. If you're planning to really get to grips with the language, the best teach-yourself book is *Colloquial Danish* (W. Glyn Jones and Kirsten Gade). For serious students of the language, the *Danish Dictionary* (Anna Garde and W. Glyn Jones, eds) is excellent; while for grammar, you can't do better than *Danish: A Comprehensive Grammar* (Philip Holmes, Robin Allan and Tom Lundskær-Nielsen).

Words and phrases

Basics

Danish **pronunciation** is a confusing affair, so for the phrases below we've explained in brackets how to pronounce them.

Taler de engelsk? (tayla dee ENgellsg)	Do you speak English?	**Hvor er?** (voa ea?)	Where is?
Ja (ya)	Yes	**Hvor meget?** (voa maYETH?)	How much?
Nej (nye)	No	**Hvad koster det?** (vath kosta day?)	How much does it cost?
Jeg forstår det ikke (yai fusTO day igge)	I don't understand	**Jeg vil gerne ha...** (yai vay GERna ha)	I'd like...
Værså venlig (verso venli)	Please	**Hvor er toiletterne?** (Voa ea toalettaneh?)	Where are the toilets?
Tak (tagg)	Thank you	**Et bord til...** (et boa te...)	A table for...
Undskyld (unsgul)	Excuse me	**Må jeg bede om regningen?** (moah yai beyde uhm RYningan?)	Can I have the bill/ check, please?
Hi (hye)	Hello/Hi		
Godmorgen (goMORN)	Good morning		
Goddag (goDA)	Good afternoon		
Godnat (goNAD)	Goodnight	**Billet** (bill-led)	Ticket
Farvel (faVELL)	Goodbye		

Numbers

0	Nul	18	Atten
1	En	19	Nitten
2	To	20	Tyve
3	Tre	21	Enogtyve
4	Fire	30	Tredive
5	Fem	40	Fyrre
6	Seks	50	Halvtreds
7	Syv	60	Tres
8	Otte	70	Halvfjerds
9	Ni	80	Firs
10	Ti	90	Halvfems
11	Elleve	100	Hundrede
12	Tolv	101	Hundrede og et
13	Tretten	151	Hundrede og enoghalvtreds
14	Fjorten		
15	Femten	200	To hundrede
16	Seksten	1000	Tusind
17	Sytten		

Days and months

Monday	Mandag	March	Marts
Tuesday	Tirsdag	April	April
Wednesday	Onsdag	May	Maj
Thursday	Torsdag	June	Juni
Friday	Fredag	July	Juli
Saturday	Lørdag	August	August
Sunday	Søndag	September	September
		October	Oktober
January	Januar	November	November
February	Februar	December	December

Some signs

Entrance	Indgang	Closed	Lukket
Exit	Udgang	Arrival	Ankomst
Push/pull	Skub/træk	Departure	Afgang
Danger	Fare	Police	Politi
Gentlemen	Herrer	No smoking	Rygning forbudt/ Ikke rygere
Ladies	Damer		
Open	Åben	No entry	Ingen adgang

Food and drink

Basics

Kniv	Knife	Ost	Cheese
Gaffel	Fork	Bøfsandwich	Hamburger
Ske	Spoon	Pølser	Frankfurters/
Tallerken	Plate		sausages
Kop	Cup	Smørrebrød	Open sandwiches
Glas	Glass	Det kolde bord	Help-yourself cold
Salt	Salt		buffet
Peber	Pepper	Pålæg	Open sandwich
Sukker	Sugar		toppings, typically
Nudler	Noodles		cold cuts
Ris	Rice	Sildebord	A selection of spiced
Brød	Bread		and marinated
Rundstykke	Crispy roll		herring
Fuldkornsbrød	Wholemeal bread	Spegesild	Salted and marinated
Rugbrød	Rye bread		herring
Småkage	Cookie	Leverpostej	Liver paté
Kiks	Biscuits	Spegepølse	Salami
Wienerbrød	"Danish" pastry	Remoulade	Mayonnaise-based
Mælk	Milk		condiment with
Skummetmælk	Skimmed milk		chopped pickles
Smør	Butter	Ristede løg	Crisp roasted onions
Is	Ice cream	Rulepølse	Rolled pork belly
			with herbs

Egg (Æg) dishes

Kogt æg	Boiled egg	Røræg	Scrambled eggs
Omelet	Omelette	Spejlæg	Fried eggs

Fish (Fisk)

Forel	Trout	Rogn	Roe
Gedde	Pike	Rødspætte	Plaice
Helleflynder	Halibut	Røget sild	Smoked herring
Hummer	Lobster	Sardiner	Sardines
Karpe	Carp	Sild	Herring
Klipfisk	Salt cod	Søtunge	Sole
Krabbe	Crab	Stør	Sturgeon
Krebs	Crayfish	Store rejer	Prawns
Laks	Salmon	Torsk	Cod
Makrel	Mackerel	Zander	Pike-perch
Rejer	Shrimp	Ål	Eel

Meat (*Kød*)

And(ung)	Duck(ling)	Kanin	Rabbit
Oksekød	Beef	Kylling	Chicken
Dyresteg	Venison	Lammekød	Lamb
Fasan	Pheasant	Lever	Liver
Gås	Goose	Skinke	Ham
Hare	Hare	Svinekød	Pork
Kalkun	Turkey	Vildt	Venison

Vegetables (*Grøntsager*)

Agurk	Cucumber	Majs	Sweetcorn
Artiskokker	Artichokes	Majskolbe	Corn on the cob
Asparges	Asparagus	Peberfrugt	Peppers
Blomkål	Cauliflower	Persille	Parsley
Bønner	Beans	Porrer	Leeks
Champignoner	Mushrooms	Ris	Rice
Grønne bønner	Runner beans	Rødbeder	Beetroot
Gulerødder	Carrots	Rødkål	Red cabbage
Brune bønner	Kidney beans	Rosenkål	Brussels sprouts
Hvidløg	Garlic	Salat	Lettuce, salad
Julesalat	Chicory	Selleri	Celery
Kål	Cabbage	Spinat	Spinach
Kartofler	Potatoes	Søde kartofler	Sweet potatoes
Linser	Lentils	Turnips	Turnips
Løg	Onions	Ærter	Peas

Fruit (*Frugt*)

Abrikoser	Apricots	Jordbær	Strawberries
Ananas	Pineapple	Kirsebær	Cherries
Appelsiner	Oranges	Mandariner	Tangerines
Bananer	Bananas	Melon	Melon
Blommer	Plums	Pærer	Pears
Blåbær	Blueberries	Rabarber	Rhubarb
Brombær	Blackberries	Rosiner	Raisins
Citron	Lemon	Solbær	Blackcurrants
Ferskner	Peaches	Stikkelsbær	Gooseberries
Grapefrugt	Grapefruit	Svesker	Prunes
Hindbær	Raspberries	Vindruer	Grapes
Hyldebær	Elderberries	Æbler	Apples

Danish specialities

Biksemad	Diced leftover roast pork fried with onion and potatoes, eaten with pickled beetroot	Boller i karry	Meatballs in curry sauce served with rice

Brune kartofler	Small boiled potatoes glazed in buttery sugar
Flæskesteg	A hunk of roasted pork with crackling, hot pickled red cabbage, boiled potatoes and gravy
Fiske frikadeller	Fish meatballs
Frikadeller	Pork meatballs
Grillstegt kylling	Grilled chicken
Bøf med bløde løg	Thick minced-beef burgers fried with onions
Kalvobryot i frikasseé	Veal boiled with vegetables and served in a white sauce with peas and carrots
Kogt torsk	Poached cod in mustard sauce with boiled potatoes
Medisterpølse	A spiced pork sausage, usually served with boiled potatoes or stewed vegetables
Røget sild	Smoked herring
Sild i karry	Herring in hot curry sauce

Skidne æg	Poached or hard-boiled eggs in a cream sauce, spiced with fish mustard and served with rye bread, garnished with sliced bacon and chives
Skipper labskovs	Sailor's stew: small squares of beef boiled with potatoes, peppercorns and bay leaves
Stegt flæsk med persille sovs	Thinly sliced fried pork with boiled potatoes and a thick creamy parsley sauce
Stegt ål med stuvede kartofler	Fried eel with diced potatoes and white sauce
Æbleflæsk	Smoked bacon with onions and sautéed apple rings
Æggekage	Scrambled eggs with onions, chives, potatoes and bacon pieces

Drink (*Drikke*)

Appelsinjuice	Orange juice
Appelsinvand	Orangeade
Chokolade (varm)	Chocolate (hot)
Citronvand	Lemonade
Eksport-Øl	Export beer (very strong lager)
Fadøl	Draught beer
Guldøl	Strong beer
Husets vin	House wine
Hvidvin	White wine
Kaffe (med fløde)	Coffee (with cream)
Kærnemælk	Buttermilk

Letmælk	Semi-skimmed milk
Mineralvand or Danskvand	Soda water/ mineral water
Mælk	Milk
Rødvin	Red wine
Sødmælk	Full-fat milk
Te	Tea
Tomatjuice	Tomato juice
Vand	Water
Vin	Wine
Æblemost	Apple juice
Øl	Beer

Glossary

Båd	Boat	**Kyst**	Coast
Bakke	Hill	**Landsby**	Village
Banegård	Train station	**Lille**	Little, small
Borg	Fortified castle	**Lufthavn**	Airport
Bro	Bridge	**Museet**	Museum
By	Town	**Nørre**	Northern
-et/-en	suffixes denoting "the"	**Ny**	New
		Plads	Square
Fælled	Common (as in "communal ground")	**Port**	Gate
		Rutebilstation	Long-distance bus station
Færge	Ferry	**Rådhus**	Town Hall
Folkeafstemning	Referendum	**Sankt/Skt/Sct**	Saint
Dansk Folkekirke	Organization of the Danish state church	**Skov**	Forest, wood
		Slot	Castle
Folketing	Danish Parliament	**Sø**	Lake, sea
Gade	Street	**Sønder**	Southern
Gammel	Old	**Stor**	Big
Genbrug	Recycling	**Stræde**	Street
Gård	Yard	**Strand**	Beach or shore
Have	Garden	**Tårn**	Tower
Havn	Harbour	**Tog**	Train
Hus	House	**Torv**	Square
Kanal	Canal	**Vandrerhjem**	Youth hostel
Kirke	Church	**Vej**	Road
Klint	Cliff	**Vester**	Western
Klit	Dune	**Ø**	Island
Kongens	King's, royal	**Øster**	Eastern

Small print and
Index

A Rough Guide to Rough Guides

Published in 1982, the first Rough Guide – to Greece – was a student scheme that became a publishing phenomenon. Mark Ellingham, a recent graduate in English from Bristol University, had been travelling in Greece the previous summer and couldn't find the right guidebook. With a small group of friends he wrote his own guide, combining a highly contemporary, journalistic style with a thoroughly practical approach to travellers' needs.

The immediate success of the book spawned a series that rapidly covered dozens of destinations. And, in addition to impecunious backpackers, Rough Guides soon acquired a much broader and older readership that relished the guides' wit and inquisitiveness as much as their enthusiastic, critical approach and value-for-money ethos.

These days, Rough Guides include recommendations from shoestring to luxury and cover more than 200 destinations around the globe, including almost every country in the Americas and Europe, more than half of Africa and most of Asia and Australasia. Our ever-growing team of authors and photographers is spread all over the world, particularly in Europe, the US and Australia.

In the early 1990s, Rough Guides branched out of travel, with the publication of Rough Guides to World Music, Classical Music and the Internet. All three have become benchmark titles in their fields, spearheading the publication of a wide range of books under the Rough Guide name.

Including the travel series, Rough Guides now number more than 350 titles, covering: phrasebooks, waterproof maps, music guides from Opera to Heavy Metal, reference works as diverse as Conspiracy Theories and Shakespeare, and popular culture books from iPods to Poker. Rough Guides also produce a series of more than 120 World Music CDs in partnership with World Music Network.

Visit www.roughguides.com to see our latest publications.

Rough Guide credits

Text editor: Ann-Marie Shaw
Layout: Pradeep Thapliyal
Cartography: Karobi Gogoi, Swati Handoo
Picture editor: Emily Taylor
Production: Rebecca Short
Proofreader: Stewart Wild
Cover design: Dan May, Chloë Roberts
Photographer: Roger Norum and Helena Smith
Editorial: London Andy Turner, Keith Drew, Edward Aves, Alice Park, Lucy White, Jo Kirby, James Smart, Natasha Foges, Róisín Cameron, James Rice, Emma Traynor, Emma Gibbs, Kathryn Lane, Monica Woods, Mani Ramaswamy, Harry Wilson, Lucy Cowie, Lara Kavanagh, Alison Roberts, Joe Staines, Peter Buckley, Matthew Milton, Tracy Hopkins, Ruth Tidball; **Delhi** Madhavi Singh, Lubna Shaheen
Design & Pictures: London Scott Stickland, Dan May, Diana Jarvis, Mark Thomas, Nicole Newman, Sarah Cummins; **Delhi** Umesh Aggarwal, Ajay Verma, Jessica Subramanian, Ankur Guha, Sachin Tanwar, Anita Singh, Nikhil Agarwal, Sachin Gupta.

Production: Liz Cherry
Cartography: **London** Ed Wright, Katie Lloyd-Jones; **Delhi** Rajesh Chhibber, Ashutosh Bharti, Rajesh Mishra, Animesh Pathak, Jasbir Sandhu, Alakananda Roy, Deshpal Dabas
Online: **London** Faye Hellon, Jeanette Angell, Fergus Day, Justine Bright, Clare Bryson, Aine Fearon, Adrian Low, Ezgi Celebi; **Delhi** Amit Verma, Rahul Kumar, Narender Kumar, Ravi Yadav, Debojit Borah, Rakesh Kumar, Ganesh Sharma, Shisir Basumatari
Marketing & Publicity: **London** Liz Statham, Jess Carter, Vivienne Watton, Anna Paynton, Rachel Sprackett, Laura Vipond; **New York** Katy Ball, Judi Powers; **Delhi** Ragini Govind
Reference Director: Andrew Lockett
Operations Assistant: Becky Doyle
Operations Manager: Helen Atkinson
Publishing Director (Travel): Clare Currie
Commercial Manager: Gino Magnotta
Managing Director: John Duhigg

SMALL PRINT

Publishing information

This second edition published June 2010 by
Rough Guides Ltd,
80 Strand, London WC2R 0RL
14 Local Shopping Centre, Panchsheel Park, New Delhi 110017, India

Distributed by the Penguin Group
Penguin Books Ltd,
80 Strand, London WC2R 0RL
Penguin Group (USA)
375 Hudson Street, NY 10014, USA
Penguin Group (Australia)
250 Camberwell Road, Camberwell, Victoria 3124, Australia
Penguin Group (Canada)
195 Harry Walker Parkway N, Newmarket, ON, L3Y 7B3 Canada
Penguin Group (NZ)
67 Apollo Drive, Mairangi Bay, Auckland 1310, New Zealand
Cover concept by Peter Dyer.

Typeset in Bembo and Helvetica to an original design by Henry Iles.
Printed in Singapore
© Rough Guides, 2010
Maps © Rough Guides

328pp includes index
A catalogue record for this book is available from the British Library
ISBN: 978-1-84836-517-9

The publishers and authors have done their best to ensure the accuracy and currency of all the information in **The Rough Guide to Denmark**, however, they can accept no responsibility for any loss, injury, or inconvenience sustained by any traveller as a result of information or advice contained in the guide.

1 3 5 7 9 8 6 4 2

Help us update

We've gone to a lot of effort to ensure that the second edition of **The Rough Guide to Denmark** is accurate and up-to-date. However, things change – places get "discovered", opening hours are notoriously fickle, restaurants and rooms raise prices or lower standards. If you feel we've got it wrong or left something out, we'd like to know, and if you can remember the address, the price, the hours, the phone number, so much the better.

Please send your comments with the subject line "**Rough Guide Denmark Update**" to ℮mail @roughguides.com. We'll credit all contributions and send a copy of the next edition (or any other Rough Guide if you prefer) for the very best emails.

Have your questions answered and tell others about your trip at ℗ www.roughguides.com

www.roughguides.com

Acknowledgements

Lone Mouritsen would like to thank Nina for being an outstanding research assistant (probably the world's best). Also a big thank you to Mette, Mor & Paul, Far & Ingjerd, Jan, and Hanne for housing and feeding me and Pepe while on the road.

Roger Norum would like to thank Anne Marie Barsøe and Astrid Ruffhead at Visit Denmark, as well as Henrik Thierlein at Wonderful Copenhagen, who was a super source for good tips and great lunches, and Lone Østergaard in Odense, who was as helpful as ever with everything Fynske. Thanks, too, to Kirsten Skovgaard Aggersborg at the Axel Guldsmeden, Turgut Firat and René Olsen at the Sct Thomas Hotel and Karen Nedergaard and Karina Living at the Absalon, who have always been so hospitable and welcoming. And to my dear CPH friends – Søren Nissen, Juan and Tommy Hein, Sine Midtgaard Hansen, Katrine Sonne, Sofus and Anders Midtgaard, Martin Hansen, Nicolas Servide, Kristine Vinther and the good folks at the Roskilde Festival press office – would definitely not have been fun without you around.

Caroline Osborne would like to thank Roy and Lise for all their help and hospitality over the years; Roger and Lone for being great co-authors; and our editor, Ann-Marie Shaw, for her patience and good nature under pressure!

Readers' letters

Thanks to all the readers who have taken the time to write in with comments and suggestions (and apologies if we've inadvertently omitted or misspelt anyone's name):

Jane Davey; Lieve Leroy; Raymond Maxwell.

Photo credits

All photos © Rough Guides except the following:

Title page
Grisetaodde lighthouse, Neno-Sund, Limfjord, North Jutland © Jochen Tack/PhotoLibrary

Introduction
The Øresund Bridge between Denmark and Sweden © Niels Poulsen/Alamy
Beach house in Zealand © Bruno Ehrs/Corbis
Beach huts © Trond Hillestad/PhotoLibrary
Black-tailed godwits © Steen Drozd Lund/ PhotoLibrary
The museum of modern art, Arken © Niels Poulsen/Alamy

Things not to miss
02 Jutland Beach © Michael Damsgaard/ VisitDenmark.com
04 Hans Christian Andersen Museum © Courtesy of The Hans Christian Andersen Museum
07 Vikingeskibmuseet © John Sommer/ VisitDenmark.com
08 Viking fortress grounds © Jan Winther/ VisitDenmark.com
09 Gudenå river canoes © Courtesy of Gudenå River Canoes
10 Koldinghus Slot © Dorte Krogh /VisitDenmark.com
11 Frederiksborg Slot © http://www.flickr.com/ photos/chad_k/157589865/
16 Rundkirke Bornholm © http://www.flickr.com/ photos/micahmacallen/19014493/
17 Roskilde Festival © http://www.flickr .com/photos/auravox/3701522511
18 Queen's Tapestries © Jørgen Schytte/ VisitDenmark.com
19 Sort Sol © Ribe Turist/VisitDenmark.com

Denmark's great outdoors colour section
Burial site near Aarlborg © Bob Krist/Corbis
Trekking path on Møn © Pixonnet.com/Alamy
Chalk cliff on Møn © Werner Bollmann/ PhotoLibrary
Red deer © Picture Press/Alamy
Kite-surfing © Picture Press/Alamy
People sunbathing at Amager Strandpark, Copenhagen © imagebroker/Alamy

Danish food and drink colour section
Smoked herring in a smokehouse, Bornholm © Ken Gillham/PhotoLibrary
Søgaards Bryghus microbrewery © Michael Damsgaard/VisitDenmark.com

Black and whites
p.100 Trelleborg © Reiner Büchtmann/ VisitDenmark.com
p.134 Hammershus castle © Cees van Roeden/ VisitDenmark.com
p.152 Land art by Alfio Bonanno, TICKON Park Langeland © OJPHOTOS/Alamy
p.186 Kite flying on the beach, Rømø © Picture Contact/Alamy
p.208 Moesgård Museum © VisitDenmark.com
p.240 Grenen - Shifting sand dunes, Råbjerg Mile, Jutland © Dr Wilfried Bahnmoller/PhotoLibrary
p.266 Elia sculpture © Wedigo Ferchland/ VisitDenmark.com

www.roughguides.com

Index

Map entries are in colour.

www.roughguides.com

INDEX

www.roughguides.com

Map symbols

maps are listed in the full index using coloured text

– – –	International border		⧫	Point of interest
– – –	Chapter boundary		@	Internet access
▬▬▬	Expressway		ⓘ	Information office
══	Major road		⊠	Post office
—	Minor road		⊞	Hospital
▬▬	Pedestrianized street		ⓟ	Parking
⚎⚎	Steps		◉	Accommodation
—•—	Railway		⚠	Campsite
- - - -	Path/cycle route		⛳	Golf course
——	Coastline/river		⚱	Museum
— —	Ferry route		⚔	Castle/fort
⊠—⊠	Gate/entrance		🏛	Stately home/palace
)(	Bridge		⚘	Fountain/gardens
▲	Peak		✡	Synagogue
⁂	Rocks		⚮	Church (regional maps)
⚡	Lighthouse		⊞	Church (town maps)
⚘	Windmill		▮	Building
✈	Airport		⬚	Market
Ⓜ	Metro station		⬭	Stadium
Ⓢ	S-Tog station		⊹	Cemetery
⚲	Boats		▦	Park
★	Bus stop		▦	Beach

MAP SYMBOLS

So now we've told you about the things not to miss, the best places to stay, the top restaurants, the liveliest bars and the most spectacular sights, it only seems fair to tell you about the best travel insurance around

WorldNomads.com
keep travelling safely

Recommended by Rough Guides